NEIL FORSYTH is Professor of English at the University of Lausanne.

THE OLD ENEMY

The Old Enemy

SATAN AND THE COMBAT MYTH

by

NEIL FORSYTH

PRINCETON, NEW JERSEY
PRINCETON UNIVERSITY PRESS
MCM · LXXXVII

LIBRARY OF CONGRESS CATALOGING IN PUBLICATION
DATA WILL BE FOUND ON THE LAST PRINTED PAGE OF THIS BOOK

ISBN 0-691-06712-0

THIS BOOK HAS BEEN COMPOSED IN LINOTRON BEMBO

CLOTHBOUND EDITIONS OF
PRINCETON UNIVERSITY PRESS BOOKS
ARE PRINTED ON ACID-FREE PAPER, &
BINDING MATERIALS ARE CHOSEN FOR
STRENGTH AND DURABILITY. PAPER-
BACKS, ALTHOUGH SATISFACTORY FOR
PERSONAL COLLECTIONS, ARE NOT
USUALLY SUITABLE FOR
LIBRARY REBINDING

PRINTED IN THE UNITED STATES OF
AMERICA BY PRINCETON UNIVERSITY PRESS
PRINCETON, NEW JERSEY

For my mother
Alice
&

in memory of my father
James Forsyth

CONTENTS

ABBREVIATIONS

ANET   *Ancient Near Eastern Texts Relating to the Old Testament*. Edited by J. B. Pritchard. 3rd ed. Princeton: Princeton University Press, 1969.

ANF   *The Ante-Nicene Fathers*. Edited by A. Cleveland Coxe. 10 vols. New York: Christian Literature Co., 1885–96. This American series is based on the Edinburgh edition, called the *Ante-Nicene Christian Library*, edited by Alexander Roberts and James Donaldson (1867–72). It has now been reprinted by Wm. B. Eerdmans Co. (Grand Rapids, Michigan, 1981–83).

CTA   *Corpus des tablettes en cunéiformes alphabétiques*. Edited by A. Herdner. 2 vols. Paris: P. Geuthner, 1963.

PREFACE

To determine the nature and function of the Devil, is no contemptible province of the European Mythology. Who, or what he is, his origin, his habitation, his destiny, and his power, are subjects which puzzle the most acute Theologians, and on which no orthodox person can be induced to give a decisive opinion. He is the weak place of the popular religion—the vulnerable belly of the crocodile.

So Shelley claimed in an essay called *On the Devil, and Devils*. Later in the essay he blames the Christians for the devil:

Like panic-striken slaves in the presence of a jealous and suspicious despot, they have tortured themselves ever to devise any flattering sophism, by which they might appease him by the most contradictory praises—endeavouring to reconcile omnipotence, and benevolence, and equity, in the Author of an Universe where evil and good are inextricably intangled and where the most admirable tendencies to happiness and preservation are for ever baffled by misery and decay. The Christians, therefore, invented or adopted the Devil to extricate them from this difficulty.

How much truth there may be in Shelley's charge is the question that has led me to write the later parts of this book, but his own equivocation—"invented or adopted"—already shows that he sensed where, historically, the problem might lie.

Personally, poetically, Shelley's problem lay elsewhere. As he goes on to say: "The Devil . . . owes everything to Milton." Shelley wrestled with the Miltonic angel, and if his best poetry came from the struggle, he also found it hard to see beyond Milton's language. So has it been for most of us, and indeed it was Milton who kindled my own interest. Yet the traces of Satan's lineage are clear in *Paradise Lost*. Epic poetry, even for Milton, is traditional poetry; it establishes its subject not by isolating but through the large inclusive comparison.

> Thus Satan talking to his nearest mate
> With head uplift above the wave, and eyes
> That sparkling blazed, his other parts besides
> Prone on the flood, extended long and large
> Lay floating many a rood, in bulk as huge
> As whom the fables name of monstrous size,

Titanian, or Earth-born, that warred on Jove,
Briareos or Typhon, whom the den
By ancient Tarsus held, or that sea-beast
Leviathan, which God of all his works
Created hugest that swim the ocean stream.   (1.192–202)

The passage makes little distinction between the fables (Hesiod, Homer, Virgil, the mythographers) and the biblical beast. Leviathan, the passage continues, is a creature of sailors' yarns, the monster that seamen oft mistake for an island, fixing their anchor in his "scaly rind." Others besides Shelley have been led to wonder "whether Milton was a Christian or not, at the period of the composition of Paradise Lost."

The doubt is ill-founded. Milton is reflecting accurately the essential ambivalence of the Judeo-Christian tradition when his narrator piles up the classical parallels and the folklore. As the earlier parts of this book will show, Satan emerged from the ancient mythological tradition, and he never quite shook off the signs of his origins. Indeed, it is my chief point of attack here that Satan is to be conceived not as the principle of evil but as a narrative character. No doubt because my competence is in literary rather than theological matters, I have presumed to argue that the writers of "scripture" and the early church fathers were mainly interpreters, even tellers, of stories. Since the word śāṭān means "adversary," I follow the story in which the Adversary is most fully himself—the combat myth—from its earliest discernible stages in the third millennium B.C. until it became the framework of the Christian belief-system.

I have written for readers who will be inquiring and intelligent but who, like myself, are not necessarily specialists in the fields of study brought together here. For this reason, I have often explained more about essential concepts, ongoing disagreements, or the latest findings than would be appropriate for experts. For the same reason, abbreviations have been kept to a minimum in the footnotes and references, and apart from certain key terms, all quotations are in English.

Translations by others are acknowledged fully on the first occurrence and often thereafter by "trans." or fuller discussion in the footnotes. For the ancient Near East, I have quoted ANET where feasible, but have frequently referred to other sources and translators as well. For biblical quotations, I tried to use the King James Version (KJV), but its familiar beauties often had to be sacrificed for accuracy, usually to the Anchor Bible or the Revised Standard Version (RSV) and infrequently to the New English Bible (NEB), but also to the other translations mentioned in the footnotes or to my own versions. For other texts also I have sometimes made my own renderings, either for polemical purposes or because no decent English version was available.

Specific editions of classical or patristic authors are cited only if a particular point in my argument is at issue, but in those cases I have always tried to give the reader the fullest possible references from which to follow up my sources. Titles of such works are given according to the form in current use, whether in the original or translation, or in the form least likely to cause confusion. Modern works and editions are referred to by the author-date system, because in some of the fields explored here, particularly Gnosticism, research has been advancing rapidly.

If he who sups with the devil should use a long spoon, he who writes about him should watch his words: Tertullian thought Satan was especially good at interpolation. I have tried to fortify myself and my text by wide reading, but I am conscious of a large debt to the help of friends and the advice of experts. For reading parts of the manuscript at various stages, I am thankful to Cater Chambliss, John Coolidge, Philip Damon, John Day, John Foley, Thorkild Jacobsen, Jim Larson, William Nestrick, Alain Renoir, Jeffery Russell, Wayne Shumaker, Steve Vaughn, and Jayne Walker. For advice on particular subjects or encouragement of other kinds, I have especially to thank Norman Austin, Jay Blair, Alan Dundes, Richard and Maria Ellis, Norman Gottwald, Richmond Lattimore, Michael Nagler, Thomas Rosenmeyer, Tony Tanner, and Richard Waswo. Marc Faessler helped with transliteration of Hebrew words. No doubt I shall rue the occasions when I have failed to follow their counsel, and none of these good people should be held responsible for the follies that remain.

Sanford Elberg was Dean of the Berkeley graduate school when I was beginning research for this book. His resourcefulness kept Ford Foundation money flowing my way at an important stage. I am especially grateful to the President and Fellows of Bryn Mawr College for the patience they showed in extending for an extra year my Mellon Postdoctoral Fellowship in Comparative Literature. The librarians at Bryn Mawr and at the Faculté de Théologie in Geneva have been most helpful. And living now in a francophone environment, I have been lucky to find so cheerful and accurate a typist as Shirley Schilly. I also owe a special debt to the meticulous copyediting of Peggy Hoover, and to the encouragement of Mrs. Arthur Sherwood, at Princeton University Press. Finally I thank my wife, Catherine, to whom I have been able to look steadily for lively intelligence and good humor.

THE OLD ENEMY

INTRODUCTION

THE DEVIL'S STORY

A s is the way with centers of pilgrimage, the castle of Wartburg probably still has a black stain on the wall of the room in which Martin
Luther flung his inkhorn at the devil. The devil, we are told, also threw
ink at Luther, but I am not sure any traces of that survive. On other occasions the two antagonists seem to have contented themselves with ex-
changing verbal blows, although once, when Lutheran doctrines could
not win the day, the devil was finally routed *"mit einem Furz."* The devil
is also said to have used a similar weapon, and it left "a train of foul odour
in the chamber for several days afterwards."[1] To the psychoanalyst, the
fart will seem the most significant weapon, revealing subconscious links
between anality and our dealings with the devil; to the theologian, the exchange of doctrine will take precedence; to the structuralist, the ink will
be seen to "mediate" nicely between the other two weapons (it is black, it
makes words) and will open large vistas of speculation. From the point of
view argued in this book, however, what is important is not the weapons
so much as the fact that the story is told at all. Luther imagined his experience as part of the perpetual combat with Satan and his kingdom which
was the core of his own and indeed of much Christian belief.[2] By flinging
ink at the devil, Luther was not only following the biblical injunction to
put on the whole armor of God, he was reenacting the central Christian
narrative. His act was an *imitatio Christi.*

To begin with Luther's inkhorn is not to imply that this book sets out
to throw more ink at the devil. Rather, it is to establish firmly the way the
argument here presented differs from previous histories of the devil, of
which there have been too many.[3] The traditional approach to Satan, at

[1] The Wartburg legend is repeated, e.g., by Summers 1973:231, Rudwin 1931:51, and
Bamberger 1952:221. (The castle is now in East Germany.) For the other, mostly scatalog-
ical, stories, see Melanchthon in Bourke 1891:163; Erikson 1958:40, 58–62, 121, 187, 243–
50; and N. O. Brown 1970:208. Full data on all works referred to will be found in the "Bibliography and References."

[2] Cargill-Thompson 1980:42–59.

[3] Jewett 1890; Carus 1974 (1st ed. 1899); Graf 1931 (1st ed. 1899); Turmel 1929; Garcon
and Vinchon 1930; Rudwin 1931; Murray 1931; Bamberger 1952; Bruno (ed.) 1952; Papini
1955; Robbins 1960; Masters 1962; Ricoeur 1967; H. A. Kelly 1974—a representative sample

least among those who take the subject seriously and not merely as the occasion for titillation or proselytizing, has been to treat him as the embodiment of evil and to proceed quickly to the more rigorous and respectable analysis of the nature of evil, an abstraction better suited to the vocabulary and methods of philosophers and theologians.[4] My own position, however, is that Satan is first, and in some sense always remains, a character in a narrative. For Satan is a character about whom one is always tempted to tell stories, and one may best understand him not by examining his character or the beliefs about his nature according to some elaborate and rootless metaphysical system, but rather by putting him back into history, into the narrative contexts in which he begins and which he never really leaves. That is, we must try to see him as an actor, or what Aristotle called an "agent," with a role to play in a plot, or *mythos*.

The essential role of Satan is opposition. Both the Hebrew word *śṭn* and the Greek *diabolos* have root meanings akin to that of the English word "opponent"—someone or something in the way, a stumbling block. Both words came to mean much more, of course. The Greek word also means "slanderer," for example, and hence a prosecutor or accuser in a court of law. But curiously enough the word "slander" is akin to "scandal," and in Greek *skandalon* means, again, an obstacle, especially a trap laid for an enemy.[5] The root idea in Satan's name, then, is an important clue to his narrative function. He is the Adversary, in much the same way that we talk of the Hero, the Donor, or the Companion, in the kind of narrative analysis pioneered by the Russian formalist Vladimir Propp.[6] He took his function for his title, however, so Satan's name is both paradoxical and tragic. It defines a being who can only be contingent: as the adversary, he must always be a function of another, not an independent entity. As Augustine and Milton show, it is precisely when Satan imagines himself independent that he is most deluded. His character is, in this sense of the word, a *fiction*.

Satan is by no means the only name by which the adversary is known in Jewish and Christian literature, but of the various names and titles— Semihazah, Azazel, Belial, Lucifer, Sammael, Beelzebub, Apolyon, "god of this world," "father of lies"—it was Satan, with its Greek equivalent,

among which both quality and point of view vary widely. Rudwin, Bamberger, and Kelly were the best general surveys before Russell's recent books (1977, 1981, 1985).

    [4] E.g., Buber 1952, Ricoeur 1967, Hick 1966, Boyd 1975, and O'Flaherty 1976.
    [5] Lattimore 1962. See below, Chapter 5.
    [6] Propp 1968. See Appendix and esp. Propp 1984: 82–99.

diabolos, which emerged as dominant, either displacing the others entirely or demoting them to inferior beings and to subordinate aspects of the general character. This was in part because both *diabolos* and the vocalized form *Satanas* occur frequently in the New Testament, in part because they are the most general terms, but also because the church fathers who built up the most thorough analyses of Satan's activities were alert to his main narrative function.

In trying to tell the Christian story, the church fathers were also trying to construct a coherent mythological and theological system with which to oppose their various rivals, whether pagan, Gnostic, or Manichaean. That system had to include, and to make narrative sense of, several apparently separate tales. On the face of it, the serpent of one tale had little to do with the rebel of a second, the tyrant of a third, the tempter of a fourth, the lustful voyeur of a fifth, or the mighty dragon of a sixth. Even when these identifications were made, a process we shall be studying in detail later, there were still difficulties, of both narrative and theological kinds. As recent analyses of more distant mythological systems have shown, the characteristics of a given hero or god will be adapted to the plot in which he functions (a good Aristotelian principle) and so may contradict the characteristics of that same figure in another plot. Edmund Leach's well-known analysis of Ganesha, one of Shiva's sons in the Sri Lankan religious system, shows that the qualities attributed to this figure, especially the sexual ones, "depend upon context and, generally speaking, are the opposite of those attributed to his father, Shiva, or to one or another of his two brothers, Skanda and Aiyanar. As Shiva varies so also Ganesha varies, but in the inverse direction."[7] Louis Dumont's similar analysis of one of those two brothers, the god Aiyanar, shows that his form in any given narrative or ritual depends upon his particular relation with demons on the one hand and with goddesses on the other. Dumont concludes that "a characteristic does not exist except in relation to its opposite."[8] What is true of these distant deities is true *a fortiori* of *the* Adversary himself: his character, indeed his very existence, is a function of his opposition to God, or to man, or to God's son, the god-man. But he may appear as tempter, tyrant, liar, or rebel, each time taking on the characteristics appropriate to his role. If he appears as the opponent of God, he is (eventually) the rebel, and if God is good, as is often but not invariably

[7] Leach 1972:303.
[8] Dumont 1972:194.

the case, then he is evil: if he appears as the opponent of man, then he is the tempter, or the tyrant. The roles overlap, of course. In the New Testament wilderness episode, Satan can tempt Christ only because he has the power to offer Christ an earthly kingship: Satan is already the tyrant, the "god of this world." And like Christ himself, who is both man and god, Satan too can be evil man or "fallen" deity: Satan "enters into" Judas for the betrayal scene, while in the Book of Revelation he is the dragon, cosmic opponent of an angel, Michael.[9]

What held all these various tales together in the developing Christian system was not simply the identification of the main character with Satan. As Aristotle said of the *Odyssey*, it is not because all the incidents happen to one man that the poem has a structural unity. Rather, each tale was seen as an episode in one larger and continuous narrative which itself has a unity of action. The separate devil-tales were all seen as cases of one basic opposition, that of Christ and Satan, and that opposition was conceived throughout the whole of the early Christian period in the terms provided by one of the most widespread of Near Eastern narrative patterns, the combat myth. Whatever disguises Satan, or Christ, might adopt for their various local encounters, they retained their main narrative functions as opponents in the Christian variant of a full-bodied cosmic myth, pitting gods against gods, in which the human condition was at stake.

This glib assertion will need severe qualification when we come to argue the particular ways in which the early Christians conceived and adapted this basic narrative. The term "myth," for example, will need careful scrutiny and definition, given the hostility it has always tended to arouse, both among early Christian apologists like Origen and among contemporary theologians. In any case, most of the interest of the argument about relations between Christian and more ancient narratives lies in the play of variation among the different versions, and finally in the peculiarity of the Christian transformation. Nonetheless, a focus on the devil's role in Christian tradition, by liberating us from the god focus of *theology*, will clarify both the informing structure of the Christian story and the kinds of connection that existed between the Christian drama of salvation and its precursors or rivals.

From our perspective, the Christian version of the plot is something like this: A rebel god challenges the power of Yahweh, takes over the whole earth as an extension of his empire, and rules it through the power

---

[9] Luke 22.3; John 12.31; Rev. 12.7–9.

of sin and death. He is the typical death-dealing villain who causes consternation among his subjects, and his depredations and cruelty make them long for a liberator. This dark tyrant, the "god of this world" as Paul called him, is eventually thwarted by the son of God (or man) in the most mysterious episode of the Christian story, the crucifixion, which oddly combines both defeat and victory. As Luther could testify, the struggle with Satan continues, however, and we wait still for the end of his story in the end of history. The function of Christ, in almost the technical narrative sense of function, is to be the potential liberator of mankind from this tyranny, while the function of Satan is to be the adversary in this Christian variant of the ancient Near Eastern combat narrative.

This bald and inadequate summary of the story is nowhere contained in the scriptures. Versions of it are implicit in the New Testament,[10] but its obscurity and fragmentation there, its presence as an assumed truth rather than a revealed truth, has made it possible for centuries of rationalizers, from the early allegorists to the latest liberal or humanist Christians, to ignore or avoid the devil's role in the Christian system. Luther was an important exception, and the devil has often, as a result, seemed more prominent in Protestant than in Catholic thinking.[11] But although Luther's theory of the Atonement, in which the devil figures large, had considerable impact on Reformation thought,[12] Luther's preoccupation with the demonic is not especially more notable than that of the gospels themselves,[13] and his Atonement theory is essentially a restatement of the combat myth implied by the chief passages of scripture, usually Pauline, which Luther cites.[14] It is arguable, furthermore, that the devil attained his greatest power over the Christian imagination during the witch-hunts of the fifteenth, sixteenth, and seventeenth centuries, and these were encouraged, if not inspired, by the Dominicans and especially the papal bull of 1484.[15] A shift of focus from God to Satan helps to clarify the mythological foundations of the whole Christian system. "No Devil, no God," as John

---

[10] Versions of the myth are studied, e.g., by Gunkel 1895, Caird 1956:70–71, Anderson 1967:161–70, Pelikan 1971:95, and 149–150, Starobinski 1974, and Talbert 1976.

[11] Obendiek 1931:180, Tillich 1948:xx–xxi.

[12] Aulén 1969:1–15.

[13] R. Yates 1977. See below, Chapter 15.

[14] E.g., Col. 1.13, 2.15; 1 Cor. 15.24–26; 2 Cor. 4.4; Gal. 1.4. See Aulén 1969:61–80, 101–22, and Caird 1956:39–53.

[15] K. Thomas 1978:521, by far the best book on the subject. On witchcraft, see also the readings in Marwick (ed.) 1970 and the intelligent survey by Mair 1969.

Wesley put it,[16] but this idea is not a peculiarity of the devil-soaked Protestant imagination; it is basic to the Christian story.

It is mainly Satan, in fact, who gives to Christianity the mythological dimension that has been so much at issue in modern theology, from the "demythologizing tradition" initiated by Rudolf Bultmann[17] to the book which a few years ago disturbed the quiet waters of English theology, *The Myth of God Incarnate*.[18] The depredations and tyranny of Satan are what motivate the incarnation story and that against which the activities of Christ are directed. The myth is most evident in those parts of the Christian testament which are explicitly apocalyptic, but it is present wherever the Satan figure or his demonic allies appear. In Luke, Christ sees Satan fall like lightning from heaven, and the implication is that the struggle of the disciples with demon opponents is an episode or manifestation of the larger myth. Similarly, when we are told that Satan enters into Judas, the human tale of treachery is transformed into another stage of the cosmic battle being waged between Christ and his adversary; such battles are the stuff of myths.

Myths are the kinds of story that have informed and validated most of the world's religious systems. In this sense the word defines a particular kind of narrative and distinguishes it from legends or folktales.[19] The word does not speak to the question of objective truth, but only to the

[16] Rudwin 1931:106. Cf. *The Trial of Maist. Dowell* (1599, p. 8), "If no devils, no God," cited in K. Thomas 1978:559.

[17] Bultmann 1958a and 1958b; Bartsch (ed.) 1961; Jaspers and Bultmann 1958.

[18] Hick (ed.) 1977. Since 1984, David Jenkins, the new Bishop of Durham, has been keeping the waters stirred up. See below, Chapter 16.

[19] Bascom 1965. The usefulness of these distinctions should not be arbitrarily limited by Bascom's unfortunate use of the word "prose," on which see Tedlock 1972. See Ben Amos 1969 and Dundes 1975. The distinctions are mainly but not entirely functional. They are ignored in French structuralism, to its detriment; see Lévi-Strauss 1966–70, Vickers 1973, and Kirk 1974:13–68. Classicists have some reason to feel uncomfortable in that the word "myth" is often used by them, as by the ancient Greeks, in several other senses. Indeed, the most basic meaning of *mythos* in Greek, common in Homer, is simply "utterance," and later, as one can see from its use in Aristotle's *Poetics*, "story" or "plot." Most classical "myths" are, according to Bascom's distinctions, in fact legends, but there is little point in trying to change the usage of centuries. The term "mythology" has a similar range in classical scholarship, being simply a collective noun for all the traditional narratives of Greece and Rome. It will be used in this book in the more restricted sense of a system of stories designed to give a complete account of the organization of the cosmos. It thus overlaps with the term "cosmology," but its focus is on the narratives rather than on the cosmic structure implied in them. Like any definitions, those adopted here will pose difficulties in the particular case, but we shall find interesting reasons where our definitions prove inadequate. It is best to begin with a tolerably clear set of terms.

question of whether teller and audience of a particular narrative regard it as true or sacred. The difficulty with the word "myth" in the discussion of our present subject arises from the various attempts in both Jewish and Greek cultures to distinguish "myth" from "history" and to elevate one at the expense of the other.[20] The same tendency is evident in the "de-mythologizing" tradition of modern theology: comparative study establishes the existence of multiple versions of a narrative pattern or incident (the virgin birth, for example), which in turn means that the pattern or incident is folklore and therefore unworthy of literal belief.[21]

We cannot pretend that this effort to distinguish myth from history on the basis of "truth-value" has never existed and does not now affect biblical scholarship.[22] What we can do, perhaps, is redefine its terms and suggest what consequences flow from that redefinition. The "truth-value" of a given narrative has always been a vital issue in the Judeo-Christian religious system because the formative stories of both Jews and Christians, the Exodus and the Incarnation, are said to have taken place within historical rather than mythological time.[23] Instead of a narrative that is situated in the creative time of the beginnings when the world was being formed, the narratives about Moses and Jesus take place in the recent past, when the world was physically as it is now. Strictly speaking, this means that those formative stories are not myths but legends. Both myths and legends claim (unlike folktales) to be "true," but legends are not necessarily sacred. What distinguishes both Jewish and Christian religious systems, then, is that they elevate to the sacred status of myth narratives that are situated in historical time. Both therefore claim the continuing activity of God in history and so sanctify ordinary human time.

In practice, a special tension exists in the Judeo-Christian tradition between myth and legend and thus between the explanatory claims of each. In the Old Testament local Israelite variants of widespread Near Eastern

---

[20] See, e.g., Childs 1960, Kirk 1974, Frei 1974, and Hick (ed.) 1977:148–66. Difficulties also arise from other sources: the various Greek meanings of the word *mythos*, differing conventions among different scholarly disciplines, the attitudes of rationalists, and the romantic (German-inspired) reaction. See also n. 26, below.

[21] Strauss 1973:10, and Dibelius 1935. But see esp. Bultmann 1958a and 1958b and Jaspers and Bultmann 1958 (a book with the subtitle *An Enquiry into the Possibility of Religion Without Myth*), Bartsch 1961, Ogden 1961, and Dundes 1977:3. Good surveys of the various approaches are Perrin 1974:21–34 and Kee 1977:9–39.

[22] Hick (ed.) 1977:163. Cf. Bidney 1967.

[23] Anderson 1967:115; Anderson 1970; Childs 1959:196. The distinction is most thoroughly formulated in the writings of Eliade (e.g., 1959), whose term *illud tempus* or *in illo tempore* has been widely used.

myths[24] coexist with the special sense of a historical covenant that in their eyes defined the Jews as different from their neighbors. This tension persisted into Christianity once the firm canonical link had been forged with the Jewish scriptures. The tension shows itself, for example, in alternative modes of explanation for the generally miserable character of human life: one, the mythological mode, ascribed evil to the activities of an independent cosmic principle loose in creation—Satan or the devil; the other, the historical mode, set sin before evil and spoke constantly, in the prophetic tradition, of a falling away from the human obligations of the covenant— a failure not of the cosmos as such, but of the human response. Many of the theological disputes of early Christianity may be seen as stressing one or the other of these alternative modes of explanation. They are efforts to insist on one kind of narrative rather than another—myth rather than legend, or "historical" legend rather than myth.

The distinction of myth and legend helps to account for the ambivalent status of Satan within the Jewish and Christian traditions. Although the adversary of the ancient Near East does not appear only in myths, the Satan of Jewish and Christian belief owes his existence to the resurgence of mythic narratives during the apocalyptic period. Once human life is seriously viewed as conditioned by a struggle between divine forces, it becomes difficult to insist on human responsibility. Yet human responsibility was essential to both religions. So we find the rabbinic and the Pauline traditions, for example, trying to construct a version of the narrative that would allow for a separate principle of evil and yet confine its power. The notorious difficulties of Paul's theology, particularly his murky concepts of the Law, Sin, and Death, may be seen as his efforts to combine the implications of myth and legend. And what, after all, to cite a similar kind of difficulty, does it mean to say that Satan "entered into" Judas?

One way of conceiving Satan's importance in the Christian tradition, then, is to see that, when he enters the narrative, he transposes legend into myth. Of course, several kinds of narrative are contained in the canon— parables, miracle stories, the passion narrative, infancy stories, the Easter narrative—to name some of the categories used by form-critical scholarship[25]—but it was the cosmic myth that validated those other kinds

[24] Childs 1960. See also Cross 1973, which develops Albright's ideas (e.g., 1957) in the fascinating ways made available by the Ras Shamra discoveries and oral epic theory. Cf. Culley 1976 and esp. Alter 1981.

[25] See, e.g., Dibelius 1935. A useful summary and development of Bultmann's and Dibelius' impact is Doty 1972. For the OT see Rast 1972. I wish N. Frye (1983:xvii) had not been so contemptuous of such approaches in his otherwise fascinating book.

of tale and elevated them to the extraordinary status they have come to occupy in the Western tradition.

By the time he becomes a character in the Christian story, then, the presence of the adversary is enough to align that story with other and comparable myths of the ancient world. But the narrative pattern of a combat between hero and adversary is by no means confined to myths, and indeed the earliest story in which we find a predecessor of the Satan figure, the Sumerian poem about Gilgamesh and Huwawa, would be in folklorists' terms a legend. In fact, most heroic poems fit the category of legend, in that they take place in a time when the world was much as it is now, and are told about figures believed to have lived in the recent past rather than in the mythological time of the beginnings. In the Gilgamesh texts, gods are present and indeed take decisive action, as in the Homeric epics, yet the principal interest of the narrative lies in the exploits of the (mostly) human heroes. Like Achilles, Gilgamesh is, in some variants, of partially divine parentage (two-thirds, in fact, a biologically curious anomaly), yet the Gilgamesh poems do not seem to have played a special role in religious life. The narrative is akin to myth in its concern with the well-being of the people and the establishment of orderly life, yet it shares also the common folktale characteristics of the difficult journey, the cleverness of the hero, a mysterious sleep, and magical helpers. Such incidents can, of course, occur in various kinds of narrative, as in the gospels.

What connects them is a narrative pattern or paradigm that persists from the time of our earliest records,[26] whether its particular form is a

---

[26] For the ontological questions raised by the persistence of patterns of this kind, see the discussion in Dundes 1977:12, 45–46, 80–83. See also Dundes' introduction to Propp 1968:xiv. Most of the narratives I here consider were brought together by those British and American myth-ritualists, followers at one or more remove of Sir James Frazer, who found seasonal conflict and vegetation rites wherever they looked. Some of this work (e.g., Frazer 1919 or Gaster 1961) has been widely influential and continues to be cited in such disciplines as psychology or literary criticism. In a general way, these scholars were Proppians before Propp (see Appendix), in that their ideas of a four- or five-act structure for *dromena* or *legomena* depend on a similar idea of narrative sequence. But their underlying historical premises, especially the notion of forgotten links with "primitive" ritual, have not worn well and lack the essential Proppian concept of "function."

Another group of thinkers, mainly theologians, have also made quasi-formalist arguments about ancient combat narratives and are clearly influenced by the myth-ritual school. See Ricoeur 1967 and Anderson 1967, books that share, in different ways, the ethnocentric view of primitive or early Near Eastern myth as ritual-based. Although they analyze many of the narratives here considered as if they are all concerned with cosmogony, both books are very useful and both make the connection with the Christian Satan.

On the myth-ritual school, see Kluckhohn 1942, Bascom 1957, and Fontenrose 1966. For its application to ancient Near Eastern myths, and for the four-act structure theory, see esp.

myth-poem sung or chanted at a religious festival, like the Babylonian *Enuma Eliš*, a secular hero-legend composed at court for the glorification of the king like the various Gilgamesh poems, a widespread folktale like the story of the Dragon-Slayer,[27] or a subject of learned theological dispute. The pattern persists because the tradition we are following is continuous, despite major historical and cultural shifts, and because the story of the adversary, whatever its local form, answers a basic human need—to cope with anxiety by telling ourselves stories in which the *archē* or origin of the anxiety may be located and defined and so controlled.

The closer we get to the sources upon which our study is based, the harder it becomes to discern any such entity as those to which we sometimes refer—"*the* story," "*the* combat myth," "*the* Christian narrative," or indeed even "Christianity." In the later parts of this book especially, we shall often seem to be exploring nothing but a confusion of sects, orthodoxies, and heresies replacing each other with bewildering rapidity, all competing with each other to offer the one true version of the central myth, and none ever quite succeeding in imposing itself upon the whole of the *soi-disant* world of Christendom. But the general historical perspective from which we approach the world of the New Testament and the church fathers will help us to see the local quarrels of the early churches as the continuation of a historical process with a very long past in the mythologies of the ancient world. From a certain critical distance we may perceive a narrative paradigm within the broad structural limits of which the variants take their places.

Christianity was at first one among several apocalyptic sects, and it is in the battle myth of apocalyptic thinking that we find the clearest echoes of Near Eastern mythology. One of the chief characteristics of Jewish apocalyptic literature is the revival, both during and after the exile, of ancient mythological modes of thought. Some of these mythological modes were no doubt learned fresh in Babylon itself, or borrowed from the successive oppressors, Persian, Greek, and Roman, but for the most part they had come from Canaanite sources and had been carried, whether as allusion or metaphor, within the sacred texts of Judaism itself. Those sacred scriptures must now be seen in the whole context, made available by the archaeologists, of ancient Near Eastern mythological systems. From these

---

Gaster 1961 and Hooke 1958 and 1963. The beginnings of the theory are found in W. Robertson Smith 1889. Examples of the continuing influence of the school, apart from Ricoeur and Anderson, include N. Frye 1957, an enormously influential book among literary critics, and Jungian myth analyses, such as Henderson and Oakes 1963.

[27] Aarne and Thompson 1964, Type 300. Cf. S. Thompson 1946:23–35. See Appendix.

ancient systems, a continuous series of transformations leads to the various Christian efforts to tell the story of Christ's struggle with Satan.

The texts we have to consult are of many kinds—clay tablets containing the verse narratives or "epics" of the ancient Near East; the biblical documents themselves; noncanonical works of the Jewish and Christian traditions, whether preserved from antiquity in such languages as Syriac or Coptic or newly available through archaeological finds like the Dead Sea Scrolls or the Nag Hammadi library; and finally the works of the early Christian theologians, culminating with Augustine. They may well seem to fall into two basic categories, according to whether they tell or interpret the stories: either they are mythology or theology. In fact, however, this is a misleading distinction, fostered both by the prominence of theology and by the mistrust of myth within the Christian tradition. In the Jewish tradition there is an intermediate category, known as midrash, in which a given tale is interpreted not by explicit commentary, like the works of the church fathers, but by retelling, often with long and free interpolations or alterations. A good deal of the story of Satan is contained in this kind of midrash. Even when the fathers of the church go to work to interpret the biblical texts, they often do so by retelling the story in such a way as to refute a rival version. In practice, then, theology is often a kind of narrative, even when disguised as hermeneutics. Conversely, the art of traditional narrative itself is always the interpretation and adaptation of previous stories. Theology merely extends the inherent potential of narration by incorporating deliberate exegesis into its structure.

It frequently happens, in fact, that the theologians of the early church are driven to invent, to rediscover, or simply to reintroduce stories that are implied by, but not actually told in, the biblical documents they are supposedly expounding. The various books of Enoch, for example, were not, finally, canonized by the Western church, but several of the narratives about a rebel angel which were thereby excluded from the canon reappear in the commentaries on Isaiah or Ezekiel of an Origen or a Tertullian and thus became part of the Christian tradition. So even when he is the subject of a learned discourse, Satan remains a narrative character, and the effort to understand him produces a retelling of his story.

For the most part, Satan was conceived not as a context-free repository of various beliefs but as an active character in a drama that was still unfinished and in which everyone was an actor. Satan was an agent in a myth, and the object of the church fathers' intellectual efforts was to ensure that the myth made good narrative as well as theological sense. So we find

such men as Irenaeus, Origen, or Augustine doing what Aristotle had rec-
ommended for the Greek dramatist. Only when the separate incidents are
arranged into a unified *mythos* is the inner meaning of the imitated action
revealed. The complex cosmological systems of the fathers are in essence
elaborations of that basic plot whose structure had been proved through
countless transformations, the myth of combat with a supernatural adversary.

The narrative interests of these theologians are perhaps most clearly revealed when they discuss the apparently philosophical problem of the origin of evil. What they tried to do was to find narrative answers, to construct a story that would situate the devil in time and so explain their own
relations to him and to his adversary, God. Here, for example, is Lactantius repeating a variant of the divine brothers motif (one that we also find
in the stories of Cain and Abel or of Jacob and Esau) and thus accounting
for evil.

> Before creating the world, God the Father produced a spirit similar to him-
> self and filled with his virtues. He then made another on whom the mark of
> divine origin did not remain. For he was tainted with the poison of jealousy
> and thus passed from good to evil by his own will. . . . He is the black fount
> of all evils. For he was jealous of his elder brother who, remaining attached
> to God the Father, obtained his affection. This being who, from the good
> which he was, became evil, is called Devil by the Greeks.[28]

Lactantius may not be the most intellectually stimulating of the fathers,
but we also find Augustine following similar methods.

Most of Augustine's theology takes the form, at either first or second
remove, of the interpretation of biblical texts long canonized. His goal
was to construct (or rather to discover after God constructed) a theological system that would answer and outdo the rival systems abroad at the
time. For reasons we shall explore later, the devil had to play a major role
in this system, and yet Augustine was faced, as many before and after have
been faced, with the problem that the Bible says very little about the devil,
and that mostly obscure and allusive. Furthermore, texts which did apparently mention the devil—far more of them than a modern commen-
tator would consider—seemed to give contradictory informtion about
him. Augustine, for example, thought that Ezekiel 28 was essentially
about the devil, though its manifest subject was the Prince of Tyre. At one

[28] Lactantius, *Divine Institutes* 2.9.3–5. See discussion in Turmel 1929:4, Hartwell
1929:186, and J. B. Russell 1981:56, 149–59. See also below, Chapter 22.1.

point Ezekiel says: "Thou hast been in Eden the garden of God. . . . Thou wast upon the holy mountain of God. . . . Thou wast perfect in thy ways . . . , till iniquity was found in thee" (28.13–15, KJV). Like many before him, Augustine took this to be a reference to the fall of the angels from heaven, an apocryphal narrative with thin biblical support. Yet the narrative would have posed fewer problems of interpretation had there not been another text, in John's gospel, that appeared flatly to contradict it. John says, "[The devil] was a murderer from the beginning, and abode not in the truth, because there is no truth in him" (8:44, KJV). Did the devil, or didn't he, enjoy the blessed life of an angel before he fell? The issue was of some importance, because if John were right the devil must have been created as a murderer and a liar, and that would impute the creation of evil to God, a conclusion that Christians from Paul on have generally tried to avoid, often with some slippery arguments. Augustine vacillated on the point, now taking John to be right and so interpreting Ezekiel to fit it, now taking Ezekiel to be right, with John the text to be wrestled down. Ultimately, the Ezekiel text would win out, and Augustine would go into extraordinary linguistic and logical contortions to reveal the meaning of John's dangerously loose form of words. But what concerns us here is that Augustine's argument about this cardinal point of doctrine is really an argument about a narrative, about what he plainly took to be two different versions of the same narrative which had somehow to be reconciled. And since he did not have the freedom of the literary critic to accept both versions of the narrative, he was forced in the end to tell his own version of the story, in the guise of interpreting Genesis 1.3 about the separation of light from darkness on the second day. Thus doctrine, as the interpretation of narrative, becomes in turn a new narrative.

It was not only as a theologian, however, that Augustine could not allow himself the freedom of a modern literary critic simply to compare, without reconciling, what he took to be two versions of the same narrative. No storyteller with certain deliberate exceptions like Sterne can allow himself that freedom. Unless you are a postmodernist, you cannot tell a story and allow for this indeterminacy: the oral singers of tales, even when denouncing their rivals, generally insist that this is *the* version, that it is the same as other versions, even if it is better.[29] The conventions of narrative are too strong: one thing happens, and then another thing becomes possible or probable, and finally certain once it is related in the

[29] Lord 1965:28–29. See Chapter 1, nn. 3, 49, 50, and Appendix.

story. This is the way it happened. The certainty of narrative about this is so strong, indeed, that we owe the notion of fate to analogy with the shape of narrative inevitability; one projects onto the cosmos the shape that personal events have achieved once they become narrative events, once the tale is told. In a Christian context, as we shall see in Augustine's *Confessions*, God is understood as the ultimate author of this narrative reasonableness.

Paradoxically, however, this power that we accord to the shape of narrative means that traditional stories must change. In spite of the insistence of the theologian or a singer of tales that it is the same old story, it never is. For stories, especially the life-forming important stories, are always being interpreted, not simply told. As tales travel and time passes, gaps appear in the plausibility and accessibility of the tale, gaps that need to be filled in the new telling, and the new version exposes fresh gaps, and so on.[30] Traditional narratives generate their own variants by the process of telling and responding to tales which is always at work. And writing does not freeze this process, even though the compilers and defenders of the canon need to think that it does.

"Why did he do that?" we ask about characters in stories, and the answer will change quite radically as ideas of what motivates people and gods change. In the Genesis flood myth, for example, Yahweh loses patience with the moral degeneracy he sees on earth, but in the Babylonian predecessor, contained in the *Atrahasis* epic, the senior gods, like irritable parents, decide that mankind is making too much noise. The result in both cases is the deluge, but its agent has different motives. The answer to the question of what makes a character act as he does may also take the form of an expanded story, even the mixing of one plot with another. In later versions of the flood myth, man's rebellious nature is incited by angelic beings who are themselves corrupted by lust for women. This story, a typical midrash on the terse biblical phrases about how "the sons of God saw the daughters of men that they were fair," as the King James Version puts it (Gen. 6.2), is in turn the context in which the story of the rebellious angel first develops.

Of the puzzles posed by the combat narratives, the question of the villain's motivation has generally been the most fruitful in generating new stories. Judas the Betrayer does it for money in Mark and Matthew, but in Luke and John, Satan prompts him. This in turn poses the question

[30] Kermode 1979:81–99; J. A. Sanders 1981.

about Satan's own reasons for acting, and the solutions were several parallel elaborations of the basic combat pattern in both the Jewish tradition and the Christian tradition. The ideas of lust, envy, or pride were each attached to different narratives, often curiously combined.

External pressures are also at work in the process of narrative change. New social conditions require fresh versions of stories, whether because an alien tale needs to be adapted to local conditions, or because an old story is no longer fully understood. The rise of kingship is an obvious instance of this kind of pressure, and indeed has much to do with the popularity of combat myths in general. The local king, or his supporting god, becomes the new name of the hero. Ninurta becomes Marduk becomes Assur as empires succeed each other in Mesopotamia and Syria, and the Davidic kingship seems to have encouraged the combination of Canaanite battle myths and the Israelite tradition of Exodus. The characteristics of the hero's adversary are also suitably adapted, so that Red Sea and Egyptian pharaoh combine in the mythical enemy Rahab.

Usually the external and internal pressures for change work together. The narrative and theological problem of the origin of evil in a perfect universe, or from a benevolent God, threatens to pose an internal contradiction in the plot, but it is also affected by struggles between rival religious groups. Puzzling out a coherent answer to such a question would satisfy the self-respect, or perhaps the God-respect, of the storyteller, but it could also serve to trounce the heretical version. Tertullian complains that "the question of the origin of evil" was a favorite preoccupation of heretics,[31] yet "orthodox" theologians have rarely been able to ignore it—among them Tertullian.

Christianity extends in its own special ways the narrative traditions of the ancient world, and this book is as much concerned with the epic poetry of the ancient Near East, in which most of the relevant narratives are told, as with the emerging Christian system. We follow the basic plot of the combat narrative from our earliest surviving examples in the Gilgamesh tradition, on into the various mythological systems of the Near Eastern world and their Greek counterparts, then into the Hebrew scriptures. The most important links are those uncovered by the archaeological exploration of Ras Shamra in modern Syria, the ancient city of Ugarit, where various Semitic as well as Indo-European speaking cultures jostled each other and exchanged ideas and stories in a metropolis that must have

[31] Tertullian, *Adversus Marcionem* 1.2.1–2. See below, Chapter 13.

been something like Dickensian London or modern Marseilles. The next section of the book concentrates on the growth of the apocalyptic movement in Judaism, following the Babylonian exile. This is the context in which a character named Satan first begins to appear, although the main records are in documents that were not canonized either by Jewish or Western Christian authorities, and so tended to disappear from the central traditions of Western Christendom. Some survived elsewhere, especially in the various books of Enoch, whether in Ethiopic or Greek translations, and have had continuing impact on subsidiary or other local forms of Christianity, particularly in the Slavonic churches. These books are especially important for the story of the Satanic rebel and help to clarify much that is otherwise obscure in the New Testament and the church fathers. Recent scholarship, such as the work of J. T. Milik on the Aramaic fragments of the Dead Sea Scrolls, and also new understanding of the Slavonic material,[32] make the separate historical stages in the development of the Satan story much clearer; indeed, in some respects, all previously published accounts of this development are simply wrong. The final sections of the book take the history of Satan on into the quarreling sects of the early Christian centuries. Again, new archaeological discoveries have made important changes in the overall picture. The Gnostic library of Nag Hammadi has helped us see how important were the struggles of what came to be called "orthodoxy" and "heresy" for the growth of the Satan myth. It was in this context, for example, that he became the father of lies, the arch-heretic. Doctrinal adversaries were inspired by the narrative adversary, and this link in turn led to fresh versions of biblical narrative, especially in the work of Origen and Augustine.

One result of the constant transformation of old into new stories is that, if we study a long enough historical span, the more recent versions will be unrecognizable to the first storytellers and their audiences. Without a knowledge of the intervening modifications, one might not notice the relation of Satan to the old Sumerian enemy, Huwawa.

[32] Milik 1976:308. See below, Chapter 12.8.

Part One

ANCIENT ENEMIES

ONE

HUWAWA AND GILGAMESH

To the english ear at least, Huwawa (or Humbaba) is a splendid name for a monster:

> To safeguard the Cedar Forest,
> As a terror to mortals has Enlil appointed him:
> Humbaba—his roaring is the flood-storm,
> His mouth is fire, his breath is death.[1]

Roaring floodwaters, a dragon, guardian of the sacred cedar trees, and bringer of death—such is Gilgamesh's great adversary. All these characteristics persist in the combat myth tradition in connection with many other enemies than Huwawa and recur in modified form with the Christian Satan.

These lines also pose several scholarly problems. They occur in the late Assyrian version of the Gilgamesh epic, but the fourth line has to be restored from a Neo-Babylonian fragment.[2] The initial words of the first two lines are also found on the Yale tablet of the Old Babylonian version, but the rest of the lines there are illegible. The same lines (though not always together) occur at least three times in that version, which suggests that they are formulaic and raises the question whether the Gilgamesh epic, like the Homeric, is a product of oral composition, and if so of what kind.[3] Similar lines, including the dragon and flood ideas, but adding that

---

[1] ANET 79, Assyrian version II v; cf. Old Babylonian III, iii, 18–20. ANET is Pritchard 1969, in which E. A. Speiser's translation of the various Babylonian fragments is the most accessible text. The standard edition in English is R. C. Thompson 1930, but Professor Aaron Shaffer of Jerusalem is preparing a new edition of all the Gilgamesh material. *Humbaba* is the Assyrian form, *Huwawa* the Sumerian and Old Babylonian, while the Hittite is *Hibibi*. An earlier version of this chapter is Forsyth 1981.

[2] On these problems, see Heidel 1949:1–16, Garelli (ed.) 1960, Jacobsen 1976:195–219, and Tigay 1977 and 1982.

[3] Falkenstein 1960; Alster 1972, 1975. Cf. Oppenheim 1964:252–62. The conventional approach is exemplified by Johannes M. Renger in Oinas (ed.) 1978. In a book otherwise packed with discussions of oral epic theory and folklore methods, Renger's contribution alone shows no knowledge of either subject. Instead, he merely asks of Mesopotamian epics, "Were they written and recited for pure entertainment, or did they have other functions?" (p. 37), at best a naive question. For a critical review of approaches to oral poetry in general, see Finnegan 1977 and Ong 1982. See below, nn. 49 and 50, and Appendix.

"his face is the face of a lion,"[4] also appear in the earliest version, a Sumerian poem, which dates from some 1,500 years earlier than the Assyrian text. What is the connection? These are actually elementary forms of the difficulties that regularly face those who try to reconstruct ancient Near Eastern narratives, and similar problems, relegated where possible to footnotes, will crop up again and again as we piece our picture together.

There are good reasons for beginning our study with Huwawa, although they are not those that led an earlier generation of scholars and enthusiasts to compare the Gilgamesh cycle with Judeo-Christian narratives. It is true that Gilgamesh is a god-man who tries to overcome death, that he tries to do so by liberating his people from a monstrous tyrant, that he collects companions to help him, and that after death Gilgamesh lives on as a figure of worship. Such similarities are suggestive, but usually rather vague. The only parallel that retains any clear historical significance is the close connection between the biblical flood myth and the story of Utnapishtim on the eleventh tablet of the Babylonian epic.[5]

By contrast, the relation that concerns us here, that of Huwawa to Satan, has not received any attention. There is a demonstrable connection, though of a rather indirect and complex kind which will take a good deal of argument to unravel. The clearest tangible link is probably the discovery of the names Gilgamesh and Humbaba among the Aramaic fragments of the Dead Sea Scrolls. To this we might add the fragment of the Gilgamesh epic itself that was unearthed at Megiddo in Palestine.[6] Jews had daily contact with Babylonian tradition during the exile, but by then the stories about Gilgamesh had spread to many other cultures, and via Hittite variants were known to Indo-European speakers as well as Semites. Gilgamesh, in fact, was still a familiar name in the Roman period.[7]

For the moment, however, it is not the putative historical links that chiefly interest us. Rather, since the Gilgamesh stories had enormous impact on the cultures of the ancient Near East, as the evidence of art as well as literature attests, these popular tales provide, first, an excellent way to get a feel for the ancient narrative traditions. Second, the way the ingre-

---

[4] Kramer 1947:17, line 100. See below, n. 11.

[5] Heidel 1949:137–269, a skeptical and one-sided survey. On the flood, see Kilmer 1972, Lambert and Millard 1969, Mallowan 1964, and Fontenrose 1945.

[6] Milik 1976:313. Schofield in Thomas (ed.) 1967:319 dates the fragment to Stratum VIII, 1550–1150 B.C., when Megiddo was under Canaanite and Egyptian control.

[7] Heidel 1949:4. See below.

dients of Gilgamesh tradition, including the early Sumerian poems, were brought together into the longer and more complex Babylonian epic offers an instructive case study of how traditional tales can change and be incorporated into larger narrative structures. Third, this process provides illuminating parallels with the efforts of various Christian interpreters to mold a coherent mythology out of originally disparate elements, something we shall be looking at closely later on.[8] Fourth, the story of Gilgamesh and Huwawa is an early example of the kind of narrative that informs Christian belief. It has many parallels and analogues, both in the ancient world and in such apparently unrelated contexts as the medieval quest of Seth for the oil of mercy,[9] and it will help us to see how the structure of such tales persists across diverse and widely separated cultures. Finally, since it is probably the oldest combat narrative we possess,[10] it will bring us as close as we are ever likely to get to the beginning of the Adversary's history. For what mainly counts here, as with Satan later, is the function of Huwawa as a supernatural adversary, which is the essence of his role in the plot.

In barest outline, the plot of the Sumerian poem is as follows. Gilgamesh and his companions go on a long journey to the land of the cedar forests; they meet and finally kill the monster Huwawa, who had been appointed guardian of the trees by the high god Enlil himself. The heroes take the severed head of Huwawa in triumph to Enlil, but find themselves reprimanded or cursed for violating the god's domain. If this is in fact how the story went—and there are missing, indecipherable, or problematic lines at crucial places—then it is not only the first combat narrative but also the first use of conventional folktale plot-structure to produce a heroic poem of different, even tragic, implications.

1. The Gilgamesh Tradition

"Gilgamesh and Huwawa"[11] is one of several separate Sumerian poems about Gilgamesh, poems that go back at least to the accession of the Third

---

[8] See below, Chapters 19, 21, and 25.

[9] Quinn 1962:21–24. See below, Chapter 12.

[10] "Gilgamesh and Agga" may be older, but it does not fit the pattern discussed here. See Kramer 1949 and Kramer 1959:192; but cf. Limet 1972.

[11] Kramer 1947 is still the only edition. He has twice published slightly revised translations in Kramer 1959 and in ANET 48–50. Line numbers in the text correspond to ANET. Other texts and fragments have been published in the interim, esp. by Van Dijk in Garelli (ed.) 1960:69–81. See now Shaffer 1984.

Dynasty of Ur, around 2100 B.C. The kings of this brilliant dynasty, builders of ziggurats, also cultivated the arts, especially those that would bolster their own rule. Gilgamesh they claimed as the most glorious of their own ancestors, and we probably owe the Gilgamesh poems, the oldest known literature, to the court poets of this period.

Gilgamesh himself seems to have been a historical king of Uruk (biblical Erech) between 2700 and 2600. Indeed, some of the personages associated with Gilgamesh in the poems are attested by contemporary inscriptions, and the custom of burying a ruler's court with him, implied by the poem "The Death of Gilgamesh," is evident in the Royal Tombs of Ur but was abandoned thereafter.[12] The Gilgamesh tradition must have developed very soon, for we have funerary offerings dedicated around 2400 at a sacred place called "The River Bank of Gilgamesh." According to a recent analysis of the Gilgamesh material, he was soon credited both with an extraordinary military ability and with great magical powers to ensure fertility and plenty. He was exceptionally good, that is, at both the magical and the military aspects of the office of *en*, the priest-king.[13] Some of the surviving narratives laud his role as liberator of his people from political dependence or as builder of the walls of Uruk; others represent him as the powerful judge in the land of the dead or as able to protect against ghosts and other evils. Some laments even mention him as a form of the dying god, Dumuzi. Both aspects of the Gilgamesh tradition must have been carried orally, in heroic song, in legend, and in religious belief, before the court poets composed the versions of the narratives that have survived for the archaeologist's spade. No doubt the oral and literary traditions continued to influence each other, until Gilgamesh became the hero of the Old Babylonian epic, perhaps 1600 B.C.[14]

The story of Gilgamesh's struggle with the monster Huwawa survives in several versions and in various languages. There are considerable differences between these versions, especially between the Sumerian and Semitic sources on the one hand, and the Indo-European Hittite version on the other. Such differences are hard to explain by the more conventional kind of scholarship with its pronounced literary bias. It is now becoming clear, however, that each of the major cultures of the ancient Near East had its own highly developed tradition of epic song and that there was

---

[12] W. G. Lambert in Garelli (ed.) 1960:49–50.

[13] Jacobsen 1976:209–11 and n. 347.

[14] Jacobsen 1976:195, 257 n. 340; Tigay 1977 and 1982.

considerable influence and overlapping among them. Even in its oldest Sumerian form, the poem here called simply "Gilgamesh and Huwawa" survives in at least two versions, one considerably longer than the other. It is the long form we follow here.[15]

Combat narratives generally begin with a motivating incident, or at least some statement of the fundamental situation. What this will be depends on the detail and mood of the story that follows, and there is considerable variety among the possibilities, which Propp baldly labeled either "Lack" or "Villainy."[16] Different versions of our Gilgamesh story illustrate most of the possibilities and also some of the difficulties of interpretation.

In the Sumerian poem, the initial situation fits Propp's "Lack" function well. Aware that he has not yet made a name for himself, Gilgamesh tells his servant Enkidu of his plan to go to the cedar forest. This forest is clearly a magical place, and it is also known as "the Land of the Living," or simply "the Land," or even, because it is where Huwawa lives, as "the Mountain Where the 'Man' Dwelt."[17] Enkidu advises Gilgamesh to inform Utu, the sun god, who has charge of the cedar country, and so Gilgamesh makes sacrifice and appeals to Utu to be his ally. Death will come to Gilgamesh, as to all men, he says, and he wants to raise up his name in "the Land" before he dies. But in his speech Gilgamesh also seems to offer Utu a different motive for his project:

> In my city man dies, oppressed is the heart,
> Man perishes, heavy is the heart,
> I peered over[?] the wall,
> Saw the dead bodies . . . floating on[?] the river;
> As for me, I too will be served thus; verily tis so.[18]

These words seem to refer not simply to death in general but to some catastrophe that has afflicted the city and caused dead bodies to float down the river. Perhaps this is no more than a vivid picture of death, yet the

---

[15] Van Dijk in Garelli (ed.) 1960:69–81, supplementing Kramer 1947. The Van Dijk text is from Larsa Senkereh; Kramer's, a "composite," is based on tablets from various sites. See below, nn. 49, 50, and Appendix.

[16] See Appendix and Dundes 1962b.

[17] Jacobsen 1976:197. On the meaning of *kur*, see the forthcoming Geneva dissertation of Françoise Bruschweiler.

[18] ANET 48, trans. Kramer.

words imply a more specific motivation than the desire for fame: a need to rid the city of its oppression. Huwawa, however, is not yet mentioned.

In the very late Assyrian version, on the other hand, Huwawa's villainy is the explicit reason for the expedition to the cedar forest. There Gilgamesh says to Enkidu:

> In the forest resides fierce Huwawa.
> Let us, me and thee, slay him,
> That all evil from the land we may banish.[19]

By this time, then, Huwawa has become the "devastating monster" or the "death-dealing demon" who is so common a figure in combat myth and folktale,[20] and his depredations are the motive for the journey to his land. This might suggest a clear progression from the earliest to the latest versions of the story: explicit "Villainy" gradually replaces "Lack" as the motivating incident. Unfortunately, the situation is a good deal more complicated.

For one thing, the words quoted from the late Assyrian version probably also occurred in the Old Babylonian epic, on which the Assyrian text is based.[21] The tablet is damaged at this point, so we cannot be sure, but Speiser follows Schott in restoring these words to the Old Babylonian text. Furthermore, Gilgamesh's speech to Utu in the Sumerian poem already implies something like the villainy of the later epic. Propp's "Lack" and "Villainy" are alternatives for the motivating function, but our Gilgamesh story suggests that they can coexist in the same tale: each version has some of each—both desire for a heroic reputation, and the monster's "evil." Which one is emphasized depends on how the rest of the story

---

[19] Speiser in ANET 79 and n. 65. See esp. Tigay 1982:79.

[20] Fontenrose 1959:10, and below, n. 58.

[21] We assume the following dates: Sumerian 2100 B.C., Old Babylonian epic 1600 B.C., Assyrian recension 1100 B.C. See Jacobsen 1976:195 and Matous in Garelli (ed.) 1960:83–94. The terminology may be confusing to the uninitiated. *Sumerian* is a non-Semitic language with no known congeners, gradually displaced by the Babylonian conquerors. The spoken languages of Mesopotamia subsequently were various, but the most widespread is called *Babylonian*, soon divided into a southern dialect, *Akkadian*, and a northern, *Assyrian*. The language of the epic texts is special dialect of Akkadian, also called "standard Babylonian," but differing from the spoken forms. In this respect, it is like the Homeric dialect and preserved many archaic forms. The "Assyrian" recension of the Gilgamesh epic is so called because it comes from Ashurbanipal's library at Nineveh, but it is a copy of a version in the standard Babylonian or literary dialect, made around 1100 B.C. by one Sin-liqi-unninni. It was this text in which George Smith suddenly, one day at the British Museum in 1872, recognized the flood myth, a discovery that led him, so the story goes, to take off all his clothes, a rare enough event in the British Museum.

goes, and the Sumerian poem treats the heroes' motivation ironically, so that we come to view the stated motives with some distance. There is also a further motive, not yet stated, which the rest of the poem implies—the city's need for the timber that Huwawa protects.

It is as well, then, to distinguish between motive and the motivating incident, or initial situation. In the Sumerian poem, the lack of a heroic name dominates, and although Huwawa's activities are no doubt in the background, his villainy could not have been made so explicit: Gilgamesh himself does not know what faces him when he begins his quest for heroic status.

The initial situation has, at any rate, identified the hero, whose emergence is confirmed by the appeal to the sun god. Utu agrees to help in some way (a variant of the donor sequence), perhaps by putting seven weather demons at his disposal.[22] Gilgamesh then gathers fifty volunteers for the journey, supplying all with weapons. Apparently the companions now cross "the seven mountains" before Gilgamesh leads them to "the cedar of his heart." Gilgamesh then fells this tree, and the companions lop and trim the branches, piling them into heaps. This action seems to arouse Huwawa, the guardian of the trees, since he now appears to afflict Gilgamesh with a deep sleep, during which he dreams and from which someone (Enkidu?) barely succeeds in awakening him. These events may be a variant of a common sequence that involves the initial battle, defeat of the hero, enemy ascendant, hero recovers—itself an anticipatory form of the main combat sequence. Certainly the medium of the later conflict is attack and defense of the trees. It is not entirely clear, however, that this nightmare-filled sleep is Huwawa's doing, and it may simply represent the supernatural preparation of the psyche for the contest to follow. The episode clearly suggested to the Old Babylonian poet the magnificent dream sequence of the expanded epic—premonitory dreams that test the interpretive abilities of the heroes and probe their readiness—and there the dreams are merely preliminary to the main battle, not a variant of the champions' temporary defeat.[23]

The Sumerian poem now follows with a fully realized variant of the hero's initial defeat. After being awakened, Gilgamesh puts on like a gar-

---

[22] Kramer in Garelli (ed.) 1960:64, as against his earlier view. In Kramer's shorter and more fragmentary version, which he called B, Enki, the trickster god, is behind Gilgamesh's decision to travel to "the Land."

[23] On Gilgamesh's dreams, see Jacobsen 1976:200, who thinks that Enkidu rashly misinterprets as favorable omens what are in fact terrifying warnings of disaster.

ment his "word of heroism" and makes a bold speech about his determination to fight Huwawa. Enkidu tries to dissuade him, for he has seen Huwawa before, we now learn, and knows how formidable he is. But Gilgamesh urges him to put aside his fears. The effort to dissuade the hero from his task is another common feature of such encounters, a kind of initial test of his will. The result, however, is less than encouraging, for Huwawa spies the companions advancing and fastens upon them his "eye of death." At first Gilgamesh succumbs and is unable to move, "frozen with terror." Finally he manages to save himself by pretending that he has come not to fight but to get to know the mountains and to offer Huwawa his sisters in marriage.[24]

Clearly the champion has recovered himself by now, but the text is too uncertain for a reliable understanding of what happens next.[25] Where the text becomes legible again, we find the champions converting Huwawa's trees into lumber; once the seven trees have been lopped and bundled, Huwawa begs for mercy. Thereupon Gilgamesh is inclined to be merciful, but Enkidu, with what Jacobsen calls "peasant's distrust,"[26] urges that he be killed. Incensed at this, Huwawa replies angrily to Enkidu, who promptly cuts off his head. The illegible part of the text is clearly important for understanding this sequence, since here the battle is rejoined.[27] As the text stands, however, we cannot see exactly what happens, and there are two alternative possibilities: force or guile.

According to Jacobsen's interpretation, "Huwawa is taken in, divesting himself of his armor of rays of terror. Thus defenceless he is set upon by Gilgamesh, who smites and subdues him."[28] So Huwawa complies voluntarily with Gilgamesh's deceitful offer of his sisters, and the episode reads like one of the Stupid Ogre tales, reminiscent, for example, of the Polyphemus episode in the *Odyssey*.[29] Kramer, however, sees a genuine combat here and assimilates the scene to the more heroic tale-types of the Supernatural Adversary, which include the "Dragon-Slayer."[30] In his

---

[24] This summary is based upon my correspondence with Thorkild Jacobsen, to whom I am indebted for several points in this chapter.

[25] For differing views about the key Sumerian words, see Forsyth 1981:16, 27 n. 12.

[26] Jacobsen 1976:200.

[27] See Appendix.

[28] Jacobsen 1976:200.

[29] Aarne and Thompson 1964, Types 1000–1199. Cf. S. Thompson 1955–58, Motif G520, "Ogre Deceived into Self-Injury." On variants of the Polyphemus tale, see C. S. Brown 1966, Dion 1969, and Glenn 1971.

[30] Aarne and Thompson 1964, Types 300–399.

popular works he compares Gilgamesh and Hercules, and includes the
Huwawa tale in a chapter entitled "The First St. George."[31] This diver-
gence between two of the greatest Sumerologists is an interesting example
of the pressure of one's own assumptions about how such tales ought to
go, and it suggests how types and genres get mixed in the telling. The
Stupid Ogre and "Dragon-Slayer" types are similar in structure: the essential difference is simply the question of means—force or guile—either
of which fits the same narrative slot. Thus the same basic plot can generate
a trickster tale or a hero legend, and the Gilgamesh poem suggests elements of both.[32] This convergence of two tale types has interesting ramifications later, when we find the early interpreters of the Christian myth
arguing about whether the devil was deceived by Christ.

The crux of the matter in the Gilgamesh poem is the nature and source
of Huwawa's power. He is, we know, guardian of the sacred trees, and
we also know that when the companions arrive at Huwawa's
"chambre"[33] he has no weapons left: the trees have been cut down. This
implies that Huwawa's power lies somehow in the trees themselves. Perhaps Huwawa is a kind of personification of the great trees' resistance to
the axe, conceived as a magical radiance that he cannot (or will not) acti-
vate as the companions advance toward him. One of the Sumerian words
for this power is *ni-te*, whose root idea is probably something like
"glow," and thus the word comes to mean "self" or "aura."[34] The real
self of a supernatural creature is viewed as his radiance, that which has
power to immobilize or terrify human beings. Given the context, then,
Huwawa's self or his powers are the great trees he embodies and without
which he is forced to sue for mercy.[35] Thus the significance of the companions' persistence in cutting down the trees is finally clear, for this is the
actual medium of the conflict.

But how do the companions manage to immobilize Huwawa's power
and so cut the trees? Narrative analysis helps here also, for just as the companions attack the trees seven times, so we recall that Utu provided Gilgamesh with seven magical powers during the donor episode, and it is

[31] Kramer 1959:170–81; Kramer 1972:13.

[32] Propp 1968:99–100; Dundes 1962b:98–99.

[33] Van Dijk in Garelli (ed.) 1960:74.

[34] Wilson in Garelli (ed.) 1960:110; Oppenheim 1949. For a more extended discussion, see
Forsyth 1981:17–19, and now Shaffer 1984.

[35] Wilke 1969:98 n. 106 translates: "Er schenkte ihm [Var. streckte ihm entgegen] da-
ranfhim seine erste 'furcht,' " but adds that "die sieben *ni-te* Huwawas als Baume vorge-
stellt."

normally at this point, the combat itself, that the magic gifts from the donor are used. They are perhaps, as Kramer suggests, "the seven demons in charge of destructive weather phenomena," one of which seems to be lightning. We should thus have here a magical conflict conceived on the model of a storm god theophany.[36]

Unfortunately for a neat analysis, Utu's gifts do not seem to reappear at this point in the poem. Gilgamesh seems to have only his determination with which to confront Huwawa. The gifts of Utu may do no more than get the companions across the seven mountains. If so, then it seems as if the magical conflict, the cutting of the trees, takes place because Huwawa is deceived by Gilgamesh's deceitful offer and withdraws his radiance from the trees. We have then a story that has elements of both force and guile, but at the crucial moment Gilgamesh becomes like the trickster heroes of folktale, from Odysseus to the Anglo-Saxon Jack or the Russian Ivan, characters who outwit rather than defeat their Goliaths in pitched battle.[37]

In the subsequent tradition, however, a heroic encounter is suggested at this point. The Hittite version, probably here following the Old Babylonian, seems to collapse donor sequence, initial confrontation, and final combat into one. When Gilgamesh cuts down the first tree with his axe, Huwawa is alerted to the violation of his trees and gets angry, but Shamash, Babylonian equivalent of Utu, speaks encouragement from heaven and then attacks Huwawa with his mighty winds. Huwawa is immobilized and begs for mercy.[38] This time, then, the hint in the Sumerian poem that Utu's gifts might be useful for the attack on Huwawa is fully developed. Indeed, the sun god is now explicitly responsible for Gilgamesh's victory, and the model of a storm god theophany is clear.

The texts of the Babylonian epic are even more fragmentary at this point than the Sumerian. But its composer added a heroic doublet to the Huwawa episode, the slaughter of the Bull of Heaven. Ishtar, piqued by Gilgamesh's rejection of her charms in the earliest known variant of the Potiphar's wife tale, begs the Bull from the high god Anu and sends it against Uruk, where its snorts are enough to open pits in the ground, big enough for two hundred young men to fall into.[39] Again the battle scene

[36] Kramer in Garelli (ed.) 1960:64; Van Dijk in Garelli (ed.) 1960:74–76. See below, Chapter 4.

[37] See nn. 22 and 29, above.

[38] ANET 83, lines 21–26 (end of Tablet v).

[39] ANET 505. The Bull of Heaven episode is also based on a Sumerian poem; see Kramer

itself is too mutilated for decipherment, but it ends with a sword thrust twixt the Bull's neck and horns in proper bullfighting fashion. Gilgamesh and Enkidu (who has now graduated from servant to friend, like the Homeric Patroklos)[40] tear out the Bull's heart and present it to Shamash. Stupidly, however, Enkidu throws the Bull's right thigh in Ishtar's face, an insult that, coupled with the killing of Huwawa, leads eventually to Enkidu's death.[41] To judge from these two developments, then, it seems that the guile idea we find implied in the Sumerian poem has been suppressed in favor of a heroic battle with a monstrous creature.

According to our expectations of combat narratives, the next and concluding scene of the Sumerian poem ought to be the triumphant return of the heroes, with the reestablishment of order and peace. That is what Gilgamesh and Enkidu seem to expect as they go to visit Enlil, lord of heaven and king of the gods. Like the hero of the "Dragon-Slayer" folktale, they carry with them the severed head of the slain monster; they kiss the earth before the mighty god and unveil the head. But instead of congratulating them, Enlil is angry, and the heroes realize they have killed Enlil's own servant. The high god now transfers the seven powers, the *me-lam*, of Huwawa to other forces, to the flooding rivers, to a lion, to the mountain, and possibly to the dread goddess Nungal. The terrors persist, even when the monster, their temporary embodiment, is destroyed.[42] And Enlil further insists that Gilgamesh and Enkidu share a portion of their food and drink as an offering to Huwawa's ghost in the netherworld.

The sobering conclusion of the tale was not entirely unexpected before publication of the longer, more complete text, since Kramer already left open the possibility that Enkidu, at least, was brought to judgment before Enlil.[43] But the ending is certainly unusual if we base our expectations too squarely upon the folktale patterns. Like *King Lear*, the narrative evokes a pattern of expectations that are then deliberately violated by the tragic conclusion.[44] Any number of ancient narratives do end with the antici-

---

1959:190, Kramer 1947:45, Wilson in Garelli (ed.) 1960:108–11, Matous in Garelli (ed.) 1960:83–94, and Jacobsen 1976:195. See also below, nn. 50 and 51. On affinities between the Babylonian poem, the Heracles-Kyknos legend, and the Ugaritic Aqhat myth, see Fontenrose 1959:167–76, who discusses the Potiphar's wife motif (K2111 in S. Thompson 1955–58).

[40] Jacobsen 1976:214. On similarities with the *Iliad* (Enkidu/Patroklos), see Gresseth 1975, and on the similarities with the *Odyssey*, see Nagler 1977.

[41] ANET 85.

[42] Van Dijk in Garelli (ed.) 1960:78 n. 110.

[43] Kramer 1947:46 n. 253.

[44] *King Lear* is based on the "Love Like Salt" and "Cap o' Rushes" variants of the Cinder-

pated success and triumph. The best known is probably the Marduk myth told in the Babylonian *Enuma Eliš* epic, which ends with the celebration of Marduk's triumph and a long recital of his fifty powers. Even there, however, the monster Tiamat, chaos demoness and symbol of the primal waters, cannot be utterly destroyed, and the epic's conclusion also contains a prayer that her forces may somehow be kept back for another year.[45] The Huwawa tale has apparently no specific religious context, and so the singers no doubt felt freer to dwell on the ambivalent, even tragic, implications of the struggle with the adversary.

2. *Variants of the Huwawa Narrative*

There is a likely parallel to this plot structure in another of the Sumerian Gilgamesh poems. In our Huwawa poem the following lines are repeated seven times during the tree-cutting episode:

> The sons of his city who accompanied him
> Cut down its crown, bundle it,
> Lay it at the foot of the mountain.

The first words recur in the poem now known as "Gilgamesh, Enkidu, and the Nether World."[46] Gilgamesh agrees to help the goddess Inanna (Ishtar's Sumerian name) to get the wood of her special *huluppu* tree. She had planted the tree herself and had been waiting for it to grow so that she could use the wood to make herself a table and a bed, but she now finds she cannot get at the tree because it has become the home of various monsters—the Anzu-bird in the branches, a *lillu*-demon in the trunk, and the snake "who knows no charm" at the roots. Gilgamesh gallantly takes up arms for Inanna, including a special axe like the one he carries in the Huwawa poem, drives off the demon and the Anzu-bird, and kills the serpent. Then "the sons of his city who had accompanied him cut down its

---

ella pattern (Aarne and Thompson 1964, Types 923 and 510). In Type 923 the Cordelia figure is banished for saying she loves her father as fresh meat loves salt. Though the play thwarts the reconciliation of father and daughter which the plot anticipates, the play was rewritten in the eighteenth century by the notorious Nahum Tate to conform to the folktale expectations. See Briggs 1964:172 and Dundes 1976c.

[45] ANET 72, Tablet VII, lines 132–34.

[46] For a general description, see Kramer 1959:195–99, and for the text, see Kramer 1938. But see mainly Jacobsen 1976:212 (using Shaffer), followed here.

crown."[47] They then present the timber to Inanna, and Gilgamesh makes for himself a hockey stick and a puck out of the roots.

Again a sacred tree is protected by fearsome monsters, again Gilgamesh does battle with them, accompanied by men from his city, and again the conversion of the tree into items of culture entails unforeseen and tragic consequences. Gilgamesh's new playthings, the hockey stick and puck, fall into the underworld; Enkidu volunteers to get them back, but finds that he cannot return, except as a ghost.

To a student of oral poetry, this parallel will have great significance. Not only are the plots similar,[48] but the parallel verse suggests that the tree-cutting episode is formulaic, narrated in standard words in whatever context it happens to occur.[49] The two episodes look like variants of a traditional type-scene carrying its own formulaic language about the felling of sacred trees and its untoward consequences.

The Babylonian singer of the Gilgamesh epic[50] may also have noticed

---

[47] Kramer 1938:10, line 99 and n. 43.

[48] Fontenrose 1959:172 and 192, who also draws a parallel with the Egyptian tale of two brothers, in which Bata is killed by felling the cedar tree on which his heart lay. This is Motif E710, "External Soul," which may also fit Huwawa's case.

[49] One variant of the line in the Netherworld poem is identical to the line in the Huwawa narrative, but Kramer relegates it to his footnotes and implies that his "scribe G" was simply quoting inappropriately from the Huwawa poem (Kramer 1938:63 n. 132; cf. Wilson in Garelli [ed.] 1960:110). For another similar passage in two Sumerian poems, see Kramer 1947:45 n. 251. Again the passage occurs in only one variant of the Huwawa poem, and Kramer calls it "inserted." He may be right, but the argument smacks of the kind of editorial tinkering that bedeviled Homeric studies before the development of oral epic theory. For defense of such a suspected passage on grounds of oral composition, see Forsyth 1979. There are no doubt scribal errors, as in the transmission of Homeric manuscripts, but variants should not simply be excised in the interests of constructing a "correct" or "composite" text, however useful such may be in showing us generally how the story went. The edition of *Atrahasis* (Lambert and Millard 1969) is a model in this respect. Compare Alster 1972:130. See above, n. 3, and Appendix.

[50] The assumption that such an epic existed already in the Old Babylonian period, despite the lateness of any reasonably complete text (above, n. 21), is well argued by Tigay 1977 and supported by Shaffer. See Jacobsen 1976:257 n. 340. On the use of the term "epic," see Sasson 1972. There is no evidence that the separate Sumerian poems formed part of a longer epic before this period (Kramer 1959:193), but it needs to be remembered, in view of the strong probability of oral composition, that our evidence is necessarily limited to those versions that were written down; see above, n. 3. On the relation of oral to written forms, there is much more to be said than the Parry-Lord idea of "oral dictated texts" (Lord 1965), about which Hillers and McCall (1976) are rightly skeptical. Apart from Finnegan 1977:16–24 and 73–87 on the relation of memorization to composition, see especially Adam Parry 1971:i–lxx; and for a recent review, see Foley 1985. For the skepticism that prevails among Assyriologists, see Laessoe 1953, but contrast Falkenstein 1960, Alster 1972, and Berlin 1981. See also Appendix.

the parallel between these two Sumerian Gilgamesh tales, for he seems to
have woven together the two plots. The curse of Enlil, from the Huwawa
poem, leads ultimately to the death of Enkidu, from the *huluppu* tree
poem, and Enkidu's ghostly description of the underworld has become,
in the new epic, dream-like premonitions of his death. The new role of
Enkidu, as beloved friend rather than servant of Gilgamesh, is the key to
this Babylonian transformation of the Sumerian stories. Besides adding a
fresh motivation for the journey to the cedar forest, the friendship makes
Enkidu's death the central event, prepared by all that precedes it and the
occasion for what occupies the rest of the poem, Gilgamesh's grand but
futile quest for immortality. That quest, which takes him beyond the human world to his meeting with Utnapishtim, to a struggle with sleep, and
finally to an encounter with the serpent who steals the plant of youth, is
itself a transposition, from a major to a minor key, of the initial expedition
to the mysterious land of Huwawa, the death-demon. Indeed, the poem
turns on the ambivalence of the human attitude to death: Gilgamesh first
courts heroic death in battle and then seeks to avoid it altogether.[51] We
may see the outline of that later tragic figure in the Sumerian Gilgamesh
of the Huwawa poem, blind until too late to the real nature of the adventure he seeks.

[51] The structure of the Babylonian epic, ignoring the extraneous Tablet XII, is as follows:

I. Uruk: Enkidu introduction, fight and friendship	2. Siduri
	3. Boatman
II. Heroic combats	4. Utnapishtim (Sumerian source)
1. Huwawa (Sumerian source)	5. Vain struggle with sleep
2. Bull of Heaven (Sumerian source)	6. Plant of youth
III. Death of Enkidu (Sumerian source)	7. Serpent
IV. Quest for Immortality	V. Uruk: the city as the
1. Scorpion man	achievement

Cf. Kirk 1970:141–52, who makes sensible remarks about the nature-culture opposition
throughout the poem, borrowing Lévi-Straussian ideas, but does not ignore the narrative
sequence. See Sasson 1972 and Jacobsen 1976:207.

The standard account of the relation between Sumerian and Babylonian versions is Kramer 1944, repeated in 1959:182–99. See also Matous in Garelli (ed.) 1960:83–94, Jacobsen
1976:195–219, and Tigay 1982. Into the Babylonian epic four separate Sumerian poems, or
the oral traditions they represent, have been worked. Of these the flood story is unconnected
to Gilgamesh. The remaining three are blended together in II and III of the structure outlined
above. The Huwawa episode begins the sequence. Its central theme, the encounter with the
adversary, is then repeated in the Bull of Heaven story, and both contribute to the next
event, the death of Enkidu. The rest of the poem then takes up the same theme as Gilgamesh
tries to overcome his final adversary, death. Cf. Kirk 1970:147.

The composition of the Gilgamesh epic during the Old Babylonian period (early centuries of the second millennium B.C.) is only the most striking instance of the Babylonians' reverence for the culture of their Sumerian predecessors, similar in some respects to the Roman reverence for Greece. They adopted the cuneiform script and preserved in their schools the alien forms of the Sumerian language. But the Babylonians also adapted and often improved what they inherited. From the various Sumerian traditions about Gilgamesh, singers created an epic comparable to the Homeric poems in its beauty and profundity, and one only wishes we knew as much about the antecedents of Homer as we know through the Sumerian tablets about the early forms of the Gilgamesh cycle. These unknown singers of Babylon changed and invented much, but they were also faithful, as is the nature of oral epic singers, to the spirit of the Sumerian beginnings of the tradition, which had by then been carried in oral and written form for at least a thousand years. Just as the German heroic poems are concerned mainly with heroes of the Burgundians and the Goths, nations that had long disappeared, or the Anglo-Saxon Beowulf poem tells the story of one of the Geats from southern Sweden, setting the scene entirely in Scandinavia, so the hero of the greatest Babylonian poem belonged to a long-vanished polity, and his exploits were told in an already archaic language.

The popularity of the Gilgamesh tradition is clear from the number and variety of versions found. An Akkadian version was found at the Hittite capital, modern Bogazköy in Turkey, and versions exist also in the Hurrian and Hittite languages. A small fragment of the Akkadian version has also been found at Megiddo in Palestine, which raises the intriguing possibility that the poem was known to the singers of the various epics now incorporated into the Hebrew Bible.[52]

The existence of a Hittite version, dating from the middle of the second millennium, is especially significant. Not only does this mean that the tradition was known in an Indo-European language, and hence perhaps to other Indo-European speakers, like the Mycenaean Greeks, who had frequent commercial and political contact with the Hittite empire, but the Hittite version itself shows an interesting and significant variation. The Huwawa episode fills a large portion of the otherwise compressed narra-

---

[52] On the Hurrian and Hittite fragments, see ANET 85–86 and Otten in Garelli (ed.) 1960:139–43. On Megiddo, see above, n. 6.

tive. No doubt this was partly because the scene of Huwawa's "land" could easily be understood as Syria and Lebanon, the land of cedars (Greek *lebanon*, cedar), so the story had a certain local interest.[53] But this Hittite version also represents the Hurrian tradition (non-Indo-European predecessors of the Hittites, from whom they borrowed many tales) in which the actual hero of the narrative, even though the outcome is the same, was not Gilgamesh but the local Huwawa himself. In the Hittite version, for example, Huwawa helpfully offers to supply Gilgamesh with timber as part of his plea for mercy.[54] Such a transformation is not without parallel among traditional narratives: the story of Ingeld in *Beowulf* is told from the point of view of his enemies, but Saxo tells the same tale at length from the other side, and a reference in one of Alcuin's letters suggests that Ingeld was the hero of some vanished English poems. Similarly, the popular tale of Brynhild and Gudrun is told from opposite points of view in the *Thithreksaga* and the *Nibelungenlied*.[55] And it was not the English romantic poets who first made a hero out of Satan, for some Gnostic sects, calling themselves Ophites or Naasenes (names based respectively on the Greek and Hebrew words for serpent) had long preceded them.[56] Indeed, the ambivalence of the enemy figure is essential, as we have seen, to the Sumerian Huwawa; he is a monstrous adversary, yet his death calls down a curse on his slayers.

3. *Huwawa and His Trees: The Ambivalence of the Adversary*

> So architects do square and hew
> Green trees that in the forests grew
> —MARVELL, "A Dialogue of Soul and Body"

Now that we possess the sobering conclusion of the Huwawa narrative, we can make more of the curious ambivalence that surrounds the monsters and their trees in all these poems. The "huluppu tree" is sacred to Inanna—indeed, she planted it herself—yet when she wants the wood from it she finds it inhabited by awesome monsters. Though she gets the

---

[53] Hansen 1975 argues instead for Elam, but we should perhaps not try any harder to locate precisely Huwawa's forest than we should Polyphemus' cave or Calypso's island. However, Tablet v, line 13, of the Old Babylonian version says that "at Huwawa's noise Hermon and Lebanon [trembled]."

[54] Speiser in ANET 83, lines 21–26. See also Gurney 1954:180 and esp. Otten in Garelli (ed.) 1960.

[55] Chadwick and Chadwick 1932: vol. 1, 82; Hatto 1972:388.

[56] Förster (ed.) 1972: vol. 1, 84–99, 261–82; Jonas 1970:92–94.

wood through Gilgamesh's chivalry, the by-product of the wood, hockey implements, leads ultimately to Enkidu's death. Huwawa himself is both devastating monster and servant of Enlil.

Huwawa's ambivalence is best explained by his function as guardian of the trees. It is clear from the tale's ending that some especially sacrosanct quality attaches to these trees. That is why they are protected by a divinely appointed watchman. Yet the forests were one of the basic items in the economic systems of the Near East. Given the shortage of timber in the lowlands of Sumer itself, the forests of Lebanon and Syria to the northeast or of Elam to the west were valuable resources, and securing the timber routes was a constant preoccupation. Hence such kings as Gudea and Naram-Sin made so much of their "opening" of the forests in their royal inscriptions:

> Gudea, the great *en*-priest of Ningursu, made a path into the Cedar moun-
> tains which nobody had entered before; he cut its cedars with great axes.
> . . . Like giant snakes, cedars were floating down the river.[57]

In the Babylonian Gilgamesh epic, the need for wood to build up the city, especially the temple of Shamash, is a major reason for the journey to Hu-wawa's forest. And even in the Sumerian poem, Enkidu urges Gilgamesh to kill Huwawa by warning him that Huwawa will "block the mountain road, he will make the mountain paths impassable," a well-known characteristic of such monsters in myth and folktale,[58] but especially significant given the importance of the timber route. Van Dijk argued that Gilgamesh's journey reflects a kind of imperialist and missionary venture, the desire to establish Sumerian gods in barbarian territory,[59] and no doubt the participants and organizers of such expeditions could easily convince themselves of the importance of such motives. But the Sumerian and

---

[57] Roux 1966:154.

[58] Vana Dijk in Garelli (ed.) 1960:73, lines 90–91. See S. Thompson 1955–58, Motifs G346 and B11; Propp 1968, Functions 8.3, 8.19; and Fontenrose 1959:10, Theme 4f. On the "death-dealing demon," see also Motifs A310, A1111, B11.7.1, B16, E272, F402.1.2, F531.3.4.2, G317, G346, H541.1.1, and H1362, and compare A531, A928, and B11.11. The very length of this list shows the flaw in atomistic motif analysis like Thompson's, since all these categories fit Propp's structural function, "Villainy." See Armstrong in Maranda (ed.) 1972:173–93, and Dundes (ed.) 1965:207. For Huwawa's characteristics, see Kramer 1947:17, lines 100–105 (dragon, lion, flood, death) and 120 ("eye of death"). Compare the "Irra" creature of the Akkadian poem (Kramer [ed.] 1961:127) and the lion-serpent "Labbu" (Heidel 1963:141–42).

[59] Van Dijk in Garelli (ed.) 1960:80.

Babylonian kings probably understood well enough the political and economic advantages.[60]

There is an obvious paradox here, which has to do with the very basis of civilization, of living in cities. On the one hand, the wood from the trees is essential for economic well-being; on the other hand, the cutting of the trees is a violation of sacred territory. Though necessary for the great building programs of the third millennium, the trees of the ancient world were treated not simply as a "resource." They contained or represented the power of the gods, and in the basic fertility rituals of the earliest period were the focus of considerable reverence. Damu was one god who seems to have embodied the "power in the sap in trees and vegetation," and one ritual lament for him contains such lines as

> O you my tamarisk, fated not to
> drink water in its garden bed,
> whose top formed no foliage in the plain,
> my poplar, who rejoiced not at its water-conduit,
> my poplar torn up at the root:
> my vine fated not to drink water in the garden.

His mother laments him as "her provider" and goes searching for him. When she eventually finds him in the underworld, she addresses him as "my brother, luxuriantly sprouting in appearance, luxuriantly fruitful in appearance." In another song, his mother identifies herself as a cedar tree:

> My sides are cedar, my breast is cypress,
> O nurse, my limbs are sap-filled cedar,
> are sap-filled cedar, are of the Hashur mountains,
> are black wood of island Dilmun.[61]

These ancient rituals persisted well into the era of kingship and empire, and the songs that accompanied the rituals came to incorporate the places and names of the times. The composition from which we have just been quoting, for example, mentions Uruk and the temple of Eanna there and was probably sung at a sacred cedar tree in the temple compound marking the god Damu's birthplace. So the paradox of the trees was actually represented in the temple itself; around a sacred cedar representing the god was a temple constructed in part from the very substance of the god. The

[60] Hansen 1975; Vana Dijk in Garelli (ed.) 1960:77.
[61] Trans. Jacobsen 1976:63, 66–70, but my "sap-filled" for his "sappy."

temple was an effort to resolve the paradox, to use the wood for building yet restore its sacred character.

An illuminating Hittite text provides an excellent example of this paradox. It contains instructions for the ritual words to be spoken when the time comes to roof a new palace with timber, and almost the entire first column of the tablet is concerned with the business of procuring this timber, which is to come from the "Mountain where the Throne rules." First the king is to placate this "Throne" (probably the *genius loci*): "Stay thou behind the mountains! Thou must not become my rival, thou must not become my in-law! Remain my equal and my friend!" Then the king is to present his credentials and insist that he has been asking the storm god for the timber "which the rains have made strong and tall." There follows an address to the trees themselves:

> Under the heavens ye grew. The lion would rest beneath you, the panther would rest beneath you, the bear would hide in you. The Storm-god, my father, kept evil away from you. Cattle pastured beneath you, sheep pastured beneath you. Now I, the Labarnas, the King, have claimed my share of you. I hailed the Throne, my friend, and said: "Art thou not a friend of me, the king? Let me have that tree that I may cut it down!" And the Throne answers the King: "Cut it down, cut it down! The Sun-god and the Storm-god have placed it at thy disposal."
>
> Now come ye up from that country of yours! The Storm-god has placed you at the King's disposal. They will assign work to you. He will procure experts for you and they will pronounce charms over you.[62]

This text shows that the sacred quality of the tree itself will be preserved on its conversion to timber, since the gods have granted the king authority over it, have even been growing the tree strong and tall so that it may fulfill its royal purpose. But the text also reveals obvious anxiety about cutting down the tree, an anxiety that the ritual is designed to dispel.[63]

The ancient agricultural and fertility system was profoundly disturbed in the third millennium by the new institution of kingship and the organized state that it embodies.[64] War, victory, and defense of the state order become dominant motifs in art, and a new form of literature, the oral and then written epic, emerges to celebrate the powers of the ruler.[65] In these

[62] Trans. Goetze in ANET 357.

[63] Firth 1963 and esp. Homans 1941 and Kluckhohn 1942 all discuss the relation of anxiety and ritual, combining the insights of Freud and Malinowski.

[64] Service 1975; F. M. Cross 1973:219–64.

[65] Jacobsen 1976:79.

epics, a basic tension is obvious between the energetic, active powers of
the new rulers, gods and men, and the older "intransitive" forces of nature on which the earlier religion was based. The king of Aratta challenges
the will of Inanna with some success, and Gilgamesh himself defies her in
the story of the "Bull of Heaven."[66] In the poem to which we referred earlier, the death of Enkidu is ultimately caused by Gilgamesh's defiance of
the sun god, Utu, even though, in defying Utu, Gilgamesh champions
Inanna herself. Conflict, not seasonal change, is the stuff of the new literature. In a later narrative, *Atrahasis*, the lesser gods go on strike and riot
outside the palace of the ruler god Enlil.[67] This new epic genre is partly,
like Greek tragedy later, an effort to cope with rapid changes in social and
economic conditions, and the disruptions of the older established way.
Gilgamesh's adventure in the cedar forest is in this sense a typical product
of its period. It begins simply with the hero's urge to make a name for
himself, and this prompts his invasion and destruction of the ancient and
sacred land of the cedars.

As we have seen, however, there is more to this invasion than the uncomplicated desire for adventure. For one thing, the place where the cedars grow is called "the land of the living," a metaphor that suggests the
symbolic meaning of the trees as the power of growth in nature and so
implies that Gilgamesh's journey there is an effort to harness that power
in more than simply the economic sense. The "land of the living" may
actually mean, or allude to, Dilmun, the wooded island of eternal paradise, with which the tree god's mother associates herself in the song
quoted above.[68] The expedition to the cedar forest may represent, then, in
a rudimentary way, the quest for the source of extrahuman power that became so prominent a feature of the later Gilgamesh material. There was
certainly a need to unite, if possible, the power of ruler and the power of
nature.

Gilgamesh himself, in fact, is the chief cultural symbol of these two aspects of power, since he represented both the magical and the military aspects of the priest-king. In the Huwawa poem, for example, Gilgamesh
functions in both roles. He issues his followers weapons from the state armory, but he also takes along the power of the weather demons he receives from Utu.

As the tradition developed, we even find Gilgamesh in association with

[66] Kramer 1959:190.
[67] Lambert and Millard 1969:47–57. Cf. Finet (ed.) 1973.
[68] Kramer 1947:45 n. 252.

the tree god himself. In the same composition from which we quoted above, Damu is identified with Ningishzuda, "Lord of the Good Tree," and the song goes on to list the kings of Ur who became incarnations of the tree god after death, providers of food and drink and of the materials of culture (cattle pens, irrigation canals, etc.). In a lament that goes back at least to the beginning of the second millennium, we find Gilgamesh as a form of the dying god, Dumuzi and side by side with the tree god, Ningishzuda.[69] Such associations are suggestive because they help to fill out the context in which the adventures of Gilgamesh with various trees came to be understood.

It is not in Gilgamesh himself, however, but in the historical king Gudea of Lagash, that we find the actual identification of ruler and the "Lord of the Good Tree." Gudea's personal god was Ningishzuda, and he was told in a dream that the tree god would provide him with materials from all over the world to build the temple of Ningirsu, the god of Girsu, Gudea's capital city. Here, in Gudea's dream, is the ultimate blending of old and new notions to make a sacred temple that would itself be the symbol of that unity. It is not surprising, then, that in the inscription commemorating his great project Gudea should claim for himself the opening of the cedar forests which the tradition attributed to Gilgamesh's expedition against Huwawa: ". . . he cuts its cedar with great axes. . . ."[70] Clearly the Huwawa narrative represents an earlier form of this effort to resolve the basic paradox of tree as sacred and tree as timber.

A curious sympathy seems to develop between Gilgamesh and his enemy, the embodiment of this paradox. Huwawa's appeal for mercy is moving enough to elicit Gilgamesh's pity, and the long episode of hesitation about whether to kill him helps involve the heroes in the enemy's ambivalence. The heroic Gilgamesh would show mercy to his humbled enemy and so avoid, though he does not yet know it, Enlil's wrath. In fact, Enkidu's two warnings, the first to desist entirely and return home, the second not to spare the defeated enemy, emphasize the contrasting character of Gilgamesh. Like Roland's companion, Oliver, Enkidu here represents the voice of ordinary common sense, while the real hero has a different set of values, which mark him both for greatness and for tragedy. Foolhardy in the face of his companion's worldly anxieties, open and generous where others are suspicious and vengeful, he is also alert, in a

[69] Jacobsen 1976:69, 71, 209–11, and n. 347.
[70] Roux 1966:154. See above.

way his companion is not, to larger meanings. At the moment of crisis, Roland insists on blowing his Oliphant when Oliver would practice a foolish consistency. At the moment of their crisis, Enkidu acts as the conventional folktale hero, whereas Gilgamesh, seeing more in Huwawa than simply "the adversary," would be merciful, aware of their mysterious kinship.

The ambivalence of the adversary is a recurring feature of the ancient combat myths, and we shall meet it several times in the course of our study. It is even more marked in the Babylonian epic, because there the elevation of Enkidu's status to friend allows the two attitudes toward the enemy to be clearly embodied in two characters whose separation leads to the tragic conclusion: Enkidu's death and Gilgamesh's futile quest for the plant of eternal youth. Already in the Sumerian poem, Huwawa's world is complex. On one level it is a real forest, on another level it is the dark wood of a later tradition, but it is also a tragic world in which good intentions produce their opposite: a world of uncertain moral values, even beyond good and evil, with the qualities that make the world's great epics stand out from the rest. This is not simply because Huwawa represents a world of personal nightmare, important as that is to the power of the poem, but because he embodies one of the basic dilemmas of civilization itself.

We do not know who was responsible for the moving transformation of the conventional folktale pattern into the Sumerian poem, but if we recognize Huwawa's significance, it is not difficult to account for the poem's popularity or for the considerable expansion of its meanings in the Babylonian epic. If it is the earliest it is also one of the finest and most subtle tales of the battle between culture hero and monster, and it suggests most of the themes that are more grandly explored in the structurally similar myths of combat between champion god and chaos monster.

Gilgamesh seems to have remained a type of the hero well into Roman times. Aelian, a Greek writer of A.D. 170–235, tells about Gilgamesh a variant of the Danae story of the birth of Perseus.[71] No earlier source attests to any connection between this tale and Gilgamesh, but the tale is a variant of the miraculous-birth-of-the-hero motif,[72] and Gilgamesh too fits this pattern. In the Sumerian king list his father is called a "*lillu*-de-

---

[71] Aelian, *De natura animalium* 12.21.

[72] S. Thompson 1955–58, Motifs A500 and T500–549. See also Rank 1959 and Dundes 1977:13.

mon,"[73] and in the Babylonian epic he is two-thirds divine and one-third human. In view of the obvious relationship between our Gilgamesh story, the Perseus type of hero legend, and the "Dragon-Slayer" folktale,[74] it is not surprising that a Greek writer should have assimilated Gilgamesh to the standard Greek type. He continued, it seems, for over two thousand years, to fit the combat pattern of oral narratives.

It even seems possible that Huwawa survived with him as the archetypal antagonist. If J. T. Milik has correctly interpreted a fragment from Qumran,[75] then Gilgamesh and Huwawa, perhaps even these mysterious trees as well, there became characters in the Jewish "Book of Giants." This work in turn was adapted by Mani for his radical cosmic dualism, in which the battle of light and dark explains the whole universe, and it was this Manichaean system against which Augustine developed his own narratives of the adversary.

[73] Jacobsen 1939:84. Lambert in Garelli (ed.) 1960:48.

[74] Aarne and Thompson 1964:89, Type 300 and cf. Type 550, and Fontenrose 1959:265, both using Hartland 1894–96. For a survey of literature on hero patterns, including Raglan, see Dundes 1977:6–13, esp. his remarks on the relation of Propp's morphology to legend studies.

[75] Milik 1976:313. See below, Chapter 10.

TWO

THE DRAGON AND THE SEA: ANCIENT NEAR EASTERN COMBATS

1. Cosmogony or Kingship?

THE ESSENTIAL paradigm we discover in the story of Gilgamesh and Huwawa is found also in other kinds of narratives and in many other cultures. The pattern itself is constant, while its context and even its inherent implications may vary radically. In all the narratives collected in this chapter, the hero is a god, the adversary also a god of some kind, and so the narratives may be classed as myths. But in many previous studies, particularly those with a focus on biblical narratives, it has also been generally assumed that the combat pattern is always bound to cosmogony, at least in its oldest forms.[1] Our first example shows that assumption to be mistaken.

The Labbu myth survives in two versions, an Old Babylonian and a later Assyrian, but unfortunately both are so fragmentary that they defy complete analysis. Curiously, however, the older version begins with the same situation as the Gilgamesh poem:

> The cities sighed, the people. . . .
> The people decreased in number. . . .
> For their lamentation there was none to. . . .
> For their cry there was none to. . . .
> "Who brought forth the serpent-dragon?"
> "The sea brought forth the serpent-dragon."
> Enlil drew a picture of the dragon in the sky.[2]

The text now describes the dimensions of the monster (very big indeed: "six cubits his mouth," for example) and continues:

> At sixty cubits he can snatch [?] the birds;
> In the water nine cubits deep he drags;

---

[1] The original argument of Gunkel 1895, still found, e.g., in Anderson 1967. See also Cross 1973:16, Ricoeur 1967:175–210, and now Day 1985:1–61.

[2] Trans. Heidel 1963:141–42. He thinks the last line refers to the Milky Way, but surely a comet is the obvious astronomical analogy. Ellipses here represent damaged or missing text; Heidel's translation indicates further doubts not noted here.

He raises his tail. . . .
All the gods of heaven. . . .

In spite of the fragmentary text, the Labbu is clearly an early prototype of the dragon of Revelation, whose tail swept down a third of the stars of heaven, and cast them to the earth."[3] The Babylonian gods are terrified at this apparition, and appeal to the moon god, Sin, who calls for volunteers. Tishpak is appointed, but apparently declines to challenge the dragon. The tablet now becomes indecipherable, but a further fragment tells of the defeat of the Labbu: a storm is stirred up, and then the hero, whoever he is, shoots an arrow and slays the beast.

Like the Sumerian Gilgamesh–Huwawa poem, this Babylonian myth is very close to the folktale type: a devastating monster threatens the city and its people, but a hero emerges to liberate the people from their danger.[4] Unlike in the Gilgamesh poem, however, the gods themselves are also cowed by the monster, and to judge from the fragments (together with other parallels to be discussed below) the hero who finally emerged after Tishpak's refusal must himself have been a god. We can tell that the victorious hero was offered the kingship as his prize, presumably the kingship of heaven, as in the later Marduk-Tiamat variant.[5] Unlike Huwawa, the Labbu monster *is* a dragon, not merely dragon-like, and he comes from the sea, a widespread motif with many parallels in other combat narratives. We might remember, however, that after his death one of Huwawa's powers appears to be transferred by Enlil to the sea—and that he himself was like the roaring flood.

Since the city and its inhabitants are already there at the beginning of the story, the Labbu myth is clearly not cosmogonic. It has to do with the preservation rather than the creation of orderly life. But it shares with the cosmogonic variants both the gods as chief actors and the reward of the kingship, with which it is more commonly connected. The combat paradigm, in fact, seems to have generated the central myth that supported and justified the kingship in many different societies of the ancient world. The same appears to have been true about the Canaanite myths which are so vital in the process of transmission. They too have cosmic, but not cosmogonic, implications—and are mostly about who is to be king.

[3] Rev. 12:4. See below, Chapters 13 and 16.

[4] Even in its fragmentary form, it shows slots α-β-γ and ι-λ-μ of our schema. See Appendix.

[5] Littleton 1969b discusses various kingship myths with a useful table of variants and themes.

2. *Canaanite Battles with Sea*

The discovery in 1928–29 of the ancient city of Ugarit some 800 meters
from the present coast of Syria at the mound of Ras Shamra has revealed
a culture of high order in close contact with many other areas of the ancient world. Indeed, what first called attention to the importance of
Ugarit was that a Syrian peasant's plow struck against a Mycenaean
tomb. The myth-poems unearthed at Ras Shamra are vital for understanding the links between the Hebrew scriptures and other ancient cultures. The tablets themselves are in a variety of languages, as well as the
local West Semitic dialect, including Sumerian, Akkadian, Egyptian,
Hurrian, and Hittite. They contain, among many other genres, letters
from the local king, Niqmed, to his own lord, Shuppiluliumash, the great
Hittite king, letters that help date the site to the first half of the fourteenth
century B.C., the same period as the important letters from El Amarna.[6]

The texts of the myths take the form of a series of epic poems showing
characteristic features of oral composition and performance.[7] The principal characters are the storm god Baal and his sister/consort Anat, herself
a great warrior with strong connections to the Sumerian Inanna and Babylonian Ishtar.[8] Unfortunately, it is not possible to piece together from
the surviving fragments a clear picture of the sequence in which the events
associated with Baal were understood to have occurred.[9] More likely, the
tablets represent parts of a whole cycle of narratives told about Baal and
the other members of the Canaanite pantheon. These narratives, as in
other comparable cultures, may well have been inconsistent with each
other.

The key Canaanite myth that confirmed the power of Baal is the story
of his battle with Yamm.[10] The name Yamm means "sea," and the other

[6] On the discovery and dating of Ugarit, see Driver 1956a:1 and Gordon 1962:128ff. Most
of the important texts are translated in ANET, but they will be cited here from various sources
with appropriate cross-references. See Clifford 1972:193–99 for a synoptic table of the various systems for designating the separate fragments, and below, n. 10.

[7] Cross 1973:112–13. The arguments of Cross and his students for oral composition follow the lines set out by his Harvard colleagues, Parry and Lord, and are generally assumed
in what follows. See Appendix.

[8] Hallo 1968:21; Pope 1972:605–11.

[9] Driver's sequence (1956a:11) is followed by Anderson 1975:142 but has not won wide
acceptance. Cf. Gordon 1949:9 and 1961:191. What we have are presumably the local Ugaritic forms of the myths.

[10] The texts are nos. 68 and 137 in Gordon 1949 and 1955 (= III AB A and III AB B in Virol-
leaud's [1957] original numbering, used by Driver 1956a and by H. L. Ginsberg in ANET
= CTA 2.4, 2.1, the system of Herdner 1963 used by Cross 1973 and others).

name by which this adversary is known, Nahar, means "river." Like his many counterparts, from the Akkadian Labbu to the Skamander of *Iliad* 21, he embodies the chaotic, disintegrating power of water, whether as raging sea or flooding river. He is the enemy of good order in the husbanding of nature or in the governing of the state. In one of the contemporary El Amarna letters, for example, the Egyptian official representative at Jerusalem complains to Pharaoh, the spiritually inclined and politically inept Akhenaton, that with all the 'Apiru raids on his territory in Canaan he is "like a ship in the midst of the sea," surrounded on all sides by anarchy and opposition.[11]

This Sea-enemy, Yamm, sends a message to El's council of the gods sitting on the cosmic mountain at the gates of heaven and the entry to the abyss. He demands that Baal be given over to him as his captive and that his own lordship be acknowledged. Unfortunately, given the fragmentary state of the texts, the specific motivation for this message is unclear, but another text[12] tells of a struggle about whether Yamm shall have a palace built for him. El is determined that his "son,"[13] Yamm, should have a palace (in the far north) and sends for the divine craftsman, who lives in Egypt or Crete (a clear sign that this is not a cosmogony). But another god, Athtar, gets wind of the work and takes the construction of the palace, the ultimate sign of kingship, to be an act of rebellion. Apparently El insists on Yamm's right to regal power, and in another text Athtar is deprived of his authority.[14] The sun-goddess warns that Yamm is favored and prophesies Athtar's downfall.[15] At any rate, in the Baal-Yamm text, Baal too seems to be challenging the right of Yamm to rule, charging him with presumption, and this challenge immediately precedes Yamm's message to El's council on the cosmic mountain.

The divine council is terrified at the message, and El readily agrees to its terms: "Baal is thy slave, O Sea."[16] Thus Baal comes under the power of Yamm-Nahar. But the craftsman Kothar-and-Khasis, whose role as

[11] ANET 487–89, letters 286–90. On the question of whether the 'Apiru were the Hebrews, see generally Bright 1972:92–94.

[12] Driver 1956a:75–79 (III AB C = CTA 2.3 = Gordon 1949: no. 129).

[13] In the Greek version of this story, Yamm (or "Pontos") is the great-grandson of El, a sign of the confusion over generations common to most of these myths, especially when they overlap with theogonies. See below, Chapter 3. The term "son," however, often indicates not kinship but status.

[14] Driver 1956a: 111 (I AB = CTA 6.1.63 = ANET 140). See below, Chapters 3.1, 6.3.

[15] Driver 1956a:77 (III AB C); ANET 129.

[16] CTA 2.1.36 (= Driver 1956a:81, III AB = Gordon 1949: no. 137); ANET 130.

palace-builder clearly makes him an important figure in the kingship struggle, prophesies that Baal will subdue Sea-River and drive him out from his dominion. He fashions a weapon (club or mace) for the purpose. Baal thereupon does battle with Yamm and smites his foe:

> Then soars and swoops the mace in Baal's hand,
> Even as an eagle in his fingers.
> It smites the head of Prince Sea [Yamm].
> Between the eyes of Judge River [Nahar]. [17]

Baal then becomes lord himself: "Sea verily is dead, Baal rules."[18] In another text, El decrees for Baal the great palace and temple on Mount Zaphon, an episode that possibly follows Baal's defeat of Yamm.[19]

3. *Marduk and Tiamat*

Closely related to this Canaanite Baal-Yamm myth is the well-known Marduk-Tiamat portion of the Babylonian poem *Enuma Eliš*. Indeed, Thorkild Jacobsen has argued that the Babylonian myth is a variant of the Canaanite, since for one thing the inhabitants of the Mesopotamian region had no significant contact with the sea, and yet Tiamat is so clearly the sea, like her Hebrew counterpart *tehōm* (the "deep" of the King James Version).[20] In spite of the long preliminaries in this epic, which amount to a Babylonian theogony-cosmogony, the main event in the poem is the defeat of Tiamat by Marduk; the battle is described at length, and the episodes follow the same sequence as the other narratives we have discussed. The poem concludes with the gods gathering for a banquet in the new Marduk temple in Babylon, itself freshly constructed like Baal's palace by the grateful gods.

In the *Enuma Eliš*, the gods also cower at the challenger, but Marduk, like Baal a storm god, the "rider-on-the-clouds," controlling wind, cloud, and lightning, takes up the challenge, goes forth to smite the foe, and tangles with her in single combat.

[17] CTA 2.4.24–25 (III AB A); ANET 131. The translation follows Gray 1965:25. Cf. Anderson 1967:24 and Day 1985:9.

[18] CTA 2.4.32; Cross 1973:116. Cf. Gordon 1949: no. 68, line 24. Baal relents, ashamed, and contents himself with receiving Yamm's homage.

[19] CTA 4.5–6 (= II AB). See ANET 135 and below, Chapter 3.1.

[20] Jacobsen 1968. His argument does not depend, *pace* Day 1985:11, on an Amorite origin for the Marduk-Tiamat combat. See also Clifford 1972:40–41.

> Tiamat opened her mouth to devour;
> He drove in the tempest lest she close her lips,
> The fierce winds filled her belly,
> Her insides distended and she opened wide her mouth,
> He let fly an arrow, it split her belly,
> Cut through her innards and gashed the heart,
> He held her fast, extinguished her life.[21]

Like Baal, Marduk also splits the enemy's skull with a club, one of the special weapons he is given. Since Tiamat is a female monster (Propp's inversion), the Babylonian text, developing the sexual implications of the imagery, takes the splitting a stage further than the Canaanite, as the above quotation demonstrates. Marduk then splits Tiamat open "like a mussel [?] into two parts," of which one becomes the sky and the other the earth. He then has a temple built to celebrate his victory.[22] As in the Huwawa tradition, wild intractable nature (trees, waters) is converted to manageable culture, represented by the temple.

Now although Tiamat is soundly defeated and even split in two, the myth also allows her, in her capacity as the primeval waters, to continue existing, so that at the conclusion of the poem there is a prayer that the violence of her flood threat shall continue to be restrained for another year at least. In this respect the Babylonian myth appears to differ from the Canaanite. Yamm-Nahar represents the forces of Sea and River in general, but there is no obvious cosmogonic connection, nor do the fragments imply the kind of politico-religious festival that is so important as a context for the Babylonian epic. Insofar as Yamm is simply another of the gods among whom the struggle for kingship takes place, he is regarded, like Baal himself, as a "son" of El. Tiamat, however, is a different kind of being; her symbolic role as a constant threat to order is more heavily stressed, but she is also, unlike Yamm, the primeval waters of the cosmogony. We might infer, from the coupling of Yamm with Nahar, that is, of salt with sweet water, and from the text in which Baal relents and does not kill Yamm, that the Canaanite enemy had a similar cosmic function. But the surviving texts give it no emphasis.

As the primeval waters, Tiamat belongs to an older generation of gods who are to be supplanted by their descendants. There are clear parallels with this generation battle in Hittite and Greek texts, but it is no necessary

---

[21] Trans. Jacobsen 1968:106, except that "distended" in line 100 I take from Heidel 1963:40, following Landsberger. Cf. Anderson 1967:20 and ANET 67.

[22] ANET 501–503, and see below, Chapter 3 n. 29. On inversion, see Propp 1984:90.

part of the combat myth—though, conversely, all the succession myths seem to include and even to presuppose a combat. Another essential difference, then, between the Canaanite and Mesopotamian myths is that the combat pattern is adapted, in Babylon, not only to a cosmogonic function but also to the succession myth.

Lambert's redating of the *Enuma Eliš* to the Kassite period, around 1100 B.C., the time of Nebuchadnezzar I, would allow time for a myth like that of Baal-Yamm to have had some impact on the Babylonian epic.[23] Tiamat would then represent a fusion of two distinct conceptions: one the native Mesopotamian idea of the primeval waters (rain and rivers) from which all else is generated but which must be severely contained, as by irrigation, for civilization to continue,[24] the other, the imported idea that the chaotic forces of the sea, Canaanite Yamm, are the enemy in the hero god's battle for kingship. Indeed, the opening lines of the epic speak of the mingling of Tiamat's waters with those of her consort, Apsu, so that she can continue to represent his fresh waters after his defeat, and Marduk later makes clouds and water from her spittle.[25]

It is clear, in any case, that Tiamat is a composite monster. Much of the mythological material retold in the *Enuma Eliš* is a good deal older than the reign of Nebuchadnezzar I. The Hurrian myths, for example, are certainly older than 1100, yet they show considerable Babylonian influence. And the central conflict with Marduk has several Babylonian precedents. One is the Labbu myth discussed above, but the most important are the many narratives about battles between Ninurta, god of the thunderstorm and the spring flood, and various monsters or dragons.

4. *Ninurta and the Anzu-Bird*

The motivating incident for the story of the conflict between Ninurta and the Anzu is fortunately preserved in some detail in an Assyrian recension from Ashurbanipal's library at Nineveh. If it does indeed preserve the old text, then it is the earliest version of the combat pattern in which the initial incident was an explicit rebellion among the gods, a motive that

[23] Lambert 1964, but contrast Jacobsen 1976, who dates the text to ca. 1250 B.C. Lambert argues against Canaanite influence: see Day 1985:11–12.

[24] Heidel 1963:42, line 140. See below, Chapter 7.

[25] ANET 60, 501.

will have many consequences in the subsequent tradition. The passage is worth quoting in full for the vivid sense of the rebel's motives it gives:

> And all the decrees of the gods he [Enlil] directed.
> To convey them he dispatched Anzu.
> Enlil entrusted to him the [. . .] of the entrance to his shrine.
> The [. . .] ing of pure water before him.
> The exercise of his Enlilship his eyes view.
> The crown of his sovereignty, the robe of his godhead,
> His divine Tablet of Destinies Anzu views constantly.
> As he views constantly the father of the gods, the god of Duranki [i.e., the
>   Temple Tower at Nippur],
> The removal of Enlilship he conceives in his heart.
> As Anzu views constantly the father of the gods, the god of Duranki,
> The removal of Enlilship he conceives in his heart.
> "I will take the divine Tablet of Destinies, I,
> And the decrees of all the gods I will rule!
> I will make firm my throne and be the master of the norms,
> I will direct the totality of all the Igigi."
> His heart having thus plotted aggression,
> At the entrance of the sanctuary, which he had been viewing,
> He awaits the start of day.
> As Enlil was washing with pure water,
> His crown having been removed and deposited on the throne,
> He [Anzu] seized the Tablet of Destinies in his hands,
> Taking away the Enlilship.[26]

This is a simple but brilliant piece of characterization. Even the repetitions, inherent in this kind of oral poetry, reinforce the tension of the passage. Constantly seeing the source of power before him every day, Anzu can finally restrain himself no longer; the temptation to make off with the Tablet while its rightful owner is bathing and disrobed is too great. In none of the subsequent transformations of the rebellion scene is the motivation so clear or so convincing, even in Milton. Anzu comes to his decision, awaits his moment cunningly, and then flees with the Tablet to his mountains.

The theft has a stunning effect on the gods that is reminiscent of the initial effect of the similar challenges in the Baal text and the *Enuma Eliš*. El

---

[26] ANET 112–13, trans. A. K. Grayson with the substitution of "Anzu" for "Zu" or "Imdugud," following Hruška 1975.

and his pantheon in the Ugaritic poem see the messengers of Yamm and "drop their heads Down upon their knees,"[27] while the gods in the *Enuma Eliš* "lapsed into silence and remained speechless."[28] In the Anzu poem,

> Stillness spread abroad, silence prevailed.
> Father Enlil, their counsellor, was speechless;
> The sanctuary took off its brilliance.[29]

Soon, however, the gods rally and hold a council, and Anu calls for volunteers or nominations: "Which god will slay Anzu, So that his name will remain the greatest of all?" Adad is nominated, the storm god or "Irrigator" (equated with Baal in Ugaritic texts, forming the composite name Baal-Hadad), but he prevaricates, and Anu will not let him undertake the mission. Precisely the same thing happens with another god, and then with Shara, Ishtar's first-born son. Each time, as is normal in oral epic, the same words are used, and the speeches are given in full, not summarized.

Finally Ninurta is chosen and goes forth to the mountains to do battle. His initial attack is repelled because Anzu is able to use the power of the Tablet of Destinies to neutralize the assault: "But the arrow could not approach Anzu, it turned back." Apparently Anzu is even able to reduce the arrow back to its constituent elements, for he calls out to it:

> O arrow that has come, return to thy canebrake,
> Stave of the bow, return to thy wood,
> Return bow-gut, to the sheep's rump, return wings to the birds.

Nonplussed, Ninurta calls to Adad and tells him to go back and report these proceedings to Ea, the wily god. As ever, Ea has a plan: Attack his wings with the south wind, he says, and then cut off the wings and scatter them. Anzu will be very upset at the loss of his wings and will cry, "Wing to wing" (clearly a play on the bird-cry, Akkadian *kappi*).[30] That is the moment to shoot the arrow. "Slit his throat, vanquish Anzu." Adad carries back these instructions, and presumably Ninurta hitches the winds and carries out the instructions, though no text is more than fragmentary at this point.

Apart from the obvious similarity of plot, the contention that the Mar-

---

[27] ANET 130, trans. H. L. Ginzberg, Tablet III AB B, line 23 (= CTA 2.1; Gordon 1949: no. 137).

[28] ANET 61, trans. E. A. Speiser, Tablet I, line 58; cf. II, line 6.

[29] ANET 113, lines 23–25.

[30] ANET 516–17, Tablet II, lines 61–65 (= 76–80, = 92–96) and 110 = 132. See Speiser's note to the Gilgamesh epic, Tablet VI, line 50, ANET 84.

duk story is in part a reworking of this myth is supported by another fact. In the *Enuma Eliš* the Tablet of Destinies also plays a role. After the defeat of Apsu in the first combat (with Ea), Tiamat hands over the Tablet to Kingu, whom she now makes her consort (though he was apparently one of her sons). On the defeat of Tiamat, Kingu is killed; Marduk gets the Tablet and presents it to Anu.[31] Furthermore, Lambert has made the acute suggestion that the eleven monsters who are allied with Tiamat in the battle are a covert allusion to the eleven monsters whom Ninurta had slain, implying that Marduk could do quite as well as the older god and so was fit to replace him.[32]

The Anzu-bird myth survives in several versions from different epochs. The earliest version is Sumerian, and the hero who defeats Anzu is apparently Lugalbanda, the father of Gilgamesh, who seeks to overcome Anzu with intoxicants.[33] In the Old Babylonian version (from Susa), the hero's name is Ningirsu, "Lord of Girsu," but this is simply a local variant of Ninurta.[34] It is the Assyrian version, from Ashur, which calls the hero Ninurta throughout. Finally, a hymn of Ashurbanipal celebrates Marduk as "the one who crushed the skull of Anzu." Since the earlier versions refer to slitting Anzu's throat, the crushing of the skull may represent a fusion with another myth, perhaps even the Canaanite Baal myths, in which this is the method for disposing of Yamm (Baal's weapon being a club or mace, rather than arrows or a knife).

Curiously enough, Jacobsen thinks that the Anzu-bird is actually an earlier form of Ninurta himself, from a period when gods were still represented in animal form: Anzu is the third-millennium thunderbird, the god of "heavy rain." The growing dislike of the nonhuman form for the gods eventually led to the displacement of the bird form onto the enemy figure of the combat pattern, "much as the god of the fresh waters, Enki/Ea, captured his own nonhuman form, Apsu, the fresh waters underground."[35] In his human form, the god is represented on Old Babylonian

---

[31] ANET 63, Tablet I, line 5 and p. 502, Tablet V, lines 69–70. I do not see the force of Lambert's contention that this episode is inconsistent with the passage in which Marduk demands that he be allowed to determine the fates. There is no mention at that point of the Tablet of Destinies. See Walcot 1966:34–35.

[32] Cited in Walcot 1966:39. Cf. Jacobsen 1976:167.

[33] The interpretation of this text is in doubt, and it may be that Lugalbanda is trying to curry favor with the Anzu. See Kramer 1959:203, Text CT XV, plates 41–42. Grayson in ANET 113 makes it an attempt to conquer him.

[34] Jacobsen 1976:127–28.

[35] Ibid., p. 129.

cylinder seals with the defeated form, Anzu-bird, hitched to his chariot and with rain pouring from its mouth. Thus the power of kingship has harnessed the powers of nature.

5. *Ninurta and the Azag Demon*

The Anzu story has no cosmogomic associations, but a parallel myth about Ninurta's battles, this time strongly cosmogonic, is related in the epic text entitled "King, Storm, the Glory of Which Is Noble."[36] The poem begins with Ninurta's special weapon, named Sharur, addressing Ninurta with fulsome praises of his heroic abilities and urging him to do battle against Azag. At first, Ninurta seems to be defeated and "flees like a bird," but after some more urging from his Sharur, he attacks again and manages to destroy Azag. He now proceeds to organize the complex irrigation system of Mesopotamia, a formative act for the whole civilization, and this is represented as harnessing and controlling the "waters of the earth," so that, for example, the Tigris will rise properly in the appropriate season. The most important of Ninurta's acts is the building of a wall of stone, so that "the mighty waters followed along the stone. Now these waters do not rise from the earth into the eternal mountains." Ninurta then presents this high stone wall to his mother, Ninlil, who thus becomes Ninhursag, "lady of the foothills." Finally, Ninurta sits in judgment over the various stones who were his enemies.[37]

This myth of Ninurta's victory over the water demon was so important in the ancient world that there are several allusions to it from many disparate places. Presumably, the *Enuma Eliš* echoes it when Marduk organizes the universe, in a kind of second creation, and the trial of the rebel Kingu with the allotment of administrative responsibilities to various defeated gods may be reminiscent of the judging of Ninurta's enemies, the stones. But the allusions go back much earlier than this. The prologue to one of the Sumerian Gilgamesh poems, "Gilgamesh, Enkidu, and the Nether World," discussed above, runs quickly through some cosmogonic events, including the battle of Enki (instead of Ninurta) against the

---

[36] Kramer's title is "Deeds and Exploits of Ninurta" in Kramer 1959:172–74. A new edition is in preparation by E. Bergmann and J. J. Van Dijk. For texts, see Kramer 1972:117 n. 76 and Jacobsen 1976:248 n. 85.

[37] Jacobsen 1976:130–31, 167. For Kramer 1959:172, Azag is simply "a sickness demon," but Jacobsen identifies him with hailstones. Cf. Landsberger 1961 and the opening of the Anzu poem, Tablet I, line 10, in ANET 514.

primeval waters. Enki sails out in a boat into the waters, which proceed to throw stones at him, probably the same stones with which Azag is identified. The waters then fling themselves at the boat. That is all we hear of the story in this poem, but we may assume the same conclusion as the Ninurta version, victory for the hero, since the poem immediately goes on to tell how the *huluppu* tree could now be planted on the banks of the Euphrates. The poem continues, we remember, with the difficulties of this beautiful tree and the valiant offer of Gilgamesh to rescue it for Inanna from the terrible beasts who have taken up residence: the serpent at its roots, a *lillu*-demon in its trunk, and the Anzu-bird in its branches. Following the normal practice of tale-singers, the poet begins his poem with the Enki allusion, both to enrich the mythological context and to suggest the kinds of ramifications we are now exploring. Specific combats are all variants of each other, just as the *nostoi* of Greek tradition were variations on the one great return story.[38]

Although the Ninurta variant of this combat with the water demon is first known from copies dating to about 1800 B.C., there is probably an allusion to it in a prayer of Gudea of Lagash, about 2100 B.C. Gudea records for us how he went into the house of Ninurta and prayed to him, beginning, "Lord, who held back the savage waters. . . ."[39] He also tells us that the god appeared to him in a dream, in which he seemed "from his wings to be the Anzu-bird, but from his lower parts a flood," another instance of the king-god taking over the characteristics of his enemy. It may be that the king's dream becomes everyone else's myth, but the king himself dreams according to the common images. This example shows how easily in this dream-like world the allomorphs of a given pattern may be combined with each other, so that the adversary becomes a composite figure, part Anzu-bird, part "mighty waters."

6. Ninurta, Akhenaton, and Psalm 104

The Ninurta form of the myth is so clearly related to the irrigation system of Mesopotamia that this must have been its original home. Nevertheless, it spread well beyond the region, as far away as Egypt, and it had an im-

---

[38] The oral poet's awareness of "roads not taken" in the course of a narrative is clear from, e.g., the allusions to Agamemnon in the *Odyssey*. On the *Iliad* as a specific *Dios boulē*, another of which was the flood story, see Kilmer 1972, and below, Chapter 7. Cf. Frame 1977 and Nagy 1979.

[39] Lambert 1965:296.

pact on the Old Testament. In the hymn of Akhenaton to his revolutionary sun god, Aton, we find a curious conjunction of mountains and waves, evidently not fully understood by those who knew only Egyptian topography:

> All distant foreign countries, thou makest their life [also],
> For thou hast set a Nile in heaven,
> That it may descend for them and make waves upon the mountains,
> Like the great green sea,
> To water their fields in their towns.
> How effective they are, thy plans, O lord of eternity!
> The Nile in heaven, it is for the foreign peoples
> And for the beasts of every desert that go upon their feet;
> [While the true] Nile comes from the underworld for Egypt.[40]

The rising of the waters to the mountains, a disaster in Mesopotamia which Ninurta was able to prevent by his wall of stone, has here been reinterpreted in the light of the beneficial annual flooding of the Nile: the "Nile in heaven" is clearly that rarity in Egypt, rain. Similarly, the primeval waters of the Mesopotamian tradition are envisaged as simply "the great green sea."

The singer of Psalm 104 may also have known some variant of the Ninurta myth. It used to be argued that he was directly influenced by Akhenaton's hymn, but more recent views have favored Canaanite mediation of the Egyptian source.[41] However, the imagery coincides even more closely with the Sumero-Akkadian than with the Canaanite or Egyptian. The psalmist praises Yahweh as follows:

> You cover yourself with light as with a garment,
>   You have stretched out the heavens like a tent,
> You stored with waters the upper chambers,
>   you set your chariot on the clouds,
> You ride on the wings of the wind,
>   you make the winds your messengers,
>   fire and flame your ministers.
> You placed the earth upon its foundations,
>   lest it should ever quake,
> You covered it with the deep like a garment
>   and upon the mountains stood the waters.

[40] ANET 371, trans. J. Wilson.
[41] Breasted 1933:366–70; Nagel 1950; Cross 1973:162–69.

At your roar they fled,
　at the sound of your thunder they took flight.
They went up to the mountains,
　they went down to the nether chasm;
　to the place which you appointed for them.
You marked a border they should not cross,
　lest they cover the earth again.[42]

Several features of these verses have analogues in the Ninurta myth: Yahweh rides his chariot "on the wings of the wind," like Ninurta's chariot on cylinder seals; the waters stand upon the mountains in that curious verse (6) in which *mayim* (waters) are made the equivalent of *tehōm* (ocean, the deep), cognate with Ugaritic *thm* and with Akkadian Tiamat; and a limit is established so that the waters are allotted their appropriate places according to the Sumero-Akkadian system—above the mountains and below the earth. This Yahweh image and the Ninurta myth appear to be the only occasions in the ancient Orient on which a god holds back savage waters as a means of organizing the world. Here at least there is a strong probability of direct Babylonian impact on the Hebrew tradition before the exile.[43]

Yet here too Canaanite influence is discernible. Baal, after all, also rides the clouds and manifests himself in thunder against the chaos waters. Now that the importance of the discoveries at Ugarit has been recognized, it is more likely that the link connecting these three traditions—Babylonian, Egyptian, Hebrew—is to be found in Canaan. We know that the Amarna period was highly syncretic and that Ugarit was a prime center for the exchange of religious and narrative concepts. For example, a Hurrian hymn to the goddess Nikkal, Sumerian Ningal, was translated into North Canaanite at Ugarit, and an Egyptian scribe wrote for his employer, one Abilmiki of Tyre, a letter back to his Egyptian suzerain comparing the pharaoh Akhenaton to Baal:

Seven and seven times I fall at the feet of the king, my lord. I am the dirt under the feet of the king, my lord. My lord is the Sun-god who . . . sets

---

[42] Ps. 104.2–9; for the translation, see Dahood 1970:31 and the arguments in Day 1985: 28–29.

[43] Lambert 1965:296. The image reappears in Job 26.8, 38.8–11, and Prov. 8.29; see Nagel 1950 and Dahood 1970:33–36. For the influence on Gen. 1.7, see Day 1985:51–53. For the link with the Red Sea tradition, see below, Chapter 4.

the whole land at peace by his might, who utters his battle-cry in heaven like
Baal, so that the whole land quakes at his cry.[44]

This shows that Baal's name needed no footnote for a contemporary
Egyptian audience, and the compliment could be immediately understood. Indeed, a Canaanite myth about Anat (or Astarte) and the Sea (presumably Yamm) is known from an Egyptian papyrus of the period,
though unfortunately it is not well preserved and no text has come to light
at Ugarit for comparison. The myth seems to have to do with the question of whether Sea shall rule over all of earth and heaven and whether the
gods shall be made to pay tribute to him—the common theme of several
Ugaritic texts.[45]

7. *Syncretism in the* Enuma Eliš

The composers of the *Enuma Eliš* took this religious syncretism a stage
further. They blended a traditional Sumero-Akkadian myth, particularly
the Ninurta versus Azag variant, with the Canaanite myth of a combat
between Yamm and Baal. Marduk has an elaborate array of weapons—
bow and arrows, lightning, a net, several winds, the flood-storm, and a
club, most of which he manages to find a use for in the ensuing battle—
and this strongly suggests an effort to include and outdo all previous heroes by taking over their special weapons.[46] Tiamat herself becomes the Sea-
enemy (from the Baal epic) as well as an aspect of the primeval watery
chaos and ancestor of the younger gods. Like the Anzu or Azag adversaries of Ninurta, she retains the characteristics, both animal and watery, of
an earlier notion of godhood, one that must now be overcome by the
more anthropomorphic deities who represent the institution of kingship.
The combat myth provides the obvious and convenient form in which
this victory may be expressed.

Marduk splits Tiamat into earthly and heavenly parts, according to the
version of Berossus,[47] the priest of Bēl Marduk at Babylon who inter-

---

[44] ANET 484. Trans. W. F. Albright and George Mendenhall. On the syncretism, see Albright 1957:211.

[45] See ANET 17–18, where Hittite parallels and similarities with the *Enuma Eliš* are also
mentioned.

[46] Marduk has either four or seven winds, the latter apparently an effort to emulate Ninurta. Compare ANET 514–17 (Tablet II, lines 3, 31, 148–50)—the Anzu myth—with ANET
66 (Tablet IV, lines 42–47)—the *Enuma Eliš*.

[47] Text quoted in Heidel 1963:77–78. For the *Enuma Eliš* see ANET 67, 501–503.

preted his native traditions for the benefit of the Greek-speaking world around 275 B.C. But what Marduk actually does in the cuneiform text is far from clear. He seems to make the heavens from half of her body and orders the waters to stay there so as not to cause another flood, but he now proceeds to use her body all over again to make the earth. Such confusion may well be due to the efforts of the Marduk priests to conceal the upstart origins of their god by superimposing Marduk as the creator upon a myth in which the world is already made by the previous generations and divided into fresh and salt water.[48]

Marduk's victory over Tiamat was apparently represented every year during the New Year festival. The statue of Marduk was carried in procession to the Akitu House and was there set upon a dais symbolizing Tiamat. "Bēl sits in the middle of the Sea [Tiamat] in the Akitu," says one late magical text, using the form of the god's name, cognate with Baal, common in the later period,[49] while a description of cultic structures in Babylon explains: "Tiamat [Sea] is the seat of Bēl on which Bēl sits." In another epic text, Marduk's son Nabu appears to insist on performing his father's duties. Among other things, "He set his feet on the rolling Sea [Tiamat]."[50] This language for the image of the god's victory will reappear frequently in the Old Testament. Sennacherib substituted the name of his god, Ashur, for Marduk in the late Assyrian period, and the Old Testament writers substituted their god, Yahweh.

Marduk's plundered statue was restored to Babylon by Nebuchadnezzar I around 1100 B.C., and the New Year rite, as well as the epic text of the *Enuma Eliš*, may date from this time. In their syncretic character, the rite and the epic, though they may not have been as closely linked as used to be thought, both illustrate a common tendency in the ancient Orient. Traditional motifs and narrative patterns were taken over from older or rival religions and adapted to the new god. So widespread are these themes that it is often impossible to trace the paths of direct influence. It remains possible that the *Enuma Eliš*, now thought to be contemporary with the oldest texts in the Hebrew tradition, had some direct impact on them, but the obvious source of Old Testament combat language is the Canaanite myths.

---

[48] For more discussion of such syncretistic problems, see below, Chapter 6.1.

[49] Jacobsen 1968:106 n. 10.

[50] Lambert 1963; Roux 1966:360–64. Fontenrose 1966 demolishes the arguments of Heinrich Zimmern and of Langdon (1923:34–59) about the *Enuma Eliš* ritual, but the influence of the myth-ritual school is still found in Ricoeur 1967:175–210.

8. *Death and the Dragon*

The combat pattern seems to have been popular at Ugarit, for there are several other Canaanite variants. In one myth, Baal takes on and is finally victorious over Mot, the death king, who is like Yamm, a "son of El." This narrative is a good deal more complicated than the Yamm epic, both in its structure and in its apparent cultic context. The Enemy this time represents not so much the forces of disorder that threaten chaos in the state, but the blight of death that threatens agricultural fertility. In one manifestation, it seems clear, Baal embodies catastrophe, whether the annual rebirth so dear to the myth-ritualists of the vegetation school or the seven-year sabbatical period argued forcefully by Cyrus Gordon.[51] In this myth, Baal goes down to fight the underworld ruler, Mot, and is actually killed, a common elaboration of the combat pattern[52] and the feature that gave rise to the hypothesis of a "dying and rising god" archetype.[53]

On his death, Baal's warlike sister/consort Anat comes to the rescue, and a bloodthirsty warrior she proves to be.

> She seized El's son, Mot.
> With a sword she sliced him;
> With a sieve she winnowed him;
> With a fire she burnt him;
> With millstones she ground him;
> In the field she scattered him.[54]

Granted that this episode clearly reflects some kind of agricultural magic, still, the myth-singer must have relished this wonder-woman's military prowess, for he has her elbowing through slain troops knee-deep in their blood and exulting in her triumph. The result of her victory (obscure in the tablets as we have them) is that Baal lives again. "Mighty Baal lives, lord of earth."

These two battle epics, one with Yamm, the other with Mot as antagonist, are the only two about Baal which survive in any substantial form from Ugarit. There are enough scattered allusions to other, lost traditions for us to know that they existed, but we have only fragments, glimpses,

---

[51] A succinct statement is Gordon 1961, more extensively argued in Gordon 1962. The seasonal pattern is argued most thoroughly in Gaster 1961.

[52] See Table 1 in Appendix, slot ζ.

[53] On this question, see Heidel 1963:16 n. 14. For Tammuz, see Jacobsen 1970.

[54] Trans. Cross 1973:118. The text is CTA 6.2. 30–35. See ANET 140.

not enough to know in full, only enough to tantalize. One text actually lists several such narratives, in typical, oral-formulaic style, as a proud boast by Anat about her many exploits. Every one of Anat's enemies in her catalog is a well-known variant of the adversary. She begins claiming the victory over Yamm which the surviving epic attributes to Baal, and her list continues with other familiar enemies:

> Did I not crush the beloved of El, Yamm,
> Did I not destroy River, the mighty god (*rabbīm*)?
> Did I not raise the dragon (*tnn*)?
> I smote the crooked serpent,
> Šhilyaṭ with seven heads.
> I smote Ars beloved of El,
> I put an end to El's calf Atik.
> I smote El's bitch the Fire,
> Destroyed El's daughter the Flame.
> I will wrest the silver, plunder the gold
> Of the one who would drive Baal from the heights of Zaphon,
> Causing him like a bird to flee
> His lordship, expelling him from his royal throne,
> From the dais, from his powerful seat. [55]

The last enemy in this catalog sounds remarkably like the rebellious Anzu-bird, but it also connects with another rebel figure in Canaan, Athtar. The language is clearly formulaic for that situation or type-scene.

Another text, perhaps a fragment of an incantation to Anat, tells us a little more about Anat's battle with the dragon, including the important detail of what happened to him:

> . . . [the dragon] swirled the sea,
> His double tongue licked the heavens,
> His twin tails churned up the sea.
> She fixed the dragon on high.
> She bound him to the heights of Lebanon. [56]

[55] Trans. follows Clifford 1972:59 and Day 1985:14. The text is CTA 3.3.35—4.47 (= V AB = ANET 137). For "River, the mighty God," see May 1955; for the name Shilyat, see Caquot and Sznycer 1970:396 n. 7. It is possible that the word means simply "tyrant," as others take it. The word *šbm* in line 37 is translated as "raise," not the more usual "muzzle," following J. Barr as cited in Day 1985:14; see the next quotation, in which the parallelism makes better sense of the passage. For the rebel language, see below, Chapter 6.

[56] The translation follows Clifford 1972:60, Cross 1973:119, and Day 1985:15–16. The text is Virroleaud (ed.) 1957, II 3.3–11.

Here we learn that the dragon, as in the Labbu myth, is explicitly connected with the sea, not simply in poetic parallel with it as in the previous
quotation. So we have a precedent in Canaan for the blending of monster
and Sea-enemy that we find in the *Enuma Eliš*—and that we shall find in
the Hebrew tradition. Second, we learn that the dragon's punishment was
to be bound to a mountain height, anticipating the fate of other adversaries, including Prometheus, Typhoeus perhaps, and also the Scandinavian
Loki. Unfortunately that is all we know from the texts so far unearthed
about this version of the battle with a dragon.

We do, however, possess another and very similar allusion to the
dragon battle; now the dragon is named and Baal replaces Anat as the victor. The allusion occurs within the poem about Baal and Mot, and the
passage is repeated verbatim a few lines later. Its context is unclear, but it
uses some of the same formulae as the Anat version:

> When you [Baal] smote Lôtān the ancient dragon,
> Destroyed the crooked serpent,
> Šhilyaṭ with the seven heads,
> Then the heavens withered and drooped
> Like the hoops of your garment.[57]

The Lôtān (*ltn*) of this text is vocalized differently, but is still recognizable
as the biblical Leviathan. The root (*lwh*) means "twist" or "coil" (Hebrew
lwy, wreathe), and so this famous name signifies originally the "twister,"
a natural term for a serpent and destined to take on the various tricksterish
implications of the English word.[58] The meaning even survives in the
same formulae as the Ugaritic texts: "Leviathan the twisting serpent, Leviathan the crooked serpent."[59] And the Old Testament also preserves
catalogs of Yahweh's victories, similar to Anat's, which place the various
enemies in parallel: Yamm, *tannīn*, Leviathan, rivers (*nehārōt*).[60]

The Book of Job is especially rich in allusions to the combat: it is, after
all, about a man's conflict with God. In one of his complaints, for example, Job asks Yahweh,

---

[57] Cross 1973:118–19, 149–50 (CTA 5.1.1–5 = Driver 1956a:103; Gordon 1949: no. 67).

[58] Emerton 1982; Day 1985:4–5.

[59] Isa. 27.1. On Leviathan, see now Day 1985:62–87. The seven heads of the Ugaritic text
survive in *Odes of Solomon* 22.3, *Pistis Sophia* 66, and *Kiddushin* 29b, as well as in Rev. 12.3,
13.1, 17.3.

[60] Ps. 74. 13–15. See below Chapter 6.7. See also Dahood 1969:199–205, Wakeman
1973:62–63, and Day 1985:22–25.

> Am I the Sea or the Dragon
> That you set a guard over me?[61]

while Yahweh himself brags comically about his feasts. Presenting himself as a divine fisherman or crocodile catcher, he asks Job,

> Can you draw out Leviathan with a hook,
> Press down his tongue with a cord?
> Put a cord through his nose,
> Pierce his jaw with a hook?[62]

From such scattered allusions as these we can piece together a tradition of various monster battles that the singers and tale-tellers seem to have regarded as multiforms of the same plot, whether the adversary were Sea/River or sea-born dragon or Death himself.

The linking idea in these myths is the struggle with dangerous waters, but so rich is the motif that it appears in many guises. In Mesopotamia the source of all rivers was the primeval water that Ninurta organized to prevent the disastrous flooding when the rains came. To this conception, represented by Apsu in the *Enuma Eliš*, was added the saltwater ocean, Tiamat. The two figures are distinct but closely aligned with each other, both in the *Enuma Eliš*, where Tiamat takes over her consort's function and their waters mingle, and in Canaan, where Nahar (River) is often merely an alternative name for Yamm. Of course it is disastrous if the sea invades an irrigation system, whether in Mesopotamia or Canaan, and this is one of the side-effects of bad floods in low, marshy areas, but in most cases these ideas are more mythical than naturalistic. It is on the mythological level that the waters mingle, so that the sea and the primeval waters come to be thought of as a great river surrounding the known world, a conception that survived in Greece as Okeanos and that is often represented as a serpent biting its tail. This encircling river was also connected with the river that must be crossed in order to pass from this world to the other. The idea is familiar from the Greek tradition of the Styx and occurs also in the Babylonian Gilgamesh epic, where the ferrymen, Urshanabi, is a prototype of the Greek Charon. And the river itself seems to have tested

---

[61] Job 7.12; trans. Pope 1965:56–60.

[62] Job 41.1–2; cf. Job 26.5–14 in Pope 1965:163–66, 266–78. See below, Chapter 21, for Origen's use of this passage. Other allusions to combat in Job are 3.8; 7.12; 9.8, 13; 26.5–14; 38.8–11; 40.1–2; and indeed the whole passage at 40.15—41.34.

the souls who wanted to cross—hence Nahar is known in some Ugaritic
formulas as "Judge Nahar."[63]

9. *The Voice of God*

The heroes who oppose these monsters use a wide variety of weapons,
knives, nets, arrows, clubs, spears, and the like. For the Hebrew Yahweh,
however, most of these material aids have disappeared. On occasion Yahweh uses his hands, but if the source of his power is specified at all, it is his
voice. Sometimes it is heard in the wind or in the thunder, for he remained, like Baal and Marduk, a storm god, but often enough all he needs
to do is roar. One of the words for this idea, *gʻr* (verb) or *gᵉʻārāh* (noun), is
often rendered "rebuke," but this is too weak a term. The word occurs,
for example, in Psalm 104 ("At your roar they fled, at the sound of your
thunder they took flight"), a text we have already linked to the combat
myth, and it occurs elsewhere in the Old Testament, each time with the
same connection.[64] A passage from Job will illustrate further and draw together the various ideas:

> The Shades beneath writhe,
> The waters and their inhabitants.
> Naked in Sheol before him,
> Abaddon has no cover.
> He stretches Zaphon over the void,
> Suspends the earth on nothing.
> He binds the waters in his clouds,
> But the clouds burst not with the burden.
> He covers the face of the full moon,
> Spreading his cloud over it.
> He marks a circle on the face of the waters
> At the boundary of light and darkness.
> The pillars of heaven tremble,
> Stunned at his rebuke (*gᵉʻārāh*).

[63] The Euphrates performs this function in a text from Ashur. See Heidel 1963:75, line 7;
cf. below, Chapter 3.1 nn. 18–19. On the question of "primal waters," see also Lambert
1965:294–95.

[64] Ps. 18.15 = 2 Samuel 22.16; Isa. 17.13, 50.2; Nahum 1.4. See also Kee 1968 and Day
1985:29. The word occurs in Ugaritic (Gordon 1949:13, 16, and 1955: nos. 68.28 and
137.24), not in Baal's battle itself but in the rebuke of the cowardly gods who yield to
Yamm's threatening visit and in Anat's rebuke of Baal for killing Yamm. Baal's weapon is
called *ygrs*, "drive out," which shares a common root (Driver 1956a:165; Cross 1973:115).

By his power he stilled the Sea.
By his cunning he smote Rahab.
By his wind the heavens are cleared,
His hand pierced the twisting serpent.
Lo, these are but the outskirts of his power;
What a faint whisper we hear of him!
Who could understand his mighty thunder?[65]

In this text, which like several others in Job is probably based on a psalm, Yahweh defeats the various enemies of the Canaanite myths, including Rahab, another name for the dragon Leviathan, as well as the Shades, linked to Mot but writhing like a snake. He clears the dragon from the sky, like the hero of the Labbu myth, he pierces the serpent, and he restrains the primeval waters. He strips naked Abaddon, "perdition," but he also covers or obscures the moon in eclipse. The binary opposition merely serves to increase the scope of the god's power. The passage recalls strongly the syncretic heaping of weapons onto Marduk, but it moves toward a focus on Yahweh's voice. In previous myths it was often the enemy whose voice, like Huwawa's, struck terror: "His roaring is the floodstorm, his mouth is fire, his breath is death." Like previous heroes, then, Yahweh takes over the enemy's characteristics. His voice, like Baal's, is still parallel with the thunder; it is not yet the abstract idea of the creative word, but the way is prepared for that development.

We should not, however, like some interpreters, make too much of Yahweh's special voice. The Old Testament text that dwells most insistently on the voice of God, Psalm 29, has long been recognized as an ancient Canaanite hymn, modified only slightly to accommodate Yahweh rather than Baal. The psalm opens with the standard "Address to the Divine Council," calling on the gods in formulaic phrases to worship the Glory of Yahweh. The Hebrew word for the Glory, kābōd, in verses 3 and 9, is generally taken as parallel to the Sumero-Akkadian me-lam, the god's essence revealed in his shining.[66]

The voice of the Lord is upon the waters;
the God of glory thunders,
the Lord, upon many waters.

[65] Job 26.5–14. For the translation and further discussion of the mythological content, see Pope 1965:164–67 and Day 1985:38–39.

[66] Cross 1973:153. See above Chapter 1, for Huwawa's aura. For the kābōd in the throne-mysticism that developed from exegesis of such texts as Ezek. 1.26 and Isa. 40.5, see Scholem 1960:40–79 and Quispel 1983.

The voice of the Lord is powerful,
　　the voice of the Lord is full of majesty.
The voice of the Lord breaks the cedars,
　　the Lord breaks the cedars of Lebanon. . . .
The voice of the Lord flashes forth flames of fire.
The voice of the Lord shakes the wilderness,
　　the Lord shakes the wilderness of Kadesh. . . .
　　and in his temple all cry "Glory!"
The Lord sits enthroned over the flood;
　　The Lord is enthroned as king for ever.[67]

Like the voices of other great heroes from Gilgamesh to Achilles, the voice of Yahweh is celebrated for its power over many of the enemies we have brought together, from the great trees in the forest to the dragon in the flood.[68] In hymn form the combat myth was often reduced to its essentials: the shining power, the decisive battles, the triumph, and the enthronement.

[67] Ps. 29.3–10 (RSV); see Dahood 1966:174–78, Cross 1973:155, and Day 1985:57–60. Among various parallels with line 10, the Babylonian passages cited for Marduk above should be added to their other references.

[68] For representation of the combat in the visual arts, see the Sumero-Akkadian cylinder seals in ANET, illus. nos. 671 and 691. See also Amiet 1953, Finet 1973, and now Teyssèdre 1985a:45–87. For Gnostic and Christian extensions of the tradition, see below, Chapters 12, 13, 16, 18, and 21, Jonas 1970:116–18, and Cooper 1983.

THREE

GREECE AND THE NEAR EAST

UNTIL THE discovery of the Ugaritic texts, and in fact until a good many years afterward, most classical scholars found it convenient, indeed almost obligatory, to discount as fabrications the considerable ancient evidence for contact between the Near East and early Greek literature and philosophy. The prejudice that lay behind this Greco-centrism was akin to that which led most theologians to insist on the uniqueness of the Israelite religious vision in spite of the obvious similarities with neighboring peoples. Although both prejudices still linger in many minds, and although the character and extent of the contacts is fiercely argued, there has by now been a remarkable shift among both classicists and biblical scholars. In this chapter we shall concentrate on Greece.

Although the first discovery at Ugarit was a Mycenaean tomb and subsequent excavations have revealed many foreign settlements, often quite large, it has been the discovery and decipherment of Hurrian-Hittite texts at Bogazköy that have made classical scholars begin to pay attention.[1] The reason is obvious. The Hittites spoke a language related to the same Indo-European family as Greek, and they even referred to the Greeks of the Mycenaean period as "the people of Ahhiyawa," a term that corresponds to Homer's "Achaeans." Furthermore, some of the Hittite myths bear a strong resemblance to the Greek traditions related in Hesiod's *Theogony*. The succession myth, in particular, looks much like Hesiod's, and it even includes an episode, absent from the Mesopotamian and Canaanite texts as we know them, in which the defeated generation of gods produces a monster to challenge the power of the new ruler. Hesiod's Typhoeus already looked suspiciously similar to the Babylonian Tiamat, but now here was a monster, Ullikummi, who, like Typhoeus, represented the final effort of the older gods to reassert themselves. When we add that the Hittite myths appear to be adaptations of the older Hurrian traditions (another case of *Graeca capta*, since the Hurrians were conquered by the Hittites)

---

[1] Even then, the meticulous German, Ferdinand Sommer, who published and first edited the Hittite texts in 1932, rejected any link with Greece. On the whole subject, see Page 1959:1–19.

and add too that both Hurrians and Hittites had settlements at Ugarit, then it was clearly time for Greek scholars to take notice.

Many books and articles have since argued the details of the connections. Major contacts took place during the Minoan-Mycenaean periods.[2] The Greeks then domesticated the Near Eastern traditions and handed them on to subsequent ages in the form of oral epic. The process probably continued even after the fall of the great palaces of the Mycenaean period, and certainly from the eighth century on there was renewed contact with the easterly neighbors, especially the trading Phoenicians. But by then the main combat myths of Greece, particularly the Titan battle and the Typhoeus story, had long been current in the Greek tradition as a part of the myth-singers' repertoire.[3]

The specific channels of transmission, and the particular versions of myths transmitted, are impossible now to disentangle. In fact, there seems to have been a good deal of overlapping at both ends: Hurrian myths were known at Ugarit, the Hittites adopted myths from others besides the Hurrians, while Mesopotamian and even Egyptian traditions were also borrowed and blended. In Greece this complex tradition, at least from the time of Hesiod or soon after, was fertilized by fresh contacts with its disparate ingredients. Hesiod became especially important for the subsequent history of the adversary figure: many later writers, from Apollonius to Milton, adapted his versions of tradition for their own narratives. But there were many other variants of the adversary battles current in the archaic period. Most of these are lost or exist only in fragments, but in some cases it is possible to document the connections between other Greek writers and the Near East.

1. *Pherecydes and the Canaanite Connection*

One of the connections mentioned in the ancient sources but ignored by an earlier Greco-centric scholarship was the plain statement in Eusebius that Philo of Byblos (A.D. 64–ca. 140), one of that heterogeneous and industrious band of ancient scholars often summarily dismissed as "mythographers," actually translated into Greek a Phoenician (i.e., Canaan-

---

[2] West 1966:18–47. See Gordon 1962 and contrast Walcot 1966, who argues for the main links during the archaic period. In my view this is a false dichotomy.

[3] On Hesiod's oral tradition, see Peabody 1975, Nagy 1979, and now Foley 1985.

ite) text by one Sanchuniathon.[4] Unlike some modern scholars, Eusebius actually pursued this piece of information to see what value it might have and found a statement by the philosopher Porphyry that Sanchuniathon was a native of Beirut who had obtained records of the Baal temple from a priest called, appropriately enough, Hierombalos; furthermore, his Phoenician history had been submitted to and accepted by Abibalos, king of Beirut, and his experts. Porphyry calculated that, based on the Phoenician king list to which he had access, Sanchuniathon must have lived before the Trojan War and near the time of Moses, which puts him close to the period of the Ugaritic texts.[5] This is not an improbable date. And Sanchuniathon's work survives, at least in the fragments of Philo's Greek translation preserved by Eusebius. One is the more inclined to trust at least parts of this precious document because the myths it tells are sufficiently close to those recovered by the archaeologists, both to the Hurrian-Hittite and to the Canaanite. Indeed, though Sanchuniathon is said to have written a Phoenician—and therefore presumably Canaanite—history, he tells a variation of the widespread succession myth which is closest to the Hittite form.[6] This means either that the West Semitic Canaanites themselves told a similar version of the myth, or at least that Sanchuniathon took the Hurrian-Hittite tradition to be a native Phoenician one. The Ugaritic texts have not, however, yielded a variant of the succession myth in the West Semitic dialect. As we have seen, the Ugaritic texts contain several combat myths, but none attached either to cosmogony or to the battle between the generations of gods.

What does this tradition tell us about Greece? Philo of Byblos himself is late. He is, like Berossus, one of many shadowy figures who helped transmit Canaanite and other Near Eastern material to the Greek-speaking world of the Hellenistic period. But Philo also tells us that a much earlier Greek writer, in fact one of the earliest prose writers, the sixth-century Pherecydes of Syros, had been inspired by Phoenician material, possibly even Sanchuniathon's, in his cosmogonic account of the world. The *Suda*, a source that might otherwise be highly suspect, also states that Phere-

---

[4] Eusebius, *Praeparatio evangelica* 1.10.44. Cross 1973:13 cites and uses his student's Ph.D. dissertation on Sanchuniathon (Clapham 1969). Skeptical accounts of Philo's report are Kirk and Raven 1966, Barr 1974, and A. I. Baumgarten 1981.

[5] Walcot 1966: 17–18; West 1966:24–28.

[6] Both Sanchuniathon and the Hurrian-Hittite Kumarbi text, for example, have a god (Eliun, Alalu) before the sky god in the sequence of generations (ANET 120–21). For tabular comparisons, see Littleton 1969b and cf. West 1966:20–28. Even Kirk and Raven (1966:31–32), while dismissing "the whole farrago," accept this detail as authentic local tradition.

cydes obtained "the secret books of the Phoenicians."[7] In recent years both Peter Walcot and M. L. West have built a strong case for the dependence of Pherecydes on the Near East, especially the Phoenicians, just as Philo of Byblos (itself on the Syrian-Lebanese coast south of Ugarit) had said.[8] Specifically, says a fragment preserved by Eusebius, Pherecydes followed the Phoenician version of a battle between Kronos (understood as Chronos, time), chief god of the pantheon, and Ophioneus, a dragon-like adversary similar to Hesiod's Typhoeus.[9]

Pherecydes' work, unfortunately, survives only in disparate fragments, but so important a clue to possible connections between Greece and the Near East deserves to be followed up. M. L. West has mentioned many possibilities in his wide-ranging study, but here we shall explore one particular thread that may indicate a connection with Canaanite myth.

We may best begin with one curious detail that has puzzled previous scholars. The defeated adversary Ophioneus falls into Okeanos, which Pherecydes calls Ogenos, and Ogenos is said to possess "mansions" (*domata*).[10] These *domata* West calls "a mystery."[11] Now in general Greek tradition, Okeanos-Ogenos was the mythical river believed to encircle the earth.[12] Pherecydes mentions it and its mansion during the description of the robe that Zas (Zeus) gave to his bride Chthoniē (Earth) on the third day of their marriage.[13] The robe is decorated with a kind of cosmic map, and, like Achilles' shield at *Iliad* 18.607–8, it shows the world surrounded by Okeanos-Ogenos and the mansions. What is their significance?

We do not know much about the context of this fragment except that is is clearly an account of the divine wedding. But if we allow for the well-

---

[7] The ancient evidence is collected by Kirk and Raven 1966:48–72, Barr 1974, and A. I. Baumgarten 1981, all with different purposes. Kirk and Raven regard the Phoenician connection as an "unlikely story, indeed," although they admit to some "oriental motifs" in Pherecydes' thought (p. 52).

[8] Walcot 1966; West 1971.

[9] Philo of Byblos in Eusebius, *Praep. evang.* 1.10.50; Kirk and Raven 1966:68. Cf. Fontenrose 1959 and below, n. 53. For Kronos-Chronos, see Klibansky et al. 1964:139, 196.

[10] Papyrus fragment B2, West 1971:16.

[11] Ibid., p. 19.

[12] Ibid., pp. 18, 50; Kirk and Raven 1966:11–19.

[13] The description of the robe is probably an *ekphrasis*, a convention of Greek narrative tradition best known from Achilles' shield. Kirk and Raven 1966:62, followed by West 1971:12, think that the wedding was actually the occasion for Zeus' demiurgic activity, during which he turned his bride, Chthoniē, into the earth as we know it. In that case, the *ekphrasis* would be a clever way of describing cosmogony itself, the wearing of the robe become a metaphor for creation. This is only a guess, and the parallel with Achilles' shield suggests otherwise—global vision rather than cosmogony.

attested connection with the Near East, particularly with the Ugaritic myths, then we may suggest a plausible hypothesis. The Ugaritic epics recount various power struggles among the gods and the resulting apportionment of authority, the most important of which seems to have been the enthronement of Baal. And the central requirement of authority, stronger even than a coronation ceremony and the official annunciation by the supreme god, El, seems to have been the building of a special palace. One lengthy Canaanite myth simply recounts the difficulties in getting Baal's own palace built following the destruction of his enemies by Anat, his sister/consort. In a repeated formulaic passage we learn: "No house has Baal like the gods, no court like the sons of Asherah." Whereupon Anat, a formidable and determined female, says:

> Let the bull El attend unto me and I will tell him
> let him attend unto me and I will repeat to him:
> I will kick him indeed like a lamb to the ground
> I will make his hoar hairs to run with blood, the hoar hairs of his beard
> with gore, if he gives not a house like the gods, a court
> like the sons of Asherah to Baal. Anat planted
> her feet and the earth did quake.[14]

Eventually the order is given to fetch the divine craftsman Kothar-and-Khasis (the equivalent, according to Philo of Byblos, of Greek Hephaestus),[15] and the palace finally gets built.

Several other narratives also turn on the importance of the palace, among them the legend of Keret[16] and a curious myth of Athtar. In this myth, which forms a kind of prelude to the long narrative about Baal and Yamm, the divine craftsman is again summoned, this time to build for Yamm "a palace of gold . . . , a mansion of silver" in the recesses of the north; he agrees, proceeds to the palace of El, and announces his plans. Athtar, however, hurries to El and tells him about the construction work, claiming that to build "a mansion of Yamm, . . . a palace of Judge Nahar," is an act of rebellion. The Sun-goddess Shapash now intervenes and breaks the news to Athtar that El has decided to depose him and deprive him of his power "before Prince Yamm, . . . Judge Nahar."[17] It is unclear

[14] Driver 1956a:89, slightly adapted. See ANET 131–38 (II AB, V AB = CTA 4.4.50–51, 3.3. 1–2).

[15] Eusebius, *Praep. evang.* 1.10.35b–c.

[16] Driver 1956a:5, ANET 142–49.

[17] Driver 1956a:75–79 (III AB C = Gordon 1949: no. 129). See above, Chapter 2.2 and below, Chapter 6.3 nn. 21–23.

precisely what authority rested in Athtar before, or why Yamm's should threaten it, but he complains that he himself has no such palace or court. El is unmoved, and simply insists on the bestowal of authority on Yamm-Nahar. At this point the text becomes too fragmentary to make sense of.

Of these various kingly mansions, Baal's is merely a necessary ingredient in his accession to the kingship, but Yamm's is the motivation for an entire myth of its own, since the question of whether Yamm is to have a palace is made the focus of the struggle for power. Yamm's mansion, then, has a definite function of its own in Canaanite mythology. Yamm is Sea or "the deep," much like the Greek Pontos, which is what Philo's Greek calls him.[18] But Yamm's other name, Judge Nahar (River), links him, like Styx herself, with the world-encircling Ocean. In fact, all these ideas are difficult to separate either historically or genetically.[19] It is possible, then, that Yamm-Nahar's great palace of gold and silver, symbol of his authority granted by El, survived to become the mansions of Ogenos, granted him on the occassion of Zas' wedding in Pherecydes.

The palace or mansion as a sign of power is obvious in Greek tradition generally, whether in the heroic and Mycenaean context of Homer or in Hesiodic myth. In the *Theogony*, indeed, Zeus honors the river Styx, oldest (line 777) daughter of "back-flowing" (i.e., circular) Okeanos, with "very great gifts" (line 399) for her support against Kronos and the Titans, and takes her children to live in his own palace. As Hesiod puts it in a curious phrase reminiscent of the importance of dwellings as a sign of authority in the Ugaritic texts, "These have apart from Zeus no house, nor any seat, nor path except where the god leads them, but always they have their seat with Zeus the loud-thunderer" (lines 386–88). Styx herself, however, does have a palace, somewhere beneath the earth but attached to her father's waters, a tenth of which she is (line 789); she lives apart from the gods in a glorious palace (*kluta domata*) roofed by great rocks. All around, in fact (and this is odd for a subterranean house), it is supported by silver pillars reaching up to heaven (line 779). Furthermore, in order to get to her palace, Iris, the gods' messenger, must cross the "broad back of the sea." Clearly, Hesiod fuses a description of a mythological domain beyond the waters at the edge of the world with a subterranean idea (as well

[18] Since Pontos in Hesiod is one of the first generation of divinities, brought forth by Gē and then mating with her to produce a diverse brood that includes Nereus and all the monsters of Greek legend, this suggests a further link with Babylonian Tiamat, herself a primordial figure and mother of many monsters.

[19] Driver 1956a:12 n. 7, and above, Chapter 2.8.

as with the description of the beautiful waterfall of the Arcadian river Styx), but the prototype for the palace of Styx may well have been her father's mansions in Canaanite myth. Homer's Okeanos at *Iliad* 14.202 also lives in mansions (*domoi*) with his wife Tethys.

The Ugaritic Yamm, however, has a role well beyond the geographical and progenerative functions of the Greek Ogenos/Okeanos. As we have seen, he is also the monstrous adversary of Baal, and traces of this combat myth also survive in Greek tradition. There are many variants of this combat, but here we are interested in the survival of something like the Yamm variant in Greece. Is there, specifically, any trace of a myth in which the adversary figure, like Yamm-Nahar, is conceived as the Sea, or Okeanos the river?

In Hesiod, we know, Kronos is represented as supplanting his father Ouranos after the famous castration scene. But a story preserved in Apollonius shows that combat with a monster must have formed part of "the lost mythology of Kronos."[20] In Apollonius' story, which he attributes to Orpheus (a legendary poet-sage who is often saddled with tales for which no better authority can be found in the Greek tradition), Kronos took power not from Ouranos (Heaven) but from "Ophion," who previously held sway over snowy Olympus. Now Ophion, like Ouranos, had a consort, one named "Eurynome, dauther of Okeanos,"[21] who was forced to yield to Rhea, as Ophion to Kronos. That Eurynome is an Okeanid is confirmed by Hesiod (*Theogony* 358), where she is one of the daughters of Okeanos and Tethys, in the same generation as Styx herself (line 361), and by Homer at *Iliad* 18.398–405.[22] There Hephaestus tells how it was Eurynome and Thetis (herself a Nereid, often confused with Okeanids, and so granddaughter of Pontos) who caught and saved him at the time of his "great fall" (*tēle pesonta*) and nursed him in their cave for nine years "while the stream of Okeanos flowed on unceasing, foaming and murmuring around us" (lines 402–3). Though the mansions of Okeanos have here become a cave, this is not necessarily a demotion, for Greek tradition is full of wonderful caves used as dwellings, like Calypso's in *Odyssey* 4:557, which is huge (*megara*). Indeed, Hesiod seems to think of Styx's palace as also a cave.[23] At any rate, Eurynome's parentage and dwelling place sug-

[20] Kirk and Raven 1966:67.

[21] Apollonius Rhodius, *Argonautica* 1.503–4.

[22] Compare the same formulae at *Theogony* 776 and *Iliad* 18.400: *thugatēr apsoroou ōkeanoio*, the one for Styx, and other for Eurynome.

[23] *Theogony* 778, "roofed by great rocks."

gest that Ophion-Eurynome may have replaced Okeanos-Tethys as the original pair, a tradition that survives in Homer and Plato.[24]

Parents-in-law, sympathy with fallen adversaries, and a mansion-like cave by Ocean do not amount to very strong connections, perhaps, between Ophion and the Sea-Adversary, but we must now add the curious detail that, on his defeat by Kronos, Ophion and his wife fell into the waves of Okeanos. That, presumably, is where they stayed. Nonnus says that Ophion and Eurynome have a house at the outermost edge of Okeanos, perhaps the same place where Eurynome secreted Hephaestus after his fall.[25] The later allegorizers appear to have identified Ophion and Okeanos, and they may have had some Greek mythological precedent, the traces of which we have just been enumerating.

The "Ophion" of Apollonius, however, has a much clearer pedigree than this putative association with Okeanos. He derives quite obviously from Pherecydes or the tradition he represents. Pherecydes, we are told, "relates a myth of army drawn up against army and gives Kronos as the leader of one, Ophioneus of the other; he tells of their challenges and contests, and that they agreed that whichever of them fell into Ogenos were the losers, while those who drove them out and conquered should possess heaven."[26] Ophioneus, furthermore, is obviously a serpent-monster, not only from his name (Greek *ophis* = serpent) but also from the plain statement of Philo again, who says that both the Egyptians and the Phoenicians recognized the divine nature of serpents and "from the Phoenicians Pherecydes too took his beginning and told of the god whom he called Ophioneus and the Ophionidae."[27]

Presumably, Ophioneus had the same wife in Pherecydes as in his imitator, Apollonius, since Eurynome would be known to him from both Hesiod and Homer, where aside from being the daughter of Okeanos she is also one of the many wives of Zeus and the mother of the Charites, one of whom, in turn, is married to Hephaestus. Genealogical or marriage connections were often the way Greek myth-tellers expressed their sense of the relationship or grouping of narratives, an organizing device to bring order to the immense number of stories. Although he is apparently speaking for Thetis' benefit, Hephaestus is actually addressing his wife,

---

[24] Homer, *Iliad* 14.201, 246; Plato, *Timaeus* 40e.

[25] West 1971:23. Cf. Ap. Rhod., *Argon.* 1.506. On Hephaestus in the combat tradition, see below and Chapter 6.

[26] Celsus in Origen, *Contra Celsum* 6.42. See also below and Chapter 21.

[27] Philo in Eusebius, *Praep. evang.* 1.10.50; Kirk and Raven 1966:68.

Charis, daughter of Eurynome, when Homer has him tell the story of his confinement in Eurynome's cave. This family connection may imply that the story of Hephaestus' fall, of which Homer gives us two different versions, was a variant of the combat myth, perhaps connected with the Titan battle, or more likely a rebel variant like the one Greek tradition usually attached to Prometheus. At least there seems to have been a story that Hephaestus met his bride (when he was not married to Aphrodite) while he was exiled to Eurynome's cave, where he stayed for nine years.[28] Indeed, Aphrodite herself, for whom a Grace (Charis) is a standard replacement in epic tradition,[29] was a sea-born creature and, like Hephaestus, the product of one parent not two. Eurynome, then, connects Hephaestus, Okeanos, and Ophioneus.[30]

What begins to emerge from these scattered details? Clearly, the Greeks inherited the combat tradition and, like their Near Eastern neighbors generated local versions for their own gods. In some of these versions a connection with the Near East is palpable. Greece seems to have known some form(s) of a narrative in which a pair of monstrous creatures associated with the Sea did battle with the supreme god and lost. Either they themselves were originally in authority but yielded on their defeat, as may have been the case with Yamm and is suggested by several of the Greek references, or they challenged the power of the chief and were put down. Yamm himself is not represented as a serpent, but we know that the Phoenicians of Ugarit had such a myth, for Anat, as we have seen, cites the victory over the serpent Leviathan along with her defeat of Yamm-Nahar as evidence of her military prowess. What seems to have happened is that the variants of the combat myth influenced and transformed each other in the course of transmission, the generation battle and the serpent-monster battles merging, as in the Ophioneus figure, or Tiamat, to produce a new variant, but remaining also as separate myths as we find them at Ugarit or in Hesiod.

So Pherecydes' serpent enemy Ophioneus fits a widespread pattern. He is a variant of the adversary (part serpent, part other beasts) whom we have discovered in Babylon and especially in the crucial Ugarit texts. Unfortunately, no myth text that actually recounts the story has yet been discovered at Ugarit. What we have instead is Anat's proud list of her con-

[28] *Iliad* 18.400.

[29] Forsyth 1979. See also Nagler 1975:52–53.

[30] Eurynome was herself apparently worshiped as a "mermaid" at Phigalia (Pausanias 8.41.4).

quests, including the Leviathan dragon and the serpent with seven heads, and another allusion to similar myths, perhaps with Baal as victor. That adversary in turn appears on Sumero-Akkadian cylinder seals[31] and is probably related also, if distantly, to the Greek Hydra defeated by Heracles. In fact, the Heracles cycle seems to have strong Near Eastern connections and is probably a variant, at the level of heroic legend, of the god battles we have been pursuing in the myths,[32] just as the Sumerian Gilgamesh cycle, particularly the Huwawa poem, was a variant of narrative patterns that could also appear in folktale or myth.

The association of Ophioneus with the world-encircling Okeanos links him too with a whole range of combat myths in which the enemy of the victorious gods is a giant or monster who becomes, upon his defeat, the serpent Ocean, or at least takes up his abode in the mythical waters at the edge of the cosmos. Such myths are found in Indian and in Norse tradition.[33] Just as Thor sails out and catches the Midgard serpent on the end of his fishing line in one Norse myth related by Snorri,[34] so Yahweh appears to have drawn out Leviathan with a fishhook, even put a rope in his nose and pierced his jaw with a hook, according to Job 41.1–2.[35] Thus Leviathan looks like a reflex of a similar narrative, and we might connect him with a seventh-century Phoenician cup from Praeneste on which are represented a wide range of human activities all surrounded by the serpent with its tail in its mouth.[36] One thinks again of the common epithet for Okeanos, *apsorroos*, "back-flowing." Once again, then, we find a convergence of adversaries, with Sea-River and serpent-dragon as the dominant and linked forms.

2. Hesiod's Theogony: *The Glorification of Zeus*

For scholars unfamiliar with folkloristic methodology and the transmission of oral traditions, it has always been essential to establish the kind of literary dependence that the plain statement of Philo of Byblos attests: Pherecydes of Syros imitated, or otherwise drew upon, Phoenician documents, and this demonstrates the presence in archaic Greek circles of

[31] Cross 1973:119 and above, Chapter 2.8. Cf. ANET, plates 671 and 691, and Amiet 1953.

[32] Brundage 1958; Fontenrose 1959; Carter-Philips 1978.

[33] West 1971:45–48 gives a useful summary. See also O'Flaherty 1976.

[34] J. I. Young 1966:79–80.

[35] See above, Chapter 2.8. In *Enuma Eliš*, Tablet I, line 72, ANET 60, Ea takes Apsu's squire Mummu, mist, by a nose-rope after his victory. Cf. Wakeman 1973:65.

[36] The parallel is suggested by West 1971:41. Cf. Jonas 1970:116–17.

Near Eastern, and specifically Canaanite, myths. Once that connection is clearly established, it is easier for the scholar trained in texts and the methods of textual transmission to accept the presence in similar accounts, such as Hesiod's, of Near Eastern material, even though Hesiod's poetry is probably a hundred years or so earlier than Pherecydes' prose cosmogony. Indeed, a close relationship between Hesiod and the myths of the ancient Near East has been widely discussed, though not universally accepted, in the past thirty years.[37] When we couple Hesiod and Pherecydes and add certain allusions in Homer which show close parallels in the ancient Near East,[38] it becomes clear that the Greek mythological tradition shows obvious similarities to its Eastern neighbors as far back as our earliest sources. But if we are willing to stress the importance of oral tradition and transmission of narratives, especially in the light of the evidence that both Homer and Hesiod were either themselves oral poets or very close to oral epic tradition, then the scant evidence of documentary dependence becomes both easier to understand and much less of a problem. The documentary evidence is indeed scant, though highly revealing, but it should serve now rather as a control on our other speculations, not as our only evidence. The mythological parallels themselves are the vital ones.

Since Pherecydes survives only in scattered fragments, he is important chiefly for showing various kinds of connection between Greek and Near Eastern traditions, and it is impossible to say much about what he himself made those traditions into. The case with Hesiod's *Theogony* is very different. Here we have a more or less complete poem that is of seminal importance for the Greek and subsequent traditions and that shows a reasonably clear interpretive tendency of its own. That is, Hesiod does not simply collect many twice-told tales; he tells them with a specific purpose in mind. Just as composers of the *Enuma Eliš* created a version of the combat narratives that would glorify their own god, Marduk, so Hesiod made the focus of his poem the emergence and establishment of the power of Zeus. Like Marduk, Zeus had to struggle against adversaries before his power was assured. In the light of the Near Eastern parallels that have attracted so much scholarly attention, it is possible to see more clearly how Hesiod adapted the narratives to suit his overriding purpose.

[37] See, e.g., Vian 1960:17–37, Kirk and Raven 1966:33–37, Walcot 1966, and West 1966:18–39. Kirk 1970:213–26 has a general survey of similarities and differences.

[38] Webster 1958 pointed to the Enkidu-Patroklos parallel, e.g., explored further by Gresseth 1975. On Siduri-Circe, see Nagler 1977. See also Boman 1960, Gordon 1962, Kirk and Raven 1966:13–14, and Nagy 1979.

The general shape of the poem is fairly clear. The universe begins from Chaos and, more important, it begins with a female divinity (Gaia, Gē, or earth) generating by herself two male figures, Ouranos and Pontos, with whom she then gives birth to the subsequent generations. For a while she manages to exert considerable influence over affairs, but as the generations proceed, so she loses significance until finally Zeus becomes the locus of authority and the world is systematically structured. So the overall structure of the poem represents the shift from chaos to order and from female power to male power. Each of the three generations of male rulers gains in importance over the previous one, and Hesiod expresses this progression by a clear increase in the male power to generate: Ouranos, Kronos, and Zeus each generate offspring by themselves, rather than simply impregnating females (a common and widespread fantasy well known to anthropologists, for example in male initiation rites that assert the primacy of male over female, of culture over nature, by imitating the female birth process and claiming to repeat it on a higher symbolic level).[39] Ouranos, of course, is castrated by his son, following Gaia's instructions and encouragement, but from his severed member Aphrodite is born—one of the classic and formative stories of Western culture. The male birth in the next generation shows a more active role for the god. Kronos himself determines to swallow all his offspring to prevent them growing up to dominate him, but he is outwitted by his wife, Rhea, just as Gaia had proved too much for Ouranos, and Zeus (it seems, though the exact meaning of the text is unclear) overpowers him and forces him to disgorge his offspring.

The third generation completes the series. Zeus is told that he too will have offspring to outdo him, so instead of waiting for the children to be born and then swallowing them, he takes up the dangerous wife, Metis, and swallows her while she is pregnant. Eventually, Athena is born from his head. This story makes little sense if we assume that Zeus' act literally puts a stop to the sequence of generations and the consequent changes in

[39] Dundes 1962a and 1976a. The transference of power from the axis of nature to the axis of culture is also a clear organizing principle of the *Enuma Eliš*. Apsu, the primeval waters, is defeated by Ea, the god of those waters, who then builds himself a temple, which he calls "Apsu." He thus not only takes over Apsu's power but actually constructs it. Marduk does the same later, but now the power of the supreme enemy, Tiamat, the waters *and* the destructive mother, is included within Marduk's new dispensation, and he proceeds to appoint tasks to all those whom he has defeated. On the nature/culture progression, and opposition, which derives from widespread anthropological thinking, not just Lévi-Strauss, and ultimately from the Greek *nomos/physis* pair, see also Kirk 1970:132–71 and above, Chapter 1.3.

authority, since it was not Athena, we may assume, who was destined to overcome Zeus. In fact, it seems to have been Achilles, or at least the child Achilles would have been if Zeus had not prudently married Thetis off to the mortal, Peleus, since Thetis was destined to bear a child who would be greater than his father. And Thetis, we may remember, is a Nereid, that is, a daughter of the Old Man of the Sea, and thus a granddaughter of Pontos, the Sea, a figure who, being the ultimate ancestor of most Greek monsters, in this respect plays a role in Hesiod similar to that which Tiamat-Apsu played in the Babylonion cosmogony. But the birth of Athena does make sense if we take the sequence of male-birth myths seriously— beginning with a birth from a castrated member, moving through a forced regurgitation in which the male himself takes a more determined role, to the swallowing and so the literal incorporation of the generating and threatening female herself. It is the swallowing of the parent, not the actual birth of the child, which is significant in this symbolic sequence. The parent's name, of course, helps a good deal, Metis being Greek for something like "wisdom" or "intelligence," cognate perhaps with "measure," and this suggests that Hesiod himself intended the obvious allegorical implication.[40]

This is the context, then, in which Hesiod chose to tell the myths of Zeus's combat with his adversaries. Greek tradition probably also had a variant of the combat in which Kronos was the hero—certainly the Pherecydes story suggests as much—but Hesiod ignores it in favor of the Zeus stories. As a result, the Kronos portion of his poem contains several obscurities, even contradictions. What, for example, happened to Kronos after his defeat? Did he go down to Tartarus with his allies, the Titans, or did he go off to rule over the Islands of the Blest? From the *Theogony* we would assume that he was bound in Tartarus with his allies, the Titans (lines 717, 729–35), and indeed line 851 makes this explicit, but a peculiar and corrupt passage of the *Works and Days* (lines 168–74) tells us he rules over the race of heroes in the Islands of the Blest.[41] And who was responsible for the trick that made Kronos vomit up the stone substituted for Zeus and so allowed Kronos' children finally to be born? It was Gaia's idea, clearly ("beguiled by the cunning schemes of Gaia," line 494), but then comes a line so apparently intrusive that one editor of Hesiod,

[40] For the blending of Metis with Jewish *Hokhmah* speculation to produce the Gnostic Sophia, see below, Chapter 18.2.

[41] A further suspicious line then reconciles the two versions by claiming that Zeus released him (173b). The lines survive only in two papyri. See West 1978:194–96.

Heyne, excised it as disagreeing with what has just been said about Gaia:
"conquered by the devices and force of his own son" (line 496). Unfortunately, Hesiod does not explain how this was done, though the later tradition certainly made up for the gap. Apollodorus has Zeus give Kronos
an emetic, Nonnus makes the stone itself an emetic, and apparently an
Orphic variant reintroduced the castration motif from the earlier generation: Zeus gets Kronos drunk on honey, ties him up, and castrates him.[42]
But what necessitated these further elaborations was not so much the
brevity of Hesiod's language as the vagueness. *Nikētheis technēsi biēphi te*,
"conquered by tricks and by force," tells us both nothing and too much.
The phrase is itself a variant of a common epic formula—"by force or
guile" as Milton would translate it—and the line has all the appearance of
an afterthought as Hesiod suddenly remembers the main point of his
story: Zeus must somehow get the credit.[43]

Even when he tells the story of Zeus' own battle for supremacy, the Titanomachy, Hesiod is not entirely explicit, and for this there seem to have
been good reasons. The narrative begins suddenly at line 617, and in the
tenth year. This was the conventional Greek length for great wars to last,
and if Homer is typical, the narrative would also begin there. But later
Homer tells us some of the things that had happened in the previous nine
years of the Trojan War, whereas Hesiod tells us nothing. Is this because
Zeus had been incapable of winning the war without the help of the
Hundred-Handers? Certainly that is the way it sounds from Hesiod's account, especially lines 626–34, but he carefully avoids saying that Zeus actually needed the help. In his account of the war itself, he writes a long and
glowing passage about what Zeus does, hurling lightning and making the
earth and ocean seethe, and even Chaos feels the heat, and it is all winds
and thunderbolts and the shafts of great Zeus. But nothing happens. The
narrative switches instead to the Hundred-Handers fighting in the front
ranks, and suddenly the war is over and the Hundred-Handers are guard-
ing the Titans down in their own ancient prison of Tartarus.[44] Of course,
they are kept down there, as Hesiod carefully tells us, by the "will of
Zeus" (line 730), but Zeus has had little to do with putting them there.

As Hesiod tells it, then, the combat was a standoff until the Hundred-
Handers intervened. Zeus' special weapons are no help until now either—

---

[42] West 1966:302. I use West's work with gratitude throughout this chapter.

[43] See line 73, *karteï nikēsas*, and line 490, *biēi kai chersi damassas*.

[44] West 1966:363, lines 734–35, suggests that the Hundred-Handers too were banished
back to Tartarus.

indeed, it is made to seem as if Zeus did not even have those special weapons until now. Over two hundred lines earlier Hesiod has told us that Zeus received thunder, lightning, and the thunderbolt from the Cyclopes in gratitude for their release from prison, and that must have been at the same time Zeus released their brothers, the Hundred-Handers (though Hesiod does not say so). Clearly, the part about Zeus needing special weapons is part of the combat tradition—we find the same story told of Baal in the combat with Yamm—and indeed the motif is common as a sign that this is the true hero, the one who can wield these weapons. But Hesiod separates it from the combat part of the narrative in order not to stress the dependence of Zeus on outside help. Hesiod tends to emphasize Zeus' generosity in freeing these monsters from their bonds, not his obligation to do so.[45] The poet's convictions lead him to bend the tradition as far as he can.

But why has he not bent it further? Was there something so sacrosanct about the ten-year standoff and Zeus' need for extra help at the end of that time? Is there some reason other than the convention about ten-year wars that prevented Hesiod from having the whole victory take place in one glorious engagement? One editor says merely that Hesiod tries clumsily to reconcile the defeat of the Titans by the Hundred-Handers with his own "tendency to glorify Zeus more than the facts of mythology warranted."[46] Plausible as this sounds, it does not give Hesiod much credit. We need to find a more satisfactory account of the problem that Hesiod faced.

The first clue is a curious passage in Homer, a typically Homeric device (known as a *paradeigma*) whereby Achilles justifies asking his mother, Thetis, to intercede for him with Zeus by referring to a previous story.[47] Once, says Achilles, Zeus found himself in a desperate plight, being in fact imprisoned by the will of Hera, Poseidon, and Athena. But Thetis came to his aid, and as we have already seen, Thetis belonged to an earlier and powerful generation, so her help was worth having. What she did was summon to Olympus the Hundred-Handers, or one of them at least—Briareos. His sudden arrival was enough to throw the ranks of Zeus' ene-

---

[45] Walcot 1966:32.

[46] West 1966:355, line 711. Milton's narrative abilities have been subjected to adverse criticism at the same point of the story.

[47] *Iliad* 1.396–406. An argument has recently been gaining ground that Homer invented his own special versions of these *paradeigmata* as it suited his plot. See Willcock 1964 and Gaisser 1969, but cf. Nagy 1979.

mies into a panic so Thetis could free him from his bonds. Therefore, says Achilles to his mother, you have a claim on his gratitude. Sensibly, Thetis does not remind Zeus of this embarrassing episode when she comes before him to make her plea, yet Zeus himself seems to remember it, for he begins his reply by saying—and the absence of the conventional address formula reveals his agitation—"This is a disastrous affair, in that you set me on to conflict with Hera" (line 518). In the Iliadic context this means that the human war is to be repeated among the gods. In fact, the theomachy does become a fully realized episode in the *Iliad*, books 20 and 21, where both the battle among the gods aligned on either side of the Trojan War and Achilles' own struggle with the river Scamander are epic variants of the mythical combat tradition. But what Thetis' earlier aid to Zeus reveals for the student of Hesiod is that there was a Greek tradition, not just some barbarian tale, in which Zeus was at a standoff with the enemy, in fact a prisoner, until the intervention of the Hundred-Handers.

Admittedly, the opponents in Homer's *paradeigma* are Hera, Poseidon, and Athena, not the Titans of Hesiod. Still, the episode shows the vulnerability of Zeus when faced with divine opposition. Indeed, Poseidon, as Fontenrose remarks, "is the Olympian equivalent of Ocean" and "often represents the wild and hostile sea of chaos rather than the orderly sea of the cosmos."[48] It is Poseidon, of course, in this aspect of wild and unruly adversary, who opposes the return of the hero Odysseus. Hera's opposition to Zeus is a commonplace of Greek tradition, best exemplified in the *Dios apatē* episode of *Iliad* 14, when she seduces him and then leaves him in a deep sleep while she aids the Trojans. Athena appears oddly as the third opponent of Zeus in Homer's allusion, but we should recall that it was she who initially opposed the return of the heroes from Troy.[49] Homer's brief story of Zeus tied up, then, may well be an intra-Olympian variant of the combat tradition, adapted to the quarrel theme of the *Iliad*. Certainly it shows Zeus in a very weak position.

Greek tradition also knew other versions of Zeus' combats than those which Hesiod tells us. After the defeat of the Titans, Hesiod says, their mother, Gaia, bore another monster, Typhoeus, with a hundred serpent heads. Had Zeus not noticed him in time, he would have taken heaven, but Zeus managed to defeat him without great difficulty (*Theogony*, lines 820–68). But in the *Homeric Hymn to Apollo*, lines 305–55, we hear that the

---

[48] Fontenrose 1959:314.
[49] *Odyssey* 1.327 (Phemios' Song); see also 13.317–21.

mother of Typhon (the creature's name has various forms) was Hera herself, angry at Zeus for giving birth to Athena all on his own. Hera therefore decides to emulate this feat. She prays to Gaia, Ouranos, and the Titans for another child, but what she produces is the monster.[50] In Hesiod,
we remember, this role is taken by Hephaestus,[51] he who was hurled from
heaven and recuperates *chez* Eurynome and Oceanos in the Homeric narrative. At *Iliad* 1.591 it was Zeus himself who threw Hephaestus out, but
at 18.397 it is Hera's will; as in the *Homeric Hymn*, Hera is the mother of
Hephaestus, and she is angry that he was born lame. It seems that there
were at least two different versions of the fall of Hephaestus. In one he is
himself a rival of Zeus; in the other he simply plays a role in Hera's rivalry,
like Typhon in the *Homeric Hymn*. It begins to look as if Hephaestus and
Typhon were alternative adversary figures in the Zeus tradition, and both
could be assimilated to the standing quarrel of Zeus and Hera.[52]

The *Homeric Hymn* tells nothing about the actual combat, although it
does add that Typhon was put out to nurse with the Delphian dragoness,
Apollo's Pythian adversary.[53] But we learn a little more of this story, or a
close variant, from the B-scholium on *Iliad* 2.783. Typhon's parent here,
though indirectly, is Kronos. Hera this time is made angry at Zeus by Gē
(Gaia), who is frustrated by the defeat of the Giants, and so Hera goes to
Kronos for help. He gives her two eggs covered with his semen. Once she
buries these eggs, a demon is to be born who will usurp Zeus' throne and
so get revenge for Kronos' defeat. Here again it is clear how much the
Greek generation struggle has to do with the male fantasy of giving birth,
which in turn produces direct conflict with the mother figures, Gaia or
Hera. In this story, however, before the demon is born, Hera and Zeus

---

[50] The birth of Ophioneus also formed a separate episode in Pherecydes, to judge from the
summary in Maximus of Tyre (Kirk and Raven 1966:62).

[51] *Theogony* 924–29. Cf. the Chrysippus fragment, West 1966:401–3, lines 886–900.

[52] Ovid, *Fasti* 5.229–58, makes Ares play this role. See also West 1966:411–13, lines 922
and 927. Milton too, though on different grounds, asserted that Mulciber "fell long before"
(*Paradise Lost* 1.748).

[53] *Homeric Hymn to Apollo* 305, 353. The story of Typhon (Typhaōn here) is contained
within the ring of these two lines, and the effect is to blend Typhon with Python, the dragoness. This shows, if any demonstration were needed, that the singers of tales were aware
of the parallels among different combat narratives. The conjunction of Python and Typhon
here is the starting point for Fontenrose 1959, a far-reaching collection of these parallels.
Apollo kills the Python, supported by the sun god Helios, just as Gilgamesh kills Huwawa
with the help of Utu-Shamash. The Python too is the devastating monster of folktale (on
which see above, Chapter 1 n. 58), here elevated to the level of foundation legend; see below, Chapter 13, on her reappearance in Revelation.

are reconciled, so she warns him in advance and he easily defeats Typhon. This variant is interesting in part because it shows how the battle with a monster could be assimilated both to the struggle of the generations and to the quarrel with Hera. Hesiod chose to tell separate stories, giving the whole tradition his own kind of shape. But he may have known and suppressed these other versions. For example, Gē and Tartarus rather than Kronos and Hera are the parents of Typhon, yet this is the only occasion in Hesiod where Tartarus is a being, not a place, and he may function simply as a metonymy for the figure imprisoned there (if Kronos is indeed imprisoned in Tartarus like the other defeated Titans). The scholiast's version brings Typhon closer to the Hittite-Hurrian Ullikummi, also the final effort of the deposed god (Kronos-Kumarbi) to regain power.[54]

The most interesting variant is told by Apollodorus. He begins with the same story as the scholiast, at least insofar as Gē is angry at the defeat of the Giants. But she mates now with Tartarus, as in Hesiod, and bears Typhon.[55] He attacks heaven, hurling stones and breathing fire, and the terrified gods flee to Egypt. This motif, the flight of the gods, appears also in Pindar's version, in which the gods turn themselves into animals to get away.[56] Zeus, however, stands firm. The episode is reminiscent of the Canaanite gods' reaction to Yamm. Zeus attacks Typhon with thunderbolt and sickle, and Typhon flees to Mount Casius in Syria. Now this mountain, where in classical times there was a cult of Zeus, was identified with the spn (Ṣaphon or Zaphon) of the Ugaritic texts. Here there was a cult of Baal, and Baal-Zaphon seems to have been continuous with Zeus-Casius.[57]

Typhon and Zeus now do battle again in Apollodorus, but this time Typhon gets hold of Zeus' sickle and severs his "sinews." He then carries the lamed and impotent god to Cilicia, where he hides him in the Corycian cave. Eventually, the sinews are recovered by Hermes and Pan, and Zeus is rescued. He renews the battles, mounts his chariot, and hurls more thunderbolts. Typhon makes another stand in Thrace, hurling whole mountains at Zeus, but Zeus turns them aside, as in the Ninurta myth, and finally traps Typhon under Etna.

It has been argued that this elaborate version, in which Zeus is actually

---

[54] Güterbock 1952; comparison in Walcott 1966:1–26 and Kirk 1970:213–20.

[55] Apollodorus, Bibliothēkē 1.6.3.

[56] Pindar, frag. 91; cf. West 1966:380.

[57] Pope 1966; Clifford 1972:60, 135–36. For discussion and other references, Childs 1974:231–32.

defeated by Typhon before the ultimate victory, only came to Greece in the Hellenistic age.[58] Yet in view of the other elements in the story that have earlier parallels, there is no obvious reason to think this, and indeed the parallels with the Hittite story of Illuyankas, the dragon, and the weather god, Teshub, suggest a much earlier link.[59] The Hittite myth is an Indo-European variant of the Near Eastern combat tradition, and its connection with Canaanite variants is widely accepted. The combat narrative in its complex generational form had long been a part of the Greek tradition, entirely naturalized except for occasional oddities like Homer's placing of Typhon among the *Arimoi*, probably Aramaeans (like Abraham). So it is odd to want to exclude the defeat motif from the early Greek tradition, so widely attested as it is in both the Hurrian-Hittite and the West Semitic contexts.[60] If we can accept, then, that some earlier form of Apollodorus' version existed already in Greece, we can begin to understand both how much Hesiod concealed and why he could not conceal it more thoroughly.

3. Zeus the Rebel

There may have been another reason why Hesiod was reticent about the earlier part of the war. In fact, he alludes to the beginning of the war in one place only, and there not at all to its motivation. Hesiod is explaining about Styx and her allegorical children (Zeal, Victory, Strength, Force; lines 386–403) and why the children have no house or path apart from Zeus. It was because Styx with her children was the first to answer Zeus' summons to come to Olympus and take on the Titans; to all who would help, Zeus promised honors and privileges. This is the only passage where Hesiod says anything about how the war began. When he describes the war itself, as we saw, he begins in the tenth year. And the reason is not far to seek. It sounds very much from the passage about Styx's children— although Hesiod is careful not to say so—as if Zeus and the younger gods were the aggressors.[61] Otherwise they would already have been on

[58] Vian 1960:28–31, supported by West 1966:392.

[59] Fontenrose 1959:73–74; Walcot 1966:15–26. For the defeat, see Appendix, column ζ in the table.

[60] West 1966:380, eager to exclude as many "foreign" elements as possible from his discussion of the Typhoeus myth, has to admit that the Egyptian parallel is as early as Hecataeus and Pindar. Contrast his statement on p. 19 that "a connexion is incontestable" (of the succession myth) with his note on line 853.

[61] Ibid., p. 273, line 391. Cf. Aeschylus, *Prometheus Vinctus* 201–3.

Olympus. The passage reminds one of the common practice of usurpers, like those well-known figures in the archaic Greek world whose designation was the original of the word "tyrant." They would collect around themselves a group of underprivileged whose only allegiance would be to the leader and who would be entirely dependent for advancement on his favor. Zeus, then, is the rebel, not the heroic defender of order against the forces of chaos. Indeed, the logic of Hesiod's own story demands this. The Titans, after all, are the older gods, their leader is Zeus' father, Kronos, who had himself usurped power from his predecessor, and what we need now is a fresh attempt to wrest power from Kronos.

Hesiod nowhere describes how Zeus himself came to power, though he is not so crude a storyteller as simply to ignore the problem. Instead, he implies that Zeus took power through the trick that forced Kronos to regurgitate his children. Immediately after Kronos is thus outwitted, Zeus puts as a memorial at Delphi the stone that had replaced him in Kronos' belly, the released brethren in their gratitude give Zeus thunder and lightning and the fiery thunderbolt, and "relying on these, he rules over men and immortals" (line 506). This fusion of two distinct episodes, the deception of Kronos and the gift to Zeus of his special weapons, allows Hesiod to make the Titan battle seem like a rebellion against Zeus. As we shall discover later, Hesiod was by no means the last poet or theologian to blur the issue of who rebels against whom, and the controlling idea is always the same—whose side the storyteller is on.

The difficulties in Hesiod's narrative must have been clear to most of his many successors and imitators, the many storytellers of one form or another who told their own versions of these traditional tales. A later version of the Titanomachy, for example, tries to clarify this obscure place in Hesiod's narrative by separating and rationalizing what Hesiod had merged. Zeus first dethrones Kronos, because of his oppressive behavior toward his relatives, and then, once Zeus has taken charge of Olympus, the Titans revolt.[62] This is clearly the impression Hesiod tried to create, but without unduly violating the tradition.

It was especially the Prometheus story that was changed in later tellings, until he became the heroic rebel of the handbook versions. Hesiod already found difficulty with the story, intent as he was upon the glorifi-

---

[62] Hyginus, *Fabulae* 150; B-scholium on *Iliad* 15.229, commenting on the fight there would have been between Zeus and Poseidon if "he who encircles the earth" (Poseidon-Okeanos) had not disappeared into the sea. Those "other gods who are assembled about Kronos beneath" (i.e., Titans) would certainly have heard of that fight. Cf. West 1966:337.

cation of Zeus; indeed, it is a good question why Hesiod chose to tell the story at all. Perhaps it had become so integral a part of the tradition that he could not ignore it. For one thing, it is the necessary preliminary to the Pandora tale (not named as such in the *Theogony*), and that story Hesiod clearly wanted to tell very badly. It explains the origin of woman and therefore, to Hesiod's misogynist mind, the ills that flesh is heir to. One part of the story gave Hesiod special trouble. Just as Zeus outwitted Kronos, so Prometheus is said to outwit Zeus, first by fooling him into taking the bones and sinews, not the meaty part, of animal sacrifices, and second by stealing fire. From this curious tale Hesiod manages to draw the moral that Zeus is not to be outwitted nor his will thwarted. He can always inflict a greater ill—in this case, women.

Though there are hints even in Hesiod's account, it was chiefly Aeschylus (or the author of *Prometheus Bound*, whoever that was) who was responsible for the development of the heroic dimensions of Prometheus' character, sacrificing himself to his terrible fate in order to wrest the basic necessities of life (cooking, craftsmanship, warmth, medicine) from the glowering and tightfisted "father of gods and men." Of all the tales told by Hesiod, it was the Prometheus and Pandora stories that were to have the most far-reaching effects on the development of Christian tradition, once the Hellenistic fusion of Mediterranean and Near Eastern religious systems had taken place. Once Eve overlapped with Pandora, or Prometheus with Satan, the separate stories would never be successfully parted again. Hesiod's misogyny infected the Eve of the Christian tradition, and the heroic rebel could never again be entirely untwined from the character of Satan.[63]

One of the attacks that quickly followed upon the dissemination of Christianity in the wider, Greek-educated world was that Christians had simply adapted, debased, and taken too literally various classical Greek myths. These the philosophers had long converted, by allegory, into intimations of profound and abstract truths. Origen, for example, refers to the philosopher Celsus thus:

> He wants to give an account of the "enigmas" which he thinks we have "misunderstood" when we teach the doctrine about Satan, saying that the ancients hint at a sort of divine war. For Heraclitus speaks as follows: "But one must know that war is a mutual thing, and justice is strife, and that

[63] See, e.g., Glasson 1961:65; Pearson 1969; Delcor 1976:24, 53; P. D. Hanson 1977:227–32; and Nickelsburg 1977:399–404. See also below, Chapters 7 and 21.

everything comes into being through strife and necessity." And Pherecydes, who was far earlier than Heraclitus, relates a myth of army drawn up
against army—the story of Kronos and Ophioneus.

Celsus goes on that "this is also the meaning contained in the mysteries
which affirm that the Titans and Giants fought with the gods, and in the
mysteries of the Egyptians which tell of Typhon and Horus and Osiris."
Homer too hints at these same truths, says Celsus, and refers to the Hephaestus story at *Iliad* 1.590.[64] Origen's response to this interesting piece
of comparative mythology is that, far from imitating the Greek and other
pagan myths, the Christian scriptures, by which Origen means here the
Old Testament only, are actually the true account that these pagan myths
reflect:

> It is the writings of Moses, which are not only far older than Heraclitus and
> Pherecydes, but even earlier than Homer, which taught the existence of this
> wicked power who fell from heaven. Some such . . . doctrine is hinted at in
> the story that the serpent, the origin of Pherecydes' Ophioneus, was the
> cause of man's expulsion from the divine paradise, and deceived the female
> race with a promise of divine power and of attaining to greater things; and
> we are told that the man followed her also.

In this curious and influential passage, Origen makes an assertion that was
to become standard doctrine among Christian apologists: that the scriptures were the original of the pagan myths, the archetype of which the
classical and Egyptian narratives were pale reflections or distortions. He
thus manages to turn Celsus' argument on its head, though in order to do
so he must assert the sanctity and antiquity of the Hebrew scriptures
rather than that of "more recent" Christian ones. The argument between
the two philosophers boils down to competing assertions about which of
the two has the older, and thus primary, text/doctrine.

The question of relations among ancient narratives is a good deal more
complicated than this, but given the limits of their respective philoso-
phies, both Origen and Celsus will turn out to be partially right. As we
have seen in this chapter, Greek variants of the combat myth, including
Pherecydes', did indeed depend upon Semitic sources, if not quite the Hebrew documents that Origen had in mind. Conversely, the Hesiodic tradition bequeathed several fresh variants to the syncretistic world in which

---

[64] Origen, *Contra Celsum* 6.42, trans. Chadwick 1953:357–59. See below, Chapter 21.5.

Jewish apocalyptic and thus Christianity grew. Before we follow these developments any further, however, we need to consider how the Semitic traditions themselves were passed on from Canaan and Babylon to the Hebrews whose history is recorded in what Christians call the Old Testament.

FOUR

COMBAT AT THE RED SEA: THE
EXODUS LEGEND

1. *The Survival of Tradition*

THE MESOPOTAMIAN and Canaanite combat myths date in their preserved forms from the second millennium B.C. How then could they
have anything to do with the mythology of Satan, which does not date
back beyond the third century B.C.? In order for us to establish more than
a casual or accidental similarity between two sets of myths from such
widely separated periods, we need to know whether and how the myths
of the ancient Near East were transmitted (and transformed) during the
intervening millennium.

Several kinds of evidence are available for the longevity of the ancient
myths. The first kind is simply the antiquarian enthusiasm of subsequent
ages. Philo of Byblos was by no means alone in wanting to preserve a
1,000-year-old tradition, the Phoenician history of Sanchuniathon. Nor
was this zeal confined to the Greek world. If Porphyry is right, then Sanchuniathon himself had also obtained access to the temple records to write
his history.[1] We know too that Ashurbanipal, the seventh-century king of
Assyria, organized teams of scribes to collect and collate as many ancient
texts as they could find, especially in Sumer and Akkad.

The results of this Assyrian taste for erudition are especially revealing.
Huge numbers of texts from local archives went to make up the famous
library at Nineveh discovered by Sir Henry Layard in 1849, as well as several smaller collections throughout the empire, as far afield as Sultan-Tepe
near Harran in Turkey. Once they arrived in the libraries, the texts were
preserved and copied, some adapted to the contemporary literary fashion
and script but others exactly transcribed to the point that blanks were left
where the original tablets were damaged. The scribes would add in the
margin such phrases as "I do not understand" or "old break."[2] In addition
to scientific and historical records, these texts included many myths, leg-

[1] See above, Chapter 3 n. 4.
[2] Roux 1966:324.

ends, and folktales, among them the Labbu myth, the Gilgamesh epic, the *Enuma Eliš*, the Anzu myth, the legend of Naram-Sin, and the Etana and Adapa stories. Contemporary enthusiasm for these ancient texts was such that Ashurbanipal himself boasted his scholarly as well as military training: "The art of the master Adapa I acquired: the hidden treasure of all scribal knowledge. . . . I have read the artistic script of Sumer and the obscure Akkadian, which is hard to master, taking pleasure in the reading of the stones from before the flood."[3] Transcriptions are often remarkably accurate where it is possible to check: whereas the Hurrian or Hittite versions of Gilgamesh were widely divergent, it is often possible to reconstruct the Babylonian "original" from the Assyrian recension.

In 612 B.C. the palaces of Nineveh collapsed in flames, but those responsible, the Chaldean kings of Babylonia, fortunately retained some of the antiquarian zeal of their Assyrian predecessors, and thus the Jews who came in exile found a flourishing literary culture in the beautiful Babylon of the brilliant if short-lived Neo-Babylonian period. Cyrus the Persian, who captured Babylon in 539, to the delight of Second Isaiah, also took pride in preserving local traditions, so that such sources were still available, for example, to Berossus for his history of Babylon in 275 B.C. Berossus had documents to hand which told the stories of *Enuma Eliš* and *Atrahasis*, the Babylonian flood epic, but it is notable that he calls the flood hero by his most ancient, Sumerian name.[4]

The scholarly preparation needed to understand and edit these ancient cuneiform texts was formidable, as Ashurbanipal's boast amply reveals, and the very scale of his efforts might lead one to suppose that it was the sheer difficulty and inaccessibility of the traditions which led him to take such pride in the undertaking. But the wealth of texts available suggests otherwise, and fortunately there are other bits of evidence, in some ways better, for the viability throughout the first millennium of the ancient Semitic combat myths.

In some of the Assyrian versions of *Enuma Eliš*, the Babylonian Marduk's name was changed to the Assyrian god's, Assur. This suggests the adaptation of still-living tradition, not the passivity characteristic of scholarly revivals. In fact, the *Enuma Eliš* had continued to be recited in the Babylonian temple, and the change of name shows an active appreciation of the poem's value—almost a canonization. On the other hand, the

---

[3] Ibid., p. 309.
[4] Below, Chapter 7. For the two Berossus summaries of the flood myth, see Heidel 1949:116–19 and Lambert and Millard 1969:134–37.

radical changes we have noted in the Hurrian-Hittite Gilgamesh stories
point to an equally vital but mostly oral or unfixed secular tradition,
where local adaptation seems to have made the enemy Huwawa into the
hero. But the best evidence for the survival of the ancient myths is the major text that has come down from the period, the book known to Christians as the Old Testament. It contains documents that span the millennium, from the twelfth-century Song of Deborah to the second-century
visions of Daniel. Here if anywhere the continuing relevance of the old
myths should be demonstrable.

Most biblical scholarship in recent years has tended to discuss this issue
in the same terms in which Herman Gunkel posed it—the connection between combat myth and cosmogony.[5] If one recognizes, however, as I
have been insisting in this book, that the narrative pattern of the combat
may be but is not essentially linked to "creation," then we may quite simply dispose of what is a pseudo-problem. Combat was more frequently
linked to the triumph or enthronement of the king than to cosmogony,
and the traditions that had most impact on the Old Testament, the Canaanite, show little interest in cosmogony. This might be just an accident
of preservation, or it might reflect the local peculiarity of Ugarit. But it
seems more sensible to recognize that the combat tradition could be realized in and adapted to a variety of contexts. The Old Testament shows an
interest in both the kingship and the cosmogonic possibilities, but not
necessarily both at once.

For some time there has been general agreement on a broader issue with
which we are here concerned, namely, that Israel's own developing understanding of its covenant relationship with Yahweh entailed frequent
tension with the mythological belief systems of its various neighbors and
competitors. The tension may be succinctly described as that between a
people who saw themselves as agents of history and who defined themselves principally by a historical (or legendary) event, the Exodus, and
those neighbors who viewed the process of nature and the events of political life primarily as aspects of a mythological system. But this tension is
not simply external, between Israel and its rivals, for the dominant mythological thinking of the whole Near East strongly affected Israel's own
belief system: the tension of history or legend with myth is present in the
texts of the Old Testament itself, sometimes simply in the choice of met-

---

[5] Barton 1893; Gunkel 1895. Cheyne (1895) claimed precedence in his review of Gunkel.
Gunkel's line was followed by, e.g., Driver 1907:30, Speiser 1964:9–13, and von Rad 1972.
Lambert 1965:287–88 reviews the controversy, and see now Day 1985:50–51.

aphor or allusion but also in the very roots of Israel's self-conception. The balance could shift, as with the rise of apocalyptic thinking, beginning in the period of the Babylonian exile, when old myths done up in fresh colors often shaped the dominant belief systems, not merely the occasional metaphor. Yet there is a continuity between these apocalyptic visions and the earlier vocabulary of prophecy, and both in turn draw on mythological concepts. There was never a time, it seems, when the typical patterns of the combat myth were entirely buried by the peculiar Hebrew emphasis on history, on the human struggle with political enemies and with God.

2. Dry Ground Through Sea and River

A good way to understand the functions of the combat myth and thus the implications of the tension between myth and history in Hebrew traditions is to study the transformations of the central legendary event itself, the Exodus.[6] If the peculiarity of the Bible is that it takes history seriously as the sphere of God's self-disclosure and of man's authentic existence, the narrative focus of that singular view is the escape from Egypt and eventual arrival in a new land flowing with milk and honey. This political series of events remained in the historical memory of the people, and its structure—Exodus : Covenant : Conquest[7]—continued to shape the experience of Israel and to be typologically repeated in subsequent events like the Exile, and then in the new Christian cult, ultimately even in the recent political history of Israel.

This historical credo is expressed in Deuteronomy thus:

> A wandering Aramean was my father; and he went down into Egypt and sojourned there, few in number; and there he became a nation, great, mighty, and populous. And the Egyptians treated us harshly, and afflicted us and laid upon us hard bondage. Then we cried to Yahweh the God of our fathers, and Yahweh heard our voice, and saw our affliction, our toil, and our oppression; and Yahweh brought us out of Egypt with a mighty hand and an outstretched arm, and with great terror, with signs and wonders; and he brought us into this place and gave us this land, a land flowing with milk

---

[6] I use the term "Exodus" in the broad sense throughout; I am not here concerned with the traditio-historical problem of the relation between the event, the wilderness, and the Passover. See Anderson 1967:27 and Childs 1974:221–24.

[7] Cross 1973:85.

and honey. And behold, now I bring the first of the fruit of the ground, which thou, O Yahweh, hast given me.[8]

This thanksgiving liturgy, despite its role in the harvest festival, is not connected with creation or indeed with any myth. Instead it stresses the historical events that, according to the Hebrew legend, summoned the people of Israel into being.[9] A legend, we recall, distinguishes itself from myth precisely by this claim to historical status.

Among the events in this legend the most dramatic is the crossing of the Red Sea. But in the earliest source there is little sign of the miracle that the later tradition imagined here, the separation of the waters to allow the Israelites to pass and the subsequent drowning of the Egyptian pursuers when the waters came together again. What led to this remarkable invention?

The earliest biblical passage about the Red Sea event is the cult-hymn preserved in Exodus 15.1–18, the "Song of the Sea." The hymn may belong to the late twelfth or early eleventh century,[10] that is, before the monarchy in the time when the political organization of Israel was a loosely connected grouping of tribes. The first part of the hymn describes how Yahweh defeated the Egyptians at the Red Sea by blowing up a storm:

> At the blast of thy nostrils the waters piled up,
> the floods stood up in a heap;
> The deeps congealed in the heart of the sea . . .
> Thou didst blow with thy wind, the sea covered them,
> they sank as lead in the mighty waters.[11]

There is no reference in the hymn to the drying up of the sea or to "the waters being a wall before them on their right and left," as the sixth-cen-

---

[8] Deut. 26.5–10 (RSV).

[9] Von Rad 1966:159. See above, Introduction.

[10] Cross 1973:121–24, accepted by Anderson 1967:37, as against Rozelaar 1952. If v. 17 refers to Solomon's temple (cf. 1 Kings 8.13), the song would be tenth century, still the earliest reference to the Red Sea. See below, Chapter 7 n. 1, for more discussion of the dating problems.

[11] Exod. 15.8–10 (RSV). On the verb *qp'w*, translated as "foamed" by Cross 1973:128, see Childs 1970:411–12, Cross' response in a footnote, and then Childs' edition of Exodus (1974:242–70), where he modifies his position in the light of Cross' further argument. Cross and Childs agree on the general thesis advanced in this chapter, which draws much from these two authorities. Gunkel 1895 already noticed the major points of contact between the combat myth and the Exodus.

tury Priestly editor puts it.[12] It is true that "the waters were heaped up" and "the swells mounted up as a hill," but anyone who has been in a storm at sea will feel the aptness of these metaphors. As it stands, preserving through the fixity of its form the oldest version of the tradition, the Song of the Sea represents the event at the Red Sea as a realistic storm (attributed to Yahweh's breath, to be sure), and the enemies are historical and human.

Yet it is also true that the waters themselves get an extraordinary emphasis in the hymn's language, and this deliverance is chosen to symbolize the very creation of Israel as a people with a special mission. Exodus 15.16b reads:

> While your people passed over, Yahweh,
> While your people passed over whom you have created.[13]

Furthermore, this creation is the result of the enemy's defeat, and the waters are called the "deeps" (tehōmōt) in verses 5 and 8, the same word we find for the creation myth in Genesis 1.7 (and for the flood at Gen. 8.2), a word that is found in Ugaritic and is cognate with Akkadian Tiamat.[14] Finally, the result of the victory is what it is in the Baal texts and the Enuma Eliš—the building of a temple and "eternal" kingship. Clearly the hymn alludes to the combat of the Divine Warrior with his watery enemy, but while the allusions tap the power of that symbolic narrative, they reveal the difference between the original meaning and the new context: far from being the potential enemy of Yahweh, these waters are a passive instrument of his historical purpose.[15] The Song of the Sea provides an excellent example, given its ancient Near Eastern context, of the way in which, even in a hymn such as this—apparently not a narrative genre—the telling of a story is also the interpretation of a story: narrative is also theology.

[12] Exod. 14.22. See below, Chapter 7 n. 13.

[13] Cross 1973:103, 130; Anderson 1967:37. Cf. Deut. 32:6 and Humbert 1958:166–74 ("Qana en hébreu biblique"). Childs 1974:241, however, prefers the RSV translation, "purchased," and so links the verb to the long history of the ransom idea, on which see below, Chapter 19.1.

[14] For Ugaritic thm or thmt also meaning "cosmic waters," see Day 1985:50 and above, Chapter 2.8.

[15] Anderson 1967:37, 50, 128; Cross 1973:131–32. Gaster 1952:82 makes a similar argument but with a different purpose. Childs 1970:413–14 argues against any "demythologizing" in this text, but that term, derived from Bultmann's work on the New Testament (e.g., 1958b; see above, Introduction, n. 17), has the wrong implications for what I suggest is a complex set of literary allusions to other uses of the same language.

This firm relationship between legend and myth, in which the mythological pattern is broken and suppressed within the new historical context, is easy to misunderstand. There is no question here of a modern historian's rigorous objectivity and patient sifting of "facts." Rather, the
significant contrast is between a people who took the legend of a definite
(and recent) political event as the focus of their faith, and the surrounding
cultures that viewed themselves and their activities in terms of the actions
and reactions of gods, in terms of their myths' plots. The difference lies
not so much in religious behavior but in the kind of event that the Israelites took to be significant and in the special relation to their God they discovered there. Like their neighbors, the early Israelites probably held an
annual renewal festival, but what they celebrated was not so much the renewal of order and fertility as the renewal of the covenant. The Song of
the Sea may have been used as a cult-hymn for this festival.[16] If we consider this ritual context, we shall be less inclined to overemphasize the
contrast between Israelite religious behavior and the common practices of
the ancient Near East.

F. M. Cross has reconstructed the hypothetical outline of this annual
festival from traditions preserved in Joshua 3–5. In his view, the ceremony preserved the ancient tradition of holy war based on the theophany
of the storm god as warrior—a tradition common to both Canaanite and
Israelite belief and indeed widespread throughout the ancient world.[17]
The focus of the Israelite ceremony, however, was the triumphant crossing of the waters. At one point in the ritual, the Ark of the Covenant was
borne in solemn procession across the Jordan, which was "divided" for
the purpose. Apparently this act recapitulated two legendary events: the
deliverance of the sea (under Moses) and the crossing of the Jordan (under
Joshua). So sea and river were symbolically paired, which is exactly what
we found in the myth of Baal's battle with Prince Sea and Judge River.
Other scholars have expressed doubts about this reconstruction, but even
one of the most skeptical, Brevard S. Childs, allows that "some sort of
cultic rite did succeed in joining elements of the Jordan crossing with the
Red Sea tradition."[18]

The subsequent tradition often maintained this ritual pairing in the formulaic manner of traditional poetry. Psalm 66.6 reads:

[16] Pederson 1940:vol. 4, 726–37; Childs 1970:415; Cross 1973:91–144; Day 1985:18–38.
[17] Cross 1973:86, 91–111, 156–94.
[18] Childs 1970:415; cf. Coats 1967; Day 1985:97–101. The importance of this image in Israel's tradition is also to be seen in 1 Kings 18–19—the story of Elijah's struggle with Baal.
The chapters show the traits of oral composition and include the dramatic parting of the Jordan by Elijah (Cross 1973:191–92).

> He turned the sea into dry land,
> men crossed the river on foot.

And in Psalm 14 there is a clear allusion also to the combat myth:

> When Israel went forth from Egypt,
> the house of Jacob from a people of strange language,
> Judah became his sanctuary,
> Israel his dominion.
> The sea looked and fled,
> Jordan turned back . . .
> What ails you, O sea, that you flee?
> O, Jordan, that you turn back?[19]

Here the myth language has reasserted itself, if we compare this passage with the archaic Song of the Sea. Yet there is no sense that the psalm alludes to an alien myth. The pairing of Sea and River, of Exodus and entrance to the Promised Land, has become as natural to the Hebrew tradition as to the Canaanite.

It is even possible to discern dimly the early stages of this transformation from realistic storm to mythical combat. Although the Song of the Sea seems to be the oldest surviving version of the Red Sea story, the oral epic tradition probably had its own variants in the early period. One of these versions, preserved by the "Elohist" and then finally worked by the Deuteronomist editor into the text of Joshua, shows no trace of the later development but remains fairly close to the hymn narrative:

> Then I brought your fathers out of Egypt, and you came to the sea; and the Egyptians pursued your fathers with chariots and horsemen to the Red Sea. And when they cried to the Lord, he put darkness between you and the Egyptians, and made the sea come upon them and cover them.[20]

The "darkness" is new here,[21] but otherwise the episode is represented as it is in the hymn: a storm drowns the pursuers, and there is no mention of the means the Israelites used to cross over.

In other versions of the epic tradition, however, possibly dependent on the 'Yahwist," the Jordan story seems already to have influenced the Red Sea crossing. One result is that the function of the storm-wind (Yahweh's

---

[19] Ps. 14.1–5 (RSV). See the discussion in Driver 1956a:76–83, as well as Cross 1973:113–20, 138.

[20] Josh. 24.6–7 (RSV); see Cross 1973:133–43. On the "Elohist" and "Yahwist" and the recent controversy about these and other terms used here, see below, Chapter 7 n. 1.

[21] See Cross 1973:164, on the possible connection between the cloud of darkness and the storm-god theophany. Cf. Exod. 14.19–20.

breath) is entirely different: while the wind blows, the Israelites can cross, but when it stops the Egyptians are drowned—the reverse of the effect in the Song of the Sea. The Priestly editor tells the story thus:

> Then Moses stretched out his hand over the sea; and the Lord drove the sea back by a strong east wind all night, and made the sea dry land, and the waters were divided. And the people of Israel went into the midst of the sea on dry ground, the waters being a wall to them on their right hand and on their left. The Egyptians pursued, and went in after them into the midst of the sea, all Pharaoh's horses, his chariots, and his horsemen. . . . Then the Lord said to Moses, "Stretch out your hand over the sea, that the water may come back upon the Egyptians. . . ." So Moses stretched forth his hand over the sea, and the sea returned to its wonted flow when the morning appeared; and the Egyptians fled into it, and the Lord routed the Egyptians in the midst of the sea.[22]

The intruder that produced this transformation of the tale may well have been the notion that the Israelites crossed the Red Sea the same way they crossed the Jordan—on dry ground.[23] Here the sea is still a passive instrument of Yahweh's will, rather than the mythical enemy. But the mingling of Jordan and Red Sea traditions has turned the turbulent storm waters of the oldest source, metaphorically piled in a heap, into a miraculous wall of water that left the "dry ground" exposed.[24]

3. *Kingship and the Myth Language*

There was also a second, political reason for the transformation of the Red Sea crossing into this miraculous walk and eventually into a new myth. In the tenth century, David and Solomon had established the new institution of kingship, alien to the social structure of the old Tribal League. The focus of the revised religion was now to be Jerusalem and Zion. This entailed a new kind of covenant, between God and king, and as in the Near Eastern counterparts, a new emphasis on heroic combat myths. One example is the David and Goliath story, in which the widespread folktale of a boy and a giant is adapted to the new heroic context.[25] Other examples

---

[22] Exod. 14.21–27 (RSV); cf. 14.29 and 15.19, the editor's transition back from the old song to the Yahwistic narrative.

[23] Cf. Josh. 3.11–17, where the word "heap" (*nēd*) also occurs.

[24] The increased importance of Moses is a striking feature of these versions. In the quoted passage, however, we may attribute it partly to the Priestly squeamishness about granting a body to God: it may be the Lord's will, but it has to be Moses' hand stretched out.

[25] Types 300, 1028, 1197, in Aarne and Thompson 1964. Cf. Jason 1979 and Rank 1959. For other aspects of the political questions, see Service 1975 and Gottwald 1979.

are found in various royal psalms. Psalm 110, probably composed in this period, adapts the Ugaritic language and makes use of the common image of the victor with his enemies under his feet.

> Yahweh's utterance to my lord [David]:
> "Sit enthroned at my right hand,
> A seat have I made your foes,
> A stool for your feet."

Archaeology has turned up examples of such artifacts, footstools or seats with writhing enemies carved around the base and reminiscent of the "Tiamat" used in the Akitu festival at Babylon. The New Testament writers would later make extensive use of this verse as messianic prophecy, but in its original context it already adapts the myth language to a statement of regal triumph.[26] The psalm then announces that the Davidic king is to be "a priest forever after the order of Melchizedek." As we know from Genesis 14.18, Melchizedek was a Jebusite (i.e., pre-Israelite) priest of the god El-Elyon in Salem (Jerusalem). This cult was a local form of Canaanite religion blending features of the Ugaritic El and Baal. The new Davidic king of the place takes over the old cult and turns its combat myth to the service of Yahweh and the Davidic monarchy. The rest of the psalm uses this mythology as support for the inviolability of Zion in the conflict with the nations.[27]

In the same way, the new monarchic mythology transformed the Red Sea crossing. In the premonarchic Song of the Sea, the mythical allusions are strictly subordinate to the physical event and the Egyptians ordinary human enemies. But now the Egyptians become Rahab, a variant of the adversary figure, and the sea again takes on its cosmic character.

There is a good deal of biblical evidence by which we may trace this shift in emphasis. An early psalm, perhaps from the tenth century, combines the old and new meanings in two parallel verses:

[26] Ps. 110.1. See Dahood 1970:112–17, whose view of the tenses and text I follow in the midst of considerable disagreement; cf. above, Chapter 2.8. The New Testament quotations, Matt. 22.44, Mark 12.36, Luke 22.42–43, Acts 2.34, and Heb. 1.13, are discussed by Hay 1973:59–154. For the Pauline allusions, see Carr 1981:89–93 and below, Chapter 14.2.

[27] This widespread view has recently been challenged by Van Seters 1975:306–8 and passim and by Clements 1980:73–81, but see Emerton 1971 and now Day 1985:125–38. A thorough study of the question, including its role in the myth-ritual school's thinking, is Horton 1976:12–53. For the later Melchizedek tradition and his conflict with a demonic rival, see Milik 1972, and for the references in Heb. 5.6 and 6.19–7.28 and in Gnostic works, see Horton 1976:87–172. See also below, Chapter 10.3.

> You rule the raging of the sea: when its
>   waves rise, you still them.
> You crushed Rahab like a carcass, you scattered
>   your enemy with your mighty arm.[28]

The same psalm goes on to equate god and king, as is the way with royalist mythology: Yahweh promises to protect him from "the enemy" and from the "son of wickedness," to crush his foes and strike down those that hate him. He then undertakes the following, in effect making David another Baal and pairing Sea with River:

> I will set his hand on Sea,
>   His right hand over River.

As Cross remarks, "The mythological allusion to the victory of the divine warrior over the watery chaos has been applied to the king, a natural transfer in the ideology of Canaanite kingship but remarkable in an Israelite context."[29] It is hardly surprising that the psalm continues with the most extreme form of the new royal covenant ideology:

> Forever I will keep faith with him,
> And my covenant with him shall endure.
> I have established his seed for ever,
> His Throne as the Days of Heaven.

Yahweh's promise to David and his house is *unconditional* and permanent.

From the early monarchy also comes Psalm 77, in which the allusion to the combat myth is explicit, and the link made clear with the Exodus and the Conquest:

> The Waters saw you, Yahweh,
> The Waters saw you and writhed;
> Yea the Deeps shuddered. . . .
> Your way was through the sea, Yahweh,

[28] Ps. 89.9–10. For the text and translation, see Wakeman 1973:56, except that I follow Cross 1973:135n, who reads ʿwybk, your enemy, in v. 11. Cf. Ps. 93.1–4 in Dahood 1969:279. Rahab is one of the Hebrew names for the mythological beast who opposes Yahweh. It may have been understood to mean "the one who has been stopped," as in Isa. 30.7, but its root probably means "to be agitated, excited"—appropriate, as Pope 1965:70 points out, for a marine monster. Since it sometimes does duty for Egypt, as in Ps. 87.4, "Among those who know me I mention Rahab and Babylon, behold Philistia and Tyre, with Ethiopia" (RSV), mention of Rahab will usually be an allusion to the Exodus tradition, conceived mythically. H. G. May 1955 discusses the link between Rahab and watery chaos enemy. Cf. Job 9.8–13, 26.5–13, and Day 1985:18–28, 90.

[29] Ps. 89.25; see H. G. May 1955:15 and Cross 1973:258–62.

Your path in the deep waters,
Your tracks beyond our understanding.[30]

There are strong connections between this psalm and another early song, the so-called "Psalm of Habakkuk," implying either literary dependence or a common oral tradition.[31] Here we find both similar cosmic ideas and the "anointed one" of the royalist context. Yahweh's anger against the historical enemies of his people is equated with his anger at the mythical combatants. There is an explicit allusion to the Canaanite Baal myth, and we find the same pairing of River and Sea that we noted in the covenant renewal ceremony:

Was not your wrath against River, Yahweh,
Your anger against River,
Your ire against Sea,
When you drove your horses,
The chariot of victory . . .
You marched through the land in anger,
You thrashed the nations in indignation . . .
You trampled Sea with your horses,
The surging of many waters.[32]

The last verse above is heavy with mythological allusions. The term "many waters" (*mayim rabbīm*) has been shown to have many close relatives in the Old Testament, and its connotations are usually of the cosmic adversary,[33] while the expression "trampled" suggests the victorious storm god with his foot on the enemy's back, like Marduk in the *Enuma Eliš*, David in Psalm 110, or Yahweh in Job:

Alone he stretched out the heavens,
Trod on the back of Sea.[34]

[30] Ps. 77.6, 19; trans. Cross 1973:136. Dahood 1969:233 calls this "a demythologized allusion to the Canaanite sea-god Yamm," but not necessarily to creation, as Cross thinks. See also Childs 1959:189, who calls attention to the mythological implications of "shake" in verse 19; cf. Wakeman 1973:118.

[31] Albright 1950 argued for literary dependence on Ps. 77; see H. G. May 1955:9–10. My own bias is for oral preservation as a song in a cultic context, given the musical notations of vv. 1, 19; see Day 1985:104–9.

[32] Hab. 3.8, 12, 15; my translation follows both Anderson 1967:98–99 and Cross 1973:140.

[33] H. G. May 1955. In Ps. 93.1–5, *mayim rabbīm* is in parallel with *nᵉhārōṭ* and *yām*; cf. Ezek. 32.2 and below, Chapter 6 n. 72.

[34] Job 9.8, trans. Pope 1965:67–70. Cf. *Enuma Eliš*, Tablet IV, line 104, Deut. 33.29, Amos 4.13, Mic. 1.3, and Isa. 63.3, but see now Day 1985:42.

Another early psalm, perhaps datable to the reigns of David or Solomon before the division into two kingdoms, makes explicit the combination of all three ingredients we have been tracing—the crossing itself, the ritual "division" of the waters, and the combat myth:

> He split Sea and brought them across,
> He made the waters to stand as a heap.[35]

Here the verb *bq'*, "split," gives us the clue we need to piece together the change in the Red Sea tradition. It derives from the battle of god and sea-dragon, whether in its Mesopotamian form (Tiamat was actually split in two by the victorious Marduk) or its Canaanite form (the same verb is used in parallel with the crushing of Leviathan's head in Ps. 74.14–15). In the early monarchy already, then, the Red Sea was no longer the passive instrument of Yahweh's will, but the enemy who had to be crushed. The same verb recurs in the Priestly version of Exodus 14.16 and 21 and in the Chronicler's late prose recasting of the traditions:

> And you split the sea before them and they crossed over in the midst of the sea on dry ground and their pursuers you threw into the deeps like a stone in the mighty waters.[36]

Thus, the parting of the waters so that the Israelites cross on dry land between two "walls" of water, derives in part from the ritual equation of the river Jordan and Sea (itself a parallelism found in the Ugaritic texts) and partly from the splitting of the Adversary in combat mythology. The human enemies of the early Song of the Sea have come to include the very waters themselves, and the Red Sea crossing has become the main Israelite variant of the combat myth.

4. *Exodus Typology and Redemption*

The royal covenant theology had profoundly changed not only the Exodus tradition but also the whole religion of Israel—it had in fact introduced the notion of the "kingdom of god" with its center in Jerusalem (or Zion) at the Temple. To religious conservatives this meant that Israel had become "like the nations," a political state with a king requiring submission to his power and supported by cosmic myths, not the special people

[35] Ps. 78.13. For the early date, see references in Cross 1973:134.
[36] Neh. 9.11, trans. Cross 1973:132. See above, n. 22.

God bound together by covenant allegiance. This conservatism continued as a powerful force throughout the next four hundred years in the voices of many of the prophets, beginning perhaps with Nathan's opposition to the temple and carried on in Elijah's challenge to Baal's priests. But when the kingdom was lost and the people were transported to exile in the alien land of Babylon, they tended to look back to the special place they had come to know, and to Zion as its heart and symbol. And they also looked forward to the day of their return. From these tangled and disturbed political events emerged the beginnings of a new movement in the thought of Israel, apocalypticism. Many scholars indeed refer to the writings of the immediate pre-exilic period, and the Exile itself, as "proto-apocalyptic." Not yet the end of the world, perhaps, but certainly a new dawn was eagerly anticipated, and it was natural that this hope also should present itself to the Israelites in the terms of the Exodus. To the historical and mythological dimensions of the old story were now to be added a third level of meaning, one that pointed to the redemptive future instead of the creative past.

Second Isaiah understood the rise of Cyrus of Persia to be a part of Yahweh's plan of history, Yahweh who calls the generations from the beginning (Isa. 41.4). He anticipated the imminent overthrow of the Babylonian Empire, Israel's return from exile, and the restoration of Zion, but he viewed all these events in the light of Israel's prophetic and Zionist heritage. These dramatic events were to recapitulate the basic history of the people, as told in the Exodus story, but with a fresh and heightened meaning: there will be none of the old struggle and suffering in the desert, for example, since Yahweh will prepare a superhighway through the wilderness and convert the desert into a new Eden. All this is a sign of divine forgiveness, of a new grace bestowed on Israel, and what is more, of the extension of salvation to all the nations. It is in light of this message of universal hope, of international redemption, that we must read the following famous and stirring prophecy:

> Awake, awake, put on strength,
>   O arm of the Lord;
> awake, as in days of old,
>   the generations of long ago.
> Was it not thou that didst cut Rahab in pieces,
>   that didst pierce the dragon?
> Was it not thou that didst dry up the sea,
>   the waters of the great deep;

that didst make the depths of the sea a way
   for the redeemed to pass over?
And the ransomed of the Lord shall return,
   and come to Zion with singing;
everlasting joy shall be upon their heads;
   and they shall obtain joy and gladness,
   and sorrow and sighing shall flee away.[37]

In this passage all the elements of our tradition are blended into a new vision of the meaning of history. Second Isaiah anticipates a renewal of the divine warrior's epiphany, the same warrior who defeated the dragon, or the beast Rahab, who overcame the chaos of the Deep in the cosmogonic combat myth, making the waters dry up so the people could proceed. Here the historical event of the crossing and the mythological combat have become identical, when viewed from this typological perspective. Deep, Rahab, Red Sea—all are parallel forms of the cosmic and historical adversary. And this great drama is about to be repeated when the people return to Zion, now "redeemed" and "ransomed," not simply from their old bondage to Egypt or their current Exile, but from the guilty history of apostasy and backsliding denounced by the prophets. And in this redemption all mankind will be emancipated from spiritual bondage.[38] This proto-apocalyptic passage in Second Isaiah is the clue, the necessary link, between the ancient combat myth and its transformation into an eschatological hope, the basis of the Christian message.

One further development would take place—the linking of the ancient story of cosmic rebellion with the Old Testament figure of the Satan—before this transformed combat myth would be the basis of the New Testament apocalypse. Otherwise, these writhing waters and twisting serpents were ready to become the narrative character to whom the Book of Revelation alludes when it identifies Satan as "the grand dragon, that old serpent, . . . the deceiver of the whole world." It follows this up with a beast rising from the sea and a vision of the end-time in which there will be no more sea.[39] That conjunction of images gathers together and preserves the language of the ancient combat transmitted in the Old Testament Exodus tradition.

[37] Isa. 51.9–11 (RSV); cf. Job 26.12–13. For the dependence of this passage on Ps. 89, see Day 1985:92.

[38] Anderson 1962 is the best account of this typological development in Second Isaiah. Cf. Cross 1973:99–111 and Hanson 1975.

[39] Rev. 12.9, 21.1. See below, Chapters 13 and 16.

Part Two

REBELLION AND APOCALYPSE

FIVE

THE SATAN OF THE OLD
TESTAMENT

T HE WORD *śṭn* and a character with the title "the Satan" appear several times in the collection of documents that came to be canonized and known to Christians as the Old Testament. The word never appears there as the name of the adversary in the combat myth, a link that was made only in uncanonical apocalyptic texts and in the New Testament. Rather, when the Satan appears in the Old Testament, he is a member of the heavenly court, albeit with unusual tasks, and the historian must be able to explain how this subordinate if dangerous character ever came to be identified as the cosmic adversary. The explanation must begin from the momentous religious and political events that form the background to the prophecy of Second Isaiah we considered in the previous chapter. We can discern in the Babylonian exile and its aftermath the roots of a striking change in the nature of Hebrew religion, and especially in the nature of God.

Second Isaiah is the prophet to whom the Hebrew religion chiefly owes its new character as "a light to the nations."

> "I Yahweh do all these things; I alone stretched out the heavens; I laid out
>   the earth; who was with me?" . . .
> He says to the Ocean, "Dry up; I will make your streams waterless."
> He says of Cyrus, "My shepherd; he will accomplish all that I wish,"
> Saying to Jerusalem, "She shall be built," and to the temple, "You will be
>   founded."[1]

The connection here is explicit between Yahweh's power as creator, the typological vision of the Exodus crossing as a mythological combat, and the current historical instrument of Yahweh's will, Cyrus the Persian. Cyrus now becomes what the Israelite kings had been in preexilic times, "the anointed of Yahweh" (Isa. 45.1), a term that passes into Greek as "Christos" and into English as "Messiah."

It was a bold move for the prophet to insist even in the dissolution of

---

[1] Isa. 44.24–28, trans. McKenzie 1968.

the nation of Judah that he saw Yahweh at work in this murky and disturbed political struggle between two pagan empires. But he does not flinch from the radical implications of this idea. Instead, he composes a "call to Cyrus," in which he imagines Yahweh himself stressing his own omnipotence and uniqueness:

> I have called you by your name; I have ennobled you, and you did
>   not know me.
> I am Yahweh; and there is no other; besides me there is no god; I have
>   armed you, and you did not know me,
> That they may know from the east and from the west that there is
>   none besides me,
>   I am Yahweh, and there is no other.
> I form light, and I create darkness; I produce good and I create
>   evil;
>   I Yahweh do all these things.
> Drip down, heavens, from above, and clouds, pour down
>   righteousness;
> Let the earth open and blossom with victory, and let righteousness
>   sprout with it;
>   I Yahweh have created it.
> Woe to him who strives with his maker—an earthenware vessel with
>   the potter!
> Does the clay say to the potter, "What are you doing? Your work
>   lacks skill"?[2]

These words perhaps contain an allusion to Cyrus' own Zoroastrian religion, in which the opposition of the twin primordial "spirits" in their efforts to establish life or nonlife is regulated by the supreme power, Ahura Mazda.[3] In any case, Second Isaiah affirms a single-minded faith that God

[2] Isa. 45.4–9. In v. 7, 1QIs[a] from Qumran reads *tōb* (good); see McKenzie 1968:77. The resemblance to Job 10.8–9 is discussed below, and that to Rom. 9.20–24 is discussed in Chapter 14. Gnostics took Yahweh's claim to be a lie, on which see Chapter 12 n. 53 and Chapter 18 n. 33.

[3] *Yasna* 3.3–4 in Duchesne-Guillemin 1963:105. Zaehner 1961:55 cites *Yasna* 44.5, in which Ahura Mazda creates both light and darkness, as in Isa. 45.7; cf. Isa. 54.16. The oversimplified version of the Zoroastrian tradition that lies behind earlier comment on Second Isaiah needs to be qualified; see the discussions in Pfeiffer 1948: 469, Duchesne-Guillemin 1958, Winston 1966, and R. N. Frye 1975. Recent work has helped to make direct connections more probable, but on the other hand the lack of reliable dates for the various stages of Zoroastrian belief makes assessment difficult. Both Job and Second Isaiah sound at times like *Yasna* 44, and all three texts may date from the same period. Sixth- and fifth-century inscriptions of the Achaemenian kings open with formulas such as "A great god is Ahura Mazda, who created this earth, who created that sky, who created man" (Dresden 1961:337), words that echo Zarathustra's insistence on the creator. (Following Dresden

forms both darkness and light. So the result of extending Yahweh's power in this dramatic way to all history is a corresponding increase in the power of one God, the most radical statement in the Bible of Hebrew monotheism. In particular, Yahweh creates evil.

The only other biblical writer who espouses so uncompromising a version of monotheism is the author of the Book of Job, in which a God who can create darkness and evil is submitted to the most profound philosophical protest: "Your hands molded and made me, and then turned to destroy me. Remember it was of clay you made me; and back to dust will you return me?" (Job 10.8–9). The ambivalence of God, the presence in him of a destructive as well as creative side, Job challenges, and only in the final revelation does he get free from his anguish and allow the monstrous and fearful side of God. Job suffers personally from the same God whom Second Isaiah announces as the lord of history.

Unfortunately, the experts have not reached any agreement about the date or provenance of the Book of Job, but the parallels with Second Isaiah have led many to argue for a relationship between the two.[4] Indeed, many scholars ancient and modern have suggested, though in the absence of any obvious evidence, that the sufferings of Job are an allegory of the troubles of Israel, just as on occasions the Suffering Servant of Second Isaiah is to be identified with the nation of Israel.[5] The final insight, then, "I know that my redeemer liveth," would apply both to the personal world and the political world—an emotional certainty with enormous repercussions for

---

and others I use "Zarathustra" for the prophet himself, and "Zoroastrian" for the subsequent tradition.) But there is nothing in either Job or Isaiah like the doctrine of the two spirits from *Yasna* 30, a passage that seems to be earlier than its Qumran analogues (discussed below, Chapter 10). The passages about Angra Mainyu, "Destructive Spirit," known afterwards as Ahriman, all seem to be late, whether Zervanite or not (Zaehner 1955:312–20), although his opponent, "Augmentative Spirit," Spenta Mainyu, occurs in *Yasna* 47.3 as the son of Ahura Mazda, who creates all things (44.7) through him (Duchesne-Guillemin 1963:67, 99). The absolute dualism of two primordial beings, Ormazd and Ahriman, as opposed to Zarathustra's own ethical dualism, seems to occur only in the late Pahlavi texts, from the Sassanid period, third to seventh centuries A.D., and thus its origins are difficult to disentangle from Gnostic or Manichaean developments. See, further, Dresden 1961, Zaehner 1955 and 1961, Duchesne-Guillemin 1953, Widengren 1946, Schmidt 1951, and Dumézil 1945. For the types of dualism, see Pétrement 1946.

[4] Pfeiffer 1948:467–80, developing Pfeiffer 1927, is the best argument I have seen for the impact of Job on Second Isaiah: the Suffering Servant of Isaiah is in part a response to the dilemma of suffering on Job. It would be strange if Job's author knew the doctrine of vicarious suffering and yet failed to make use of it. Pope 1965:xxxiii, whose translation I follow, also finds Pfeiffer convincing. More recent editions of Pope's *Job* have appeared but the points I borrow have not been changed.

[5] Anderson 1975:457–60, referring, e.g., Isa. 49.3. For the nationalistic Job, see the references in Pope 1965:xxxiv.

the political revival of Israel after the defeat of Babylon by Cyrus. Though such a view of Job is too simpleminded, besides begging the question of date, one can readily see the parallels, and indeed it may have been partly this view that led to the canonization of the dangerous Book of Job within the sacred scriptures.[6]

Hebrew monotheism rarely attained either the philosophical profundity of Job or the passionate clarity of Second Isaiah. It was not long before this integrated version of God would break apart. The sixth- or fifth-century editor of the Priestly traditions, known to scholarship as "P," blurred the issue on which Second Isaiah pronounced himself so clearly. By a crucial syntactical ambiguity, P modified the inherited form of "primeval history" and so hedged on the question of whether God himself created the darkness. All that P specifically and incontrovertibly states is that God said "Let there be light."[7] Soon the darkness, indeed evil itself, would take on an independent existence, hostile to the very being that Second Isaiah claims created it.

Even in the Book of Job we may discover the seeds of this later development, in "the Satan" of the folktale frame with which the text as we have it begins. Though the major part of the book is set entirely on earth, and we are allowed to see Job's troubles from his own, his friends', and his wife's points of view, the book opens after a brief prologue with a scene in the heavenly court and the wager between God and the Satan. The word "Satan" is here a title, rather than a proper name, since it appears with the definite article, roughly equivalent to "Attorney General" or "Public Prosecutor." The Satan is represented as one of the *benē 'elō-hīm*, the "sons of God" familiar from the Ugaritic texts, who are generally

---

[6] On the date of Job, see Pfeiffer 1948:675–78 and Pope 1965:xxx–xxxvii. On the place in the canon, see Pope 1965:xxxviii–xxxix. Pope favors a date in the seventh century B.C., at least for the Dialogue, but is alert to the many problems and to the Babylonian and Canaanite parallels.

[7] Gen. 1.3. The grammar of these sentences, both in Hebrew and in the Septuagint, allows for various interpretations. Speiser 1964 adopts the view that Genesis opens, like the *Enuma Eliš* or the Yahwist version (Gen. 2.4b), with a temporal clause: "When God began to create. . . ." This view means that the darkness and the deep (*tehōm*) were already existent. On the grounds that this is not theologically defensible, Anderson 1967:111 argues for a strict reading of the Greek syntax, so that "In the beginning" refers to an absolute temporal beginning (cf. Eichrodt 1962). Childs 1960:30–42 has a good discussion of the ambiguity but thinks the Priestly author is trying to break with the pagan view, not to leave it implied. See, however, Day 1985:49–53. I prefer to insist on the ambiguity rather than to argue for the writer's "intentions," unlike Kapelrud 1974. On "P," see below, Chapter 7, and on the relation among the mythological ideas in P, Second Isaiah, and Job, see Day 1985:54–56.

conceived in the Hebrew tradition as the members of the heavenly court.[8] These are the beings who, upon the threat of the adversary, panic and fall silent. In the Baal-Yamm poem, we recall, the gods "drop their heads Down upon their knees,"[9] and the *'ēlīm* in Job have a similar reaction to Leviathan: "Were not the gods cast down at sight of him? . . . When he raises himself, the *'ēlīm* are afraid."[10]

Like its mythical and earthly counterparts, the heavenly council of Yahweh suffered occasional threats to its harmony. A key member of this court was a spirit who was usually given the name *mal'āk Yahweh*, herald or messenger of god. The stem of this word is *l'āk*, emissary, cognate with Arabic *la'āka*, to send on a mission. To this is prefixed the *ma-*, which indicates an abstract noun form, feminine in gender.[11] In some Old Testament passages, this spirit is simply an aspect of Yahweh himself; it is what appears to Moses in the burning bush,[12] before Yahweh himself takes over two verses later. It appears also as the pillar of fire and cloud that gives darkness to the Egyptians but light to the camp of Israel.[13] Here especially the idea is akin to that of the "radiance" of Sumero-Babylonian gods. Elsewhere, however, the *mal'āk Yahweh* is a separate entity doing God's will, usually translated *angelos* in the Septuagint. It appears, for example, to Hagar,[14] announcing the birth of that outcast wild man, Ishmael, or, in one version of the Passover legend, it is the destroying angel whom the Lord has to restrain from indiscriminately slaughtering the Israelites.[15] A similar figure is the spirit who appears as "evil" or "lying" in several passages of the Deuteronomic historian. Yahweh makes a breach between Abimelech and the citizens of Shechem by sending an evil spirit;[16] he provokes trouble between Saul and David by making Saul prophesy against his will and hurl a javelin at David;[17] and in the impor-

---

[8] Cross 1953. Pope 1955:47–49 collects the Ugaritic references, and Pope 1965:xxxv, 9, the biblical. Parallels are at Job 38.7 and Ps. 29.1, 89.6–8. For I Kings 22.9–23 and Gen. 6.2, 4, see below; cf. Ps. 82.1, where they are called simply "gods." Cross 1973:186–90 discusses the various "council of Yahweh scenes" and also Isa. 40.1–9, "Comfort ye, comfort ye, my people."

[9] See above, Chapter 2.4 n. 27.

[10] Job 41.9, 25. See Pope 1965:280–82 and Day 1985:62–72.

[11] Klüger 1967:58; cf. below, Chapter 9, on Mastema.

[12] Exod. 3.2. See Childs 1974.

[13] Exod. 14.19, 24. See above, Chapter 4.2, and below, Chapter 21.2.

[14] Gen. 16.7–12.

[15] Exod. 12.23. See below, Chapter 21.6, for Origen's interpretation.

[16] Judg. 9.22–23. Klüger 1967 brings together these passages.

[17] I Sam. 16.14–16, 18.10–11, 19.9–11.

tant episode that leads to the foundation of the temple, he is the angel of pestilence: "The angel stretched out his arm toward Jerusalem to destroy it, but the Lord repented of the evil and said to the angel who was destroying the people, 'Enough! Stay your hand.' "[18] We note here an angel who wants to do more than the Lord will finally allow, a potential clash of wills that is to be vastly developed in the later tradition. The temple of Jerusalem is to be erected on the spot where the angel stopped his destruction, a foundation legend as ambivalent as the narratives we earlier linked to the temples of Sumer and Babylon.

An episode with remarkable parallels to the Job prologue concerns a minor prophet in the time of Ahab, Micaiah ben Imlah. He has a vision of

> the Lord seated on his throne, with all the host of heaven in attendance on his right and on his left. The Lord said, "Who will entice Ahab to go up and fall at Ramoth-Gilead?" One said one thing and one said another; then a spirit came forward and stood before the Lord and said, "I will entice him." "How?" said the Lord. "I will go out," he said, "and be a lying spirit in the mouth of all his prophets." "You shall entice him," said the Lord, "and you shall succeed; go and do it."[19]

When Micaiah explains this to Ahab, that the Lord has "spoken evil" concerning him, one of these lying prophets steps forward and smites Micaiah on the cheek. Ahab has Micaiah imprisoned, takes the advice of the lying prophets, and is killed at Ramoth-Gilead.

In each of these passages, the angel or spirit of the Lord is associated with some conflict, but in each case, hostile as he may show himself to particular men, he remains a servant of the divine king, a shady but necessary member of the Politburo. In other cases, indeed, he is even presented as a supporter of the potentially "good" side of the conflict.[20] The primary function of the heavenly court was judgment, and it thus mirrored the conflicts it was called on to judge and would eventually be unable to restore its own unity.[21] It was in the Satan figure, himself a member of this court and in many ways parallel to the *mal'āk Yahweh*, that the tensions within the monotheistic faith would emerge most clearly.[22]

---

[18] 2 Sam. 24.16.

[19] 1 Kings 22.19–22 (NEB). The parallel with the lying dream of Agamemnon in *Iliad* 1 is also remarkable. For further development of this story, see below, Chapter 10.3.

[20] See below on Num. 22.22; Zech. 3.1–10.

[21] See Cross 1973:189–90, on the prophetic role of the divine messenger.

[22] For parallels in the later Qumran texts (e.g., 4QAmram), see Vermes 1975:260, and for the *Testament of Abraham*, see Stone (ed.) 1984:63.

The Hebrew word *śṭn*, vocalized as *śāṭān*, means something close to the English word "opponent" in its root sense of "to place in the way," "to obstruct." In the curious episode of Balaam's ass, for example, Yahweh's angel, the *mal'āk Yahweh*, stands in the road and blocks the way, *le-śāṭān-lō*, "as an obstruction to him."[23] Since Balaam's journey to Moab was unauthorized, the angel is simply doing God's will, and the prudent donkey has the sense to see this, despite the promptings of his rider, who is unaware of the obstruction. The Septuagint (the Greek version) here uses the word *endiaballein*, whose root meaning, again, is "to set something across one's path." A *diabolos* is one who performs the action signified by the verb *diaballein*.[24] Despite the parallel progress of the words *śāṭān* and *diabolos* toward their invidious denotations, the episode of Balaam's ass shows that no necessary evil attaches to either. If the path is bad, an obstruction is good.

The converse, however, became the normal situation. A "stumbling block" is usually bad in English (though it may conceivably spur one to greater efforts), and the words "stumble" and "fall" are often related—as in the progress of the Hebrew and Aramaic root *nphl* toward the grandiose meaning of "the Fall."[25] The Greek for "stumbling block" is *skandalon*, which gives us not only "scandal" but also "slander," another well-known activity of a *diabolos*. The root meaning of Satan survived into New Testament times, as we may see from a passage that contains both Greek and Hebrew words. In Matthew 16, Jesus explains to the disciples the path that lies before him—toward the cross. Peter is horrified and tries to dissuade him from his course, whereupon Jesus replies, "Get thee behind me, Satan. For you are a *skandalon* in my way."[26]

Most uses of the root *śṭn* in the Old Testament already suggest this kind of darker meaning; the assumption is usually that the path is right and the opponent wrong. But the word does not necessarily refer to spiritual adversaries. In 1 Kings, for example, the word refers to an ordinary earthly enemy: "And Yahweh stirred up an adversary [*śāṭān*] to Solomon, Hadad the Edomite." In the same chapter, Rezon, king of Damascus, is called "*śāṭān* to Israel all the days of Solomon."[27]

[23] Num. 22.22; Klüger 1967:38.
[24] Lattimore 1962; cf. Kittel (ed.) 1951–76, s.v. *diabolos*.
[25] See below, Chapter 10.1.
[26] Matt. 16.23; see Lattimore 1962, below, Chapter 15 and the relevant entries in Kittel (ed.) 1951–76, esp. *skandalon* (Eng. trans. vol. 7, pp. 339–48).
[27] 1 Kings 11.14, 25; Klüger 1967:34.

In the Book of Job, however, we find a subtle play on words that suggests a more complex idea. When the Satan and the other members of the court present themselves to Yahweh, he says to the Satan:

> "Where did you come from?"
> The Satan answered Yahweh,
> "From roaming the earth,
> And strolling about on it."[28]

There follows Yahweh's question about whether the Satan has seen his servant Job, "a blameless and upright man who fears God and shuns evil," and then the Satan's challenge and Yahweh's acceptance of it. The same passage is repeated when the Satan returns to Yahweh after his first attempt on Job fails, and Yahweh authorizes him to turn the screw. But what exactly was the Satan doing "roaming the earth and strolling about on it"? Much later these words would be incorporated into the composite picture of the roving devil at liberty to tempt and subvert, but we are still a long way from that time. The Satan of Job is certainly no "fallen angel."

The clue in the Hebrew here is the word for "roam," šûṭ. Hebrew or Arabic are languages that lend themselves to puns much more readily than English because of the absence of vowels in the earlier written forms, so we must not necessarily assume any profound significance whenever we meet such a Derridean play on words. Yet in this case at least, the author of Job has brought into resonance with the generic notion of "adversary" a more specific concept. Herodotus tells us that the power of Persia depended heavily on an elaborate system of intelligence agents, some of whom were known as "The King's Eye" or "The King's Ear."[29] The system was a kind of secret police structure, rather like Savak or the KGB, and its purpose was to maintain surveillance of the satraps, to detect and report any seditious move. Xenophon quotes the proverb "The King has many ears and many eyes." So the Hebrew pun alludes to a system that must have been especially irksome to subjects of the Great King and may suggest that at least the Satan part of the Book of Job was composed in Persian times. To this word šûṭ is added the parallel verb "stroll" (hithallēk), cognate with an Akkadian word applied to the evil eye or to evil spirits that rove about seeking to do harm.[30]

---

[28] Job 1.7; trans. Pope 1965:1.

[29] How and Wells 1928: vol. 1, 108. Tur-Sinai 1957 was the first to develop this line of thought.

[30] Pope 1965:11, citing parallels in Prov. 24.34.

The word šûṭ, to rove or roam, also occurs in a similar context in Zechariah 4. Again we have a vision of the heavenly court and again the Satan is present, but here the "eyes of the king" are not brought into direct connection with the Satan. Instead, God is represented as a seven-branched candlestick, and the seven lamps, here the symbol of Zerubbabel's kingship, are "the eyes of the Lord which rove through the whole earth."[31] This part of Zechariah has been convincingly dated to the early Persian period, to around 520 B.C., and thus may well be more or less contemporary with the composition of the Satan episode in Job.

The Satan's role in Zechariah has an extra ingredient missing from Job: he is rebuked by Yahweh's angel (the mal'āk Yahweh) for his opposition or prosecutor's role, as if he has gone too far and needs to be restrained. For the first time we sense a genuine danger to the solid monotheism of Second Isaiah. This public official entrusted with the duties of seeking out and accusing unjust men now threatens to exceed the limits of his office, a J. Edgar Hoover or a CIA director who no longer clears his every move with the president but imperceptibly at first begins to act on his own initiative to plan the harassment of a Martin Luther King Jr. or to develop subtle stratagems to poison Fidel Castro's cigars. We still have some way to go before this politically useful official is disgraced and becomes the scapegoat for an unsuccessful or unpopular policy. But already the Satan of Zechariah's vision has taken on more color and character than the simple obstruction that waylaid Balaam's ass. The word śāṭān of the Balaam episode is merely in grammatical apposition with the mal'āk Yahweh, whereas in Zechariah the Satan is a separate being with his own official duties and is directly opposed to the mal'āk.[32]

The political context of the Zechariah passage illuminates considerably the Satan's role. Following the return to Jerusalem after the exile, various groups with differing religious agendas contended for power. One such group was the inhabitants of the former Assyrian province, Samaria, inheritors of the northern kingdom's Mosaic traditions.[33] Since the secession of the northern kingdom under Jeroboam, there had been long and bitter rivalry between Israel and Judah, and many Samaritans seem to have regarded the Babylonian exile of Judah as a divine judgment on the

---

[31] Zech. 4.10. On the dating, see P. D. Hanson 1975:249.

[32] Compare the Abraham scene in the *Book of Jubilees* 17.15–18.12, where the mal'āk and Mastema are similarly opposed. See below, Chapter 9.

[33] Anderson 1975:480, 490. On the whole question I follow P. D. Hanson 1975, but cf. Carroll 1979a and 1979b.

heretical direction of its monarchist theology. Now, however, the Samaritans were willing to help with the rebuilding of the temple. Another group consisted largely of the "people of the land," those who had remained in the area of Jerusalem after its destruction in 587. They too looked with suspicion on the returning exiles and clung to the vision of a prophet such as Second Isaiah that Yahweh was himself about to inaugurate a new age of peace and national reconstruction. But the group that eventually won the struggle, composed now chiefly of the Zadokite priesthood and its supporters, who had been scattered during the exile years, strongly espoused the rebuilding of the temple as the focus for a new and powerful monarchy.[34] More significant, this priestly group, asserting that Yahweh himself had removed to Babylon with themselves during the exile,[35] refused to allow its rivals any part in the rebuilding program and organized the temple cult so as to exclude the rivals from any but the most perfunctory participation.

This rebuff of Samaritans and of the "people of the land" sent both groups off in separate political and theological directions. The Samaritans would eventually build their own temple on Mount Gerizim overlooking Shechem, the earliest center of the Israelite confederacy, and so emphasize their own adherence to the Mosaic covenant expressed in the Torah, the only part of the Hebrew scriptures they regarded as sacred.[36] The visionary "people of the land," on the other hand, unable yet to remove themselves from the new temple cult that had disenfranchised their faith, would become the medium through which the eschatological fervor of the prophetic movement sustained itself and was transformed, through sects like the Essenes, into a cosmic and apocalyptic vision of the last days.

Zechariah and Haggai together tried to harness the prophetic tradition and its eschatological message to this priestly temple cult, although once the struggle had been won and the new temple was in the exclusive control of the priestly elect, there evolved a new theology that focused strictly on the Torah and on ritual observance and neglected the passionate vision

---

[34] Ezek. 11.14–21, 40.46, 44.15; cf. 1QS^{b}3.22 and below, Chapter 10.1, on "the sons of Zadok, the priests" at Qumran. The Zadokite tradition would later be the basis of the Sadducees' claims to legitimacy.

[35] Ezek. 1.1–7, 11.16, 43.2. On this subject, see D. S. Russell 1964, but esp. P. D. Hanson 1975:241–42, whose argument I follow here. For a review of further scholarship, see Stone (ed.) 1984:383–88.

[36] The temple was destroyed by John Hyrcanus in 129 B.C. On the subsequent development of the Samaritans, see MacDonald 1964 and Kippenberg 1971. For bibliography, see Scobie 1973, but see also Hick (ed.) 1977:64–86 and Schenke in Layton (ed.) 1981.

of an eschaton. This entailed abandoning the inherently revolutionary stance of prophecy vis-à-vis the monarchy and identifying it instead with the ruling circles, the Davidic monarch and the high priest. The passage about the Satan in Zechariah reflects the early stages of this conflict, before the priestly tradition had fully established itself and while the opposition to these returned fugitives was still strong among the people. Thus Zechariah's night visions bear a similar relationship to the political ruling class as had the combat myths to the kingship in other Near Eastern cultures, or for that matter the ancient Davidic monarchy itself.[37] The visions are infused with the royalist ideology and tend to legitimate its institutions.

It is this position that the Satan opposes, and he is therefore a cosmic projection of the groups hostile to the temple hierocracy. The radical groups had made several extreme charges of uncleanness against the Zadokite priesthood,[38] and these are apparently the charges the Satan makes against the candidate for high priest, Joshua, in the heavenly court:

> Then he showed me Joshua the high priest standing before the angel of the Lord, with the Satan standing at his right hand to accuse him. The Lord said to the Satan, "The Lord rebuke you, Satan, the Lord who has chosen Jerusalem rebuke you. Is not this man a brand snatched from the fire?" Now Joshua was wearing filthy clothes as he stood before the angel; and the angel turned and said to those in attendance on him, "Take off his filthy clothes." Then he turned to him and said, "See how I have taken away your guilt from you; I will clothe you in fine vestments"; and I said, "Let a clean turban be put on his head." So they put a clean turban on his head and clothed him in clean garments, while the angel of the Lord stood by.[39]

Although Yahweh rebukes the Satan, it was presumably his charge of defilement which led to the ceremony of purification here witnessed by Zechariah in his vision. The charges have apparently led to a trial before the heavenly court, with a prosecutor, the Satan, and a public defender, the *mal'āk Yahweh*. The verdict exonerates Joshua and cleanses him, promising that if he will walk in the ways of the Lord he will "judge my house, and keep my court." In this and the subsequent vision, Zerubbabel, the nominee for Davidic king, is also granted his authority. Together Joshua and Zerubbabel are represented as the two olive trees who stand

---

[37] P. D. Hanson 1975:251–55. See above, Chapters 1 and 4, and see Lambert 1978.

[38] As reflected in Third Isaiah (56–66).

[39] Zech. 3.1–5. On the relations of Zech. 3–4 and Ezek.40–48, see Stone (ed.) 1984:385 and, in general, Collins 1979.

on either side of Yahweh (the candlestick with its seven eyes) to guard his dominion over the restored community.[40]

Throughout the Persian period, the Zadokite ascendancy and control of the temple cult seem to have prevailed, though not without such bitter strife at times that Ezra apparently had to be sent by the Persian overlords to restore calm. The excluded groups probably continued to expect some grand demonstration of Yahweh's power, following the visionary expectations of Second Isaiah and his use of the Divine Warrior imagery from earlier times. It was probably among these groups that fully apocalyptic and otherworldly fantasies developed, although once the Zadokites had been deposed during the second century we find them equally given to apocalyptic fervor, as the Qumran text known as the Damascus Covenant (or Zadokite Document) demonstrates.[41]

The temple-centered ritual of the new dispensation, which depended on Persian tolerance for its continued ascendancy, could not halt the progressive splitting of the concept of God. Indeed, the new Judaism of ritual and political accommodation may well have hastened the process. Around 400 B.C. we find the Chronicler[42] attempting in a tolerant spirit to unite the contradictory elements with an idealized and conciliatory vision of the past. He uses both northern and southern historical traditions, for example. He ignores the bitter power struggle between Zadokite priests and Levites that must have been still vividly remembered (indeed, he is careful to accord their proper honors to the Levites, and even allows at one point that they "were more upright than the priests in sanctifying themselves,"[43] a matter of special concern for this obsessively ritual-minded author). And he incorporates several allusions to the holy war tradition popular among dissident prophetic groups. So it is surely significant that here and only here in the whole of the canonical Old Testament do we find a reference to an independent spiritual force named "Satan," minus the definite article and minus any identification with the heavenly court.

---

[40] Zech. 4.2–14; P. D. Hanson 1975:255–56, 264, 270.

[41] See P. D. Hanson 1975:259 and below, Chapter 10. An important linking text is the eschatological holy war of Deutero-Zechariah 14 (P. D. Hanson 1975:369–73).

[42] Myers 1965:lxxxvii–lxxxix discusses various suggestions for the dating of the Chronicler (Ezra, Nehemiah, 1 and 2 Chronicles). He is followed by P. D. Hanson 1975 in proposing 400 B.C. as the best possibility. Cf. R. K. Harrison 1969:1153–57, but contrast Pfeiffer 1948:811–12 and Williamson 1977. One of Myers' arguments for the earlier date is the large number of Persian words.

[43] 2 Chron. 29.34.

Conciliation within the group will proceed more smoothly if there is an enemy without.

The Chronicler retells the whole of Israel's history from the beginnings to his own time, but fortunately we are not entirely dependent on this unimaginative priest (if such he was), since one of his principal sources for the preexilic period survives also: the so-called Deuteronomic History (Deuteronomy to 2 Kings). Comparison of the two works reveals how much the Chronicler revised the older historical traditions according to the spirit of the priestly code. The David of Samuel-Kings, for example, is essentially a political leader of genius, capable both of wide vision and of self-serving, corrupt uses of power; the Chronicler's David is a proto-priest, the organizer of Israel as a worshiping community who made Jerusalem his religious center, conceived the first temple according to a plan direct from on high,[44] assigned the priestly duties, and established the liturgy.

One result of this ecclesiastical transformation of David is the omission of his less creditable acts. The Chronicler ignores the unsavory episode of Uriah the Hittite and Bathsheba, as he also passes over another masterpiece of the earlier history, the moving and tragic story of Absalom's revolt. Given the Chronicler's pro-Persian stance and his political moderation, a revolution that is so compelling and dangerous is the last thing to which he would want to call his reader's attention, and still less the ruthless methods provoked by that civil war among the members of the holy family. But there was one sin of David's that could not be passed over: the taking of the census. This episode could not be avoided, because its aftermath was the revelation of the site on which the temple was to be built. But the story still underwent a striking change in the hands of the Chronicler.

In the Deuteronomic History the story begins thus: "And again the anger of the Lord was kindled against Israel, and he moved David against them to say, Go, number Israel and Judah." After the census was completed, however, David repented of his sin and begged the Lord to take away the iniquity:

> And David's heart smote him after he had numbered the people. And David
> said unto the Lord, I have sinned greatly in that I have done: and now I be-

[44] 1 Chron. 28.19; cf. Ezek. 25.9, 40–48, and Zech. 2.5–9. See Hamerton-Kelly 1970. Cf. also Rev. 21.9–27 and below, Chapter 13.

seech thee, O Lord, take away the iniquity of thy servant; for I have done very foolishly.[45]

The Lord then offered David a choice of three ways to work off the sin, and David chose three days of pestilence that killed seventy thousand people. Just as "the angel of the Lord" was about to strike Jerusalem, however, the Lord "repented him of the evil" and called a halt right where Araunah the Jebusite had his threshing floor. This became the site of the future temple.

This version of the story makes Yahweh the cause both of David's sin and of his punishment. A further difficulty for the pious and patriotic Chronicler was that no immediate cause of Yahweh's anger is given, though the Lord would have been able to cite several actions of David recounted in previous chapters had he been called on for justification.[46] At any rate, the Chronicler could not accept a Yahweh who inflicts both sin and punishment, so his account begins: "And Satan stood up against Israel, and provoked David to number Israel."

Now that he has squarely attributed the initial transgression to "Satan," the way is clear for him to write:

> And God was displeased with this thing: Therefore he smote Israel. And David said unto God, I have sinned greatly, because I have done this thing: But now, I beseech thee, forgive the iniquity of thy servant. For I have done very foolishly.

David thus retains the holy character with which the Chronicler endows him, since Satan is responsible for his sin. Similarly, Yahweh is protected from blame, and his punishment is not simply malicious; it fits the theory of just reward and punishment that had become crucial to Judaism. David sees the angel of the Lord above Jerusalem, falls down on his face, and cries as one who understands this theory well:

> Is it not I that commanded the people to be numbered? even I it is that have sinned and done evil indeed; but as for these sheep, what have they done? let thine hand, I pray thee, O Lord my God, be on me, and on my father's house. But not on thy people, that they should be plagued.[47]

[45] 2 Sam. 24. 10 (KJV). For the taboo on a census, see Exod. 30. 11–16 and Frazer 1919: vol. 2, 555–81.

[46] Pfeiffer 1948:353 suggests that in the earliest source of the Deuteronomic history the census story may have been the sequel to the adventures of the ark related in 1 Sam. 4.1–7.2.

[47] 1 Chron. 21.1–17 (KJV).

A God who punishes men for their sins had long been integral to Israel's covenant theology, but in the Deuteronomic History the sins were collective and the punishment was often delayed or indirect. The kings of the northern secessionists after Jeroboam, for example, are regularly censured because they "did what was evil in the sight of Yahweh, and walked in the way of Jeroboam and his sin which he made Israel to sin,"[48] but the particular king is essentially the embodiment of his people, and the historian cannot deny that the northern kingdom flourished for an extended period. The Chronicler, however, converts this still-supple theory into a rigid doctrine of individual reward and punishment, precisely the position of Job's friends: if you suffer, you did wrong. The misfortunes of Saul, Jehoram, Uzziah, Josiah, and Zedekiah are all divine punishments for their sins, but the Chronicler cannot take the further step that his predecessors had taken and infer that Yahweh may be, for his own long-term historical purposes, the cause of the sin itself. Certainly he cannot follow the author of Job to the profound conclusion that Yahweh could make a just man suffer. David, the otherwise spotless ruler, is therefore "provoked" by Satan to sin, and thus God's treatment of him is justified. God himself had nothing to do with the sin, and it is even a sign of David's magnanimity that he should accept responsibility for a sin to which Satan had provoked him.

For the first time, then, we find in the Chronicler a Satan who acts independently of divine permission. In this simpleminded theodicy, Satan substitutes for God as the *agent provocateur* in human affairs; indeed, he ceases to be an agent of God at all and acts on his own initiative. He has in fact replaced God. We are fortunate that the source of the story is extant in 2 Samuel, for it reveals both the change that had come over the Hebrew tradition in the new context of Judaism and the reason why Satan's role became necessary—the moralistic desire to free God from blame. There had always been a rebellious undertone in the relation of the people to God, a questioning of his acts or of his failure to act promptly. But now the need to justify God's ways to men has resulted in a disastrously circumscribed conception of the deity. Rarely may the problem of suffering be approached with the insight of Job's author, who balances a rebellious Promethean defiance against a God who, as the omnipotent creator, finds the merely human notion of justice absurd. But the Chronicler, and many after him, were incapable of seeing the presumptuous quality of their

[48] E.g., 2 Kings 10.29; 13.2, 11; 14.24; 15.18.

newly moral view of God, the pride that, as Job had finally understood, would try to fashion God in the human image. Gnostic arguments would later expose the shallowness of the Chronicler's theology, for if one takes his idea seriously, then God has indeed become Satan. Gnostics had at least this precedent for their view of the wicked and irascible God of the Old Testament as a jealous and ignorant demiurge.[49] Certainly the way was now open for the rapid and spectacular rise to power of the independent evil ruler of human affairs.

The final stage in the transformation of the Satan from official of the heavenly court to independent adversary had not yet been reached. The passage in Chronicles is isolated, and one such reference is not enough to indicate a common belief. It was the apocalyptic movement in its most extreme form that completed the metamorphosis of subordinate official into rebellious angel, of *agent provocateur* into a sinister and mysterious spirit at loose in the universe. A revealing illustration of the difference is the following brief, almost casual allusion in the New Testament. The First Letter of Peter concludes with a standard series of injunctions to the young churches of Asia Minor, one of which is: "Be pure, be on the watch: for your adversary the devil [*ho antidikos humōn diabolos*], like a roaring lion strolls about [*peripatei*], seeking whom he may devour."[50] The Greek verb *peripatei* is equivalent to the Hebrew verb for what the Satan does at Job 1.7, *hithallēk*, to stroll or walk about. And in the context of the lion seeking prey, the whole passage may be an allusion to Job, who at 10.16 berates Yahweh because "Bold as a lion you stalk me." But notice the contrast. In Job the Satan is still in God's service; he roams (*šûṭ*) and strolls about with God's permission. Furthermore, it is Yahweh whom Job compares to a lion stalking his prey. But by the time we reach the New Testament, the adversary has become entirely separate from Yahweh, an independent threat for the faithful to beware. Peter has no need to explain further, for by then everyone knew about the devil—to be on guard. But Job still thinks of God himself as the persecutor.

Certain affinities between this development of the Satan in the Old Testament, particularly the divided God suggested by the Chronicler, and the religion of the Persian overlords have suggested to many scholars that regular contact with the Zoroastrian system had begun already to influence Jewish belief. The genuine affinities are slight, however, and there is

[49] Grant 1959:34; Dahl 1981. See below, Chapter 18.4.
[50] 1 Pet. 5.8.

no trace yet of the Persian idea that both good and evil spirits participated in the creation.[51] And perhaps the best argument against a strong Persian influence is the fact that the developing Satan concept had not yet been linked with combat mythology, a process we shall find at work in the apocryphal literature of the next centuries. Rather, the name of Satan for a supernatural being developed originally within the Canaanite-Jewish conception of the heavenly court and is linked exclusively to the legal and judiciary proceedings of that court. (It was chiefly from this function that the Greek translation, *diabolos*, accuser, is derived.) Satan is not yet, for example, the bound dragon inherited from Canaanite myth, nor the monstrous chaos that opposes El or Baal in that same context or in Old Testament allusions.

[51] See above, n. 3. See Albright 1957:359–64, Gordis 1965:69–71, and Klüger 1967:157. See also below, Chapter 10.2.

SIX

THE ADVERSARY
AS REBEL

THE RISE of an independent Satan as we have followed it in the previous chapter took place during the same period as a rebellion variant
of the combat myth was becoming popular in apocalyptic and often dissident circles. In general, the point of these stories in which the adversary
is a rebel against his overlord was the imminent demise of the rebel—the
end of the story, not its beginning. Nevertheless, the question of motivation, of how and why the adversary rebels, was a part of the plot from
its earliest form. It was this problem that now came to exercise the new
myth-makers of Jewish apocalyptic literature and was to lead to the fusion
of the Old Testament Satan with the adversary of the combat tradition.
The figure who links them, who attracts both to himself, is also, we shall
see, a lapsed member of the heavenly court.

1. Rebellion as Combat Motive

Up to this point in our inquiry, we have been adopting a rather Aristotelian view of narrative, recognizing the dominance of plot over character,
and we have occasionally borrowed Propp's terminology to show the
transformations and variations in the combat mythology of the ancient
Near East. From this point of view it is a secondary and contingent matter
what particular form the enemy figure takes, its sex, its origin, its moral
status, and whether it is sea god, monster, or chaos demon. What counts
is simply that the figure is the adversary within the *mythos*, the generic plot
structure.[1] But this concentration on plot has led us to minimize the question of *ēthos* or motivation: what leads the enemy to be an enemy in the
first place?

Such a question seems to be a major reason for the variations among
different realizations or performances of a given plot. Sophocles and

---

[1] Jones 1962:31 and passim is the best exposition of this characteristic difference between
ancient and modern literature. Cf. Kermode 1979:75–78.

Euripides, for example, had very different conceptions of Electra, different both from each other and from their model, Aeschylus. This in turn led them to compose rather different versions of the *Oresteia* plot. Meditation on the situation of the characters, on their likely feelings and resentments, is chiefly what gives rise to changes in the crucial details that both adapt the plot to the different preoccupations of the author or to a new cultural environment and at the same time extend the life of a given plot beyond its putative origin. Why did he do that? A satisfactory answer, not necessarily a complete one, will make the old plot acceptable in a new and alien context. This is precisely what happens to European tales taken over by other groups. Cinderella among the Zuñi becomes a tragic figure who forgets her primary obligation to feed her turkeys in favor of staying too long at the ya-ya dance and is punished when the turkeys fly away, leaving her in disgrace and without a livelihood. Hamlet was severely castigated by an African tribe for failing to have proper respect for his father's brother. Eve becomes an adulterous wife among the Limba of Sierra Leone, the serpent her seducer.[2]

Among the narratives we have so far considered, few of them pay much attention to the question of motivation. Even those variants of the combat pattern that begin with some explicit villainy—an attack on the city or palace, an overt challenge to the gods—do not usually explain this event. Yamm, like Mot, appears merely to issue his demand that Baal be his servant; Huwawa is simply there and conducting his depredations. In this respect the narratives are akin to the generic folktale pattern we find in Propp. The first slot in the schema is a lack or an explicit villainy, but its function is simply to get the action moving, not to probe the background of the enemy's character. Yet it is this lack of probing which proves the undoing of Gilgamesh and Enkidu in the Sumerian poem, for they discover at the end that Huwawa's function is sacred and sanctioned by Enlil himself, a case of a folktale convention being usefully exploited in a different medium.

To this generalization there are exceptions. Tiamat has been roused to attack the younger gods by the defeat and death of her husband, Apsu, and by the promptings of her brothers.[3] Apsu too is provided with a motive for the malign intent which provokes the first, magical battle, and it is one that reveals most clearly the way myths project the ordinary preoc-

---

[2] Benedict 1935: vol. 2, 259, and cf. Tedlock 1972:65–73 for a recent performance of this "Cinderella" tale. For Hamlet, see Bohannan 1966, and for Eve, Finnegan 1967:267–70.

[3] ANET 62, Tablet I, lines 111–23. See above, Chapter 2.3 and 2.7.

cupations of human beings to the cosmic level: his children are noisy, and their racket will not let him rest.[4] The chief exception, however, is that variant of the combat pattern in which the adversary is some kind of rebel.

In this rebel type, a quite explicit and elaborate motivation scene is often a part of the combat narrative, since the combat consists in the act of rebellion itself or its martial consequences, and the victory is the suppression of the rebellion. We have already cited one such plot, the Sumerian myth of Anzu, in which the villain, Anzu, steals the Tablets of Destiny from the high god, Enlil, after being placed in a position of trust that subjects him to intolerable temptation.[5]

Unfortunately, the myth of Anzu is the only moderately well-preserved instance of this rebel type in a pure and elaborated form, but there are enough fragments and allusions in other contexts to encourage the assumption that the rebel plot was indeed a common variant of the combat pattern. Anat mentions her victory over a rebel among the catalog of her exploits,[6] and it is possible that the challenge of Yamm to Baal implies this rebellion theme; one student of the text calls it "a clear-cut grab for power."[7]

2. *Which One Is the Rebel?* Enuma Eliš

We have already noted that the *Enuma Eliš* is likely to have been influenced by the Baal-Yamm myth. This makes the *Enuma Eliš* a revealing example of intertextual variation among combat myths. Apparently the imaginative priests responsible for the composition of this poem recognized in the Baal-Yamm epic about the struggle for kingship a plot that could be adapted to their purposes of glorifying Marduk.[8] According to the Babylonian cosmogonic tradition, Ea, the god of the waters, had already defeated and replaced Apsu, the personification of those primal waters, much as Ninurta had defeated and replaced Anzu, his own earlier form. To this story the author now added the Marduk-Tiamat myth. Unlike the Canaanite Yamm, however, the Babylonian Tiamat was not simply the Sea-enemy, for she also represented the primal salt waters and was one of the progenitors of all the gods. She therefore has an obvious reason for her

---

[4] ANET 61, Tablet I, lines 37–40. See below, Chapter 8.
[5] See above, Chapter 2.4.
[6] See above, Chapter 2.8 and n. 44. See also Clifford 1972:59.
[7] Miller 1973:28.
[8] See above, Chapter 2.4 and Chapter 4.1.

hostility to the younger gods, since they had put her husband, Apsu, the primal fresh waters, to death. This linking of the Ea-Apsu plot with the Marduk-Tiamat plot was undoubtedly suggested by the extra connotations of Tiamat as primal mother within the Babylonian religious system, but its principal literary effect, given the brevity with which the Apsu episode is treated, is to provide Tiamat with a motive for her attack, which Yamm's had lacked.[9]

Unfortunately, the distinction is not nearly so clear as the preceding analysis implies.[10] The tablet that appears to begin the Baal-Yamm story is damaged at the top, but one possible reading of some of the lines has Baal apparently issuing a challenge to Yamm's kingship:

> . . . Said Baal the Powerful:
> May you be driven from the throne of kingship,
> From the seat of dominion![11]

Furthermore, several commentators see a connection between this tablet and another[12] that they assume preceded it. On this tablet the story of the building of Yamm's palace is recounted, and if indeed this tablet did precede the Baal-Yamm struggle, then Baal would be the rebel, a rising young god, like Marduk, seeking advancement.

This uncertainty may not be due entirely to our inability to relate the Ugaritic tablets definitively to each other. We may compare the uncertainty in the *Enuma Eliš* about the earlier distribution of power before the kingship is bestowed on Marduk. Anu is generally represented as the king of the gods, though he plays little role in the epic, and Ea, as Marduk's father, receives more attention. Enlil, the previous king of the pantheon in other texts, is suppressed entirely until a cursory mention at the end of

---

[9] But some way had still to be found to replace Ea, the hero of the first challenge, with the new hero Marduk. The solution was close at hand in the epic convention whereby several gods prove inadequate to a threat until the hero emerges, a convention we have seen to be native to the Babylonian tradition from the myth of Anzu. So Ea simply becomes one of those inadequate gods. Like Enlil in the Anzu myth, he "lapsed into dark silence and sat right still" (ANET 63, Tablet II, line 6). He then goes for advice to Anshar, his forefather, who reminds him of his heroics against Mummu and Apsu and urges him to try again. He declines, and Anshar turns to Anu, who does set out but quickly returns terrified. Finally Anshar bethinks himself of Marduk, and so Ea, Marduk's father, summons him. After making sure he himself receives the kingship, Marduk sallies forth and wins a great victory. See above, Chapter 3 n. 39.

[10] Lambert 1965:294–95 points to the uncertainty about identifying Tiamat.

[11] See ANET 130 (III AB, B = Gordon 1949: no. 137; CTA 2.1).

[12] Driver 1956a:77 (III AB, C = Gordon 1949: no. 129; CTA 2.3). See also H. L. Ginsberg in ANET 129, and above, Chapter 2.2.

tablet 4, in which Marduk gives him his "place." Furthermore, the usual sign of the kingship in Babylon, the Enlilship as it is known from earlier texts, was the Tablets of Destiny, and yet Tiamat still appears to have them to bestow on Kingu as a challenge to Anu's right to the kingship.[13] It is possible that the author of the poem simply did not take the Tablets seriously by this time, yet the frequent reiteration of them suggests otherwise, and Tiamat's retention of them is the chief symbol of the political crisis her hostility causes.[14] The problem of who is to be king, now that Tiamat has established Kingu as a rival and Anu has proved inadequate to the task, is resolved only by calling in another earlier generation of deities, Lahmu, Lahamu, and the Igigi, to a big feast and assembly at which the kingship, but not the tablets, is bestowed on Marduk:

> O Marduk, thou art indeed our avenger.
> We have granted thee kingship over the universe entire.
> When in assembly thou sittest, thy word shall be supreme.
> Thy weapons shall not fail; they shall smash thy foes.
> O lord, spare the life of him who trusts thee,
> But pour out the life of the god who seized evil.[15]

The situation looks like a projection of some human political crisis in which the Queen Mother, so to speak, a kind of Livia or Agrippina figure, retains enormous power and some actual rights.[16] To represent her as a rebel against the established order is merely one way of looking at the problem she poses, though the poet makes it coincide with her general characterization as the adversary. Indeed, a similar motivation is provided for Apsu in the earlier plot, borrowed apparently from the Babylonian Flood epic, *Atrahasis*, so that his desire to dispose of his own children will appear to justify the seizing of power from him. Hesiod's tradition, we know, played a similar trick by representing Kronos as the swallower of his offspring, and the Titans as rebels against Zeus. The logic of the plot, however, demands the opposite, that the younger gods shall seize power from their elders, and this is apparently what the Titan battle earlier represented—the successful rebellion of Zeus.[17] This uncertainty about who is rebelling against whom will prove to have important repercussions in

---

[13] This formulaic passage occurs at I.156 = II.46 = III.47 = III.104.

[14] W. G. Lambert, as cited by Walcot 1966:39.

[15] ANET 66, Tablet IV, lines 13–18.

[16] On this subject generally, see Finet 1973, Lambert and Millard 1969:23–25, and below, Chapter 8, on the *Atrahasis* epic.

[17] See above, Chapter 3 and n. 61, and West 1966:273.

the subsequent transformations of the combat myth. Just as in the parallel human situations, the rebel may justify himself by appealing to a higher or an older authority, by casting the ruler as a tyrant, or by representing his rebellion as the opposite—an effort to reestablish rightful authority and order against rebellious opponents.

In those cases where the battle is between generations of gods, as in the Babylonian, Hittite, and Greek myths, the ambiguity about who is the real rebel may also be explained in psychological as well as political terms. Otto Rank's theory of "projective inversion" argues that the child converts his own resentment at his father into a fantasy that the father wants to destroy the child.[18] Kumarbi, in Hittite texts deriving from a Hurrian myth, seems to reflect both aspects of this ambiguity. In one text he attacks his father Anus (the name is a transliteration, not a translation), the king of heaven, and castrates him, but is thereby impregnated with three deities—the Tigris River, the storm god, and his attendants—all fearsome and destructive creatures in their own right. Eventually his rebellion is put down and his punishment is foretold: "In the end thou shalt have to strike the rocks of the mountains with thy head."[19] Another text tells of a rebellion by this same Kumarbi, but this time against his own son, the storm god Teshub, who has somehow become king of heaven. Kumarbi descends to earth, impregnates a stone, and a diorite giant is born, one Ullikummi, who becomes a variant of the standard "devastating monster" figure. Aid comes to Teshub from Ea, who eventually takes an axe to this huge stone giant, the same axe that originally separated heaven and earth, and manages to cut him loose from his dominant position atop the Atlas figure Ubelluris. Teshub then charges in and defeats him and apparently retrieves the kingship.[20] Kumarbi, like Kronos, is a threat to both the older and the younger generation.

The examples discussed so far, from the myth of Anzu to Hesiod, suggest some of the ramifications of the rebellion theme and show that it was a common solution to the narrative problem of the enemy's motivation, whether the rebellion was described in the acute and elaborate way represented by the myth of Anzu, whether it is merely implicit, as in the

---

[18] See Rank 1959, a brilliant but neglected study; cf. Dundes 1977. Readers inclined to scoff at such Freudian interpretation of myths might care to consider the recently discovered Babylonian myth from the obscure town of Dunnu, in which myth each generation of gods slays their fathers and marries their mothers (Lambert and Walcot 1965).

[19] Güterbock 1948:124. Cf. Walcot 1966 and P. D. Hanson 1977:204.

[20] The most convenient account of these myths is by Güterbock in Kramer (ed.) 1961:139–180.

Yamm story, or whether, as in some of those cases in which the combat myth is linked with a struggle between generations of gods, the enemies of the ultimate victor are simply characterized as rebels, however high their previous status and whatever their venerability. It seems the combat myth has a tendency to include the link between adversary and rebel whenever the ultimate function of the myth is to stress the power and authority of the victor—whenever, in fact, that power is threatened.

3. *Athtar: The Rebel in Canaan*

Embedded within the Canaanite Baal-Mot cycle of myths we find the following curious story. It must have also been a separate myth of its own, to judge from its fascinating links with Hebrew and Greek allomorphs, but unfortunately the only form in which it survives among the Ugaritic texts is in this truncated, undramatic version. Baal has been (provisionally) killed by Mot, and Anat, his ultimate rescuer, sets up an ironic cry, calling on El's wife, Asherah, to rejoice now that one of her own "brood of young lions" can become king. El takes her at her word, and Asherah immediately proposes one of her sons for the job. Following the well-established convention we have met in the combat context, El rejects him as too weak to compete with Baal and therefore, we presume, too weak to take over his position. Asherah then proposes another son, known as Athtar the Rebel, whereupon:

> Athtar the Rebel went up to the reaches of Zaphon.
> He sits enthroned on the throne of Aliyan Baal.
> His feet did not reach the footstool,
> His head did not reach the top.
> And Athtar the Rebel said,
> "I will not reign on the reaches of Zaphon."
> Athtar the Rebel came down.
> He came down from the throne of Aliyan Baal.
> And he reigned over the whole of the vast earth.[21]

In this version Athtar goes up to the sacred mountain but finds that when he sits on the huge throne of kingship his feet will not reach the footstool, nor his head the top (a delightful scene that recalls the memorable flashback to the hero's youth in Eisenstein's *Ivan the Terrible, Part II*). Athtar therefore appears to relinquish the throne voluntarily, though there may be something petulant about his words: "I will *not* reign on the reaches of

[21] CTA 6.1, 55–65, trans. Clifford 1972:164–65. Cf. ANET 140.

Zaphon." At any rate, he is then given power over the vast earth (although this may mean no more than that he became god of underground streams and irrigation)[22]—which compensates for the adaptation of the story to the need for a preliminary defeat before the real hero (Anat) appears.

Elsewhere we find Athtar similarly engaged in trying to push his own merits at the expense of others. A text summarized before[23] turns on the building of Yamm's palace, to which Athtar takes objection as a rebellious act. The sun goddess Shapash tells Athtar that El is going to depose him and bestow authority on Yamm-Nahar. This narrative may be linked to the story of Athtar's own rebellion, for which it provides splendid motivation, and of exactly the kind that would later drive Satan to protest and rebellion. But in their current form the various fragments do not seem to fit together in this way.[24]

Like Marduk, and possibly Baal himself, Athtar seems to have been a young god bent on self-advancement. Unlike the others, however, he seems to have aspired beyond his powers. The second of the two texts described above seems to imply, further, that one form of Athtar may have been the planet Venus, attempting every morning to ascend the heavens but always thrust down again by the rising of the sun. At least this hypothesis would explain neatly the role of Shapash in the myth. Athtar's namesake in Arabic tradition was certainly the planet.[25]

The same conception of the planet Venus as a rebellious figure seems to be implied by yet another Ugaritic text, in which two wives of El give birth simultaneously to Šaḥru and Šalimu, Dawn Light and Evening Light.[26] These two young gods, "beautiful and gracious," are immediately very hungry, and they suck "the breasts of the lady . . . and there

---

[22] See Caquot 1958, McKay 1970:461, and P. D. Hanson 1977:206, who considers *ba-arsi* as either earth or underworld, in either event the lower realms from the point of view of Athtar's aspirations. The parallel with Satan's reward and punishment is striking. Cf. Grelot 1956.

[23] See above, Chapter 3.1 n. 17.

[24] The possibility is there, however, and we should remember that the Athtar myth survives only as a part of the Baal cycle. The breaking and reforming of traditional narratives is a very common occurrence, and may well have happened here. At any rate, the parallel with Satan's later act of rebellion, as in the Latin Adam book or in Lactantius, both having Gnostic connections, is a strong one, and not to be explained solely by the Isa. 14 passage that links the two stories. See below, and Chapter 12.7.

[25] Grelot 1956:31; Caquot 1958:55; McKay 1970:455, 462; Kaiser 1974:38–40; P. D. Hanson 1977:206–7. The links all make sense through the assumption that Athtar is something like "a son of the Dawn," as are his congeners in Greek and Hebrew. See below.

[26] CTA 23; Clifford 1972:165–68.

entered into their mouths the birds of heaven and the fishes of the sea."[27] In spite of running about eating right and left, they remain unsatisfied and so gain admittance to the "field of El," that is, the paradise garden on El's mountain, where there is plenty of bread and wine. How the story ends is unclear, but if the two gods are really to be identified with Venus, then what are we to make of the common astronomical dogma that the identity of the morning and evening stars was not known, at least in Greece, until the sixth century? The two names may mean no more than "Dawn" and "Twilight"; certainly the Hebrew cognate šaḥar means "dawn" rather than the planet.

4. Phaethon: The Rebel in Greece

What makes these questions important, and the uncertainty of our evidence so frustrating, is the possible impact of these Canaanite myths in subsequent tradition. A plausible connection with the Greek figure Phaethon has been traced by a number of scholars. The well-known version of his myth derives from Ovid's *Metamorphoses*, but this in turn goes back to a lost play of Euripides recently reconstructed from fragments by James Diggle.[28] Euripides himself, however, seems to have invented the romantic story aboout Phaethon's quest for the real father, Helios, and the gentlemanly but disastrous promise made to him. In an earlier form, certainly in Aeschylus' lost play, the *Heliades*, and perhaps also in a lost work of Hesiod, Phaethon stole the chariot of the sun without his father's consent, a clear act of rebellion paralleled most closely in the theft of the Tablets of Destiny by the winged creature Anzu.[29] Indeed, Phaethon, Typhon, and the Titanomachy are linked by the later Greek tradition, and Ovid apparently noticed the parallel between the disastrous fires caused by Zeus' thunderbolts at the destruction of Phaethon's chariot and the similar incident in the story of the Titans.[30] Some late sources even make Phaethon's rebellion the occasion for Zeus to destroy the world with a flood or fire, a tradition that goes back, through the *Cypria*, to Near Eastern flood myths.[31] Phaethon too was identified with the planet Venus in the later Greek tradition, but this may well be an invention of the Hellen-

[27] Ps. 73.9 may be an allusion to this line (Dahood 1969).

[28] Diggle 1978.

[29] West 1966 on *Theogony* 987. But cf. Diggle 1978:27, and for the plot of Aeschylus' play, see his sensible remarks on p. 30.

[30] Diggle 1978:21, 22 n. 1; Ovid, *Metamorphoses* 1.253–61.

[31] Kilmer 1972. Cf. J. Hansen's essay in Oinas (ed.) 1978. See also below, Chapter 7.

istic poets, whose fondness for catasterisms is well known.[32] Certainly
Hesiod regarded Phaethon and Heōsphoros, the dawn star, as separate en-
tities, though he grants them the same mother, Heōs the dawn.[33] But
Phaethon's name means "Shining," and as an adjective it was applied to
Jupiter, Saturn, even the sun itself.[34] The name was associated with Dawn
in Homer, being one of the two horses of Heōs,[35] and in the feminine
form the same two names, Phaetousa and Lempetiē (Gleaming) were the
two daughters of Helios, the sun, corresponding in both cases perhaps
with the two morning stars, Venus and Mercury.[36]

But there was also a persistent association of Phaethon with his mythological father, Helios the sun,[37] and the earliest form of Phaethon as
Rebel has him challenging his father's power. "Shining One" is a natural
enough name for the Sun's son, as for any number of other astronomical
phenomena. What is significant about Phaethon is not the potential identification with a particular astral being,[38] but his character as a variant of
the cosmic rebel.[39] The river into which Phaethon plunges on his failure
is called Eridanos. A later tradition identified this river with the Italian Po,
but originally it seems to have been another name for the mythical Okeanos, the same river into which the Ophioneus rebel figure of Pherecydes
is hurled on his defeat by Zeus. In Greece at least the two stories seem to
have been variants of the same plot and thus instances of that popular
Greek theme of *hybris*. At the level of legend, the presumption and the
fatal plunge of Ikarus are a further variant of the same pattern.[40]

[32] Diggle 1978:14, on Wilamowitz' now discredited hypothesis about the lost Hesiodic
and Euripidean versions.

[33] Hesiod, *Theogony* 987 and 378. I follow West 1966 and Nagy 1973 in assuming a traditional relationship between Phaethon son of Helios and Clymene, and Phaethon, son of
Heōs and Cephalos. Diggle's caution (1978:10–15) seems to me excessive.

[34] Diggle 1978:15 n. 2. On *me-lam* and *kābōd*, see above, Chapter 2.9, on Ps. 29.

[35] *Odyssey* 23.246.

[36] Grelot 1956, but see below, n. 41.

[37] The Phaethon story is well known on the North Pacific Coast of America (S. Thompson 1946:314) and the motif is A724.1.1. Luomala 1940, who studied the distribution of the
Sun-Snarer myths, with which Phaethon might seem related, concluded that the Oceanic,
American, and Africana analogues were all separate and unrelated traditions. The psychological implications of the rebellion plot help us to see why it occurs so widely.

[38] Nagy 1973 and Grelot 1956 take different views on the identification.

[39] The Hesiodic story about Phaethon that we do possess, as opposed to the lost text, is
actually a variant of the widespread "snatching" tale, in which a goddess, often Heōs herself
but also Aphrodite as in this tale, rapes a beautiful youth and carries him off to serve in her
temple.

[40] *Hybris* is an action, not a state like pride (Lattimore 1964:18–28).

5. *Lucifer: The Rebel in Isaiah*

These possible links between versions of the Phaethon myth and the rebel
figures of Ugaritic texts gain an extra fascination from the obvious parallels with a third tradition, that represented by the famous poem contained in Isaiah 14. From our present point of view, the myth alluded to
in Isaiah looks like a blending of the Ugaritic traditions with a story very
much like the Phaethon myth; the three together look like variants,
adapted to their several purposes, of one common rebel plot.[41]

The following part of Isaiah's famous taunt represents the shades of the
dead kings in Sheol, the Waste Land, greeting a new arrival (much as the
shades of the Greek dead greet Odysseus or the suitors in Homer):

> Have you too become weak like us,
> Have you become like us?
> Your pride is brought down to Sheol,
> The sound of your harps:
> Maggots are the bed beneath you,
> And worms are your covering.
> How are you fallen from heaven,
> Helel ben Shahar (Shining One, son of Dawn)!
> How are you felled to earth,
> Conqueror of the nations!
> You said in your heart:
> "I will ascend to heaven
> Above the stars of El.
> I will set my throne on high,
> I will sit enthroned
> On the mount of assembly,
> On the recesses of Zaphon [in the far north].
> I will ascend upon the high clouds,
> I will become like Elyon!"

[41] I agree with Astour 1967:269 that McKay's (1970) hypothesis, direct influence of the
Greek myth in Syria and Palestine, is extremely unlikely at this period (cf. Kaiser 1974:40).
I am equally loathe to posit a theory based on common observation of a natural phenomenon, the gradual dimming of the planet Venus in the dawn sky. In order to view that phenomenon as a rebellion, one must first have a rebellion plot well embedded in one's tradition
and consciousness, an objection that applies to much naive interpretation of myth. The nature myth theory was espoused by Gunkel 1895:133 and is in that respect a child of the nineteenth century. See Dorson 1965. Nagy 1973 argues that Phaethon is a solar myth preserved
from Indo-European tradition, but this ignores the strong connections with Semitic counterparts.

But you are brought down to Sheol
to the depths of the Pit.[42]

Such a view of the land of the dead is rare in the Old Testament, though it does occur in several passages, notably the summoning of Samuel's spirit by the witch of Endor,[43] and it is similar to the view contained in the Gilgamesh cycles or in the *Nekuia* of Odyssey 11. It looks as if this conception, which lies behind the taunt that this new arrival has become "weak" like the other dead, a mere shadow of his former self, was consciously suppressed in the written Israelite tradition[44] as a part of that whole set of notions associated with the myth and cult of the surrounding peoples from which the Jews tried to distinguish themselves. In this respect the mythological allusions and the world of the dead itself are both used as ironic metaphors to express the helplessness of this great but foreign potentate, the king of Babylon. But even though the allusions themselves form part of the taunt and are firmly held within a historical and political frame, the myth has an imaginative and evocative power that threatens to fracture this container, and it is developed in considerable detail. The ambitious thoughts of the rebel allude to some figure like the Ugaritic Athtar, who also went up to the "reaches of Zaphon" to challenge the king (though Baal, not El, in the version we have), and the name of this mythological rebel, "Shining One, Son of Dawn," makes him an exact equivalent of the Greek Phaethon.

Šaḥar, in various Hebrew contexts, preserves some of its old mythological meaning as a feminine dawn goddess,[45] and the original of this feminine dawn may well have been the Indo-European goddess Usas, the Heōs of Homer and Hesiod, perhaps blended now with Semitic Ishtar.[46] Her son, Helel, may possibly be the sun itself, and indeed *Šaḥar* may mean the rising sun, according to an older school of thought,[47] or *Hêlēl* may be

---

[42] Isa. 14.10b–15, trans. Clifford 1972:161–62; cf. Kaiser 1974:28–29. The heavenly council sits on "the mount of assembly."

[43] 1 Sam. 28; cf. Ps. 88.13 and Eccles. 9.5.

[44] Kaiser 1974:35, with note citing the extensive literature on this subject.

[45] Ps. 108.2, 110.3, 139.9, in which dawn has wings and can fly to the uttermost parts of the sea, though still within God's domain; cf. Song of Songs 6.10 and Job 3.9, 41.10, and see McKay 1970:457–59.

[46] Despite the caveat in n. 41 above, Nagy's work and that of his students is a brilliant exploration of the Indo-European dawn goddess and her numerous descendants (Nagy 1973, 1979; Boedeker 1974; Clader 1976; Frame 1977). Ishtar announces herself as goddess of morning when she descends to recover Tammuz (McKay 1970:461 n. 2).

[47] May 1937; Dorson 1965.

an allusion to the planet Venus, as most modern commentators on the passage believe.[48] Whether or not the composer of the Isaiah passage made this explicit identification, the Greek translators of the Septuagint certainly did, since their translation of *Hêlēl ben Šaḥar* as *Heōsphoros ho prōi anatellōn* clearly combines the astronomical identification with Hesiod's Heōsphoros, son of Heōs, the dawn-bringer, Venus. The Greek was in turn rendered by the Latin vulgate as *Lucifer, qui mane oriebaris,* and the name has stuck to the rebel ever since.

We have seen it to be a characteristic of the rebel variant of the combat myth that the rebel habitually fails, or rather that if he succeeds he automatically ceases to be a rebel and becomes instead, like Hesiod's Zeus or the Babylonian Marduk, the legitimate hero who himself puts down a rebellion. Clearly this phenomenon is linked to, if not exactly caused by, the common ideological use to which the combat myth was turned: celebration of the king's authority. Isaiah's manner of introducing his myth also presupposes this connection and that his audience will recognize the allusions. Zaphon, El, Elyon need no further explanation,[49] and the myth is used specifically to refer to an earthly potentate. But Isaiah reverses the common implications of such mythology: "Is this the man who made the earth tremble, who shook kingdoms, who made the world like a desert, and overthrew its cities?"[50] Just as the form of the song is a lamentation for the dead but now inverted as parody,[51] so the point of the comparison between monarch and god is now derision.

Whether he has a specific original in the period, or whether he is the generic representative of all such kings—a more likely assumption—this particular Babylonian king apparently led a glorious life, but he is here aligned with the upstart rebel, not the successful repeller of aggression, as if to suggest that all such earthly rule is a kind of rebellion that will inexorably lead to the Pit. The true king, against whom there can be no successful rebellion, is the equivalent of the myth's El, head of the Canaanite pantheon ("the stars of El"), and the redactor of this text, the man responsible for its inclusion in the Isaiah scroll, has no doubts about who this is. He introduces the poem with the following prose words addressed to the

[48] Grelot 1956; McKay 1970.

[49] "Zaphon" is here on its way to becoming the "heavens" of Job 26.7, above the clouds ("Yahweh stretching Zaphon over the void *tōhu*"), but it is familiar enough from other Old Testament passages as the mount of the divine assembly in the far north (Pope 1965:165 and esp. Clifford 1972). Elyon was another Canaanite deity (Day 1985:129–38).

[50] Isa. 14.16–17 (RSV).

[51] Kaiser 1974:32–33. Compare the restored trees at 14.8, quoted below.

Israelites: "When Yahweh has given you rest from your pain and turmoil and the hard service with which you were made to serve, you will take up this taunt against the king of Babylon."[52] By extension, then, the hero of the Hebrew combat myth, radically historicized as it now is, continues to be Yahweh, while the kings, even those who temporarily tyrannize the people of Israel, are equated with the cosmic rebel. This identification now becomes increasingly important in Hebrew tradition. The tyrant of apocalyptic mythology, whoever his temporary embodiment may be in the troubled history of these centuries, is often regarded as a usurper of the throne, not the true king.

It is generally agreed that the poem we are discussing does not come from the genuine Isaiah of Jerusalem, the great eighth-century prophet. Isaiah seems to have founded a school of prophecy, and many of the documents bound together in the Isaiah scroll, including Second Isaiah's grand vision, appear to come from the hands of later members of the school who kept the Isaiah tradition alive, even on into the postexilic period. Probably our poem comes from some sixth-century hand who would have had an immediate interest in the downfall of Babylon,[53] but was then reworked and incorporated into the general section in which it now stands, the oracles against the nations. Whoever composed the poem was alert to the dominant themes of the genuine Isaiah's ministry: the coming of the dark and destructive "Day of Yahweh" on which "the pride of men shall be humbled,"[54] the close link with Jerusalem and its royal covenant theology, the vision of Yahweh as the high king presiding over his heavenly council. In particular, the poem echoes the genuine Isaiah's preoccupation with the Assyrian emperors as the "rod of Yahweh's anger" sent to punish a godless nation, as the instrument of God's judgment, but finally, once the purpose is accomplished, as the symbol of monarchy's weakness: "When Yahweh has finished all his work on Mount Zion and in Jerusalem, he will punish the arrogant boasting of the king of Assyria and his haughty pride."[55]

For Isaiah, the Assyrian enemy who comes from afar, from "the end of the world" with chariots like the storm wind, was also "the enemy from the north."[56] This expression recurs in other Old Testament passages

---

[52] Isa. 14.3–4 (RSV).
[53] Childs 1959:196 n.26. It is also possible that it was first used against Sargon.
[54] Isa. 2.17.
[55] Isa. 10.12. See Anderson 1975:323.
[56] Isa. 5.26–30; 10.5, 12, 24–34. See Childs 1959:191.

from the preexilic era, especially Jeremiah,[57] and these passages in turn have other parallels, for example, in Habakkuk and Nahum.[58] In all these cases the enemy in question has the characteristics of a human agent, of specific political foes. But it is likely that the "enemy from the north" tradition originated in the figure of Baal-Zaphon in Canaanite mythology and was radically historicized within the Old Testament until only a trace of the myth remained.[59] The reference in our poem to Zaphon itself, the mountain of the far north, is thus both a continuation of this tradition, and also one of the first signs of the revival of explicitly mythological language and imagery in the time of the exile.[60]

Identification of the king of Babylon, the power responsible for the fall of Jerusalem and the exile of the Jews from their homeland, with the figure of the cosmic rebel was to have considerable effect on the thinking of subsequent writers. In the previous chapter of Isaiah (part of the same oracle against Babylon, at least in the form we now have it, and perhaps from the same hand), Babylon and the world power hostile to Yahweh are inextricably linked in the prophecy of the final catastrophe when Yahweh and "his weapons of indignation" will destroy the earth.[61] Long after Babylon itself had ceased to be an important power on the world scene, its king would be the symbol of the world ruler to be destroyed on the Day of Judgment, and its name would be the generic designation for all such powers, even when the particular empire that roused the indignation of the people was, as in the Book of Revelation, Rome.[62] Henceforward, kingship mythology could be turned against those who used it for ideological support, such as the various opponents of the Jews who called themselves by the names of Baal or his Babylonian equivalent, Bel-Marduk, such as Merodach-baladan (Marduk-apal-iddina),[63] or the Belshazzar who figures in the "prophecies" of Daniel. So the author of our poem and its companion prophecies dramatically transformed the implications of the kingship theme, and he was clearly aware of doing so.

One result of the removal of this Babylonian tyrant from the land of the

---

[57] Jer. 1.14–15; 4.6; 6.1, 22.

[58] Hab. 1.5–11; Nah. 2.2–10, 3.1–3.

[59] Childs 1959, with the literature cited there, should now be updated by Clifford 1972, the definitive study of the subject. Note also the presence of the tree-enemy again in Isa. 10.33–34, a common motif. See below, nn.65 and 66.

[60] Childs 1959:196–97.

[61] Kaiser 1974:8–9.

[62] Rev. 14.8; 16.19; 17.1ff.; 18.2ff.

[63] 2 Kings 20.12 = Isa. 39.1. See Kaiser 1974:15 and Jacobsen 1968.

living is that now "the cypresses rejoice at you, the cedars of Lebanon, saying, 'Since you were felled, no hewer has come against us.' "[64] This is a clear allusion to precisely those achievements for which the great Babylonian emperors had been eager to reap praise, following the Gilgamesh tradition, emperors such as Sargon or Gudea, and even the great enemy Nebuchadnezzar himself, who boasted like his predecessors:

> What no former king had done, I achieved: I cut through steep mountains, I split rocks, I opened passages and constructed a straight road for the transport of cedars. I made the Arahtu float down and carry to Marduk, my king, mighty cedars, high and strong, of precious beauty and of excellent dark quality, the abundant yield of the Lebanon, as if they were reed stalks carried by the river.[65]

We have seen that the Hittites may well have made the guardian of those great trees into the hero of their version of the Huwawa story, treating him as a local deity of their own.[66] Now a Hebrew poet makes a similar reversal of the received tradition, and we hear the trees' point of view. They become an eloquent symbol of what the oppressed suffer under the rule of a tyrant who rebels against Yahweh.

6. *The Rebel Princes in Ezekiel*

We find a similar link of cosmic rebel with earthly king in a passage in Ezekiel, a book that presents itself as contemporary with the Babylonian exile. Here, more explicitly than in the Isaiah poem, the point of Ezekiel's denunciation becomes the identification of king with god common to the combat myth. Ezekiel hears the word of Yahweh, instructing him to transmit the message to the Prince of Tyre:

> Because your heart was proud and you have said, "I am god (*'ēl*), I sit in the seat of Elohim in the midst of the seas";
> yet you are but a man and no god, though you consider yourself to be as wise as a god.
> You are indeed wiser than Daniel and no secret is hidden from you; . . .
> Because you think yourself equal to God,
> therefore behold, I will bring strangers upon you, the most terrible of the nations. . . .

[64] Isa. 14.8.
[65] ANET 307, trans. A. L. Oppenheim. See above, Chapter 1.3.
[66] See above, Chapter 1.2. For later developments of this image, see below, Chapter 10.1.

They shall thrust you down into the Pit. . . .
Will you still say, "I am a God," in the presence of those who will slay
    you?[67]

The allusion here must be to some myth like those we have been discussing from Ugarit. The Athtar text gives us the rebel who would be equal with god (Baal), while the Yamm text has a beautiful palace built for the sea god and foretells his overthrow. Yet in Ezekiel the point of the allusion becomes the whole set of exaggerated notions of a king's status implied by the use of such myths for an earthly king's glorification, and the exalted hero is a mere man after all.

Ezekiel then proceeds to announce the downfall of the king of Tyre and, like the similar passage in Isaiah 14, the poem is cast as a lamentation:

You were full of wisdom, perfect in beauty;
You were in Eden, the garden of God, every precious stone was your
    covering . . .
With the guardian cherub I placed you; you were on the holy mountain of
    God, in the midst of the stones of fire you walked.
You were blameless in your ways from the day you were created, till
    iniquity was found in you.
In the power of your trade you were filled with violence,
And when you sinned I cast you from the holy mountain of God
And the guardian cherub drove you out from the midst of the stones of fire.
Your heart was proud because of your beauty, you corrupted your wisdom
    for the sake of your splendor.
I cast you down to the ground,
I exposed you before kings to feast their eyes on you.[68]

As in the Ugaritic texts, the paradise of El is on the holy mountain, and the stones of fire (jewels, stars, lightning) indicate an astral conception similar to the other variants we have discussed. The brightness and beauty of the king's cosmic counterpart fit well with the son of Dawn figure to whom the Isaiah poem alludes. Though the guardian cherub occurs elsewhere in the Jewish tradition,[69] the combination with the garden of God, Eden, the holy mountain, original wisdom, and hidden secrets also implies an overlapping allusion to some variant of the myth we know from Genesis 2 about a primal man. If so, this would be the first of many occasions on which the Eden myth and a cosmic rebellion myth influenced

---

[67] Ezek. 28.1–9. See esp. Zimmerli 1983 and also Clifford 1972:171. For the rebel's possession of secrets that turns out worthless, see below, Chapters 8.2, 19.4.

[68] Ezek. 28.12–17. I have modified the RSV slightly in the light of Eichrodt 1970:389.

[69] Eichrodt 1970:393; McKenzie 1956.

each other.[70] As in the Genesis version, the cherub is the symbol of the hero's separation from the bright garden.

Following his denunciation of the ruler of Tyre, Ezekiel goes on to prophesy the fall of the Egyptian pharaoh, but now, as if it were equivalent, he uses the dragon form of the combat myth, such as we have met it in Babylonian and Canaanite texts, in the Psalms, in Job, and in Second Isaiah.

> Behold, I am against you, Pharaoh king of Egypt,
> the great dragon [*tannīn*] that lies in the midst of his streams,
> .that says, "My own are my streams, I made them."
> I will put hooks in your jaws . . .
> and I will draw you up from the midst of your streams . . .
> And I will cast you forth into the wilderness,
> you and all the fish of your streams;
> you shall fall upon the open field. . . .
> To the beasts of the earth and to the birds of the air
> I have given you as food.[71]

The passage is soon repeated with variations of its basic formulae: "You are like a dragon in the seas and you burst forth in your rivers."[72] Instead of the hook, Yahweh will use a net, like Marduk faced with Tiamat. Again the enemy will be given to birds and beasts to eat.

> I will strew your flesh upon the mountains,
> and fill the valleys with your carcass.
> I will drench the land even to the mountains with your flowing blood,
> and the watercourses will be full of you

—lines that recall the fate of Tiamat, Mot, and Prometheus. Then Ezekiel immediately recurs to the rebel form:

> When I blot you out, I will cover the heavens and make their stars dark;
> I will cover the sun with a cloud
> and the moon shall not give light.

[70] Other possible allusions to a grove of the gods are the Gilgamesh epic, ANET 169–70, the Babylonian Adapa myth, both still current at this period as we have seen (above, Chapter 4; Eichrodt 1970:394), and the garden in the Canaanite Šaḥru and Šalimu text (CTA 23; Clifford 1972:167–68). Cf. McKenzie 1956, which links the Ezekiel passage with Gen. 2–3 but unconvincingly separates it from the Isaiah myth. See also Isa. 51.3. For later assimilation of the two variants, see below, Chapter 12.2.

[71] Ezek. 29.3–5 (RSV slightly modified). For the parallels, see above, Chapter 2, and Day 1985:93–95. The dragon's claim that he made his streams himself brings him very close to the Gnostic form of the rebel, the demiurge, on which see below, Chapter 18.

[72] Ezek. 32.2. The Hebrew brings together *tannīn*, *yammīm*, and *nehārōt*.

> All the bright stars of heaven I will make dark over you,
> and I will put darkness upon the earth.[73]

And the multitude of Egypt is to be cast into the Pit to lie with the other mighty of the nations. In these chapters of Ezekiel the rebel myth and the general combat myth against the powers of chaos, dragon and water enemies, are combined into one great cosmological symbol of contemporary historical events.

7. From Prophecy to Apocalypse

Following the tradition of Isaiah of Jerusalem, Ezekiel understood the historical enemies of the Jews to be a sword in the hand of Yahweh, punishing Jews and foreigners alike for their rebelliousness. For Isaiah the rod of Yahweh's anger was the contemporary Assyrian monarchs; for Ezekiel it was apparently the king of Babylon, Nebuchadnezzar himself. Following the prophetic tradition before him, Isaiah had understood the covenant of Yahweh with his people as conditional, not as the unlimited and eternal covenant of the Davidic monarchy. The condition, as ever, was the obedience of the people to Yahweh's will:

> If you are willing and obedient,
>   you shall eat the good of the land;
> But if you refuse and rebel,
>   you shall be devoured by the sword.[74]

Similarly with Ezekiel, the fall of Jerusalem to Babylon was a sign of the general apostasy for which he berated his contemporaries. Indeed, the oracles against the nations (Ezek. 28–32), from which we have been quoting, are simply an extension of Ezekiel's earlier denunciation of the Israelites themselves. The continuity between the sections of Ezekiel's prophecy is clear, and this makes Ezekiel an important key to any effort to understand the popularity of the rebel myth at this period of the exile. In essence, Ezekiel's pseudo-divine rebel is simply a cosmic illustration of the human propensity to apostasy—and his sin is the same as Eve's in the garden, Eve who succumbed to the serpent's false promise, "Ye shall be as gods."

In both cases, then, where a variant of the cosmic rebel plot appears in

---

[73] Ezek. 32.2–31 (RSV). See below, Chapter 7 nn.26, 28.
[74] Isa. 1.19–20 (RSV). See Anderson 1975:331.

the Old Testament, Isaiah and Ezekiel, the myth functions mainly as metaphor; the focus in each case is on human enemies and human sins. Both examples, however, have a kind of imaginative power, an expansion of detail, so that, like Homeric similes, they take on a life of their own. Far more than mere allusion, their evocative language threatens the balance of historical and mythological points of view that we have seen to be characteristic of Old Testament narrative. Soon, and perhaps partly because of the visionary power these passages represent, that traditional balance would be lost, and the mythological language, the cosmic aspect of the double prophetic vision, would dominate.

There is one other characteristic of these passages which we have so far ignored but which is closely linked to this shift from history back to cosmology. In each case these myths refer to eschatological events. Ezekiel is instructed to say that the pharaoh and the ruler of Tyre will soon be cast down; the pseudo-Isaiah gloats over the downfall of the king of Babylon at least partly in the future tense ("All of them will speak and say to you: 'Have you too become weak as we?' "). Now insofar as the primary focus remains the realm of political and historical events, the anticipation of future events is no more than the continuation of the prophetic tradition, of the concept of the "Day of Yahweh," for example, familiar from Amos or the genuine Isaiah. Eschatology itself seems to have originated among the prophets, as they interpreted for king and people contemporary events in the light of their religious vision. But now the fall of Jerusalem and the terrifying physical and psychological experience of the exile seem to have stimulated a new kind of visionary, of whom Ezekiel, in spite of his evident peculiarities, is genuinely representative. It had always been characteristic of prophetic eschatology to claim a direct witness of events transpiring in the divine council of Yahweh and his heavenly court, to see the divine plan and then to translate that plan into the terms of "plain history."[75] But now the events of plain history had become both so awesome and so incomprehensible to the canny but ordinary mind that only the visionary language, not its political translation, made any coherent sense. Ezekiel and the pseudo-Isaiah still made the effort, but it would not be long before the Jewish eschatological vision became almost entirely cosmological—and apocalyptic. The loss of nationhood produced a profound disillusion with and indifference to the day-to-day world of poli-

[75] P. D. Hanson 1975:11; Stone (ed.) 1984:384–92. See the story of Micaiah, above, Chapter 5.

tics, and the language of vision ceased to have the kind of immediate historical relevance that it still held for the prophets, even for the mad Ezekiel. It would soon remain entirely cosmic, and the restoration of the people become entirely a cosmic event.

This shift in eschatological meanings did not happen so suddenly as this brief account may seem to suggest. We have already noted in Second Isaiah the revival of mythological imagery to express the coming return to Zion, but that event itself was regarded as imminent and genuinely and politically possible, given the rise of Cyrus of Persia and the resulting historical situation. Second Isaiah had been able to avoid the kind of literal-mindedness that goes with fully apocalyptic thinking. Similarly, in the cases of Isaiah 13–14 and Ezekiel 28–32, the historical references were sufficiently specific to allow for considerable mythological elaboration without a complete shift of interest to the cosmic realm. The seeds of apocalyptic are here and they have germinated, but they have not yet produced the plants that would eventually choke the real sense of human and political possibility. Second Isaiah's typological shift of Exodus language to the imminent future still envisioned a genuine human liberation from tyranny.

The resurgence at this time of the popularity of the rebel myth is only one of the signs of the general revival of mythological language. The old songs of the wars of Yahweh, such as we find in Amos, for example,[76] now came to express the hope for establishment of Yahweh's universal rule. The new conquest used the terms of the old, and the new world was to be a new creation, a revival of the golden age: "For lo! I create a new heaven and a new earth."[77] The Urzeit, and indeed the whole of Israel's history, becomes Endzeit.

To illustrate this shift, juxtapose two texts that allude to the combat. One is a psalm, a lament for the destruction of the temple in 586 B.C. It cries to Yahweh for aid and reminds him of how he defeated the dragon, Yamm, and Leviathan:

> How long, O God, will the adversary blaspheme you,
>   the foe revile your name, O Conqueror? . . .
> Destroy, O God, the kings from the East,
>   achieve victory in the middle of the earth!
> You broke apart Yamm by your might:

[76] Amos 1–2.7. See Cross 1973:99–111.
[77] Isa. 65.17.

you shattered the heads of the dragon on the waters.
You crushed the heads of Leviathan,
    you gave him as food to be gathered by the people of the wilderness.
You released springs and brooks,
    it was you who turned primordial rivers into dry land.[78]

If you could do that, goes the lament, then why are you not doing it again now to these historical enemies?

In the following passage, from the so-called Isaiah Apocalypse, probably a later text than the psalm, this logic is taken a step further. Yahweh will indeed repeat that primordial victory.

In that day, Yahweh will punish
    with his hard and great and strong sword
Leviathan, the twisting serpent,
    Leviathan, the crooked serpent,
    and he will slay the dragon in the sea.[79]

What the Psalmist had prayed for the prophet confidently anticipates: recapitulation of the primordial victory in the imminent future. But where the Psalmist's enemy was still the political foes of Israel, the Isaiah Apocalypse wants another mythological battle and triumph, and the enemy is once again the dragon.

The growth of this eschatological thinking poses an obvious problem, which is akin to the historical problem that generated it. If Yahweh defeated the dragon enemy in the primordial battle, why should he have to do it again now? Did Yahweh not win after all? Unthinkable, yet logical, almost an inevitable corollary of the shift from Urzeit to Endzeit. Possibly this logic offers a further reason for the popularity of the rebel variant of the combat in this period. The more the various kings of historical empires came to be viewed, even in metaphor, as cosmic tyrants, the more too a kind of narrative logic demands that they also be seen as cosmic rebels—and Yahweh is simply biding his time until he puts down the rebellion once and for all. The tyrants have to be rebels because of the common procedure we have noted earlier in this chapter: rebels have no legitimate

---

[78] Ps. 74.10–15, trans. Dahood 1969:199–205; cf. Wakeman 1973:62–63 and Day 1985: 22–25.

[79] Isa. 27.1. See above, Chapter 2 nn.58, 59. The Isaiah Apocalypse also brings together earlier and later stages of my argument, since it blends Baal and Noah themes. Compare Isa. 24.18–19 with Baal in CTA 4.7.25–32 (Day 1985:145–46) and with Gen. 7.11, 8.2 (Kaiser 1974:191).

authority, such as must be granted, by the Hebrew imagination, to Yahweh. Babylon, once simply a historical power, becomes a cosmic upstart.

We should not, however, make the mistake of reading into these proto-apocalyptic texts the full cosmology that was to be invented by Christianity, though that was precisely what the church fathers were to do. For the moment, all these myths merely grouped themselves, as available metaphor, around an essentially historical center. Take away that center, and the various myths may coalesce in the cosmic vision of the end-time: monstrous enemy, a Leviathan or a Rahab, dragon or serpent, can be merged with the essentially political figure of the cosmic rebel. With the rise of apocalyptic thinking this is precisely what happens. Torn loose from its historical anchor, mythological speculation came more and more to dominate many branches of Jewish tradition. The roots of such thinking in genuine prophetic eschatology are forgotten.[80]

[80] My arguments in this and the previous chapter follow the line of P. D. Hanson 1975. For a critique, see Carroll 1979a, and for some of the larger issues, see Bruns 1984.

SEVEN

THE SONS OF GOD AND THE
DAUGHTERS OF MEN

THE COSMIC rebel of the Old Testament was more or less confined to metaphor. In the apocalyptic and largely apocryphal literature, however, he escapes from these narrative limits and becomes a character in his own story. "Religion," said Santayana, "is the poetry in which we believe," and we now follow the transformation of cosmic rebel from imaginative extension and poetic intensification of belief to an object of belief himself.

In the period between the Exile and the rise of Christianity, the theology of Judaism, as Hebrew culture now came to be called, became more and more dualistic. "Dualism" is a complex and confusing term, but if we approach it from a literary as much as a theological point of view, we may be able to make better sense of this important change in the direction of Hebrew tradition. The narrative terminology about the battles of the divine warrior, inherited from the earliest days of the Tribal League, now referred vaguely if at all to any historical enemies. Instead, its inherently cosmological meanings reasserted themselves, and the people of the post-exilic period believed themselves to be witnesses to, even participants in, a vast cosmic struggle that would end only with the glorious victory of the final days. Many Jews continued to translate this combat myth back into political terms. The Maccabean Revolt or the elaborate military detail of the Qumran *War Scroll* are sufficient testimony to that; the seeds of the Zealot movement against the Romans may be there also. But the actual language in which the struggle was envisaged developed directly from combat mythology, and the opponents were divine beings as much as human.

If the full story of this ongoing war were to be told, however, then the story had to start somewhere, and the obvious place to look for such a narrative beginning was to the myth of cosmic rebellion. If the hostile forces of the adversary army were cosmic beings, their origin had to be explained in cosmic terms also. The enemy could not simply be *there*, at least for an inquiring mind informed by the Hebrew tradition of mon-

otheism. Yet as the complex history of the narrative will reveal, this solution was not worked out once and for all, to be passed on intact to subsequent generations. The rebellion myth never disappeared from the
Jewish tradition once it had gained currency in the Babylonian, Palestinian, and Egyptian areas of dispersion, yet the forms in which it appears are
so various that they seem to owe as much to fresh meditation on the narrative problems as to inherited tradition. To a long succession of thoughtful religious myth-makers, from the anonymous authors of the extra-
canonical Enoch books to Milton, cosmic rebellion would seem the most
suitable solution to the narrative problem of how to begin the story. Once
the rebellion itself was so conceived, however, the particular motivation
of the rebel himself could still be quite variously understood, and rarely
was the story told with the subtlety of the Babylonian myth of Anzu. The
versions that do achieve such plausibility leave ineradicable marks on the
subsequent traditions.

The initial impulse for the development of the rebel myth, then, was
not so much the effort to account for the origin of *evil*, viewed as an abstraction, though the myth certainly served that function, but to answer a
narrative question of more general and more fundamental interest: how
do I begin my story? Is it a villain who is responsible for the "lack"—and
if so, where does he come from? In the Jewish context it is impossible to
separate that question from the more immediate form of the question:
how did we get here?

The rapid development and popularity of the rebellion story among the
various sects of apocalyptic Judaism entailed some serious theological
problems that can be reduced to one essential question: was history within
the scope of human responsibility, or was it simply the battleground for
superhuman forces? The part of this question of most immediate concern
for the growth of the rebel myth was whether man or god was the cause
of human suffering. Isaiah and Ezekiel, we saw, both used the rebel in
ways consonant with the history-centered character of the Yahweh faith.
The cosmic rebel was still a projection of human rebelliousness, an image
raised to celestial proportions of the *hybris* of kings. The magnification is
ironic; it functions to diminish the human rebel. But when the rebel became an object of belief, then if the thoughtful storyteller were not careful
the rebel's activity could explain, and then excuse, human sinfulness. A
cosmic evil, beyond human control, would raise the difficult problem of
the relationship between evil and sin.

The rebellious angel and his followers begin their long career through interpretation and elaboration of Genesis, in particular the "primeval" history that makes up chapters 1–11. Until the last decade it was widely accepted that the earliest stratum of this part of Genesis came from a writer of genius known to scholarship as "J" or "the Yahwist," together with some fragments from "E" or "the Elohist." These designations derive from the two principal names for god and refer to the authors of Israel's two national epics. Composed in the ninth or tenth centuries, these epics were, it was held, later edited and incorporated by one "P" or "the Priestly writer," perhaps with some refinements from a later "Redactor," or "R." This view of the growth of Genesis, the Graf-Wellhausen or documentary hypothesis, has been seriously challenged on several counts, although it still has many supporters.[1] Some would abandon the documentary hypothesis entirely, others would redate the Yahwist to the seventh century and so make him a contemporary of D, the "Deuteronomic historian," and others have fought for various modifications of the hypothesis in view of the stronger arguments of the critics.[2] At the moment, any solution that does not ignore the whole issue must be merely provisional, but at least for the primeval history the differences between J and P parts are so striking that they require separate designation, however we account for them. I here assume that the Priestly writer composed, in the sixth or perhaps the fifth century, the text we have, incorporating much traditional material—disparate stories about the first human family, the great flood, and even a myth about the origin of languages. This traditional material had already been brought together in an older text that the Priestly writer used and greatly respected. The author of this older text, whatever his date, was a writer whom we may as well call the Yahwist.

Whatever the ultimate source of these myths, the Yahwist appears to have organized them according to his own subtle version of the covenant faith, and this organization the Priestly writer respected, even if he did not agree with its implications. Each of the stories seems designed to illustrate

[1] The consensus had already been challenged by earlier iconoclasts like Cassuto 1964 (and cf. Harrison 1969), but it still held good for P. Ellis 1968 and even for Anderson 1975 and 1978. The main attacks came from T. L. Thompson 1974, Van Seters 1975, Schmid 1976, and Rentdorff 1977. There has since been much anguished but often stimulating discussion. In essence, Van Seters argued that all the patriarchal narratives were late, postexilic reconstructions of the past, written with the recent supremacy of the Neo-Babylonian empire very much in mind. The view adopted here is akin to that of Clements 1977, a long review of Rentdorff.

[2] Both Clements 1977 and Luke 1977 are flexible but, if I understand them, conservative responses to the new chaos.

the human propensity to violate the limits imposed by the covenant with Yahweh, even though they are set in the primordial time before any formal covenant existed. Each story, in fact, establishes the need for the covenant, at least in general moral terms, since the heart of the Yahwist's "epic" is the story he goes on to tell, the Exodus—deliverance from Egypt, guidance in the wilderness, the covenant, and the conquest of Canaan. These are the decisive events by which Yahweh established the special status and responsibility of Israel.

Since the recovery through archaeology of analogous political treaties establishing feudal relations between people and lord, the particular meaning of the covenant has been a hot topic in Old Testament studies. Scholarship has uncovered, for example, the profound difference between the tribal covenant of the league and the royal ideology of David. In the Sinai covenant, the great acts of Yahweh for the people placed them under an obligation to serve their covenant Lord but did not constrain him to continue the relationship if the people proved unfaithful.[3] In the Davidic theory, on the other hand, Yahweh had bound himself not to abandon the royal line or its subjects, a position that religious conservatives like the great prophets (except Isaiah of Jerusalem) protested strongly. The Yahwist's theology would seem to be, at least in part, a return to the Sinai tradition, for it is not the presence of the Ark in Jerusalem which symbolizes the relation to God, but the signs of Yahweh's special interest in Israel revealed in the Exodus. Nevertheless, the royalist ideology affected him, for he also tells the story, elaborated later by the Priestly editor as the rainbow episode, of Yahweh's promise not to destroy his people again.

> As Yahweh smelled the soothing odor, he said to himself, "Never again will I doom the world because of man, since the devisings of man's heart are evil from the start; neither will I ever again strike down every living being as I have done.

> So long as the earth endures,
> Seedtime and harvest,
> Cold and heat,
> Summer and winter,
> And day and night
> Shall not cease."[4]

[3] Mendenhall 1955:44–50. See above, Chapter 4.3.
[4] Gen. 8.21–22, trans. Speiser 1964.

To be sure, the Yahwist inherited something like this with the tradition of the flood itself, Yahweh only says this "to himself," and this is far from a positive promise to protect Israel in perpetuity. Nevertheless, we may detect something of the kingship's ideology, appropriately muted given the stage of human history being told, in the limits Yahweh here imposes on his own freedom.[5]

The Yahwist tells these primordial stories, then, with the covenant faith as their informing principle. In each case that faith is violated as man oversteps the limits the covenant with Yahweh imposes, and so the stories each illustrate in a different way human rebelliousness. Rebellion itself is a political term (*re-bellum*, renewing war), but for the special Hebrew tradition, rebellion was a symptom of a more general sinfulness conceived as the human tendency to break the covenant relationship. The result of this rebelliousness is divine wrath and inexorable punishment. From Eden to the Tower of Babel, each myth in the Yahwist's primeval history illustrates this premise, in the same way as Yahweh himself demonstrates the principle to Abraham by the destruction of Sodom and Gomorrah.[6]

There are a number of interesting precedents for the Yahwist's epic in other Near Eastern texts, and it will help to understand his special perspective if we glance briefly at one such parallel, the closest of all, in fact: the Babylonian flood epic, known as *Atrahasis*.[7] The parallels have been so widely canvassed[8] that I need only point to one aspect of the striking similarities, the reason given in each source for the decision to send the flood. Though the problem in *Atrahasis* is posed in the picturesque and charming language about the sheer noise that men are making down there, so much that Enlil cannot sleep, Anne Kilmer has elegantly and convincingly shown that the real issue is overpopulation: "The people multiplied, the land was bellowing like a bull."[9] The problem is finally resolved not by the flood, which Atrahasis and his family manage to escape, but by the introduction of stringent forms of birth control.

[5] Clines 1979 takes the view that the Yahwist generally opposes the kingship ideology, specifically in the sons of God episode, but this ignores the subtleties summarized in the text below.

[6] Gen. 18.17–21. For the narrative parallels between flood and fire destructions, see Fontenrose 1945 and below, Chapters 12.7 and 20.

[7] Lambert and Millard 1969, a splendid edition of the numerous fragments.

[8] A convenient summary is Heidel 1949:224–69, if one allows for his dismissive interpretations.

[9] Kilmer 1972. See esp. Lambert and Millard 1969:72, Tablet II.1.2–3. Cf. Moran 1971, P. D. Hanson 1977, and Clines 1979.

As we have seen in our discussion of the *Enuma Eliš*, this overpopulation motif was borrowed by the priestly composers of that epic for Apsu's annoyance at the younger gods and his decision to wipe them out. In neither case is the issue one of rebellion, though one might loosely describe the offending behavior as rebellious. In its original context, the *Atrahasis* epic, the noisy children motif refers, like its Yahwistic counterpart, to the difficult relation of gods and men, not as in its adaptation to the *Enuma Eliš*, to the relations among generations of gods.

This episode in the Babylonian flood story is clearly the ultimate source of the curious episode of "the sons of God and the daughters of men" that introduces the Yahwist's version. This episode was destined to have an influence out of all proportion to the meager four verses it gets at the beginning of Genesis 6. Speiser translates them as follows, calling the passage "Prelude to Disaster":

> [1]Now when men began to increase on earth and daughters were born to them, [2]then divine beings saw how beautiful were the human daughters and took as their wives any of them they liked. [3]Then Yahweh said, "My spirit shall not shield man for ever; since he is but flesh; let the time allowed him be one hundred and twenty years."
>
> [4]It was then that the Nephilim appeared on earth—as well as later—after the divine beings had united with human daughters. Those were the heroes [*gibbōrīm*] of old, men of renown.

There are numerous interpretive problems here.[10] As it stands, verse 4 appears to intrude as a kind of etiological gloss, to which some more words appear to have been added ("Those were the heroes") as yet a further explanatory comment. Verse 3 would appear more logically if it were a continuation of the Priestly genealogies that constitute chapter 5 of Genesis, but in that case verses 1–2 are intrusive—and anyway, what has man done that his life should be so circumscribed? Such problems made this passage a perfect focus for midrashic interpretation of the kind that all such difficulties spawned in the subsequent hermeneutic tradition. Indeed, the reinterpretation started as early as the Greek translation of the Septuagint, perhaps even as early as Ezekiel and the Priestly editor. But since the recovery and explanation of the *Atrahasis* epic, one thing at least should now be clear that was never very clear to the previous legions of

---

[10] The seminal discussions of Robert 1895, Jung 1926, Lods 1927, and Kraeling 1947 should now be supplemented by P. D. Hanson 1977, Nickelsburg 1977, Petersen 1979, and Barthelmus 1979. See Dexinger 1966 and Delcor 1976:4 for fuller bibliography.

interpreters. This passage is a genuine "prelude" to the flood story, not a separate fragment inappropriately tacked on from some other myth, for the main point of the two opening verses—as of the more elaborate story in the Babylonian epic—is the problem of overpopulation: "Now when men began to increase on the earth."

In the Yahwistic context this motivation was but dimly understood. Indeed, it is remarkable that it has survived in the Genesis version at all, since, when the Yahwist's epic was edited by the Priestly writer, the instructions of God after the flood became exactly the opposite of the Babylonian concern with more careful population control. The Priestly God (Elohim) says, "Be fruitful and multiply." These words echo the conclusion of the first creation, another Priestly addition (1.28 = 9.1–2), and thus turn the flood story into a second creation myth, with the watery chaos of tehōm now given dramatic elaboration.[11] So striking a modification of the Babylonian story has even been seen as a direct repudiation of that alien tradition.[12] If the majority of modern scholars are correct,[13] the Priestly writer lived either during or shortly after the Babylonian exile, and his assemblage of the epic and Priestly traditions would be likely to reflect a certain antipathy to the conquerors' own religious tradition, with which the exile had made many Jews only too familiar. But the injunction to "be fruitful and multiply and fill the earth" is entirely appropriate to the hope for national revival after the decimation of the population during the turmoil and war that preceded the fall of Jerusalem. We do not need to posit a Priestly writer who knew and understood the overpopulation theme of Atrahasis. The reversal of the Babylonian conclusion to the flood myth is another curious example of what can happen when a narrative is adapted by a different culture.[14]

Whether or not the Priestly writer understood the central idea of the Babylonian epic, his addition of the "be fruitful and multiply" theme to his version of the Yahwist's epic certainly helped to obscure the traces of

[11] I here follow the sensible arguments of Cross 1973:305 and Andersen 1978 that the scholarly fiction "R," putative redactor of the J and P material, should be identified with P. Alter 1981:141–47 has a splendid discussion of the advantages that accrue to the critic once he makes that assumption.

[12] Childs 1960; Moran 1971; Kapelrud 1974. Others have proposed, plausibly, that the Priestly writer is "demythologizing" his own tradition, such as Ps. 104, and thus only indirectly the Babylonian. See Day 1985:49–57. Cf. Alter 1981:27–35.

[13] Kaufman 1960 challenged this consensus, placing P before D, the Deuteronomic historian, but see von Rad 1966.

[14] For a different view, see Kikawada 1975.

the overpopulation concern. The new theme may well account for the loss of connection between verses 2 and 3. Indeed, only with the recovery of the *Atrahasis* text was it recognized that Yahweh's apparently unmotivated decision to limit the life span to 120 years is a direct response to the threatened population explosion that would result from indiscriminate copulation between "divine beings" and human women.[15] The structure of the Priestly writer's flood myth is chiastic, a carefully wrought design that a literary critic would call "ring composition."[16] Though it incorporates the Yawhist's version, it has its own shape. The narrative moves in toward its center, the focus on Noah and the minute remnant of creation adrift in the Ark: "God remembered Noah and all the beasts and cattle that were with him in the Ark, and God caused a wind to sweep across the earth. The Waters began to subside." The wind (*rūaḥ*) recalls the "wind from God" with which the same writer had begun the first creation.[17] It starts the movement out that reverses the order of the inward sequence. Given this structure, the theme of repopulating the earth not only echoes the first creation (8.17, 9.1 = 1.28) but also is the counterpart of the acts by which God had destroyed. But this skillful literary use of the "multiply" theme obviously precluded finding the cause of the flood in overpopulation, even assuming that this had been an option for the writer. He therefore added to the Yahwist's epic the verses about violence or lawlessness (*ḥāmās*) and corruption of the earth (6.11–13), in order to allude to the Yahwist's earlier stories about disobedience, fratricide, and Lamech's revenge. The injuncton against murder (9.6) then picks this up again as a further ring to enclose the main narrative.[18]

Even in the Yahwist's original epic, the Babylonian concern had probably become virtually unrecognizable because his theological convictions were so different. One may wonder, indeed, why he should have preserved what traces he did of the theme. A possible answer is to be found in a comparison with the other myths he adapted to his primeval history.

Three of these myths have more in common than the general resentment of Yahweh's instructions. The Eden and Babel stories both recount separate examples of human efforts to transcend the barrier between gods

---

[15] Kilmer 1972; Moran 1971; Clines 1979:39.

[16] Cassuto 1964:30–31. See McEvenue 1971.

[17] Gen. 1.2. On the *rūaḥ 'elōhīm*, see now Day 1985:52–53. For the later use of this feminine word for "spirit" in Gnostic versions of the trinity, and the substitution of *pneuma*, a neuter, in orthodox Christianity, see Pagels 1979:52.

[18] Cross 1973:306; Anderson 1978:31–39.

and men, and in this light the copulation of women with "divine beings" serves the same function.[19] The truth of the serpent's claim "Ye shall be as gods" is confirmed by Yahweh's anxious response. He agrees that "the man has become like one of us" and ejects him from the garden lest "he put out his hand and taste also of the tree of life and eat, and live forever" (3.22), which would apparently have completed the magical transformation. The Babel myth is an obvious, almost allegorical example, as the Yahwist tells it, of the same aspiration. It seems to be based on the religious idea that informed the Babylonian ziggurat, that one could walk up this imitation mountain and meet with the gods.[20] The overpopulation myth, though it retains its Babylonian position as the introduction to the flood story, now becomes a matching instance of the same transgression.

The Yahwist seems to have noticed, however, that the form of the myth he adopted might be taken to represent this transgression from the opposite point of view—gods trying to cross the barrier from their side. So in order to make sure that the myth fit his dominant theme, he added the following verses to establish the connection with the punishment that ensues. In his mind it is not overpopulation, still less the "noise" of mankind, which prompts Yahweh to destroy.

> When Yahweh saw how great was man's wickedness on earth, and how every scheme that his mind devised was nothing but evil all the time, Yahweh regretted that he had made man on earth, and there was sorrow in his heart. And Yahweh said, "I will blot out from the earth the men that I created, man and beast, the creeping things, and the birds of the sky; for I am sorry that I made them." But Noah found favor with Yahweh.[21]

Undoubtedly the Yahwist's narrative instincts were right, since the guilt of mankind is not a conclusion that the unprejudiced reader of the previous verses would inevitably be driven to adopt. He seems also to have seen that his brief allusion to the "diving beings" and their activity might at least mitigate the human fault. So he makes sure that Yahweh's displeasure is properly explained and places the moral responsibility firmly on human shoulders before he proceeds. The sexual behavior is intended merely to illustrate, not to excuse, human sin. It is not so large a

---

[19] P. D. Hanson 1977:214. On the later development of the "mixing" theme, see below, Chapters 19.2 and 23.2, and Stroumsa 1984:31–35.

[20] This idea lies behind Ezek. 28.2, "I am a god (*'el*), I sit in the seat of Elohim," the boast of the Prince of Tyre, above Chapter 6.6, according to Cross 1973:44.

[21] Gen. 6.5–8, trans. Speiser 1964.

step from the Yahwist's severe interpretation of the myth to the antifeminist version, in which alluring females cause the great catastrophe,
though this version of the story does not appear until much later in the
development of the Genesis tradition.

Who, then, are these "divine beings"? Since the discovery of the Ugaritic texts, there is little mystery here either. These are the *benē 'elōhīm*,
members of the divine council, the gods of Canaan taken as a group.[22] The
phrase takes on a different coloring in the monotheistic context. In the
two renderings of the Greek Septuagint, for example, it becomes either
hoi huioi tou theou, sons of god, just like the "sons of El" of Ugarit, for
Genesis 6.2, or *hoi angeloi tou theou*, for Genesis 6.4, a phrase that makes
them God's messengers and identifies them with the *mal'āḳ Yahweh*.[23]
These are the same beings who sing hymns of praise to Yahweh at the creation.[24] In the Genesis passage, the phrase simply refers to this group of
"gods" who appear in the divine council around Yahweh, the council that
often formed the object of prophetic visions. Apparently these beings, or
some of them at least, found the beautiful creatures of the earth to their
liking and mated with them, like their counterparts in Greek mythology.

Such a parallel clearly occurred to one of the transmitters of this story,
for he added the gloss about the *nephīlīm* and the origin of the heroes, the
men of "name," the *gibbōrīm*, thinking perhaps of themes like the partly
divine parentage of Gilgamesh in the Babylonian epic, a man who also
made a name for himself.[25] Whether or not this was the Yahwist himself,
another tradent, or the Priestly editor, the text is too inextricably entangled to say. But we know that a tradition survived in Israel similar to the
one recorded by Hesiod in the *Works and Days*, for Ezekiel alludes to a belief that heroes who die in battle are treated with honor in Sheol:

> And they [i.e., those who die in disgrace, like the Egyptian pharaoh] do not
> lie with the heroes, the giants of old, who went down to Sheol with their
> weapons of war, whose swords were laid under their heads and whose
> shields are over their bones, for the terror of the heroes was in the land of
> the living.[26]

[22] See above, Chapter 5 n. 8, and Delcor 1976:7–12.
[23] Cf. Ps. 29.1, 89.7, Alexander 1972, and Wickham 1974. See also above, Chapter 5
n. 11.
[24] Job 38.7.
[25] See above, Chapter 1, Lods 1927:204–5, Bamberger 1952:8, and Clines 1979:34–35.
[26] Ezek. 32.27, trans. Eichrodt 1970. For Hesiod, see Vernant 1966 and Nagy 1979.

The Hebrew words are *gibbōrīm* and *nōpelīm*, the same as in Genesis 6.4. Whoever added the gloss there was thinking of the same tradition about ancient heroes and so made the passage into an etiological story about their origin.

In the Hebrew of the Genesis and the Ezekiel passages, then, there seems to be no trace of political rebellion, and still less of a disgrace or "fall" of these heroic beings or their divine ancestors. Rather, on the one hand we have a story of sexual desire, on the other a simple heroic tradition.[27] It must have been because of the honor done to dead heroes, for example, that Ezekiel's pharaoh and his like do not get to lie beside these honored men of the past. But when these passages were translated into Greek by the authors of the Septuagint, we find a very different interpretation. The Greek translator of the Ezekiel passage, for example, omits the qualifying negative before the verb and so produces the following transformation: the Egyptians "lay beside the giants, those who had fallen in former times and had gone down to Hades with their arms." For this remarkable version there are two principal reasons. First, the Greek translator is following the Targumist interpretation of the term *nephīlīm* as cognate with *nāphal* "to fall."[28] Second, he clearly has in mind the Greek myth of the proud Titans, often confused with the proud giants.[29] This identification became common thereafter, as in the *Sibylline Oracles*, which picture the archangel Uriel leading to judgment "the Titans and the giants and such as the flood destroyed."[30] The Greek translator of Genesis also rendered *nephīlīm* by *gigantes*. That the *nephīlīm* were thought to be superhuman in size we may conclude from Numbers 13.33: "And there we saw the *nephīlīm* [Greek *gigantes*], sons of Anak, and we were in their sight as grasshoppers."

As soon as the Hebrew scriptures were translated into Greek *koinē*, then, we find these obscure passages rendered explicable by reference to Greek traditions about the giants, Titans, and cosmic battles. This was

[27] Kraeling 1947. P. D. Hanson 1977 sees here a political rebellion as a reflex of the cosmic rebel myth. There is no trace of a cosmic battle either; see Petersen 1979:52–53 and Bamberger 1952:8. On the further development of this passage, see below Chapter 8.

[28] Isa. 14.12 "How you fell [*naphalta*] from heaven." Cf. the Targum of 13.10, where the word is applied to constellations or meteors. See also Fitzmyer 1971:81, Delcor 1976:14, 22, 28, Stroumsa 1984:22, and below, Chapter 10 n. 12.

[29] *hyperthumos* at Hesiod, *Theogony* 718, and Homer, *Odyssey* 7.59.

[30] *Sibylline Oracles* 2.231 in Charlesworth (ed.) 1983:351; cf. *Sib. Or.* 1.98–124, where the Jewish and Greek traditions are blended. See also Delcor 1976:15 and Collins in Stone (ed.) 1984:357–81.

natural enough, given the general effort to render special Hebrew conceptions in the language of the conqueror, but it posed fresh problems, akin
to those that troubled Christian interpreters.[31] Josephus has no qualms
about this procedure, and he paraphrases these verses of Genesis thus:
"Many of the angels of God united with women and engendered proud
offspring, disdainful of all virtue because of the faith they placed in their
own power; in fact, the actions attributed to them by our tradition resem-
ble the bold exploits which the Greeks recount about the Giants."[32] As we
have just seen, there is a good reason for this apparent similarity. The tradition is Greek in origin, whatever it may owe to other sources as well.
Philo, however, felt the need to warn against this kind of parallelism, intent as he was on making Judaism palatable to a sophisticated and philosophically trained audience in Alexandria. In his treatise *De Gigantibus* (58)
he comments on Genesis 6: "Someone may think that Moses here makes
allusion to the poets' myths about the giants, even though myth-making
is totally foreign to him and he proceeds by the light of the inner Truth.
. . . Therefore, far from offering a myth about the giants, he wishes to
(express) the idea that some men belong naturally to the earth, others to
heaven, and others to God"—a curiously obscure "clarification."

In view of the many parallels between Greek and Near Eastern mythology, often due to the influence from Canaanite, Hittite, or other
sources of dissemination, we must not make too much of the impact of
Greek mythology on Jewish tradition following Alexander's conquest.[33]
Many of the myths of the Near East were carried in the Hebrew tradition
itself, as we have seen in the case of the Red Sea legend, or in the Isaian
rebellion myth. This suppressed mythological tendency was clearly reac-
tivated by the new and direct contacts with neighboring religious systems
during and after the exile—Babylonian, Persian, then Greek—but the as-
tonishing resurgence of mythological conceptions in Jewish apocalypticism must not be attributed solely to "alien" ideas.[34] It was often the very
resistance to alien systems in the preexilic period that was paradoxically
responsible for the preservation and transmission of those traditions. Indeed, our brief Genesis myth may well be an instance of this dialectic,

[31] On Origen and Celsus, see below, Chapter 21.

[32] Josephus, *Antiquitates Judaicae* 1.3.1.

[33] For different views, see Glasson 1961, Delcor 1976, and Nickelsburg 1977. See also below, Chapter 8, and Boman 1960.

[34] For the place of the *Sybilline Oracles* in this process, see Collins in Stone (ed.) 1984 and
Charlesworth (ed.) 1983:81–83, 317–34.

since the Yahwist and his editors not only change the theological implications of the myth but also seem to find it distasteful. One scholar even
discovers a subtle polemic against the mythological tradition in Yahweh's
categorical assertion that man "is but flesh."[35] Divine and human cannot
mix their substance as the myth of the *benē 'elōhīm* and its many analogues
imply.

We have now identified the following stages in the development of this
seminal passage in Genesis. Its origin lies in the Babylonian *Atrahasis* epic,
and it is thus a genuine prelude to the flood myth. Hebrew epic tradition
adapted and shortened the episode to fit the Yahwist's moralized view of
the cause of the flood and so obscured the original idea of overpopulation.
For the Yahwist the story of sexual desire between divine and human extends his theme of hybris. The Priestly editor of the sixth or fifth century,
who may have known the *Atrahasis* story, then incorporated the Yahwist's
text into his own version, which made the flood story into a new creation. His addition of the "be fruitful and multiply" theme completely reversed the Babylonian idea, perhaps consciously. At some point a gloss
was added to account for the ancient tradition of heroes and to locate the
story in time. The Greek translators read the passage, the implications of
which were already obscure, in the light of Greek traditions, not simply
of heroes but also of Titans, giants, and cosmic battles. Philo felt it necessary to correct this reading, but in practice the passage could rarely be
separated henceforth from the combat theme, being itself so deeply
embedded in the Hebrew tradition. Indeed, as we are now to discover, the
story of the sons of God and the daughters of men became a variant of the
rebel myth even without the intervention of the Greek language and its
combat traditions.

[35] Childs 1960:42–48; Bamberger 1952:263n, citing Cassuto 1964, vol. 2. But see below,
Chapter 8, for a more cogent connection with Hesiod.

EIGHT

REBELLION AND LUST:
THE WATCHER ANGELS IN THE
ARAMAIC ENOCH BOOKS

ALTHOUGH there is no apparent allusion to a cosmic rebellion in the
Genesis text, it was through the subsequent rewriting of the flood
myth that the Jewish rebellion myth developed. The earliest stage was
probably the composition in Hebrew of a "Book of Noah," perhaps as
early as the fourth century, of which only fragments survive.[1] To judge
from these fragments, the Book of Noah was an apocalyptic work that
told a fuller version of the flood myth interpreted along the typological
lines of Second Isaiah's eschatological version of the Exodus. Just as God
had destroyed the world in the time of Noah in order to replace it with a
more successful creation under the sign of the rainbow, so he would again
wipe out all the evil and corruption of the present through some new cat-
aclysm at the end-time and make a new world to grow from the ruins of
the old. A miraculous birth story is attached to Noah, as to other hero figures, and he becomes both the saving remnant and the savior who cleanses
the earth.[2] The fragments also show that the Book of Noah, like its apocalyptic cousins, reveals some confusion about past, present, and future
time.[3] Following the general tendency of apocalyptic literature to ascribe

[1] The Noah fragments are incorporated into *Enoch* at 54.7–55.2, 65–67, 83–84, and 106–7,
but *Enoch* 6–11 probably derives from it also. See Charles (ed.) 1913: Vol. 1, 168–74, J. P.
Lewis 1968:12–15, Dimant 1978, Milik 1976:56, and now Black 1985:8–9. The Qumran
fragments are translated in Barthélemy and Milik 1955.

[2] The miraculous birth story, *Enoch* 106–7, with its play on the name of Noah as "rest"
("remnant" or "relief," Gen. 5.29), occurs also in the Latin fragment (Charles [ed.] 1913:
vol. 2, 278–79; cf. below, Chapter 11 n. 6) and is repeated with variation in the Qumran
Genesis Apocryphon (1QGenAp 2–5 in Fitzmyer 1971:51–55 and Vermes 1975:216–17). For
the parallels, see Gen. 21 (Isaac), Judg. 13 (Samson), 1 Sam. 1 (Samuel), Matt. 1.18–25 (Jesus), and 2 *Enoch* 72 (Melchizedek; Charlesworth [ed.] 1983:211 and Vaillant 1952:65–85).
See also Stone (ed.) 1984:93–95, 407–8, and contrast the birth of Cain story, below, Chapters
12.6 and 17.1.

[3] Typological linking of flood and end-time is explicit in *Enoch* 106.18 and 107.1 (cf. 91.5–
9). It recurs throughout the tradition and is found, e.g., in Matt. 24.37–38, Luke 17.26, or 2
Pet. 3.5–7. For the echo of Noah's dove in the Paraclete, see Kikawada 1974.

events to active spirits, this Noah story also connects the catastrophic events more clearly than does Genesis to the activities of the sinful angels with the daughters of men.

The next stage of development was probably incorporation of the Book of Noah or the tradition it represents into the Enoch literature. Most of this does survive, at least in Ethiopic translation, and it has been the focus of intense debate in recent years.[4] In postexilic times among the disenfranchised sects of Palestine, a group of writings, chiefly visions of the transmundane world, was composed and attributed to Enoch. Enoch appears in Genesis 5 as the seventh of the primordial patriarchs between Adam and Noah, but he has a curious double in Genesis 4.17, the alternate or Yahwist genealogy. This Enoch is the son not of Jared, as in 5.18, but of Cain. What is more, Cain is said to have built the first city and to have named it "Enoch" after his son. I argued earlier that the ambivalence of the adversary is linked to a fundamental uneasiness about living in cities. Here we find a further illustration of the point, and a further reason why the pseudo-Enoch knows so much about adversary angels.[5] Indeed, the existence and preservation of these two genealogies, in each of which Enoch, Methuselah, and Lamech appear, reflect the same kind of ambivalence. One makes Cain the parent of subsequent humanity, the other substitutes a new son of Adam and Eve, called Seth, to whom we may trace our origins.[6]

The obvious reason, however, why Enoch was thought to have special knowledge about the origins of humanity is that, as we are told in Genesis 5.24, "Enoch walked with God, and then was no more, because God took him." He also lived exactly 365 years. The Priestly genealogy that cites

[4] Charles' splendid pioneering work (1893, 1912, 1913) has been updated by recent studies and new editions. See Black (ed.) 1970 and 1985, Milik 1971 and 1976, Knibb 1978, and Charlesworth (ed.) 1983. For reviews of recent scholarship, see Stone (ed.) 1984. The *Ethiopic Enoch*, called *1 Enoch* in Charles and the *Book of Enoch* or simply *Enoch* here, is to be distinguished from *2 Enoch* (*Book of the Secrets of Enoch*, discussed below, Chapter 12.8) and from the medieval Hebrew *3 Enoch* (Odeburg 1973). That the complete text of the original Enoch books survives only in Ethiopic translation is a sign of the disfavor into which this literature fell from the fourth century A.D. For its popularity in the early church, see below, Chapter 20, Lawlor 1897, and Charlesworth (ed.) 1983:8–9. The Greek text survived through the Middle Ages (Kaske 1971), and substantial portions were quoted by George Syncellus (808–870), to which Scaliger called the attention of the Renaissance. They include most of *Enoch* 6–10, the meat of the rebellion myth, which was therefore available to Milton. See Denis 1970:17–20, Black (ed.) 1970, and Charlesworth (ed.) 1983:98–103.

[5] See above, Chapter 1.3, on Huwawa. Pseudo-Philo, *Antiquitates Biblicae* 2.3, identifies the two Enochs and has him marry Seth's daughter; see Bowker 1969:301.

[6] See below, Chapters 12.6 and 17.1, on the genealogies in subsequent tradition.

these two curious bits of information may indicate that some of this remarkable body of legends had already begun to develop in the exilic years. The number 365 is too obvious a number to be entirely unrelated to Babylonian astronomical speculation, an important aspect of the Enoch literature, and Enoch's translation to the divine realms without dying points to the use of a Mesopotamian tradition like the one associated with Ziusudra-Utnapishtim-Atrahasis. Berossus, we are told, wrote that Xisouthros (Ziusudra) "disappeared . . . did not appear to them anymore . . . he was going to dwell with the Gods because of his piety." Furthermore, like the Enoch figure, he transmitted antediluvian wisdom to later generations by burying his books secretly in the foundations of Sippar-Suruppak.[7] Enoch's visionary journeys may well have been inspired by the overlapping of Israel's own prophetic traditions with such Babylonian narratives as the otherworldly expedition of Gilgamesh.[8]

The oldest texts we now have of the Enoch literature are the Aramaic fragments found in the Qumran caves, the earliest of which date from the first part of the second century B.C. But one part of this literature, the "Book of Watchers," which comprises the first 36 chapters of the Ethiopic *Book of Enoch*, clearly incorporates older material in its central part, chapters 6–16. This part, the "Visions of Enoch," contains material that goes back at least to the third century B.C.[9] and in turn takes over some of the Hebrew Book of Noah.[10] The "Book of Watchers" also alludes to another work, the "Astronomical Book of Enoch," preserved both in Qumran fragments and as chapters 72–82 of the Ethiopic *Enoch*, and this astronomical material seems to go back to Mesopotamian astron-

---

[7] Lambert and Millard 1969:136–37; Milik 1976:33. See also J. P. Lewis 1968:12–15 and now Stone (ed.) 1984:392. For buried or secret books in the Sethian Gnostic context, see below, Chapter 12.7.

[8] Grelot 1958a; Milik 1976:30–31. Greenfield 1973:xiv thinks this "a bit much," but he allows the 365 years to have a "primal mythological reference" without specifying further. Speiser 1964:43, ad loc, links Enoch and the Sumerian Enmeduranna, who instituted the solar year, a suggestion supported by Greenfield. Milik 1976:31–32 wants to extend his argument to make Gen. 6.1–4 refer to Enochic traditions or even to the *Book of Enoch* itself; Greenfield rejects this redating, as do Beckwith 1981 and Neugebauer 1981 (now in Black 1985). Note that "sons of heaven" (*Enoch* 6.2) replaces "sons of God" (Gen. 6.2), to which Hellenistic Judaism objected (Lods 1927). Barthelmus 1979:22–24 thinks Gen. 6.3 is an interpolation based on the Enoch book. The tangles of literary and oral tradition are difficult to sort out here, but my own argument follows Greenfield 1973 (against Milik 1971 and 1976) on this point.

[9] P. D. Hanson 1977:197; Stone 1978. Black 1985:13–17 gives a slightly different reconstruction.

[10] Charles (ed.) 1913: vol. 2, 14, above n. 1; Charlesworth (ed.) 1983:7.

omy.[11] The Enoch tradition, then, is archaic and often bears striking resemblance to such Babylonian traditions as the wisdom genres, frequently "letters" from antidiluvian sages to the king.[12] A schematic presentation (Figure 1) may help us grasp the complex history that seems to lie behind the Enoch material.

The parts of the Enoch material that concern us are those that convert the Genesis flood myth, by midrash or retelling, into a rebellion of angels. Unfortunately, the story is not entirely coherent, and the sections where it is presented most fully, chapters 6–11, reflect more than one stage in the growth of the tradition. The general outline is as follows. A group of angels join with their leader in a plot to violate their assigned role; they descend to the earth and have sexual intercourse with the daughters of men; as a result, the earth is corrupted and eventually cries out in its agony to heaven; God intervenes and sends down good angels, among them Michael, to put a stop to the goings-on and imprison the rebels; at the same time, God foretells the ultimate end of all this—after seventy generations in prison, the rebels will be permanently locked away in torment, while all wrong is destroyed from the earth and a new world is born in righteousness and peace. When we look at the details of this myth, we discover several inconsistencies, the most glaring of which is that the rebel leader is alternately *Šemiḥazah* (Semjaza in Ethiopic; hereafter anglicized as Semihazah) or *ʿAśaʾel* (Azazel; hereafter anglicized as Asael).[13]

1. *Semihazah: The Mixing of Angels and Women*

The earliest story seems to be the one about Semihazah, and it may go back to the Book of Noah.[14] The author first repeats the Genesis verses

[11] Milik 1976:15–22; cf. Beckwith 1981. For more discussion of the various "Books," see now Stone (ed.) 1984:395–406.

[12] On the wisdom genre, see Lambert 1960 and Stone (ed.) 1984:283–322. In Fig. 1 the distinction between A and B texts of *2 Enoch* is explained below, Chapter 12.8; see also Charlesworth (ed.) 1983:96.

[13] Nickelsburg 1977:383–86 and P. D. Hanson 1977:220 proposed different solutions: Asael's story is a secondary elaboration through interpolation or organic growth. My own solution is compatible with either; see below. For further discussion, see Collins (ed.) 1979, Dimant 1978, Barthelmus 1979, and Newsom 1980. Milik 1976 and Knibb 1978 were not available to Nickelsburg and P. D. Hanson in 1977, although both cite Milik 1971—an indication of how difficult it is even for experts to stay abreast of developments in these fields. See Stone (ed.) 1984 for an excellent review of recent scholarship.

[14] Charles 1893 (ed.) and 1913 thought that all of *Enoch* 6–11 was derived from the Noah book, since Enoch is nowhere mentioned within these chapters. But see above, n. 1.

FIGURE I. *The Enoch Tradition*

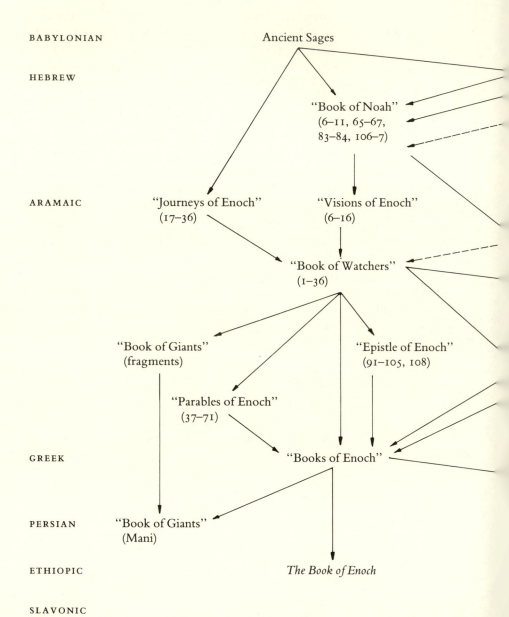

BABYLONIAN   Ancient Sages

HEBREW
                                          "Book of Noah"
                                          (6–11, 65–67,
                                          83–84, 106–7)

ARAMAIC   "Journeys of Enoch"   "Visions of Enoch"
                      (17–36)   (6–16)

                                          "Book of Watchers"
                                               (1–36)

           "Book of Giants"   "Epistle of Enoch"
             (fragments)   (91–105, 108)

                      "Parables of Enoch"
                           (37–71)

GREEK   "Books of Enoch"

PERSIAN   "Book of Giants"
              (Mani)

ETHIOPIC   *The Book of Enoch*

SLAVONIC

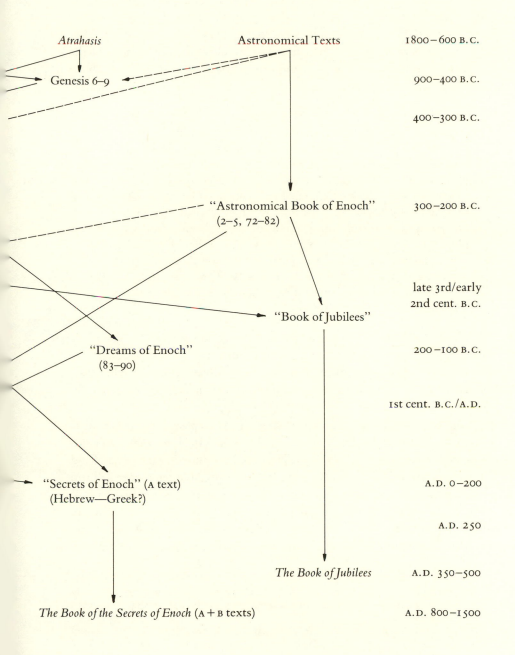

Atrahasis	Astronomical Texts	1800 – 600 B.C.
Genesis 6–9		900–400 B.C.
		400 –300 B.C.
	"Astronomical Book of Enoch" (2–5, 72–82)	300–200 B.C.
		late 3rd/early 2nd cent. B.C.
	"Book of Jubilees"	
"Dreams of Enoch" (83–90)		200 –100 B.C.
		1st cent. B.C./A.D.
"Secrets of Enoch" (A text) (Hebrew—Greek?)		A.D. 0 –200
		A.D. 250
	The Book of Jubilees	A.D. 350–500
The Book of the Secrets of Enoch (A + B texts)		A.D. 800–1500

about the sons of god and the daughters of men and then goes on to tell an elaborate myth to explain that tantalizingly brief allusion. In the process, the whole of the Genesis flood myth is reworked into a full vision of history, with the apocalyptic and eschatological perspective dominant. That is, primordial events are reinterpreted as typological anticipations of the end-time, according to the common hermeneutical principle of Jewish apocalyptic. It begins thus:

> And it came to pass, when the sons of men had increased, that in those days there were born to them fair and beautiful daughters. And the Watchers (angels), the sons of heaven, saw them and desired them. And they said to one another: "Come, let us choose for ourselves wives from the daughters of earth, and let us beget for ourselves children." And Semihazah, who was their leader, said to them: "I fear that you will not wish to do this deed, and that I alone will pay for this great sin." And they all answered him and said: "Let us all swear an oath, and bind one another with curses not to alter this plan, but to carry out this plan effectively." Then they all swore together and all bound one another with curses to it. And they were in all two hundred and they came down in the days of Jared on the summit of Mount Hermon. And they called the mountain Hermon because on it they swore and bound one another with curses.[15]

It is clear from this passage that the author has converted the Yahwist's theology of transgression into a genuine conspiracy. The Watchers are fully aware of the implications and possible consequences of what they conspire to do. The passage does not, however, make explicit what decrees their plot violates.

One key to this radical transformation of the Genesis passage is probably to be found in the term "Watcher," by which the *benē 'elōhīm* of Genesis are now designated. Two new ideas are here added to the general and ancient theme of the heavenly court. We have already seen that in Job and Zechariah one member of the court was known as a Satan and that his task was to go to and fro upon the earth as the "Eye of the King."[16] It is likely that the term "Watcher" derives in part from this security function of certain officials in the heavenly court. The Satan now has subordinates to

---

[15] *Enoch* 6.1–6, trans. Knibb 1978:67–69, supplemented by Milik's "Watchers" from the Aramaic fragment of this portion. Translations throughout are from Knibb 1978, but using Milik 1976 where possible and occasionally adapted to Isaac in Charlesworth (ed.) 1983 and now Black 1985.

[16] Above, Chapter 5. The title "the satan" is not used in the Aramaic portions of the Enoch books. See below, Chapter 9, and on *Enoch* 40.7, 54.6, see Chapters 10.3 and 12.1 and Black 1985 ad loc.

help him with the business of keeping an eye on human affairs. These Watchers appear again with a similar function in a second-century apocalypse, the Book of Daniel, in which the Watchers and the Holy Ones give the decree against Nebuchadnezzar.[17] It is clear that they function there as agents of God.[18]

The Watchers also have by now a second function, one preserved most clearly in a later elaboration of this myth in another second-century apocalypse, the *Book of Jubilees*. There is it made plain that the rebel angels had been given the task of watching over mankind, in the sense of protecting them, and their duties included instructing "the children of men to do judgment and uprightness on the earth."[19] This additional function of the Watchers provides another link with older Near Eastern traditions. Enki, for example, is the Sumerian god who instructs mankind in useful arts, a function taken over by his Babylonian equivalent, Ea (who is also the god who saves Atrahasis from the flood), and by "Oannes," the seventh antediluvian sage-king in Berossus.[20] If this benign function did originally attach to the term "Watcher," little is left of it in *Enoch*. In this version of the myth, the *benē 'elōhīm* are corrupt from the beginning of the story.

The relations so far explored between this part of the Enoch text and Genesis offer as clear a case of the link between theology and narrative as one will be likely to meet. A new story results from interpretation of the old in the light of new hermeneutic principles and of other narrative traditions. The mystery in the Genesis flood myth, namely, the apparent lack of connection between the mixing of gods with women and the subsequent flood, is now clarified through the retelling of the story as a rebellion myth. The angels conspire to sin, in conscious violation of their assigned tasks. One result is that responsibility for the catastrophe is now placed precisely where the Yahwist had deliberately *not* placed it—on the heavenly beings. The new story thus presents a radically different theology.

There is still no sign that at this stage of its development the rebellion

[17] Dan. 4.17. For the antiquity of this tradition and links with the Qumran "Prayer of Nabonidus," see Nickelsburg in Stone (ed.) 1984:34–37.

[18] Dan. 4.13–25. See below, Chapter 10.1. The word for "Watcher" is *'ir* (Aramaic plural *'irin*, Hebrew *'irim*). It is translated in Greek as *egrēgoroi*, a form based on the strong perfect of *egeirō*, *egrēgora*, to be awake, watchful. This word appears as *Grigoroi* in *2 Enoch*.

[19] *Jubilees* 4.15. See below, Chapter 9. There is probably a link with the late biblical idea, found in Dan. 10.13–21, of guardian angels for the nations (Bamberger 1952:12).

[20] Grelot 1958b:23–25, Milik 1976:29, and P. D. Hanson 1977:229 argue persuasively that this benign teaching function is older, even within the Hebrew tradition, than the destructive impact evident in *Enoch*. See below, Chapter 9.

myth shows any Greek influence. It is rather the combination of various elements already current in Hebrew, and now Aramaic, tradition. Mount Hermon, for example, is a form of the cosmic mountain familiar from the Gilgamesh epic, as well as Ugaritic and Old Testament texts,[21] and the descent of the angels at this point thus represents symbolically, an attack on the throne of the Divine King.

Nevertheless, this new narrative brings the Semitic tradition of the flood very close to Greek traditions about the giants and the Titans. Hesiod, for example, told the following story in his *Eoiae*, part of which turned up on the Berlin Papyrus from Oxyrhynchus:

> Now all the gods were divided through strife; for at that very time Zeus the thunderer was contemplating marvellous deeds, to mix up a tempest all across the boundless earth, and already he was eager to wipe out the race of articulate humans, declaring that he would destroy the lives of the demigods so that the children of gods might not mate with wretched mortals, and that they should see their fate with their own eyes; henceforth, even as before, the blessed ones would have their life and their dwelling away from men. On those who were born of immortals and mortals Zeus laid toil and sorrow upon sorrow. . . . From high trees the fair leaves fell in abundance to earth, and the fruit fell to the ground at the fierce blowing of Boreas by the will of Zeus; the deep seethed and all things trembled at his blast.[22]

Then the arrows of Zeus overcome the dread and violent (*hybristēn*) serpent. Zeus' action here is not explained, at least as the papyrus fragment stands, but it seems to be connected with the "strife" among the gods and with Zeus' desire to separate mortal and immortal again. The scholiast on *Iliad* 1.5 preserves a few lines from the *Cypria* in which Zeus decides that men should destroy each other (in the Trojan War) because of overpopulation.[23] Thus the Greek tradition clearly carried narratives about the destruction of the world by Zeus, in the one case through a tempest like the one that causes the flood, in the other case through having the heroes kill each other.

The Enoch book, probably the Book of Noah too, brought two such

[21] Judg. 3.3; Ps. 133.3 (Hermon/Zion); 1 Chron. 5.23 (Baal-Hermon). See Lipinski 1971, Clifford 1972, and P. D. Hanson 1977:199. For Gilgamesh, see above, Chapter 1 n. 53, and below, Chapter 10.1.

[22] Hesiod, *Eoiae* B3–34, in Evelyn-White (ed.) 1914:198–203. See Glasson 1961:60, Nickelsburg 1977:395, and *Enoch* 10.12 and 15.10, cited below.

[23] Evelyn-White (ed.) 1914:496. Cf. Kilmer 1972, J. Hansen in Oinas (ed.) 1978, and above, Chapter 7.

stories together, explaining the Genesis flood myth by means of the giant variant of the combat myth. The Semihazah version of the rebellion myth goes on to tell the fulfillment of the angelic conspiracy in such a way that it seems to echo this Greek tradition. Probably the Greek and the Jewish myths are variants of a common tradition represented also by the Ugaritic myth of the two huge sons of El: Dawn and Dusk.[24] Angels and women mate, and this is what follows:

> And they became pregnant by them and bare giants three thousand cubits high . . . , and they devoured the entire fruit of the labour of the sons of men and men were unable to supply them. But the giants conspired to slay men, and to devour them. And they began to sin and to do violence against all the birds and beasts of the earth, and reptiles which creep upon the earth and creatures in the waters, and in the heaven, and the fish of the sea, and to devour the flesh of one another, and they were drinking blood. Then the earth made the accusation against the lawless ones.[25]

The resurgence here of the overpopulation theme, the Babylonian cause of the flood, almost obscured in Genesis, is quite remarkable and may be due to the renewed contact with Babylonian tradition during the exile. The fantasies represented are common—devouring giants or monsters, fear of indiscriminate sexuality, the subsidiary bestiality—but their particular form here suggests a creative blend of Babylonian, Canaanite, and Genesis myths similar to the overlapping of war and flood traditions in Greece. Just as the Trojan War could substitute in Greece for the flood catastrophe, so we find that the Genesis text has been almost pushed out in the Enoch literature by the battle theme. The only reference to Noah occurs almost as an aside at 10.1–3 (an angelic warning to hide himself, for the deluge is coming cf. 10.6), and even there he is simply "the son of Lamech." That is also the only reference to the flood in the whole myth, so much has the eschatological fantasy, a revival of the mythological combat, come to dominate.

The theological shift from the Yahwist or the Priestly writer is equally remarkable. In Genesis the flood was a punishment for men's sin. Here the destruction of the world is benign, God's response to the cry of the earth. Whereas Noah was clearly distinguished from all other men by his right-

---

[24] See above, Chapter 6, and below, n. 28. Cf. Delcor 1976:24 n. 2.

[25] *Enoch* 7.2–6 in Milik 1976:151, citing his "Copy 1"; cf. Black 1985:28, 126. For the corresponding fragments from the "Book of Noah," see Barthélemy and Milik 1955, nos. 19 and 19bis. For the "lawless ones," Greek *anomoi*, cf. 2 Thess. 2.8 and below, Chapters 14.6 and 17.1, one of the ingredients of the Antichrist figure.

eousness, in *Enoch* we have heard nothing about a wicked humanity. Instead, all human suffering is attributed to the angelic revolt and the sins of their giant brood. We may detect here a cosmic projection of contemporary political events, perhaps the wars of the Diadochi, inheritors of Alexander's empire, during which Palestine changed hands at least seven times in twenty-one years (323–302),[26] but the *Enoch* author conceives of the mighty of this world in cosmic, mythological terms as principalities and powers.[27] The end will come only when Michael and his angels come down to take on the wicked spirits and deliver the earth from their influence.

If indeed the Canaanite myth of the sons of El lies behind this story, then there too an equally radical transformation has taken place. This miraculous growth myth was apparently, in its Canaanite context, a celebration of the sexual powers of El, though with a strong hint about the dangers implied by the voraciousness of his offspring.[28] In *Enoch*, however, the blending with the Babylonian flood myth and its primary cause, overpopulation, together with the theological independence of these Judaic myth-makers, has led to a new focus on the sheer wickedness of the angelic transgressors.

The earth cries out in its agony, reminding us of Gilgamesh's complaints about the depredations of Huwawa, and the high god, like Utu-Shamash, finally responds to this appeal by sending down Michael to confront Semihazah. At this point we should expect, according to our schema of the combat plot, a battle, victory, triumph, perhaps with complications. We shall see that later the battle and victory of Michael do become a part of the story.[29] But in this text God's intervention is apparently sufficient, and Michael's task is simply to announce the punishment. Indeed, God's speech to Michael foretells the rest of the story—an early instance of apocalyptic discourse in which the future becomes the tense of narrative closure. God's word itself is enough to make the events happen.

The punishment does, however, include a kind of displaced combat. Michael is to inform[30] Semihazah that he will watch his sons destroy one

[26] Nickelsburg 1977:391. More complex dating is in Barthelmus 1979:154–83.

[27] See below, Chapter 14, for these Pauline terms. See also Nickelsburg 1977:389 and Stone (ed.) 1984:92.

[28] Clifford 1972:166–68 (CTA 23). See above, Chapter 6.3.

[29] See below and Chapter 13 on Rev. 12.9. For Michael, see Collins 1975, Day 1985:141–78, and Beasley-Murray 1983.

[30] Milik 1976:175 and Black 1985:137 prefer *dēlōson* from the Gizeh papyrus, but Charles (ed.) 1893:28 n. 15 preferred Syncellus' *dēson* (bind).

another on the earth, just as in the Hesiodic variant. Indeed, this process
has already begun in the internecine strife of the giants. Michael is then to
imprison Semihazah for seventy generations until the final judgment. The
punishment episode thus extends itself backward, through the power of
prophecy, to include the battle and victory. This is a normal development
in apocalyptic contexts; the end-time came to be seen as almost entirely
combat and punishment.

This mixing of time-schemes, of prophecy with the event foretold,
tends to scramble the chronology on which conventional Proppian analysis depends. Henceforth it becomes more difficult to discern the steps of
a given narrative, and this difficulty itself becomes the occasion of further
narrative elaboration. The question of when the punishment of the adversary takes place, or the combat itself, will be variously answered in the
subsequent tradition. Even in this text Semihazah's punishment is
stretched a good deal. He first watches his offspring destroy one another,
then waits seventy generations in chains before his final and permanent
torment begins. What happened during those seventy generations? At this
point the text is silent, although the question is addressed, as we shall soon
see, in the next part of the book.

The apocalyptic context has thus changed more than the theology of
the flood myth. As soon as the command of God to his angel intervenes,
the narrative itself is disrupted. What looks at first like a speech within a
tale becomes the tale itself. The final destruction of all wrong is foretold
as well as the flowering of "the plant of righteousness" (Israel) and the
messianic kingdom that will follow the final judgment. The flood itself is
simply forgotten.

Before the prophetic discourse intervenes, however, the Semihazah
narrative seems to have had a fairly straightforward logic connecting angelic lust with the origin of evil. Intercourse ("mixing") of angel with human naturally produces offspring, those voracious giants whose strife
symbolizes the suffering of humanity at the hands of the mighty. But
when this material from the Noah tradition was incorporated into the
"Visions of Enoch," someone evidently did not understand the symbolic
connection, or else felt the need to establish a more theologically explicit
link between primordial giant brood and present evil. So in a confused
way the Lord explains to Enoch during one of his visions that the giants
will be called "demons" or "evil spirits" (*pneumata ponēra*) on the earth
and that on the earth shall be their dwelling. Apparently they are to be
spirits because "from the holy watchers is their beginning and primal or-

igin," but to make sure of the connection the author also says that the spirits come from the bodies of the giants, perhaps when they die. These spirits continue to "oppress, destroy, attack, do battle, and work destruction on the earth, and cause trouble; they eat no food and do not thirst, and are not observed. . . . And these spirits shall rise up against the children of men and against the women, from whom they came forth."[31] In this way the persistence of evil after the imprisonment of the rebel angels is explained as the constant work of invisible evil spirits, condemned to live on the earth because that is where they were born: "The dwelling of the spirits of heaven is in heaven, but the dwelling of the spirits of earth . . . is on earth."[32] This expansion of the Yahwist's theology again comes oddly close to the Hesiodic variant cited above.[33]

2. Asael and Forbidden Knowledge

Meditation on the origin of evil seems to have produced another complication within the Semihazah narrative, and again the impulse for this further layer of meaning seems to have been the effort to interpret the text of Genesis in the light of the fresh contact with Babylonian tradition. Here the origin of evil is connected with human access to forbidden knowledge. Immediately after the angelic conspiracy is conceived, the narrative lists the names of the twenty leaders, beginning with Semihazah the chief, and including Asael as the tenth. It then proceeds thus, as preserved in two almost identical copies from Qumran:

> Those two hundred and their leaders all took for themselves wives from all
> that they chose; and they began to go in to them, and to defile themselves

---

[31] *Enoch* 15.9–12, trans. Black 1985:34, 152–53. Cf. Charles 1893:36, esp. his interpretation of *sōmatos*. See below, Chapters 9 and 20, and cf. Lods 1927:146–47. For an indication of the theological problems, see, e.g., the insistence of Knibb 1978:101 that "the clause [15.9] explains why *spirits* came out of the flesh of the giants, not why *evil* spirits came out." In the Hesiodic variant (above, n. 22) the soul (*psyche*) of the snake survives.

[32] *Enoch* 15.10—the beginnings of the idea, developed by Philo and Origen in the Platonic tradition, of a descent of spiritual into corporeal forms. See below, Chapters 18 and 21.

[33] On "mixing," see above, Chapter 7, and below, Chapter 22.2. This section of the "Book of Watchers" (*Enoch* 12–16) was already present in the "Visions of Enoch" but apparently not in the "Book of Noah." It contains an elaborate sequence in which Enoch himself becomes prominent. He substitutes for Michael and is instructed, like Ezekiel, to announce the punishment of the rebels, who here become like disobedient priests from the heavenly temple. We may discern here an early form of the tradition, discussed below (Chapter 10.3), associated with Melchizedek. The result of this extended revenge fantasy is to make the wicked angels tremble at their fate, another form of the substitution of prophecy for event; cf. Suter 1979 and Stone (ed.) 1984:93.

with them, and they began to teach them sorcery and spellbinding and the cutting of roots; and to show them plants. And they became pregnant by them and bore giants.[34]

Thereafter the theme of secret teachings (introduced here) continues in parallel with the giant plot. The earth complains and accuses the rebels of their teaching; men perish and cry out to heaven (7.6–8.4). The angels intercede and complain to God, both about lawlessness and the teachings for which Asael and Semihazah are responsible (9). Then God responds with an indictment both of the giants and of the teachings and plans the punishment of the angels. At times, as in the above quotation (7.1–2), the two themes are so entangled that they appear to explain each other. Similarly, at 9.6–9 of the Ethiopic version (part of which is also preserved at Qumran)[35] we read:

> See then what Azazel has done, how he has taught all iniquity on the earth and revealed the eternal secrets [Qumran: which were kept in heaven, so that the experts among the sons of men should practice them.] And Semjaza has made known spells, he to whom you gave authority to rule over his companions. And they have gone to the daughters of men of the earth, and slept with them, having defiled themselves by females, and revealed to them these sins. And the women bore giants, and thereby the whole earth has been filled with blood and iniquity.

Thus the text as we have it ascribes the teaching to both Asael and Semihazah.[36]

In this form the myth is an instance of a widespread mythological theme, the beginnings of human culture in the instructions of divine beings, which was current among Jews at least in the moralized form of

---

[34] *Enoch* 7.1–2 in Milik 1976:167, copy 2; cf. 151 for copy 1, where "herbs" replaces "plants." Knibb 1978:77 has "trees," and the Gizeh Greek has *botanas*. Nickelsburg 1977 and P. D. Hanson 1977 both argue that the teaching motif, here mentioned for the first time, is part of the later Asael elaboration. Thus 7.1, from "they began to teach," would be added to the original text. True, the Greek text of Syncellus also omits these words, but it includes the first part (sorcery and spells) at the end of the next verse. In any case, Syncellus does not represent an independent tradition, though he occasionally agrees with the Qumran fragments against the other Greek and Ethiopic readings.

[35] Milik 1976:158; cf. Knibb 1978:81.

[36] Because they think that *all* the Asael and teaching references are part of a later elaboration of the original Semihazah narrative, Nickelsburg 1977 and P. D. Hanson 1977 are forced to argue that the associations of Semihazah with "spells" and teaching are *tertiary* elaboration, *after* the addition of the Asael material; see the critique of Collins 1978 and Dimant 1978.

"instructing unto righteousness."[37] But the results of that teaching are now wholly destructive, a transformation whose historical origins are obscure but which obviously owes something to Yahwistic and Priestly theology. In particular, the phrase "showed them plants" ("trees" in the Ethiopic version) may show the influence of the Genesis story about the tree of prohibition, with "sorcery" as the linking idea. Thus the myth links the origin of culture and the origins of evil in the world. The plot logic works as follows. Lust causes the transgression of the boundary between divine and human;[38] this results in humans learning forbidden mysteries, and this in turn leads to the corruption of the earth.

Those teachings associated with Semihazah have to do with "plants," the cutting of roots, and magic generally.[39] But the teachings associated with Asael are more elaborate, and this may have led to his elevation to chief of the rebels to replace Semihazah. Indeed, the elaboration of the forbidden knowledge theme in the original Semihazah narrative may perhaps be traced to a desire to specify more exactly both what the teachings were and how they could be so damaging. The first stage of this elaboration is probably to be found in the list of the teachings at 8.1–3. The list of angels here differs considerably from the earlier list, and further changes took place in the process of translation into Greek and Ethiopic.[40] Though the list begins with Asael this time, Semihazah and others are also mentioned.[41] Each of the angels apparently has a special skill. Semihazah, for example, taught "spell-binding and cutting of roots"; Hermoni, named after the mountain on which they descended, taught "the loosing of spells, magic and sorcery," Baraqel "the signs of thunders," Kokabel "the signs of the stars," and so forth. Asael, however, begins the list, and the special knowledge he imparted was

> to make swords of iron and breastplates of bronze, and he showed them
> metals which were dug out, and how they should work gold to fashion
> [adornments], and concerning silver, to fashion it for bracelets, and for

---

[37] See *Jubilees* 4.15 and S. Thompson 1955–58, Motif A541: "Culture Hero Teaches Arts and Crafts."

[38] Elaborated in *Enoch* 15.4–10.

[39] *Enoch* 7.1, 8.3, 9.8, where only Syncellus adds to the generic "sins" the words "and they taught them to make hate-producing charms" (Charles [ed.] 1893:21 and Nickelsburg 1977:397 n. 63).

[40] Milik 1976:152–59; Knibb 1978:79–84; Black 1985:120–24.

[41] Syncellus, apparently aware of the problem this caused, adds after Asael's name that he was the "tenth of the leaders" (Black [ed.] 1970:22).

other adornments of women. And he showed women about antimony, and eyeshadow, and all precious stones, and dye-stuffs.[42]

What has caused the teachings associated with Asael to be presented so fully, and to be elevated to the head of the list?

First of all, we should notice that Asael's special skill, the working of metals, allows the author to introduce a further midrash of a passage in Genesis, this time the brief reference to Tubal-cain as the "forger of all instruments of bronze and iron."[43] Tubal-cain, one of the patriarchs, appears in Genesis as part of the progressive degeneration of the human race from the beginning until the flood, so the negative connotations of his teaching are suitably transferred in the *Book of Enoch* to the rebel angels. Once again this new theology substitutes angelic for human responsibility.

In this new context, Asael's skill with metallurgy could now provide a more coherent connection between the two results of the angels' lust— forbidden knowledge and giant progeny. It is here, I think, that we discover a narrative explanation for the further emphasis on the Asael story, and the resulting contradiction whereby Semihazah survives as leader in some parts, while Asael replaces him in others.[44] The clue to this Asael development is contained in the two metallurgical or minerological skills that he has to teach. One is the making of implements of warfare, which accounts for the terrible destruction wrought by the giants when they turn on each other and so become symbols of all human strife. The other is the secret knowledge he gives to women about how to lure men, such things as gold and silver ornaments, precious stones, dyes, and especially eyeshadow. On the one hand, Asael's gifts lead to war; on the other, the secrets of feminine adornment link the initial lust with the resulting knowledge. And both, in the view of these Judean authors, are the causes of human misery.

Once the forbidden-knowledge theme has been elaborated and so linked to the strife of the giants in this coherent way, Asael would tend to

---

[42] *Enoch* 8.1–3; Syncellus here seems to have rendered the text more accurately than the other Greek or Ethiopic translators. See Milik 1976:167–68, Knibb 1978:80, and Nickelsburg 1977:397 n. 64.

[43] Gen. 4.22, a very ancient passage; see Speiser 1964:37.

[44] Semihazah at 10.11 and 14, e.g., Asael at 9.6, 10.4–10. See below, Chapter 10.1; cf. Milik 1976:314 on the "Book of Giants," and pp. 248–52 on an early Hebrew work, perhaps fourth century, in which, Milik thinks, Asael is also the chief angel and the main cause of mischief.

replace Semihazah as the focus of the rebellion story. God therefore announces that "the whole earth has been ruined by the teaching of the works of Asael and on him [*ep' autōi*] write down (to him ascribe) all sins."[45] He also receives a separate punishment from Semihazah and the other angels. Whereas they are to witness the destruction of their sons and then to be "bound in the valleys of the earth" until the end of time, God tells Raphael to

> Bind Asael hand and foot, and cast him into the darkness; and make an opening in the wilderness that is Doudael; and cast him there. And lay jagged and sharp rocks beneath him; and cover him with darkness, and let him dwell there forever; and cover over his face, and do not let him see the light. And on the day of the great judgment, he will be led away to the conflagration.[46]

The combination of motifs now associated with Asael begins to make him sound very like Prometheus. In Aeschylus' version, at least, he too is chained hand and foot to a cliff, and then, according to Hermes' prophecy, Zeus will open the rock and imprison him within it.[47] Prometheus too was a culture hero who taught mankind useful arts, including, again in Aeschylus, metallurgy. Through the seductive Pandora, in Hesiod's version, Prometheus' gift of fire is ultimately responsible also for all human evils, and in both contexts the teaching is certainly a rebellion against Zeus. It is possible, then, that the Greek Prometheus story, perhaps through some handbook version combining Hesiod and Aeschylus, influenced the Judean (or possibly Samaritan) author of the Asael material.[48] Against this, however, are the possible early date of the development and links with Babylonian material.[49] The motif of punishment on the rocks of a mountain is common also to Canaanite and Hurrian-Hittite tradition.[50] Probably it is better to posit, as in the case of the flood-giant elaboration, the parallel development of Near Eastern tradition in Greece and in the Jewish world.[51] In both contexts, we should add, the rebellious ad-

[45] *Enoch* 10.8, in the Greek of both Syncellus and the Gizeh mss. See Black (ed.) 1970:25.

[46] *Enoch* 10.4–6. The Greek text has "*hypothes autōi.*" See Black (ed.) 1970:25. Knibb 1978 renders the Ethiopic as "throw on him jagged rocks." Cf. Black 1985:134 and below, n. 66.

[47] Aeschylus, *Prometheus Vinctus* 1016.

[48] Nickelsburg 1977:399–404 argues strongly for the impact of the Prometheus myth here; cf. Barthelmus 1979.

[49] Milik 1976:248–52; see above, n. 44.

[50] Güterbock 1948:124; P. D. Hanson 1977:204.

[51] West 1966:314–15 argues for the origin of the bound giant/Titan motif in the Caucasus, following Axel Olrik's *Ragnarök.*

versary of the god becomes an ambivalent figure once he is associated with the culture-hero tradition and so with the special knowledge that distinguishes mankind. Prometheus gets a very different press in Hesiod and Aeschylus—for one the hero is Zeus, for the other it is Prometheus—and the same is true of Asael in the later Jewish tradition.[52] By then, Prometheus had become associated with the Judeo-Christian rebel, and once that happened the ambivalence of the adversary would be as much an aspect of Satan as of Huwawa.

In the Enoch material, however, scarcely a trace of the benign teaching function remains. Indeed, in a passage from the accompanying "Visions" section, even the secrets themselves turn out to be worthless. Enoch is sent explicitly to Asael (Semihazah is never mentioned here) to announce the punishment of the fallen Watchers, and he gloats thus over their plight: "You were in heaven, but its secrets had not yet been revealed to you and a worthless mystery you knew. This you made known to the women in the hardness of your hearts, and through this mystery the women and the men cause evil to increase on the earth."[53] Clearly this refers to the specifically feminine secret (and alludes at the same time to the rebel of Ezek. 28), but the general suggestion here that the mystery was a worthless one, showing only the ignorance of the Watchers and Asael in particular, was destined to take on much more elaborate detail in the Gnostic movement.[54]

The details of the Asael development can be explained in the same way we accounted for the other developments of the rebellion myth, as internal elaboration of elements already carried by the Hebrew tradition. Asael's name, for example, means "God has made,"[55] and thus embodies his manufacturing skills, just as the names of other angels refer to astronomical or meteorological functions. It may have a Phoenician origin,[56] or even go back to a Canaanite source as the name of one of his brother Watchers, Daniel, certainly did.[57] But Asael's elevation to leadership of the Watchers was surely encouraged by another similar name, and one that made possible a further development of his story, again as a midrash of a biblical passage. Asael is very like Azazel, which is the name of the

---

[52] Milik 1976:131 cites *Sybilline Oracles* 2.215 and the *Testament of Solomon* 7.7; see Charlesworth (ed.) 1983:350, 969.

[53] *Enoch* 16.3 in Knibb 1978:102–3. Black 1985 renders "unspeakable."

[54] Below, Chapters 12.7 and 18. For Ezekiel; see above, Chapter 6.6.

[55] Milik 1976:153 and Knibb 1978:73, *contra* Klüger 1967:41–50.

[56] Milik 1976:156.

[57] Ibid., p. 29; cf. Ezek. 28.3, 14.14–20: "Noah, Daniel, Job."

desert place to which the scapegoat of the Yom Kippur ritual was banished.[58] Indeed, it has often been suggested that this Azazel was once the name of a desert demon to whom a goat was sacrificed, just as another goat is dedicated to Yahweh in the ritual. In any case, this overlapping could now provide a natural conclusion to the rebel angel story. The scapegoat of the ritual had all sins ascribed to him (literally, "written on him"), and he was then cast out into the desert. This idea was now taken up into the myth: God announces that the ruin of the earth is all the fault of Asael. "On him write down all sins." Such words could apply logically only to the leader of the revolt, not just to the tenth in a list of angels. Apocalyptic eschatology thus transforms the powerful and ritually sacred words of Leviticus: "For on this day shall atonement be made for you, to cleanse you: from all your sins you shall be made clean before the Lord."[59] In the *Book of Enoch* this is no longer an annual ritual but the final act of a cosmic drama. The Day of Atonement has become the Day of Yahweh.

The merging with the Leviticus ritual also adds a detail to the angel's punishment. Like the rebels of earlier traditions, Asael is to be bound "hand and foot" by Raphael.[60] We recall that Anat "fixed the dragon on high. She bound him to the heights of Lebanon."[61] Thus Raphael, whose name means "God is a healer," but which here includes a pun on *rapha*, to tie, is to bind Asael and place under him "sharp and jagged rock."[62] Ninurta, we recall, heaped up stones against the defeated Azag demon.[63] In *Enoch*, this detail suggests a playful etymology of Asael's name; *'aza'zel* is translated in the Targum as "rugged and severe," while the wilderness is called "rocky." This folk etymology has been taken over into the punishment episode.[64]

The full punishment of the rebel angel, in both Semihazah and Asael layers, alludes to the passage about the pharaoh's ignominious end in Ezekiel and to the downfall of the astral rebel in Isaiah 14. Ezekiel 32,

---

[58] Lev. 16. See P. D. Hanson 1977:221–23 and Delcor 1976:35–37. At *Enoch* 69.2 the form in all texts is Azazel.

[59] Lev. 16.21; cf. Ricoeur 1967:50–99.

[60] *Enoch* 10.4 in Milik 1976:162. See above on the "binding" of Semihazah.

[61] Above, Chapter 2.8 n. 56; Cross 1973:119; Day 1985:14. Cf. Job 41.1 and Delcor 1976:27. The link with Ps. 69.23, proposed by P. D. Hanson 1977:224, is rejected by Day 1985:113–19.

[62] Milik 1976:316, and see above, n. 46.

[63] Above, Chapter 2.5. Teyssèdre 1985b:133, proposes Azag for the etymology of Azazel, which is as unlikely as he implies ("aucune garantie de sérieux").

[64] P. D. Hanson 1977:220–24, citing Pseudo-Jonathan on Lev. 16. See Nickelsburg 1977:401–2; his objection has no force.

which combines dragon and rebel adversaries and echoes the fate of Tiamat and Mot, is especially close to the *Enoch* text: "I will throw my net
over you. . . . And I will strew your flesh upon the mountains and fill the
valleys with your carcass. . . . All the bright stars of heaven I will make
dark over you, and I will put darkness upon the earth."[65] Similarly, Asael
is to be covered with darkness, "that his face may not see the light," while
the Lord tells Michael to "bind" Semihazah and his cronies "for seventy
generations in the valleys of the earth until the day of their judgment."[66]
On the great Day of Judgment, they are to be thrown into the fire. Semihazah especially is for it; he is to be thrown into "the abyss of fire and
torture and perpetual imprisonment."

There are other echoes of these astral rebels in *Enoch*. In one of the visions worked into the text of the "Book of Watchers," Enoch travels
around in cosmic realms seeing all the workings of the universe, the store-
houses of the winds, great rivers flowing from their sources, the abyss itself—all expressions that seem to derive from the apocalyptic revival of
Canaanite and Babylonian mythological imagery. In one terrifying place
beyond the abyss, beyond heaven and earth, a desert with no water or
birds in it, he sees

> seven stars of heaven bound and cast together in it, like great mountains and
> burning with fire. Then I said, "For what sin have they been bound, and
> why have they been thrown here?" Then spoke Uriel, one of the holy an-
> gels who was with me—and was chief over them—and he said to me, "En-
> och, . . . these are some of the stars which transgressed the command of the
> lord, and they have been bound here till ten thousand years have been com-
> pleted, the period for their sins."[67]

In this elaboration of the punishment episode in the rebel myth, the astral
aspects of the rebel we noted in Isaiah and Ezekiel (the "stones of fire")
have reasserted themselves in quite explicit form. Once again, Babylonian
conceptions may be detected here, perhaps also in the Ezekiel and Isaiah
variants, for in the cuneiform writing system the sign for "god," *ilu*, may
also be read as "star," *kakkabu*.[68] But the principal concern of the author

[65] Ezek. 32.2–8. See above, Chapter 6.6 n. 72.

[66] *Enoch* 10.12 in Black (ed.) 1970:25. The Ethiopic has "under the hills," showing the influence of the Titan myth and the fates of Atlas and Typhoeus.

[67] *Enoch* 21.3–6; cf. 18.12–19.2. Black 1985:15–16 has a good discussion of the journey sequence here. Reflecting the Isaiah and Ezekiel texts, the passage immediately goes on to describe Hades; see Charles (ed.) 1893:46.

[68] Cf. Kokabel, the name of an angel in *Enoch* 8.2, above, n. 42; at Job 38.7, *kōkebe bōqer*,

here was probably to bring within the same narrative reinterpretation of
Genesis the "stars of God" and "stones of fire" allusions in the texts of
Isaiah and Ezekiel.

In another of the Enoch books, also represented by Qumran fragments,
we find a further elaboration of this identification between rebel angels
and stars. This work, the "Dreams of Enoch," may be dated fairly closely
by historical reference within it to 164 B.C., during the Maccabean revolt,
which thus makes it contemporary with the only canonized Jewish apocalypse, the Book of Daniel. As we should expect, the book is a series of
symbolic and eschatological visions, during which the author recapitu-
lates the rebellion story from the "Book of Watchers." Asael is pictured
as the first star to fall from heaven. Now we may also see, surely, the impact of Greek myths about the sexual escapades of Zeus in various animal
forms:

> Behold, a star fell from heaven, and it arose and ate and pastured among
> these bulls. And after this I saw the large and black bulls, and behold, all of
> them changed their stalls and their pastures and their heifers, and began to
> moan one after another. And again I saw in the vision and looked at heaven,
> and behold, I saw many stars, how they came down and were thrown down
> from heaven to that first star, and amongst those heifers and bulls; they
> were with them, pasturing amongst them. And I looked at them and saw,
> and behold, all of them let out their private parts like horses and began to
> mount the cows of the bulls, and they all became pregnant and bore ele-
> phants and camels and asses. And all the bulls were afraid of them and were
> terrified before them, and they began to bite with their teeth, and to devour,
> and to gore with their horns. And so they began to devour those bulls, and
> behold, all the sons of the earth began to tremble and shake before them,
> and to flee.[69]

Properly terrified by this remarkable barnyard orgy, the sons of the earth
flee until angel-like beings in white, corresponding to the archangels of
the "Book of Watchers," come down and bind the miscreants and throw
them into "a chasm of the earth."[70] This Animal Apocalypse may also allude more generally to the animal form in which Egyptians and Canaan-

---

"the morning stars," are in parallel with bene 'elōhīm, "the sons of God." See Clifford
1972:161.

[69] Enoch 86 in Knibb 1978:196–97 and Black 1985:301. Isaac in Charlesworth (ed.) 1983:63
translates "cows" instead of "bulls," which makes the allegory closer but probably sorts out
the sexes too clearly. For the links with Dan. 10–12, see Nickelsburg in Stone (ed.) 1984:103.

[70] Enoch 88.1–3 picks up several passages from the earlier text, e.g., 10.4, 8.1, and 7.5: "So
they began to sin against birds, wild beasts, reptiles, and fish."

ites, for example, pictured their gods. El the Bull was a common designation of the chief Canaanite god, and the bull figure in Solomon's
temple, constructed by Phoenician craftsmen, represented the same idea.
The contemporary Book of Daniel also pictures the enemies of Israel in
animal form, just as the "Dreams of Enoch" goes on to review the history
of Israel in the guise of sheep and wolves, lions and tigers.

In the apocalyptic Enoch literature, the Near Eastern rebellion myth
thus became an integral part of the Judaic tradition. The punishment episode adapts the Canaanite tradition of the dragon's imprisonment on the
mountain. The angels themselves, beings of heavenly origin, do not yet
have any characteristics of monsters, even if their offspring commit the
typical depredations of the Huwawa figure, but the Animal Apocalypse
suggests that what was intended as allegory might easily become identification.

In a passage parallel to the one that identifies rebel angels and stars, we
find a curious shift in the implications of the lust theme. Unfortunately,
we have no Qumran fragment that preserves this verse, and the Greek
text differs in a slight but significant way from the Ethiopic here. Only the
Ethiopic translation has this curious feature, so we cannot know how old
it is, but it forms part of the "Visions of Enoch" section we have seen to
be early. Uriel explains to Enoch the sins of the angels who were promis-
cuous with women and adds, "And their wives, having led astray the angels of heaven, will become Sirens."[71] Clearly the story has overlapped
with Greek mythology, but the curious thing about the passage is that the
women have now become responsible for the sin—they "led astray the
angels of heaven." We have already seen the Yahwist make a similar shift,
though with a clear theological intention, but here the verse seems to be
merely a gratuitous piece of antifeminism. Elsewhere in the Enoch literature, the rebel angels have so far been the ones whose lust led humans
astray, but now the women become equally responsible. It is possible that
a theological point similar to the Yahwist's is concealed here but, as the
tradition develops, antifeminism of this kind will continue to surface as
long as the lust of angels and women is the story that explains the origin
of evil. And this antifeminism will often seem to support the theology.
Wherever we find a writer troubled by the theological implication of the
rebel story and so trying to shift the blame back to man, where the Yahwist had put it, "man" is often in fact woman.

[71] *Enoch* 19.2; Charles (ed.) 1893:51 n. 49 made the brilliant and plausible "Sirens" emendation, but see now Black 1985:36, 161.

NINE

THE CONVERGENCE OF
SATAN AND THE WATCHER ANGELS:
The Book of Jubilees

THE QUMRAN discoveries have yielded other texts that help us trace the development of the rebellion myth, among them fragments of the original Hebrew of the influential *Book of Jubilees*. An important source for the study of heterodox Judaism, this work tells its own version of the rebellion, in some ways more logically than the Enoch material, which the author of *Jubilees* used. Although it may have been initially composed at some point during the third century, *Jubilees* was edited and thoroughly revised before the extant version—which survives complete, like the *Book of Enoch*, only in Ethiopic translation—was set down in the last quarter of the second century, sometime before 104 B.C.[1] Like the canonical Book of Chronicles, the apocryphal *Book of Jubilees* rewrites history to conform to the new and strict understanding of the Law characteristic of postexilic Judaism. What Chronicles did for Samuel and Kings, *Jubilees* does for Genesis and Exodus.

Chronicles, we have seen, protects God by attributing to Satan what God did in Samuel. In the same way, we learn from *Jubilees* that the less savory acts attributed to Yahweh in the Torah—for example, the demand for the sacrifice of Isaac and the attempt to kill Moses[2]—were in fact prompted by the prince of the hostile angels, whose name in *Jubilees* is usually "Mastema." This term means "enmity" and is an abstract nominal form of the verb root *śṭm*, hate. This verb in turn is cognate with *śṭn*, and so Mastema and Satan are related names.[3] Indeed, *Jubilees'* version of the sacrifice of Isaac opens with a confrontation between Mastema and the angel of the presence, clearly modeled on Job 1–2 and Zechariah 3.

[1] Milik 1976:58 dates the whole to 125 B.C. and Charles (ed.) 1913: vol. 2, 6, to 109–105 B.C. Davenport 1971:13–14, 16–17, dates the final redaction to 140–104 B.C. and suggests that it may have been composed at Qumran. Cf. Van der Kam 1978 and Stone (ed.) 1984:101–3.

[2] Gen. 22 (cf. *Jubilees* 17.15–18.12); Exod. 4.24 (cf. *Jubilees* 48.1–3).

[3] Above, Chapter 5. See Gordis 1965:216–17 and 1978:14.

The composer of *Jubilees* tells us explicitly that he used the Enoch books and the "Book of Noah": "for thus I have found it written in the book of my ancestors, likewise in the Words of Enoch and in the Words of Noah."[4] It appears from the material worked into the *Jubilees* text that its author(s) knew the "Book of Watchers" (*Enoch* 1–36), the "Astronomical Book" (*Enoch* 72–82), and the "Dreams of Enoch" (*Enoch* 83–90).[5] But the author's theology, though definitely apocalyptic, is dominated by the supremacy of the Law, and this leads him to adapt the rebellion myth in certain crucial respects. Furthermore, his rigorous chronological scheme, dividing all history until the giving of the Law on Sinai into periods of forty-nine years each (seven times seven), makes for what is in some ways a more coherent narrative. *Jubilees* preserves, for example, a more archaic variant of the rebel myth, in which the angels descend first to "instruct the children of men, that they should do judgment and uprightness on the earth," whence they may derive their name, the "Watchers."[6] This original descent is synchronized with the days of Jared, the father of Enoch (i.e., the year 461), but the corruption of these angels through lust is dated to the twenty-fifth jubilee, that is, shortly after the year 1200.

One of the chief causes of confusion in the Enoch books was the overlapping of Urzeit and Endzeit in apocalyptic typology. Indeed, in the "Book of Watchers" this apocalyptic perspective has gone so far as actually to contradict the Genesis text. In the Genesis flood story, God promises never again to destroy his creation; the sign of this convenant is the rainbow. But in *Enoch* the expansion of the flood myth into an angelic rebellion intended to account for the corruption of the whole earth in all time leads to the announcement of an impending destruction in the end-time.[7] A further result of this temporal confusion in *Enoch* is a kind of double punishment of the rebels. On the one hand, it is synchronized with the flood, from which only the son of Lamech escapes; on the other hand, it is to happen at the final destruction of the world. In the first case, the rebels are bound and thrown into prison; in the second case, they are consigned to the fire and burned up. Yet the imprisonment of the rebels does not seem to inhibit their ability to do harm to mankind, an oddity that is explained in one passage of the "Visions" section by the idea that "de-

---

[4] *Jubilees* 21.10 in Milik 1976:56. See above, Chapter 8.1.

[5] Charles (ed.) 1913: vol. 2, 18, on *Jubilees* 4.17–23, which is cited from this version unless otherwise stated.

[6] *Jubilees* 4.15. See above, Chapter 8 nn. 16-18.

[7] P. D. Hanson 1977:195.

mons" issued from the bodies of the slain giants and continued the work of corruption between the initial rebellion and the final judgment.[8]

The *Book of Jubilees* clarifies this confused picture by its more systematic, less symbolically allusive scheme of world history. For example, Noah's importance is restored, and the anticipations of the end-time become simply warnings to follow the Law in the new world that follows the flood. The purpose of the narrative is to turn its readers back to the Torah. The new version of the myth is as follows.

After the Watchers have begun their corruption, and lawlessness increases on the earth, the Lord decides to destroy all men except Noah. God is also wroth with the angels and determines to root them out of creation. He has their sons destroy each other with the sword while the fathers watch, and then he binds the angels in the depths of the earth until the last judgment (*Jub.* 5.1–10). So far the story is similar to the Enoch versions. But God's decision is now elaborated in order to dwell on the consequences of not abiding by the Law in the new creation after the flood, a moralizing episode rather than a conflation of Urzeit and Endzeit. The narrative reinforces the point by switching back to the judgment on all the men who were found unfaithful before the flood, that is, all except Noah, whom God saved as he will save all who follow the Law. The story of the ark's construction, the ensuing flood, and the new creation is now told. A considerable portion of the narrative is devoted to various festivals instituted at that time, all to be kept with legalistic and calendrical strictness (5.19–7.39). But the angels are clearly punished at the same time as the men—the angels by watching their children slay each other, the men themselves by the flood—and the two episodes are viewed as cosmic and earthly parallels. *Jubilees* thus restores the flood to its rightful place and at the same time confirms our hypothesis that flood and war are traditional alternatives for world destruction, obscurely fused in *Enoch.*[9]

Up to this point in the narrative, however, the rebellion myth in *Jubilees* does not do what it was designed to do in *Enoch*, namely, explain the origin of evil and its continuation until the end-time. The flood intervenes and cleanses the world. So the author now duplicates the story of the Watchers, but in a different form and synchronized with his historical time chart. Following the restoration of the world, Noah and his sons and

[8] *Enoch* 15.8–9, 16.1. This passage, separated from the "Book of Noah" version of the rebellion myth (6–11), is a retelling of the story with Enoch himself in the role of god's messenger to the angels. See Charles (ed.) 1893:36n, 1913: vol. 2, 27n, and below, n. 14.

[9] See above Chapters 7 and 8, and Van der Kam 1978.

grandsons divide up the earth among them all (year 1569). But once again things go wrong. The sons of Noah complain to their father that "unclean demons" are leading the family astray and "blinding and slaying his sons' sons" (10.1–2). The wars of the angels' giant brood are thus transferred to the human descendants of Noah, and henceforth war and bloodshed, along with the eating of blood (forbidden by God in the covenant with Noah)[10] and idolatry, are to be the chief signs of human depravity (11.2–7). Noah now prays to God that the demons be imprisoned, reminding God of what the Watchers were like and that these demons (spirits) are their descendants.

> Thou knowest how Thy Watchers, the fathers of these spirits, acted in my day; and as for these spirits which are living, imprison them and hold them fast in the place of condemnation, and let them not bring destruction on the sons of thy servant, my God; for these are malignant, and created in order to destroy. (10.5)

God hears these prayers and instructs his angels to carry out the imprisonment order.

It is possible that *Jubilees* may here be preserving an earlier version of the story than the Enoch books, perhaps deriving directly from the old "Book of Noah." If so, then the Enoch books transformed this eminently human episode into the vague but poetically effective story of the "earth" crying out against the depredations of the giants and the evil teachings of the Watchers. In *Enoch*, the cry prompts God to send down Michael and the other archangels and so anticipates the eschatological battle and punishment. *Jubilees* restores some measure of narrative logic to the episode by locating it after the flood as a problem that is separate though similar to the one faced by Noah "in his day," and by the idea that the demons are descendants of the Watchers. Yet if the imprisonment order were actually to be carried out as planned, we would still have no reason for the continuation of the earth's corruption beyond the time of Noah's appeal.

Jubilees solves that problem with the insertion of the following crucial episode, made necessary by the abandoning of the Urzeit-Endzeit typology. We are now still in the Urzeit, and so some way must be found to explain the connection between beginning time and the present. Therefore, just as the imprisonment order is about to be carried out, the chief of the evil spirits, Mastema, makes a final, desperate plea:

---

[10] *Jubilees* 6.4–10; see Gen. 9.1–17. On this theme, see Teyssèdre 1985b:123–30.

Lord, Creator, let some of them remain before me, and let them hearken to
my voice and to all that I say unto them; for if some of them are not left to
me, I shall not be able to execute the power of my will on the sons of men;
for these are for corruption and leading astray before my judgment, for
great is the wickedness of the sons of men. (10.8)

God apparently approves of the privileges Mastema claims here, for he instantly agrees to the proposal: "Let the tenth part of them remain before
him, and let nine parts descend into the place of condemnation" (10.9).
The response represents an interesting narrative compromise with the
Enoch versions. There the "spirits" that issue from the bodies of the dead
giants are introduced almost as an afterthought, a confused means of solv-
ing the problem of continuing corruption. Here in *Jubilees*, not only do
these "demons" warrant a whole new episode, a doublet of the earlier
punishment, but the author has devised a means of having it both ways.
Nine-tenths of the fallen angels are punished, so completing the rebellion-
punishment theme, but a tenth part remain unpunished until the end-
time, so explaining the continued decline of Israel.[11] To compensate, God
charges his angels to show Noah the secrets of medicinal herbs, so reviv-
ing the benign aspect of secret and angelic teaching obscured in *Enoch*.
Noah dies content. The episode reminds us that the Sumerian and Babylonian flood heroes, Ziusudra and Utnapishtim, were also purveyors of
secret wisdom, even a plant of youth. It surely suggests the borrowing in
this part of *Jubilees* from the "Book of Noah."

The function of Mastema's spirits, despite God's ready compliance
with his request, is not clear. From the last clause of Mastema's speech, it
would appear that they are merely to search out and expose human sin,
"for great is the wickedness of the sons of men" (10.8). Yet the previous
clause has said that their purpose is actually "corruption and leading
astray," which sounds much more like what their forebears, the Watcher
angels, had done—actually to initiate evil. Nor is the difficulty cleared up
in the rest of *Jubilees*. The next chapter, for example, begins with a section
on the sins of Noah's descendants, dwelling particularly on the wars they

[11] In the Christian tradition that stems from the Watcher story, angels and demons are not
always separated in this way. The idea here is that the angels produce the giants, who then
produce the demons (spirits) from their dead bodies. Justin ignores the giants but distinguishes angels and spirits, as do Athenagoras and Tertullian (below, Chapter 20). On the
other hand, Lactantius, *Divinae Institutiones* 2.15, regarded the demons simply as wicked angels (Charles [ed.] 1893:21, 36n, and below, Chapter 22 n. 6). See also Chapter 15, and for
the *Book of Enoch*, above, n. 8.

fight with each other. Once again the author is adapting the Enoch story of the giants' battles to this postdiluvian world. The spirits under Mastema all take part in these sins, but the language leaves it unclear whether they can initiate them or not:

> [men] began to make graven images and unclean simulacra, and malignant spirits assisted and seduced [them] into committing transgression and uncleanness. And the prince Mastema exerted himself to do all this, and he sent forth other spirits, those which were put under his hand, to do all manner of wrong and sin, and all manner of transgression, to corrupt and destroy, and to shed blood upon the earth. (11.5)

The theological problem here, namely, where ultimate responsibility lies for human wrongdoing, would henceforth prove desperately difficult for generations of theologians.

This point is an important one, and worth a moment's elaboration, since previous interpreters of *Jubilees* have usually read their own theology into the text. Bamberger, for example, says quite blandly that *Jubilees* is clear on the point: "Nor does he [Mastema] initiate the process of sin. Men must take the first step in doing evil: only then can Prince Mastema and his evil spirits lead them on to greater wrongdoing." But he cites the same passage I have just quoted as illustration of his point. In his translation of *Jubilees*, Charles makes a similar mistake in an effort to protect God. At 15.31 we read that God has made "many nations and many peoples, and all are His, and over all hath he placed spirits in authority to lead them astray from him." According to Bamberger, the passage is interesting as the first reference to "guardian angels" who watch over nations and individuals, but if so, then they do a remarkably poor job. Charles, however, takes another line, arguing that the "ultimate result" (leading them astray) is here treated as if it were the "immediate purpose of God's actions."[12] It is true that the statement here does not accord well with the apparent reason for introducing a character like Mastema in the first place, namely, to protect God from the possibility that he may be responsible for evil, as Second Isaiah and Job had allowed. But this is precisely the kind of theological inconsistency to which the invention of such an intermediary figure leads. Fallen angels are not, in the end, a very useful solution to the problem of evil; they merely push the problem back a stage.

Mastema himself is a curiously indefinite figure in *Jubilees*. He does not seem to have emerged from the dead giants, like his followers, yet we find

[12] Bamberger 1952:29–30; Charles (ed.) 1913:37n.

no other account of his origin. To judge from his speech to God, he seems to have no fear that he himself will be imprisoned along with the spirits, like the Semihazah or Asael of *Enoch*. And he seems to expect that God will know what he means when he refers to "my will"—"if some of them are not left to me, I shall not be able to execute my will on the sons of men."

The answer to this problem may well lie in his name, Mastema. Since it is etymologically linked to *śāṭān*, it may thus carry connotations similar to those that we discovered for the Satan of the Old Testament. "Adversary" or "opponent" (*śāṭān*) here becomes "enmity" itself (*maśṭēmā*), an abstract idea corresponding to the abstract form of the word. Thus the role of the Satan as accuser, prosecutor, and tempter is included within the more general function of enmity to Israel.

Jubilees' version of the Red Sea episode will illustrate this function. In Exodus 14.8 it is "the Lord" who hardens the heart of the pharaoh and induces him to pursue the Israelites. This potentially malicious act of the Lord is attributed, in the *Jubilees* midrash (48.12–18), to Mastema, not God, even though its purpose, devised by God, is to "smite the Egyptians and cast them into the sea." Mastema thus tries to be an "obstacle" to the exodus, and angels are required to restrain him from accusing the Israelites. The theme of "accusation" has little relevance to the Red Sea story, but it strongly suggests the Job figure of the Satan. Of course it was relatively easy, in this instance, to account for Mastema's enmity, since the result is so clearly a demonstration of God's power over Israel's traditional foe, the Egypt-Rahab of the Old Testament. But where, as in the passage quoted previously, Mastema's role is to provoke the Jews themselves to sin, the theological difficulty is more serious. In keeping with the role of the Old Testament Satan, Mastema mostly seems to work within the limits ordained by God. But no clear idea emerges from *Jubilees* of what those limits are. The ambiguity about how far Mastema could go corresponds to the ambiguity about the Satan's role in Job, Zechariah, and Chronicles, and the ambiguity allows for a gradual loosening of the reins which hold them in.

The *Book of Jubilees* does, however, differentiate between Mastema and Satan. The word *śāṭān* (or its Ethiopic transliteration, *shay-ye-tay-nah*) occurs four times in the work. On three of these occasions the word could readily be taken as a common noun, meaning "enemy" or "adversary" in general. Of these three, two are apocalyptic and refer to the grand new world that will follow the final judgment on the sinners, when people start to follow the Law again:

> And all their days they shall complete and live in peace and joy,
> And there shall be no Satan nor any evil corrupter;
> For all their days shall be days of blessing and healing.[13]

This passage is echoed later:

> And the jubilees shall pass by, until Israel is cleansed from all guilt of fornication, and uncleanness, and pollution, and sin, and error, and dwells with confidence in all the land, and there shall be no more a Satan or any evil one, and the land shall be clean from that time for evermore.[14]

The third reference to Satan seems to be a kind of projection backward in time from these happy days, back to the earlier time when Israel enjoyed some prosperity in Egypt in the days of Joseph:

> The children of Israel multiplied in the land of Egypt, and they became a great nation, and they were of one accord in heart, so that brother loved brother. . . . And there was no Satan nor any evil all the days of the life of Joseph which he lived after his father Jacob, for all the Egyptians honored the children of Israel.[15]

Given the Urzeit–Endzeit typology of apocalyptic literature, it is not surprising to find Golden Age and Future Age pictures duplicating each other in this way, and once again we find the common idea of *Jubilees* that war is the chief symptom of sin and that peace and brotherly love are the signs of its absence. In all three cases, Satan seems to be a personification of the hostility Israel experienced from Gentiles, who are the chief source of trouble throughout history in this patriotic author's opinion. Even the marriage of the Watchers with human females seems, to this writer, analogous to marriage between Israelite and Gentile and so an obvious defilement. To such a crude level has the lofty theology of the Yahwist been reduced.

The other reference to Satan in *Jubilees* is more precise. It is closely linked with Mastema and thus shows that here, for the first time, we are seeing the convergence of the rebel angel tradition with the Old Testa-

---

[13] *Jubilees* 23.29, part of an eschatological poem. Charles translates Ethiopic *zah-yeh-may-shen* as "destroyer," but I follow Davenport 1971 in substituting "corrupter."

[14] *Jubilees* 50.5. Compare the *Assumption of Moses* 10, cited below, Chapter 13 n. 9.

[15] *Jubilees* 46.1,2. See Davenport 1971:39.

ment idea of the adversary. This convergence helps account for the obscurity of Mastema's origin. After God has given his permission to Mastema to keep a tenth of the spirits beside him to help with the work of corruption, the good angel who is telling the whole story to Moses continues: "And we did according to all his words: all the malignant evil ones we bound in the place of condemnation, a tenth part of them we left that they might be subject before Satan on the earth"(10.11). Elsewhere in *Jubilees* the word "Satan" occurs as part of a stock phrase, "There will be [was] no Satan and no evil [corruptors]." But here the link with Mastema is explicit, so that this Satan is conceived not simply as the personification of hostility but as a cosmic force behind the earthly enemies of Israel and the aggressive sins to which they are tempted—a force with power over the angelic adversaries. The contemporary Book of Daniel similarly envisages angelic powers acting through the great empires of history,[16] one of the key features of apocalyptic thinking. This close narrative relation of Satan to Mastema illustrates what we have said about the linguistic relation of the two terms. A distinction is implied, but it is little more than that between the abstract idea of "enmity" and its embodiment in "the enemy," Satan. The fusion of Satan with the combat myth has confirmed his status as a hostile cosmic power, even if his function is still vague.

It is clear from *Jubilees'* use of Enoch material that the name "Mastema" has replaced the Semihazah or Asael of *Enoch*, the leaders of the rebellion. *Jubilees* has confused the picture, however, by duplicating the rebellion-punishment story, telling one variant of it before the flood and another after. The result is that Mastema does not appear in the narrative until the second variant, after the flood. His connection with the first rebellion of the Watchers is obscured, and indeed the first generation of Watcher rebels has no apparent leader. The effort to clarify one theological and narrative problem, how evil could continue when God had ordained the flood to destroy it, gets the author of *Jubilees* into further difficulties. He fails to account for the origin of Mastema, and he also fails to give a coherent explanation of why he is allowed to continue his corrupting work. Is it to make men go astray, or merely to capitalize on their own tendency to do so? Furthermore, Mastema himself is virtually pushed aside by the new Satan figure, as if the general hostility is now to be embodied in the generic adversary, or perhaps in the accuser of Job.

---

[16] Dan. 10.13–21, 12.1. See Caird 1956:6–11, Bamberger 1952:12, above, Chapter 8 nn. 17, 18, and below, Chapter 10.1

Occasionally *Jubilees* substitutes the name "Beliar" for "Mastema." This is the Greek equivalent of the Hebrew *Beli'al*, which means simply worthless, also translated as *anomia* in the Septuagint. *Benē Beli'al* ("Sons of Belial") is a common expression, a casual curse, often meaning little more than "worthless fellows"[17] and *Jubilees* uses the expression in this sense for those who go uncircumcised (15.33). But we also find Moses praying that God will not forsake Israel:

> O Lord, my God, do not forsake Thy people and Thine inheritance, so that they should wander in the error of their hearts, and do not deliver them into the hands of their enemies, the Gentiles, lest they should rule over them and cause them to sin against Thee. Let Thy mercy, O Lord, be lifted up upon Thy people, and create in them an upright spirit, and let not the spirit of Beliar rule over them to accuse them before Thee, and to ensnare them from all the paths of righteousness, so that they may perish from before Thy face. (1.19–20)

This passage occurs in the preamble to *Jubilees* and may have been added later. But it is typical in that it sets historical and spiritual enemies in parallel with each other, and the spiritual enemies are conceived as satanic, on the Old Testament model of "accusers." Between the two parallel sentences, however, there is no theological link. In the first, men sin through the "error of their hearts" (the *yēṣer hāra'* of the later rabbinic theology),[18] while in the second, sin is ascribed to the spirits of Belial, who accuse and ensnare men and keep them "from all the paths of righteousness."

The theological ambivalence would prove highly troublesome to more rigorous minds. Cosmological dualism, which is to say some variant of the combat myth, was influencing the mythology of Israel more and more, and hence the problem of evil became more difficult to resolve. Job may ultimately have come to see that what humans experience as evil is the darker aspect of God, but in the combat myth God and his adversary are radically distinct. The idea of an adversary of man who works somehow with God's permission, obvious enough in Job, becomes less conceivable when the adversary becomes a rebel against God himself. Only such men as Augustine and Milton would be capable of the act of intelligence necessary to understand this idea, and so to reintegrate their own rebellious instincts.

[17] Bamberger 1952:28. See below, Chapter 10, n. 19.
[18] See below Chapter 10.2.

TEN

THE ANGEL OF LIGHT AND THE
ANGEL OF DARKNESS

WE SAW in the previous chapter that the composite figure of person-ified hostility, Mastema-Satan-Belial, in the *Book of Jubilees* took over the role of the rebellious Watcher leader, but left unclear the question of his own origins and power. A further reason for this confusion is the mixing of time periods, avoided in *Jubilees* but common to most apoca-lyptic texts, so that the great battle of the end-time appears also to have taken place in the beginning, and even to be going forward in the present. The rebellion, after all, is a mere episode in the combat story, and it was rarely told as fully as in the Enoch tradition. More often, it occurs simply as an allusion, and in an abbreviated form, within the more immediately interesting narrative of the apocalyptic final battle. Among the men of Qumran in particular, the eschatological battle was eagerly awaited, and thus the Watcher story, with its ensuing conflict, formed only one part of a larger cosmic vision. They looked forward in their hymns to another flood, when "the rivers of Belial burst their high banks," the great abyss is opened, and the enemy waters, "the floods of Belial, burst forth unto hell itself, when the depths of the abyss are in turmoil," and when there will be "warfare the like of which has never been seen," even in the days of the giants.[1]

1. *Giants and Trees: The Moralized Myth*

In Cave 4 at Qumran, further Enoch fragments were discovered which their editor assigns to a separate work, the "Book of Giants." Also appar-ently attributed to Enoch, this book seems to have been composed, like the "Epistle of Enoch," after the *Book of Jubilees*, since neither is there mentioned among Enoch's works. The fragments are not many, but they

---

[1] Gaster 1964:146 (1QH 3.19–36). The language of this passage recalls, and indeed resumes, the Divine Warrior tradition, concentrated now on the end-time. Vermes 1975: 159 replaces Belial with Satan, as often; *caveat lector*. As a rule I follow Gaster's translation, with refer-ences given to Vermes and occasionally to Burrows 1968.

come from several different copies, suggesting that the book was a popular one, and they allow us to see that the core of this "Book of Giants" must have been a further transformation of the Watcher myth.

What makes these fragments especially interesting is that the "Book of Giants" was previously known only in the later form it was given by the hand of Mani, the young and ascetic Christian aristocrat who founded the new religion of Manichaeism in the third century A.D. Mani's version itself survives only in fragments, pieced together from their various languages in the 1930s and 1940s by W. B. Henning.[2] It now appears that the original book was a part of the Enoch literature current among the Essenes of the desert.

This time, in what looks like parts of dialogue, the story is told—in considerable detail—in the voices of the giants themselves, offspring of the union between angels and women. For example, Semihazah's son, Ohyah (Og), complains:

> I have shown myself more powerful. And by the might of my sturdy arm and by the strength of my power, I had attacked all flesh and I have made war with them. But . . . I do not find any support to strengthen me, for my accusers . . . they dwell in the heavens and they live in the holy abodes, and I will not win my cause, for they are more powerful than I.[3]

The book seems to have contained fairly clear references to the knowledge of mysteries, to impiety on the earth, and to the giants' massacre of men. The giants themselves seem to be mainly responsible for the corruption of the world, insofar as one can tell from the meager fragments, although apparently Asael-Azazel is also punished, in keeping with his expiatory function in Leviticus. "Then he punished not us, but Azazel, and has made him . . . [the sons] of the Watchers, the giants, and all [their] beloved ones will not be spared . . . he has imprisoned us." Milik thinks this fragment goes on to allude to the combat of the archangel Michael with the chief of the demons. Michael as a punisher of the Watchers is present already in the earlier Enoch texts, but if Milik is right, then he here becomes for the first time the battle hero best known from the Book of Daniel and the Christian Book of Revelation.[4]

---

[2] Henning 1943–46 and 1977. On the dating, see Milik 1976:58–59, 298–321, and Greenfield and Stone 1977.

[3] Milik 1976:308. In a Parthian fragment, Ohyah is linked with Leviathan in internecine struggle, apparently including Raphael also (Henning 1943:71).

[4] Collins 1975. For Michael in Canaanite texts and as the son of man in Dan. 7, see now

Among the giants listed by these Qumran fragments occur two more familiar names: Gilgamesh and Humbaba. Gilgamesh is simply listed as a giant, but Hobabes (as he appears here) also recurs as Hobabis in a Middle Persian fragment of the Manichaean adaptation: "Hobabis [*hwb'byš*] robbed *'hr* . . . of *nxtg*, his wife. Thereupon the giants began to kill each other and to abduct their wives. The creatures too began to kill each other."[5] We cannot know how these two characters were transmitted to the Jewish author of this "Book of Giants," but their incorporation into this new context suggests some familiarity with the Mesopotamian traditions. The passage may thus be a direct allusion to the best known of the Babylonian *gibbōrīm*, the heroes of old mentioned in Genesis 6.4 but now sources of destruction and corruption. Humbaba's theft of someone's wife suggests adaptation of the devastating-monster motif from a folktale context like those in which a dragon, bear, or devil steals the king's daughter.[6] It is even possible that the passage refers to the (false) offer of his sister by Gilgamesh to Huwawa.

In one of the new Aramaic fragments, we find the Watcher enemies in general identified as trees. A dream vision of a garden in which two hundred trees "came out" is explained thus by Enoch: ". . . and the trees that came out, those are the Watchers and the giants that came out of the women." This garden is ultimately destroyed by water and fire, which recalls the list of Yahweh's achievements in, for example, Psalm 29, where he takes over the glory of Gilgamesh or Gudea.[7] The association of trees and heroes is common enough in heroic traditions; one thinks of Homer's several tree similes or Amos 2.9: "Yet destroyed I the Amorite before them, whose height was like the height of the cedars, and he was strong as the oaks." So we should not press too far a possible link to the association of Humbaba and trees in the Gilgamesh cycle. The dominant allusion is probably to Ezekiel's grand vision (31.1–18) of the destruction of the world-tree of paradise, contiguous as it is with the catching of the sea-monster (32.1–16) and the descent to hell of Egypt's ruler (32.17–32). By now there is probably some connection, already implied in Ezekiel, between enmity and the tree of prohibition.

Day 1985:167–78. For parallels between Daniel and Revelation, see Yarbro-Collins 1976 and Beasley-Murray 1983.

  [5] Milik 1976:311–14.

  [6] Propp 1984:96–98. See above, Chapter 1, and Appendix.

  [7] Milik 1976:303–6; Stroumsa 1984:167. For Ps. 29, see above, Chapter 2 n. 67. Compare also the fragment of Hesiod's *Eoiae* cited above, Chapter 8 n. 22, where a tree also appears suddenly as the object of Zeus' destructive activity.

Even though it represents Egypt, Ezekiel's "world-tree" is a stately cedar nourished by the waters of the deep, whose rivers (*nehārōt*) pour forth
around the place where the tree is planted—an unusual scene in Egyptian
landscape. The passage (Ezek. 31.1–4) recalls the trees of Genesis 2.9–14,
with the four rivers that flow out from the garden as soon as God planted
the trees. Yahweh nonetheless destroys the great tree, and will make the
deep mourn and restrain its many waters, the rivers (Ezek. 31.15), just as
he destroyed the garden itself. Ezekiel, it seems, adapts to his proto-apocalyptic language the same tradition that occurs in Genesis, but in Ezekiel
the echoes of the ancient myths are clearer: his great tree recalls strongly
the *huluppu* tree that Gilgamesh cut down for Ishtar, which led finally to
Enkidu's death in the Sumerian poem "Gilgamesh, Enkidu, and the
Nether-World." It towers above the trees of the forest, all the birds nest
in the branches, and the beasts of the field reproduce beneath it, such that
even the trees of Eden envied it and the cedars in the "garden of God"
could not rival it (31.8–9).[8] It is possible, then, that the traditions preserved in Ezekiel were brought together in the Aramaic "Book of
Giants," and the traditional enemies of Yahweh were represented as trees,
as giants and heroes of old (*nephīlīm* and *gibbōrīm*), and as descendants of
the Watcher angels. In the apocalyptic context, however, the depredations of the giants would be represented as outside history, or rather in the
present and future as well as in the distant past.

In another vision, almost a doublet of this one, Ezekiel hears an allegory
about an eagle breaking off a twig from the top of the cedar of Lebanon.
The twig is replanted in the land of merchants and becomes a spreading
vine. The eagle represents the king of Babylon, the twig the people of the
exile—and the point of the story is that the Lord God will plant a tree on
the mountain height of Israel.

> It will become a noble cedar, and under it will dwell all kinds of beasts; in
> the shade of its branches birds of every sort will nest. And all the trees of the
> field shall know that I the Lord bring low the high tree, and make high the
> low tree, dry up the green tree, and make the dry tree flourish (Ezek. 17.23–
> 24).

Drawing on these traditions, Daniel presents a similar vision of the destruction of a great tree. Nebuchadnezzar dreams he saw

[8] See above, Chapter 6.5, H. G. May 1955:18–21, McKenzie 1956, and Childs 1959:
196–97.

a tree in the midst of the earth; and its height was great. The tree grew and became strong, and its top reached to heaven, and it was visible to the end of the earth. Its leaves were fair and its fruit abundant, and in it was food for all. The beasts of the field found shade under it, and the birds of the air dwelt in its branches, and all flesh was fed from it. . . .

And behold, a watcher, a holy one, came down from heaven. He cried aloud and said thus, "Hew down the tree and cut off its branches, strip off its leaves and scatter its fruit; let the beasts flee from under it and the birds from its branches. But leave the stump of the tree in the earth, bound with a band of iron and bronze, amid the tender grass of the field."

The dream contains its own interpretation, reinforced by Daniel afterward: "the Most High rules the kingdom of men, and gives it to whom he will" (Dan. 4.17, RSV). Although the Watcher has here become a "holy one," as often, the passage is a close parallel to the Enoch fragment, and it too echoes Ezekiel and such texts as Psalm 29. Daniel, however, moralizes: "Break off your sins by practicing righteousness, and your iniquities by showing mercy to the oppressed" (4.27). Detached from one context, reinserted in another, the great world-tree has lost most traces of the struggle—for power and control of natural resources—with which it was once connected. It is now, both in Daniel and in the "Book of Giants," a subject for dream—and its function is to point a moral.[9]

In another related text, the so-called *Zadokite Document* or *Damascus Covenant*,[10] we find a similar association of ideas—great trees and mountains, heroes of old and giants, the Watcher angels, and the generation destroyed by the flood. Put together with the "Book of Giants," with which it is probably contemporary, the passage suggests that although some of the Babylonian heroic traditions survived at Qumran, as in the texts of Genesis or Ezekiel, they occur now as in the Book of Daniel, in a radically transformed context that turns the rebellion myth into a homily.

The relevant passage from the *Damascus Covenant* runs as follows:

[9] Cf. Judg. 9.8–15; *2 Baruch* 36; *2 Esdras (4 Ezra)* 4.13–19. A connection with the vision of Zarathustra in the *Bahman Yast* is plausible (Collins in Stone [ed.] 1984:361). For further discussion of the world-tree motif, see Widengren 1951 and Butterworth 1970; cf. Forsyth 1985. See also the *Book of Sirach* 24.12–34 for the world-tree as Sophia, and the Qumran hymn 1QH 5.20–6.35 in Gaster 1964:159–60.

[10] This text was first made known through medieval copies found in the Genizah (storeroom) of the Old Cairo synagogue in 1896–97 and published in 1910. It was seen to derive from a Qumran original as soon as the Dead Sea Scrolls came to light. On the date, not later than 100 B.C., see Milik 1976:58 and Dimant in Stone (ed.) 1984:490–91, *contra* Delcor 1976:21. Milik thinks it may quote from the "Book of Giants."

I will open your eyes to see and understand how God acts, so that you may choose what he has desired and reject what He has hated, walking blamelessly in all his ways and not straying after the thoughts of guilty lust or after whoring eyes. For many there be that have strayed thereby from olden times until now, and even strong heroes have stumbled thereby.

Because they walked in the stubbornness of their hearts, the Watchers of heaven fell; yea, they were caught thereby because they kept not the commandments of God.

So too their sons, whose height was like the lofty cedars and whose bodies were as mountains. They also fell.

So too "all flesh that was upon the dry land" [Gen. 7.21–22, the generation destroyed by the flood]. They also perished. These became as though they had never been, because they did their own pleasure and kept not the commandments of the Maker.[11]

The passage clearly alludes to the opening of the flood myth in Genesis, but the problem posed by the Genesis text and its subsequent midrashic development in *Enoch* and *Jubilees*, namely, the obscure narrative connection of the various parts—sons of God or Watcher angels, heroes of old or giants, man's wickedness—this problem is now resolved in a new way. The Priestly morality about God's law, into which the older Yahwist's epic had been absorbed, is now the dominant, and indeed only, narrative link. All the episodes of the *Jubilees* story are now resumed as simple instances of the one moral flaw, not keeping God's commandments, and the only link between them is the moralizing "they also fell."

While one must not ignore the distinction of genre—narrative and moral exhortation overlap but are not identical—it is nonetheless significant that the Watcher myth can be used in this way. The idea found in the Targum that *nephīlīm* is cognate with *nāphal*, to fall, has already taken root.[12] The angels and their sons, the giants, "fell" through their stubbornness. And for the first time the parallel between angelic and human conduct is made explicit. The point of the story, like an exemplum in a homily, is its "moral." The word *nāphal* retains barely a ghost of its narrative meaning in Isaiah's or Enoch's vision of stars falling from heaven. It is now a metaphor, the dramatic equivalent of "stray" and "stumble," which is what even strong heroes do, through guilty lust and

[11] *Damascus Covenant* 2.14–21, trans. Gaster 1964:73; cf. Vermes 1975:98–99.

[12] Above, Chapter 7 and Delcor 1976:14, 22, 28. "Jared," in whose days the Watchers came down, father of Enoch, is taken to mean "descend" here (*yrd*), a traditional etymology known also to Origen for "Jordan." See below, Chapter 21.

whoring eyes. Soon, perhaps already, the word can be used as a catch-phrase for what happened to Adam and Eve—the Fall—where no physical movement from heaven down to earth is implied.[13]

The *Damascus Covenant* extends this moralized conception of the Watcher story to the whole of history. It alternates God's judgment of the wicked, "flames of fire and angels of destruction appointed for them that turn aside from his way," with praise for the righteous remnant, the "sons of Zadok." So, for example, the story of Moses and the Exodus now illustrates this conflict, but the opposition that interests the sect most is not so much the struggle with the Egyptians as the quarrel of true with false prophecy. The Angel of Lights supports Moses and Aaron, while "Belial in his cunning set up Jannes the apostate against them." This is the earliest known reference to a widespread Jewish legend, and it follows from the retrospective application of dualism to the whole of history.[14] Belial continues to ensnare Israel, but the remnant also persists until the final visit of God to requite the wicked and reward the faithful. The Watcher story is one example among many of the moral struggle whose resolution is eagerly expected. We are not far here, either in time or in approach to narrative, from the complete allegorization of the Watcher myth that we find in Philo.

History for Philo is the story of the descent of heavenly spirit into earthly substance and the progressive degeneration of the resulting hybrid. This Platonizing conception can be illustrated just as well by the Eden myth as by the Watchers—and neither episode is conceived as a historical moment, a beginning, but simply as a convenient paradigm of the general fall into matter. "When the light of thought is veiled and obscured, the companions of darkness, who had taken over the world above, united themselves with the weakened, effeminate passions, which are called daughters of men, so as to produce children for themselves and not for God."[15] These perverted beings, who merely abused the name of angels, had sought out the pleasures of the senses rather than of right reason. Entirely detached from its historical moment, the story has been con-

[13] See above, Chapter 7 n. 28. This development is complete by the first century A.D. See *2 Esdras* 7.118 (below, Chapters 12 and 14): "Adam . . . the fall was not thine alone, but ours also who are thy descendants."

[14] *Damascus Covenant* 2.2–5.18 in Gaster 1964:72–77. See Ginzberg 1910–38: vol. 2, 335, vol. 5, 425, and vol. 6, 144; and cf. A.T. Hanson 1966:93, 2 Cor. 11.13–15, 2 Tim. 3.8, and below, Chapter 14 n. 19.

[15] Philo, *Quod deus sit immutabilis* 3; cf. *De gigantibus* 17. See Stone (ed.) 1984:353 n. 123, Stroumsa 1984:27–28, Teyssèdre 1985b:309, and below, Chapters 12.1, 21.3, and 25.1.

verted to the Platonic function of "myth," as illustration or exemplum, a focus for imaginative philosophizing.

2. The Two Spirits

The moralistic context of the rebellion story in the *Damascus Covenant* also contains a further clue to the contemporary meaning of the combat myth within the Qumran community. The above passage introduces the Watcher story with the admonition "Open your eyes . . . and choose what he [God] has desired and reject what he has hated." From what is now known about Qumran theology, this injunction may be seen to allude to an issue of much moment among the Brotherhood. "What [God] has desired" and "what he has hated" are "the Two Spirits."

We find this conception in several different places among the Qumran texts. The doctrine of the two spirits, because of its dualistic and deterministic implications, has aroused a good deal of controversy, and some lame, defensive commentary, among modern scholars. In the Watcher passage from the *Damascus Covenant*, the author appears to take a position in favor of free will, insisting on the power of choice, yet the doctrine itself is hard to reconcile with personal liberty, as were most current uses of the rebel myth.

What seems to have happened at Qumran, or in those sects of apocalyptic Judaism for which the Qumran scrolls provide evidence, the Essenes in particular, is this: the combat terminology of many Old Testament passages, related as it was to several of the surrounding religions, has now become a radical apocalyptic myth of an ongoing battle between two rival forces in the cosmos, led by the spirit of light and the spirit of darkness. We may probably detect here the influence of Iranian mythology. The Jews had been subject for two centuries to the authority of the Persian Empire, once Cyrus had liberated them from Babylonian exile. A cosmic struggle between light and darkness was already implied by such myths as Baal's battle with Mot, the lord of death, but it was in the Zoroastrian tradition that this kind of narrative came to be seen as an all-encompassing cosmic conflict in which the ordinary man takes sides according to explicit moral principles.

We have seen, however, that Zarathustra's own teaching may not have implied the absolute dualism later identified as the central Zoroastrian concept. Indeed, the theological problems inherent in the combat myth seem to have troubled the Iranian tradition also.[16] At Qumran the Zo-roastrian ideas seem to have been absorbed at the same time the difficulties of the rebellion myth were becoming apparent, and in any case the teach-ings about cosmic conflict, whether indigenous or Iranian, were trans-formed by the special circumstances of the Essene sect.

The men of Qumran saw themselves as charged with the special task of maintaining the Law and Covenant of God at a time when most Jews had, as they saw it, turned away into apostasy. In this sense, the Essenes pro-vide a close analogy to the Puritan wing of Protestantism. They were en-lightened men, preparing the way in the desert[17] for the new kingdom to be born out of fiery destruction of "this world." As the *Rule of the Com-munity* makes clear, the Qumran sect felt quite explicitly that the world they had left behind was entirely dominated by the adversary, usually called by them "Belial"—and that they were in fact living in "the last days." The annual review to be conducted by the Qumran priests is intro-duced by this matter-of-fact statement: "The following procedure is to be followed year by year so long as Belial continues to hold sway.[18] As a re-sult, Essene literature is rich in references to the eschatological war and the apocalyptic hopes of the Community. We may note as of special interest for our argument the fragment of a *pesher*, or commentary, on 2 Samuel 7.10–14, God's advice to David. Part of the fragment says,

> And as for his saying to David, "I will give thee rest from all thine ene-mies," this means that God will [then] give them rest from all those "sons of Belial" who put stumbling blocks in their way in order to encompass their rack [and ruin], i.e. from all who will [then] enter into the counsel of Belial and lay stumbling blocks for [the Sons of] Light, devising devices of Belial against them, so as to make them yield to Belial because [their hearts] have been led astray.[19]

[16] See Zaehner 1955:312–20 and Zaehner 1961:55; see also above, Chapter 5 n. 3. Cf. Win-ston 1966:200–210 and R. N. Frye 1975, *contra* Osten-Sacken 1969:239–40. For a recent re-view, see Stone (ed.) 1984:386.

[17] Isa. 40.3, quoted both in the Qumran *Rule of the Commuity* (or *Manual of Discipline*) 1QS 8.17 and in John 1.23. See Gaster 1964:64 and Vermes 1975:86.

[18] *Rule of the Community* 1QS 2.19. See Gaster 1964:49 and Vermes 1975:74. Like many of the Qumran texts, this one dates from the late second and early first centuries B.C.; see Di-mant in Stone (ed.) 1984:498.

[19] 4QFlor 1.7–13. See Gaster 1964:338, with notes; cf. Dan. 11.31–32. On possible ety-mologies for Belial, see Gaster 1970. The most likely is *beli ya'al*, without profit, hence "worthless," but the rabbinic view was *beli 'ol*, without yoke, so "unrestrained." For some interesting speculations, see Teyssèdre 1985b:232–37 and Burrows 1958:287–89. The name Belial is substituted for that of Mastema in material from *Jubilees*. *Damascus Covenant* 4.12–

The story of David is now read in the light of texts from elsewhere in the scripture, here of Balaam's worship of idols—a preoccupation that reappears in the New Testament also.[20] The political, flesh-and-blood enemies of David in Samuel have now become the generic "enemy"; like the Satan they are "stumbling blocks," and these satans are now the demonic forces controlling "this world." Furthermore, as the next verses show, David himself has now become the Branch or Plant of David, a messianic figure in the eschatological age.

The *Rule of the Community* provides a full picture of the cosmological narrative in its heavily moralized form. The work contains careful instructions, anticipating Gnostic teachings, "for the man who would bring others to the inner wisdom." This section, known as "The Treatise of the Two Spirits," consists of a series of abstract statements expanding the words of Deuteronomy, "See I have set before thee this day life and good, and death and evil."[21] These biblical words are taken, like the passage from Second Isaiah discussed previously, to refer to the Essene teaching of two conflicting "spirits" (*rūaḥ*). The relevant passage is worth quoting at length, for it shows a further development of Mastema-Satan-Belial into the Angel of Darkness, while the Essenes themselves have now become "the sons of light." The theological difficulties here are acute.

> This is for the man who would bring others to the inner wisdom, so that he may understand and teach to all the sons of light the real nature of men . . . touching the reasons why they are now visited with afflictions and now enjoy periods of well-being.
>
> All that is and ever was comes from a God of knowledge. Before things came into existence He determined the plan of them; and when they fill their allotted roles it is in accordance with his glorious design. . . . Nothing can be changed. . . .
>
> Now this God created man to rule the world, and allotted to him two Spirits after whose direction he was to walk until the final Inquisition. They are the spirits of truth and of error.
>
> The origin of truth lies in the Fountain of Light, and that of error in the Wellspring of Darkness. In the hand of the Prince of Lights is dominion over all the sons of righteousness; in the ways of light they walk. And by

---

13 echoes *Jubilees* 49.2, and 5.18–19 echoes *Jubilees* 48.9, but Mastema remains in a direct reference at 16.1. The form Beliar (e.g., 2 Cor. 6.15) is due to Syriac pronunciation.

[20] Num.: 31.16, 25.1–2; Rev. 2.14. See below, Chapter 17.1. For Balaam as magician, see the entries in Ginzberg 1910–38: vol. 6, 55–56.

[21] Deut. 30.15; Gaster 1964:40, 107. Cf. on Isa. 45.7, above, Chapter 5, and Ps. 1.6 and Prov. 4.10–19.

the Angel of Darkness is all dominion over the sons of error; and in the way of darkness they walk. And by the Angel of Darkness is the straying of all the sons of righteousness, and all their sin and their iniquities and their guilt and their deeds of transgression are the result of his domination; and this by God's inscrutable design will continue until the time appointed by him. Moreover, all men's afflictions and all their moments of tribulation are due to this being's hostility [*maśṭēmā*]. All of the spirits that attend upon him are bent on causing the sons of light to stumble. . . . It is God that created those spirits of light and darkness, and made them the basis of every act. . . .

All men are born to these spirits. . . . It is in these ways that men needs must walk and it is in these two divisions, according as a man inherits something of each, that all human acts are divided throughout all the ages of eternity. For God has appointed these two spirits to obtain in equal measure until the final age.

Between the two categories He has set an eternal enmity. Deeds of error are an abomination to truth, while all the ways of truth are an abomination to error; and there is a constant jealous rivalry between their two regimes, for they do not march in accord. Howbeit, God in his inscrutable wisdom has appointed a term for the existence of error, and when the time of Inquisition comes, He will destroy it forever. Then truth will emerge triumphant for the world, albeit now and until the time of the final judgment it go sullying itself in the ways of wickedness owing to the domination of error.

. . . [God] foreknows the effect of their works on every epoch of the world, and He has made men heirs to them that they might know good and evil. But at the Inquisition he will determine the fate of every living being in accordance with which of the two spirits he has chosen to follow.[22]

This is a thoroughgoing dualistic assessment of the state of the world, yet because the preacher has transformed the cosmic combat, in the manner of the *Damascus Covenant*, into a moralistic sermon, he hedges on the question of its deterministic implications. Words like "inherit," "allot," and "dominion" strongly suggest that a man can only behave according to his inheritance, ordained by God.[23] But the homily seems to end with the insistence that every man's fate will be judged according to which of the spirits he *chooses* to follow.

---

[22] *Rule of the Community* 1QS 3.13–4.26 trans. Gaster 1964:50–54; cf. Burrows 1968:374–76 and Vermes 1975:75–77. See also H. G. May 1963, Osten-Sacken 1969:17–27, 165–84, and 1QH 1.5–38, 13.1–12, 1QM 10.11–16.

[23] H. G. May 1963:3–4; Osten-Sacken 1969:78–80. On the whole question, see Merrill 1975 and esp. the sensible summary by Dimant in Stone (ed.) 1984:534–35. Collins 1981 shows that *rūaḥ*, spirit, has the whole range of meanings by now, from a cosmic entity to a human quality.

Parallel doctrines occur in the works collectively known as *The Testaments of the Twelve Patriarchs*, fragments from some of which have been found at Qumran. Most of the relevant passages simply extend the ethical dualism of biblical texts into an elaborate opposition of virtues and vices, but often a metaphysical or angelic dualism is implied also. Belial is mentioned in eleven of the twelve books, but Satan occasionally replaces him. The *Testament of Dan* says "the spirit" moves at the right hand of Satan (3.6) and claims to find in the *Book of Enoch* that the prince of the spirits is Satan.[24] Here the human inclination and the angelic power seem generally to function in parallel, and the stress throughout is on the human situation, not on the cosmic conflict.

In the *Testament of Judah*, however, the deterministic implications are more firmly resisted—significantly by the introduction of a third "spirit." Having read in "the books of Enoch the righteous" what is in store, Judah tells his children to guard against sexual promiscuity and greed. Love of money leads to idolatry, he claims, as it did in his own case: "The prince of error blinded me, and I was ignorant."[25] Again the human and the cosmic are parallel, but he then goes on to say:

> Two spirits wait upon man—the spirit of truth and the spirit of error. And in between is the spirit of understanding of the mind [the conscience], which inclines as it will. And the works of truth and the works of error are written in the hearts of men, and each of them the Lord knows.[26]

It is clear that conversion of the combat myth into an explicit teaching troubled many of these apocalyptic thinkers, both within and beyond the Qumran community.

One way that the teachers of Qumran could resist the radical dualism implied by the myth and perhaps current in Persian contexts was by attaching the doctrine to Genesis 1.3–5, in the Priestly version of the creation myth. They then interpreted that passage in such a way that God

[24] *Testament of Dan* 5.6; Kee in Charlesworth (ed.) 1983:809. Cf. Collins in Stone (ed.) 1984:336, *Testament of Asher* 6.4–6, and *Gad* 4.7.

[25] *Ho archōn tēs planēs* is a phrase that recalls the language used for Satan in the New Testament. In fact, the phrase may be a translation of Sammael, god of the blind. See below Chapters 12.6, 14.3, and 17.1, and see Black in Logan and Wedderburn 1983:71–72 and Barc 1981.

[26] *Testament of Judah* 20.1–3 in Charlesworth (ed.) 1983:800; cf. Stone (ed.) 1984:336–44. These texts seem to have been composed in Greek, although the Qumran Aramaic fragments point to a multilingual oral and literary tradition.

creates both the spirit of light and the spirit of darkness, even though the Priestly text itself implies the preexistence of darkness.

Nevertheless, the rabbis of the Talmudic period found it necessary to condemn the doctrine of the two spirits as a dangerous heresy. They insisted instead on the doctrine of the two natural tendencies: the *yēṣer-hārāʿ*, the potentially evil imagination of men, as opposed to the *yēṣer-tōb*, the inclination to good.[27] In the scholarly argument about the Qumran theology, those who assert that the texts imply no cosmic or dualistic ideas betray more anxiety than insight, but at least they take the bull by the horns. Their opponents, though recognizing the dualism and determinism, merely insist vacuously that the men of Qumran "did not permit their 'system' to deny the responsibility of man."[28] Josephus, at least, thought the Essenes determinists; for them, he says, fate governs all things, and nothing happens to men that is not according to its determination.[29]

The most dramatic form of the combat myth at Qumran was the vision of the eschatological battle for which the brotherhood was preparing itself, a vision contained most fully in the text known as the *War Scroll*, or the *War of the Sons of Light and the Sons of Darkness*. There we learn that the spirits of truth are under the rule of the prince or angel of light, while the angels of destruction are under the dominion of Belial.[30] The *War Scroll* develops the prophecies of Ezekiel about the final battle with Gog of Magog and Zechariah's apocalyptic eschatology ("Then shall the Lord go forth and fight against those nations, as when he fighteth on a day of battle . . . and all the Holy ones with him") into a full-scale military description, replete with details of maneuvers and battle standards after Hellenistic and

[27] Tennant 1903:78, 113–17, 169–76; Williams 1927:51–91; Moore 1929: vol., 474–96. Cf. Gen. 6.3, above, Chapter 6, and for a possible quotation in the New Testament, James 4.5. For a Christian parallel to the Qumran doctrine, see the *Epistle of Barnabas* 18–21, where the angels of God and Satan rule over the ways of light and darkness. The Jewish-Christian affinities of this text, Revelation, and the Pseudo-Clementines, for example, point to the context in which the combat myth had most impact in the early Christian centuries. See Yarbro-Collins 1976 and below, Chapters 13, 17.1, and 22.

[28] H. G. May 1963:5, and nn. 1 and 2. Cf. Merrill 1975 and Dimant in Stone (ed.) 1984:534.

[29] Josephus, *Antiquitates Judaicae* 13.5.9; cf. *Bellum Judaicum* 3.12. The *Book of Sirach* 15.11–20 makes an effort to sort out the theology of this doctrine.

[30] 1QM 1.2, 13.2, 4–6. For Belial as angel of evil, see also 1QS 1.18, 24; 2.5, 14; 1QM 1.1, 5, 13; 4.2, 11.8, 13.2; and *Damascus Covenant* 4.13–15; 5.18; 8.2; 12.2; 19.14. The angel of light shares most characteristics with Michael, the angel of Israel in Dan. 10.1 and 12.1, but the texts mention several other angels as well, e.g., 4Q 177 12–13.1, 7, mentions an angel of truth; see Stone (ed.) 1984:521.

Roman models.[31] The text seems to allude to the Enoch material on the defeat of the rebels, instructing the various battalions to carry standards marked with the names of the four archangels—Michael, Gabriel, Sariel, and Raphael.[32] During the projected exhortation to the troops, the commander is also to invoke several of the battle texts we have been discussing, the David and Goliath combat, the Holy War tradition and the battles with "Kittim" (a collective name for successive enemies: Egyptians, Assyrians, Seleucids, and Romans), the prophetic battles such as those seen by Enoch and Daniel, and of course the Red Sea combat: "Thou hast done unto these as thou didst unto Pharaoh and the captains of his chariots at the Red Sea."[33] The whole army of the sons of light is imagined as organized after the model of the Exodus and the wilderness wanderings.

The odd thing about the War Scroll is that, despite its evident apocalyptic and eschatological implications, the battle itself is conceived in realistic terms, such that the Israeli General Yadin, who edited the text, found it eminently practical for a military campaign. In this respect, the War Scroll reverses the common tendency of apocalyptic thought to conceive the final battle exclusively in cosmic and mythological terms. The imagery of the eschatological combat myth has become so real to these intense desert exiles, and the anticipation of the final days has become so vivid, that something like the Old Testament relation between history and myth is curiously restored. Qumran theology may have developed a deterministic bent, but in the practical matter of the preparation for war, the men of Qumran were quite ready to play their role in the coming victory. Granted that they were sustained in this attitude by the conviction that they alone had maintained the covenant with Yahweh and were therefore the preordained allies of the Prince of Light, still they conceived of this final battle as an engagement with real human armies. We do not know

---

[31] Ezek. 38–39; Zech. 14.2–5. Cf. Isa. 25.6. On Gog's mythological background, see Childs 1959:195–97. Unfortunately, Gog is no relation to Og, son of Semihazah. On the *War Scroll*, see Yadin 1962, and for more recent views, see Stone (ed.) 1984:426, 516–17. Some parts at least must now be dated to the second century B.C.

[32] 1QM 9.17. Cf. esp. *Enoch* 40.9–10, although the reconstruction is uncertain here. On this section of *Enoch* (chaps. 37–71), known usually as the "Parables," or "Similitudes," later than the books so far discussed but preserving older traditions, see below, Chapter 10.3, and Knibb 1979. A likely date is late first century B.C. The archangels appear also in *Enoch* 9, 10, and 20 (above, Chapter 8). Sariel warns Noah about the flood, Raphael confronts Asael, and Michael confronts Semihazah, while the fourth angel, who rounds up the offspring, must be Gabriel.

[33] 1QM 11.12 in Gaster 1964:315; cf. Vermes 1975:138. For the Kittim, see Num. 24.24 and Dan. 11.30. For the wilderness, cf. Exod. 18.25, with *Damascus Covenant* 13.1–2, 20; 14.3.

whether these Essenes actually engaged in military training or kept up the military practices of the Maccabean revolutionaries. But the *War Scroll* reveals that they certainly identified the cosmic adversaries of the combat mythology with the imperial powers and their traitorous allies who were the material cause of their suffering and exile, whether Greek, Seleucid, Hasmonean, or Roman.

In such circumstances, it is not difficult to see how the descendants of those Jews who returned to Zion from the Babylonian exile to find themselves the clients of a Persian satrap could have adapted the Iranian system of belief to their own prophetic, and now apocalyptic, combat traditions. The Iranian system itself shows affinities with the older Babylonian traditions from which the Jews had long been borrowing. The demon of wrath and fury, Aeshma Daeva, will ravage the earth much as the demon Irra devastated Marduk's Babylon, but at the end a new teacher will appear, Truth will emerge triumphant, and the world will be renewed.[34] Just so the scrolls look forward to the end of the present "Era of Wrath," when a teacher will arise to introduce the new age, when truth will be made manifest and all things renewed.[35] The withdrawal of the faithful to the desert, ostensibly to preserve the purity of their own heritage, may actually have helped them reread their tradition in the context of the radical antagonism characteristic of the Persian doctrines. The obvious motive for going into voluntary exile in this way is to reestablish contact with the God of Israel, whom many patriarchs and prophets had traditionally found in the desert. The exiles thus confirmed themselves as the "saving remnant" of the covenant, "the elect of his favor."[36] They no longer had to believe that an outraged God had revoked his covenant with them. What they were now suffering was no more than a temporary setback in the long struggle between the forces of Good and Evil. As Gaster explains it, the momentary triumph of Evil would be followed inevitably

> by the final discomfiture of Falsehood (*Druj*), the condign punishment of all
> who had espoused it, the reward of the partisans of Truth or Right (*Asha*),

[34] *Yasna* 29.1–30.6, 31.8, 41.12; *Bundahesh* 30.17, 32.8; Duchesne-Guillemin 1963. See above, Chapters 2 and 5. The *aeshma daeva* appears as the foul-smelling Asmodeus, he of the "fishy fume," in the *Book of Tobit*, datable to perhaps 200 B.C. and important at Qumran.

[35] *Rule of the Community*, 1QS 4.19–25; *Hymns of Thanksgiving* 3.34, 11.13–14, 12.11–13; see Gaster 1964:26–27.

[36] *Rule of the Community*, 1QS 8.1–19 in Gaster 1964:64 and Vermes 1975:85. Cf. Isa. 65.9, Ps. 105.43, 2 John 1, 1 Pet. 2.9, and Rev. 17.17.

the dissolution of a corrupt world in fire and brimstone (*ayah khshusta*), and the eventual emergence of that new world.[37]

None of these concepts needs to have been borrowed from Persia, but the complex we find among the Qumran sect makes the argument for Persian influence persuasive. In Persian belief, sectarian Judaism found an extreme version of the combat myth which most closely fitted the needs of the times and, dressed up with suitably portentous theological terminology, often coincided with their own traditions.

One form of Persian belief in particular would have corresponded closely with the developing views of apocalyptic sects. The Zervanite myth of a god of time and destiny who rules over even the warring gods Ormazd and Ahriman, the fathers of light and dark, shows a structure of belief similar to that which caused the introduction of a third "spirit"— the understanding of the mind—in the *Testament of Judah* version of the "two spirits" doctrine. J. Duchesne-Guillemin, a distinguished Indo-Europeanist, adduces the Zervanite myth as the most likely source of this doctrine even in the *Rule of the Community*. There could be an easy consonance between this idea and the Hebrew term *rūah* for the spirit of God that moves on the face of the waters in Genesis.[38]

The same scholar also compares the doctrine common to the Qumran texts and the New Testament, that Belial or Satan is the "prince of this world," with the Zervanite myth. At the conclusion of this myth, Zervan the great god above all says to Ahriman, "I have made Ormazd to rule above thee," meaning that Ahriman is the prince of this world, but Ormazd, the spirit of light, rules the world above.[39] Relative dating is difficult, but Zervanism seems to have been a concurrent response to the hardening of Zarathustra's ethical dualism into the radical opposition of Ahriman and Ormazd.

3. The Prophet and the Satanic Priest

It is characteristic of apocalyptic thinking to erase or collapse history. The "saving remnant" concentrates on the end-time, and all past time anticipates or mirrors the present. The battle lines are drawn, and the sons of

---

[37] Gaster 1964:25.

[38] Duchesne-Guillemin 1958:94. Cf. Zaehner 1955, Winston 1966:205, West 1971, and Collins 1981.

[39] Duchesne-Guillemin 1958:95–96. For Gnostic parallels, see below, Chapter 18.

Belial are soon to be consigned, with the Watchers, to eternal fire.[40] By a curious but frequent twist of thought, the very "domination of Belial" is the sign of how soon the end must come; he can hold such power because he will not have it long.

An interesting illustration of the Qumran tendency to read all history in the light of the "two spirits" doctrine is found in the work known as the *Martyrdom of Isaiah*. It survives only because it was worked into the opening chapters of a later Christian composition, the *Ascension of Isaiah*, but the original Jewish work was readily discernible even before the Dead Sea discoveries.[41] It can now be seen to reflect the Qumran ideology even though no copies have been found there.

The work opens with a scene in which Isaiah prophesies his own death at the hands of Manasseh. Manasseh was the son of Hezekiah, and his story is told in 2 Kings 20.16–21.18 and again in 2 Chronicles 32.32–33.20. He was the king whose long reign steered Israel through the period of Assyrian domination by adopting certain cults, notably that of Moloch in the Vale of Tophet. For this he became notorious in the Jewish tradition; his name and apostasy were synonymous. But in the *Martyrdom*, Isaiah explains not that Manasseh shall have dealings with heathen but that

> Sammael Malchira shall serve Manasseh and execute all his desires, and he shall become a follower of Beliar rather than of me. And many in Jerusalem and in Judea he shall cause to abandon the true faith, and Beliar shall dwell in Manasseh, and by his hands I shall be sawn assunder.[42]

The prophecy soon begins to be fulfilled. Manasseh serves Satan and his angels, and turns Jerusalem into a hotbed of occultism, fornication, general lawlessness, and persecution. Isaiah withdraws to the wilderness, where he lives on wild herbs with a faithful group of fellow prophets.

Now a key figure in the story emerges, the false prophet Belchira. He brings before Manasseh three charges against Isaiah: that he predicts the fall of Jerusalem and the captivity of the people, that he claims to have seen God and so contradicts Moses, and that he calls Jerusalem "Sodom" and its leaders "the people of Gomorrah." Manasseh has Isaiah seized, because Belial "dwelt in the heart of Manasseh." As Isaiah is being sawn asunder,

---

[40] *Rule of the Community*, 1QS 2.7; cf. Mark 9.43 and Matt. 18.9.

[41] Charles (ed.) 1913: vol. 2, 155–58. See Flusser 1953 and Stone (ed.) 1984:52–56. The *Ascension of Isaiah* had something like canonical status among some groups in the third century A.D.; see Horton 1976:103.

[42] *Martyrdom of Isaiah* 1.7 in Charles (ed.) 1913: vol. 2, 159. On the form Beliar, see above, n. 19.

Belchira, mouthpiece of Satan, tries to get him to recant. But Isaiah refuses, aided as he is by the Holy Spirit, curses Belchira and the demonic powers that control him, and dies. Isaiah's fellow prophets, however, get away without being martyred.

The conflict between true and false prophecy is given a specific biblical anchor in the figure of Belchira. He is said to be a descendant of that Zedekiah ben Chenaanah, who, possessed by "a lying spirit" from Yahweh, smote Micaiah ben Imlah on the cheek at 1 Kings 22.19–22.[43] Like Isaiah, Micaiah had a vision of God upon his throne surrounded by the heavenly court, and like Isaiah he was punished for his opposition both to king and to false prophets. But now the real conflict is between the Holy Spirit, who sustains Isaiah in his moment of trial (as it sustained Daniel in his) and the various adversary figures who inhabit Manasseh and Belchira: Sammael, Malchira, Belial, and in several passages, Satan.

Beyond this deliberate genealogical link between the two false prophets, the story has little biblical or traditional basis. (There is nothing to suggest that the historical Isaiah lived beyond the reign of Hezekiah.) Instead we have a patent fiction, dressed up with biblical allusions, which serves as a virtual allegory of the situation of the Qumran community, or one very like it, during the first century B.C. The retreat into the desert, an intrusive item in the story, was basic to the Qumran sect, and the motives were similar—to escape the wickedness of the king and his priests in Jerusalem, now seen as Sodom and Gomorrah. The conflict between true and false prophets parallels the Qumran opposition of the Teacher of Righteousness to the Spouter of Lies and the Wicked Priest. One opponent of the sect was even referred to as Manasseh.[44] But the most significant parallel is the more basic conflict between the two spirits, the forces of the Prince of Light and the Angel of Darkness.

Among the Qumran texts themselves, the adversary is usually known as Belial, as we have seen. But in the *Martyrdom of Isaiah* many names occur in parallel with each other. There is Sammael, which means "the blind god" or "god of the blind," a common figure in rabbinic and Gnostic texts who is probably the "god of this world" that Paul denounces for blinding unbelievers.[45] There is also Malchira, a name that has now been plausibly connected with the Milki-resa, a Watcher angel denounced in

---

[43] See above, Chapter 5.

[44] 4QpNah 3–4 III 9–12 in Vermes 1975:233–34. See Dimant in Stone (ed.) 1984:509–11, 543, and also 13 n. 58 for references to the Wicked Priest.

[45] 2 Cor. 4.4. See above, n. 25.

some Qumran fragments as the ruler of darkness; it means "my king is impiety" and is the counterpart of Milki-sedeq, better known as the Melchizedek of Hebrews 7.[46] And then there is Satan himself.

In the *Book of Jubilees*, Satan's status was vague, still in part a generic adversary rather than a definite being with a name and character of his own. But now, in the Qumran literature itself and in the *Martyrdom*, he is clearly himself. Though only one among several names, he is worshiped by the wicked king and his priest, who functions as his mouthpiece, and he is in conflict, a losing one, with the Holy Spirit for the soul of a prophet. The story is similar to the legend that first appears in the *Damascus Covenant* that the Angel of Lights helped Moses and Aaron against Belial's support of Jannes the apostate, and it recalls also the conflict between Michael and Satan over the body of Moses, to which allusion is made in Jude 9. It also anticipates the form that the combat myth was soon to take on in Gnostic and Christian circles. What counts in the struggle between God's forces and Satan's is truth and lying, orthodox and heretical interpretations of dehistoricized narratives. The persecution of prophets became a common motif in the New Testament, and a sign of the approaching end in the figure of Antichrist.[47]

A parallel rise in the frequency of the name Satan for the adversary occurs in another text, probably also from the first century B.C. or early in the next century. This text has been handed down as chapters 37–71 of the *Book of Enoch*, known as the "Parables" or "Similitudes of Enoch," but no fragments have appeared from the Qumran caves, and it seems to be a later reworking of the stories told in older books.[48] Plural satans occur in two places. In one, which may go back to a Noah book, Noah is worried by the sinking of the earth and goes off to get an explanation from his ancestor. He learns that the flood is to come because "men have learned all the secrets of the angels and all the violence of the satans and all their secret powers.[49] Here it looks as if the word is used for the sons of the Watchers, the Giants, who had fallen to warring on and killing each other. Another passage uses "the satans" for those demons who "accuse" the in-

[46] For Milki-resa and his counterpart, see Vermes 1975:252–54, 260–61, 265–68; Horton 1976; Stone (ed.) 1984:55, 521; and Day 1985:131.

[47] See I John 2.18 and below, Chapter 17.1. Cf. 2 Thess. 2.3–9; Matt. 5.12, 23.29–37; Luke 13.33–35, and Acts 7.35–37, 52.

[48] Black 1985:181–93 dates it to pre-A.D. 70. See below, Chapter 12.1 n. 4, and cf. Stone (ed.) 1984:398–403.

[49] *Enoch* 65.6. On the Noah fragments, see above, Chapter 8 n.1.

habitants of earth before the Lord of Spirits, where the Satan of Job and Zechariah has clearly influenced the Enoch narrative.[50]

Satan appears twice in the singular in another passage. Enoch sees the angels of punishment in a deep valley preparing the instruments of torture for Satan, and in a valley of fire preparing the chains for the troops of Asael, for the demons who, by inciting mankind to sin, had acted as servants of Satan.[51]

In these two texts, the *Martyrdom of Isaiah* and the "Similitudes of Enoch," we thus find an important transitional development. In each case the name Satan appears in parallel with the figures he is soon to replace in the Christian tradition. In the first, he stands at least on equality with the powers of darkness in the texts produced by the men of Qumran, while in the second he is linked to the rebel angel figures of the apocalyptic tradition. And his consignment to the bottomless pit, the chains and the fire, is already preparing. It was to continue preparing for a very long time.

[50] *Enoch* 40.7; See Black 1985:200, and above, Chapter 5.
[51] *Enoch* 53.3 and 54.4–6.

ELEVEN

ANTIFEMINISM AND THEOLOGICAL
DILEMMAS

THE DUALISTIC and determinist implications of apocalyptic eschatology are troublesome, we have seen, when the Angel of Darkness has
as much independence—indeed control of the whole world—as in some
Dead Sea scriptures. These theological problems are especially difficult to
avoid once the origin of evil is attributed to the rebellion version of the
combat myth. From the theological point of view, the difficulty raised by
the rapid growth of the rebellion myth boils down to the question
whether angelic beings or humankind are to bear the ultimate responsibility for evil. Yet this question often took a special form. Because the
story of the Watchers was still in essence an elaborate midrash of Genesis
6.1–4, its central theme was sexuality; that is to say, lust was the cause of
the initial rebellion and corruption. The myth therefore could attract to
itself all kinds of sexual neuroses, in particular male fear of women. In fact
the myth, with a slight change of emphasis from its earlier forms, could
become a perfect vehicle for denouncing the female of the species, since
human males play no part in that brief Genesis text. Sex takes place only
between angels and women.

We have already noted a few of the passages where the responsibility is
shifted from angels to women, and since this version of the myth would
have a profound effect on the subsequent development of the tradition,
indeed on Western civilization as a whole, we may here follow briefly
some of its ramifications. The antifeminine emphasis was especially useful
for a male theologian who wished to place the blame for evil squarely on
human shoulders.

Possibly the Yahwist himself had given some encouragement to this
view by the severe position he takes immediately after the intercourse episode: "When Yahweh saw how great was man's wickedness on earth"
(Gen. 6.5), a sentence that reappears frequently in *Enoch* or other apocalyptic literature. But the obvious place where the antifeminine tradition
begins is with the development of the Asael variant of the rebellion myth.
Asael became the leader of the rebellion, we have seen, partly because the

skills he taught included the secrets of female adornment—jewelery and cosmetics of various kinds, especially eye shadow. Enoch at one point in the "Visions" section denounces Asael and his followers because they revealed heavenly, but worthless, mysteries to women: "This you made known to the women in the hardness of your hearts, and through this mystery, the women and the men cause evil to increase on the earth."[1] To be sure, the men are also responsible here, but women are the conduits, if not the sole cause.

In a later passage of the "Visions," possibly added only in the course of Greek translation, Uriel explains to Enoch that "their wives, having led astray the angels of heaven, will become Sirens."[2] Those are the only two passages in the earlier Enoch books in which the women share or take over the blame from the angels, although the barnyard orgy of the "Dream" section[3] suggests similar sexual fears.

But in one of the *Testaments of the Twelve Patriarchs*, we find a most virulent form of this new version. In the *Testament of Reuben*, the first of the twelve, the brief mention of Reuben's sin at Genesis 35.22 has been expanded into a bitter attack on women. In Genesis, Reuben simply "lies with" Bilhah, his father's concubine. Jacob then denounces him for defiling his father's bed (Gen. 49.3–4). That is all we learn from Genesis. But in Reuben's *Testament* this brief incident becomes the occasion for a long tirade against women and a warning to his sons on the grave dangers of fornication: do as I say, not as I do. As he tells the story here, Reuben once caught sight of Bilhah's naked body while she was bathing in a covered place, could not get the memory out of his mind, and then, when he found her lying naked in a drunken stupor, somehow managed to rape her without her waking up (in the *Jubilees* version of the story, she does wake up and cries out).[4] His conscience still troubles him, he says, and he reminds his sons of the good Joseph, who managed to resist a woman's wiles no matter what kinds of Egyptian magic they tried. Bilhah, we might note, had not exactly been active in seducing Reuben, unless we imagine (what the text does not state) that she somehow contrived to expose herself just where Reuben would see her. Nonetheless, despite Bilhah's apparent innocence, Reuben goes on, "women are evil, my children," and proceeds with a long series of common male fantasies about

[1] *Enoch* 16.3 in Knibb 1978:102–3.
[2] *Enoch* 19.2. See above, Chapter 8 n. 71.
[3] *Enoch* 86 in Knibb 1978:196–97. See above, Chapter 8.2.
[4] *Jubilees* 33.4–7.

women—they are weaker so they use wiles, even magic if wiles won't work, they are "overcome by the spirit of fornication more than men," or so an angel has told him, they adorn themselves to beguile, and through "the accomplished act" they take men captive. "Every woman," he explains, echoing the Enoch literature on the fate of the Watchers, "who uses these wiles has been reserved for eternal punishment." Reuben now tells his own variant of the Watcher myth:

> For thus they allured the Watchers before the Flood. As they continually beheld them, they lusted after them and conceived the act in their mind; they changed themselves into the shape of men and appeared to them while the women were making love with their husbands; and the women, lusting in their minds after these apparitions, gave birth to giants, for the Watchers appeared to them as reaching up to heaven.[5]

This passage contains two widespread ideas—most obviously the incubus fantasy whereby husbands are replaced by demons in the act of love itself, and also the common folk idea that what a woman thinks of when she conceives will determine the shape or nature of her baby. But most important, the Watcher story has here become a kind of homily on the nature of women. It points the moral that follows immediately: "Beware, therefore, of fornication; and if you wish to be pure in mind, guard your senses from every woman."

In a fragmentary Qumran text, dating from the turn of the era and known as the *Genesis Apocryphon*, we find a slightly more ambivalent extension of a parallel story. As in *Enoch* 106.6, Lamech, the father of Noah, is suspicious, believing that his baby boy could not glow so much if he were not of angelic parentage. Here, however, the suspicion leads to a long and emotional scene, absent in the *Book of Enoch*, in which Lamech denounces his wife for infidelity with one of those cursed Watchers. He tries to get her to confess, but she swears that the seed was planted by Lamech and no Watcher or Son of Heaven. Lamech is unconvinced. He gets his father, Methusaleh, to go and have a word with his father, Enoch, who by this time dwells with angels. Enoch is able to reassure him.[6]

    [5] *Testament of Reuben* 4–5.7, trans. Kee in Charlesworth (ed.) 1983:784. See above, Chapter 10 nn. 24, 26. Bamberger 1952:31 cites this passage but then says a number of unusually obtuse things about it.

    [6] *Genesis Apocryphon* 2.3–18, in Fitzmyer 1971:51–55 and Vermes 1975:215–17. See Stroumsa 1984:23–27 and Nickelsburg in Stone (ed.) 1984:104. Cf. above, Chapter 8 n. 2. The story is adapted for Joseph's similar complaint about Mary in the *Gospel of James*; see Hennecke and Schneemelcher 1963–65: vol. 1, 381.

The same could happen to Eve as happened to Bilhah, Noah's poor mother, or the Watchers' women. Nakedness and the fig leaf are present already in the Genesis version of her story, and by now the women of Greek mythology were affecting Jewish tradition. We have already noted those seductive sirens, and Eve would similarly overlap with Hesiod's misogynistic picture of Pandora. Prurient interest of this kind would soon drive Eve into the arms of the devil.[7]

In parts of the New Testament, we find the same sexual implications we find in *Reuben*, or in the later Enoch tradition. The pseudo-Pauline First Letter to Timothy denounces women in a similar though less virulent way, and at one point immediately proceeds to Adam and Eve:

> In like manner also, [I will] that women adorn themselves in modest apparel, with shamefacedness and sobriety; not with braided hair, or gold, or pearls, or costly array. . . . Let the woman learn in silence with all subjection. But I suffer not a woman to teach, nor to usurp authority over the man, but to be in silence. For Adam was first formed, then Eve. And Adam was not deceived, but the woman, being deceived, was in the transgression.[8]

This implies Eve's guilt rather than Adam's, and shows a chain of associations similar to those that from time to time characterize the Watcher myth.

In the First Letter of Peter, those associations appear to become quite explicit. The third chapter of this letter begins with a similar and lengthy admonition to women—for example, "whose adorning let it not be that outward adorning of plaiting the hair, and of wearing gold, or of putting on of apparel." Before long, the writer is talking of Christ, of the apocryphal descent into hell, and of the Watcher legend (here Christ has taken over Enoch's role):

> By which also he went and preached unto the spirits that were in prison; which sometime were disobedient, when once the long-suffering of God waited in the days of Noah, while the ark was a preparing, wherein few, that is, eight, souls were saved by water. The like figure whereunto even baptism doth also now save us.[9]

[7] Below, Chapter 12. A possible counterexample is the allusion to Titans and giants in Judith (16.6): The people congratulate her for overcoming Holofernes "by the beauty of her face" and not with the methods of "sons of Titans" or "proud giants."

[8] 1 Tim. 2.9–14 (KJV).

[9] 1 Pet. 3.19–21 (KJV). For further discussion, see below, Chapter 21. For the date, ca. A.D. 90–110, see N. O. Kelly 1969:234, 237, and (for 1 Peter allusions to *Enoch*) 155.

These two passages show that, even into the late New Testament times represented by these two letters, antifeminism was likely to be linked with the transformations of the Watcher myth. Together with the passages from the *Testament of Reuben* and the *Genesis Apocryphon* they show that, in the homiletic or moralizing context in which the Watcher myth tended now to occur, it could draw to itself plentiful parallels in Greek or other traditions, and that it could also transform the story of Adam and Eve.

It is hardly surprising that antifeminism should arise in the course of moralizing about a myth that traces the origins of evil to lust. Blaming women is an uncomplicated solution for men suspicious of their own sexual needs. This antifeminine tendency would not always assume the virulent form we find in Reuben's homilies or in the harsher parts of the New Testament. Sometimes it is barely recognizable within the more clearly theological dilemmas posed by the Watcher myth. It was surely these dilemmas, rather than a revulsion against such simple antifeminism, that led to the gradual demotion of the Watcher myth within more orthodox Jewish circles.

An interesting illustration of this demotion is the first-century A.D. *Apocalypse of Baruch*, which survives in Syriac translation. Together with the *Apocalypse of Ezra*, or *4 Ezra* (*2 Esdras* in the Vulgate appendix), the Syriac *Baruch* reflects the dark period after the destruction of the second temple (A.D. 70) and represents a more determined reassertion of the basic covenant theology than any of the other products of apocalyptic Judaism. It contains many of the ideas now found in rabbinic Haggadah ("something told," i.e., the body of popular legend, often midrashic in form, taken over by the synagogue preachers and destined to make up a large part of the Talmud). What is especially interesting here is that the origins of sin and death are traced not to the lustful angels but to Adam's sin. The culpability of human sin is reinforced by the rabbinic doctrine of the *yēser hāraʿ*:

> Though Adam first sinned and brought untimely death upon all, yet of those who were born from him each one of them has prepared for his own soul torment to come, and again each one of them has chosen for himself glories to come. . . . Adam is therefore not the cause, save only of his own soul, but each of us has been the Adam of his own soul.[10]

---

[10] *2 Baruch* 54.15, 19, in Charles 1913 (ed.): vol. 2, 511–12. Cf. *2 Esdras* 7.116–18, cited below, Chapter 14 nn. 33, 34. On these two works, see Stone (ed.) 1984:408–14.

The author then goes on to tell the Watcher myth, but with a striking change of emphasis and an implied link with the Adam story. After Adam's sin,

> Sheol kept demanding that it should be renewed in blood, and the begetting of children was brought about, and the passion of parents produced. . . . And the darkness of darkness was produced. For he [man] became a danger to his own soul: even to the angels he became a danger. For, moreover, at that time when he was created, they enjoyed liberty. And some of them descended and mingled with the women. And then those who did so were tormented in chains. But the rest of the multitude of the angels, of which there is no number, restrained themselves. And those who dwelt on the earth perished together with them through the waters of the deluge. (56.6–11)

The author knows the Enoch tradition and expects his readers to know it. But now it is mankind who has become a danger to the angels and caused some of them to fall. As in the Qumran context, the Watcher myth here illustrates the extent of human corruption, rather than its origin.[11] By now, it seems, the only solution to the theological difficulties of the Watcher myth was dramatically to reassert human responsibility and thus to substitute Adam's sin for the Watcher's lust. In this passage at least, antifeminism, if present at all, is only incidental to the theological statement of man's responsibility for suffering, sin, and death. Adam's sin, rather than Eve's, is what produces the consequences earlier attributed to the Watcher episode—war and sacrifice (Sheol renewed in blood), and "the passion of parents" and "the darkness of darkness."

This theological shift is all the more remarkable because the Syriac *Baruch* still insists dramatically on the apocalyptic combat myth itself. In the end-time to come, when the Messiah is revealed, the earth will be menaced by a new flood of black waters, and the waters will rain down from a cloud that rises from "a very great sea" (53.1). This idea follows the Qumran tradition in bringing back together the Enoch story of an eschatological flood with the watery adversary of Canaanite myth. The menace of the new flood is parallel with the reappearance of Behemoth and Leviathan, who "shall ascend from the sea." Just as the final flood will be subdued, so will these chaos monsters. In fact, they are to be food for the great messianic banquet to be shared with the "saving remnant."[12]

---

[11] See Bamberger 1952:43 and above, Chapter 10.1. See also Stone (ed.) 1984:413. For the theological and sexual confusion in Josephus' version, *Antiquitates* 1.69–71, see Stroumsa 1984:131.

[12] *2 Baruch* 29.3–4. The vision of these two monsters derives via Job from Canaanite myth.

The explanation offered for the existence of these adversaries, however, does little to solve the problem of their origin. The text adds, returning to Behemoth and Leviathan, "those two great monsters which I created on the fifth day of creation and shall have kept until that time." The echo of Genesis 1.21, "So God created the great sea monsters," does not explain the conflict within creation, although the obvious intention is to bring the combat tradition back within monotheistic confines. But that, in turn, means abandoning or demoting the Watcher myth. Adam's sin might here account for human sin, death, even angelic corruption, but not the source of the hostility itself. That would require a much more elaborate version of Adam's story and an Eve who was still more the repository of antifeminine spite.

On Behemoth, Leviathan's helper, see Day 1985:80–82; he proposes that Behemoth in Job goes back to the Ars, beloved of El and smitten by Anat (CTA 3.3.40–41, above, Chapter 2.8). See also CTA 6.6.50: "In the sea are Ars and the dragon." Parallels occur in the "Parables of Enoch" (60.7–9) and in *2 Esdras* 6.49–52; see Ginzberg 1910–38: vol. 5, 26, 43–46. It is possible that the eating of the enemy goes back to the fate of Mot in Canaanite myth, but its more immediate source is biblical; the passage alludes to the catalog of Yahweh's victories in Ps. 74:13–15 (above, Chapter 2.8), in which the heads of Leviathan are given as food to the people of the wilderness—now the "saving remnant" in the Qumran tradition. Cf. Isa. 28.2–8, Ezek. 29.3–5, and Cross 1973:99–111. See also above, Chapter 6.6.

Part Three

GNOSTIC AND CHRISTIAN MYTHOLOGY

TWELVE

THE ADAM BOOKS AND THE SERPENT'S IDENTITY: GNOSTIC DEVELOPMENTS FROM JEWISH APOCALYPTIC

CHRISTIANITY began as one more Jewish apocalyptic sect with a peculiar messianic belief, but its rapid expansion, and especially the decisive struggles between "orthodox" and "heretical" wings, caused the informing combat tradition to undergo several significant mutations. Broadly speaking, the combat narratives developed now in two main directions, but in the earliest period the two are not easily distinguishable. Both depend upon the Jewish sectarian movements responsible for apocalyptic ideology, but one of the tendencies, what soon came to be called Gnosticism, is ultimately a more radical departure, while the other, which evolved into Catholic Christianity, identified itself as anti-Gnostic and tried, in particular, to preserve the covenant tradition of the Old Testament scriptures. As the quarrel between the two tendencies grew, we find the issue joined more and more frequently around one central narrative and theological problem: which myth accounted for the origins of suffering, and was it human or angel, the sin of a broken covenant or the evil of a cosmic power, which had caused the trouble? Once again, we shall follow the transformations of the narratives to understand the theological arguments.

The origins of Gnosticism probably pre-date the earliest Christian records, Paul's letters. On this question there is still considerable debate, since it has been customary for students of early Christian history, following the early fathers, to regard Gnosticism as an aberrant form of Christianity. Historians of religion have often challenged this concept but until recently had not gained much of a hearing in Christian circles. New discoveries, however, especially the Gnostic library unearthed at Nag Hammadi in Egypt since 1945, have now led most scholars to allow for the existence, in at least preliminary form, of a Gnosticism independent of

Christian influence although growing up in similar conditions and from similar origins—sectarian Judaism.[1] Both Gnostic and Catholic religions are strongly dualistic and have much to say about the world tyrant of the combat myth, both have redemption theologies, and both show a remarkable development of the brief Yahwist myth of Adam and Eve. In fact, these three ingredients are closely connected. Before we follow the transformations of apocalyptic Judaism in Christianity, we shall look at some of the independent connections of Judaism and Gnosticism, following the same thread as before: the rebellion variant of the combat myth. It is in this independent development that we find the link developed with the story of Adam that played so large a role in Christian narrative.

1. *The Watchers and Eve*

The story of the Watchers, developed in the Enoch literature, was still the tale that accounted for the imperfect state of the world and thus the origin of the world tyrant figure of apocalyptic mythology. But there are signs that, during the first century B.C., the story of Adam and Eve began to be connected with the Watcher narrative. In the third-to-second-century *Book of Jubilees*, of course, the two tales are still widely separated, since the structure and apparent chronology of Genesis is deeply respected by that work's author. But soon after, it seems, the structural parallels of the two stories—and the beginnings of redemption theology—led to the linking of the two, and eventually to the displacement of the Watcher by the Eden story.

A passage in the *Book of Sirach* (180–75 B.C., an apocryphal work also known as *Ecclesiasticus*) says that death is the consequence of a woman's sin,[2] a remark that forms part of a contrast between good wives and bad and that reflects the antifeminism often implied in the Enoch and later literature. But the actual reference of the remark is uncertain. Perhaps the allusion is still to the story of the Watchers, but it is sufficiently ambiguous to suggest that already the story of Eve's temptation had been drawn

[1] Gnosticism is also discussed below, Chapter 18. On the dating question, note that even the generally cautious Wilson 1968:135–39 admitted the likelihood of pre-Christian Gnosticism; see Pearson 1980. For reviews of the scholarship in this rapidly moving field, see Bianchi (ed.) 1967, Rudolph 1969 and 1971, Charlesworth 1976, Layton (ed.) 1981, Barc (ed.) 1981, and Stone (ed.) 1984. The bibliography of Scholer 1971 is annually supplemented in *Novum Testamentum*. A good introduction for the nonspecialist is Jonas 1970 or Pagels 1979.

[2] *Book of Sirach* 25.24, for which see the RSV; cf. below, n. 15.

toward the lustful angel incident, especially if the singular "woman" is not to be taken as a general reference to womankind.

Similarly, when the *Wisdom of Solomon* (second to first centuries B.C.) says, "God created man for immortality, and made him the image of his own eternal seed; it was the envy of the devil [*diabolos*] that brought death into the world, and they that belong to his world experience it,"[3] the reference may be either to the Watcher story or to Eden and its aftermath—Cain's murder of Abel. It implies the idea of an independent cosmic tyrant who opposes the will of God, developed already in apocalyptic circles, and may be the earliest explicit connection between the adversary and the origin of death. Death follows upon the rebellious Watchers' lust (the slaughter of their giant offspring), but it is the story of Eden which most clearly makes death the consequence of sin. This passage may thus be an instance of the overlapping of the two tales.

Soon there is definite evidence of this link. A late section of the Enoch literature, not found among the Qumran scrolls but eventually included as chapters 37–71 of the Ethiopic *Enoch*, probably dates from late in the first century B.C. or early in the first century A.D. In this section, which is known as the "Parables" or "Similitudes of Enoch,"[4] the Watchers have new names, and one of them, Gadreel, takes over the function of Asael in the Aramaic texts—the invention of war and the teaching of metallurgy. But he also gets a further credit:

> Gadreel: this is the one who showed all the deadly blows to the sons of men; and he led astray [seduced] Eve, and he showed the weapons of death to the children of men, the shield and the breastplate and the sword for slaughter.[5]

What is significant about this casual but momentous addition to the activities of the lustful Watchers is that, first, Eve is seen to be parallel to the "daughters of men" who attracted the angels, and second, that the tempting serpent is simply absent. Eve's seducer too is an angel.

This figure normally became Sammael in the Targum and in rabbinic

---

[3] *Wisdom of Solomon* 2.24. See the RSV and Clarke (ed.) 1973; cf. D. S. Russell 1964:200. The passage may be an early version of the Cain-Seth contrast, on which see below. The opposition of the Qumran texts between sons of light and sons of darkness is now being read into the text of Genesis.

[4] On the dating, see Greenfield 1973:xvii, *contra* Milik 1976, and cf. Knibb 1979, Stone (ed.) 1984:398–403, and Black 1985:183–89. The question is of some importance because the "son of man" passages are found only here in the *Book of Enoch*.

[5] *Enoch* 69.6 in Knibb 1978:161. Milik 1976:98 uses the word "seduced." On the name, see Black 1985:246.

tradition, but in a text known as the *Apocalypse of Abraham*, preserved only in Slavonic translation but datable to the same period that inspired the Syriac *Baruch* and the *Apocalypse of Ezra*, the seductive angel is called Azazel. As in the Enoch tradition, this is the evil being who "scattered over the earth the secrets of heaven and rebelled against God" and who is banished to the bowels of the earth (chap. 14). But the visionary here is Abraham, not Enoch, and he sees a world much more firmly divided between the forces of God and the Adversary. Some people, the descendants of Abraham, are set apart at the right side of the picture, but those on the left are mostly assigned for vengeance and destruction at the end of the world. The pageant of human history concentrates on the consequences of Adam's sin and includes a vision of "fornication and those who desired it" stuck in "the lower depths of the earth" (24.5–7).[6]

Once the identification between the lustful angels and the seducer of Eve was made, it proved difficult henceforth to dissociate Eve's sin from lust, whether her own, the angel's, or occasionally Adam's. And this angelic intrusion into the Eden story brought with it not only the overriding sexual interest of the Enoch literature, but also (and oddly) the ideas of perfect wisdom, of teaching, and of narcissism that we have followed as they evolved in the rebel angel tradition from the Ezekiel passage about the Prince of Tyre: "You were full of wisdom, perfect in beauty. . . . Your heart was proud because of your beauty: you corrupted your wisdom for the sake of your splendour."[7] Ezekiel may have been thinking of Adam when he wrote his splendid denunciation of that hybristic prince, but if so the later tradition referred the passage to the rebellious angels; almost no one else, certainly not those who read the Yahwist with any attention, thought of Adam in this way. Adam makes no other significant appearance in the canonical scriptures of Judaism, and his story, until these apocalyptic developments, had nothing to do with the subsequent

---

[6] See Bamberger 1952:46–49. On the dating of *Apocalypse of Abraham*, see Stone (ed.) 1984:416–18. Azazel is equated with "impiety" and "perdition" (29.7). At one point he is depicted between Adam and Eve, with wings, a dragon's body, and human hands and feet (23.9–11), but the latest editor, R. Rubinkiewiecz in Charlesworth (ed.) 1983:684, takes this to be a Bogomil-influenced elaboration. For Sammael in the Targum, see Etheridge 1862:164–70 and Bowker 1969:132, 142; for Pirke Rabbi Eliezer, see Evans 1968:58 and Nickelsburg 1981:529. On the dating, see Jung 1926, Bowker 1969:14–35, Vermes 1970, Alexander 1972, and Segal 1977. See generally Tennant 1903:174–237.

[7] Ezek. 28.12–17. See above, Chapter 6.6. Cf. Ezek. 1.26: "and upon the likeness of the throne was the likeness of man ['adam, anthrōpos] above it." On the tradition of throne and Merkabah mysticism which depends from this verse, see Scholem 1960:40–77 and Quispel 1983.

fate of mankind. How then did this remarkable fusion of the Adam and Eve myth with the Watcher rebellion come about?[8]

2. Adam and Original Wisdom

The key is the growth within apocalyptic Judaism of a new kind of literature, the Adam books. These Adam books seem to have developed in the context of redemption theology and are probably echoed in the link of Adam and Christ in Paul's theory of redemption.[9]

Again, the immediate precursor of this development would seem to have been the Enoch literature, for it is there that the Edem myth, like the flood myth, receives unexpected modifications. The story is still not the one it would become in a Gnostic context, but it is already heading in that direction. In one of his visionary journeys, Enoch says,

> I came to the Garden of Righteousness, and saw beyond those trees many large trees growing there and of goodly fragrance, large, very beautiful and glorious, and the tree of wisdom whereof they eat and know great wisdom. . . . Then I said, "How beautiful is the tree, and how attractive its look." Then Raphael the holy angel, who was with me, answered me and said: "This is the tree of wisdom, of which thy father old and thy aged mother, who were before thee, have eaten, and they learnt wisdom and their eyes were opened, and they knew that they were naked and they were driven out of the garden."[10]

In this apocalyptic context, then, the tree of knowledge was now understood to confer not the moral consciousness of good and evil, but rather wisdom.[11] Any reference to a prohibition on this wisdom is omitted, and the expulsion from the garden seems to result from Adam and Eve lamenting their nakedness. The prohibition is similarly omitted from the version of the story in the *Book of Jubilees*, which is here as anxious as we have seen in its use of Mastema to protect God from any embarrassment. It also omits the questioning of Adam and Eve after their meal, which might imply God's ignorance and the fears he expresses lest they eat of the tree of life and so become immortal, which certainly imply his jealousy. The tree that caused the trouble is simply "the tree in the midst of the gar-

---

[8] For a detailed account from a different point of view of the relations of Adam and Watcher stories, see now Stroumsa 1984:17–35, 82–88.

[9] Brandenburger 1962 is the fullest discussion. See below, Chapter 14.

[10] *Enoch* 32.3–6, in Charles (ed.) 1913: vol. 2, 207.

[11] Widengren 1951. See above, Chapters 1.3 and 10.1, for ambivalent trees.

den." The result of eating from this apparently harmless tree is again that Adam and Eve know their nakedness and leave the garden ashamed. Paradoxically, however, this is presented as a blessing to man, since the wearing of clothes puts him above the animals and enables the author to criticize the Gentiles who "put off their clothes"—that is, the Greeks who were introducing naked gymnastics.[12] The author is actually so anxious to get mankind clothed that he has Eve dress herself in fig leaves before she passes on the fruit to Adam.

The stress on wisdom rather than obedience or moral consciousness owes more to the Priestly editor's insistence that Adam was made in the image of God than to the childlike, naive pair of creatures represented in the Yahwist's original story. It is this perfectionist version of Adam and Eve[13] which, with certain important exceptions,[14] dominates the tradition henceforth, especially as Adam, Eve, and then their son Seth take over some of the functions of Enoch as visionary and teacher of revealed wisdom. The *Book of Sirach*, for example, taking the development a step further, claims that at their very creation God endowed Adam and Eve with "insight and understanding" and even "taught them good and evil."[15] This kind of midrash clearly reverses the ideas in the Yahwist's myth and makes it difficult to see how such wise people could have fallen for the serpent's trick. Indeed, the perfectionist Adam did not develop without misgivings among certain theologians. Another tradition was also current, as in the *Apocalypse of Abraham*, which developed the idea of Adam and Eve as the first sinners, if not as the cause of subsequent sin. Obviously, since the new interest in Adam developed within the context of redemption theology, Adam must have done something that required redemption. But Adam the hapless sinner, whom we soon meet in some Jewish and Christian contexts, was difficult to reconcile with the wisdom tradition; indeed, it would take considerable ingenuity to bring them together. The new Adam literature includes both aspects, but it is the wise father of mankind who dominates it, the Adam, for example, of the *Wis-*

---

[12] *Jubilees* 3.31. Charles 1913: vol. 2, 17, compares 1 Macc. 1.13–14.

[13] Tennant 1903:242–43. Williams 1927:43, Jervell 1960:52–69, and Evans 1968:11–25 all discuss the resulting diverence between "maximalist" (perfectionist) readings, deriving from P, and 'minimalist," deriving from J. See the references in Kittel (ed.) 1951: vol. 2, 394–97, on *eikon*, image, esp. in Philo. The contradiction is between Gen. 1.26–27, where man (and woman) is made in God's image, 2.7, where Yahweh himself makes Adam out of earth (the "golem"), and 2.21–23, where he uses Adam's rib to make Eve. Cf. Moore 1927–30: vol. 1, 479, and Segal 1977:53–57.

[14] For Irenaeus, see below, Chapter 19.

[15] *Book of Sirach* 17.1–11; but cf. the antifeminist passage cited above at n. 2.

dom of Solomon, where we learn that Sophia (Wisdom) "kept guard over
the first father of the human race, when he alone had yet been made; she
saved him after his fall, and gave him the strength to master all things."[16]

3. Origins and Texts of the Adam Books

The first Adam books may have been composed as early as the first century B.C. and probably circulated among some of the same sectarian Jewish groups (scattered throughout the diaspora but especially strong in Palestine itself and in Alexandria) among whom the Enoch literature was
popular.[17] It seems to have been the development of redemption theology
in sectarian circles like Qumran which encouraged this new emphasis on
Adam and his brood. On the one hand, these Adam books show strong
links with the apocalyptic Enoch tradition; on the other, they already contain many of the redemption ideas that were soon to be so radically developed in Gnosticism.

Most of the Adam books are preserved only in late Syriac, Armenian,
Ethiopic, Slavonic, or even Arabic versions, considerably altered by
Christian editing from their original states and so of little use for argument about the original nature of the cycle. There is one Syriac text, called
the *Testament of Adam*, whose first half at least may go back to pre-Christian sources, perhaps even to the Qumran community.[18] The original
work from which the Slavonic *Book of the Secrets of Enoch (2 Enoch)* derives
may also have come from the same sectarian Jewish circles. At one point
it actually refers to a "Book of Adam and Seth."[19] But the chief surviving
works upon which the reconstruction of the Adam books must depend
are the *Vita Adae et Evae* (Life of Adam and Eve) and the misnamed *Apocalypse of Moses* (divergent redactions, in Latin and Greek respectively, of a
common Hebrew or Aramaic original), and the recently discovered Nag
Hammadi text, the *Apocalypse of Adam*. The latter is definitely Gnostic,
though probably early, since it lacks any obvious Christian allusions or
elaborate speculation about "archons" and "aeons" so common in other

---

[16] *Wisdom of Solomon* 10.1–2. But note that, although Adam here introduces a catalog of
seven righteous men, he is the only one who is not called "just."

[17] For the links between the Enoch and Adam traditions, see Nickelsburg 1981:526–33.

[18] Denis 1970:11 and Charlesworth 1976:912, but see now the caution of Stone in Layton
(ed.) 1981: vol. 2, 556. Nickelsburg in Stone (ed.) 1984:111 makes a good case for seeing an
earlier "Testament of Adam" beneath the Greek version.

[19] Until now, however, the importance of this Slavonic work has been seriously overes-
timated, and I argue in the Excursus below the reasons for excluding it as evidence for the
early Satan tradition.

Gnostic texts. It seems to refer to, or depend upon the prior knowledge of, certain sections of the original work upon which the Latin *Vita* and the Greek *Apocalypse of Moses* are based.

This original book, written in either Hebrew or Aramaic, we shall henceforth call the "Book of Adam." The quotation marks, rather than italics, should warn the unwary that the book does not actually survive in its original form.[20] Unfortunately, the difficulties of reconstructing the book have some bearing on our argument, so we must be clear how tentative our more precise conclusions are. But we can say generally that the book told a midrashic story of the lives of Adam and Eve after their expulsion from Eden until their deaths.

The first problem is that the two translations of the book differ very widely from each other, although with considerable overlap. We are especially interested in three of the stories told, but they are not all contained in both versions. Second, the Latin version, the *Vita Adae et Evae*, already shows several Christian interpolations in its earliest version, which cannot be definitely dated much before the fourth century. Third, the story it tells about Satan, absent from the Greek version, has been seriously misunderstood in the past. Some of these problems will become clearer as we proceed, taking up each of the three stories in turn and following them through their transformations. The Greek version probably dates from the first century A.D., so we shall begin with a story told in that version and see how it has changed in the Latin.

4. Seth and the Oil of Mercy

The Greek book is the oldest known source for the popular medieval story of Seth and his quest for the oil of mercy,[21] a story that in Christian circles was eventually linked with the history of the holy rood.[22] Briefly, the story is as follows. Adam, being now 930 years old and ill, is approaching death. He summons his sons to him, of whom the third-born,

---

[20] On the date of this original Adam book, perhaps even first century B.C., see Sharpe 1973 and Charlesworth 1976:74. Milik 1976:45 pointed to evidence of "second Adam" speculation already in the second century B.C., now supported by Black 1985:20 on *Enoch* 90.37. Nickelsburg 1981:525–30 points to evidence of more than one "Book of Adam," although his argument seems unnecessarily complicated. On the Gnostic *Apocalypse of Adam*, see below.

[21] If Quinn 1962:27 is right, the very term "oil of mercy" may have originated in the Greek book.

[22] The earliest extant Western version combining Seth and Holy Cross legends is ca. A.D. 1170. See Quinn 1962:11, and 97 for an older Slavonic version.

Seth, offers to get the fruit of Paradise to heal him. Adam does not want this fruit, however, and tells Eve and Seth to get instead "the tree out of which the oil floweth." They are to put earth on their heads as a sign of penitence and pray. On their journey they meet a wild beast, but "the image of God" in Seth overcomes his ferocity. When they arrive, God sends the archangel Michael to refuse Seth the oil of mercy and to promise instead that it shall be given to the people of God at the end of time.[23]

Sources or analogues for this tale are numerous and widespread. Apart from the Canaanite *Epic of Keret*[24] and the folktale known in the Grimm version as "The Water of Life,"[25] they also include the story of Gilgamesh's journey to "the Land" where the supernatural trees are guarded by a bestial creature whose ferocity is mysteriously dispelled. Like the Sumerian Gilgamesh tale, the conclusion of Seth's expedition is also ambivalent—no oil now but a promise of deferred success.[26] This conclusion fits well the apocalyptic eschatology—it is clearly a midrash on the exclusion of Adam from Paradise lest he eat the tree of life, and it has several apocalyptic parallels[27]—but the quest itself has all the earmarks of spiritual allegory. The tree is no longer the great cedars of the magical "Land" or the mysterious but inaccessible tree of Genesis; it is the mystical tree of life.[28] Oil from this tree was used for the anointing in Gnostic ritual, and also suggests the names Messiah and Christ.[29]

Part of the interest of this story concerns the role of Seth. His only mention in Genesis is as the third son of Adam, but in sectarian Jewish and then in Gnostic contexts he became, as the favored third son of folktale,

---

[23] *Apocalypse of Moses* 9.3–14.3, cf. 27.2–28.4.

[24] ANET 142–49. Cf. Virroleaud 1941 and Cross 1973:180 for links with the rebel tradition.

[25] S. Thompson 1946:107–8 and Bolte and Polivka 1913–32: vol. 2, 394–401, 511, where the possible links with the Seth story are discussed. See also Aarne and Thompson 1964:92 (Types 550–51) and S. Thompson 1955–58, Motifs E80, FI11.

[26] Above, Chapter 1. Nickelsburg 1981:517 calls this the "kerugma," the essential message of the book: Adam (and all mankind) must learn to bear the consequences of his sin and die. Nickelsburg also notes the parallel with the probably earlier *Testament of Abraham*, in which Death becomes a satanic figure in the heavenly court; cf. Stone (ed.) 1984:63.

[27] *Testament of Levi* 18.11 (now know from Qumran fragments) has the Messiah "give to the saints to eat from the tree of life," while *Enoch* 25.4–5 says the tree of life at the judgment "will be given to the righteous and the humble [and] . . . the chosen" (in Knibb 1978:113–14 and Black 1985:171). The sequence of allusions begins in Ezek. 47.12.

[28] See Butterworth 1970 for general discussion. Cf. Widengren 1951 and above, Chapter 10.1. The A text of *2 Enoch*, on which see the Excursus below, has a similar great tree with oil flowing from its roots, another sign of probable links between the original of this work and the "Book of Adam."

[29] *Gospel of Philip* 73.15–19 in Robinson (ed.) 1977:144. See also Ginzberg 1910–38: vol. 5, 119 n. 113, Chadwick (ed.) 1953:342 n. 2, Quinn 1962:26, and Pagels 1983:168.

the type of righteousness. Indeed, the three sons of Adam were identified by some Gnostics, both Sethian and Valentinian, with the three classes of men and with the three kinds of substance: the material (Cain), the psychical (Abel), and the spiritual (Seth).[30]

How far this elevation to cult status had gone by the time of the "Book of Adam" is unclear, but the figure of Seth represents quite clearly the evolution in a mystical direction of the apocalyptic Enoch. In the Enoch books, Michael gives Enoch the promise of the tree of life he here gives to Seth[31] and the allusion to "the book of Adam and Seth" in the oldest part of 2 Enoch gives both Seth and Enoch the same function as recorders of the truth for future generations, originally the task of the antediluvian sages of Babylon.[32] In addition, Enoch and Seth exchange places as the organizers of Adam's funeral.[33]

Unlike Gilgamesh, who defeats the adversary either by a trick or by force, Seth quells the "wild beast" who gets in his way (probably an allusion to the root idea of ś*ṭn*, to oppose or obstruct) by means of "the image of God" in himself. Genesis says that Seth was made in the image of Adam, but since it also says Adam was made in the image of God it required no grand metaphysical speculation to draw the obvious conclusion. Nonetheless, the idea of God's image in man acquired important philosophical implications in Philo and in Paul, while among the Gnostics it supported the concept of a mystical connection between the highest god, called Anthropos or Adamas, and the divine part of man.[34] The donor episode of our basic narrative pattern thus became the vehicle of a vital spiritual doctrine.

Seth's quest for the fruits of paradise, and especially Michael's promise

[30] Below, Chapter 18 n. 29. See Pearson 1980:152; Layton (ed.) 1981:506 and passim; Hippolytus, *Refutatio omnium haeresium* 5.20; Irenaeus, *Adversus haereses* 1.7.5; and Pearson 1981:473–75. The link between the favored third-son motif, as in AT 550–51, and Seth's prominence has not been explored. On the Cain-Seth contrast, see below and Chapters 17.1 and 18.4.

[31] Above, n. 27. See also Quinn 1962:27–30, Nickelsburg 1981:526–29, and Stone (ed.) 1984:114.

[32] Berossus in Heidel 1963:117–18; J. R. Smith 1975. See above, Chapter 8. See also now Stroumsa 1984:108–10, and below, n. 73.

[33] See Ginzberg 1910–38: vol. 5, 158 n. 59, 126 n. 137; *Apoc. Mos.* 35–43, *Vita* 46–48. Cf. Altmann 1944.

[34] Gen. 1.26–27, 5.3. See n. 13, above, and 1 Cor. 11.7, 15.45–49, 2 Cor. 4.4, and Col. 1.13–15, where the idea applies to Christ. On the Gnostic development, see Schenke 1962 and now Stroumsa 1984. Cain is made in the image of the devil; see below and Chapter 18.1 on John 8.44 and 1 John 3.9. On Philo's view of Seth, see Kraft in Layton (ed.) 1981: vol. 2, 437–38, and Pearson 1983.

that the oil from the tree will be given at the end of time to God's people, shows that the Adam story was already developing in the context of apocalyptic redemption theory. The further elaboration of the story shows this even more clearly as the narrative takes on definite Gnostic, and then Christian, meanings.

The Gnostic *Apocalypse of Adam* consists of a revelation received by Adam and passed on to Seth. Adam explains how he and Eve fell into the power of death and of the despicable creator God.[35] Heavenly angels, however, came and woke him from the "sleep of death" to teach him true knowledge. This was passed on to Seth and his seed and is to be preserved until "the Illuminator" comes "to leave for himself fruit-bearing trees" and to rescue the true believers from "the day of death."

In this work, Seth does not himself go on a quest to Paradise, except in the sense in which he, like other Gnostics, is told by Adam that "those who reflect on the knowledge of the eternal God in their hearts will not perish, for they have not received a spirit from this kingdom alone; they have received it from the holy angels."[36] Instead Seth's function is to preserve and hand on the Adamic revelation—as usual in Gnostic contexts, the revelation *is* the redemption.

In the second or perhaps third century A.D., however, the quest story reappears in the "Descensus ad Inferos," which draws an obvious narrative and theological parallel between Seth's unsuccessful journey and Christ's descent to redeem the righteous dead and harrow hell: Christ is to deliver to Adam the very oil Seth sought.[37] In the "Descensus" version of Seth's story, Michael prophesies that the son of God shall baptize Adam

[35] See below, Chapter 18, for discussion of the demiurge.

[36] *Apoc. Ad.* 78.8–27, trans. in Robinson (ed.) 1977:256–74. Most subsequent quotations from the Nag Hammadi texts are from this collection.

[37] See Hennecke and Schneemelcher 1963–65: vol. 1, 445–81, for texts and related documents, such as the *Epistle of the Apostles*, ca. A.D. 160; cf. M. R. James 1953:166–86. The "Descensus Christi ad Inferos" is a Christianized form of midrash, based on Heb. 13.20, Eph. 4.8–9, Rom. 10.7, Rev. 1.18, and esp. 1 Pet. 3.19–20, in which Christ replaces Enoch and preaches to the "spirits in prison" who were once disobedient "in the days of Noah." See Reicke 1964 ad loc. and above, Chapter 11. See also Irenaeus, *Adv. haer.* 4.16.2, 36.4, and below, Chapter 19. The myth has many Near Eastern parallels. See Cooper 1983 for a basic version in exegesis of Ps. 24. Just as Seth took over Enoch's role among some Gnostic groups, so did Christ among other sects, perhaps under the influence of Gnostic myth-making. The "Descensus" was probably composed in Christian Gnostic circles in the second century. It was then incorporated by the fifth century into the *Gospel of Nicodemus*, which survives in both Greek and Latin manuscripts and is the source of the popular medieval story of the Harrowing of Hell. See J. B. Russell 1981:120–22, but also Layton (ed.) 1981: vol. 2, 521, 553, and Stone (ed.) 1984:116–17.

in the Jordan and anoint him with the oil of mercy. He is then to bring him back to Paradise, to "the tree of mercy."[38]

The idea that Christ was actually to redeem Adam himself goes much further than Paul, who cites Adam's life simply as a parallel and cause of Christ's. The idea of Adam's redemption seems to have developed in Gnostic and Manichaean circles. One Manichaean document expressly says that Christ awakened Adam, baptized him, and gave him to eat of the tree of life.[39] The idea had an obvious appeal at both the popular level and the Gnostic level, where Adam was seen to have a mystical identity with all mankind. In any case, it remained part of the Seth story when, perhaps in the fourth century, the "Descensus" version was incorporated into the Latin adaptation of the "Book of Adam," the *Vita Adae et Evae*.[40] There Michael again prophesies that Christ will baptize Adam, anoint him, and then lead him back to Paradise and the tree of mercy. In addition, since baptism does not in itself constitute redemption, a further motif was later added to the Christianized *Vita* story: Seth returns from Paradise with a twig that becomes the wood of the cross, the sign of genuine and complete redemption.[41] So the Seth story continued to evolve as it incorporated the necessary ingredients of redemption within the Christian system, but already in its earliest non-Christian form it contained the redemptive promise.

5. The Serpent and Satan

Other stories told in the original Jewish "Book of Adam" also represent interesting development of the Enochic literature, and confirm the impact on the Adam story of the apocalyptic combat myth and the promise of redemption in the end-time. Here at last the serpent of Genesis is linked to the apocalyptic adversary, and his name is explicitly Satan.

Early in the *Apocalypse of Moses*, Adam briefly tells the story of his expulsion from Paradise, but there is no mention yet of the serpent, only of

---

[38] Hennecke and Schneemelcher 1963–65: vol. 1, 182. Cf. James 1953:126–27 and *Gospel of Nicodemus* 19. On parallels with the Armenian *Penitence of Adam*, see now Nickelsburg 1981:521 and Stone (ed.) 1984:114–15, 117.

[39] Widengren 1946:123.

[40] For discussion of the Greek and Latin texts, see Denis 1970. The translation and commentary of L.S.A. Wells in Charles (ed.) 1913: vol. 2, 123–54, prints the versions in parallel columns, but see Nickelsburg 1981:520. I have not had access to the new version in Charlesworth's second volume.

[41] Quinn 1962:86–101. The *Vita* version of the quest forms chaps. 30–44.

an "enemy."[42] Soon, however, Eve herself tells a much longer version of the story. She tells of her temptation by Satan, who appears first as an angel and then as a serpent, but she tells this only after a long account of the seduction of the serpent by Satan. "Be my vessel," says Satan to snake, "and I will speak through thy mouth words to deceive her." As she tells her story, then, Eve ought to be quite clear who the enemy is.[43]

She and Adam had been given charge of separate parts of the garden, she explains (thus accounting in typical midrashic fashion for the puzzling detail of Adam's absence), and they had, moreover, been given angels to guard them. But "[the serpent] hung himself from the wall of paradise, and when the angels ascended to worship God, then Satan appeared in the form of an angel and sang hymns like the angels. And I bent over the wall and saw him, like an angel."[44] Eve then reports their conversation:

> He said to me, "Are you Eve?" and I said to him, "I am."
> "What are you doing in Paradise?"
> And I said to him, "God set us to guard and to eat of it."
> The devil [diabolos] answered (through the mouth of the serpent), "You do well, but you do not eat of every plant."

The Armenian recension of this work omits the phrase "through the mouth of the serpent," so avoiding the abrupt transition from angel back to snake. But the phrase is there in the Greek. In fact, it is probably the author, rather than the transcribers of the text, who is having difficulty deciding whether the one talking is the serpent hanging on the wall or Satan the chorister over the wall. We have already heard that Satan will speak through the serpent's mouth. Perhaps the two are supposed to be working in cahoots, one on each side of the wall.[45] What is clear is that the real tempter is now the devil. *Diabolos*, we have seen, was the word used generally in the Septuagint to translate the Hebrew *śṭn*. By now both words imply the whole apocalyptic combat myth. The tempter is the cosmic adversary.

Eve goes on to relate the actual event, and here we may spot the final fusion of the Watcher angel tradition of lust between women and angels

---

[42] *Apoc. Mos.* 7.2; cf. *Vita* 33.2.

[43] *Apoc. Mos.* 16.5. The text seems a bit muddled, however, and it is not clear whether Eve is still the narrator.

[44] *Apoc. Mos.* 17.1.

[45] For the recurring problem of whether the devil-serpent could actually have been inside Paradise, see below, Chapter 25.2. For the relevance of the inside–outside dilemma to the story, see below, Chapter 15.

with the Eden story. Literal seduction by an angel is here combined with the story of the tree and its fruit. Eve opens the gate to Satan. Then the tempter gets Eve to swear she will persuade Adam to eat too, whereupon "he went and poured upon the fruit the poison of his wickedness, which is lust, the root and beginning of every sin, and he bent the branch on the earth and I took of the fruit and ate."[46] This ingenious combination of the two tales succeeds in explaining why the fruit of the Eden tree was so harmful, but only at the expense of transforming the tree itself. It is no longer the tree of the knowledge of good and evil, but any "branch" that the serpent has poisoned with his lust.

As in the wisdom tradition, the sin of the Yahwist's tale, violation of the prohibition on the knowledge of good and evil, is absent from the "Book of Adam." To the philosophically inclined, ignorance was not an acceptable state for this first pair of humans, and thus neither ignorance nor knowledge could have caused the Fall. Lust, however, with its conventional implications of an opposition between mind and body, would be more appealing as an explanation of the Fall within this sectarian, ascetic, and proto-Gnostic context. Indeed, most subsequent commentators, from the rabbis to Augustine (at times), would allow the disobedience of the prohibition in the Yahwist's story to be pushed aside or replaced by lust as the grounds of the Fall.[47]

This version of Eve's temptation is akin to, and perhaps derives from, the overlapping in the later Enoch literature (not found at Qumran) between the lustful Watcher and the Eden story. The "Parables of Enoch," in which the parallel is explicitly drawn, is probably more or less contemporary with the "Book of Adam" and may even derive from similar sectarian circles. But in Eve's narrative in the "Book of Adam," Semihazah-Azazel-Gadreel-Sammael has finally become the devil, Satan.

Eve's seduction by Satan also influenced another contemporary development of Old Testament narrative. The Job story evidently continued popular among certain Hellenistic-Jewish groups. The Greek Septuagint text differs and shows considerable development from the Hebrew text that underlies the Masoretic version. The story is quoted as an instance of patience in the New Testament letter of James (5.11), and a variant of it survives in a work called the *Testament of Job*, composed in Greek around

[46] *Apoc. Mos.* 19.1–3.

[47] On the prevalence of the lust theory among the rabbis, see Tennant 1903:156–60 and Bamberger 1952:106–34. For the Gnostic link of Eve and Sophia in the "lewd Prunikos" figure, see Dahl 1981:706–12, and below, Chapter 19.1.

the turn of the era, perhaps in Egypt. Its writer feels compelled to insist that Satan derives his limited authority from God,[48] whom he "implores" to allow access to Job's property. But that word is all that is left of the scene in the heavenly court.[49] Instead the Satan figure has now become the enemy of contemporary dualism rather than the licensed prosecutor of the Bible. He is called "the devil" (3.3, 17.1), "the evil one" (7.1), the deceiver and an idol (3.6), and the battle enemy (18.5),[50] as well as Satan.

At times he is a comic character in this text. He spends his first three chapters treating with Job via the doormaid because Job locks himself away and refuses to see his caller. He disguises himself as a beggar, as king of the Persians, as a whirlwind, or as a bread-seller who trades his wares for the hair on Job's wife's head (23.11) and then follows her stealthily home. By the time his role in the book is over, he is a rather pathetic figure. Job here responds to his wife's "Curse God and die" speech with some eloquent praise of patience, and then says, "Do you not see the devil standing behind you and unsettling your reasoning so that he might deceive me too? For he seeks to make an exhibit of you as one of the senseless women who misguide their husbands' sincerity."[51] Job is thus represented as a second Adam figure, but one who will not fall for the ruses of his wife and the devil this time. Quickly this scene too becomes comic. Satan is so cowed by now that he hides behind Job's wife, a parody of the Sammael scene in Eden, and Job has to call him to show himself. Eventually he comes out and says, "Look, Job, I am weary and I withdraw from you, even though you are flesh and I am a spirit. You suffer a plague but I am in deep distress. We are like two athletes wrestling, and you have me pinned." The athlete-of-Christ idea is common enough in certain New Testament contexts, chiefly Johannine, but here Job seems to function as a prototype of the would-be initiate in an early form of throne-mysticism.[52] At one point Satan himself seems to have a throne, but other textual variants make it Job's throne throughout. Since this is the point at which Satan appears as wind while Job is sitting on his throne, one wonders if this is not an advance version of Martin Luther's encounter with the devil.[53]

[48] *Testament of Job* 8.1–3 in Charlesworth (ed.) 1983:842.
[49] Cf. *Test. Job* 20.2–3. On the testament genre, see Stone (ed.) 1984:325–55.
[50] *Test. Job* 47.10 also mentions the adversary, but may be a later addition when the work was taken up by the Montanists (Spittler in Charlesworth [ed.] 1983:835). Cf. Kee 1974.
[51] *Test. Job* 26.6. With Job 2.9, cf. *Test. Job* 24–25.
[52] Kee 1974; *Test. Job* 27.2–5.
[53] *Test. Job* 20.5 (in Charlesworth [ed.] 1983:847). Cf. above, Introduction, n. 1.

6. The Birth of Cain

The Adam book nowhere tells the Watcher story. Instead it is Eve's narrative that accounts by implication for the subsequent state of mankind. Adam is told, for example, that he will henceforth have to suffer the hostility of "wild beasts," and Seth's return to Paradise was indeed impeded by one such beast.[54] This hostility generalizes the enmity forecast by Genesis 3.15 between the seed of serpent and woman, a verse that we know from other allusions could now be read in terms of the apocalyptic combat myth.[55]

This combination also gave rise to another narrative episode by an all-too-easy step. Eve was seduced by the serpent-devil, and the result was Cain. Seth, however, was Adam's own son, and the difference in "seed" continued to be reflected in their descendants. The story of Cain's adulterous conception occurs in the Targum, is implied in the New Testament, and is common in Gnostic contexts. In the *Apocalypse of Adam*, for example, which probably derives it from the "Book of Adam," we hear Adam reassuring Seth that he is indeed his son[56] but that the demiurge "created a son from himself and Eve your mother." At this point, unfortunately, three lines are missing, but when the text is legible again Adam is feeling "sweet desire" for Eve as a result of the (missing) thoughts he has been having.[57] It is possible that this story is already implied by the barnyard orgy scene at *Enoch* 85–90, since by contrast Seth is there represented as a pure-white bull.[58] Certainly the gulf between Cain and Seth is already equivalent to that between the sons of darkness and the sons of light at Qumran.[59] In Philo, Seth becomes allegorically the "seed of human virtue," sown from God, and he is placed in deliberate antithesis to Cain.[60] It looks as if Philo knows and opposes a more literal, and extreme, form of the antithesis. The Greek version of the "Book of Adam" also appears to refer to this story of Cain's birth.[61]

---

[54] *Apoc. Mos.* 24.4, cf. *Vita* 37.1.

[55] See below, Chapters 14.2 and 19; Nickelsburg 1981:517. For the homology with Christian martyrdom (e.g., "I realized I was to fight not with beasts but against the devil," *Passio Perpetuae* 10.14), see J. B. Russell 1981:72.

[56] *Apoc. Ad.* 66.4–7. See below, Chapters 17.1 and 18.4.

[57] *Apoc. Ad.* 66.25–67.4 in Robinson (ed.) 1977:257. Cf. Dahl 1981:695.

[58] See above, Chapter 8.2, and Pearson 1981:491.

[59] On the children of God idea, see also R. E. Brown 1982:384–93.

[60] Philo, *De posteritate Caini* 172–73, commenting on Gen. 4.25. See Kraft in Layton 1981:457–58, and Pearson 1980 and 1981.

[61] *Apoc. Mos.* 2; see Nickelsburg 1981 for this interpretation.

The narrative sequence of the Eden story was thus made parallel with that of the Watcher myth; angelic lust for woman leads to the "mixing" of the two and so to the birth of offspring (giants/demons/Cain) whose murderous deeds represent, and even account for, the subsequent state of the world. It looks as if the traditions represented by the "Book of Adam" were shifting the focus of human loathing from the Watcher angels of the Enoch books to the supernatural adversary who was now being read in the Eden story—Satan.

7. Satan's Envy of Adam: A Gnostic Allegory

Although the devil of Eve's narrative in the *Apocalypse of Moses* has the characteristics of the cosmic adversary, there is no suggestion, as there was in the Enoch tradition, that the angelic rebellion was actually caused by the angels' lust. Instead, Eve's story presupposes a being who is already hostile and who brings with him "the poison of his lust." A new story was needed to fill the breach left by the suppression of the Watcher tale, and this was quickly supplied. The story is absent from the Greek but present in both the Armenian and the Latin versions of the "Book of Adam."[62] In some ways it is a variant of the story given to Eve in the Greek version, but now Gnostic ideas have definitely intervened. The angelic rebellion is explicitly linked to the Adam and Eve story, and the motivation is not lust but envy.

The context of the story is as follows. After their expulsion, Adam and Eve separate, and once again Eve is tempted by the devil. Disguised this time as a shining angel,[63] he persuades her to abandon her penance and leads her back to her husband. Adam reproaches Eve bitterly for being deceived a second time, and amid much lamentation Eve asks the devil why he keeps persecuting them.

The devil now explains to them, patiently and at length, that Adam and Eve are the cause of his own expulsion from heaven. His story blends in a most ingenious and plausible way the figure of the rebellious Shining One, Son of Dawn, from Isaiah 14 with the creation of mankind.

---

[62] Nickelsburg (1981:524–25 and in Stone [ed.] 1984:115–16) takes the Armenian *Penitence of Adam* to be an intermediate stage of development between Greek and Latin forms. The devil's story fills the opening chapters (1–22.2) of the *Vita* and concludes with a more elaborate version of the birth of Cain. God then sends Adam seeds to grow food, which looks like an effort to allegorize, or de-Gnosticize, the Seth story.

[63] *Vita* 9.1. See below, Chapter 14.3 at n. 16. The shining angel is a reminiscence of Lucifer; see above, Chapter 6.5.

When thou wast formed, I was hurled out of the presence of God and banished from the company of angels. When God blew into thee the breath of
life and thy face and likeness was made in the image of God, Michael also
brought thee and made (us) worship thee in the sight of God. . . .

And I answered, "I have no need to worship Adam." And since Michael
kept urging me to worship, I said to him, "Why dost thou urge me? I will
not worship an inferior and younger being (than I). I am his senior in the
creation, before he was made I was already made. It is his duty to worship
me." When the angels, who were under me, heard this, they refused to
worship him, and Michael saith, "Worship the image of God, but if thou
wilt not worship him, the Lord God will be wroth with thee." And I said,
"If he be wroth with me, I will set my seat above the stars of heaven and
will be like the highest."

And God the Lord was wroth with me and banished me and my angels
from our glory; and on thy account were we expelled from our abodes into
this world and hurled on the earth. And straightway we were overcome
with grief, since we had been spoiled of so great glory. And we were
grieved when we saw thee in such joy and luxury. And with guile I cheated
thy wife and caused thee to be expelled through her (doing) from thy joy
and luxury, as I have been driven out of my glory.[64]

The devil here constructs, on the basis of the fresh command to "worship
the image of God" in man (Gen. 1.27), a highly plausible account of his
motives. Like the Canaanite Athtar, he is moved to rebel because his authority has been bestowed on another, and like Tiamat, or Kronos and his
Titans, he can claim to be of an older generation. He goes on to stress the
connection between his own punishment and that of Adam and Eve, and
so accounts for his continuing hostility both to God and to man. The story
is a resurgence of an old Near Eastern myth pattern. It is adapted now by
scattered allusions to the Old Testament, but the plot itself has no canonical foundation.

Gnostic literature, on the other hand, offers close parallels. Broadly
speaking, Gnosticism split the biblical God into a transcendent being and
a lower creator being or demiurge. In doing so it carried to a radical conclusion widespread tendencies in Jewish theology to stress the transcend-
ence and unknowability of God.[65] Genesis 1.27 was understood to imply
a link between the true god, Anthropos, and man's image, while conversely the hated demiurge of Gnostic theory was also based on scriptural

[64] *Vita* 13.2–16.4 in Charles (ed.) 1913; vol. 1, 123–30. For parallels, see above, Chapters
2.2 (Yamm), 3.2 (Hephaestus), 6.2, and 6.4.

[65] E.g., Josephus, *Contra Apionem* 2.167. See Pearson 1980:154 and Chapter 18, below.

exegesis. His ignorance, jealousy, and sin are ultimately a midrash on key texts from Exodus and Isaiah where Yahweh boasts he is the only God "and beside me there is no other."[66] In Gnostic systems, the boast is false, and he is variously rebuked from on high: "Man exists, and the Son of man" is one such rebuke that clearly parallels Michael's command to worship man in the *Vita* story.[67] Because of the "inbreathing" of the heavenly spirit, man (Adam) is in fact higher than the demiurge, as Adam explains to Seth in the *Apocalypse of Adam*.[68] Therefore the demiurge tries to keep man imprisoned in the world of death and continues his persecution.

These Gnostic ideas depend heavily on Old Testament citations, but the scriptural allusions are reassembled into a radically new system. The Gnostic attitude to Judaism is one of alienation and revolt.[69] At least in the earliest stages the Gnostics could be called people who were "no longer Jews," a phrase applied by Irenaeus to the Basilidian Gnostics.[70]

The closest parallel, then, to Satan's narrative in the *Vita* is the opening of the Gnostic *Apocalypse of Adam*. Given the Gnostic mythology and thus the exchange of demiurge for devil, this passage could be the same narrative told from Adam's point of view:

> Listen to my words, my son Seth. When God had created me out of the earth along with Eve your mother, I went about with her in a glory which she had seen in the aeon from which we had come forth. She taught me a word of knowledge of the eternal God. And we resembled the great eternal angels, for we were higher than the God who had created us and the powers with him, whom we did not know.[71]

As in the *Vita*, Adam and Eve are angelic and glorious, "higher" than the demiurge and his powers, who correspond to "the angels who were under me" in the *Vita*. The passage continues with the reaction of the demiurge to his discovery of Adam and Eve:

[66] Exod. 20.3–5 = Deut. 5.7–9; Isa. 45.5–6, 46.9. See above, Chapter 5. Cf. *Apocryphon of John* 11.20, 13.9, in Robinson (ed.) 1977:105–6, and Dahl 1981.

[67] *Apocryphon of John* 14.14–15 in Robinson (ed.) 1977:106. See Schenke 1962:64–68, 84–107.

[68] *Apoc. Ad.* 64.14–19 (cf. 15.1–20.31) in Robinson (ed.) 1977:107–10: "And his thinking was superior to all those who had made him."

[69] Jonas 1970:250–53 (on the Greek sources) and Jonas in Bianchi 1967:90–108 (on the Jewish). Cf. Grant 1959:27–38, on which see Pearson 1980:244. See also Rudolph 1978:291–312, Dahl 1981, and below, Chapter 18.4.

[70] Irenaeus, *Adv. haer.* 1.24.6; see Pearson 1980:155.

[71] *Apoc. Ad.* 64.1–19 in Robinson (ed.) 1977:256–57; cf. Nickelsburg 1981.

Then God, the ruler of the aeons and the powers, divided us in wrath. Then we became two aeons. And the glory in our heart(s) left us, me and your mother Eve, along with the first knowledge that breathed in us. . . . After those days the eternal knowledge of the God of truth withdrew from me and your mother Eve. Since that time we learned about dead things, like men. Then we recognized the God who created us. For we were not strangers to his powers. And we served him in fear and slavery. And after these events we became darkened in our heart(s).

The punishment by the demiurge is typically Gnostic, but it parallels the continuing hostility between devil and mankind in the *Vita*. The withdrawal of eternal knowledge corresponds to the expulsion from "joy and luxury," while the new life of fear and slavery under the Gnostic tyrant, with its learning "about dead things," corresponds to the tyranny of death that results for Adam, Eve, and all mankind.[72]

There is other evidence of a relation between the Gnostic *Apocalypse of Adam* and the growth of the original "Book of Adam." The efforts of Seth to find a remedy for death are common to both, and the survey of subsequent history, including the three periods of destruction by flood, fire (Sodom and Gomorrah), and the catastrophe of the end-time, also shows a common tradition. Indeed, the motive for recounting this history is the same in both: the need to preserve the revelation in written form through the catastrophes that will follow.[73] This constant emphasis on Adam's special knowledge is a development of Hellenistic wisdom literature, as we have seen, and it involved a peculiar transformation of the Yahwist's tale. Now Adam is even blessed for his love of knowledge, and in the *Vita* version he is enabled to foretell the future because, he explains, "the rest of the secrets were revealed to me when I had eaten of the tree of the knowledge, and knew and perceived what will come to pass in this age."[74]

The difficulty of more closely dating these various texts makes it impossible to say with certainty what relation the devil's story of his rebel-

---

[72] For the relations among the texts, see Perkins 1977:385–86 and contrast Shellrude 1981. A useful summary now is Stroumsa 1984:98–103.

[73] Perkins 1977:387–90; Stone (ed.) 1984:470–74. These motifs are sometimes identified; see above, Chapter 8, and Fontenrose 1945. The arrangement into three consecutive stages is paralleled at Luke 17.26–32 (cited below, Chapter 13) and 2 Pet. 2.4–10 (cited below, Chapter 20). But see Klijn 1977:121–24 and now Stroumsa 1984:103–13, who shows that the link with the three stelae of Seth goes back to the ancient tradition of buried writings, discussed above, Chapters 1 and 8.

[74] *Vita* 29.2. All of chaps. 25–29, Adam's revelation to Seth, is absent from the Greek version and looks like a reaction to Gnostic ideas.

lion in the *Vita* bears to the Gnostic *Apocalypse*. Perhaps we should posit no more than the independent development, in separate "normative" and radical directions, of a common tradition derived via the original "Book of Adam," from Near Eastern myth and apocalyptic. Yet there seems typically to have been a kind of dialectical relation between Gnosticism and "orthodoxy," whether rabbinic or Christian. The Gnostic defines himself *against* the received tradition of Judaism, and the mainstream, in turn, reacts with a revised or tamer version of the Gnostic idea—gradually defining itself as "orthodox" in the process. Christianity, moreover, would soon find itself in the peculiar position of defining itself against both Judaism *and* Gnosticism. It is therefore tempting to argue that the story of Satan's rebellion in the *Vita* is a deliberate reaction to the Gnostic narrative expressed in the *Apocalypse of Adam* and similar texts. For the Gnostic demiurge who actually created Adam and Eve and then tried to keep them in subjection, the *Vita* substitutes the less subversive idea of a corrupt adversary who in his jealousy tries to challenge the creator, both by setting "his seat above the stars of heaven" and by interfering with the creation on earth when the first plan fails.[75] Otherwise the *Vita* retains the shape of the Gnostic story, and the result is a radically new version, both of the Eden story and of the rebellion myth. Since the devil's narrative contains no definite Christian reference, its author was probably a Jew, if not the original author of the "Book of Adam." But the story would have an obvious appeal to the later Christian editors to whom we owe the Latin *Vita*. For by then, Gnosticism had become a more serious challenge to Catholic Christian theology.

In this chapter we have been able to perceive the context within which the combat myth and the Adam story were first linked. That context was a further development of the sectarian traditions which were linked to the Enochic literature but in which rabbinic Judaism, apocalyptic beliefs, and proto-Gnostic ideas could all still coexist. From a narrative point of view, the Adam story gradually came to substitute for the Watcher story as an account of the adversary's motivation since it could account much better for the adversary's hostility, not so much to God as to mankind. But this narrative thinking was inseparable from the theological idea of redemption from the adversary's tyranny, about which Adam and Eve frequently complain.

[75] See below, Chapters 17–19, for further discussion. My view of this dialectic has certain parallels in, e.g., Schenke 1962:92–94, J.N.D. Kelly 1960 and 1979, Pagels 1976, Segal 1977, and Dahl 1981.

It is possible that the *Vita* story of Satan's fall was intended to connect with an apocalyptic idea already present in the Greek version of the "Book of Adam." We there find for the first time the belief that Adam is eventually to inherit the glory originally possessed by Satan. Adam's soul appears after his death before the throne of God, who promises him that he will set Adam on the throne of his deceiver. "And he shall be cast into this place to see thee sitting above him; then shall he be condemned, and they that heard him, and he shall be grieved sore when he sees thee sitting on his glorious throne."[76] It would certainly not be the first time that Urzeit ideas had developed, in apocalyptic literature, by extrapolation from Endzeit expectations. Thus the final defeat of the adversary was linked to the redemption of Adam, and this link in turn required a further motivation at the beginning of the whole cosmic plot. Given the eclipse of the Watcher story, that motivation was now established by the double, and parallel, falls of Adam and Satan.

If this reconstruction of the elements that make up the *Vita* story should prove accurate, it means that we owe the first recognizably modern version of the Satanic rebellion to Gnostic redemption theory and its narrative context. The idea that Satan's specific sin was the refusal to worship Adam had no impact on standard Jewish literature, but it became the accepted account of the fall of "Iblis" (*diabolos*) in the Quran.[77] It also exerted considerable influence, through the *Vita*, on the Christian Middle Ages.

8. *Excursus: Satan in the Slavonic* Book of the Secrets of Enoch

Almost all discussions in the twentieth century of the early traditions about Satan and fallen angels have made extensive use of a work known as *The Book of the Secrets of Enoch*. It now appears, however, that all the parts of this work that refer to Satan, Satanail, or Sotona are the additions of a late reviser or editor, possibly a fifteenth-century Slavic scholar of the Bulgaro-Serbian school around Vladislav the Grammarian. Whatever sources he used to expand the original text, these additions can hardly be used as evidence for the growth of the Satan myth in the apocalyptic period.

Manuscripts of this work first came to light in the nineteenth century and became known to Western scholars through the edition and Latin

---

[76] *Apoc. Mos.* 39. For the *kābōd* or "glory" in throne-mysticism, see Quispel 1983, and for Ps. 29.3, above Chapter 2.8.

[77] Quran 7.11–24, also 2.30–36, 15.28–44, etc. See Bamberger 1952:112–17.

translation of Matvei Sokolov (1899), the English translation of W. R. Morfill (1896), and a German version by G. N. Bonwetch (1922). R. H. Charles included a revised translation in his *Apocrypha and Pseudepigrapha of the Old Testament* (1913). On the strength of this edition, the book also became known as *2 Enoch*, and most scholars working in other disciplines have continued to refer to Charles.[78] Charles' translation and assumptions, however, are now seriously out of date.

The manuscripts of the *Book of the Secrets of Enoch* are written in the language known as Old Church Slavonic; the earliest dates from the fifteenth century. They preserve the work in two versions: a long form and a short form. The original editor, Sokolov, believed that the long form was the more authentic and that the short form was an inferior abridgement. He further assumed that the long form was a translation of an original Greek work, composed during the first Christian century. It was this assumption that also informed Charles' interpretation that the work was a genuine record of primitive Christianity.

The only scholar to pose a serious challenge to Charles' interpretation before the 1950s was Leo Jung (1926). Jung rejected the supposed date of the original *2 Enoch* because an astronomical argument convinced him that the book could not have been composed before the fifth century and was probably the work of Bogomil heretics between the twelfth and fifteenth centuries.[79]

The Bogomils inherited the Gnostic and Manichaean idea of an independent Being, a satanic adversary, who helped create the world and who was in fact the source of the material universe. The belief owes something to the early penetration into the Slavic world of Manichaeism, and it is connected with local variants of the widespread "Earth-diver" creation myth, which survives today in Eastern Europe.[80] Thus it was logical for Jung to connect the extreme dualism of at least the Satan passages in *2 Enoch* with this heretical tradition.

Meanwhile, a fuller text had been published. It was translated into Hebrew by A. Kahana together with several arguments for a Hebrew original dating from the first century B.C. This work, Kahana believed, was then expanded in a Greek translation, which in turn formed the basis of

---

[78] Charles (ed.) 1913: vol. 2, 425–69. See, e.g., Revard 1980:31, Quinn 1962:25–30 and n. 40, Evans 1968:31–36, 87, 295, and Bamberger 1952:32–34; but now H. A. Kelly 1985:18n.

[79] Maunder 1918; Jung 1926; cf. Rubinstein 1967.

[80] See Hennecke and Schneemelcher 1963–65: vol. 1, 68, 487, Loos 1974, and Dundes 1962a; cf. Long 1963.

the Slavonic version. The Russian scholar N. A. Meshchersky also argued for a Hebrew original of the short form.[81]

In 1952 the French Slavicist André Vaillant published a new edition and translation of the Slavonic texts, in which he showed that the long form was a fifteenth-century expansion of the short form. The short form, then (which differed somewhat from the one given by Charles), was the real translation from the Greek and was thus the only version that could shed any light on the apocalyptic era. The additions of the reviser appear as an appendix on pages 86–119 of his book and contain all three of the passages normally cited in the growth of the Satan legend.[82] Vaillant thus confirmed that all the Satan passages are late and probably owe much to the Bogomil dualists.

Vaillant further assumed, however, that the short form represented the composition of an early Christian, partly because it is apparently cited by Origen[83] but chiefly because Vaillant detected in the constant adaptations of the earlier Enoch books a Christian opposition to Jewish ideas. For example, whereas the Jewish Enoch angrily damns the fallen Watchers at one point, this Enoch manages to reconcile them with God. It is unclear, however, on what grounds Vaillant takes this notion to be Christian: it was in fact rejected as an Origenian heresy by the Council of Chalcedon (A.D. 543).[84]

Vaillant's assumption has been challenged forcefully on several fronts. J. T. Milik has argued that all of the Slavonic 2 Enoch must date from the ninth or tenth centuries, and assumes that the author was a Greek monk.[85] I find his "lexical argument," based on the nonoccurrence before the ninth century of one putative Greek word in the (perished) original, to be singularly unconvincing. On the other hand, I find the arguments of the great Gershom Scholem far more congenial.[86] He sees in 2 Enoch an adaptation, in a more obviously Gnostic direction, of the visionary journeys in the earlier Aramaic Enoch books. He dates the original (for which he too thinks Hebrew a likely language) to early in the Christian era, but finds no real traces of Christian influence or doctrine. Indeed, the argu-

---

[81] See references in Bamberger 1952:289–90 and in Charlesworth (ed.) 1983:94.

[82] The three passages in Charles 1913: vol. 2, 425–69, are 18.3–6, 29.4–5, and 30.11–31.8. See Vaillant 1952:93, 99, 101–3 and also n. 90, below.

[83] Origen, De principiis 1.3.2: "Sed et in Enoch his similia describuntur," referring to the creation, not described in 1 Enoch.

[84] Vaillant 1952:x. See below, Chapter 21, and Andersen in Charlesworth (ed.) 1983:96.

[85] Milik 1976:107–15.

[86] Scholem 1960:40–79 and Scholem 1962:62–64.

ment of S. Pines seems to confirm the origin of the work among sectarian Jewish circles, perhaps related to the Qumran sect and sharing certain concepts with the Zervanite movement in Zoroastrianism.[87] The short form of the book cites the "Book of Adam and Seth," which points to an origin among groups of sectarian Jews similar to those studied earlier in this chapter. But however legitimate that assumption may be, we cannot now assume that 2 Enoch is the primary text used by the other works. Still less can we argue the primacy of the long form, as Charles constantly did.[88]

What we thus lose, above all, is the early date for a theory of pride as the cause of Satan's fall. For this there may be hints in the Adam books, but we must wait until Origen, perhaps even Augustine, for a fully developed theory.[89] But the link between the Luciferan rebel and the lustful angels, argued by previous scholars from the long form of 2 Enoch, I have traced instead in the earlier Enoch and Adam traditions. There is no need to abandon it.

I would also suggest that the sources of what the putative fifteenth-century editor added may also be found in Jewish or Jewish-Gnostic literature. There is, for example, a long passage about Adam's creation and fall through the devil's envy,[90] which results in God's curse on ignorance. This seems to derive from a version of the "Book of Adam," since the informing idea is similar to the devil's narrative in the Latin *Vita*. Here, however, as in the Greek version, the devil is already fallen. The absence of any reference to the serpent also recalls the Alexandrian Jewish wisdom tradition. In its present form this passage involves two Slavonic puns and so must be original with that language. The devil will become a demon (*běsi*) because he fled (*běže*) from heaven, and he will become Sotona because his name was Satanail. Not only does this second pun appear to be obscure to modern editors, but it changes in different manuscripts, a sure sign that it was obscure to the copyists too. However, it seems to involve play with the verb "to create" (*sŭtvori, sotvori*). One manuscript makes this character create a demon, others a "heaven." So the obscurity or uncertainty has collected around exactly the issue on which Gnostic and orthodox teachings diverged—demiurge or devil, creator god or fallen angel. The manuscript confusion at this point is regrettable but

---

[87] Pines 1970. See further, Greenfield 1973:xviii–xxi and Stone (ed.) 1984:406–8.
[88] Andersen in Charlesworth (ed.) 1983:94 hedges on this question.
[89] Schmidt 1951, but see Russell 1977:194–95 n. 34.
[90] 2 Enoch 30.11–31.8; Vaillant 1952:101–3; Andersen in Charlesworth (ed.) 1983:152–54.

understandable—great anxiety attached to the issue. From the psychological point of view this anxiety is expressed and contained in myths of anal birth or abortion, common in Gnostic systems,[91] but from the historical point of view, as I argue below, it is the principal reason for the devil's rise to power, and the Slavonic scribes would be aware of the Bogomil heresy.

The devil's own fall is given two accounts in *2 Enoch*. One is simply a retelling of the Watcher story, also present in the short form and very close to the version of *1 Enoch* 6–11[92] but with the name of the leader added in the long form: Satanail. The other is a variant of the rebellion myth, interpolated into the creation account. The second day, Monday, is devoted entirely to making armies of angels, including stars. Rock produces fire, which in turn produces angels, "the bodiless ones." The combination recalls Ezekiel's stones of fire, but the procedure seems to be conceived as the striking of fire from flint. Thus far the short and long forms agree, but then the long form adds:

> I [God] gave orders that each should stand in his own rank. But one from out of the order of archangels deviated, together with the division that was under his authority. He thought up the impossible idea, that he might place his throne higher than the clouds which are above the earth, and that he might become equal to my power. And I hurled him out from the height, together with his angels. And he was flying around in the air, ceaselessly, above the abyss. And thus I created the entire heavens. And the third day came.[93]

This story uses language reminiscent of the Isaiah or Ezekiel rebellion myths (throne, equal to God), but the prominence of fire, absent in Genesis and different from Ezekiel, suggests the pressure of some myth of a fire-stealer like Prometheus. The leader is nameless, except for the secondary chapter headings of one manuscript, where he becomes Satanail. The rebellion here has no motive; it is merely attached to the second day of creation because the angels were made then. In this respect, the passage differs from Byzantine lore, in which Satan fell on the fourth day,[94] but there was considerable flexibility in both Jewish and Christian speculation, the angels being absent from Genesis 1 or the related scriptural pas-

---

[91] Compare Dundes 1962a on "anal birth" with Stroumsa 1984 on "abortions."

[92] *2 Enoch* 18.3 and *1 Enoch* 6.6 have the same number (200) of princes of the Watchers, "Grigori."

[93] *2 Enoch* 29.4–6 in Charlesworth (ed.) 1983:148. Cf. Jude 6 and 13b below, Chapter 20 n. 2.

[94] Andersen in Charlesworth (ed.) 1983:149.

sages like Proverbs 8.25–29, Job 39.11, or Psalm 104.4–9. The passage in 2 *Enoch* probably reflects rabbinic and early medieval concern with the hexaemeral tradition.

The most plausible account of the history of this curious book would seem to be as follows. It was originally composed as a further addition to the Enoch literature, probably in sectarian Jewish circles of the first century A.D. The language was Hebrew, and the work represents one of the earliest stages of the Jewish throne-mysticism (ascent through the seven spheres to the final vision of the Lord's throne), that eventually became Merkabah mysticism. It was then translated into Greek like the other Enoch literature. The Greek version survived in the Orthodox church until the twelfth century at least, since it appears to be cited in a work of that date, an apologetic book entitled *Dialogue Between a Patriarch and a Roman*. The first Slavonic translation was made in the ninth or tenth century, and then an erudite antiquarian composed an expanded version of the Slavonic text in the fifteenth century. He filled out his original with many allusions to esoteric lore such as the mystical meaning of Adam's name, the true nature of Paradise, the fall of Satan and his subsequent envy of man—by now a commonplace through the popularity of the Adam book—and the Alexandrian and Gnostic tradition of God's curse on ignorance.

Although we thus lose an early date for the story of Satan's pride, we gain a more balanced sense of how the narrative could be conceived. The difference between the short and the long forms of 2 *Enoch* shows that the Watcher and the Isaiah-based rebellion stories continued to develop separately, at least in the Eastern world, even when they had already influenced each other. The Watcher story is present in the short form, but it is linked to the other myth only in the long form—and by as clear an interpolation as one could wish to find. At least within this tradition, use of the Isaiah story as an explanation of the devil's fall is a later development and needs to be reconciled (hence the interpolation) with the Watcher myth.

THIRTEEN

APOCALYPSE AND CHRISTIAN
COMBAT

"A GOOD TREE bringeth not forth corrupt fruit; neither doth a corrupt tree bring forth good fruit" (Luke 6.43, KJV). The meaning of this verse was, it seems, a "celebrated question" in the early years of the church,[1] since it assumes a world divided into good trees and corrupt trees and does not explain how some trees had originally been corrupted. It thus leaves open the possibility, apparently confirmed elsewhere in the Christian canon, that the world had been thus divided since the beginning. "He that committeth sin is of the devil," says the first letter of John, "for the devil sinneth from the beginning. For this purpose the Son of God was manifested, that he might destroy the works of the devil."[2] Echoing but intensifying the Essene language about the sons of light and the sons of darkness, the letter continues: "Whosoever is born of God doth not commit sin; for his seed remaineth in him; and he cannot sin, because he is born of God. In this the children of God are manifest, and the children of the devil [*tou diabolou*]." Given such passages, and the absence from the canonized texts of any explicit account of the origin of evil or the evil one (both *tou ponērou* in the genitive), the commentators would require considerable ingenuity to reincorporate the rebellion myth, in whatever form, into their own version of Christian doctrine. The antagonism of the sides in the apocalyptic combat myth had reached such intensity that it was a genuine intellectual challenge to imagine how things could ever have been different.

Indeed, if the dualistic adaptations of the combat myth within Jewish apocalyptic posed serious theological problems for the more reflective among the rabbis, the role of the myth in Christianity would raise even graver difficulties. It would eventually, as in the Judaic context, challenge the assumption, inherited from the covenant tradition, that mankind (or Israel) was somehow responsible for the dreadful state of the world, but it would also complicate and leave ultimately unresolvable the question of

---

[1] Origen, *De principiis* 2.5.4.
[2] I John 3.8 (KJV); see R. E. Brown 1982:384–93, and below, Chapters 17.1, 18.4, and 25.

what exactly was the mission and accomplishment of Christ. The rabbis were soon able to turn Judaism away from the dualistic narratives of the apocalyptic sects,[3] but Christian theologians were impelled to include the myth of angelic rebellion, in some form, within the orthodox tradition. For the apocalyptic combat myth is an essential informing principle of the New Testament.[4]

No doubt Christianity quickly became much more than another apocalyptic sect. There is indeed an anti-apocalyptic tendency within the Christian tradition, due partly to the impact of Greek thought and most evident in the Alexandrian speculation of men like Clement and Origen. But the first Christians of Palestine and Syria were Jews, they moved easily in the world of apocalyptic fantasy, and it was chiefly through their ingrained habits of thought that the combat myth, with its inherent difficulties, was bequeathed to the subsequent tradition.

The gospels of Matthew and Luke, drawing on a common source, whether "Q" or oral tradition, both make Jesus allude to the Enoch alignment of flood and end-time. In Matthew's version, he says, "As were the days of Noah, so will be the coming of the Son of man. For as in those days before the flood they were eating and drinking, marrying and giving in marriage, until the day when Noah entered the ark, and they did not know until the flood came and swept them all away, so will be the coming of the Son of man." To this Luke adds the typologically equivalent catastrophe, Sodom and Gomorrah, creating a three-stage history like the Adam books.[5] Matthew also makes Jesus allude to the Enoch punishment of the angels (25.41), while Luke (23.30) gives to him a saying, varied by Revelation 6.16, inviting rocks and mountains to fall on the people at the end-time. This recalls the fate of Asael.

One of Paul's letters anticipates the imminent end with the following typically apocalyptic language: "For the Lord himself shall descend from

---

[3] A good instance is the objection of the Jew Trypho to Justin's proposition that the angels could sin (*Dialogue* 79). On the decline of the Enoch literature among the rabbis, see Bamberger 1952:42–45, 89–111.

[4] This view is not universally accepted. The area of disagreement is akin to that which we have noted in Old Testament scholarship—the extent to which mythological language is taken seriously by those who use it. For a range of views, see Dibelius 1935 and Bultmann 1957, the starting point for the "demythologizing" controversy, Käsemann 1964, Förster 1964, Hartmann 1966, Conzelmann 1969 and 1973, Doty 1972, Perrin 1974, Kee 1977, and Lincoln 1981. See below, Chapter 14.1–2, for more discussion.

[5] Matt. 24.37–39, Luke 17.26–32. See above, Chapter 12.7 n. 73. For the eschatological differences between Luke-Acts and Revelation, see Conzelman 1973 and Drury 1976.

heaven with a shout, with the voice of the archangel, and with the trump of God.'' Those still alive shall be caught up together with those dead in Christ "in the clouds to meet the Lord in the air."[6] This way of thinking echoes the common fantasy of an ascent, like Enoch's, above the corrupt Watcher angels who rule in the air. In Mark, probably the earliest of the gospels, we read a passage that the other synoptic gospels repeat: "But in those days . . . the sun shall be darkened, and the moon shall not give her light, and the stars of heaven shall fall, and the powers that are in heaven shall be shaken. And then shall they see the Son of man coming in the clouds with great power and glory."[7] The stars here are familiar from the Enoch tradition, and the powers (*dunameis*) in heaven supply the connection with the rebellious cosmic powers we have already met in Jewish apocalyptic.

Apocalypses have many forms in the Jewish tradition, but one that is especially relevant to the New Testament is the "apocalyptic discourse," a speech telling what to expect when the end actually comes. This form, of which Mark 13, from which we have just quoted, is an instance, has been analyzed thus:

> There is usually a description of the "woes," the climactic catastrophes marking the death throes of human history as now known. This is followed by an account of the form of God's eschatological intervention, either directly or through an eschatological redeemer figure. Then there is an account of the final judgment itself and a description of the punishment of the wicked and the eternal blessedness of the people of God that will follow.[8]

So the standard shape of the apocalyptic discourse is very much like the general pattern of a folktale, such as we have discovered it, for example, in the Gilgamesh legend and in various forms of the combat myth. This is especially true if the "woes" are attributed to an adversary (Propp's "villainy"); the Markan apocalypse, for example (13.6–7), anticipates false prophets who "shall come in my name," as well as "wars and rumours of wars."

In a similar work, the Jewish *Testament of Moses*, a work that dates from the first century A.D., we have a model instance:

> And then his kingdom shall appear
> Throughout all his creation,

---

[6] 1 Thess. 4.16–17 (KJV). See below, Chapter 14.
[7] Mark 13.24–26 (KJV), part of the so-called Markan apocalypse.
[8] Perrin 1974:77, referring to Hartmann 1966:145–59; cf. Collins (ed.) 1979.

And then Satan shall be no more.
And sorrow shall depart with him.
Then the hands of the angel shall be filled
Who has been appointed chief,
And he shall forthwith avenge them of their enemies.
For the Heavenly One will arise from his royal throne,
Yea, he will go forth from his holy habitation
With indignation and wrath on behalf of his sons.
And the earth shall tremble, even to its ends shall it be shaken,
And then high mountains shall be made low
And the hills shall be shaken and fall.
The sun shall not give her light,
And in darkness the horns of the moon shall flee
Yea, they will be broken in pieces.
It will be turned wholly to blood.
Yea, even the circle of the stars shall be disturbed.
And the sea shall retire into the abyss,
And the fountains of waters shall fail,
Yea, the rivers shall vanish away.[9]

The discourse ends with the people of God looking down upon the destruction of their enemies. Not only is the pattern itself familiar from the ancient Near Eastern combats, but there is a remarkable continuity of imagery—mountains dissolve, the sun is darkened, the stars are disturbed, and the sea-river dries up. Above all, there is the formulaic idea, which we first met in the *Book of Jubilees*, and which is implicit throughout the New Testament, that "Satan shall be no more."

The most elaborate instance of Satan's role in Christian mythology occurs in the wilderness temptation scenes, but the one that most clearly establishes his continuity with the cosmic adversary of the Near East is in the Book of Revelation. This odd document, purportedly by one John (of Patmos), is the only full-length apocalypse that found its way into the Christian canon. In spite of frequent disapproval from churchmen, including Martin Luther, it has exerted an enormous influence. The work is a kind of palimpsest, with its various layers having both Jewish-Christian and Johannine affiliations, and it shows thorough familiarity with the Jewish apocalyptic tradition. God's wrath employs typical cosmic instru-

---

[9] *Testament* (or *Assumption*) *of Moses* 10.1–2. See Charlesworth (ed.) 1983:931–32 and Charles (ed.) 1913: vol. 2, 400. Cf. Stone (ed.) 1984:344–49, and for the parallels in the *Book of Jubilees*, see above, Chapter 9 nn. 13–15. Jude 9, the dispute between Michael and the devil for the body of Moses, may allude to this work.

ments: the four horsemen (pestilence, war, famine, death), the angels with their trumpets, and Apollyon, the angel of the abyss. Generally the influence of the Book of Daniel is evident. The adversary first appears as a wild beast (*thērion*) rising out of the abyss to attack the witnesses of God, recalling both the Leviathan-Yamm figure and the opponent of Seth in the "Book of Adam."[10]

It is chapter 12, however, that is most important for the role of Revelation in the mythology of Satan. Here is the only explicit reference in the New Testament to a war in heaven, and so the key text for the war in later tradition. Although there is some influence from Greek myths, the main source of the narrative in Revelation 12 is the apocalyptic combat of Judaism. The adversary appears here as a dragon, *drakōn*, the word used in the Septuagint to translate the Hebrew *tannīn*.[11] He has seven heads, like the Greek hydra or the Ugaritic monster *Šhilyaṭ*, and the detail suggests how archaic are the traditions preserved here; although Psalm 74, for example, mentions the many heads of the dragon and Leviathan, no Old Testament text records the number as seven.[12] The dragon's tail sweeps one-third of the stars down to earth, a passage that recalls the Labbu dragon[13] and has been frequently understood as a reference to the fall of the angels. It should be read in the light of the Enoch tradition, which in turn is linked to the myth of the rebellious son of the dawn, reflected in Isaiah 14 and in the Phaethon story. By now the connection of angels and stars was a commonplace.[14]

The dragon's function here, as in many similar folktales or myths, is to lie in wait for the child of a woman in labor, to devour it as soon as it is born.[15] This symbolism has been much disputed, but in its achieved form

[10] Rev. 11.7; cf. Dan. 7.3, 7, *2 Esdras* 11.1, and *2 Baruch* 29.4. On the whole subject, see Gunkel 1895:360–61, Bamberger 1952:62–64, and Collins (ed.) 1979. *Abyssos* is the Septuagint noun used to translate the Hebrew *tehōm*. Yarbro-Collins 1976:165–70 offers a good discussion of the beast and the Antichrist tradition, showing the mixing of oral and literary influences. See also R. E. Brown 1982:428–32 and below, Chapter 17.1.

[11] E.g., the great sea monsters of Gen. 1.21 and Ps. 91.13, 148.7.

[12] See above, Chapter 2 n. 55, 57, 60.

[13] Heidel 1963:142 and above, Chapter 2.1. Cf. Schmidt 1951, and see Motif G361.1.4 in S. Thompson 1955–58. Parallels with Dan. 8.10–11 and Nonnos, *Dionysiaca* 1.163–81, are discussed by Yarbro-Collins 1976:78.

[14] Compare Jude 6 and 13, where the fallen angels are replaced by wandering stars. See above, Chapters 6 and 8, and J.N.D. Kelly 1969. See also below, Chapter 20.

[15] For the folk traditions, see Tale Types 300, 315, and 590 in Aarne and Thompson 1964 and Propp 1972. Using Fontenrose 1959, Yarbro-Collins 1976:56–71, 245–70, argues that the dragon-woman-child narrative is derived from the Pytho-Leto-Apollo myth (Leto fused with Isis). She presents good evidence that the myth was well known in Asia Minor in the

within Revelation 12, the implications are clear: the woman is Israel and the child is Christ. The atonement theory of the early church fathers begins here.[16] In a different version, the role of the dragon is played by Herod in the infancy narratives. Here the dragon is thwarted because the moment the child is born it is caught up to the throne of God. The woman is pursued by the serpent into the desert, but she escapes, in a passage that blends various elements of the combat and the Exodus traditions, possibly even including a narrative such as Achilles' fight with the river.

> And the serpent spat water like a river from his mouth behind the woman, to sweep her away with the flood. But the earth came to help the woman, and the earth opened its mouth and swallowed up the river which the dragon spat from his mouth. And the dragon was furious with the woman, and he went off to fight against the rest of her children, who observe the commandments of God and have the testimony of Jesus. And the dragon took up his stand on the sand of the sea.[17]

We have met before, in Greek myth, a dragon who takes his stand beside the cosmic waters, and we have met connections between the monster enemy and the sea. We have met woman as earth (Gē) in the Greek tradition and, in the Anat of Ugaritic myth, a woman who opposes and overcomes the Leviathan-dragon.[18] We have seen before the blending of the Exodus "dry land" and the defeat of the cosmic water enemy. But here all these

---

first century, and the argument is persuasive. She also finds two separate sources within Rev. 12, redacted first by a Jewish writer and then by a Christian editor. I am not sure one can be quite so precise, since time scale is regularly confused in apocalyptic and the renewed strength of the adversary in Rev. 12.12 is a widespread motif, as in the Antaeus legend and S. Thompson 1955–58, Motif B11.11.1. It is also a slot in our basic combat pattern (see Appendix). There are good psychological reasons why the dragon-woman-child triangle should be so common a tale-type; see Rank 1959 and Carsch 1968:475–76. The Moses-in-the-bullrushes story is a variant, co-opted by the Christian birth and infancy legends. Another variant, which may also have influenced Rev. 12 directly, is the myth preserved in Hesiod about the Gē and Hera figures, discussed above in Chapter 3. Like the Adam myths discussed in Chapter 12, this one too has Gnostic parallels in the Demiurge-Sophia-Adam triangle, more particularly in the Demiurge-Illuminator-Seth myth of *Apoc. Adam* 78–80 (J. T. Robinson [ed.] 1977:260–62); cf. Yarbro-Collins 1976: 69–70. On the Fontenrose methodology and its limitations, see Appendix.

[16] Below, Chapters 19.1 and 21.2.

[17] Rev. 12.15–18. My translations here stay close to the familiar KJV where possible. On the apparent allusion to Gen. 3.15, see below, Chapters 16, 17.1, and 19.2. For possible links with the mysterious Qumran hymn, 1QH3.6–18 (Gaster 1964:142–44), see Teyssèdre 1985b:263–71.

[18] See Song of Songs 6.10 and Pope 1972, ad loc., on connections with Anat. See also above, Chapter 2.8 and 3.2. On the link with Isa. 26–27, see Court 1979:112.

traditional motifs are connected explicitly, if rather clumsily, with the most influential of all allusions to the combat: sandwiched between the two passages that refer to the woman, her child, and the dragon chase in the desert (12. 1–6, 13–18) comes the war in heaven itself.

> And there was a war in heaven, Michael and his angels fighting with the dragon. And the dragon and his angels fought, and he did not prevail, neither was there found a place anymore for him in heaven. And the great dragon was cast out, that old serpent, who is called the devil and the Satan, he who deceives the whole world, was cast out onto the earth, and his angels were cast out with him.
>
> And I heard a loud voice in heaven saying: "Now is the salvation and the power and the kingship of our God and the authority of his anointed, for the accuser of our brothers has been cast out, he who accused them day and night before our God. And they overcame him. . . . On account of this rejoice, heavens and you that dwell there; woe to the earth and the sea, for the devil has descended to you with great fury, knowing that his time is short."[19]

Here in one text are combined most of the elements of the mythological tradition we have been studying.

To summarize briefly, here is a fall from heaven, like that of Helel ben Shahar-Phaethon, or Hephaestus; here is a creature who was once in heaven but who no longer has a place there; here is the leader and his Watcher angels, opposed by Michael and his angels, from the Enoch literature and Daniel; here is the accuser from the court of God, the Satan or devil of Job and Zechariah; here is the wanderer, *ho planōn tēn oikoumenēn holēn*, who wanders/leads wandering, astray, the whole world—the *agent provocateur* of Job; here too is the independent Satan who challenges the power of heaven, the dragon-monster of Greek and Near Eastern tradition.

When did all these events—the war and the Fall, the accusation and the challenge—take place? The whole chapter is ostensibly a vision, beginning from the sign of a woman which appeared in heaven, and therefore the events take place in the "visionary present." But visionary tenses are notoriously slippery; the narrative past tense is dominant throughout, but the voice that speaks from heaven says, "Now is the salvation . . . ," and the speech concludes with what amounts to a future: "Woe to the earth and the sea, for the devil has descended . . . , knowing that his time is

---

[19] Rev 12.7–12. One Armenian recension substitutes "Beelzebul" for "the devil"; see Souter (ed.) 1947, ad loc.

short." We have found in other apocalyptic texts that the time is often both beginning and end, as well as visionary present, and the Book of Revelation continues the ambivalence. There is fodder for those readers who would later find here either the war of the beginning or the apocalyptic war of the end-time, even the present time of Christ's earthly appearance and the beginning of the end.[20]

"John of Patmos" follows this chapter about the dragon with two beasts, one from the sea and one from the land. The first beast derives its power from the dragon and transmits it to the second. The allusion is clearly to Job's Leviathan and Behemoth but mediated by the apocalyptic tradition, as found in *Enoch* 60.7–8 or in *2 Baruch* 29.4, where the two beasts are anticipations of the last days and where they serve as food for the faithful during the general destruction—a messianic banquet.[21] But here they have a patently allegorical and historical function. They represent the Roman Empire and its emperor (one beast deriving its power from the other), whether Nero or Domitian. Thereafter in Revelation there is only one beast, who is the Antichrist, the earthly representative of Satan as the Christ is God's. The Antichrist means generally the Roman Empire, or its specific emperor, and again we are confronted with the common apocalyptic tendency to substitute cosmology for politics.[22] The mark of the beast is placed on all who agree to worship the idolatrous image of the emperor.

Eventually, John sees the Messiah on his white horse engage the beast in battle and defeat him. The beast is supported by the kings of the earth. On his defeat he is hurled into the lake of fiery brimstone, together with the "false prophet," while his supporters are slain by the sword that issues from the Messiah's lips. This rider on a white horse has affinities with Qumran beliefs—transformations of Israel's (and Canaan's) holy war ideology.[23] This whole section of Revelation is dense with allusions to the Exodus, to the Isaian apocalypses, and to Ezekiel's parallel visions.

The beast and his followers have now been overcome, and only Satan,

---

[20] Jerome held that the war happened at the same time as the fall, but Gregory the Great dated the war to the end of time. Gregory's view predominated until the twelfth century, when Peter Lombard reverted to Jerome's chronology and Aquinas followed him; see J. B. Russell 1981:194, also Revard 1980:131–35.

[21] Above, Chapter 11 n. 12. See also Gunkel 1895:51–61, Caird 1966:161–62, Pope 1965:268–79, and Yarbro-Collins 1976:164–67.

[22] Yarbro-Collins 1976:172–84 and Court 1979:122–53. "Nero redivivus" is actually a variant of a widespread legend, applied, e.g., to Adam, King Arthur, and John F. Kennedy; see Utley 1957. For the Antichrist, see Bousset 1896, Dahl 1964, and below, Chapter 17.1

[23] See references in Ford 1975:313–25, Gray 1965:35–36, and Anderson 1967:161–62.

the dragon himself, remains. In his next vision, John sees an angel descend from heaven,

> holding in his hand the key of the bottomless pit and a great chain. And he seized the dragon, that old serpent, who is the devil and the Satan, and bound him for a thousand years, and threw him into the pit, and shut it and sealed it over him, that he should not deceive the nations anymore until a thousand years were ended. After that he must be loosed for a little while. (20.1–3)

The allusion to the Enoch tradition, in which the rebellious Asael is bound in the pit,[24] should now be obvious, and again the time scheme is obscure—narrative past, visionary present, and apocalyptic future being all combined. The text continues with a vision of the millennial kingdom to be enjoyed by the martyrs and those not marked by the beast—the first resurrection.

Then comes the final episode in Satan's career. He will be released from his prison and arouse the nations, Gog and Magog, to gather them for battle. They marched (past tense suddenly) up to lay siege to the camp of the saints and the beloved city (presumably the millennial Jerusalem). But "fire came down from heaven and consumed them; and the devil who had deceived them was thrown into the lake of fire and brimstone where the beast and the false prophet were, and they will be tormented day and night for ever and ever." (20.9–10) There follows now the vision of the Last Judgment, when Death and Hades too are thrown into the fiery lake. Then comes "a new heaven and a new earth," imitated from Isaiah 65.17, "for the first heaven and the first earth had passed away, and the sea was no more." The sea here is not the ordinary sea that sailors cross; it is the mythological enemy, the Ugaritic Yamm blended with the hostile Red Sea of the Exodus. The visionary is then carried away, like Enoch, to a high mountain from which he can see the holy city Jerusalem descending out of heaven studded with jewels (like the garden of God in Ezekiel) and reuniting God with his people. The final chapter of Revelation opens with a vision of the river of the water of life, flowing from God's throne through the city, "and on either side of the river there was a tree of life with its twelve kinds of fruits, yielding its fruit each month; and the leaves of the tree were for the healing of the nations." Night is no more. The book closes with a coda cursing those who misuse the words of the prophecy by adding or subtracting anything, and blessing those who wash their

---

[24] *Enoch* 10.4–6. See above, Chapter 8.

robes, that they may enter the city by the gates. Even here at the end, then, we find yet another allusion to the Satan tradition, namely, to the Zechariah passage in which the accused appear before the heavenly court in clean linen, and so confound the accuser.[25]

The apocalyptic imagery of the Book of Revelation continues and extends the common tendency of Judaism to project political repression onto the cosmic stage—and then to work out the fantasy of revenge in a combinaton of military and symbolic visions (the white horse and its supernatural rider).[26] It tells a story of the enemy punished and presents this ultimate event as if it were happening in the visionary's presence. Yet despite the powerful emotion of the visionary's voice, his obvious commitment to the glorious outcome, he does not present himself, even in Enoch's tentative manner, as in any way a part of the action he envisions. The events are all entirely beyond him; he is no more than a spectator of the grand drama. This is consistent with the broad combat tradition in that the events take place on a scale well out of human reach, between overwhelming supernatural forces.

The Satan of Revelation, then, represents an ontological dualism that is more extreme than anything we have noticed in the Jewish tradition. True, he is allowed, like his predecessors in Job and Zechariah, to remain in heaven and accuse the saints, at least until the angels expel him. But there is nothing in the Jewish tradition which says that, at the end of the Messiah's millennium, Satan *must* (*dei*) be released from his chains to stage his final rebellion. The text does not make clear the source of this obligation, or who is bound by it, but Satan seems to enjoy at least a limited measure of independence, and even, what would cause trouble among the church fathers, actual rights, such as could appear to limit the power of God.

[25] Zech. 3.3–5. See above, Chapter 5.
[26] On this fantasy and its subsequent history, see esp. Cohn 1977.

FOURTEEN

PAULINE ENEMIES

THE PREVIOUS chapter marshaled evidence for the impact on the New Testament of the combat myth, chiefly in its Jewish apocalyptic form. But the earliest documents included in the Christian Testament are the letters of Paul's mission to the Gentiles, and we might therefore expect them to provide the best indication of the story told by the primitive church. So naive an assumption will quickly be dissipated by a reading of modern commentaries. The strength of Paul's personality and the historical importance of his teachings are not at issue, but the meaning of his words on any given subject is very much open to debate—and the problems begin with the question of which words are actually Paul's. The only letters whose authenticity has not been seriously challenged are those to the Galatians, the Corinthians, and the Romans, but even there grave textual and interpretive problems arise. Paul's authority quickly became so vital that his followers often claimed to be writing in his name, and soon various rival theologies were fathered on him. On the question that faces us—Pauline use of the combat myth—the most divergent views have been advanced.[1]

From Paul's own account in Galatians, as well as from the less reliable traditions preserved in Acts, it appears that the first Christians were already debating the meaning of the new revelation and that one of the chief issues was the extent to which the revelation was actually new. This quarrel continues in various forms among modern theologians, although given the nature of the evidence, the argument is necessarily more about Paul than Christ. The more extreme camp would isolate Paul radically from his first-century milieu, while others would assimilate his views either to the apocalyptic tradition or to the newer Gnostic tendencies. Major historical questions are at issue. What stage had Gnosticism reached in Paul's world? What difference did the fall of Jerusalem in A.D. 70 make? How quickly did the first Christians start to wonder why the anticipated

[1] The most extensive modern studies are perhaps Bornkamm 1966 and 1971 (following Bultmann 1951 and 1955) and the commentaries of Käsemann, now available in English (1980, cf. 1964). On the combat question, contrast Caird 1956 and Carr 1981. On Paul's own "authority," see Schütz 1975.

end did not arrive? Such questions, however, are often inseparable from theological debate. What does apostolic authority amount to? What did the earliest Christians believe, and so what should their modern counterparts believe? Which among the different views of Paul or his contemporaries are indispensable to Christian faith, and which are merely part of the ground in which those views developed, or, in one of the more persistent forms of that question, what is real history and what is mere mythological dressing?

On the problem that concerns us here, the more extreme theologians take the view that, although there are frequent references to Satan there are no undeniable allusions to the hostile angels or rebellious cosmic powers within the genuine Pauline corpus. Belief in such creatures is a product of second-century Gnostic vagaries, and it was only then that Paul's language came to be understood as referring to spirit enemies. At the other extreme, second-century Christian letters and other documents are held to show only a minor development from what is already present in Paul, in spite of the major changes of the political world and the enormous and rapid growth of the various sects that called themselves Christian.[2] In each case the argument depends as much on the context in which one wishes to read Paul's language as on the reconstruction of the texts themselves.

In my own view there is little to be gained by isolating Paul so radically from the background and tradition we have been studying. Indeed, one thereby loses the sense of just how interesting and original a thinker Paul was. On the other hand, a distinction is to be made between Paul's own guarded use of the myth language and its proliferation in Gnostic (or in anti-Gnostic) contexts. Otherwise the genuine Pauline dilemma, and the subtle tensions of his language, will be lost. Paul's teaching is informed by the combat tradition, but his emphasis is on the new situation brought about by the death and resurrection of Christ. These events have radically altered the world, so that the warring forces of the older tradition, as we see them at Qumran, for example, have been reconciled by the cross. Exactly how this was done is, as Paul allows, "a mystery," but he appears to view the event of the crucifixion as a brilliantly paradoxical transformation of the old eschatological hope: death has been overcome by Christ's

---

[2] The tradition from Gunkel 1895, Dibelius 1909, Bultmann 1951 and 1955, Cullmann 1957 and 1962, Caird 1956, Grant 1959, Schmithals 1971 and 1972 (developing Bultmann's ideas about Gnosticism), and Lincoln 1981 stresses the angelic powers, while Schniewind 1951, Lee 1970, and Carr 1981 represent opposing views. See also the review of Carr by Hooker 1983.

death and resurrection. Paul's task is to disseminate this message, and the opposition he encounters is a sign of the lingering power of the adversary and of the old world-view in the human soul. Every time Paul uses the word Satan he is referring to the opponent of human salvation, not to the figure who does battle with Michael in the Book of Revelation. Satanic opposition takes the form of opposition to Paul, so completely does Paul identify himself with the Christian message. The struggle with this opposition is being won, he is confident, but not in any way that the older mythological tradition would lead one to expect, and not, therefore, in a way that nonbelievers in Paul's interpretation could be expected to understand. Paul's use of combat language is thus either muted or ironic, and these are the qualities of his teaching that are lost once his followers, including the authors of the deutero-Pauline letters, have different kinds of opposition to face.

1. Paul and Apocalypse

Pauline language often echoes Qumran terminology.[3] The Romans are urged to "cast off the works of darkness and put on the armor of light" (Rom. 13.12), while the Thessalonians are called "children of the light and children of day" (1 Thess. 5.5). The chiastic antithesis of this verse also opposes night and darkness. In the same letter, we find the passage quoted earlier which appears to anticipate "the day of the Lord" within the apostle's and his correspondents' own lifetime: "Then we who are alive and remain shall be caught up" with the dead in Christ (4.16–5.2). To that extent, at least, Paul would appear to have inherited the widespread apocalyptic hope.

On the other hand, like the rabbis whose practices he often follows, Paul was alert to the theological difficulties of apocalyptic myth in its cruder forms. He certainly will have nothing to do with the midrash we have met in *Jubilees*, whereby Pharaoh's heart was hardened not by God but by Mastema. Paul quotes the relevant Exodus texts (9.12, 16; 33.19) to the Romans (Rom. 9.14–18), and there is no trace of a hostile opponent or evil intermediary doing God's will. Paul's exposition rests on a larger view of God's historical purpose and on a characteristic use of the Book of Job: "But who are you, a man, to talk back to God?" (Rom. 9.20). Paul

---

[3] See, generally, Murphy-O'Connor (ed.) 1968, but also Vawter 1963; Hengel 1974: vol. 1, 175–210; J. Baumgarten 1975; J. A. Sanders 1977; and Lincoln 1981:169–91.

flinches neither at attributing apparent evil to God nor at adopting God's voice as his own.[4]

Equally characteristic of Paul is his cautious adaptation of the redemptive expectations we have seen developing in apocalyptic circles. The Pauline corpus contains several passages that look like early christological hymns used in baptism. Similar hymns appear also in Gnostic contexts, such as the *Apocalypse of Adam*, but the Pauline versions minimize the dualistic implications, whether apocalyptic or Gnostic.[5] According to the hymn in Colossians 1.15–20, where the language seems to have tried to accommodate the Colossian heresy,

> in him all things were created, in heaven and on earth, visible and invisible, whether thrones or dominions or rulers or authorities [*eite thronoi eite kuriotētes eite archai eite exousiai*]. . . . For in him the whole fullness [*to plērōma*] was pleased to dwell, and through him to reconcile [*apokatallaksai*] all things to himself, whether on earth or in heaven, making peace through the blood of his cross.

Everything that may have appeared hostile before is now made one. The term *plērōma*, fullness, is probably borrowed from the gnosticizing Colossians since it is common in this letter and not elsewhere, but the other Greek terms recur in various Pauline contexts, always with their mythological implications muted or their potential hostility overcome. Indeed, the hymn in Philippians omits them entirely:

> Christ Jesus, . . . being in the form of God, did not reckon equality with God something to be grasped, but emptied himself, taking the form of a slave, being born in the likeness of men. And being found in human form, he humbled himself and became obedient till death, the death of the cross. Therefore God has exalted him, and given him the name which is above every name, that at the name of Jesus every knee should bow, of those in heaven, those on earth, and those under the earth, and every tongue confess that Jesus Christ is Lord (Phil. 2.6–11).

---

[4] Job 40.2; cf. Isa. 45.9. See above, Chapter 5. Dodd 1932:170 calls Paul's argument "a false step," since it requires a deterministic and therefore amoral relation between men and God. Käsemann 1980:267–71 calls Dodd's view "crass." Thus the modern commentaries perpetuate the ancient anxieties.

[5] See Vermes 1958, Käsemann, 1964:154–62, and esp. J. T. Sanders 1971:9–15. The relevant passages are Col. 1.15–20, Phil. 2.6–11, Eph. 1.20–21, 2.14–16, 1 Tim. 3.16, 1 Pet. 3.18–22, Heb. 1.3, and John 1.1–11. Eph. 2.14 appears to add "enmity" as a clarifying gloss on the curious phrase "has broken down the dividing wall." See below and J. T. Sanders 1971:22.

The emptied Christ is a curious reversal of the fullness in the Colossians hymn and shows how flexible a weapon Pauline language might be against what looks like a similar heresy. The string of Greek abstractions is here simply "names," and there is no telling from this passage whether the creatures on three levels who are now obliged to bend the knee had previously been hostile, loyal, or indifferent.

A long succession of heroes, beginning with Gilgamesh, had set out to acquire a name for themselves, but the naming of Jesus above other names is the result of his humble human death, not of his heroic victory in battle. In fact, this event echoes not so much heroic or apocalyptic traditions as the buried myths of the Old Testament, indeed, of that most uncompromising antidualist, Second Isaiah, whose God creates both good and evil. Yahweh calls Cyrus thus (Isa. 45.4–7, 20–23): "I call you by your name, I surname you though you do not know me. I am the Lord, and there is no other, besides me there is no God. . . . To me every knee shall bow, every tongue shall swear." It is characteristic of Paul to cite an Old Testament passage that, like Yahweh's boast to Cyrus, implies but does not openly state an opposing claim.

Since the date and authenticity of the Colossian and Philippian letters are disputed, neither passage quoted provides good evidence for Paul's view about the myth of a cosmic redeemer. All the documents in which these primitive hymns have been held to appear are either late or suspect on other grounds. All seem to interpret, rather than simply quote, the hymnic language, as if some other, more Gnostic version were threatening their account of Christian triumph. Thus the tension in these Pauline texts is not only carried over from the Old Testament quotations but also the result of variant readings within the contemporary church. Indeed, the Gnostics would soon be offering a characteristic inversion of Yahweh's claim; for them, he is either lying or ignorant.

2. The Myth of Psalm 110.1

To clarify the Pauline transformation of Old Testament mythological language, we may examine the several citations of one verse from an enthronement psalm, the opening of Psalm 110. "Sit at my right hand, until I make your enemies your footstool" is the way Yahweh's words to the king were read in Paul's time, although the original may not have implied a reference to the future.[6] The psalm has various Ugaritic parallels, and is probably one of the many signs of the revival of mythological language by the Davidic kingship. The victor with his foot on the defeated enemy is a common literary and iconographic device. The verse appears frequently as a *testimonium*, or proof-text, in the New Testament, and it had already acquired a messianic interpretation in pre-Christian apocalyptic contexts.[7] Acts cites it twice, once on the lips of Stephen, martyred while Saul-Paul watched—"Behold, I see the heavens opened, and the son of man standing at the right hand of God" (Acts 7.55–56)—and once on the lips of Peter, "Sit at my right hand, until I make thy enemies thy footstool" (Acts 2.34). Mark's gospel makes Jesus himself cite the verse during his interrogation by the priests as a proof of his messianic role: I am the Christ, he says, "and you will see the son of man seated at the right hand of power, and coming with clouds of heaven" (Mark 14.62).

The letters written in Paul's name appear to use the verse five times. Once only the first part of the verse is quoted (Col. 3.1), but elsewhere the enemies from the second half are the focus, whether by direct citation of the verse or by Pauline elaboration. Yet these enemies are no more definitely cosmic adversaries than they are in the Davidic context. The old tension of myth and history is still present, and each passage could as well refer to contemporary, historical opponents. At 1 Corinthians 15.24–27, for example, Paul reminds his correspondents of the eschatological hope, and incidentally mixes the time-scheme because he tempers the forward-looking Psalm 110 with the backward-looking words of Psalm 8.6, which refer, in the original, to man's domination of creation (sheep, oxen, birds, fish) in the manner of Genesis:

> Then comes the end, when he delivers the kingdom to God the father, after destroying every principality and authority and power. For he must reign until he had put all his enemies [*echthrous*] under his feet. The last enemy to be destroyed is death. For God has put all things in subjection under his feet.

Apart from the personalization of death as an enemy, the myth language is defused or muted, and the terms "principality" (*archēn*), "authority" (*exousian*), and "power" (*dunamin*) could be and have been taken to be simply human institutions.[8]

---

[6] Dahood 1970:112–17. See above, Chapter 4.3
[7] Fully studied by Hay 1973:59–154; cf. Carr 1981:89–93 and Lincoln 1981:145.
[8] Carr 1981:91, *contra* Cullmann 1962:193 and Käsemann 1980:250–51. Cf. Conzelmann

Earlier in the same letter to the Corinthians, Paul refers to the ruler of this age as those who crucified Christ. The language here has a Gnostic ring, but there are apocalyptic affinities aplenty,[9] and again the mythological implications are muted. These rulers could just be the human authorities responsible for the execution. We do speak wisdom, Paul concedes, but

> it is a wisdom not of this age [*aiōnos*] nor of the rulers of this age [*tōn archontōn tou aiōnos toutou*] who are being destroyed. Rather we speak a wisdom of God in a mystery, the hidden wisdom which God foreordained before the ages [*tōn aiōnōn*] for our glory, and which none of the rulers of this age knew. For if they had known it, they would not have crucified the Lord of glory (1 Cor. 2.6–8).

The Greek verb that I translate "destroy" is the same in both passages (*katargeō*, to render barren, useless, impotent), though with some variation of tense and mood. Yet here the dominant contrast is not between power and impotence but between wisdom and ignorance. In Gnostic circles the ignorance of the cosmic rulers became a major topic, but so guarded is Paul's language that it is by no means clear that he is thinking of cosmic ruler at all.

When Paul quotes Psalm 110.1 in the letter to the Romans, even though he is again talking of Christ's resurrection from the dead, he does not quote the second part of the verse directly: "Christ Jesus, who died, indeed, who rose again, is at the right hand of God" (Rom. 8.34). And even though Paul goes on to give a specific list of enemies, expanding the Davidic saying, the point is again that they have been overcome, or rather that they have lost their power:

> For I am sure that neither death, nor life, nor angels, nor principalities, nor things present, nor things to come, nor powers, nor height, nor depth, nor anything else in all creation, will be able to separate us from the love of God in Christ Jesus our Lord (Rom. 8.38–39).

1975:273–74. It is worth noting that the myth language in this passage grows more insistent with the mention of *echthrous*.

[9] The Qumran parallels are well summarized by Barth 1974: vol. 1, 19–21, even though he is primarily discussing Ephesians. Conzelmann 1975:58–63 notes parallels with the wisdom tradition and discusses the consonance between wisdom and apocalyptic. On the rulers of this age, see Carr 1981:118–21. On *aiōn* as both a temporal and a spatial term at this period, see Sässe in Kittel (ed.) 1951: vol. 1, 197–209, Jonas 1970:51–54, and Lincoln 1981:172 and passim. The word thus means both "world" and "age," often pluralized by the Gnostics as the worlds in which the soul wanders lost and seeking redemption.

This language allows for the hostility of death, but immediately qualifies it by adding "nor life," and the other enemy terms are similarly defused by dispersion among other words. The dominant tone is assertive: the triumphant hope will not allow the potential hostility of these beings to thwart that hope. In all these passages, in fact, even when he speaks of the rulers who crucified Christ, Paul is immediately concerned with how his readers will react to the combat language.

Even in the probably pseudonymous letter to the Ephesians, where the myth language is already reasserting itself, when Christ appears at the right hand of God the enemies have been suppressed, as enemies, and indeed one could interpret these verses with no reference to hostile powers but simply as a variation of the hymn language we found in Philippians 2.5–11, the elevation of Christ above every name that is named:

> He raised him from the dead and made him sit at the right hand in the heavenlies [*epouraniois*] above all rule and authority and power and dominion [*pasēs archēs kai exousias kai dunameōs kai kuriotētōs*], and every name that is named, not only in this age [*aiōni*] but in the one to come; and he has put all things under his feet.[10]

The provenance of the letter to the Ephesians is much argued, but here at least we find a similar muting of the adversary language as in the parallel Corinthians passage, definitely Paul's, or in Romans 8. The milder language of Psalm 8.6 has completely pushed out the harsher conclusion of Psalm 110.1. Yet Ephesians immediately goes on to mention "the prince of the power of the air, the spirit that is now at work in the children of disobedience" (Eph. 2.2), and whatever those phrases mean exactly, they are a clear reference to the mythological adversary in a form similar to that we have met at Qumran, blurring the theological dilemma of human responsibility.[11]

There is one other Pauline passage that may allude to the first verse of Psalm 110. If so, it is the only one to name the adversary (although the play with every name that is named elsewhere may imply that the diversity of terms does not matter much). In this passage (Rom. 16.17–20) the

[10] Eph. 1.20–22. See Barth 1974: vol. 1, 152–53, esp. for the full discussion of other views. It was Marcion and the Gnostics who first accorded canonical status to Ephesians.

[11] Belial in the Scrolls is the prince of spirits at 1QS 3.23; see above, Chapter 10, and below, Chapter 15. See also Matt. 8.16, 10.1, 12.43, etc. For discussion of the syntax of the Ephesians passage, see Barth 1974: vol. 1, 215–16 and Carr 1981:102–3. The spirit (*pneumatos*) may be in apposition to air (*aēros*) only, in which case we have a being who poisons the air much as the devil encountered by Luther did.

enemy becomes the Satan *tout court*. Suddenly and oddly Paul interrupts his greetings to his correspondents:

> I beg you, brothers, to keep an eye on those who dissent and put stumbling-blocks [*skandala*] in the way, against the doctrine you have learned. Avoid them. Such people are slaves not to Christ our Lord but to their own bellies; through plausible and pious talk they lead astray the hearts of the innocent. Your obedience is known to all—I rejoice in you—but I would have you be wise as to the good, guileless as to evil. The god of peace will soon crush the Satan under your feet.

Whereas the phrase from Psalm 110.1 (*hupo tous podas*, under your feet) is elsewhere a reference to the victorious Messiah, it is here the followers of Paul to whom the promise applies.[12] Thus not only Christ but Christians generally will soon overcome the adversary—and here the adversary is the embodiment of Paul's own opponents.

However oddly these words may sit with the rest of the letter to the Romans, they are similar to what Paul often says elsewhere about his opponents.[13] Indeed, this is the context—Paul's rivalry with other teachers of the Christian message—in which the peculiar Pauline transformation of the combat myth must chiefly be situated.

3. *Paul and His Opponents*

Paul seems to have been the kind of man who is stimulated by opposition. According to his own words (Gal. 1.13–14), as well as the tradition preserved in Acts, he had once persecuted all Christians as strongly as he now opposed those whom he regarded as false teachers. At times, he took a broadly optimistic view of this situation, arguing that "there must be heresies among you, that those who are genuine may be recognized" (1 Cor. 11.19). No doubt Paul's own combativeness was partly responsible for the series of challenges to his authority and teaching. And he was not

---

[12] Hence, we might suggest, the enemy is named Satan, a word that Paul uses for the opponent of human efforts; cf. 1 Thess. 2.18; 1 Cor. 5.5, 7.5; and 2 Cor. 2.11, 11.14, 12.7. Most of these passages are discussed in more detail below. As in Revelation, Paul's Satan always has the article, except at 2 Cor. 12.7, but in Greek this does not necessarily indicate that there are other Satans. It could be either a name or a title, and Paul probably thought of it as both; cf. Cranfield 1979: vol. 2, 803. On this passage in Romans, see Dodd 1932:9–18 and Käsemann 1980:416–19; cf. Schmithals 1972:219–38. For the more commonly perceived allusion to the protevangelium of Gen. 3.15, see below, and e.g., Förster in Kittel (ed.) 1951: vol. 5, 581.

[13] Phil. 3.18–19; 1 Cor. 5.1–13, 6.12–20; 2 Cor. 10–14. See, generally, Fenton 1978.

above presenting his quarrels with other Christians in the terms provided by the combat myth, in which the adversary was now normally called Satan.

The connection of Satan with a *skandalon*, a stumbling-block, explicit in the Romans 16 warning to Paul's followers, was available, we have seen, in the etymology of the Hebrew word *sāṭān*. The bilingual Paul would no doubt be alert to the linguistic echoes. When he tells the Thessalonians, for example, that he has not been able to come to see them because Satan hindered him (*enekopsen*), the verb he chooses has the same root (*koptō*, to strike, cut, or lay waste) as *proskomma*, another word for an obstacle or cause of offense, like *skandalon*. The two words are used in parallel at Romans 9.33 for the mysterious "stone" on which the Jews are said to stumble. Quoting Isaiah 8.14 and 28.16 in a way that seems to have been common in Christian circles,[14] Paul implies that the stone-for-stumbling (*lithon proskommatos kai petran skandalou*) was the Law. This is one of several Pauline passages where the Law plays the role of a Satan. In the letter to the Thessalonians, however, there are no such complications. Paul merely shifts from the normal word for "prevent" or "hinder," *kōluō*, which he has used in the preceding verses, to the more resonant *enekopsen* (1 Thess. 2.18): Satan was in Paul's way, and he could not come.

More often, Paul uses the word "Satan" in the more developed sense of the apocalyptic combat tradition. He quickly tells the Thessalonians, immediately after the passage just discussed, that he is afraid that because he cannot get to them personally the tempter (*ho peirazōn*) may have tampered with their belief and Paul's labors (*kopos*, suffering, toil, and trouble) should be for nothing (3.5). He does not name the tempter here, but Satan is explicitly the tempter at 1 Corinthians 7.5, where Paul is advising his correspondents to marry rather than let Satan tempt them (*peirazei*). Satan can thus tempt either to heresy or to sexual indulgence, like the Watcher angels of the Enoch tradition, but Paul seems especially concerned about heresy.[15]

Paul writes to the Corinthians that he is afraid they will be deceived in the way that Eve was deceived by the serpent (2 Cor. 11.3), and he goes on to warn them that Satan transforms himself into an angel of light, so his servants may therefore be expected to present themselves as apostles

[14] Cf. 1 Pet. 2.6–8. See Dodd 1932:175 and Käsemann 1980:277–79.

[15] On Satan as tempter, see the discussion of 2 Chron. 21.1 (above, Chapter 5) and in the Adam books (above, Chapter 12). Cf. 1QS 3.20 for Belial as seducer of men (above, Chapter 10.2).

of Christ (11.13–15). It is a warning that has been frequently repeated among quarreling factions of the church, and the identification of Satan with heresy, rather than any sexual proclivities in his story, would soon become the major source of his continuing power. This is the earliest of many denunciations of heresy that imply and soon assert the link between serpent, heresy, and Satan.

The references in this second letter to the Corinthians are too brief for us to say with any certainty what version of Satan's story Paul has in mind. The proximity of the allusions to the serpent and to Satan makes it possible that the story is the one told in the Adam books. The Greek *Apocalypse of Moses* makes Satan appear as serpent and in the form of an angel to tempt Eve.[16] The relative dating is uncertain, however, and in any case the Adam book says nothing about Satan as an angel of *light*.

This term has obvious affinities with the Qumran literature. The *Rule of the Community* describes at length the opposition of the two spirits in man and attributes their antagonism to angels of light and darkness. The *War Scroll* extends and dramatizes this conflict, developing the rebellion myth of the Enoch books.[17] Indeed, we have noted that the "fall" of angels and men could be used at Qumran as the same kind of warning Paul here issues to his Corinthian flock. The *Damascus Covenant*, which contains that moralizing allusion to the rebellion myth, views the history of Israel as a falling away from the covenant, in fact, as a sharp struggle between those who maintain it and those who oppose it: "When, in the old times, Israel was first delivered, Moses and Aaron maintained their charge, through the help of the angel of lights, although Belial in his cunning sets up Jannes the apostate against them."[18] The legend that Jannes opposed the Mosaic teaching is widespread in Jewish circles, although the oldest reference is the one just quoted.[19] It follows from the application of apocalyptic combat dualism to the whole of Israel's history. The legend recurs in 2 Timothy 3.8, also a warning against false teachers, but in none of its versions does the adversary transform himself literally into an angel of light, unless we take "angel" in its less developed sense of "messenger."

---

[16] *Apocalypse of Moses* 17.1, quoted above, Chapter 12.5.

[17] *Rule of the Community*, 1QS, 3.13—4.26, discussed (with the *War Scroll*) above, Chapter 10.2.

[18] *Damascus Covenant* 5.18 in Gaster 1964:77; cf. below, Chapter 17.

[19] Ginzberg 1910–38: vol. 6, 144. For "Jambres" the "brother" of Jannes as really *mambres* (= "the apostate"), see A. T. Hanson 1966:93 and below, Chapter 22. Cf. Hennecke and Scheemelcher 1963–650: vol. 1, 456, and above Chapter 10 n. 14.

The angel of light could be an allusion to the rebellious light-bearer, *Heōsphoros–Hêlēl-ben-Šaḥar*–Lucifer, whose "fall" might give some ironic point to the "transformation" of Satan. Apart from this passage, Paul uses the verb *metaschēmatizō*, transform, only twice, and it does not occur elsewhere in the New Testament.[20] But here Paul uses the word three times, both for Satan's transformation and for that of his servants. It is likely that, as with the word *plērōma*, fullness, in Colossians, the stress is so heavy here because Paul is turning their own word against his opponents. They make radical claims about their conversion, and Paul agrees: "Yes, and look what they have become." Of course, Paul makes equally radical claims about his own conversion elsewhere, so he is not on firm ground here. In this passage he makes a virtue of his weakness or his holy folly, in ironic contrast to the strength and wisdom of his opponents. Irony is a notoriously difficult trope to judge and for that reason is a useful and flexible weapon.[21] In the absence of clear and independent information about the precise heresy to which Paul was responding, it is difficult to tell the exact force of Paul's language. Indeed, that is a part of Paul's own argument: "transformation" or "conversion" is the common coin of religious language, so intention, context, authority will provide the only, and hardly reliable, grounds to distinguish true from false. Paul was clearly aware of the problems posed by a claim to authority, and so, when he goes on to give a summary of the afflictions he has suffered as a sign of his credibility, he hedges the tale with deprecation of his own boasting. The oscillation in this part of the letter between assumed humility and bragging is itself a fascinating sign of Paul's uneasiness, since the charge of bearing false light might as readily be made against him. Isaiah's light-bearer had, we recall, aspirations to ascend above the stars of God but was in fact brought down to the pit. If Paul wants the allusion to count against his opponents but is afraid it might be used against him, then we could understand why he does not make it more explicit but cloaks it in protective irony.

Indeed, he goes on, as if drawn to make the claim in spite of his better instincts, to mention a vision of Paradise and the third heaven, but the experience happened to "a man I know." Paul is much more reticent about this claim ("whether in the body or out of the body I do not know") than an Enoch book would have been, or John of Patmos, and Paul immedi-

---

[20] Lincoln 1981:102, citing Phil. 3.21 and 1 Cor. 4.6.
[21] See esp. Booth 1974.

ately turns this reticence to his advantage. A thorn in the flesh was given to him, a messenger of Satan, or perhaps "a messenger Satan" (*angelos Satan*, 2 Cor. 12.7), to trouble him and restrain his elation at the vision (*hina mē huperhairōmai*). "That I might not be lifted up too high" sounds like an ironic allusion both to what his opponents claim and to what Isaiah's Lucifer had tried to do.[22]

A rich scholarly literature has grown up over the identity of Paul's opponents at Corinth, extending into the domain of sober historical research the passion and heat of those first-century quarrels.[23] Probably they were Jewish Christians from a Hellenized Palestinian milieu whose claims about signs and wonders would be hard to distinguish from many another preacher of realized eschatology, even to a contemporary observer. Their views may not have been so radically different from Paul's own tendencies as he would like us to think—hence the intensity and defensiveness of his language. Both Paul and his opponents are examples of how readily the eschatological language of apocalyptic could move in a Gnostic direction.

It is tempting to assume that these rivals of Paul compared themselves to Moses as the bringer of written but veiled words from God (2 Cor. 3). This would give added point to Paul's warning about Satan transforming himself into an angel of light, since the passage quoted from the *Damascus Covenant* shows that this might be a witty allusion to Moses and Jannes. It is also plausible that Paul is using popular sayings of Jesus against his opponents. Luke records the saying that Jesus saw Satan fall like lightning from heaven, and the other synoptic gospels report the famous but problematic "Get thee behind me" as addressed both to Satan and Peter.[24]

[22] On Paul's "thorn in the flesh," see Hughes 1962:441–51. The curious phrase *angelos Satan* is the only occasion in Paul where the word "Satan" occurs without the definite article and in the alternate form *Satan* as opposed to *Satanas*. Both forms are indeclinable. This Satanic thorn may be the same as the "affliction" that prevented Paul from going to the Thessalonians, but none of the commentators appears to consider the possibility that Paul may there have been simply excusing his absence in the delicate way the French language encourages: *j'ai eu un empêchement majeur*, without further specification. Paul may also be alluding to Ps. 28.21, 71.13, or 109.4, 6, 20, 29.

[23] See, e.g., Grant 1959:156–60; Georgi 1964; Bornkamm 1961:68–77; R. M. Wilson 1968: 27–28; Schmithals 1971:70–75; Schmithals 1972; E. E. Ellis 1975 (a useful summary); Horsley 1980 ("Hellenistic Jewish religiosity focused on *sophia* and *gnōsis*"); and Wisse 1981 (who reviews the controversy in the light of Nag Hammadi).

[24] Thrall 1983 plausibly suggests that the ironic "super-apostles" and the Peter-Satan saying point to Jerusalem Christianity. See below, Chapter 15. On the Gnostic affinities of Jewish Christianity, esp. in the Pseudo-Clementine *Homilies*, see Schoeps 1964 and Bauer 1972:241–85.

When addressed to Peter, it is accompanied by the explanation "You are a stumbling block [*skandalon*] in my way." The potential pun on Peter's name would have some point if the opponents of Paul at Corinth were followers of Jerusalem or Petrine Christianity. This would also explain why Paul calls them ironically "superlative apostles."

In this engagement Paul shows a tendency that is characteristic of him. He claims visions and makes mythological allusions, just as his several opponents do, but his own terms are more cautious, muted, ironic, more alert to the dangers of the prophetic and apocalyptic traditions. Nevertheless, the very brevity of the allusions to Satan here is revealing. One does not say that Satan transforms himself into an angel of light without further explanation, even if the idea is as packed with witty allusions as I have suggested, unless some such episode is familiar to one's readers. The developed adversary of Jewish and Christian apocalyptic is a familiar figure to Paul and his audiences, and he is familiar as the agent in a story they all know.

This passage from the second letter to the Corinthians is one of two Pauline passages that make it likely that the story of Satan, the apocalyptic adversary, was already drawing the story of Eve and the serpent toward it, that they were being, at least tentatively, explained together. The other is the line we have quoted before from the letter to the Romans, also in its context a warning against heretics, that God will soon crush Satan under your feet. No serpent actually appears there, but two serpent texts seem to be exerting pressure on Paul's words. One is the curious saying in Matthew 10.16, "Be ye wise as serpents and innocent as doves," of which Paul's "I would have you be wise as to the good, guileless as to evil" (Rom. 16.19) seems to be a variant.[25] In both cases the Greek words are *sophoi* and *akeraioi*, and in both cases the context is a warning about the opposition to be expected by the faithful. Paul's next words, the promise that God will soon crush Satan under your feet, are not normally taken as an allusion to the mythological victor of Psalm 110.1 with his enemies under his feet, in the way that we have argued above. Most commentators notice only an allusion to Genesis 3.15, in which enmity is forecast between the woman's seed and the serpent's, and the woman's will "crush" the serpent's head.[26] Apparently this text was by now being used in mes-

---

[25] Irenaeus, *Adv. haer.* 5.20.1, has a more radical variant: "The wisdom of the serpent was conquered by the simplicity of the dove."

[26] Käsemann 1980:418 cites four parallel usages. Two refer to treading on evil spirits (*Test. Levi* 18.12; *Test. Simeon* 6.6) and link this with Adam. Cf. *Test. Zebulon* 9.8, which also re-

sianic contexts, and it was to become known as the "protevangelium," the first cryptic announcement within the Old Testament of the Christian gospel revealed in the New. It is likely, then, that Paul and his correspondents were aware of the alignment of the Genesis serpent with Satan and that this composite figure was chiefly understood as the tempter, both of Eve and of her descendants in the contemporary world. But if so, Paul treats the narrative with his usual circumspection. There is no serpent in his promise to the Romans that God will soon crush Satan under their feet, in spite of the allusions, and in the Second Letter to the Corinthians the references to Eve's serpent and the Satanic transformation into an angel of light are separated by eleven verses.

4. *The Adversary and the Law*

Apart from his rabbinic suspicions of apocalyptic theology, Paul had a more positive reason to be cautious in his use of the combat myth. He has his own views about the Law to promote. Indeed, some aspects of this key Pauline idea appear to be influenced by apocalyptic mythology. The Law of sin and death, as Paul calls it, is a frequent topic in his letters, yet it is a notoriously difficult idea, and we should not assume, simply because of Paul's status within the Christian tradition, that he was himself conscious of all its implications or that he was aware of its connections with the combat myth in quite the way I suggest. So widespread was the mythological mode of thought that it often tended to shape the conscious ideas of the period in much the way that the inherent characteristics of any language form and seem "natural" to its native speakers.

Like Satan, we have seen, the Law is a stumbling-stone, *petran skandalou* (Rom. 9.34). And as a continuing and powerful institution, the Law has superhuman qualities similar to those of the "powers" or "names" referred to in the Pauline hymns. Its authority is beyond that of an individual man. But unlike those superhuman powers who before Christ's coming retained, like the Satan figure, all the independence of acting normally attributed to characters in a story, the Law quite obviously preserves the connection with the human sin it is designed to expose and punish. "Thou shalt not" in the Decalogue is the heart and foundation of the Torah. Thus

---

fers, like *Test. Levi*, to victory over Beliar. For *Apoc. Mos.* 10.1–12, see above, Chapter 12.6. *Jubilees* 23.29 does not, in my opinion, allude to Gen. 3.15. On the protevangelium, see also Vawter 1977 and the discussion of Luke 10.19 in Chapter 15, below and of Irenaeus in Chapter 19.

Paul's shift of focus from the apocalyptic adversaries to the hostile Law of sin and death is not so much antimythological or antiapocalyptic thinking as it is an effort to link the common framework of apocalytic myth with the profound experience of inner transformation registered by Paul and many other Christians. Paul's Christ is not so much the victor over cosmic enemies as the one who has nullified the Law and its power over the individual conscience through guilt.

Paul refers specifically to the common idea that the Law was given by angels (Gal. 3.19), found also in the *Book of Jubilees*, in Josephus, and elsewhere in the New Testament.[27] The opposition in Paul's Greek is between the Law given by angels and the promise (*epangelia*) to Abraham, which to Paul means Christ. Christ, he tells the "foolish Galatians," has "redeemed us from the curse of the Law" (3.1, 13). But the Law was given, Paul is careful to stress, because of transgressions (*parabaseōn*), and furthermore it performed the function of a *paidagōgos*, a schoolmaster, during the spiritual childhood of the Jews between the time of Moses and Christ. Thus the source of the Law's power and its apparent hostility is firmly located in sin or spiritual unreadiness, rather than in some independent cosmic source of evil.

The idea of the hostile Law has not, however, been entirely shorn of the connotations of cosmic adversaries. Paul goes on to explain the schoolmaster idea thus: "I mean that, while the heir is a child, he is no different from a slave, even if he is the lord of everything. He is under guardians and trustees until the time set by the father. So with us, when we were children, we were in bondage to the elemental forces of the universe [*ta stoicheia tou kosmou*]" (Gal. 4.1–3). This phrase has occasioned much debate. As the vehicle of a metaphor, it refers primarily to what a later tradition called grammar, the elementary rules of language, even the alphabet itself—what a child first learns and which may often seem like slavemasters. But as tenor, the phrase seems to carry more weight than this: these are the rules of the universe, not only of the grammar book. The idea derives probably from Stoic concepts of natural law, now melded with astrological thinking, and would include the planetary owners, now known by the still current names of Greek and Roman gods (March, *vendredi*, etc.), whose function was to regulate the calendar and thus the timely working of the natural world. Thus the Law from which

[27] *Jubilees* 1.27; Josephus, *Antiquitates* 15.5.3; Acts 7.53; Heb. 2.2. Recent discussions of Paul's view of the Law which try to sort through the confusion are J. A. Sanders 1977 and Räisänen 1980; the latter is especially provocative.

Paul proclaims liberation now that school is out means not only the Torah but also the world of ordinary nature conceived in its regular and repetitive aspect, the "law" of nature. So Paul denounces the Galatians for observing "days and months and seasons and years" (4.10). In extending the idea of the Law to include the physical universe, Paul approaches Gnostic ideas about the world as a prison in which humanity is confined.[28] But whereas in Gnostic thought these elemental forces were all under the control of a hostile deity, Paul's emphasis is on the human attitude toward them, which Christ has supposedly transformed. "In those days, when you did not know God, you were enslaved to those who were not really gods. . . . How can you turn back again to those weak and beggarly spirits (*stoicheia*), whose slaves you want to be once more?" (4.8–9). Beings raised by human credulity to divine status, to whom Paul and the Old Testament refer elsewhere,[29] these no-gods or demons have now lost their power, if only human beings will stop giving it back to them.

In the more elaborate doctrine written for the Romans, Paul shows a similar concern to distinguish between the effects of the Law and its intrinsic nature. We may also discern here a buried polemic against the apocalyptic elaboration of the Satan figure, since the Old Testament Satan, as we have seen, was initially the divinely appointed public prosecutor in the cosmic court. Like Satan, the Pauline Law is the great accuser.[30] The Law also carries out the sentence and is even the tempter: "I would not have known sin, but by the Law; for I had not known lust, except the Law had said, Thou shalt not covet. But sin, taking occasion by the commandment, wrought in me all manner of concupiscence" (Rom. 7.7–8). But when the Law, like Satan, enslaves men, then the appropriate functions have been exceeded. Satan's further role as *agent provocateur* (in Job) derives from his legitimate function in the divine court, but when he becomes an independent evil power, the apocalyptic development, he has

[28] Grant 1959:156 has a sensible discussion of astrology and the "prison of this world" idea. Caird 1956:51 aptly cites Apuleius, *Metamorphoses (The Golden Ass)* 11.6, for the generalized longing to be free of the stars' domain. Enoch's ascent is one of many visions of the transmundane, and the idea is by no means exclusively Gnostic. The phrase *stoicheia tou kosmou*, or a close variant, also occurs at Col. 2.8, 2.20; cf. 2 Pet. 3.10–12. See Lohse 1971:96–99, Betz 1979:204–5, and Bruce 1982:193–205.

[29] 1 Cor. 8.4–6, 10.19–20; Isa. 45.5; Deut. 32.17, 21; Ps. 96.5, 106.37. See above, Chapter 5 n. 4, and cf. Haag 1974:349–50 and below, Chapter 15 on the "Prince Baal" (*zbl b'l*) origin of Beelzeboul. See also 2 Thess. 2.3–12, discussed below.

[30] Rom. 2.12, 3.19; Caird 1956:41–42. See also above, Chapter 5. In the passage cited in the next sentence, the Greek word for "covet" and "concupiscence" is *epithumia*; the language of the KJV gives an idea of its range of meanings.

exceeded his authority, and Paul's Christ, we remember, has overcome all authorities and powers. Just so, the Law, which should have been conceived as an instrument of the divine will, has taken on, for the pious Jew, an independent authority. It has become, like those no-gods, an idol. That captivity to the higher power of the Law, wording which echoes the Exodus typology of Second Isaiah in a further transformation, has now been annulled: "You have died to the law through the body of Christ, so that you may belong to another, to him who has been raised from the dead. . . . Now we are discharged from the law, dead to that which held up captive, so that we serve not under the old written code, but in the new life of the spirit" (Rom. 7.4–6).

In the second letter to the Corinthians, Paul connects the Law not only to the sin that has given it authority, but also to an apparent divinity who is the enemy of Christian liberation, "the god of this world" (*ho theos tou aiōnos toutou*, 2 Cor. 4.4). Once again, the singular enemy may be an ironic concession to Paul's Corinthian opponents, if the idea of an ignorant demiurge were an aspect of their teaching.[31] He can also be read as merely a personification of all the forces of this *aiōn* that would thwart the success of the Christian message. But this hostile god is a formidable opponent, and his power is like that of the Qumran Belial, or indeed Paul's Satan. On the road to Damascus, according to Acts 26, Paul saw a vision of light which prompted him to go to the Gentiles and "open their eyes, that they may turn from darkness to light and from the power of Satan to God" (26.18). Unreliable as the wording of Acts may be, in the Second Letter to the Corinthians Paul's "god of this world" blinds the minds of unbelievers to the light of the gospel. And the means he uses is again the Torah.

Paul's argument here depends both on his own experience and on his ironic references to writing. Apparently his opponents introduced themselves with written letters and may, we have seen, have compared themselves in this respect at least to Moses. Paul seizes the chance to denounce the Law, for "the letter killeth, but the spirit giveth life" (2 Cor. 3.6, KJV). Reminding his audience that we should all be forgiving of one another's faults "lest Satan should get an advantage over us, for we are not ignorant of his wiles" (2.11), Paul proceeds to contrast the effect of Moses' Law with the effect of the gospel. On descending from Sinai, Moses had to cover his face with a veil since it still shone with God's glory and the peo-

---

[31] See above, n. 23 and Chapter 12, and below, Chapter 18; cf. Barrett 1973:130–33. On *aiōn*, see above, nn. 9 and 28. For Sammael as "blind god" or "god of the blind," see above, Chapter 12.5 and Barc 1981.

ple could not bear to look on it. This practice is continued in the synagogues whenever Moses is read (Exod. 34.29–35; 2 Cor. 3.6–15). The veil remains unlifted because only in Christ is it removed. Thus the true meaning of the Pentateuch is hidden from the pious Jews who still reverence the Law. Paul refuses to follow the Gnostics in tampering with God's word (2 Cor. 4.2) and so promotes no hidden gospel. Rather, he argues, blindness to the true meaning of the published word is the work of the adversary. "If our gospel is hidden, it is hidden among those who are lost. In them the god of this world has blinded the minds of the unbelievers, so that the light of the glorious gospel of Christ who is the image of God should not shine out to them" (4.3–4). By contrast, Paul is able to read the Old Testament accurately, with the veil removed, because "the god who said 'Let light shine out of darkness' . . . has shone in our hearts to give the light of the knowledge of the glory of God in the face of Christ." So Paul manages to link together, and so condemn, his opponents' use of letters, the tablets of stone, and the power of the cosmic adversary over the interpretive abilities of his readers, for all these warnings about the letter are contained in Paul's own letter.

5. The Origins of the Struggle

The power of the god of this world manifests itself in the misreading of written texts, or scripture. So Paul provided another warrant for the link between Satan and heresy, and once his own texts became scripture they would themselves be subject to various conflicting readings. But Paul himself therefore tried to give an accurate reading of his scriptures, the history of the spiritual minority of the Jews contained in the Old Testament. Following the midrashic tradition that had generated so much apocalyptic rewriting, Paul felt the need to retell the earlier events of the cosmic-historical narrative, not simply to concentrate on the final liberating event. To that end, for example, he argued to the Galatians (3.6–9, 15–18) that the promise to Abraham has priority over the works of the Law because it preceded the giving of the Law; it was an earlier incident in the narrative. The rule of the Law occupies the historical span between the giving of the promise and its fulfillment in Christ. In effect, Paul is urging his Galatian audience to recognize where they are in the narrative. We have all now moved on to the final stage, the liberation, and so we should cease to behave as if the grand conclusion to this narrative had yet to be told. And he urges them to get the story right. Look in the Bible, he tells them, and see that Abraham precedes Moses. The prototype of the justification by faith (because Abraham believed, he was given the promise) precedes the gift of the Law, and thus distinguishes the true hero of the story from the temporary function of the Mosaic Law.

But the insistence on the Law as the Law of sin and death led Paul to go further than this reconstruction of history as narrative. To the Corinthians first, and then to the Romans in a more elaborate way, he argued that we need to know the very beginnings of the story in order to understand properly what the end signifies. The story begins in Adam's sin. The Law then came to confirm the sin and to teach men, in the manner of a schoolmaster, the implications of that sin and its condemnation. Christ now cancels that sin. As one man's sin led to judgment and death for all men, so one man's act of righteousness leads to acquittal and life for all.[32] Whether Paul had in mind any such notion as Augustine later fathered on him, the doctrine of original sin, he was clearly trying to tell a complete story, with a beginning, middle, and end, and so to clarify the doctrine that was being misread by others.

Unfortunately for those who would soon be trying to understand Paul's story, the evasions, suppressions, and ironies of his language would pose serious difficulties. In particular, the role of the cosmic adversary in this human story would be problematic. It was easy enough to see that Christ overcame the god of this world at the end of the narrative, but Paul nowhere explains how the adversary was linked with Adam's sin at the beginning. He was, we have seen, decidedly circumspect about allowing the adversary into his narrative at all.

Paul's allusions to Adam are a sign of the increasing importance of the Adam books, and so of redemption theology, that we have reviewed earlier. Corresponding uses of Adam's story occur also in first-century Jewish sources, especially in two apocalyptic works that, in the wake of the destruction of Jerusalem and the burning of the second temple by Titus in A.D. 70, try to reassert, like the rabbinic commentators, the covenant tradition with its emphasis on human responsibility. The *Apocalypse of Ezra* (*2 Esdras*) complains that Adam's fault was responsible for the terrible state of the world:

> It would have been better if the earth had not produced Adam, or else, having once produced him, had restrained him from sinning. For how does it

---

[32] Rom. 5.18, cf. 1 Cor. 15.21–22. See below, Chapters 23–25.

profit us all that in the present we must live in grief and after death look for punishment?[33]

This hapless Adam is scarcely the creature who, in the wisdom tradition, was originally perfect. It would take much narrative inventiveness to bring those two Adams together.

These two Adams correspond to the two parts of the theological dilemma about evil. On the one hand, in *Enoch* and *Jublilees*, since the lust of the angels accounts for present suffering, Adam himself could be as perfect as one liked, whatever view is taken of Eve. On the other hand, if man himself is responsible, as the covenant tradition insisted, then the stress is laid on "the daughters of men" or on Eve, or on the behavior, not the original state, of Adam himself. The above passage from *2 Esdras* goes on to emphasize human blame:

> O thou Adam, what hast thou done? For though it was thou that sinned, the fall was not thine alone, but ours also who are thy descendants. For how does it profit us that the eternal age is promised us, whereas we have done the works that bring death? And that there is foretold an imperishable hope, whereas we so miserably are brought to futility?

The idea that all men repeat the sin of Adam was to become a commonplace in the Christian tradition, but this passage is one of the few where we meet it in an independent Jewish work. The implication that man has free will and so is not deterministically subject to the whim of the bad angels is stressed even more in the contemporary *Apocalypse of Baruch*: "Adam is therefore not the cause, save only of his own soul. But each of us has been the Adam of his own soul."[34]

In these two Jewish works and in Paul, Adam's story thus replaces that of the Watcher angels as the beginning of all our woe, however much these texts may hedge on the theological issue of "cause." It is possible that these allusions to Adam imply a version of his story like those quoted in our discussion of the Adam books in which the Watchers' rebellion is linked to the seduction of Eve and so to Adam's fall. Nevertheless, Paul's suspicions of the apocalyptic myth appear to be working here also. The passages in which Paul links Adam and Christ lack any reference to the

---

[33] *2 Esdras* 7.116–17. See now Metzger in Charlesworth (ed.) 1983:541, and cf. Bamberger 1952:42–45, Altmann 1944, Brandenburger 1962, J. A. Sanders 1977, Stone (ed.) 1984: 412–14, and above, Chapter 11.

[34] *2 Baruch* 54.19, cf. 17.3, 19.8, 23.4. See Stone (ed.) 1984:409. For the later parts of the contemporary *Apocalypse of Abraham*, chaps. 21 to end, see above, Chapter 12, Scholem 1960:68–72, and Stone (ed.) 1984:415–18.

angel, or to the serpent. This absence would pose serious problems and allow ample interpretive latitude to later commentators.

6. *The Pauline Tradition*

Several letters have come down under Paul's name that many modern commentators think are pseudonymous. Almost nobody takes the pastoral letters (the two letters to Timothy and the letter to Titus) as genuine, but other letters, in particular 2 Thessalonians, Colossians, and Ephesians, are disputed. If their author was not Paul, he (or they) was someone working out the implications of Pauline language and doctrine. In each of these letters, the quarrels with heretics in the church seem to have reached a more pronounced stage than in the letters to the Romans or to the Corinthians.

Second Thessalonians looks like a deliberate imitation of 1 Thessalonians, but whereas the genuine letter looks forward to the imminent Parousia, or Second Coming, the second letter has to account for the delay. It develops quite an elaborate scenario of what must happen first[35] and so sounds as much like the Book of Revelation, with which it may be more or less contemporary, as anything in the genuine Paul. Don't be deceived, the writer tells his audience, by false letters purporting to be from me, announcing the "day of the Lord." This is rich, since the writer is claiming to be Paul. There is no trace now of the typical Pauline irony we found in the second letter to the Corinthians.

One of the things that must happen first, it seems, is the rise of a kind of Antichrist figure. He will oppose and exalt himself above every other god. He will even take his seat in the temple of God and proclaim himself God. Allusions to Antiochus Epiphanes as he appears in Daniel under the resounding title "Abomination of Desolation" become common in the period; Pompey and then Caligula play similar roles.[36] This is history as rebellion myth. The language of combat now becomes more insistent than Paul himself had allowed it to be, and the prophecy continues:

> And then the lawless one (*ho anomos*) will be revealed, whom the Lord will slay with the breath (*pneumati*) of his mouth; he will destroy (*katargēsei*) him by the epiphany of his coming (*tēi epiphaneiai tēs parousias autou*). The coming of the lawless one by the working of Satan will be in all power and with

---

[35] 2 Thess. 2.1–12, cf. 1 Thess. 4.15 (cited above, Chapter 13). Deutero-Pauline Christianity is discussed in detail by Bornkamm 1971, Mitton 1976, and in useful summary by Perrin 1974.

[36] Dan. 7, 8.13, 11.31, 12.11. Cf. Matt. 24.15 and R.E. Brown 1982:334.

false signs and wonders, and with every deception of injustice for those who are perishing because they have not accepted love of the Truth in order to be saved. Therefore God sends upon them a strong delusion (*energeian planēs*) to make them believe what is false, so that they all may be judged who did not believe the truth but had pleasure in injustice.[37]

The Greek of this passage is tangled and confused, as my translation shows. Clauses straggle and get tacked on, subjects change rapidly, words recur in different senses (*energeia*), and the coming (*parousia*) of Christ is followed immediately by the coming of the lawless one. The manuscripts reflect the confusion, so that, for example, the phrase I render as "the Lord will slay" appears with three different verbs (and three different grammatical forms for one of them), while the word "Jesus" is added in several texts. The proliferation of variants is, however, proportionate to the number of citations of the passage in the subsequent tradition. It became a major proof-text in the struggle against heresy.[38]

Who is this lawless one who is to be destroyed by the breath of the Lord? Whatever the contemporary reference may have been, the language is that of the combat myth. It echoes Paul's own words to the Corinthians. *Katargeō* (destroy) is the same verb Paul had used for the end of the enemies (principality, authority, power, death, rulers of this age),[39] but now the adversary is more definitely personal and singular. The Greek for "the lawless one" (*ho anomos*) is the word that the Septuagint often uses to translate Belial, while the famous phrase "the mystery of iniquity" (*to mustērion tēs anomias*) occurs also in this passage (2.7). But other terms crowd in insistently: "the man of sin" (*ho anthrōpos tēs hamartias*), "the son of perdition" (*ho huios tēs apōleias*), "the opponent" (*ho antikeimenos*), and of course "the working of Satan" (*kat' energeian tou Satana*). Like the Antichrist of John, this figure is under the control of the great adversary himself.[40]

[37] 2 Thess. 2.8–12. For the false "signs and wonders" tradition, alluding to Deut. 13.1–6 (cf. 26.9 and above, Chapter 4.1 n. 8), see below, Chapter 17.1, on 1 John 2–3, and cf. Mark 13.22 in the Synoptic Apocalypse, above, Chapter 13.

[38] See the textual notes in Suter (ed.) 1947, ad loc.

[39] 1 Cor. 2.6–8, 15.24–27.

[40] For the mystery of iniquity, see, e.g., Melville, *Billy Budd, Sailor*, chap. 11; for 1 John 2.18, see R. E. Brown 1982:333–37, 398–401, J. Coppens in Murphy-O'Connor (ed.) 1968:132–58, and below, Chapter 17.1. For discussion of Revelation, see above, Chapter 13. The word "Antichrist" itself is used only in the Johannine letters (1 John 2.18, 22, 4.3; 2 John 7); its prefix, "anti-," means primarily "substitute for" and then "against." Polycarp uses the word in *Philippians* 7.1 (see below, Chapter 17.1), apparently referring to these passages,

The Pauline tradition that we glimpse in this passage seems to be making a virtue of a necessity. The coming of Christ is delayed, because false teachers and false gods must arise first, to be destroyed, as the apocalyptic tradition proclaims, in the *eschaton*, the end-time. The strength of one's adherence to the new gospel must be sifted and tested before the new earth can be born. So the above passage ends with the explicit insistence that it is God himself who deludes the heretics, as he deluded the Egyptians and hardened their hearts. Yet in the same passage, a few words earlier, it was the work of Satan that was responsible for error. Indeed the phrase *energeian planēs* seems to echo *energeian tou Satana*. The dilemmas of monotheism seldom lead to such bald but revealing contradictions.

One further term used in this passage would have far-reaching repercussions later. The writer introduces the warning about the delayed Parousia by saying that the rebellion (*hē apostasia*) must come first. A standard episode in the combat myth has thus been transferred from the time of the origins to the time of the end; indeed, the awaited end cannot come without it. Rarely would the need for Satan in the Christian narrative appear so clearly, but we should note the particular form of the narrative transformation here. Satan himself is not mentioned at first. The first term is an abstraction, "rebellion" (*apostasia*), although it is followed immediately by the cluster of other terms listed above, all personal, even human (man of sin, son of perdition, opponent, aspirant to the throne of God). The movement of thought is from the general to the particular, and then, with the mention of Satan himself, to the general again, from the idea of rebellion to its human incarnation to the force that works through him. We shall find the same trajectory in the thought of Irenaeus as he tries to situate the rebel and arch-heretic in his developing system.[41]

The author of the letter to the Colossians, if it was not Paul himself, appears to have been arguing against an early form of the Gnostic heresy. To that end he develops the imagery of cosmic liberation, announcing that God "has delivered us from the power of darkness, and has translated us to the kingdom of his dear son" (Col. 1.13). In Christ the Colossians have "put off the old man [Adam] with its practices, and put on the new man, who is renewed in knowledge after the image of him that created him"(3.9–10). This is apparently an image from clothing, and the same word (*apekdusamenos*) recurs in the obscure passage that purports to ex-

---

and then Irenaeus (see below, Chapter 19) uses it in quoting 2 Thess. 2.8–12 (where it does not appear) at *Adv. haer.* 5.25.1. See on Origen also, below, Chapter 21.6 n. 48.

[41] See below, Chapter 19.1.

plain what Christ did on the cross: "he cancelled the written document [*cheirographon*] which was hostile to us," a phrase in which we can recognize the Pauline irony about the Law even if it here means specifically a book kept by angels in which sins are recorded. This document Christ seems to have nailed to the cross, and in so doing, the writer would have it, "Christ stripped [*apekdusamenos*] the principalities and powers, and made a public example of them, triumphing over them in it" (2.14–15).[42] Here the typical Pauline softening of combat language has generated much difficulty among interpreters. Three ideas seem to be mixed together to cause the confusion: the imagery of a Roman triumph in which the defeated foe might be dragged along naked to the jeers of the crowd, the contrast of Adam and Christ as the old man and the new (with appropriate clothing), and the exposure of the Law to ridicule.

The letter to the Ephesians, widely regarded as post-Pauline, combines an insistence on moral purity similar to that at Qumran with a more fully developed cosmology of the kind that was current in other spiritual systems of the period, especially Gnosticism. The allusion to the christological hymn, cited earlier, is followed by the assertion that the Resurrection has brought new life to those who were dead and so separates the past from the present.

> You who were dead in trespasses and sins he has made alive. Whereas in time past you walked according to the course of this world [*kata ton aiōna tou kosmou toutou*], according to the prince of the power of the air [*ton archonta tēs exousias tou aēros*], the spirit that works in the children of disobedience, among whom also we all had our conversation in times past in the lusts of the flesh, fulfilling the desires of the flesh and of the mind.[43]

The separation of the two powers, of darkness and light, of evil and good, is confirmed both spatially and temporally by the Resurrection. Thus, even as it offered an escape from the dreadful present (or rather the immediate past), the Pauline tradition solidified the dualistic idea of a world divided between opposing forces. And the split was both cosmic and personal. "The prince of the power of the air" probably originates in the Babylonian Pazuzu (or *pašittu*) "the king of evil spirits of the air," who spreads

---

[42] For a balanced discussion of this passage, see Lohse 1971:111–13. Carr 1981:52–85 offers a fresh construction of the Greek, but he also offers a full discussion of other views. He admits that a Roman triumph consisted in part of the exhibition of one's conquered foes, but oddly denies that this implies a battle. One fascinating problem in this passage is that, since it is Christ who is literally nailed to the cross, he is himself the "writing" that he cancels.

[43] Eph.2.1–3 (KJV). See above, n. 10.

violence and fever, a personified disease demon. We have seen how such a figure became part of the combat tradition in the Mastema of *Jubilees*.[44] Here in Ephesians he continues as a quasi-cosmic figure, revivifying the Pauline language about the rulers of this world who crucified Christ. But he is chiefly a psychological force, "the spirit who works in the children of disobedience." Reversing Paul's own emphases, the reference to Adam becomes covert, while the adversary again becomes the focus of attention.

It is hardly surprising, then, that this same letter goes on to abandon almost entirely the Pauline reticence about the apocalyptic combat myth. It offers one of the clearest versions of the moral and spiritual combat at the heart of Christian mythology:

> Put on the whole armour of God, so that ye may be able to stand against the wiles of the devil. For we wrestle not against flesh and blood, but against principalities, against powers, against the rulers of the darkness of this world, against spiritual wickedness in high places.

The language of the Authorized, or King James Version, dramatic as it is, does not bring out the full force of the last phrase, *ta pneumatika tēs ponērias en tois epouraniois*, the spirit forces of evil in the heavenlies. We find here the standard metaphors of apocalyptic military terminology, but unlike the visions of John of Patmos we find also a speaker who is directly engaged in the struggle and who encourages others to join him. These words do not require the audience to take up arms against the Roman Empire, but rather to wage war against the spiritual or angelic forces who give power to the present world rulers. This spiritual combat calls for the weapons of truth, righteousness, "the gospel of peace," the helmet of salvation, the sword of the spirit, and above all "the shield of faith, wherewith ye shall be able to quench the fire-tipped darts of the evil one [*tou ponērou*]" (Eph. 6.11–16). On many occasions, the metaphors of shield and sword have been translated back into their terrible reality. Christianity became not only a militant but a military creed, forgetting "to struggle

---

[44] *Jubilees* 10.8; cf. Targum of Job 28.7 and *Atrahasis* 3.7.1–11 in Lambert and Millard 1969:103. Lefèvre in Bruno de Jésus Marie (ed.) 1952:54 and H. A. Kelly 1974:12 cite parallels in the *Testament of Benjamin* 3.4, "the spirit of the air, Beliar," plus three from the *Ascension of Isaiah*, which also recall "the god of this world" of 2 Cor. 4.4: "Beliar the angel, great king of this world . . . shall descend from his firmament"(4.2); "And we ascend into the firmament, he and I, and there I see Sammael and his power"(7.9); "he descends into the firmament where the ruler of this world lives" (10.29). Cf. M. Barth 1974: vol. 1, 228–32. Ignoring the obvious developments from the Enoch tradition, Carr 1981 once again rejects all these parallels. On the Qumran background, see above, n. 9.

not with flesh and blood." Paul himself was probably not the author of these words, since they unequivocally abolish his reticence about the cosmic enemy. But there was good reason, not the least of which were the beginnings of official persecution and the destruction of Jerusalem, for the subsequent tradition to be troubled by and so to clarify Paul's ambivalence. The gospels, we shall now see, provided further reasons.

FIFTEEN

THE COMBAT IN THE SYNOPTIC
GOSPELS

ONE FREQUENTLY encounters the view in biblical criticism that the synoptic gospels, especially Mark, represent a Christianity of a popular, unreflective kind, a sort of basic "simple faith." I do not propose to quarrel directly with this view—it has been amply challenged in recent scholarship[1]—but simply wish to expose one of the biases that continue to foster it. The contrast implied is usually between the synoptic gospels and John or Paul, both of whom are indeed more intellectually stimulating writers, perhaps because they both argue. One focus of the contrast is usually the synoptic preoccupation, suitable for popular faith, with exorcism. Embarrassing as the topic of exorcism may be (and certainly made more so by a recent spate of films) to the liberal Christian, exorcism is nevertheless a central, even dominating concern of the synoptic gospels, and the topic may not be dismissed or excused on the grounds of its popularity. We find here a genuine continuity between the apocalyptic Christianity of the Book of Revelation, Paul's more theologically complex religion, and the world of common belief, unreflective or not. The exorcism stories are the most frequent form that the combat tradition takes in the synoptic gospels. One of the chief tasks of Jesus, as Mark, Matthew, and Luke tell it, was the struggle against unclean spirits or evil demons.[2]

The importance of the exorcism stories in Mark may be illustrated both by their number—there are twenty or more (depending on certain interpretive differences) in what is a rather brief narrative—and by the speed with which the author of this gospel[3] gets down to the telling of the first one. Immediately after his splendid preamble (the preaching of John the

---

[1] Farrer 1951, Auerbach 1953:40–49, Nineham 1963, Ricoeur 1975, Drury 1976, Kee 1977, and Kermode 1979 represent some of the more stimulating and divergent recent discussions.

[2] R. Yates 1977 is a succinct statement; cf. J. B. Russell 1977:221–49, and now H. A. Kelly 1985:17–56.

[3] For convenience he is here called "Mark," and we follow a similar convention for the other gospels.

Baptist) come variants of standard episodes in the combat plot: the baptism of Jesus himself, the descent of the dove, then Mark's oddly brief reference to the wilderness episode, followed by the gathering of the first disciples from the fishermen beside the sea. Equipped with these new helpers (and we recall that acquiring helpers was a common ingredient of such hero stories, one we have noted in the Gilgamesh narrative at a similar point), Jesus proceeds to his first public act. He goes to the synagogue at Capernaum on the Sabbath and preaches. Mark does not choose to tell us here about the teaching itself. Instead, he dramatizes the visit to the synagogue thus (we are still only at verse 23 of the first chapter):

> And there was in their synagogue a man with an unclean spirit, and he cried out, saying, "let us alone, what have we to do with thee, thou Jesus of Nazareth? art thou come to destroy us? I know thee who thou art, the Holy One of God."
> And Jesus rebuked him, saying, "Hold thy peace, and come out of him." And when the unclean spirit had torn him, and cried with a loud voice, he came out of him.

The meaning of this story is contained fairly clearly in the reaction of the audience:

> And they were all amazed, and questioned among themselves, saying, "What thing is this? A new teaching: for with authority commands he even the unclean spirits [*pneumasi*], and they do obey him." And immediately his fame spread abroad throughout all the region around Galilee.

Mark does not tell us the teaching itself, partly because he already summarized it when Jesus gathered the first disciples ("The time is fulfilled and the kingdom of God is at hand"), but also because the teaching is somehow represented by the event the people have witnessed—a new teaching: power over the spirits.

The story shows a continuity of language with the earlier combat tradition. When we translate the word *pneuma* as "spirit" we miss the connection, for the word means literally "breath" or "wind." In case we miss the point, Mark soon tells another story in which Jesus literally (or so it seems) walks upon the water and calms the storm, so repeating in a new context the action of the combat hero against his enemy. Furthermore, we should notice *how* Jesus is said to command the unclean spirits. The Greek verb in the story, translated as "rebuke" in the King James Version and frequent in the exorcism stories, is *epitiman*, and the Semitic word that it probably translates is *g'r*, found in several texts that speak of God "rebuking" the waters of chaos (Ps. 18.16, 104.7, 106.9). The same Semitic root occurs also in two of the Ugaritic texts that recount Baal's victory over Yamm-Nahar, Sea-River, texts that influenced Psalm 104, for example. In that psalm the Lord puts the waters to flight with his powerful "roar." The verb in its various Semitic contexts is probably the equivalent of the widespread motif among warlike cultures of the hero's great battle-cry— such as the supernatural shout of Achilles at *Iliad* 18.217. In the New Testament, although the idea has lost most of its explicit military associations, it still retains the connotations, as Kee suggests, "of divine conflict with hostile powers, the outcome of which is the utterance of the powerful word by which the demonic forces are brought under control." Thus, Jesus' rebuke is no mere reprimand, but "the word of command by which God's agent defeats his enemies, thus preparing for the coming of God's kingdom."[4] So this earliest stratum of New Testament miracle stories—the exorcisms—belongs not to the Hellenistic wonder-worker tradition so much as to the demonology characteristic of apocalyptic Judaism. Thus the link is clear between the explicit war language of the apocalyptic writings themselves and the general context into which Mark, and the other synoptic writers, place the daily activity of Jesus. The link is a narrative, the Christian legacy from the ancient combat myth but now transformed to history or legend, in which Jesus plays the role of hero and liberator of his people from the depredations of, now even *possession* by, the powers of evil.

The Greek verb *epitiman* is actually quite common in the gospels, and in one instance at least it seems to preserve even stronger traces of its combat connections. When Peter recognizes Jesus as the Christ, there follows in Mark's version a curious series of "rebukes."[5] First, Jesus rebukes all the disciples and tells them to keep quiet about what Peter has said. Then, when Jesus makes the first of his three prophecies of the Passion, Peter himself begins to rebuke Jesus. Mark does not tell us what Peter said, but Jesus's reaction is curious and revealing: "He turned round, looked at his disciples, and rebuked Peter, saying, 'Get behind me, Satan. For you do not think about the things of God, but the things of men.'" Jesus promptly launches into the series of paradoxical sayings about losing one's life to save it and gaining the world to lose one's soul. Now by any

---

[4] Kee 1968. See above, Chapter 2.9 n. 64, and Day 1985:29n.
[5] Mark 8.27–9.1.

reading this is an odd part of Mark's text, yet there is a reasonably clear link in Mark between the sermon that follows and the rebuke to Peter. A series of oppositions between the things of this world (of men) and the things of God is triggered by the mention of Satan, the fundamental opponent. What Jesus says in the Greek is *"Hypage opisō mou, Satana,"* where the word *opisō* preserves the sense of something in the way, opposing forward progress, which we have already noted in the story of Balaam's ass, one of the earliest instances of the word *śāṭān* in the Bible. In Matthew's version of the saying, Jesus even adds, immediately after the word *Satana:* *"skandalon ei emou"* (You are a stumbling-block to me).[6] So Peter plays a Satan, or *diabolos*, to Christ's progress on the way toward his condemnation, death, and resurrection.

Curiously enough, the word *skandalon* is, as we have seen, cognate with "slanderer," which is one of the most common meanings of *diabolos* in Greek. By now a cluster of ideas has gathered about the words used for the adversary, and they are all likely to be present at any mention of the terms "Satan" or "devil." Satan, devil, something placed in the way, opposed, opponent—all connect quite readily with "slander" or "false accusation, of the kind that creates scandal," one of the primary functions of the Old Testament Satan. Into this set of ideas the word *epitiman*, rebuke, fits easily, whether it is Peter who rebukes Jesus or Jesus who rebukes Peter. The word signals an accusation here (you ought not to do that, you are a Satan, or obstacle, to me), but the link with the combat idea of an adversary, also present in the passage, still hovers naturally in the penumbra of meaning.

Matthew attaches the Markan recognition episode to the declaration, absent in Mark, that the church is to be built on Peter, the Rock. That Christ should then call Peter "Satan" too may seem a little unfortunate if the church were to get a solid start in its history. And there have been plenty of Protestants willing to call the popes Satan or Antichrist. Indeed, the ambivalence of the idea of a church itself—its dependence on heresy or opposition—was to be one of the principal reasons for Satan's continued power in the Christian tradition. Matthew may actually have been trying to avoid such ambivalence by his addition of the phrase *"skandalon ei emou"* (you are a stumbling-block in my way). What he implies, in effect, is that when Jesus called Peter "Satan" he was using the word in its generic Hebrew sense, not denouncing his chief disciple as a follower of the devil.

[6] Matt. 16.23. See Lattimore 1962 and above, Introduction and Chapters 5 and 14.

He did not, however, do his case much good by using another version of the same saying in the wilderness episode. There Jesus speaks the words "*Hypage, Satana*" (Get thee hence, Satan) directly to the devil. The words "*opisō mou*" (out of my way, behind me) are missing, but otherwise the saying is the same. Perhaps the hypothetical "sayings source," or the oral tradition, offered two different versions of this remark in two different contexts, of which Matthew uses both, but Mark only one (the words do not occur in Luke, although they are added in the King James Version). But the remark is so much more appropriate in the wilderness context that one might suspect, on the grounds of *lectio difficilior*, that its earliest context was the Peter episode. At some point, at any rate, it was linked to the wilderness scene, where its connection with the combat tradition would be much more obvious.

The testing of the hero before his main encounter with the enemy is a common feature of combat myths, as we have seen. The wilderness episode fits this function well, but again there is a curious difference between Mark, on the one hand, and Matthew and Luke, on the other. Matthew and Luke share a tradition in which Jesus meets the temptations by quoting Deuteronomy. For example, Deuteronomy 6.16, "Ye shall not tempt the Lord your God," is cited in Matthew 4.7 and Luke 4.12, and Deuteronomy 6.13–14, "Thou shalt fear the Lord thy God, and serve him and shalt swear by his name. Yet shall not go after other gods, of the gods of the people which are round about you," becomes in Luke 4.8, "It is written: thou shalt worship the Lord thy God, and him only shalt thou serve," to which Matthew 4.10 adds, "Get thee hence, Satan." The passages in Deuteronomy concern the Jewish wanderings in the wilderness, interpreted as a testing of the people before their entry into the Promised Land and to teach them that man does not live by bread alone.[7] Despite the considerable variations between Matthew and Luke, precisely what we would expect in oral narrative tradition, the allusions to the Exodus-Conquest typology show clearly that both gospels view the wilderness episode as filling the same narrative function in the overall combat plot, although for them the battle scene has now shifted to Christ's life.

All this makes the radical variation in Mark the more mysterious. His version of the temptation episode (1.12–13) is very brief—but for the phrase "and was tempted of Satan" this would not be the well-known

---

[7] Deut. 8.2–3; Matt. 4.4; Luke 4.4. Cf. H. A. Kelly 1964 and 1974:49–56 and R. E. Brown 1965:203–7.

temptation episode at all—and the rebuke to Satan occurs in a totally different context. Is there any way to explain this?

The conventional function of the testing scene in the pattern of the combat myth, as we studied it earlier, was to confirm the hero as hero, often by explicit recognition of his status from a council of the gods. At the level of myth, we saw, the divine council may even replace the donor episode as the confirmation of the hero's status. In Mark's version, the wilderness scene itself is very brief, but it follows immediately the remarkable scene of the baptism by John and the voice from heaven, the descent of the dove establishing the identity of the hero. If the function of the testing scene is recognition of the hero, then, that task has already been performed by the baptism, and the temptation reference simply confirms it.

It may also be relevant that John is described just before as "the voice of one crying in the wilderness," which is here not only an allusion to Isaiah 40.3 but also the necessary preliminary to the recognition of Jesus in the wilderness. Furthermore, recognition as a phenomenon takes up a good deal of Mark's gospel. The paradox is that the devils and unclean spirits recognize Jesus instantly, while many others, including often enough the disciples themselves, do not. And as we saw, at the very moment when Peter recognizes the true nature of Jesus as the Christ, the Messiah, or heroic liberator of his people, Peter is called Satan (8.27–33). The story of Peter's recognition is complemented by the other story in which, at the moment Jesus announces himself as the Christ, Peter denies him.[8] Peter's own act of recognition is preceded by the story of a blind man who needs two applications of Jesus' hands before he sees clearly (the first time he sees men only as "trees walking"), and it is followed by Jesus' distinction between the things of God and the things of men. One result of all this, as Kermode demonstrates well, is that the text of Mark becomes all the more enigmatic. But we might also posit here a kind of three-level hierarchy of recognizers. The first level is the ordinary men who do not "have eyes to see," represented in the story by what the other disciples say men say Jesus is (John the Baptist, Elijah, one of the prophets). Then comes the level of the unclean spirits and Peter, who see him truly perhaps, but can only oppose what they see. Finally there is the third and highest level of recognition, implied somehow in the paradoxes about losing one's soul in order to have it and accompanied by the injunction to deny oneself, take up

[8] Kermode 1979:139.

one's cross (so everyone has a cross, and the actual crucifixion is symbolic of this?), and follow Jesus. Do the injunctions to secrecy in Mark (usually violated), coupled with the frequent statements about "they that have ears/eyes to hear/see," imply that this third level of recognition may be achieved only by what Milton calls that "sovrain eyesalve"[9] which changes the organs of perception?

It seems possible, then, that this enigmatic language with which Mark shapes his variant of the story is an effort, parallel but different from Paul's, to alter the shape and meaning of the traditional myth from a combat with external forces into a model of personal transformation. Mark has at this point already recorded the saying in which Jesus announces publicly "There is nothing from without a man that entering into him can defile him: but the things that come out of him, those are they that defile the man" (7.15). It would be rash to take this line of argument too far in relation to a text as much the subject of scholarly disagreement as Mark's is, but the idea may nevertheless give us a way to read these frequent stories of exorcism. It may show us not simply that they are variants of the combat tradition, which is fairly obvious, but how and in what direction their variation tends. After all, a burning issue of Jesus' lifetime was the question of the political leadership of the Jewish Messiah,[10] a hope that we find again and again, in symbolic form, in the apocalyptic literature, and it is this role which Jesus seems to reject decisively in the wilderness episode, whether in Matthew's version or Luke's version. The general direction of the Markan gospel, then, is away from this standard story of a war with external enemies and instead toward a more personal or inward struggle.

This central characteristic of the exorcism stories is most obvious in that of the Gerasene demoniac. Granted that this story is built up, as Starobinski has shown,[11] of a series of oppositions—between upper and lower worlds, god and demon, clean and unclean, man and animal, Jew and Gentile, this side of the lake and the other—the most striking and incontrovertibly relevant opposition is between internal and external. The demoniac is possessed by a spirit who, like the synagogue spirit, engages

[9] "If we will but purge with sovrain eyesalve that intellectual ray which God hath planted in us, then we would beleeve the Scriptures protesting their own plainnes, and perspicuity" (*Of Reformation*, p. 37 of 1641 ed. in Patrick 1967:61).

[10] Jeremias 1971: vol. 1, 71–72. Cf. Perrin 1974:143–66 and Kee 1977:121–65, each of whom takes a different view of the historical *Sitz im Leben* but all of whom stress the apocalyptic context.

[11] Starobinski 1971 and 1974; Mark 5.1–20.

in a dialogue with Jesus and tells him his name is Legion (for like Roman troops we are many). The devils beg not to be sent entirely out of the country, but instead into a herd of swine, some two thousand says Mark. As soon as Jesus expels the spirit(s) from the man, it (or they) take over the herd of pigs, who promptly rush down the hillside and drown themselves in the sea. News spreads fast, and people come out from the city to discover the possessed man in his right mind and clothed. Having heard the story, the people beg Jesus to go away. Jesus does so, but he tells the man to go about and proclaim the cure, the reverse of the normal Markan injunction to silence.

The story is made up of a series of dramatic comings and goings. Jesus crosses the sea and enters an alien (Gentile) community from outside; the spirits come out of the man and go into the pigs; the pigs so invaded plunge down the hill and into the sea; the people come out of the city and implore Jesus to go away, "out of their coasts." At the end, Jesus goes into the ship, and the man asks to come along too, but Jesus will not let him. Instead, he tells him to go back, not now to the tombs (outside and isolated) where he had previously lived, but "home to thy friends." The excluded man is thus reincorporated into his community, even as Jesus himself leaves it, and returns to the other side of the sea, that is, back to his world. And at the center of all this entering and leaving is the point of the whole episode—the exorcism of the spirits from within the man. That they take on a concrete form in the memorable spectacle of the poor pigs only serves to emphasize the main movement, from inside to outside for the spirits and so from exclusion to inclusion for the man.

Once we see that the chief point of all these exorcism stories is the dialectic of inner and outer, we may begin to see their function in the Markan theology. On the literal level, each story records a dramatic cure in which what was formerly within the sufferer becomes external to him, and thus he is no longer in its power. But the impact of the stories, their implications for their audience, are by no means as simple. Though they seem to make external what was previously internal, they also imply that the internal source of suffering is in fact an external alien force, an intruder that has taken over the motivating energy of the victim and turns it to sinful ends. Now we can begin to see why the dialectic of inner and outer in the story of the Gerasene demoniac is so complex. The cause of suffering is shown to be both inner and outer. The action of the exorcist liberates the sufferer and shows the true source of the individual pain to be an external agent, yet before the exorcist performs his miracle there was no such radical separation of inner and outer. Hence the confusion that arises in both the synagogue and the Gerasene stories about who exactly is speaking to Jesus, the human being or the possessing devil.

The exorcism stories in Mark and the other synoptic writers appear to have a double function. On the one hand, they pose the central problem of the Christian gospel in a peculiarly ambivalent or enigmatic form. Is the source of sin to be viewed as external, as in the idea of pollution, in demonology itself, in apocalyptic myth, or as internal, as in the moral sermon of Jesus in Mark, in one aspect of Paul's more articulate theology, and in the subjective experience of the demonic victim, the one possessed? This is not a question of levels of sophistication or of progress (as Ricoeur, for example, would have it[12]) from simpler to more complex, and therefore more moralistic, theology, for the issue of inner and outer is a necessary part of all such exorcism stories. On the other hand, these stories dramatize in a readily available form and in a peculiarly personal way the general struggle of the hero figure (exorcist) with his adversaries. The plunge into the sea of the demons in the Gerasene story parallels the apocalyptic end of Satan and his angels cast into the fire or the abyss. And in spite of the frequent mistranslation of *daimonia* as devils in English Bibles, the synoptic gospels do imply, in at least two instances, that the demons are a sort of loosely organized army under their general, Satan,[13] so that the conflict is more explicitly between the two main characters of the combat tradition.

The problem is as follows. The terms used generally for the alien spirits that Jesus exorcises, especially in Mark, are *pneumata akatharta* and *daimonia*, "unclean spirits" and "demons." What connection do these beings have with the cosmic adversary figure, called both Satan and *diabolos* in the Book of Revelation? In other words, are the various exorcisms to be understood simply as isolated acts of healing, each one with the tenuous connection with the ancient combat tradition for which we have been arguing, or are they various local skirmishes in a long war, the war of the last times anticipated in the apocalyptic literature? This is not an easy question to answer, although theological doctrine has long since opted for the latter solution. If we look at each act of exorcism in isolation, we cannot get far beyond remarking the survival of combat language and the absence, itself quite striking, of any magical-medical formula like that stand-

---

[12] Ricoeur 1967: 21, 46, 240.

[13] Mark 3.22–29 (Matt. 12.22–29; Luke 11.14–22), the Beelzeboul controversy, and Luke 10.17–20. See Bamberger 1952:67–69 and below.

ard in, for example, the Egyptian treatises of the period. But fortunately
the synoptic gospels raise this problem themselves, and so afford at least
tentative answers to it, even though we must not expect the theological
inclusiveness of a latter era. Two episodes are crucial here. One of them is
found only in Luke, while the other is common to all three synoptic writers—the so-called Beelzeboul controversy.

Although all three gospels represent Jesus as conferring the power of
exorcism on his disciples,[14] only Luke has the story of the mission and
return of the seventy disciples (10.1–20). The mission may well be a symbolic anticipation of the church's mission to the Gentiles, since in Jewish
thinking seventy was the traditional number of Gentile nations.[15] But the
narrative is strongly reminiscent of the visit of the two angels to Sodom
and Gomorrah (a widespread ancient story type having close associations
with the flood pattern),[16] and indeed Sodom's destruction is alluded to in
the text, as are Tyre and Sidon. The seventy are sent out in pairs to test
the various cities and prepare for Christ's coming. They are to wish peace
on each house, to accept hospitality, heal the sick, and tell their hosts that
the kingdom of heaven is nigh. They are also told to cry woe on any city
that does not receive them. They are not told explicitly to exorcise devils
(although the healing mission may well be taken to include such activity,
as in the miracles of Christ himself), but when they return the following
exchange takes place:

> And the seventy returned again with joy, saying, "Lord, even the demons
> [*daimonia*] are subject to us in thy name."
>   And he said to them, "I beheld Satan as lightning fall from heaven. See, I
> have given you the means/authority [*exousian*] to tread on serpents [*opheōn*]
> and scorpions, and over all the power of the enemy [*tou echthrou*], and noth-
> ing shall be able to harm you.[17]

The words seem to reflect an ecstatic vision, and have the same tense
difficulties as we noted in the Enoch tradition and the Book of Revelation.
In any case, the passage clearly connects the power over demons with the
combat tradition we have been tracing. Each little exorcism or act of healing is linked to the "fall" of the enemy, who is here envisaged as a heav-

---

[14] Mark 6.7; Matt. 10.1; Luke 7.1–2.
[15] Gen. 10; Targum Pseudo-Jonathan on Deut. 32.8; *Enoch*, 89.59; Perrin 1974:209. Why
else have the twelve suddenly become seventy?
[16] Fontenrose 1945. Cf. Heb. 13.2, which cites Gen. 19, and see above, Chapter 12.7 n.
73.
[17] Luke 10.17–20. See Moule 1963:206.

enly body (as in the rebel tradition), and the image of treading on the defeated foe, here represented by serpents and scorpions, is already a familiar one in the iconography of the victory scene. Inevitably, the passage was to become a much-cited proof-text in the developing mythology of Satan.

The other synoptic passage that demonstrates a link between the devils (*daimonia*) exorcised and Satan appears in different forms in all three gospels—the Beelzeboul controversy. The core common of each of the three variants is the dialogue and saying to which the story leads. This probably shows that in each case the stories are constructed to give a context for the saying and that each of the three gospel writers believed the saying to be sufficiently important to provide it with a narrative frame. The dialogue is essentially an accusation by the Jerusalem scribes that Jesus casts out demons by the power of the prince of demons, Beelzeboul.[18] Jesus' response in all three versions is to point out that for the prince of demons, whom Jesus immediately calls Satan, to cast out demons would be to turn against ("divide") his own kingdom and so bring about his own downfall. The logic of the case is that since Satan is unlikely to be so foolish the power by which Jesus works against the demons must be the power (finger or spirit) of God. But what is interesting about the response is its assumption that demons are the allies or servants of Satan and that exorcism is therefore against the adversary himself.

Various parables or sayings have accumulated around this core in Matthew and Luke, but all three continue the episode with the parable of the strong man's house. "No man can enter a strong man's house, and spoil his goods, except he will first bind the strong man: and then he will spoil his house" (Mark 3.27). The implication is that Satan is the strong man and Jesus is out to rob him. Whether we should conclude further that Jesus has already bound Satan and is now liberating his "possessions" is unclear. If so, then presumably the binding of Satan should be identified with the wilderness scene,[19] but the more likely explanation is that the exorcisms themselves are regarded as the victorious combat with Satan and

---

[18] See Kittel (ed.) 1951: vol. 1, 605; Strack and Billerbeck 1922–61: vol. 4, 515. The name Beelzeboul/Beelzebub seems to derive from *zbl b'l*, "Prince Baal." In view of Matt. 10.25 ("If they have called the master of the house Beelzeboul"), the meaning "Lord of the House" seems to be understood rather than the possible "Lord of the Dung." The form Beelzebub contains a derisive allusion to Baal-zebub, "Lord of the Flies," the pagan god of Ekron in 2 Kings 1.2. The deliberate corruption reflects the demotion of pagan god to demon, e.g., Ps. 96.5 and Deut. 32.17. I am indebted here to Dr. John Day.

[19] Best 1965:12–13; cf. Forsyth 1985.

his kingdom.[20] Matthew and Luke both add the saying "He who is not with me is against me." At any rate, it seems clear that the sayings about Beelzeboul and the strong man are included in all three synoptic gospels because of the need to situate the exorcisms in the context of the combat with Satan and so to make explicit, in our terms, that they are variants or transformations of the combat myth. Jesus liberates the victims of the devil's oppression. As the summary of his life in Acts 10.38 puts it, "He went about doing good and healing all that were oppressed by the devil [*tou diabolou*], for God was with him."[21]

The differences between Paul and the synoptic gospels have long preoccupied the commentators. Paul mentions demons only as the idols to whom pagans sacrifice (1 Cor. 10.19–22). He rarely cites the sayings of Christ, and when he does (as at 2 Cor. 7.11), he can follow it with his own saying, apparently of equal authority. The heart of Paul's message is the death and resurrection of Christ, whereas the gospels concentrate on the life, the sayings, and the Passion. Paul, the earlier writer, preaches to the Gentiles and undermines the Jewish Law, but the Jesus recorded in the post-Pauline synoptic gospels hardly transcends the categories of Judaism, even if he is at odds with some of its practitioners. Paul apparently cites with approval the christological hymn in which the heavenly Christ decides to obey God's will before he becomes the earthly Jesus (Phil. 2.5–10), whereas the synoptic gospels, unlike John's gospel, ignore Jesus' preexistence. Paul's letters, and the gospels are clearly intended for different audiences (Mark, Matthew, and Luke-Acts also differ significantly in this respect), and it is likely that by the time the gospels were set down the idea of a nonhuman Christ, the docetic heresy, required more elaborate refutation than it had for Paul.

In the terms offered by our study of the combat tradition, we can see that Paul and the synoptic gospels all make use of apocalyptic ideas but transform them in quite different directions. The hostile powers of Paul, however ambivalent they are, differ radically from the demons of the synoptic writers. Both make extensive use of the Satan, but only the problematic letter to the Ephesians mentions the *diabolos* (4.27, 6.11), and in Paul neither Satan nor the devil is linked to demons.

Radical as these differences are, they were often overlooked as the

---

[20] Aulén 1969:76; Leivestad 1954:47; Yates 1977:44.

[21] On the survival and impact of the belief in exorcism and the struggle with demons, see Harnack 1904: vol. 1, 152–80, who cites esp. Tertullian and Origen. Cf. below, Chapters 20 and 21, Cohn 1975, and K. Thomas 1978.

canon began to form and the church tried to find a unified teaching against heresies. And there was one dimly discernible narrative idea, common to Luke and Paul, that could encourage the early church to do so. Luke 10.19 connects the fall of Satan with power to tread on serpents (*opheōn*) and scorpions, while Paul mentions the seduction of Eve by a serpent (*ophis*) in the same context as the transformation of Satan into an angel of light (2 Cor. 11.3, 13–14). Romans 16.20, we saw, mentions the promise that God will soon crush Satan "under your feet." We can discern in these scattered remarks the beginnings of the protevangelium reading of Genesis 3.15 about the enmity between the heads of the serpent's descendants and the heels of Eve's. But in none of these passages, we have seen, is Satan identified with a serpent. The biblical identification of Satan and serpent rests neither on Paul nor on Luke, but on the Book of Revelation.

SIXTEEN

THE DEVIL AND THE

CANON

THE COMBAT MYTH so inextricably entwined with the origins of Christianity has often proved something of an embarrassment to liberal theologians, most obviously because of the stature and power that the myth grants to the adversary. Modern theologians, following Bultmann, have tried to "demythologize" the Christian faith and so leave a valid historical core that might be the object of respectable and rational belief. According to one group of English theologians, for example, Christians need no longer take literally the myth of a god-man as the focus of their beliefs.[1] Such progressive views received something of a setback in 1984 when York Minster was struck by lightning soon after the installation as Bishop of Durham of David Jenkins, a man who was not quite sound on the virgin birth or the resurrection. But doubts about the myth are by no means exclusively modern. In England, for example, they go back well beyond the rationalizing tendencies of the nineteenth century, not only to eighteenth-century deism but to the seventeenth-century phenomenon that has been called "the decline of hell."[2]

In the church as a whole, the problem of the adversary is much older. The power of the devil in the myth, when recast in theological terms, gave rise, for example, to the earliest of several theories of the atonement, the idea that Christ's victory had been won by paying a kind of ransom to the devil through the death on the cross. We find the theory in one form or another in Irenaeus, Origen, Basil the Great, Ambrose, and Jerome. The idea of a ransom paid to the devil could not fail to trouble the minds of several church fathers, but it was a logical extension of the combat myth that informs the earliest Christian texts. Any combat myth necessarily accords some measure of power and independence to the figure of

[1] Hick (ed.) 1977; see esp. Maurice Wiles' essay "Myth in Theology" (pp. 148–66) for a useful summary of the use of the word "myth" in theological contexts. It should be supplemented by the documents collected in Feldman and Richardson 1972. Bultmann's 1941 essay appears as "The New Testament and Mythology" in Bartsch (ed.) 1961. Cf. Jaspers and Bultmann 1958.

[2] See Walker 1964 and also K. Thomas 1978:767–800.

the adversary, even if, like Huwawa in the Gilgamesh epic or Satan in the story the church finally learned to tell, he derives his power ultimately from some higher source such as Enlil or Elohim. As theological thinking develops, this essential characterisic of the combat myth comes to be viewed in a more abstract and philosophical way as the problem of "dualism." But even though the language of debate in modern times has tended toward philosophical abstractions like "dualism," a term not used before 1700,[3] and even though several crucial points of doctrine were at issue in the great struggles of the first Christian centuries over what constituted orthodoxy, the language of the early church, as it worried over these theological issues, was generally the language of narrative or of the interpretation of narrative. Gregory of Nazianzus tried to discredit the ransom theory by asking ironic questions about its narrative credibility: "To whom was this [ransom] offered, and for what cause?" What happened, and why did it happen?—the most fundamental questions we ask about stories. When the answers are obscure or unsatisfactory, as they were for Gregory, we change the story. The problem of dualism and the quarrels about heresy that it spawned would remain at bottom narrative issues until, for example, Milton was impelled to ask his muse for similar narrative guidance at the beginning of *Paradise Lost*: "Say first what cause. . . ."

Narrative issues of this kind seem to have played a large role in the very formation of the Christian canon. Like rabbinic Judaism, Christianity is a religion based on interpretation of the Book. But there was for some time considerable argument about exactly what constituted that Book, or *Biblos*. The earliest Christians meant essentially what their Jewish brethren meant by "the scriptures": the Old Testament, more particularly, the Law and the Prophets. But early in the second century Marcion proposed his own canon of Christian writings, excluding the Jewish scriptures and limited to a severely expurgated Luke and Paul. This started a reaction, beginning with Marcion's contemporary Justin Martyr, which led eventually to the establishing of the Christian canon, with different branches of the church having differing canons. So the initial impulse to fix a canon was the work of a heretic, and the canon itself, as often, was the response of "orthodoxy" to that challenge.[4] Orthodoxy was defining itself largely by answering this and related challenges.

---

[3] Thomas Hyde apparently coined the term "dualismus" in *De vetere religione Persarum* (1700) to refer to what he thought were the heretical ideas of the Zoroastrians. See Duchesne-Guillemin 1958:10–11.

[4] Hennecke and Schneemelcher 1963–65: vol. 1, 28–60; Grant 1965. For a review of more recent work on canon formation, see J. A. Sanders 1981:373–94, who shows that the in-

Many of the documents thus excluded from the major canons survived, if at all, only in areas or languages peripheral to the Rome-dominated Western church. The *Book of Enoch*, although cited in the canonized Jude by name and supported by, for example, Tertullian, finally survived complete only in Ethiopic. Explicitly Jewish-Christian texts had to disguise themselves in such forms as the Pseudo-Clementine *Homilies*, while most of the Gnostic texts denounced by the church fathers disappeared entirely until Coptic translations were recently unearthed from the sands of Egypt. So if Christianity is the interpretation of the Book, that interpretation also defined the Book, in the literal sense of setting its limits, and we must be careful not to assume a Book before it existed.

The puzzling Letter to the Hebrews, for example, is not simply "a text of such excellence that it forced its way into the canon of the New Testament."[5] It was ascribed to Paul in the early church, but it shows few of the Pauline concerns, and Origen recognized in his commentary that its author was known only to God. The ascription was no more than an excuse to canonize the work. What, then, does it contain that would be so compelling? For one thing, it makes the clearest New Testament statement of what became the Christology of the orthodox tradition, enshrined in the creeds, that Jesus was both son of God, higher than the angels, and truly man. But in particular, as it puts forward this teaching, it offers a useful summary of the main event in the combat myth, and the relevant passage (Heb. 2.14) was "perhaps more often quoted by the Fathers than any other New Testament text."[6]

> Since then the children are sharers in flesh and blood, He also himself in like manner partook of the same; that through death he might bring to nought him that had the power of death, that is, the devil, and deliver them who through fear of death were all their lifetime subject to bondage.

The Incarnation is here understood to have had only one goal—death—and that death in turn is the victory over the adversary. The purpose of that victory is the liberation of mankind from slavery or tyranny. Through all the subsequent elaboration of this idea, it was always the paradox of triumph through death which would generate the most influential and often bizarre narratives. More generally, it was the problem of how

---

terpretive flexibility lost by fixing a text was compensated for in allegory. A good account of the processes involved is Bruns 1984; see also Vermes 1970.

[5] Perrin 1974:137.
[6] Aulén 1969:74.

to interpret this main event which would lead to the enormous growth and variety of narratives current during the early centuries of the Christian era. As the paradoxical victory in defeat became the focus of more and more controversy, so the number of narratives that tried to situate this event within a coherent narrative frame would proliferate, and other stories, once entirely independent, would now be attached and retold.

Narrative analysis of Christian belief, then, begins from the same paradox with which theology has had to cope. "It is death and Sheol," as A. Fridrichsen explained fifty years ago, "that form the scene of the redemption. And it is probably the oldest interpretation of Jesus' death that the death is the victory; the resurrection (glorification) comes as the reward, the seal, the completion, the manifestation of the result."[7] In our narrative terms, this means that the central Christian mystery is to be seen as a curious but decisive transformation of the combat pattern. Liberation from the death-dealing demon is actually achieved by the death of the hero. The resurrection is only the sign, not the occasion, of triumph. In the noncanonical literature that Christianity soon spawned, especially in the "Gospel of Nicodemus," a narrative was told of the descent to hell and its harrowing, a satisfying challenge and defeat of the devil during the three (actually two by our numbering system) days prescribed by Christian ritual observance between the crucifixion and the resurrection.[8] But this elaborate story—obvious as the need for it was—is simply a dramatization of the event that was the focus of belief: the victory in death.

The context in which this narrative event must be placed, we have argued, is the apocalyptic expectation of a conclusive battle against the world tyrant. Following the typology of Exodus, as it had been elaborated in Second Isaiah, the hero of the tale is the liberator from slavery or tyranny. The exorcism stories fit this type clearly, as does the Pauline theology of a victory over the power of death or the annulment of the Law of sin and death. Victory over death, then, is the event that fits the conclusion of the combat pattern, and in the Letter to the Hebrews that victory is specifically located on the cross. For its author, these are the last days (Heb. 1.2) of the apocalyptic hope.

We may now derive from this argument a further reason for the importance of the Adam story in Paul. If the victory over death is the conclusion, then the story that now fits best into the beginning of the combat

---

[7] Fridrichsen 1931:133, originally published in Swedish in 1920 and developed by Aulén 1969 (1st ed. 1931).

[8] See above, Chapter 12.4 n. 37.

pattern will be one that recounts the origin of death, and the biblical story that does so is the story of Adam and Eve. Most cultures have such a story, and the Eden narrative has many widespread features, including the warning not to do something and the inevitable disregard of that warning: "In the day that thou eatest thereof thou shalt surely die."[9] Paul's difficult and murky ideas about the Law of sin and death, then, can now be seen as an effort to explain in theological terms what his version of the Christ story establishes in narrative terms: Adam's disobedience near the beginning occasioned Christ's death, in obedience to the Law that thereby annulled the Law, near the end of the story.

Paul's combination of the Christ event with the Adam episode as a theory or story of the Redemption posed fresh problems, which also helped define the shape of the canon. The problems may be viewed in either theological or in narrative terms, but either way a central difficulty is how to connect the devil with the Adam episode. Even if Paul did have in mind a version of the Adam story which connected it to the angelic fall, as the contemporary Adam books did, we have already noted that there is little consistency about that tradition, and the problem was still posed about the relative responsibility of the angel-serpent or man. We have seen too that, if the Adam story replaced the Watcher story to account for the origin of evil, new explanations were required about the angelic fall.

But the letters in which Paul mentions Adam (Corinthians and Romans) do not make any link with the Watcher tale, and subsequent interpreters would have to work out new connections between human and angelic fall. Nor does the story of the happy garden in the second and third chapters of Genesis have any obvious connection with the evil tyrant, "the god of this world," from whom the believer was supposedly now redeemed.

We have noted already that the apocalyptic kind of narrative, dualistic as it is, poses serious theological problems about the responsibility of human beings, about the primacy of Evil or Sin, to use a convenient shorthand. It was this kind of problem which Paul's narrative move now raised. On the one hand, Christianity followed the Jewish tradition of a continually broken covenant in blaming mankind for the state of the world. Paul's alignment of Adam and Christ fits this tradition, and thereafter the story of a lost Eden became the most common focus of this view. On the other hand, the inherited combat myth, which meant that the hu-

---

[9] Gen. 2.17. See S. Thompson 1955–58, Motif A1335.

man Jesus was identified with the god-hero and so raised above human status, led to the objectivization, within the cosmos as a whole, of the god's adversary, and thus the location of the source of sin outside man, in personified Evil. Somehow these two views had to be reconciled; a new origin myth that would bring them together had to be found. The myth would not, of course, be really "new"—there is no such thing. Rather, in keeping with the tradition of a Bookish religion, it would take the form of "interpretation." One biblical passage or episode would be read in the light of others, until they came to imply each other—as they did for Milton. But it is remarkable how often, in spite of developments in the Adam literature, the Eden story and some version of cosmic rebellion continue to be told separately. Even when they are brought together they threaten to fall apart into their separate origins, and so the essence of the theological-interpretive dilemma would be the effort to reconcile them. A constant tension would persist within the larger story, the "new" myth, between the priority of Sin or Evil.

This tension also had its historical implications and led to at least one terrible tragedy. The apocalyptic hopes of Judaism reached a drastic climax with the Jewish War of A.D. 66–70 against the Romans. The fact of the Roman enemy was a sure sign of the externality of evil, but equally the very presence of the godless Gentiles within the holy city of Jerusalem must be due to the sins of the people of God. Deliverance could come only when the people were pure enough in God's eyes. When the Romans broke into the city to which they had laid siege, they found Jew murdering Jew in the name of this purity before God's Law.

Such internecine strife has been repeated often enough in the Christian context, and for similar reasons, namely the ambiguous relation of Sin to Evil, of internal to external causes of suffering. The enemy may be within, but where do we draw the line between inside and outside? In the above example, the logic of thought starts from the assumption that the enemy is within the city but not in me. Those other fellows are the traitors. We have noted a similar ambivalence in the exorcism stories, and the Eden story suggests the same dilemma: the serpent is within the garden, but is it therefore within Adam and Eve, or in the maker of the garden—in God himself? Such problems are the stuff of theology and the main source of strife within the developing Christian church. We can see them raised in one form or another by most of the controversies that help to define church doctrine, and most clearly in the search for a satisfactory origin myth.

We have seen that one way of linking the rebellion and Adam stories—through Satan's envy—was current in the Adam literature of Hellenistic Judaism, especially the *Vita Adae et Evae* and its congeners. Undoubtedly this narrative had an impact on the church as it tried to tell itself its own version. But there seems to have been no question of canonizing these books themselves, and the main factor that drove the church toward the identification of serpent and Satan was the political struggle with heresy which occupied so much of the energy of the young church. Some Gnostics in particular had elaborated the Adam and Eve stories current in Alexandria into their own coherent and explicit narrative. The serpent of the story was the hero and was even identified with Christ.[10] He tried to save Adam and Eve from the ignorant and tyrannical God who would deny them knowledge, represented by the tree. It was thus imperative, if Paul's insistence on aligning the two stories was not also to separate the Christian from the Jewish God, for the church to reverse the Gnostic identification. If God were to remain the hero of the story, the serpent had to become his adversary, the tyrant of the new religion.

But could it do this when the serpent of Genesis was quite plainly just that, a serpent? True, he had some odd characteristics for a snake; he could speak, for example, and he seemed to know God's mind. But Genesis nowhere says he was anything other than a talking snake.[11] One method for a religion of the Book would be to find another text that did make this identification, and then to read each in the light of the other. Only one text of those not otherwise unacceptable for canonization made explicit the requisite identification of Satan and serpent—the curious work we know as the Book of Revelation. There, in one character, the church found "the great dragon, that old serpent, called the Devil, and Satan."[12] We have already noticed that these passages bring together most aspects of the apocalyptic combat myth, from the star-like angel to the accuser at the heavenly court and the *agent provocateur* who leads astray the whole world. Perhaps the author intended the phrase *ho palaios ophis*, that old serpent, to refer to the Genesis serpent, since he seems to allude to its apocalyptic complement, the protevangelium of Genesis 3.15 at Revelation 12.17. Certainly, in view of the Gnostic identity of the serpent, the church found

---

[10] *Testimony of Truth* 47.4–49.9 in Robinson (ed.) 1977:411–12. On the Ophites, see below, Chapters 18 and 21, and for the probable link with Revelation, see below, Chapter 17.1. Cf. Barrett 1983:129.

[11] See J. M. Evans 1968 for the problems of the Genesis account.

[12] Rev. 12.9; cf. 20.2. See above, Chapter 13.

it convenient to think he did. Justin, for example, is clearly alluding to this text in his *First Apology*: "Among us the chief of the evil demons is called the serpent and Satan and the devil, as you can learn from examining our writings. Christ has foretold that he will be cast into the fire with his host and those who follow him, to be punished for endless ages."[13] Justin's appeal to Revelation as "our writings" is one of the earliest signs that the idea of a Christian canon was developing and shows that the need to identify the devil was a prime motive.

In spite of misgivings by a number of prominent churchmen, the "Apocalypse of St. John the Divine," that odd and obscure series of visions, more Jewish than Christian in content and barely relevant to a church establishment that had mostly given up its apocalyptic hopes, was assumed to be by the author of John's gospel, and was included among the holy texts.[14] For nowhere else is Satan actually called the serpent. No doubt other early Christians had the equation in mind. Paul's mention of Adam in his redemption theory even seems to require it, and one passage in his letter to the Romans (16.20) implies it.: "And the god of peace shall crush (*suntripsei*) Satan under your feet shortly." Since Paul is praising his correspondents for obedience, it is likely that he alludes to a variant of the prophecy in Genesis 3.15, the protevangelium, thus identifying the serpent with Christ's and mankind's enemy.[15] But he does not actually say that by "Satan" he means also the Genesis serpent, and indeed the church would later go to considerable trouble to insist on the equation. Without the Book of Revelation as a sanctified text, the identification of Genesis serpent with the adversary would have stood on much shakier ground.

The placing of the Apocalypse at the end of the Bible brought some advantages also for the shape of the canon. The Book of Revelation points forward to the end of time, just as Genesis talks of its beginning. The tree of life at the end of the book balances the tree of knowledge at the beginning (an echo that would not escape the acute Augustine, who planned his own *Confessions* around two equally symbolic trees). And the enemy, he who had started all the trouble in the beginning, could be seen to be finally

[13] Justin, *First Apology* 28.1, trans. E. R. Hardy in Richardson (ed.) 1970:259. Cf. Rev. 20.3, 10, Matt. 25.41, and below, Chapter 20 n. 7.

[14] Revelation was suspect especially in the Eastern church; Eusebius raised doubts even in the fourth century. Justin, himself no complex thinker, seems to apologize with his next breath for the apocalyptic message, explaining that God delays the end so that people can repent. See below, Chapter 20, and for Irenaeus' influential view, see Chapter 19.1.

[15] For interpretation of Gen. 3.15 in the light of the combat, see above, Chapters 12.5, 14.5, 15, and below, Chapter 19.2.

defeated here at the end. This means of closure gives to the whole Christian Bible the shape of the combat myth, and the felt need to do so accounts well both for the inclusion of the Book of Revelation at all and for its commanding position as the last word. And, what was to be even more significant for the subsequent history of the church, the identification of Satan/serpent as "he who leads astray the whole world" made the struggle with heresy seem to be an extension of the mythological combat.

Part Four

THE DEMIURGE AND THE DEVIL

SEVENTEEN

SATAN THE HERETIC

To CONCEIVE the earliest stages of Christianity as the steady triumph of orthodoxy (right belief) over heresy is at best simpleminded. It is the conception that many church fathers tried to impose, and it is still the view that informs the tamer historians of Christian doctrine, even the more judicious among them. For example, Jaroslav Pelikan, whose projected five-volume history of *The Christian Tradition* began appearing in 1971, allows that "heresy could sometimes claim greater antiquity than orthodoxy" (without giving any examples) but continues calmly:

> What did characterize primitive Christianity was a unity of life, of fidelity to the Old Testament, of devotion, and of loyalty to its Lord, as he was witnessed to in the Old and New Testament. Heresy was a deviation from that unity. . . . It is becoming increasingly evident that this "primitive catholicism," with its movement from kerugma to dogma, was already far more explicitly at work in the first century than was once supposed.[1]

If that were true, one might wonder why the earliest church we glimpse in New Testament letters is already alive with controversy. "O foolish Galatians, who hath bewitched you?" writes Paul (Gal. 3.1), and he frequently attacks other teachers, whether Jewish-Christian or Gnostic. His followers explicitly denounce heresies, chiefly Gnostic. Nor is it only the Pauline tendency which tries to root out false teaching, for the theme is common to the so-called catholic epistles and to the letters to the seven churches with which the Book of Revelation begins. Most of these letters already reflect a period when minor distinctions were becoming crucial points of difference and when mutual hostility intensified the hardening and elaboration of doctrine—when, in fact, the church was being formed in order to "guard the deposit, avoiding the profane babblings and contradictions of the *gnosis* which is falsely so called."[2]

In spite of occasional exaggeration of the evidence, the thesis that Walter Bauer first advanced in 1934 about the heterogeneity of early Christian

---

[1] Pelikan 1971:70, cf. Conzelmann 1973:110–11.
[2] 1 Tim. 6.20. See also Fenton 1978 and Wisse 1981, 1983.

sects and the inappropriateness of a concept such as orthodoxy[3] remains the basis of any sound understanding of the early "church." In Edessa, in Alexandria, in Antioch, in Ephesus, in Corinth flourished various forms of Christianity which were later denounced as heresy. "Orthodoxy" is that form of church organization and teaching which came to be associated with Rome and which was able to impose its authority, always imperfectly, on the rest of Christendom. The very idea of an orthodox belief is a product of the quarrel with heresy.

The struggle between competing versions of Christianity lent some of its characteristics and a vital theological function to Satan. As the prince of error and the father of lies, he became the arch-heretic, the name under which rival teachers were denounced. Thus the battle with heresy, which occupied so much of the energy of the early church fathers and to which we owe the formulation of Christian doctrine, came to be seen as the newest transformation of the ancient combat myth. What he had done in the beginning, Satan was still doing. He was the first apostate, and still the ultimate source of apostasy. The enormous diversity of sects and beliefs with which one disagreed could be comprehensively labeled "error"— and collectively damned as "firstborn of Satan." Orthodoxy came first, and then heresy twisted and distorted its pristine teaching. As Origen put it, "Heretics all begin by believing, and afterwards depart from the road of faith and the truth of the church's teaching."[4] Tertullian uses the analogy of a wild olive or fig tree that springs from a cultivated seed.[5] Just as Satan had perverted the first creation, so now he was seen to be the seductive power responsible for "deviations" from the true path established by Christ's coming.

The assumptions behind this retrospective version of early Christianity die hard. Amid all the excitement and intrigue generated by the discovery at Nag Hammadi in Egypt of various Gnostic documents, this ancient orthodoxy has revealed its continuing power. Only with great reluctance has it been conceded that one or two of these Gnostic "gospels" may derive from traditions older than the canonical gospels of Matthew, Mark,

---

[3] Bauer 1972 (1st Ger. ed. 1934), attacked, e.g., by Turner 1954 (who was generally impatient with things German; cf. the attack on Bultmann, pp. 103–10) but defended by e.g., Pagels 1979:xxxi and now Wisse 1983. The English translation contains a useful appendix on the reception of the book; see Bauer 1972:286–316.

[4] Origen, *Commentary on the Song of Songs* 3.4, trans. Pelikan 1971:69; cf. Bauer 1972:xxiii.

[5] Tertullian, *De praescriptione haereticorum* 36.6–8 and *Adversus Marcionem* 1.1.6, cited in Bauer 1972:xxiii and Pelikan 1971:69.

Luke, and John.[6] It is now possible, however, in the light of these finds and the prodigious scholarly labors they have stimulated, to recognize that the conventional picture of early Christianity was invented to serve the purposes, both doctrinal and political, of what became "establishment" Christianity.

More than any other factor, the struggle about heresy produced the story of Satan's original rebellion as a major ingredient of the Christian *mythos*. Apostasy (turning away from God, or literally, standing away) had to be experienced as disagreement about fundamental Christian doctrine before it was seen as a cosmic force. What was seen as Satan's opposition to Christ in the present was projected backward into the story of his origin. Only thus could the church construct a satisfactory account of the origin of things with which to oppose the many rival myths of the period. And in the process, Satan took on several characteristics from the heretical cosmologies that his own story was designed to discredit.

In a parallel development, the Jewish tradition took a similar step. The Targum of Palestine (Pseudo-Jonathan) adds to its rendering of the golden calf story Aaron's belief that he saw "Satana dancing among the people." When Aaron threw the gold into the fire, Satana entered in also—and out came the calf.[7]

We shall be concerned from now on with two related questions: how the dialectic of "truth" and "error" came to be viewed as an extension of the central Christian combat myth, of the opposition of light and darkness, God and "the god of this world"; and how adaptations in the Christian story of Satan resulted from the process of refuting heresy.

1. *First Born of Satan*

The association of Satan with heresy takes its cue from various New Testament texts. Among Pauline letters, the words to the Corinthians about the "god of this world" who has "blinded the minds of them which believe not" could be read in this way (2 Cor. 4.4). The letter to the Ephesians expands the idea to include the ways of the world generally. To walk "according to the course of this world" is to walk "according to the prince of the power of the air, the spirit that now worketh in the children of dis-

---

[6] See Koester in Robinson (ed.) 1977:17, on the *Gospel of Thomas*, and Pagels 1979:xvi–xvii. Cf. above, Chapter 12 n. 1. See now the Wilson Festschrift (Logan and Wedderburn 1983) for a comprehensive review.

[7] Exod. 32.24; Etheridge 1862:552. See Bowker 1969, and above, Chapter 10.3.

obedience" (Eph. 2.2). But the key text was the passage about the "lawless one," the "mystery of iniquity," in 2 Thessalonians, with its references to "false signs and wonders" and believing what is false.[8]

The idea is present in other, non-Pauline tendencies as well. The author of Jude links the "ungodly" Enoch angels, "the wandering stars," with Balaam's error (*planēi*), Korah's rebellion (*antilogia*), the way of Cain, and his contemporaries who "defile the flesh and reject authority" (Jude 8–13). The author of 2 Peter repeats all this, adding that these false prophets of the Old Testament are like "the false teachers who will secretly bring in destructive heresies" (2 Pet. 2.1).

In the Johannine letters, the false teachers are explicitly identified with the diabolic opposition to Christ expected at the end of time.

> Children, it is the last hour, and as you have heard that antichrist is coming, so now many antichrists have come; therefore we know that it is the last hour. They went out from us, but they were not of us; for if they had been of us, they would have continued with us. (1 John 2.18–19)

So these adversaries of the writer were former colleagues who now dissented. The logic of the thought is that they must have been the devil's all along. "He who commits sin is of the devil; for the devil has sinned from the beginning" (3.8). And behind this logic lies the story that Cain (and so his spiritual descendants) was the result of Eve's seduction by the devil. This explains the murder of Abel and requires another son, a different "seed," for Eve and Adam—Seth.[9]

Alluding to this story, "John" goes on:

> No one born of God commits sin; for God's seed abides in him, and he cannot sin because he is born of God. By this it may be seen who are the children of god and who are the children of the devil. . . . For this is the message which you have heard from the beginning, that we should love one another, and not be like Cain who was of the evil one and murdered his brother.

Fortunately for those, like Irenaeus or Augustine, who would later be obliged to interpret this passage, the author does not actually tell the story

---

[8] 2 Thess. 2.8–12. See above, Chapter 14.6, and compare the false prophet and blindness parallel in *Martyrdom of Isaiah*, discussed above, Chapter 10.3. The Melchireza vs. Melchizedek struggle is behind Heb. 7 also.

[9] R. E. Brown 1982:400, 428–32. See above, Chapter 12.6, and below, Chapter 18.4.

of Cain's birth.[10] He goes on with a magisterial tautology: "And why did he murder him? Because his own deeds were evil and his brother's righteous."[11] In a full Gnostic context this myth was understood to mean that the saved were essentially children of the hidden God, not the creator, but the Johannine adversaries had probably not gone quite that far.[12] The ambivalence and so the potential for quarrels about the meaning of the idea were great: the Watcher angels too were sons of God (*huioi*) in the Septuagint, such terms are common in the New Testament,[13] the Qumran community used similar phrases constantly, while Philo thinks that "if we have not yet become fit to be thought sons of God, yet we may be the sons of his invisible image, the most holy word."[14] But in the Johannine context the myth informs the explicit idea that the sign of the combat at the end of time is the sectarian quarreling of the new religion.

"John of Patmos" uses similar language in the "letters to seven churches" that open the Book of Revelation. For the first time a sect is named, the Nicolaitans, although we learn little about them except that they are active in Pergamum and in Ephesus, that the author hates them, and that whoever "conquers" will get to eat from "the tree of life, which is in the Paradise of God" (Rev. 2.7). Irenaeus links them with the Nicholas of Acts 6, who was one of the first seven deacons appointed by the apostles—not so bad as calling Peter himself Satan but still a difficulty for those who think the early church was pure in its orthodoxy.[15] In the same context, "John of Patmos" also alludes to Balaam as a false teacher, recalling that he taught Balak to put a stumbling-block (*skandalon*) in Israel's way (worship of Baal, or indifference to it), and denounces someone as a Jezebel, "who calls herself a prophetess and teaches and beguiles [*planōi*] my servants?" The son of God is speaking through John and continues, "Beloved, I will throw her on a bed [of sickness], and those who commit adultery with her [I will throw] into affliction, unless they repent of her doings. And I will strike her children dead."

Such deeds will be done not simply because Jezebel, the followers of

[10] Irenaeus, *Adv. haer.* 5.25.1, identifies for the first time the Antichrist of this passage with the man of iniquity in 2 Thess. 2.3–12. See below, Chapter 19.2; cf. Tertullian, *De resurrectione carnis* 24.18–20. For Augustine, see below, Chapter 25.3.

[11] 1 John 3.12. See R. E. Brown 1982:xx–xxii, 402.

[12] See Stroumsa 1984, R. E. Brown 1982:385–87, and below, Chapter 18.1.

[13] *Teknon*: e.g., John 1.12, 11.52, and Rom. 8.16, 9.8. *Huioi*: Rom. 8.14, 19; cf. e.g., 1.4, 9.4, and Matt. 5.9.

[14] Philo, *De confusione linguarum* 28.147, a work which likewise attacks (Jewish) apostasy.

[15] Irenaeus, *Adv. haer.* 1.26.3.

Balaam, or the Nicolaitans are heretics, but because they know "the deep things of Satan" (Rev. 2.22–24). The phrase is used only once in the fourth or middle letter, to Thyatira, but it appears to be a common saying (*hōs legousin*, as they say),[16] and Satan himself appears four more times in these few verses. The Pergamese are especially afflicted, it seems, since that is "where Satan dwells" or "where Satan's throne is" (Zeus' altar, perhaps, or Dionysus' seat in the theater), while the second and sixth letters to Smyrna and Philadelphia are linked by the repeated denunciation of those who claim to be Jews and are not, who belong instead to "the synagogue of Satan" (Rev. 2.13, 2.9, 3.9). These letters reflect a phase in which Jewish apocalyptic myth was evolving toward throne-mysticism, here adapted to a Christian context. The son promises that "he who conquers I will grant him to sit with me on my throne, as I myself conquered and sat down with my Father on his throne" (Rev. 3.21). But with their reiteration of the Satan figure, the letters echo the conquest or triumph episode of the combat myth and they prepare, as the form of the book stands, for the vision of the battle between Michael and Satan, the old serpent, and thus between the new Israel and the new heretics.

The early (apostolic) fathers echo these New Testament attitudes. Ignatius, for example, in his own warning to the Ephesians, says, "Do not let yourselves be anointed with the foul smell of the teaching of the prince of this world lest he capture you and rob you of the life to come."[17] Polycarp quotes both the Johannine and the Pauline letters in his own letter to the Philippians. "Everyone who does not confess Jesus Christ to have come in the flesh is antichrist," he avers (alluding to 1 John 4.2–3), and adds that such people are therefore "first born of Satan"—an allusion, allegorical or not, to the story of Cain's birth. Indeed, Polycarp apparently used this phrase quite freely, since he is cited by Irenaeus and Eusebius as denouncing Marcion in the same terms.[18] Justin thought that heresy was "a doctrine of demons" and that "the wicked demons have also put forward Marcion of Pontus." Later, Montanus was thought to have fallen into a satanic ecstasy, having been entered by the adversary.[19]

[16] See Barrett 1983:127–29.

[17] Ignatius, *Ephesians* 17. See Richardson (ed.) 1970:92 and Bauer 1972:68. For a good survey of the apostolic fathers' view of the devil, see J. B. Russell 1981:30–50.

[18] Polycarp, *Philippians* 7.1. See esp. Dahl 1964. The phrase *prōtotokos tou Satana* echoes both Heb. 12.23, John 8.44, 1 John 3.8, and perhaps Rom. 9.7. For Irenaeus, *Adv. haer.* 3.3.4, and Eusebius, *Ecclesiastical History* 4.14.7, see also Bauer 1972:70; and R. E. Brown 1982:333, 416.

[19] Justin, *First Apology* 58.1, trans. E. R. Hardy in Richardson (ed.) 1970:280. See also Pelikan 1971:70. The Montanus story is cited in Bauer 1972:133.

2. *Satan and Judas*

There is another New Testament idea behind the link of Satan and heresy, one with much more dramatic implications. Satan is somehow within the heretic, just as he is "in" the possessed of the exorcism stories, but more especially as he is in Judas the Betrayer.

Judas occurs in all four gospel versions of the Passion narrative, and in each case he has only one function, to betray. Indeed, with his first mention, at the end of the list of twelve disciples, he is called the Betrayer,[20] and however the four gospels develop his character, the betrayal of Jesus is always the only relevant issue. The germ of the character and his presence at the last supper is in the *testimonium* of Psalm 41.9, "Even my bosom friend, whom I trusted, who ate of my bread, betrays me," words that may allude to the betrayal of David by Absalom and Achitophel. Mark attaches to this the kiss, as well as the incident in which Judas visits the chief priests and they give him money, while Matthew adds the dialogue that took place during the visit, specifies thirty pieces of silver, and goes on that Judas later threw the money into the temple and hanged himself (like Achitophel).[21] These additions show an interest in the motivation of the incident (the money) and in the development of an important character (the suicide). But the additions of Luke and John reveal a further concern: money alone cannot be enough to motivate so momentous a deed.

Luke begins the visit to the priest with the words "Then entered Satan into Judas surnamed Iscariot being of the number of the twelve" (22.3). Luke retains the money as well, but John omits it (although he does make Judas the keeper of the money box). Instead John develops the equation of Satan and Judas much further. For the list of the twelve he substitutes Jesus' words " 'Did I not choose you twelve, and one of you is a devil?' He meant Judas" (John 6.70). And John makes the last supper itself the moment when Satan enters Judas. Judas eats the morsel of bread, "and after the sop Satan entered into him. Then said Jesus unto him, 'What you are doing, do quickly' " (13.27).

The reasoning behind these transformations of the betrayal episode is not simply the search for an adequate motive. Whereas Mark and Matthew characteristically tell the Passion narrative from the human point of

---

[20] Mark 3.19; Matt. 10.4; Luke 6.16.
[21] Mark 14.10–11, 43–45; Matt. 27.5; 2 Sam. 17.23.

view, Luke and John, who have nothing of Matthew's suicide story, are eager to connect the human passion story with the larger cosmic plot of which it forms a part. Luke is perhaps a little halfhearted about this, keeping Satan and the money side by side as parallel conceptions of the motive. But John's focus is the myth of a cosmic redeemer descending to save the world from the darkness into which it has fallen. "Now is the judgment of this world, now shall the prince of this world be cast out."[22] So he turns the betrayal, and thus the event it causes, the crucifixion, into an episode in the cosmic struggle. Jesus is well aware of what is happening, and not only prophesies his betrayal (as he also does in the synoptic gospels) but himself gives the dipped bread, Satan's means of entry, to Judas. The irony of the betrayal-crucifixion-resurrection sequence is thus made transparent. Satan thinks this is his victory, but it is actually the beginning of his defeat. At the moment he enters the human agent, by a demonic inversion of the eucharistic bread,[23] the opponent himself precipitates the events that are to undo him, moving the plot along to its necessary climax.

The differences among these four variants of the betrayal story pose in an obvious way the familiar theological problem of responsibility—was it Judas himself, or Satan using him as helpless agent, who betrayed Jesus? A parallel problem was raised, we have seen in the tradition of the Watcher myth and in the question of Eve's responsibility or the serpent's identity. In each case it was the presence of the cosmic adversary that posed the problem in its most acute form. The variation among the four gospels is a measure of the ambivalence with which the apocalyptic combat myth was treated in one of the most important episodes of the Christian story.

Nonetheless, this intersection of the human passion story with the cosmic myth was required by the need to oppose or adapt the developing cosmologies of the Gnostics. John's notion of the preexistent *logos* as redeemer already implies such opposition, and his account became central for those churchmen, like Irenaeus, who were faced with widespread, sophisticated systems of cosmic redemption. The versions of the betrayal story told by Luke and John would allow the church to identify heretics

[22] John 12.31, cf. 16.11, 14.30. For affinities with Qumran and Gnosticism, see R. E. Brown 1966: lii–lxvi. Cf. Burrows 1958:123–30, Grant 1959:163–77, and Fuller 1962:101–32.

[23] Kermode 1979:85–92. On the "twinning" of Judas and Jesus, see J. B. Russell 1977:239–240 and the Borges story, "Three Versions of Judas."

more dramatically as followers of Satan, apostates, and traitors. And just as the betrayal, like the Fall, was necessary for the redemption, so the existence of heresy, with its corresponding identification of Satan as father of lies, as "he who deceiveth the whole world," would move the church toward the development and articulation of its comprehensive story. The combat tradition may have become muted as myth, particularly in Paul, but it soon became, partly through the influence of Paul and John, the ideology of an embattled church caught in the struggle between the spirit of truth and the spirit of error. If Satan had not already existed, the church would have had to invent him.

EIGHTEEN

GNOSTICISM AND THE DEMIURGE

THE KEY figure in the linking of Satan and heresy is Irenaeus, whose passionate and meticulous attack on heretics reflects the efforts of the Rome-dominated church in the latter years of the second century to impose its views on the diverse groups who called themselves Christians. Irenaeus himself had known Polycarp in Smyrna as a boy, had read and perhaps known Justin Martyr, had spent some time in Rome, and ultimately became bishop of Lyons, the most important Roman city of Gaul and headquarters of the imperial cult through the *concilium Galliarum*.[1] Thus he had a wide knowledge of the Roman world, including its Greek-speaking areas (the language of his boyhood and of the first Christians at Lyons, and the original language of his book), but the heresies he attacks are principally those that flourished in Rome itself. Outside the one universal ("catholic") church, he declared, there is no salvation.

Irenaeus entitled his book *The Refutation and Overthrow of the Gnosis Falsely So Called*, enlisting himself in the tradition of the pastoral letters (1 and 2 Timothy and Titus). Actually, one of his chief targets, Marcion, was not a Gnostic in the strict sense. This confusion is a symptom of the process that was taking place in the church, for which Irenaeus provides such good evidence, that the dialectic of "heresy" and "orthodoxy" was teaching the church its doctrine and that the various forms of "heresy" had significance only as they opposed the orthodox view, not in themselves or vis-à-vis each other.

Amid the enormous diversity, Irenaeus sees two major targets: (1) Christian Gnostics, especially Valentinus and his followers, and (2) Marcion of Pontus, against whom the next generation of church fathers, particularly Tertullian and Origen, also wrote treatises and whose ascetic

---

[1] The importance of Irenaeus is argued from differing viewpoints by, e.g., Aulén 1969 and Pagels 1976. A judicious summary is by E. R. Hardy in Richardson (ed.) 1970:343–54. See below, Chapter 19 n. 1. Many of the writings by the church fathers cited in this and subsequent chapters are conveniently translated and collected either in ANF or Schaff (ed.) 1886–96. Where necessary and possible, however, I refer to more modern editions.

brand of Christianity continued to flourish in eastern parts of Christendom well into the fourth century. In spite of their differences, both Marcion and Valentinus were dualists, and that was enough for Irenaeus. What he especially loathes, so much that he mentions it in the first paragraph of his preface, is the "blasphemous and impious view about the Demiurge."

This term derives ultimately from Plato (meaning "world-maker"), but what it meant among these late Hellenistic spiritual movements was the idea of a creator god who had bungled his job and who was therefore unworthy of worship. There was another God beyond him, entirely distinct, who was the true object of human aspiration. The concept reflects the feelings of revulsion with which large numbers of spiritually inclined people of the time regarded matter in general, the political and social organization of the material world under the Roman *imperium*, even the stars in their regular courses, and especially the bodily functions. Marcion, for example, thought that Christ, in whom he fervently believed, could not have assumed a material body, part of the created and demiurgic world, because that body would have been "stuffed with excrement."[2]

1. *The Watchers and the Demiurge*

The Watcher angels from the Enoch tradition are one source of the demiurgic idea, and the transformed narrative provides a measure of what happened to the Jewish tradition in Gnostic contexts. No longer a midrash of Genesis, even of the elaborate kind found in the Qumran literature, interpretation has now become inversion of the original narrative. Here is the version of the Noah story from the *Apocryphon of John*, an important text for the Sethian and Valentinian tendencies in Gnosticism, and known to Irenaeus.

> And he repented for everything which had come into being through him. This time he planned to bring a flood over the work of man. But the greatness of the light of the foreknowledge informed Noah, and he proclaimed [it] to all the offspring which are the sons of men. But those who were strangers to him did not listen to him. It is not as Moses said, "They hid themselves in an ark," but they hid themselves in a place, not only Noah but also

[2] Tertullian, *Adversus Marcionem* 3.10.1. See E. Evans 1972:198 and Pelikan 1971:75. On the docetic aspect of Gnosticism, see Bianchi 1978.

many other people from the immovable race. They went into a place and hid themselves in a luminous cloud.[3]

The phrase "it is not as Moses said" echoes through this and other Gnostic texts, deliberately correcting, not covertly revising, the scripture. And here it takes two different figures, not one god as in Genesis, to send the flood and to rescue Noah. This split in the godhead is characteristic of Gnosticism, extending the tendencies of Judaism we saw in the Chronicler. Following the adapted combat myth, the two figures are now engaged in perpetual struggle. The "unmovable" or "unshakable race," loosely linked to Noah here, is the typical "saving remnant" from the Jewish tradition, but transformed now into the race of Seth, perfected or perfectible Gnostics, and so, like the Qumran children of light, inhabitants of a luminous cloud.

The *Apocryphon* continues with the story of the Watchers, which here follows the flood, inverting the narrative sequence of Genesis 6.

And he made a plan with his powers. He sent his angels to the daughters of men that they might take some of them for themselves and raise offspring for their enjoyment. And at first they did not succeed. When they had no success, they gathered together again and they made a plan together. They created a despicable spirit, who resembles the Spirit who had descended, so as to pollute the souls through it. And the angels changed themselves in their likeness into the likeness of their [the daughters of men] mates, filling them with the spirit of darkness, which they had mixed for them, and with evil. They brought gold and silver and a gift and copper and iron and metal and all kinds of things. And they steered the people who had followed them into great troubles, by leading them astray with many deceptions.

This is the Enoch story, but several things have happened to it. The demiurge and his powers (*archontes*; most of the Pauline terms or their equivalents recur in this and other Gnostic texts) do not succeed at first in mixing the worlds. So they devise two stratagems. They create an imitation spirit (*antimimon pneuma*, rendered by the Coptic as both "despicable" and "opposing"), whose function is to deceive the souls of people, and they themselves take on, after the manner of incubi, the form of the women's husbands. In the *Testament of Reuben* 5.7, where we first met this idea, it was part of an antifeminist trend, but here the evil angels are once again the focus of blame.

The opposing spirit, he who imitates the true spirit, the one who de-

[3] *Apocryphon of John* 28.32–29.12, trans. in Robinson (ed.) 1977:115. On Sethian Gnosticism, see above, Chapter 12.4 and 12.6, and Layton (ed.) 1981: vol. 2.

scended to save the world, is a typically Gnostic idea. The two worlds of above and below, good and evil, are constantly seen as mirror images of each other.[4] The roots of the idea, however, are in the Qumran doctrine of the two spirits, and it also resembles the Johannine idea of the Antichrist, he who imitates the true saviour and so deceives through the power of Satan.[5] So we find basically Jewish ideas, themselves variants of the combat myth, developing in different but parallel directions in Gnostic and Christian contexts.

The demurge's second plan is successful in the *Apocryphon of John* and now accounts explicitly for subsequent suffering.

> They [the people] became old without having enjoyment. They died, not having found truth and without knowing the God of truth. And thus the whole creation became enslaved forever, from the foundation of the world until now. And they took women and begot children out of the darkness according to the likeness of their spirit. And they closed their hearts, and they hardened themselves through the hardness of the despicable spirit until now.

We have seen that this narrative already had a similar function in apocalyptic Judaism, but now its leading character, the chief *archōn*, is the same as the figure who sends the flood. The struggle is no longer between the creator and a rebellious Watcher angel, but between the creator and the unknown god above. The creator, that is to say, has himself become the rebel, and so the demiurge. There is no evidence here of a strong Christian influence. Rather these are the traditional narratives of Judaism now fractured and recombined. But soon, and particularly in the ideas of Valentinus, the Gnostic religion was defining itself as much, if not more, in explicitly Christian terms.[6]

2. Valentinian Gnosis: The Purification of God

As the early Christian apologists conceived of the meaning of the term, a "Gnostic" was one who claimed a particular kind of spiritual knowledge.

---

[4] This is a midrash, or aggressive inversion, of Gen. 1.7, the separation of the waters above and below, itself developing Ps. 104 and the Mesopotamian myth. See above, Chapter 2.6 and Chapter 7; see also Quispel 1983:61.

[5] On the "imitation spirit" as Gnostic, see Stroumsa 1984:37, 142–43. See Pearson in Stone (ed.) 1984:453–60 on the Jewish origins of these ideas.

[6] Other allusions to the Watcher tradition in Gnostic texts are *A Valentinian Exposition* 38.22–37, *Testimony of Truth* 40.30–41.4, and *On the Origin of the World* 123.4–13, all in Robinson (ed.) 1977. See also Puech 1978: vol. 1, 271–300 and Pearson 1972.

A Gnostic did not "know" because he had gradually learned or because he had followed a system of rational inquiry along the lines suggested by Greek classical tradition from which the use of the word derives, or because, like Paul on the road to Damascus, he had been struck by a vision that came from without. The Gnostic knew because he knew himself, because he had been revealed to himself. This self-knowledge was not the Socratic knowledge that one knows nothing, nor was it the humble confession that one is full of pretense and self-deceit. It was knowledge of the inner core of one's being and the identity of that core with "the ineffable greatness." This knowledge is itself the Redemption.

The Valentinian Gnostics offered a particularly succinct statement of the questions that this kind of knowledge could answer: "who we were and what we have become; where we were or where we had been made to fall; whither we are hastening, whence we are being redeemed; what birth is and what rebirth is."[7] These questions were never peculiar to Gnosticism; they are the basic stuff of any developed religious system. Some of us are enlightened, we know the answers to these questions; the rest are ignorant. There are many parallels. For example, an early Christian letter written from Rome to Corinth enjoins the readers to consider "from what stuff we were created, what kind of creatures we were when we entered the world, from what a dark grave he who fashioned and created us brought us into this world."[8] It is not the questions themselves, but the answers to the questions, which differentiate one system of belief from another.

The answers that came to be regarded as orthodox Christian depend on faith in Christ and *his* knowledge of his origin. The Gnostic, on the other hand, knows that he is himself a spiritual being who has come to live in a soul and body, that he once dwelt in the spiritual world above but has fallen into this world of sense and ignorance. Through self-knowledge he is reborn into the spiritual world. The Valentinian system summarized this knowledge in the following way, according to Irenaeus (capitalized words indicate hypostatizations, characters in the Gnostic myth):

> Perfect redemption is the knowledge itself of the ineffable Greatness: for
> since through Ignorance came about Defect and Passion, the whole system

[7] Clement of Alexandria, *Excerpta ex Theodotou* 78.2, quoted in Grant 1959:5; cf. Pelikan 1971:91. Theodotus seems to have been writing in Alexandria around A.D. 140–160.

[8] *1 Clement* 38.3, trans. Richardson (ed.) 1970:61. This anonymous letter dates from ca. A.D. 96 and is itself an attack on a fresh "outbreak" of Corinthian Christian Gnosticism (48.5), following Paul's lead. It is an early instance of Rome's efforts to impose its views (63 and 65); see Bauer 1972:95–106.

that springs from Ignorance is dissolved by knowledge. . . . Through knowledge, then, is saved the inner, spiritual man; so that to us suffices the knowledge of universal being: this is the true redemption.[9]

The Valentinians gave this Gnostic self-knowledge a privileged theoretical and mythological foundation that turned both knowledge and ignorance into divine events. In this elaborate myth, ignorance was both the cause and the major constitutive event of the divine disaster that is creation. Sophia, the last of the emanations from the unknowable Forefather of all, strove to comprehend the greatness of the Father and thus overstep the limits of her ontological status. But the power known as Horos (Limit) stopped her and brought her back to herself. However, the passion engendered by her intention continued to subsist as a formless entity, an "abortion," cast outside the divine and original Pleroma (Fullness) by the Horos. This initial act of ignorance by the paradoxically named Sophia (Wisdom) sets in motion a chain of events that eventually results in the creation of matter and the universe as we perceive it physically.

Sophia is a ubiquitous figure in Gnosticism. She originates in a blending of various traditions. Hellenistic-Jewish *hokhmah* (wisdom) speculation had already adapted some Greek philosophical traditions that were now remythologized. One of Sophia's prototypes is Hesiod's Metis (intelligence, measure), now identified with her daughter, Athena, born from her father's head after he swallowed the mother. The Sophia story is also yet another variant, radically transformed, of the Watcher myth.[10] Her incestuous but frustrated desire for the father is a further adaptation of the antifeminist possibilities of the myth as we met it, for example, in the *Testament of Reuben*. But another aspect of Sophia and another sexual attitude will soon appear.

The demiurge is for Valentinians the son of the hypostatized passion of his mother, Sophia. He is variously called Ialdabaoth, "child of chaos," Sakla, "prince of darkness," or Sammael, "the blind god."[11] But he was

---

[9] Irenaeus, *Adv. haer.* 1.21.4. See Grant 1959:78 and Jonas 1970:131, 174–77.

[10] There are many variants, e.g., *On the Origin of the World* 108.14–22: "And when Pronoia saw the angel [Adam-anthropos] she became enamored of him. But he hated her because she was in the darkness. Moreover she desired to embrace him and she was not able" (trans. Robinson [ed.] 1977:168). The variant in the *Apocryphon of John* 28.11–32 (Robinson [ed.] 1977:115, quoted above) makes the origin in the Watcher myth clear. See Tardieu 1974, Dahl 1981, and Stroumsa 1984:62–65. On the female redeemers of Gnostic religion, e.g., *Hypostasis of the Archons* 89.11–91.1 (Robinson [ed.] 1977:154–55), see esp. Pagels 1979:48–69. On the links between Eve and Sophia, see MacRae 1970. For Metis-Athena, see above, Chapter 3.2. See also Quispel 1983:62.

[11] On the names of the demiurge as descriptive of his character, see Pearson 1980:154, Barc 1981, and below.

ignorant of the chain of events that had produced him. Ignorant even of his own mother's role in the process, he nevertheless brought forth both the material (and the psychical) universe. As the *Gospel of Truth*, perhaps a work of Valentinus himself, puts it, the demiurge, here called Error,

> became powerful; it fashioned its own matter foolishly not having known the truth. It set about making a creature, . . . preparing in beauty, a substitute for the truth. . . . Being thus without any root, it fell into a fog with regard to the Father, . . . preparing works and oblivions and terrors in order that by means of these it might entice those of the middle and capture them.[12]

Unbeknownst to this prodigal son, his mother Sophia, horrified at the results of her passion, also injected into the earthly creature called "Man" a part of her own essence, the pneumatic or spiritual substance of which she was formed. This *Pneuma* connects us back with our divine origin; it resides in us as if in a womb until it is ready to receive the *Logos*, the final "information," through *Gnosis*. So it turns out that Sophia, the mother, is actually the hero of the story, since all along she had in mind this secret aim with the demiurgical creation. At this point, the story passes well beyond its Jewish roots and becomes explicitly Christian, since the gnosis itself is brought down to mankind by Jesus unified with Christos—here the divine emanation whose function is the reunification and restoration of serenity both within the *Plerōma* and outside it. The gnosis descends like the dove upon the human Jesus at his baptism in the Jordan[13] and departs from him before his passion so that Death is deceived. As Jonas puts it:

> The suffering of the mortal Jesus had no other significance than that of a stratagem. The real "passion" was the precosmic one of the upper and lower Sophia, and it was what made salvation necessary, not what brought salvation. Nor was there ever an original sin of man, a guilt of the human soul: there was, instead, the time-preceding guilt of an Aeon (Sophia), a divine upheaval, whose reparation in its course required the creation of the world and of man. Thus the world, unbeknown to its immediate author, is for the sake of salvation, not salvation for the sake of what happened within

---

[12] *Gospel of Truth* 17.15–35 in Robinson (ed.) 1977:38.

[13] In one text (not Valentinian) the Jordan renews its function in the combat myth (see *Testimony of Truth* 30.20–23, 31.1–3; cf. Stroumsa 1984:122–23), as well as becoming an allegory of "the desire for sexual intercourse."

creation and to creation. And the real object of salvation is the godhead it-self, its theme the divine integrity.[14]

So there are two contradictory plots or purposes at work in the created world. One is the intention of the demiurge to trap spiritual light in dark matter; the other is the overriding plan of salvation whose object is the final elimination of darkness and thus the purification of God.

The Valentinians who developed this complex salvation narrative claimed to be Christians, indeed, to be the true inheritors of the faith. As in the Pauline teaching, the key to their system is the opposition and con-nection of the Fall and the Redemption, although Paul's version is based on sin, on guilt and absolution, while Valentinus' version is based on ig-norance and knowledge. Indeed, as in other versions of the Gnostic nar-rative, the figure of the ignorant demiurge is the key to the spiritual mes-sage of salvation. He it is who explains the need for redemption, and he is, will he, nill he, part of a whole redemptive process. The narrative therefore insists on its irony: the audience can congratulate itself on know-ing what the central figure has forgotten. The creation myth serves the purpose of explaining—indeed, enacting—the Gnostics' redemptive mes-sage, since the nature of the demiurge is the central "secret" that Valentin-ian Christians have to reveal.

The Valentinian thus shared with the Pauline Christian the dualistic dis-tinction between the evil "god of this world" and the good father of Christ above him. But Ialdabaoth, unlike the Pauline tyrant, was not sim-ply the evil ruler. The fierce objections of the heretic-hunters were raised by the Gnostic idea that Ialdabaoth had also created the world over which he ruled so badly. Even though, according to the Valentinians, the good God had managed to mix some of his own substance with the creation, so that ultimately it might be redeemed, the impulse to create at all had come from the ignorant tyrant. The whole of visible, physical reality was thus fundamentally repugnant to the Gnostic initiate.

Such a view could only have arisen with the collapse of the classical world and its respect for the order and beauty of creation. Indeed, the Gnostic demiurge is a *deliberate* reversal of the creation theory in Plato's *Timaeus*. Ialdabaoth fashions the material universe in ignorance of the di-vine forms, preparing in beauty a substitute for the truth.[15] This Platonic "heresy" eventually inspired the attack on Gnosticism by that former

---

[14] Jonas 1970:195–96; cf. Dillon 1977.
[15] *Gospel of Truth* 17.19–20 (above, n. 12); cf. Irenaeus, *Adv. haer.* 1.5.3.

Gnostic, Plotinus, for whereas the Gnostics viewed the activity of the demiurge and the consequent descent of spiirit into matter as a divine tragedy, the Neoplatonist conceived the creation as the positive and necessary self-expression of the divine.[16]

3. *Marcion the Literalist*

Gnostic Christians were by no means the only exponents of belief in a demiurge to threaten the integrity of Christian monotheism. Marcion of Pontus, who claimed to know no Gnostic secrets and who was an emphatic literalist in his interpretation of scripture, also believed in a demiurge, though he needed no elaborate cosmogony to account for his existence. One could read about him quite well, thought Marcion, in the God of the Jewish scriptures. Because of his textual strategies, Marcion's teaching was treated as an even more serious threat to orthodoxy, and it is symptomatic of the fear his activities inspired that Irenaeus should have made him one of the principal targets of a book whose title announced that it was an attack on Gnosticism. Marcion too, after all, believed in the dangerous demiurge.[17]

Marcion's dualism was far more radical than that of any other teacher of the period except Mani. Unlike Valentinus, Marcion denied any connection whatever between the Good God and mankind. Mankind is entirely the creation and property of the demiurge, "ruler of the universe."[18] This world-god, the Old Testament deity, has also no connection, by genealogy or history, with the Good God revealed in Christ. The Good God, like the deities of Epicurus, lived in complete tranquillity, entirely separate from the world, until in his goodness he decided to introduce himself to the alien world of creation. Christ's role is that of a purchase fee. He buys mankind with his blood and thus cancels the creator's claim to his property. That claim is "just" but not "good." The Old Testament

---

[16] Plotinus, *Enneads* 2.9. The Plotinian vision probably influenced the later church attacks on Gnosticism. Certainly Augustine, who himself opposed Gnostic dualism, especially in its Manichaean incarnation, was deeply affected by the circle of Milanese Platonists for whom Plotinus represented the pinnacle of philosophy. See Augustine, *Confessions* 7.9, *Contra academikos* 2.2.2, and the excellent discussion in P. Brown 1969:88–133.

[17] On Marcion's importance, see, e.g., Grant 1965, Nigg 1962:58–72, and Jonas 1970:136–46. If one takes the mythological system and the exegesis of texts, rather than "knowledge," as the unifying principle of Gnostic religion, then Marcion fits quite well, as Stroumsa 1984:170 points out.

[18] *Kosmokrator*, in Irenaeus, *Adv. haer.* 1.27.2. See Pelikan 1971:73.

is thus an expression of that justice, which is entirely distinct from the goodness revealed in the New Testament (or at least in that part of the Christian scriptures which Marcion allowed to be a valid manifestation of the Good God, an expurgated Paul and Luke).

Marcion rejected entirely the prophetic, figural, and often allegorical interpretation of the Old Testament by which Christian commentators attempted to marry it with the new revelation. The legalistic pettiness of the Jewish God is, according to Marcion, entirely in keeping with his character and does not need to be explained away. Marcion thereby dissolved one of the main strengths of Paul's theology, the dialectical tension between justice and mercy, between Law and Gospel. No longer the two extreme manifestations of one godhead between which a delicate balance is maintained, they become two separate and mutually exclusive principles. Marcion's position is like projecting two allegorical personifications of the mystery plays, Justice and Mercy, as literally separate figures who exist beyond the confines of the stage.

Because of this powerful simplifying literalness, Marcion's impact was profound. His separation of the Law from the gospel, of the Old Testament from the salvation news of Luke and Paul, impelled the church to form its own canon of sacred scripture, a crucial step in the effort to enforce a unified Christendom. And the early redemption theory of the church is deeply affected by him. Irenaeus, Tertullian, and Origen all wrote against him, and their idea of the devil owes much to their efforts to refute his view of the Old Testament God.

There is some confusion in the testimonies with regard to Marcion's idea of this demiurge, but this confusion is best understood as caused not by Marcion but by those who saw the devil in his creator God.[19] Tertullian says explicitly that Marcion regarded the demiurge as equivalent to the devil, even though he also tells us that for Marcion "there are two gods, one just and the other good."[20] It seems obvious that the confusion is Tertullian's, who finds Marcion's description of the just God, the demiurge or creator of the Old Testament, to be equivalent to his own view of the devil, the prince of this world.

In Irenaeus' testimony we find an intermediate step between Tertullian's two versions. He too says that Marcion thought of the Old Testa-

[19] Pace Blackman 1948:67, Pelikan 1971:74, and J. B. Russell 1981:58.
[20] Tertullian, Adversus Marcionem 5.18.12, 5.13.15, cf. 2.10 (where the demiurge is auctor diaboli) and 2.28. Apelles split from Marcion for just this reason. The demiurge was "god" to Marcion, but to Apelles he was angelus inclitus (Tertullian, De carne Christi 8.2).

ment God as "judicial," but he also tells us that Marcion called him "the author of evils, lustful for war, inconstant in his opinions, and self-contradictory."[21] This portrait is not without grounds in the Old Testament, and Marcion, Irenaeus, and Tertullian were by no means the first to transfer these unpleasant characteristics from the High God to his adversary. For Irenaeus and Tertullian, the devil is an alternative to the demiurge, and the character of the devil enables them to salvage the Jewish scriptures from these heretics who would separate the Creator of Genesis, Job, and Isaiah from the God revealed by Christ.

4. The Demiurge and Genesis

The Gnostic or Marcionite revisions of the Old Testament did not need to be as thoroughgoing as the Gnostic reversal of Platonism. There were enough spiteful deeds attributed to Yahweh (or Elohim) in the Jewish scriptures for the ingenuity of the Gnostic rationalists to identify their evil creator with the Old Testament God.

The anti-Jewish bias of Marcion and certain Gnostics, apparent even in some who were Jews by birth, derives much of its weight from the more extreme denunciations of the people by the Hebrew prophets themselves, and from such radical critics as the Qumran sect. This alienation from Judaism was felt by several other Christian writers. The author of the fourth gospel, for example, has "the Jews" claim, "We be not born of fornication; we have one Father, even God." To this, Jesus replies, "Ye are of your father the devil, and the lusts of your father ye will do."[22] So the father of the Jews, the father of Abraham, is the devil. Jesus' statement may be interpreted symbolically: he is not a racist, and he denounces not the state of the cosmos but the morals of his Jewish opponents. Nonetheless, his words are more like the attacks on the sons of Belial in the Qumran scrolls than the prophetic warnings of an Isaiah or an Ezekiel. The devil has already become a major force and the opponent of Jesus' God.

The idea that the father of the Jews is the devil may be traced to exegesis of Genesis within the Jewish tradition, in fact to the story of Eve's seduction and the birth of Cain.[23] But in the Gnostic context these basically Jewish ideas underwent riotous development. In the *Apocryphon of John*,

[21] Irenaeus, *Adv. haer.* 3.25.3, 1.27.2; cf. 3.12.12.

[22] John 8.41–44. On the revolt against Judaism in the Gnostic tradition, see Jonas in Bianchi (ed.) 1967:90–108, Pearson 1980, and Stone (ed.) 1984:443–81.

[23] See above, Chapters 12.6 and 17.1, and esp. Pearson 1972 and 1981.

for example, the demiurge perceives "the virgin who stood by Adam" and begets two sons by her, Elohim and Jahve, both ugly like their father, and these sons he calls Cain and Abel, in order to mislead. Elsewhere we hear that the archons say, "Come, let us lie with Eve, that what will be born may be ours," whereupon "they led Eve far away from Adam's face and knew her."[24] The function of these various stories is to identify in the text of Genesis the origin of the lust that keeps the world going and so imprisons the spirit. Irenaeus sums it up thus:

> The jealous Ialdabaoth wanted a plan for depriving man [of the moist nature of light] through woman, and from his own desire he brought forth a woman whom Prunikos [= Sophia] took and thereby invisibly deprived of power. The others came and admired her beauty, and called her Eve; they desired her and from her generated sons who are called angels.[25]

The obsession with lust has made Eve's story homologous with the story of the sons of God, the lustful angels. And the sequels too are parallel. Just as the giants, products of that union, turned on each other and started warfare, so Cain and Abel, Eve's son, quarreled and one killed the other. The two myths have come to seem like variants of the same narrative, summed up like this in another report: "The devil came to Eve and had intercourse with her as a man does with a woman, and begot with her Cain and Abel."[26]

This exegesis of Cain's (and Abel's) parentage is linked to another idea in Genesis, the birth of Seth. The naive reader might assume from Genesis that Seth is the third son of Adam and Eve. But Gnosticism will not brook naive reading. If Cain could become the devil's child, it was not hard for Seth to be God's child. Divine births were plentiful in the mythological tradition, and if we look closer at Genesis we can see one there too. "And Adam knew his wife again, and she bore a son and called his name Seth."[27] In the normal way, Adam could expect to be Seth's father, it would seem from this language, but the verse continues with Eve's comment, giving the reason for Seth's name. She says, "God has appointed for me another seed [*heteron sperma*] instead of Abel, for Cain slew him." All three of his children having now been fathered by supernatural creatures, whether

---

[24] *Apocryphon of John* 24.9–25 and *Hypostasis of the Archons* 89.19–30. See Segal 1977, Barc 1981:132–38, and Puech 1978: vol. I, 274.

[25] Irenaeus, *Adv. haer.* 1.30.7.

[26] Epiphanius, *Panarion* 40.5.3. See Stroumsa 1984:40–47.

[27] Gen. 4.25a. For the characteristic anxiety, see Lamech on Noah's birth, above, Chapter 8.1 n. 2.

devil or god, poor Adam, despite the biblical words, would seem to be left without progeny. But Gnostic ingenuity was equal to this problem. Genesis 5.3, after all, claims that "when Adam had lived a hundred and thirty years, he became the father of a son in his own likeness, after his image, and named him Seth"—just as man was made in God's image according to Genesis 1.26. So the divine image is what was passed on from Adam to Seth, and Adam comes back into the paternal line.[28] Another Genesis verse, 3.15, also becomes relevant here, explainable in terms of the basic combat myth, which informs these interpretations: "And I will put enmity between thee and the woman, and between thy seed and her seed." Cain and the serpent's seed are to be in constant enmity with Seth and God's. In Valentinian theology, the material beings "have the devil for father," psychic beings are his sons by intent, whereas the true Gnostic, the *pneumatikos*, was keeping the seed (and so God) pure. According to Theodotos, these three types correspond to the three sons—Cain, Abel, and Seth.[29]

Identifying the creator God of these Genesis stories as ignorant or foolish tended to oversimplify the many-sidedness of the God of Israel. For example, he no longer had to be both the impersonal being of the Priestly writer and the Yahwist's workman who scoops up the earth with his hands. For many Gnostics, the true picture was the jealous God who banishes Adam from Eden out of fear that he will eat the tree of life and become a god himself.[30] To such a God, of course, the world he created will appear "good," and the Priestly writer says he thought so: "and he saw that it was good."

As in the Jewish Haggadic tradition the interpretation of the scriptures was the medium in which to express a complete doctrine of creation. By the time we first hear of an evil demiurge, among the sects called Cainites and Ophites by the heresiologists, he is already linked to the reinterpretation of the Old Testament. In his arrogance the demiurge tried to convince the angels and himself that he was master of the universe:

And when he saw the creation which surrounds him and the multitude of angels around him which had come forth from him, he said to them "I am

[28] *Hypostasis of the Archons* 91.30–33 in Robinson (ed.) 1977:156. Cf. Schenke 1962.
[29] *Extracts of Heracleon*, frags. 44 and 46 (in Origen, *Commentary on John* 20.20–24); *Excerpta ex Theodotou* 54.1. See above, Chapter 12 n. 30.
[30] Gen. 3.22. None of those involved in these ancient controversies, whether opponents or defenders of the God of Genesis, had the benefit of the modern scholarly view that Genesis is an amalgamation of different Hebrew and other Semitic traditions, but they were reacting to similar textual problems and inconsistencies. See Segal 1977.

a jealous God, and there is no other God beside me." But by announcing this, he indicated to the angels attending him that there exists another god: for if there were no other one, of whom should he be jealous?[31]

The Eden story was one of the principal revelations of the character and actions of this god. Having created Adam and placed him in Eden so that he would be trapped in physical reality, the demiurge also prohibited the tree of knowledge, by which man might have learned of his own nature and the higher God above. The serpent, however, sometimes identified with Christ, persuaded the pair to eat of the tree.[32] So Ialdabaoth, fearful and jealous, cast them out of Paradise and gave them lust so that they should propagate and keep the divine spark confined.

Such readings of Genesis, which gave to the Ophite and Naasene sects their names, from Greek *ophis* and Hebrew *nāhāš* (serpent), understandably provoked a hostile reaction among the orthodox.[33] But by reversing these interpretations and identifying serpent with Satan, the church did not escape from the limitations of moralistic interpretation. As we have seen, these were the very limitations that allowed the Satan to escape from the heavenly council and set up on his own. The monotheists's beliefs could be preserved in the face of these dualistic attacks only if at least some of the rich ambiguity of the Old Testament God, and some of the basic tension of the Pauline equivalent, could be preserved.

The Gnostic reevaluation of the text of Genesis accords with the Gnostic attitude toward the world itself. In both there is an arrogance and a contempt for apparent, and to them superficial, meanings. To the Stoic, or to any classically inclined philosopher, the *heimarmenē*, the orderly operation of the cosmos, might seem to be the physical manifestation of the divine principle that controlled it. The orthodox Jew also celebrated the created world, in psalms, in Job, in Priestly writing. But to the Gnostic this was to fall into the malicious but skillful creator's trap. Actually this

---

[31] *Apocryphon of John* 13.5–13 in Robinson (ed.) 1977:106. Cf. Irenaeus, *Adv. haer.* 3.12.6–12, see also Grant (ed.) 1961:76–77, and Jonas 1970:134. There are many parallels for this ignorant boast in Gnostic texts, e.g., *Hypostasis of the Archons* 86.30–87.4 (Robinson [ed.] 1977:153), where the demiurge's name is Sammael, god of the blind or blind god, and this brag further evidence of his blindness. Cf. *Origin of the World* 103.11–24. See above, Chapter 12 n. 66, for the Old Testament allusions, and for the social context, see Pagels 1979:28–47.

[32] See *Testimony of Truth* 49.7–10 in Robinson (ed.) 1977:412. The passage puns on Aramaic *hewyā*, serpent, and *hawā*, instruct. It also links the serpent with Exod. 7.8–12, Num. 21.9, and a variant of Rev. 12.10—attributed to Moses! See Pearson 1972.

[33] On Origen's use of Ophite ways of reading, see below, Chapter 21. Another Gnostic sect, the Peratae, regarded Jesus as a manifestation of the "general serpent" and thus the embodiment of wisdom, Sophia (Jonas 1970:93 and Stone [ed.] 1984:457).

orderly cosmos functions as a prison for the spiritual part of man, and the creator of this smooth system is really a jailer. In the same way the Gnostic read Genesis, looking for the esoteric truth contained in those powerful but malicious words. Just as an evil deity had made the world but had in his blindness unwittingly embodied something of the truly divine substance in his creation by means of which the whole might be redeemed— that *pneuma* or spirit within the soul which all Gnostics taught—so the truth about the ignorant creator is embodied in the creation story despite the conscious intention of its author, the demiurge. Whether he was reading the Bible or the book of nature, the Gnostic was alert for the hidden sense. "For great is the blindness of those who read."[34]

[34] *Testimony of Truth* 48.2–3 in Robinson (ed.) 1977:412. There is a striking parallel here with Blake's reading of Milton, and he was led to it by the same path that had motivated his predecessors, the Gnostics: the search for esoteric truth. Milton, he thought, had unwittingly embodied the truth about this monstrous global system in his poem and was therefore a true poet, since "he was of the devil's party without knowing it."

NINETEEN

IRENAEUS: REFUTATION OF
THE DEMIURGE

T HE COUNTERATTACK against belief in a bungling demiurge took place on several fronts at once. Irenaeus himself insists on the apostolic succession (what would become an important claim to authority of the Roman papacy) and on the authority of the four "apostolic" gospels.[1] In those texts no demiurge is mentioned, and indeed the opening of the fourth gospel—the Logos doctrine—may be read as a refutation of any such idea: the divine Word was both creator and redeemer. Furthermore, the church was already in the process, stimulated by Marcion, of establishing the canon of Christian scriptures to include the Old Testament and so to bind firmly the creator God to the God revealed by Christ. This entailed a good deal of uneasiness about how to interpret the texts, since on the one hand the church had to reassert the literal meaning—God the creator *was* good, in spite of Gnostic scorn—and on the other hand the church had to allow for some interpretive latitude if it were not to fall into Marcionite literalism. If Marcion could edit the text of Luke or Paul to insist on his views, so also we learn from 2 Peter 3.16 that in Paul's letters "are some things hard to be understood, which they that are unlearned and unstable wrest, as they do also the other scriptures, unto their own destruction." This may be the earliest reference to apostolic documents as Holy Scripture in the way the Old Testament was regarded, and it demonstrates the importance of controversy in generating the very notion of a fixed canon and an established reading of it.[2]

Similar quarrels also caused the pastoral letters to be written, which at-

---

[1] Irenaeus, *Adv. haer.* 3.1–5. Irenaeus wrote in Greek. Eusebius and others quote parts of the Greek text, but the work survives complete only in Latin translation. There is also an Armenian version of books 4 and 5. I have used the edition of Rousseau and Doutreleau 1965–82 in the excellent French Sources Chrétiennes series. Another work of Irenaeus, known as the *Demonstration* or *Proof of the Apostolic Teaching*, was discovered (in Armenian translation) only in 1904. See Froidevaux 1959 in the same series.

[2] Grant 1965:31 and Conzelmann 1973:143. Note that the author of the Book of Revelation had already claimed that God would punish anyone who tampered with his text (Rev. 22.18–19).

tack "myths and genealogies" (1 Tim. 1.4) or "Jewish myths" (Titus 1.14) and which establish the Christian message for the first time in clear opposition both to Jewish apocalyptic thought and to Gnostic anticosmism. The author of these letters (who claims to be Paul just as the writers of the Gnostic gospels claim to be John or Peter, or as the writers of the Jewish pseudepigrapha claim to be Ezra or Enoch) clearly opposes a gnosis that enjoins abstinence from meat and marriage, and insists that "everything created by God is good" (1 Tim. 4.3–4). The rehabilitation of matter thus became an important weapon against the heretics, despite the excesses of the more ascetic Christians,[3] and led to an emphasis on moral struggle not to misuse the divine gift, rather than opposition to the gift itself as evil. Yet the struggle itself was intensely felt by all those early Christians, for though Satan might not be the creator, he was clearly the ruler: "the whole world lieth in the evil one" (1 John 5.19). One reason for Irenaeus' fervor is that he saw his task as a part of that struggle.

1. *Apostasy and Ransom*

Irenaeus was trying simultaneously to make three points: that Satan is the inspiration of heresy, that Satan is the arch-apostate himself, which implies a story about his origins, and that this story in its turn both refutes the Gnostic mythology and, like that rival system, indicates the means of redemption. Like Polycarp, the inspiration of his boyhood, Irenaeus regarded all heresies as instigated by Satan, and so he introduced his account of the heretical theories of redemption in the following terms: "There are as many ceremonies of redemption as there are mystagogues. This kind of person has been infiltrated [*hypobeblētai*] by Satan with a view to the denial of the baptism of rebirth to God, indeed the renunciation of the whole faith."[4] So Satan was the first Gnostic (though Simon Magus was the first in human form) and responsible for all such subsequent renunciations of the truth. The authority of Revelation is again important: Irenaeus is merely demonstrating with concrete examples that "the devil . . . leads astray the whole world." Elsewhere he says that "those who do not believe in God, and do not do his will, are called sons, or angels, of the devil, since they do the works of the devil," citing the Johannine words of Jesus

---

[3] Dodds 1965:21–36. Cf. 2 Cor. 6.14–7.1 and Eph. 2.3, but see now the salutary essay by Pagels 1983.

[4] *Adv. haer.* 1.21.1; cf. 1.25.3, 1.27.3 ("the serpent inhabiting Marcion"), 3.16.1, and 5.26.2.

and glossing them with an allusion to the Watcher angels. Magic, he tells the heretics, is something that "Satan, your father, enables you to accomplish with the help of the mighty angel Azazel."[5]

Irenaeus tries to establish the theological link between Satan and heresy by means of the key term *apostasia*, a Greek word meaning literally "standing away" and so a defection or revolt, connected with *apostatēs*, a runaway, deserter, rebel. Having no obvious Latin equivalent, the word appears transliterated in the Irenaean text. Irenaeus' immediate warrant for the term is the Pauline tradition. We have seen that the Second Letter to the Thessalonians, probably pseudonymous, uses the word as part of its attempt to explain the delayed Parousia (2 Thess. 2.3). The same passage also mentions Satan. Justin seems to have thought the Hebrew etymology of "Satan" was *sata* (apostate) and *nas* (serpent). Neither word appears in classical Hebrew, but Justin was no doubt thinking of *šūt*, to roam, and *nāḥāš*, both words we have previously linked to the Satan tradition.[6] Irenaeus repeats this etymology, since the term *apostasia* and the link with Satan serve Irenaeus' purpose of proposing an alternative to the demiurgic creation myth. He therefore uses the term when he is trying to articulate a theory of redemption.

The most revealing passage is the following, and its obscurity—whether it is Irenaeus' or the Latin translator's—is ample testimony to the difficulties of simultaneously answering heretics and developing a coherent redemption doctrine.

> We could in no other way have learned the things of God unless our Teacher, being the Word [*Logos*], had been made man. . . . He who is the almighty Word, and true man, in redeeming us reasonably [*rationabiliter* = *logikōs*] by his blood, gave himself as a ransom for those who had been carried into captivity. And though the apostasy tyrannized over us unjustly, and when we belonged by nature to almighty God had snatched us away contrary to nature, and made us his own disciples, God's Word, mighty in all things, and not failing in justice, behaved with justice even towards the apostasy itself: he redeemed that which was his own, not by violence (as the apostasy had by violence gained dominion over us, greedily seizing what was not its own), but by persuasion, as it is fitting for God to gain his ends

5 *Adv. haer.* 1.15.6; cf. *Demonstration* 18. For John 8.44, see *Adv. haer.* 4.41.2 and above, Chapter 17.1. *Adv. haer.* 4.16.2 and 36.4 allude to the condemnation of the rebel angels. For the importance of John, see below and Chapter 25.3. On Irenaeus and Revelation, see now Yarbro-Collins 1981:377–81.

6 J. B. Russell 1981:66 notes that Justin may have been thinking in his own Samaritan dialect.

by gentleness and not by violence. So neither was the standard of what is just infringed, nor did the ancient creation of God perish.[7]

The terms that Irenaeus emphasizes in this passage are "justice," "nature," and the logos creation doctrine from John. The opposition of justice and injustice in the passage also includes the equivalent oppositions of persuasion and violence, reasonable and unreasonable, ransom and depredation, freedom and captivity.

By his stress on justice, Irenaeus is trying to turn the idea of a Just God back against Marcion, its proponent. So he insists that it was the Good God who acted justly and that the apostasy had gained power unjustly. By the fact of his creation, man belongs to the true God, and the God who creates is also the God who redeems. "He . . . gave himself as a ransom for those who had been carried into captivity" and so "redeemed that which was his own." The obscurity of Irenaeus' language diminishes if we situate it in this anti-Marcionite and, more broadly, anti-Gnostic context.

For one thing, Irenaeus is here adapting Marcion's theory of relations between the two gods. What for Marcion was a simple purchase—the offering of Christ by the Good God to the demiurge in payment for his rights over mankind—becomes for Irenaeus a ransom paid to the "apostasy." But whereas in the Marcionite transaction, the demiurge, as sole creator, has just claims to mankind, in Irenaeus' view "the apostasy tyrannized over us unjustly, and, when we belonged by nature to almighty God, had snatched us away contrary to nature." The emphasis on "nature" here is deliberately opposed to the dualist idea that the natural man, indeed all nature and its God, is evil. Thus Marcion's straightforward purchase becomes a redemption, a buying back, of what had been unjustly "carried into captivity."

The passage brings together several scriptural citations, the most obvious of which are the various references to Christ as a ransom (*lutron*)—for example, Matthew 20.28 or Mark 10.45—"The Son of man is come . . . to give his life a ransom for many"—or 1 Timothy 2.6: "who gave himself a ransom for all." None of these passages, however, explains to whom the ransom was paid, and this allows for considerable latitude

---

[7] *Adv. haer.* 5.1.1. The Latin text of the crucial passage reads: "Et quoniam injuste dominabatur nobis apostasia, et cum natura essemus Dei omnipotentis, alienavit nos contra naturam, suos proprios faciens discipulos, potens in omnibus Dei Verbum; et non deficiens in sua justitia, juste etiam adversus ipsam conversus est apostasiam."

among the various atonement theories that the church has developed. Unlike Anselm, from whom the satisfaction theory of the atonement derives, Irenaeus clearly thought that the ransom was paid to the devil and that the New Testament texts implied this. So did Origen, Basil the Great, Gregory of Nyssa, Ambrose, and Jerome, although the idea caused great and angry controversy in the early church, and more recent theologians have kept up the battle.[8] Since Irenaeus' language, or that of his Latin translator, is not exactly pellucid, and many interpreters have not thought that this passage implies that the ransom was paid to the devil, I want to make the point clear. The argument depends generally on Irenaeus' obvious opposition to Gnostics and Marcion, but more specifically on another of the scriptural allusions he makes here, to typological-allegorical Exodus interpretation with its equation of Egypt-Rahab and the traditional adversary figure, the tyrant from whom Moses (now Christ) liberates the captive Israel.

The adversary, in Irenaeus' thinking, holds the people captive. Certainly that is unjust, since he has no real right to do so (Irenaeus differs here from later Greek fathers like John of Damascus or Gregory of Nyssa, who stress man's guilt by asserting the devil's rights[9]), but the problem is still how to free the faithful. The slavery metaphor is significant here. If a slave is freed by an act of violence he is not rightfully manumitted, even if the initial act of enslaving were unjust. So God acts reasonably or lawfully, in such a way that the devil has no claim against him. He is offered a fair redemption price, even though he "tyrannized over us unjustly."

The ransom theory by itself does not abolish Marcion's theological dualism. These early fathers simply maintained the Marcionite distinction but substituted God and Satan for Marcion's Christ and demiurge. This important moment in the rise of the Christian theory of the devil has received little attention as such. Yet it was an obvious enough narrative move. It extended the process we have analyzed by which Satan or some equivalent was gradually substituted for Yahweh at the more embarrassing moments of religious history. It was not now Yahweh but the old enemy who exacted such cruel price from Christ.

The new theory occasioned great debate within the church. Having

---

[8] Aulén 1969 gives the clearest exposition of these quarrels, but contrast Pelikan 1971:148–52, who disagrees with Aulén's view of Irenaeus. Cf. Rashdall 1919:233–48, 259, 364, and E. R. Hardy in Richardson (ed.) 1970:351, who regards Aulén's thesis as "most unfair."

[9] Gregory of Nyssa, *Great Catechism* 22, 24. See Schaff (ed.) 1890–94: vol. 5, 494, and Aulén 1969:45–49.

seen its logic, Gregory of Nazianzus denounced it: "Since a ransom belongs only to him who holds in bondage, I ask to whom was this offered, and for what cause? If to the Evil One, fie upon the outrage!"[10] Anselm later recognized the problem in a calmer way: the ransom theory accorded too much power to Satan by allowing him rights over man, and thus threatened a dualist heresy, so he reassessed the theory of the redemption and evolved the idea, even more akin perhaps to the underlying Marcionite doctrine of a Just God, that the two figures involved in the exchange were not God and Devil but Son and Father, two manifestations of the one godhead. Thus the sacrifice became not ransom, such as one pays to a rival power, but satisfaction, such as one pays to Justice.[11]

The outrage that Gregory fied upon and Anselm rejected was a genuine danger, largely because the ransom theory had been initially put forward as an answer to heretics for whom the world tyrant was an even more powerful figure than in the New Testament. Some scriptural warrant might be found in the repeated idea of the New Testament that Christ was incarnated so "that through death he might destroy him that had the power of death, that is, the devil,"[12] yet this phrase really suggests only the combat theme of the opposition of Christ to devil and gives no hint of the ransom relationship. It is to Irenaeus' and then Origen's extension of the combat in their quarrel with heretics that the church owed its "classic" theory of the atonement.

Given Irenaeus' main purpose in our key passage, the refutation of heresy, the most significant of the scriptural allusions is to the Johannine doctrine of the Word made flesh. It is not simply the occasion for Irenaeus' pun about God acting reasonably (*logikōs*); it is the crucial refutation of the Gnostic view of Christ, and of creation.

Irenaeus is here trying to fill a significant gap in New Testament theology, the fact we have noted before that nothing there accounts for the usurpation of the created world. This absence would encourage heretics to think that the creation itself was wicked. Irenaeus is trying to substitute

[10] Gregory of Nazianzus, *Orations* 45.22, trans. in Schaff (ed.) 1890–94: vol. 7, 431.

[11] Anselm, *Cur Deus homo?* 1.3–7. The Protestant theory derives from Anselm and became dogma within the Calvinist churches. Rashdall 1919 summarizes and expounds the theory, while himself preferring the liberal view deriving from Abelard via Socinianism and the Enlightenment that the satisfaction was obtained through a change in man. Aulén 1969 argues that Luther did not, as is generally supposed, follow the Anselmian satisfaction theory but reverted to what Aulén calls the "classic" view.

[12] Mark 10.45. Cf. Matt. 20.28, Heb. 2.14, and above, Chapters 15 and 16; see also below, Chapter 21.2.

a wicked usurper for an evil or incompetent creator, but he faces difficulties in finding appropriate texts. Paul made it necessary that the usurpation have something to do with Adam but had not made clear how the usurping tyrant and Adam's sin were linked.

Irenaeus faced a related difficulty in using John's gospel because it nowhere mentions the Yahwist's Adam and Eve tale. Why then did he need John at all? The opening of the fourth gospel was central to his argument because it explicitly identifies the redeemer with the creator by means of his Logos doctrine. The creator comes to redeem his own creation. "All things were made by him; and without him was not anything made. . . . He was in the world, and the world was made by him, and the world knew him not" (John 1.3–10). Most Gnostics could not allow that "the Word was made flesh," for Gnostic flesh, like its creator, was evil.

There is a considerable likelihood that John was consciously opposing some form of Gnostic world-view and thus defined his vision in terms that both evoke and refute the Gnostic position. John tells nothing of the synoptic tradition about Jesus' birth from Mary, the appearance to Mary of the angel Gabriel, the various visitors to the manger. The gospel begins instead with a hymnodic prologue, a poem of creation and salvation in the tradition of Genesis midrash. Genesis is here reassessed by the creator's new role, as the Christ, of redeeming his creation from the evil powers to which it has fallen victim, the darkness of this world (1.5, 10). As soon as the dove descends (1.32), the Christ is already the redeemer on his mission. This John has affinities with Jewish apocalyptic, especially with the Qumran ideas, but he is also much closer than the synoptic writers to the sophisticated religious consciousness displayed by the Gnostic leaders. Throughout the gospel there is a strong dualism of "this world" and "those who are not of this world," of the birth from flesh and the birth from spirit, of the light and the darkness.[13] The redeemer descends, as in Gnostic thought, from the unknown God above, engineers the defeat of the prince of this world, and returns exalted to open the way back into heaven. In spite of the silence about Adam, then, Irenaeus could find in John's gospel the kind of articulate cosmology he needed as an alternative to the Gnostic heresies.

Indeed, Irenaeus was sure that John had anticipated his attack. He was led to this view partly because, like other early Christians, he identified

[13] Burrows 1958:123–30 and Grant 1959:163–77. For a general review of these issues, see R. E. Brown 1966:lii–lxxvi and now Barrett 1983.

John the author of the Book of Revelation, who explicitly denounces the Gnostic Nicolaitans, with John the author of the gospel and letters:

> John, the disciple of the Lord, wished by the proclamation of the gospel to extirpate the error which had been planted among men by Cerinthus and much earlier by those called Nicolaitans, who are an offshoot of the knowledge that is falsely so called. John wished to confound them and show that there is one God who made all things by his Word. It is not true, as they say, that the demiurge is one and the Father of the Lord another.[14]

But the gospel of John lacked what Gnostic systems had in abundance, an account of how or why the created world needed to be redeemed. Despite its references to the "prince of this world," it nowhere tells how this prince had come to power. The darkness into which the light came is simply there.

Nonetheless, the Logos doctrine and the *apostasia* idea together help Irenaeus to refute the heretics. The Gnostics who in various ways would have separated the human body of Jesus from the divine Christ who descended with the dove, and would thus have denied the Incarnation, are answered, as Irenaeus thought John had answered them before him, by the Logos idea itself, the Word made flesh, so that flesh too is redeemed. Marcion is answered both by the assertion that we had been led into captivity, unnaturally alienated from our true master, and by the substitution of the "apostasy" for the Just and Separate God of Marcion's Old Testament. The ransom is thus paid not to Marcion's demiurge but to another figure intended to take his place within the structure of the ransom idea, a world ruler who is separate from God not in origin and by nature but only because he turned away, because he is an apostate.

Other aspects of Irenaeus' thought seem to draw similar inspiration from the heresies he is attacking and may shed light on the *apostasia* idea. Following Paul's alignment of Adam with Christ, and an earlier suggestion of Justin, Irenaeus set the Tree next to the Cross, and Eve next to Mary:

> For as Eve was seduced by the word [*sermo*] of an angel to flee from God, by transgressing his Word [*verbum*], so Mary by the word [*sermo*] of an angel received the glad tidings that she would bear God by obeying his Word. . . .
> As the human race was subjected to death through a virgin, so it was saved

---

[14] *Adv. haer.* 3.11.1; cf. 1.26.1. See also above, Chapter 17.1.

by a virgin, and thus the disobedience of one virgin was precisely balanced
by the obedience of another.[15]

This doctrine about Mary, which had spectacular developments in the
Middle Ages, may well have been inspired by the Gnostic teachings about
the divine mother, Sophia, and her redemptive function in the Gnostic
myth. Many Gnostic groups gave roles to women, even allowing them to
celebrate the eucharist. These practices were denounced by Irenaeus and
Tertullian, but the role of Mary, which builds on the gospel nativity legends, may be intended as some form of compensation for the inferiority
of women in the orthodox church. Thus the angel's annunciation to
Mary makes up for Eve's seduction by a different kind of angel.[16]

The alignment of Eve and Mary is a part of Irenaeus' larger theory of
"recapitulation," according to which Christ's life is a recapitulation in
perfection of the folly and disobedience of Adam's: "By his obedience to
death, the Word annulled the ancient disobedience committed at the
tree." In Irenaeus' version of the story, the creative Word "came to the
very place and spot where we had lost life, and broke the bonds of our
fetters," implying that the cross was placed where the tree of knowledge
had stood.[17] The doctrine helps Irenaeus to answer his opponents, both by
binding more tightly the Christian message to the Old Testament in the
face of Marcion's radical separation of the two and by offering him the
beginnings of a mythological view of sacred history comparable in its potential scope to the Gnostic blending of creation and redemption theory.
Apostasia is thus the counterpart to Gnostic Ignorance, and whereas the
ignorant demiurge is answered by knowledge of the hidden god, apostasia
is answered by Christ's perfect and openly proclaimed obedience.

It is thus clear that Irenaeus needs to be able to read the Adam story as
the original apostasy. Referring to the wilderness temptations, he says:

> Recapitulating everything in himself, then, Christ also recapitulated the
> battle against our enemy, provoking and defeating him who at the begin-

[15] Adv. haer. 5.19.1. For the problems of translation here, see E. R. Hardy in Richardson
(ed.) 1970:389–90; cf. Demonstration 33.

[16] Cf. Justin, Dialogue with Trypho, 100 in ANF, vol. 1, 249. On the seduction of Eve and
the heavenly compensation by the "Mother of All Living," Sophia, Barbelo, or Eve herself,
see Pagels 1979:48–69. For the importance of typology in the later tradition, see Daniélou
1950, Evans 1968:99–104, and below, Chapter 25.3. For Irenaeus, see Lawson 1948:121–45.

[17] Demonstration 34, 38; cf. Aulén 1969:29 and Adv. haer. 5.19–22. On recapitulation as already a Valentinian doctrine, see now Pagels 1983:167—the church was separated, like Eve,
from her true husband, and needs now to be reunited with the new Adam; cf. Adv. haer.
1.8.4.

ning had led us captive in Adam, trampling on his head, as you find in Genesis that God said to the serpent, "And I will put enmity between you and the woman, and between your seed and her seed."[18]

Irenaeus probably had this story in mind when he mentions apostasy in the passage we have been studying from the opening of book 5. If so, however, he found no way to articulate the idea; his focus is on the cosmic rather than the human aspect of the apostasy, and his intent is to counter Gnostic redemption cosmology with what he regards as Christian.

In fact, Irenaeus avoids the complete personification of *apostasia* as Satan. It is rather the apostasy itself which "tyrannized over us unjustly," and God acts "with justice against the apostasy itself." It is thus not an entirely separate being, and though Irenaeus is not perhaps clear about what he has in mind, we may turn to other passages in his work to see the direction of his thought. Above all, Irenaeus is eager to connect the apostasy with his own attack on heretics, whom he saw as repeating the initial apostasy and thus as the dupes of Satan. Not only was their false theory of the redemption a trick of Satan's to keep them in bondage (it was, we have noted, "instigated by Satan to lead them to renounce the baptism of rebirth to God, indeed to deny the whole faith"), but the heretics themselves are also apostates: "All of these rebelled in their apostasy much later, in the midst of the church's history."[19] Apostasy is not so much a separate cosmic being as a state of mind. It is a universal and continuing state of mind, to be sure; it belongs as much to the first deceiver as to those who continue to reject the truth. But it is rather a projection upon a universal scale of what Irenaeus took to be the recalcitrant psyche of the individual heretics.

Clearly, Irenaeus is here reaching for some definition of the primal and recurring sin, but the term "apostasy" covers too wide a ground for this. It is in essence a spatial rather than a moral term; it states the fact of "turning away" but does not define or account for it.

2. Adam and Recapitulation

In spite of the importance of *apostasia* as a refutation of the demiurge, it is unclear how Irenaeus imagined a motive for it. The status of the term as a quasi-personified abstraction makes it hard to link with the overall *mythos*.

---

[18] *Adv. haer.* 5.21.1; cf. 3.23.7, 4.40.3.
[19] *Adv. haer.* 3.4.3; cf. above, n. 4.

What the recapitulation theory compels him to do is tell some version of the Adam story which will also account for the existence of an angelic heretic. If the Gnostics can fit the Eden story to their version of the creation-redemption plot, then Irenaeus, by reversing the ideas of tempter and savior, needs to do so too. But the Adam story as he tells it only poses further difficulties that could not be solved within the system he has invented. Presumably the idea of apostasy is designed to include both Adam's disobedience and Satan's usurpation, but the ambivalence of the term never really makes this clear, and it is remarkable that Irenaeus never uses the term for Adam's sin.

The version of the Eden story Irenaeus tells derives clearly enough from the Enoch literature and the Adam books. Possibly, he follows Tatian, who suggested that God's firstborn, feeling envy of mankind, made Eve feel desire and thus introduced the first couple to sexual intercourse. The result of this, as Jesus said, was that marrying and giving in marriage increased the corruption of the world before the flood, in parallel with the end-time. Adam and Eve then attached themselves to this firstborn as being more subtle than the rest and declared him to be God.

> Then the power of the Logos banished the beginner of the folly and his adherents from all fellowship with himself. And he who was made in the image of God, when the more powerful spirit departed from him, became mortal; but that first-begotten one through his ignorance and transgression became a demon.[20]

Tatian's myth bears only a distant relationship to the story of the clever snake in Genesis. Instead, it takes elements of various apocryphal stories and creates a remarkable new narrative. The senior angel of the Adam books now tries actually to make man worship him, instead of complaining peevishly to God that he ought to. The rebellion of the Enoch tradition is now connected directly to a competition with God for man's worship, with sexuality the devil's weapon. The Johannine Logos doctrine is introduced into the Adam story for the first time, with the Logos as the opponent of this rival god. And the Gnostic idea of the ignorance of the subordinate power, the first-begotten of Sophia, accounts for his transformation into a "demon." In fact, the Gnostic influence is so strong here

[20] Tatian, *Oratio ad Graecos* 7 and Clement, *Stromata* 3.49–102, alluding to Matt. 24.37–39 (above, Chapter 13 n. 5) and 1 Cor. 7.2–5. Cf. Justin, *Dialogue with Trypho* 124. Evans 1968:81 discusses well these narrative variants. See now Pagels 1983:151–55.

that Tatian himself soon became the leader of a heretical sect with Gnostic leanings and was excommunicated.

Irenaeus, more alert to the dangers of the Gnostic heresy, revised Tatian's version and thus brought it closer to the Eden story as it appears in Genesis. He gave due weight to the notion of sin, for which Paul had used the story as an explanation; God's "firstborn" becomes simply "the angel" to avoid the taint of Gnosticism. We also find the characteristic Irenaean stress on disobedience.

> This commandment the man did not keep, but disobeyed God, being misled by the angel, who, becoming jealous of the man because of the many favors God had bestowed on the man, both ruined himself and made the man a sinner, persuading him to disobey God's command. So the angel, having become by falsehood the head and fount of sin, both was himself stricken, having offended against God, and caused the man to be cast forth from Paradise.[21]

The story of Adam thus became for Irenaeus what it was in the "Book of Adam"—the origin of all sin, both Adam's and the angel's. Prior to his jealousy and deception of Adam, the angel was unfallen.

There is one more important difference between Tatian's version and that of Irenaeus. Whereas Tatian followed the Priestly Genesis and the Alexandrian tradition in general in making Adam the near-divine creature "in the image of God," Irenaeus adopted a different view of Adam's prelapsarian nature. Following the implications of the Yahwist's tale more closely, he suggested that Adam and Eve were just children:

> So, having made the man lord of the earth and everything in it, He made him in secret lord also of the servants in it. They, however, were in their full development, while the lord, that is the man, was a little one; for he was a child and had need to grow so as to come into his full perfection. . . . Wherefore also he was easily misled by the deceiver.[22]

Children themselves, that is, Adam and Eve, "had no understanding of the procreation of children" and were supposed to wait before they started to multiply. This idea of Adam's status neatly explained the prohibition on the tree of knowledge. There was nothing wrong with it in

---

[21] *Demonstration* 16; cf. *Adv. haer.* 1.28.1, 3.23.8, and above, Chapter 12.7.

[22] *Demonstration* 12; cf. *Adv. haer.* 3.22.4, 4.38.1, and Theophilus, *Ad Autolycum* 2.25. For the impact of Irenaeus' view, see Hick 1966:217–21 and esp. the remarks of J. B. Russell 1981:82.

itself, nor was it permanently denied to him; he was just too young as yet for such heady food.

Though Irenaeus' version of Genesis had the advantage of opposing the Gnostic primal sin with a suitably Pauline story, it was open to even more objections. It cast serious doubts on the wisdom of God. What conscientious parent leaves his children to run free when there are "deceivers" around? It also failed to account for the gravity of the consequences. Why should all mankind suffer for the slip of two young children? It thus could not provide an adequate repudiation of the heretics who claimed that the creation was at best a bungled job. Furthermore, it threatened to place too much blame on the angel. Though Irenaeus had been able to reintroduce the idea of sin into his story, thus avoiding the dangerous implications of Tatian's "folly" and "ignorance," it is the angel who becomes "the head and fount of sin," the angel who "made the man a sinner."

One can sympathize with Irenaeus' difficulties. He has available to him several different stories about the origins of evil, and he has various opponents whom he must somehow discredit. All these stories, together with their corresponding redemptive ideas, sit uneasily in his mind. He has a tradition about "the prince of this world" to explain, together with a story of the corruption of the Watcher angels which had no necessary link with the Eden tale; he has the two Pauline theories of the redemption to bring together; and he must make the Adam myth central to his story of rebellion in the face of a Gnostic heresy that made it the beginning of man's salvation, and of a rationalist like Celsus, who called it an old wives' tale.[23] Not surprisingly, he was unable to pull the whole mythology-theology together into a coherent Aristotelian unity that would completely express the manner of God's participation in human history. The church would have to wait until Augustine before such a demanding structural synthesis could emerge.

One symptom of Irenaeus' difficulties is the odd use he makes of New Testament serpents. Matthew 10.16 reads, "Be ye wise as serpents and gentle as doves." So eager is Irenaeus to assert his recapitulation typology that he twists this language out of recognizable shape: "Then was the sin of the first-formed man healed by the virtue of the First-Begotten [i.e., Christ], the wisdom of the serpent was conquered by the simplicity of the dove, and the chains were broken by which we were in bondage to

[23] Origen, *Contra Celsum* 4.38. See below, Chapter 22.5.

death."[24] It is possible that Irenaeus here makes independent use of a logion from oral tradition, but it is more likely that this is typical of the textual distortion that was common in the struggle with heresy.

Despite these difficulties, Irenaeus had offered several readings of the main stories which would influence the subsequent development of Christian thought. The Adam story had been firmly established as the great crisis that accounted for the rest of human history, and the idea of apostasy had suggested a way of linking it to the liberation theory of redemption. This apostasy, the turning away from God as the primal sin, provided Irenaeus and the church after him with a means to counter the Valentinian theory of divine ignorance and the Marcionite doctrine of the total separation of two Gods from the beginning of things. He had reimagined the Eden tale in the terms provided both by the Watcher tradition and by the quarrel with dualism, and the tale had in the process taken on the necessary cosmic dimension. Though this threatened the human focus of the story—its concentration on Adam's sin of disobedience—it increased its explanatory power.

Irenaeus is thus the first important church leader to construct a version of the Christian combat myth that at least attempts to include all the relevant but disparate narratives. In particular, he managed to establish an identity for the adversary which accounted for his continuing role in the myth. In a passage that describes the devil as both a rebel and a robber,[25] Irenaeus also identifies him as the enemy of God and man, the opponent of the Logos, the apostate, and the serpent: "The Word of God, who is the creator of all things, overcame him through man, and branded him as an apostate, and made him subject to man. See, says the Word, I give you power to tread upon [calcare] serpents and scorpions, and upon the power of the enemy."[26] Irenaeus takes Jesus to be alluding to the Eden story when he promises power over serpents, and thus the recapitulation doctrine extends also to the adversary, not only to Adam/Christ, Eve/Mary, Tree/Cross. "So the Scripture says: I will put enmity between you [the serpent] and the woman, and between thy seed and the seed of the woman; he shall trample on [calcabit] thy head, and thou shalt watch [ob-

---

[24] *Adv. haer.* 5.19.1. For the translation, see Rousseau and Doutreleau 1965–82: vol. 5, pt. 1, 304–5, and E. R. Hardy in Richardson (ed.) 1970:390. For the logion, cf. Rom. 16.9 and above, Chapter 14.6 n. 25.

[25] The devil as robber is the earliest citation of John 10.1–10 as applied to the devil. In the gospel, Jesus seems to be referring to previous false messiahs.

[26] *Adv. haer.* 5.24.4, quoting Luke 10.19. See above, Chapters 12.6, 14.2, and 15, and Aulén 1969:24–26.

servabis] for his heel. This enmity the Lord recapitulated in himself, being made man, born of a woman, and trampling [*calcans*] on the serpent's head."[27] So the recapitulation theory provides firm narrative closure, since the redemption episode picks up and transforms details from the opening, the Eden story. The serpent yields to the dove.

The major change that the later church would introduce into Irenaeus' version of Genesis would be to separate Adam's disobedience from the angel's fall and then provide a new connection. Basil the Great, for example, says:

> Thus he was not instituted as our enemy from the outset; he is driven to become our enemy through envy. For, having been made aware that he is an outcast from the angelic ranks himself, he finds it insupportable to him to see man, who is of the earth, exalted to angelic status.[28]

This is virtually a summary of the story told in the "Book of Adam," and it provides a clear counter to the dualist idea of an original evil force. But since the character of Adam's antagonist has now been so magnified, Adam himself cannot remain the child he was for Irenaeus. He reverts once again to the perfectionist Adam of the Alexandrian tradition, and the devil's envy immediately becomes more plausible.

The double fall of angel and Adam derives ultimately from the needs of Paul's double theory of the redemption. But the separation of the two falls which Irenaeus had tried to bring together created a new danger. Granted that the myth of a premundane fall of Lucifer could restore Adam's princely state and so help to justify the Fall, the fall of Lucifer itself was still not fully explained. The difficulties of the Adam story were simply pushed back one stage.

Irenaeus himself avoided this danger by making the two falls, of angel

---

[27] *Adv. haer.* 4.40.3; cf. 5.21.1. Irenaeus can take the various texts to be linked partly because his Greek Bible, the Septuagint version, has the same or related verbs in each verse—*teirō* and *suntribō*, cognate with Latin *tero*. However, the Vulgate (and Irenaeus' translator) uses *calco* to translate *suntribō*. Someone misread the Greek as *tēreō*, to watch for, in Gen. 3.15, which accounts for Irenaeus' *observans*. The Hebrew *šp* was vocalized as *šū'p* (bruise) in the Masoretic text, but Gunkel 1895, followed by many since, argued for *šā'ap* (crush), both because of the combat myth allusion and because of the New Testament passages like Luke 10.19 (*patein*) and Rom. 16.12 (*suntribō*). From other texts also, it looks as if Gen. 3.15 had for some time been connected in this way to the combat myth and was becoming what theologians therefore call the *protevangelium*, a promise of the gospel or proto-gospel. See above, Chapter 14.5.

[28] Basil, *That God Is Not the Author of Evil* 8, quoted in Evans 1968:88; cf. *Hexaemeron*, Homily 2.4 in Schaff (ed.) 1894: vol. 8, 61.

and man, coincide. He knows nothing of a premundane cosmic battle. Yet it would ultimately be the Irenaean theory of apostasy that would enable the church to incorporate the divine rebellion and war into its *mythos* and still keep the focus on sin rather than on the cosmic drama of good versus evil. Augustine, for example, was to insist on this doctrine—the two falls had the same moral origin, turning away from God to the self. Satan's first sin could not continue to be identified with the temptation of Adam and Eve, as Irenaeus had tried to do, but even when that sin became again the challenge to God of the rebellion myth, the sin itself remained apostasy, the turning away.

Henceforth the Catholic church could begin to answer the heretics with its own developing cosmic system, though it had adopted much of the Gnostic mythology in order to create it. The Gnostic idea that the divine light was being redeemed *from* the darkness could be countered both by the Johannine idea that the light had come *into* the darkness and by the theory that man—the whole man, not just his "light" or spirit—was redeemed from the devil. Yet the devil himself had always to be seen, not only as an independent cosmic force but also as a projection of and thus a lesson in the human sin that Paul had located at the center of the redemption doctrine. So the story of Satan came to be a dramatized demonstration of the psychology that Irenaeus attributed to the heretics: anyone who refuses to accept the tradition of the four canonical gospels, "despises the companions of the Lord, despises Christ himself, he even despises the Father, and he is self-condemned, resisting and refusing his own salvation, as all the heretics do."[29]

[29] *Adv. haer.* 3.1.2.

TWENTY

THE WATCHER ANGELS IN THE
EARLY CHURCH

Like IRENAEUS, several other early Christians made use of the Watcher tradition to account for the adversary's origin, and it seems to have remained current even into the age of monasticism.[1] The story had the advantage that it linked angelic and human sin, but it had a serious flaw too: given its biblical context in the flood myth, one must ignore the historical relation of Adam to Noah in order to make the lustful angels responsible for Adam's sin. The story might be an example of evil, but it could hardly continue to explain its origins, once Paul's redemption theory had given such importance to the Adam story. The Watcher myth's prestige seems to have waned along with that of the Enoch books themselves, at least in the Western church. Instead, another myth, based on the ambitious rebel of Ezekiel and Isaiah, soon came to replace it. The chief reason for this seems to have been the growing awareness of the need to counter Gnostic heresy, and the key figure was Origen. What was the situation Origen faced?

There are several clear allusions to the Watcher story in the New Testament. "Depart from me, you cursed, into the eternal fire prepared for the devil and his angels" is what Matthew's Jesus will say at the Second Coming. The Letter of Jude refers to "the angels which did not keep their own position but left their proper dwelling." They have been kept in "eternal chains in the nether gloom until the judgment of the great day," and they are also "wandering stars for whom the nether gloom of darkness has been reserved for ever."[2] Revelation 12.9 and 13.14, about the devil-beast who "leads astray those that dwell on the earth," echo the *Apocalypse of Abraham* and *Enoch* 54.6 about the hosts of Azazel who are punished for "leading astray those who dwell on the earth." In each case, however, the allusions are brief and general enough that they would not guarantee the persistence of the Watcher tradition in the presence of a se-

---

[1] Bamberger 1952:74–81, Pelikan 1971:135, and now Stroumsa 1984:30.
[2] Matt. 25.41; Jude 6, 13. See *Enoch* 12.4 and 54.4–5 and cf. Rev. 20.2–3.

(349)

rious rival. Indeed, the language of these passages could apply equally well to the prideful rebel, once he was seen to be an angel.

Even though the letter of Jude is denouncing lust at the time it makes the allusion to the angels, the main point of the letter is an attack on false teachers. The letter is clearly connected with 2 Peter, which uses the same language in a more expanded form, attacking false teachers equally for their lust and their presumptuousness:

> For if God spared not the angels that sinned, but cast them down to Tartarus, and committed them into chains of darkness, to be reserved until the judgment; and spared not the old world, but saved Noah, a preacher of righteousness, and seven others, bringing a flood upon the world of the ungodly; and turning the cities of Sodom and Gomorrah into ashes condemned them to extinction, making them an example unto those that after should live ungodly; and delivered the righteous Lot, vexed with the filthy conduct of the wicked; . . . the Lord knows how to deliver the godly out of temptations, and to reserve the unjust until the day of judgment to be punished: and especially them that walk after the flesh in the lust of uncleanness, and despise government. Presumptuous are they, self-willed, they are not afraid to speak evil of the glorious ones.[3]

Both these letters have been shown to date from the early years of the struggle with Gnosticism, around A.D. 90, and both use the Watcher story, with its parallels in the Sodom and Gomorrah complex, as moralistic exempla, in the manner of the Qumran scrolls, rather than as explanations of the causes of evil.[4] Both are trying to illustrate the nature of heresy and to warn against it; neither is so explicit as to require the Enoch story in order to be understood; both try to establish a link, if indirectly, between angelic activity and false teaching, adapting the secrets of the gods which the Watchers revealed and which turned out worthless.

The most detailed version of the Watcher myth in Christian literature occurs in the Pseudo-Clementine *Homilies*. This body of literature, claiming to come from the early bishop Clement of Rome, is based on a text of Petrine Christianity, the "Proclamations of Peter," known to Origen, and provides evidence of the link between Jewish Christianity and Gnosticism in the second century. Peter tells us that the angels first came down to preach to men and call for repentance, an allusion to the originally benign function of the Watchers. Soon, however, they fell prey to the power

---

[3] 2 Pet. 2.4–10. Cf. above, Chapter 12 n. 73, on the Adam books, and *Enoch* 10.1–16, 12.3–13.3 and 64.1–69.1, for the "glorious" angels.

[4] Reicke 1964:144, See above, Chapters 10.1 and 17.1; see also Fontenrose 1945 and Justin, *First Apology* 53. Jude 14–15 cites *Enoch* 1.9 and the *Assumption of Moses*.

of the flesh and changed themselves into various precious stones, pearls and gold, to attract the women. United with the daughters of men, they lost their divine natures and were unable to return to heaven. The giants were the bastard offspring of their illegitimate "mixing," and they became the first eaters of men, poisoning the earth with bloodshed. Destroyed by the flood, their spirits, as demons, continued to lead a separate existence as punishers of unbelievers and sinners. It is likely that this story represents a buried polemic against Paul's efforts to make the Adam story responsible for evil, although the overt opponent is Simon Magus. In this text, as in Jewish Christianity generally, much is made of the constant warfare between the two kingdoms or powers. The demons, under the king of darkness, attack body and mind, but Christ's name, especially in exorcism and baptism, is the best antidote.[5] Qumran traditions have been adapted, but not very radically, to the beliefs of Jewish Christians.

The first of the apologetic fathers, Justin Martyr, shows a similar inclination to explain the demons, so common in the gospels, by reference to the Watcher angels. Originally appointed to govern the nations, like the holy Watchers of Daniel, some of these angels fell for women and produced children "who are called demons." "They enslaved the rest of the human race . . . and sowed among men murders, war, adulteries, licentiousness, and all manner of evils."[6] The narrative has been simplified and rationalized by the elimination of the giants, for example, so the offspring are immediately demons.

Elsewhere, Justin links Satan with the leader of this band:

> Among us the chief of the evil demons is called the serpent and Satan and the devil, as you can learn by examining our writings. Christ has foretold that he will be cast into fire with his host and the men who follow him, all to be punished for endless ages. God delays doing this for the sake of the human race, for he foreknows that there are some yet to be saved by repentance, even perhaps some not yet born.

This is the earliest passage, we have seen, that cites the words of Revelation as scripture in order to identify serpent and Satan.[7] It also vaguely aligns this composite enemy with the curse of Matthew 25.41. In its con-

---

[5] *Homilies* 8.11–19, discussed in Bauer 1972:117, 241–35, and Schoeps 1964. On the dualism of the *Epistle of Barnabas* and other Jewish-Christian texts, see J. B. Russell 1981:38–45, 60.

[6] Justin, *Second Apology* 5, in ANF vol. 1, 190. Black 1985:132, 161, shows how close this passage is to *Enoch* 9.9, 19.1. See above, Chapter 9 n. 4.

[7] Justin, *First Apology* 28.1, in Richardson (ed.) 1970:259; cf. ANF vol. 1, 172. Here the Greek word is the diminutive *daimonion* rather than *daimōn*. See above, Chapter 16 n. 13.

text the passage is a sly attack on the author's Roman audience. Ironically, he says, "Beside each of those whom you think of as gods a serpent is depicted as a great symbol and mystery." Justin's identification of evil demons, Satan and serpent is in fact the climax to his momentous argument that these evil demons have managed to convince everyone they are the pagan gods. He introduces this argument with a variant of the Watcher myth, even more simplified, in that the distinction between angel and demon, like that between demon and giant, has also now disappeared: "You punish us injudiciously, without deliberation," he tells his audience,

> driven by unreasoning passion and the whips of evil demons. The truth must be told. In old times evil demons manifested themselves, seducing women, corrupting boys, and showing terrifying sights to men—so that those who did not judge these occurrences rationally were filled with awe. Taken captive by fear and not understanding that these were evil demons, they called them gods.[8]

These demons were then responsible for the death of Socrates, who had tried to show people what these gods really were. In the same way they are having us Christians persecuted. In fact, pagan persecutors and heretics like Simon Magus are all the instruments of these demons.

In their disguise as pagan gods, these demons also invented another cunning trick. Anticipating that Christianity would be directed against their power, they invented myths like those of Dionysus, Perseus, Hercules, or Asclepius to imply that the Christ story was just another such "marvelous tale of the kind the poets tell."[9] The contrast Justin makes here is between classical poets and Hebrew prophets, and he triumphantly points out that, since these demons did not understand what the crucifixion was to be, no diabolical variant exists among the classical poets. So far as we know, the argument in this form was original with Justin, although it is probably based on the common Old Testament demotion of pagan gods to idols.[10] Once proposed, the idea quickly gained currency.

A fuller account that builds on Justin's argument comes from another second-century apologist Athenagoras. Athenagoras' *Plea Regarding*

---

[8] Justin, *First Apology* 5, in Richardson (ed.) 1970:244; cf. ANF vol. 1, 164. For similar concepts, see Minucius Felix, *Octavius* 26–27; and Commodianus, *Instructiones* 1, 3, 16, in ANF vol. 4, 189–90 and 203–6, discussed in Pelikan 1971:135 and 384 and J. B. Russell 1981: 104–6.

[9] Justin, *First Apology* 54, cf. 21, in ANF vol. 1, 181, 170.

[10] Ps. 96.5, "For all the gods of the nations are idols," which in the Septuagint (LXX) reads *eidōla daimoniōn*. Cf. Deut. 32.17, where the LXX has *diaboli*. See above, Chapter 15 n. 18.

Christians is addressed to the emperors Marcus Aurelius and Commodus and draws extensively on the philosophical tradition of Greece; he apparently wrote the *Plea* from Athens. This accounts in part for the curious fusion of the Watcher story with a philosophical terminology that brings his account of the Christian view of demons very close to the Gnostic view. Indeed, he associates Satan, like the Gnostics, with matter. He is aware, however, of the objections to dualism advanced by Plato and commonly used against Christians at the time. So he begins his account by disclaiming dualism. Just as the Son is the wisdom of the Father, and the Spirit is his effluence, like light from fire, so also we recognize powers associated with matter.

> Of these there is one in particular hostile to God. We do not mean that there is anything which is opposed to God in the way that Empedocles opposed strife to love and night to day in the phenomenal world. For even if anything did manage to set itself up against God, it would cease to exist. It would fall to pieces by the power and might of God. Rather do we mean that the spirit that inhabits matter is opposed to God's goodness. . . . This opposing spirit was created by God, just as the other angels were created by him and entrusted with administering matter and its forms.

Like men, angels also have free will, he explains, and so just as some men turn out faithless in their tasks, so it is with the angels. Some remained obedient, but others

> violated their very nature and office. Among them was this prince of matter and its forms, and others who were set in the first firmament. (You will note that we say nothing without authority and speak only of what the prophets have foretold.) These latter angels fell into lusting after virgins and became slaves of the flesh, while the prince of matter became negligent and wicked in managing what was entrusted to him. From those who had intercourse with the virgins were begotten the so-called giants.[11]

Athenagoras claims to find the angelic fall and the prince of matter in Genesis, but he is clearly reading the story of the angel sons of God in the light of the Enoch literature. Neither Genesis nor the *Book of Enoch*, however, associates the Watchers with the "first firmament." This sounds more like the cherub from Ezekiel who was on the holy mountain of God and who walked up and down in the midst of the stones of fire. The association of

---

[11] Athenagoras, *Plea* 25, trans. Richardson (ed.) 1970:327–28; cf. ANF vol. 2, 142. For Celsus in Origen, *Contra Celsum* 6.42, see below, Chapter 21.5.

the angels with stars was already a commonplace, not only in the Enoch literature but also in the Stoic world of astrology and in Gnostic systems.[12] The phrase suggests the kind of overlapping of the Enoch and Ezekiel-Isaiah myths that we have noted already in the later Enoch tradition.[13]

Athenagoras now continues his appeal to the Roman emperors by alluding to their common literary tradition. It is not only the sacred scriptures which mention these giants, he says, but even "the poets."

> This is not surprising, for worldly wisdom differs [from divine?] just as plausibility differs from truth. While the one is of heaven, the other is of earth; yet, according to the prince of matter himself, "We know how to tell many lies that resemble the truth."

The devil is the father of lies, said John's Jesus to the Jews, but Athenagoras here makes Satan quote the words of Hesiod's Muses.[14] The whole Greek tradition of poetic inspiration is now, it seems, available to Christian denunciation as the work of the devil. And since Hesiod's Muses are the daughters of Zeus, again the whole of pagan polytheism can be associated with demons. Indeed, it was on these grounds that Christians refused to worship at the shrines of the Greco-Roman world, something that horrified the law-abiding Celsus, a contemporary of Athenagoras, who saw in this refusal the denial of all that made for a cohesive community, united around the worship of its traditional gods—indeed, the Christians thereby rejected the very basis of "civilization" itself, the practice of living in cities.[15]

Athenagoras then summarizes the Christian view:

> Those angels, then, which fell from the heavens, haunt the air and the earth and are no longer able to rise to heavenly things. Along with the souls of the giants, they are the demons which wander about the world. Of these, there are two classes: the demons proper, who act in accordance with the natures they have received, and the angels, who act in accordance with the lusts they indulged. The prince of matter, moreover, as is clear from what happened, rules and governs in opposition to the goodness of God.

---

[12] On Celsus' recognition of the stars as divine, see Origen, *Contra Celsum* 5.54, and the notes, ad loc., in Borret 1967–76, vol. 5.

[13] See above, Chapter 9, and Chapter 12.8 on *2 Enoch* 29.4.

[14] John 8.44; Hesiod, *Theogony* 27; cf. Homer, *Odyssey* 19.203, and Justin, *First Apology* 23.

[15] Origen, *Contra Celsum* 5.51–55, and below, Chapter 21.5.

The separation of classes here is based on confused hints in the Enoch tradition,[16] but it also looks as if Athenagoras is trying to confine the lustful Watcher story to the angels and demons, servants of Satan, since he suggests negligence or forgetfulness as the cause of the fall of the prince himself. Perhaps he is here trying to reconcile the Watcher and the rebel traditions; laziness and negligence reappear as the motives of Satan's fall in other authors who use the Ezekiel-Isaiah texts for their story.[17] But though there may be some overlap in the Athenagoras version, it is still the Watcher story that dominates his account of Christian belief.

In Tertullian we find a more complex and interesting situation. As Origen's great Latin contemporary, he provides some confirmation, however different his milieu, of the narratives available in the church when Origen was writing. What we find in Tertullian is the two tales, Watcher and rebel, sitting uneasily together. He describes the "angelic apostates" as the "deserters of God, the seducers of women," and the inventors of astrology. Clearly this refers to the Enoch tradition, as does his statement that the angels' lust for the daughters of men inflamed them to the point that they forsook the presence of God and fell into sin.[18] Like Justin, he alludes to the Book of Revelation, saying that henceforth the angels dedicated themselves to leading the world astray: Satan and his angels occupied the whole world and corrupted the rest of creation.[19]

But Tertullian also makes use of the rebellion myth of Ezekiel and Isaiah, though without distinguishing its hero from the leader of the lustful Watchers. The Ezekiel passage, he says, clearly mocks the angel, not the prince of Tyre:

> for no human being was ever born in the paradise of God, not even Adam himself, who was rather translated thither; nor has any man been set with the cherub on God's holy mountain, that is, in the height of heaven, from which our Lord testifies that Satan also fell . . . [and] like lightning was cast down. None other than the very author of sin is denoted in the person of this sinful man.[20]

[16] Above, n. 6.

[17] E.g., Origen, *De principiis* 2.8.3, 2.9.2, and Jerome, *Commentary on John* 16 (referring to Origen); see J. B. Russell 1981:126–27.

[18] Tertullian, *De idololatria* 4.2, 9.1; *Apologia* 35.12. Cf. *Adversus Marcionem* 5.18.14, in E. Evans 1972:628. The other Tertullian texts are conveniently in ANF, vols. 2 and 3.

[19] Tertullian, *De virginibus velandis* 7.2; *De spectaculis* 8.9; *De corona* 6.2; *De anima* 57; *De cultu feminarum* 1.2.1: "These are the angels whom we are destined to judge; these are the angels whom we in baptism renounce." He continues by defending the authenticity of *Enoch* with an argument about 2 *Esdras* 14.37–40. See Bamberger 1952:76 and Pelikan 1971:135.

[20] Tertullian, *Adversus Marcionem* 2.10. See E. Evans 1972:114–16.

The Ezekiel passage, read in the light of Luke 10.18, is very useful for Tertullian to counter Marcion because it allows for a good being who becomes corrupt by choice, thus absolving God from responsibility and answering the Marcionite and Gnostic charge that the adversary (whether demiurge or devil) was corrupt by nature.

Tertullian's view of the devil also owes much to the parallel Isaiah passage. His most common term for the devil, *aemulus*, alludes to the son of the dawn who in envy tried to rival or ape god. This word is often linked with another, one that connects directly with the struggle with heresy—*interpolator*. "The power of that corrupting and imitative angel [*interpolatoris et aemulatoris angeli*] right from the beginning cast down mankind from its wholeness."[21] Heretics corrupt, *interpolant*, the text of scripture just as Satan corrupts God's other text, the world. The apologist's job is thus to establish a pure text (the literal meaning of canon) of scripture and to interpret it accurately in the face of heretical distortions.

So Tertullian brings together Isaiah and Ezekiel rebels and reads the Genesis serpent as the same creature. He also has in mind the New Testament Satan who leads men astray and slanders God:

> What was the origin of this malice of lying and deceit toward men, and slandering of God? Most certainly not from God, who made the angel good like all his works. Indeed, before he became the devil, he is declared to be the wisest of all; and wisdom is surely no evil. If you turn to the prophecy of Ezekiel, you will easily perceive that this angel was both by creation good and by his own act corrupt.

He goes on to assert just how good he was made—"irreproachable," in fact—and then asserts the freedom God gave him.

> For God would in no way fail to endow with liberty of choice a being who was next to himself. Nevertheless, by condemning him, God testified that he had departed from the condition of his created nature, through his own lusting after the wickedness voluntarily conceived within him. By setting a fixed term to his actions, God . . . defers the devil's extinction . . . [and so] has allowed time for a contest [*certamen*] in which man might cast down his enemy by the same freedom of choice that had led to his fall, thus proving that the blame was not God's but his own. . . . Thus the devil would be punished even more bitterly in being overcome by him whom previously he had overthrown.[22]

---

[21] *De spectaculis* 2; see J. B. Russell 1981:94–95.
[22] *Adversus Marcionem* 2.10.

This form of recapitulation doctrine, peculiar to Tertullian, uses the anticipated end of the combat myth to justify God's behavior at the beginning.
The language, while directed against the Marcionite view, seems to bring
together the Ezekiel creature and the Semihazah-Asael of *Enoch*. Indeed,
Tertullian betrays no uneasiness about this fusion. He seems to take it for
granted that the two narratives are variants of the same plot.[23] It is Origen
who finally separates them and so encourages the church to concentrate
on the prideful rebel in Satan rather than on his lust.

[23] Cf. *Apologia* 22: "We are instructed, moreover, by our sacred books, how from certain
angels who fell of their own free will [Ezekiel], there sprang a more wicked demon-brood
[*Enoch*], condemned of God along with the authors of their race [New Testament and
Enoch], and that chief demon we have referred to" (trans. ANF, vol. 3, 36). Cf. also Lactantius, *Divine Institutes* 2.15, 4.27.

TWENTY-ONE

ORIGEN'S WICKED ANGEL: UNIVERSAL FALL AND REDEMPTION

IF WE ARE right to reject the evidence of the Slavonic *Book of the Secrets of Enoch* for the early development of a rebel angel myth in Christian literature,[1] then Origen's role in the growth of Christian mythology becomes even more important than has been previously understood. It is not that he invented the story of the ambitious angel, but rather that he makes it the key element in his refutation of Gnosticism. He tells us himself that the story was already current in the churches of his time (the first part of the third century) so that he claims no originality in proposing it. Instead he wants to use it in order to supply the lack of a coherent account of evil.

> The scriptures do not explain the nature of the devil and his angels, and the adverse powers. The most widespread opinion in the church, however, is that the devil was an angel and that, once he became a rebel, he persuaded the greatest number of angels possible to revolt with them.[2]

Origen's use of the rebel narrative not only decked it out, for the first time, with sufficient philosophical and scriptural justification that it could henceforth withstand the attacks of heretics and pagans, but also supplied the church with a major offensive weapon against its rivals. The result, and something we can follow in Origen himself, was the substitution of the ambitious rebel for the lustful Watcher.

1. Origen and Interpretation

For many reasons Origen is a key figure in the articulation of Satan's story and its transmission to Christian posterity. His intellectual brilliance and

---

[1] Above, Chapter 12.8. H. A. Kelly 1964:203–4 briefly makes a similar point, on which see now J. B. Russell 1981:130.

[2] Origen, *De principiis*, pref. 6. I translate from the most recent study, a French edition, Crouzel and Simonetti (eds.) 1978–84 and from Harl et al. (eds.) 1976, a translation that includes the Greek fragments collected by Koetschau. The work survives complete only in Rufinus' Latin version of the late fourth century, on which see Harl et al. (eds.) 1976:270, Daniélou 1948:214, and below, n. 53.

Alexandrian education gave him ready access to the Greek philosophical tradition, and especially to its allegorical methods of interpreting classical Greek, Egyptian, and Jewish myths. His early training as a catechizer of pagans who wanted to become members of the Christian church led him to explain Christian doctrine in ways that would be understood by the convert and especially to dwell on the redemptive aspect of baptism. His contact with Platonic and Christian Gnostic circles led him to develop explicit doctrines about the origin of evil to oppose the Gnostic cosmogonies. His skill as a defender of Christianity against Celsus has left us the most detailed apology we possess from the early church, containing the most interesting and revealing investigation of Satan's story before Augustine. His meticulous textual scholarship made him the best qualified of the church fathers to read out this story from the scattered and obscure allusions in the scriptures. It is clear that he was deeply familiar not only with the sacred books themselves but also with the varied traditions of interpretation, both Jewish and Christian. He had read Plato and Aristotle, but also countless works now lost or fragmentary, as well as the Enoch literature, Philo Judaeus, Justin, Plutarch, and Clement of Alexandria, his own teacher and predecessor.

Like Irenaeus, Origen adapted several ideas from his Gnostic opponents. His thinking, like that of Clement, shows a considerable Gnostic influence. He believed in the existence of secret teachings, an esoteric and eternal gospel, accessible only to the "pneumatic," alongside the exoteric gospel preserved in the New Testament. In fact, he referred to *gnosis* as perfected faith. And he took over, apparently from Valentinus, the idea of a universal redemption, or apocatastasis. For this he was attacked by Augustine and he was posthumously condemned for heresy by Justinian in 543 and again apparently at the Second Council of Constantinople in 553.[3]

It is a curious irony of Christian history that the man most responsible for developing and defending the Satan story as a weapon against both pagan and heretic should himself have been declared anathema for a heresy about Satan. For apocatastasis includes the doctrine that, at the end of all succeeding aeons, even the devil would be saved.[4] Otherwise, the eternity of hell would mean the ultimate triumph of Satan.[5] The doctrine was intimately bound up with Origen's theories about the preexistence of the

---

[3] Pelikan 1971:277; J. B. Russell 1981:144–48.

[4] Kolakowski 1974. For more precise discussion, see Müller 1958 and Patrides 1967.

[5] Nigg 1962:42–57. Although universal salvation remained a tenet of the Eastern church, see the criticism of Origen in Lossky 1957:32–33, 42, 62.

immortal soul, the nature of reason, and the ultimate goodness of God. It depended also on his Platonic theory of evil, with which he opposed Gnosticism. As a falling away from God, evil could have no essence of its own and would eventually be converted back into the purity of spirit, the state in which all things begin. Nevertheless, while the church retained the rebellious angel who emerges from Origen's thinking, it condemned the philosophical doctrine on which it ultimately depended.

It is perhaps not surprising, then, that Origen should show himself a little uneasy at times with the doctrine of Satan. The point is worth illustrating because we find it repeated a good many times in the subsequent tradition: a curious defensiveness often allied with a shrill assertiveness. This is to be explained partly by the context in which the story of Satan developed in the early church—the quarrel with heresy and paganism. But if we read closely it is evident that the theorist about the nature of Satan occasionally feels himself suddenly alone, determined to follow up the logic of his thought, equally determined to avoid what he knows to be fundamental errors, but "alone without a guide." In the course of his defense of what he takes to be the Christian doctrine of Satan against the ridicule of the Stoic Celsus, for example, Origen suddenly scuttles for safety: "Although we have boldly and rashly committed these few remarks to writing in this book, perhaps we have said nothing significant."[6] Maybe he is suddenly conscious of having violated a mystery (words like "hint," "mystery," and "enigma" are common in this section of the work, as are subjunctive and optative moods: "one might learn," "one would see") or that he has not thought through the biblical passages as thoroughly as was his normal habit. Perhaps he is even aware, at some level, that the whole structure he has tried to erect is a nonsense ("nothing significant," *exethemetha tacha ouden*). At any rate, he goes on to imply that he has not been able to examine the relevant scriptural passages with his customary meticulousness and that there is probably more to be said on the subject. Then he turns on Celsus and his ilk with unusual ferocity:

> But if anyone with the time to examine the holy scriptures were to collect texts from all sources in order to give a coherent account [*logon*] of evil, both how it first came to exist, and how it is being destroyed, he would see that the meaning [*boulēma*] of Moses and the prophets with regard to Satan has not even been dreamt of by Celsus or by any of the people who are dragged

---

[6] Origen, *Contra Celsum* 6.44. See Borret 1967–76 for the Greek text; my translation usually follows Chadwick 1953 closely.

down by this wicked demon and are drawn away in their soul from God and
the right conception of him and his word.

The charge against Celsus and those like him is a common one in early
Christian literature: that heretics and opponents of the church are themselves under the influence of Satan, the father of lies. They are therefore,
like Satan, incapable of properly understanding either God or his word.
Accurate interpretation of texts is beyond them. Yet the words Origen
uses betray his own anxiety. He is aware that an account of evil must
bring together into one body (*sōmatopoiēsai*) what is scattered (*panto-
chothen*) throughout the scriptures, and the word he uses for examining
the scriptures is *basanos*. This means literally a touchstone by which gold
is proved, and thus any test to try whether something is genuine or not.
But what test can Origen apply? He has no such tangible touchstone and
so rounds on his adversary with the charge that it is he who lacks it. The
word *basanos* also came to mean an inquiry by torture, and thus anguish.
So Origen's "examination of the holy scriptures" can also mean torturing
the scriptures to extract from them a reluctant and perhaps false confession—a common practice with martyrs like Origen's own father. We still
speak of "twisting a text" and of "tortured interpretations," and Origen's
own intellectual honesty may here have led him to the sudden fear that
that was exactly what he had done in order to extract the doctrine of
Satan.

The absence of a reliable touchstone, something outside the hermeneutic circle of reader and text, against which to test the validity of one's understanding is a hot topic in contemporary literary theory, and play with
the word *basanos* might be taken a good deal further than I am willing to
do here. To the fathers of the church, however, indeed to the authors of
the New Testament books themselves, the issue appeared very different.
Disagreement over fundamental doctrine, the struggles with heresy and
with classical philosophy, even the squabbles over Montanism, Arianism,
the freedom of the will, or the nature of Christ that occupied a good deal
of the energy of the early church—none of these difficulties seem to have
prevented any of the various interpreters of Christian scripture, except in
rare moments like the one we have just noticed in Origen, from feeling
reasonably sure that they did have access to precisely that kind of reliable
touchstone. Indeed, this is one of the great benefits presumably conferred
by divine revelation. The idea of proof-texts (*testimonia*), for example,
turned on it—the discovery of passages in the Old Testament which could

now be read as prophecies and announcements of what the New Testament revealed.[7]

Origen follows in, and often pushes a good deal further, this interpretive tradition. Like other early fathers, he reads the scriptures in the light of the struggle with and eventual victory over the evil powers, the struggle announced by Christ's life and death. His thinking about baptism provides an illuminating example.

During the early years of his career at Alexandria, Origen was charged with the task of catechizing those preparing for initiation into the faith. Thus baptism became a central part of his theory of the redemption from the evil powers.[8] The complex theory depends on citations of Paul and on an explication of Paul's own adaptation of the Old Testament Exodus story to mystical Christian uses. Origen brings together, for example, two separate Pauline passages.[9] In one, Paul tells the Romans:

> As many of us as are baptized into Jesus Christ are baptized into his death. Therefore we are buried with him by baptism into death: that like as Christ was raised up from the dead by the glory of the Father, even so we also should walk in newness of life. . . . For he that is dead is freed from sin.

In the other passage, Paul explains to the Corinthians that "all our fathers were under the cloud, and all passed through the sea, and all were baptized into Moses in the cloud and the sea." Origen brings these texts together and adds an elaborate explication of the three days of Christ's death and resurrection. The first day is the Passion, the second is the descent into hell, the third is the resurrection, which Origen correlates with the three-day journey into the desert that pharaoh forbade to Moses (citing Hos. 6.3). But the most important basis of the correlation between baptism and the Exodus is the liberation from the power of the demon, the combat language already embedded in the Exodus story and echoed in the New Testament but now at a spiritual level.

> You see how much the teaching of Paul differs from the literal meaning. What the Jews think of as a crossing of the sea, Paul calls baptism; what they

---

[7] Origen himself represents Christ in exactly this way, as he who teaches the readers of texts to advance from letter to spirit (*Commentary on the Song of Songs* 3); cf. Daniélou 1948:149. For the devil as "*interpolator*" in Tertullian, see above, Chapter 20 n. 21.

[8] Origen's views on baptism are conveniently collected by Daniélou 1948:65–74. On the powers, cf. Carr 1981:153–73, and for the devil in baptism, see H. A. Kelly 1979 and now 1985.

[9] Rom. 6.3–7; 1 Cor. 10.1–2; Origen also cites John 3.5 in the same context.

believe to be a cloud, Paul says is the Holy Spirit. . . . He calls it baptism accomplished in the cloud and the sea so that you too, who are baptized into Christ in the water and the Holy Spirit, may know that the Egyptians are chasing you and want to bring you back to their service, I mean the "powers of this world" and "the evil spirits, whom you once served."[10]

Origen is here citing also from the Ephesians passage that summarizes the central Christian combat myth: "Put on the whole armor of God, that ye may be able to stand against the wiles of the devil . . . against powers, against the rulers of the darkness of this world, against the spirit forces of evil in the heavenlies."[11] Thus Origen makes baptism part of the theory of redemption as a victory over Satan.

In citing Old Testament texts as illustrations of the idea of baptism, Origen was following the method of the primitive catechism of the church, just being organized in Origen's time and to which his scholarship contributed heavily. This is traditional typology, of the kind we find in Second Isaiah, and as developed by Justin and Irenaeus, even though Origen's own interpretive strategies were different. Thus he cites the crossing of the Red Sea and the river Jordan, already traditional types of baptism, but develops them in the direction of his own mystical philosophy of initiation. The catechumen who has just abandoned the darkness of idolatry and comes to hear the divine Law has begun his redemption by abandoning Egypt. Then, as a full catechumen, he has crossed the Red Sea. Finally, when he comes to the sacramental font of baptism and is initiated into the "venerable and majestic mysteries, known only by those to whom it is rightful [fas], then, having crossed the Jordan with the mysteries of the priests, you will enter into the promised land."[12]

2. Redemption and Ransom

The theory of baptism is clearly linked with the larger theory of the redemption. This theory also has a double aspect, both objective and subjective, such as we find in Origen's theory of baptism and in the whole

---

[10] Origen, *Homilies on Exodus* 5.1, 5; Daniélou 1948:68–70.

[11] Eph. 6.11–12. See above, Chapter 14.6. The passage also cites other similar proof-texts, such as Rom. 16.20.

[12] *Homilies on Joshua* 4.1; cf. *Homilies on Luke* 24. For the idea of descent, *katabasis*, see *Homilies on Luke* 21.4, and for the homologies of *Jared* and *Jordan*, see *Commentary on John* 1.28, 6.42–44, and 6.24–25, where Origen refers explicitly to *Enoch* 9.9; see also Black 1985:177. The idea that the Jordan is thus "turned back" is Gnostic; see above, Chapter 18 n. 13.

New Testament transformation of the combat tradition. An objective event, the crucifixion, is echoed subjectively within the individual Christian soul. Origen's combat language here becomes evident. In fact, he presents the whole life of Christ as a combat with the adversary powers: "When Jesus was born . . . , because of that the powers were weakened, their magic being refuted and their works dissolved. And they were defeated not only by the angels who descended on earth because of Jesus' nativity, but by the soul [*psyche*] of Jesus and the divinity that was in him."[13] He goes on to explain the visit of the three Magi in this way. Wondering why their magic was no longer working, they realized that the man whose birth was announced by the star was more powerful than all the demons, so they came to worship him. The demons, however, still retained some power until the crucifixion, which explains why Jesus said to Peter, "Get thee behind me, Satan." It was Satan who had spoken in Peter's disbelieving words, "This can never happen."

The final dispossession by the crucifixion, the logical explanation of which has generally defeated the most acute Christian minds, Origen interprets like this:

> The Cross of Our Lord Jesus Christ was double. . . . The Son of God was visibly crucified in the flesh, but invisibly it was the devil who was fixed to the cross with his principalities and powers. This will seem true if I cite the words of Paul: "What was opposed to us, he has removed from the way, fixing it to the cross. He has stripped the principalities and powers and has boldly made an exhibition of them, in triumphing over them by the Cross." Thus there is a double aspect to the cross of the Lord: the one, of which the apostle Peter speaks when he says that the crucified Christ has left us an example; the other by which the cross was the trophy of his victory over the devil, by whom he was at once crucified and glorified.[14]

Origen also cites the story of Adam to explain another detail of the crucifixion story:

> Just as to the one who confessed him [the thief on the neighboring cross] he opened the gates of Paradise in saying: "Today you shall be with me in Paradise," and thus gave access, which he had denied to the sinner Adam, to all who believe in him—who could thus indeed escape the sword of fire which was set up to guard the tree of life and the gates of Paradise—in the same

[13] Origen, *Contra Celsum* 1.60. See the discussion in Daniélou 1948:256–65, where the following passages are also quoted.

[14] *Homilies on Joshua* 8.3, quoting Col. 2.14–15; see above, Chapter 14.6 n. 42.

way, except for him, no one else can dispossess the principalities and powers and the rulers of this world whom the apostle mentions and cast them
into the desert of hell, except for him who said, "I have conquered the
world."[15]

And in the same way, the victory is echoed in each individual: "Each of
those who is crucified with Christ dispossesses the principalities and powers and makes an exhibition of them, triumphing over them on the cross,
or rather Christ brings that about in each one."[16] So even an Origen finds
it hard to make sense of the victory-in-defeat paradox that is the central
transformation of the Christian combat myth. He tries out the idea that
invisibly it was the devil who was fixed to the cross, but instead of arguing the point, he falls back on the authority of Paul and then on the bald
assertion that the cross was a trophy of victory. What he appears to mean
by the distinction between visible and invisible crucifixions is that Christ
was indeed crucified, as every witness testified, but that, since all believers
are now liberated from death, and they can go back to the Adamic paradise, the source of the devil's power is nullified. The invisible crucifixion
is thus symbolic of its power, the extension of its triumph to all mankind.

The idea of a visible and invisible crucifixion is a sign of Origen's own
Gnostic tendencies, and it leads him toward two further arguments: one
that Christ was in disguise, or incognito, the other that the devil was
therefore deceived. He quotes Paul to this effect: "We speak God's wisdom in a mystery . . . which none of the rulers of this world knows; for
had they known it, they would not have crucified the Lord of Glory."[17]
For Origen, this implies that the devil did not understand what he was
doing and was in fact hoodwinked. He also has the idea that Christ disguised himself as an ordinary man in order to persuade the devil's pris-
oners to follow him out of the prison house.

Origen was no doubt aware that the central paradox of the crucifixion
as redemption eluded him. He insists on it, yet cannot fully explain it. In
the *Commentary on Matthew*, for example, we find him ruminating again
about the way the crucifixion could have brought about this victory over
the principalities and powers. We find here together the Irenaeus theory
of ransom (and Origen's own polemic against Marcion, preserved only in

[15] See also *Homilies on Leviticus* 9.5.
[16] Origen, *Commentary on Matthew* 12.25. On each nation and now each individual as a
battleground for a good and evil angel, see J. B. Russell 1981:34–38.
[17] 2 Cor. 2.7–8; Aulén 1969:51. See above, Chapter 14.3.

fragments, is probably in the background), with the idea of the deception of the devil.

> But to whom did Christ give his soul as a ransom [*lutron*] for many? Surely not to God. Was it then to the Evil One [*tōi ponerōi*]? For he had power over us, until the soul of Jesus was given as a ransom for us, since he let himself be deceived, thinking he could have power over that soul and not recognizing that to keep him would require a trial of strength [*basanon*] that he was not equal to.[18]

He continues by asserting that death too has been defeated, since Christ is free among the dead and all others may follow him—the idea of the invisible crucifixion represented here in the mythological language of the descent into hell.

Death and the devil are, as in Paul, alternate forms of the common enemy power.[19] The general idea here seems to be as follows. The enemy expected to triumph, but in fact the enemy was deceived, because Christ put to flight the power of death by coming back from the dead. The enemy was induced to go along with the plan by being paid a ransom, but the ransom was deceptive. The devil was tricked into accepting the living Christ and putting him to death, expecting that to be the end of the matter. Whereupon Christ rose from the dead and thus encouraged others to do the same, at least in the figurative sense.

The idea of a ransom paid to the devil, and the idea of the deceit of the devil, had spectacular developments among the later fathers, especially the Greek, and caused strong reactions.[20] But here in Origen neither idea has developed very far. Instead, he seems to hesitate between two variants of the combat tradition, one in which the adversary is overcome by force of arms (Christ's freedom from death gave him more power than the devil), the other in which the stupid ogre is deceived. We have noted before that these two tale-types are alternatives for each other and that the Sumerian Gilgamesh tale seems to have existed in both forms.[21] So here the obscurity of the means of victory in the Christian myth has produced similar alternatives to account for it. For many later interpreters this resurgence of the underlying myth was what occasioned the sharpest reactions. Anselm's satisfaction theory of the atonement was thought to be a

[18] Origen, *Commentary on Matthew* 16.8. See also Pelikan 1971:148.
[19] Ibid., 13.8–9; cf. Daniélou 1948:267.
[20] Above, Chapter 19, nn. 8–12.
[21] Above, Chapter 1.1.

great advance over such puerilities, and the English scholar Rashdall could write about the patristic idea of a transaction with the devil that "the objectionable feature in the whole system is . . . the childish and immoral way in which [the devil's] rights were satisfied or bought out by Christ's death."[22] Yet the whole tradition we have been studying implies just such narrative ideas, however uncomfortable the liberal Christian may be about them. Christians believe that Christ allowed himself to be put to death in order to break the chain of power the tyrant exercised. The problem is how? To answer that question, the early church, even a sophisticated philosopher like Origen, thought the matter out in narrative terms.

Origen's version of Satan's story, then, is an expansion of the combat myth as redemption. Liberation from an evil tyrant is the essential plot of the tale. But Origen's real contribution to the developing story lay in his demonstration that the adversary had once been a good creature who lived in light.

3. The Enoch Tradition

Origen's thinking about the beginnings of evil seems to pass through three roughly identifiable stages. In the earliest period, we still notice the impact of the Watcher story; in the second, Origen's maturity, we find (in the *Peri archōn*, or *De principiis*, as it is known from Rufinus' Latin version) an elaborate theory of the precosmic fall of Satan designed to counter Gnostic doctrine; in the third, marked by the late work *Contra Celsum*, we find the theory defended, but now against a philosopher who accuses the whole Christian narrative of a naive dualism.

At the time when Origen's career was starting, the story of the lustful angels was still popular in the church. We have noted its use in Justin Martyr, Irenaeus, Athenagoras, and Tertullian. More important, Origen's chief models, Philo and Clement of Alexandria, both make use of the story. In Philo we find an allegory of the cause of sin which fuses the Watcher and the Eden stories to make lust the basis of the angels' fall and the fall of all creatures.[23] Clement refers more explicitly to the Enoch story, though with the same Platonic emphasis, when he argues that the

---

[22] Rashdall 1919:364; cf. J. B. Russell 1981:140.

[23] Philo, *De gigantibus* 2–6, 12–18. Cf. *De opificio mundi* 151–69; *Legum allegoria* 1.17, 56–62, 2.9–11, 71; and *Quaestiones et solutiones in Genesim* 1.6–11, 37. On Philo's methods and his philosophical position, see Scholem 1960:54–57, Ginzberg 1910–38: vol. 5, 416–18, Laporte 1970, Dillon 1977:93–95, 158–60, and Stone (ed.) 1984:241–46.

real sin of the angels was that they "renounced the beauty of God for a beauty which fades, and so fell from heaven to earth."[24] Here already it looks as if the Watcher story and the Ezekiel myth about the creature whose heart was proud because of his beauty have begun to influence each other.

Origen's early difficulties with the sins of the flesh are well known. They are most obvious in the story of his self-castration. Apparently he took too literally the gospel words "There are even eunuchs who have made themselves that way for the sake of the kingdom of heaven." Perhaps the story is apocryphal. It certainly is odd to find the Christian theologian most often accused of inappropriately allegorizing the scriptures taking so momentous a text literally. At any rate, the story suggests why the Philonic allegory may have had an appeal for him. We discover the trace of this appeal in his comment on the Eden tale: the man becomes the "mind" and the woman becomes the "heart," while sin results from the "heart's" inclination toward the delights of the flesh, symbolized by the serpent. We have noted above that the Enoch tradition linked the angelic lust with a literal seduction of Eve. The Philo-Origen allegory looks like the kind of effort common in Alexandria to dress up with philosophical implications otherwise unacceptable tales.[25]

The main line of Origen's thinking, however, displaces the Watcher story to the periphery of his doctrine. He alludes to it in commenting on John 6.42 while discussing the general idea of "descent," and then later repeats the Philonic interpretation of the story when Celsus dredges it up. According to Celsus, Christians entertain the absurd belief that many angelic visitations other than Christ's have occurred, "even sixty or seventy at a time, who were perverted and for punishment were chained under the earth, whence come hot springs, their tears."[26] Origen replies that Celsus is confused:

> He cites obscure passages from the Book of Enoch, but he does not seem to have read it, nor to have known that the Book of Enoch is not generally held to be divine among the churches. . . . But let us grant him, generously, what he has not discovered in the Book of Genesis: "The sons of God saw that the daughters of men were beautiful, and took to themselves wives

---

[24] Clement of Alexandria, *Paedagōgos* 3.2 (in ANF vol. 2, 274); cf. *Stromata* 3.7, 5.1, 7.7. Satan's fall, however, was different from that of the lustful angels, but Clement does not seem to know how. See also Chadwick 1966.

[25] Origen, *Homilies on Genesis* 1.15. Cf. below, Chapter 25.1.

[26] *Contra Celsum* 5.52. Cf. Black 1985:177.

among all the ones they picked out." Nevertheless, I shall convince those who are capable of understanding the thinking of the prophet that, according to one of our predecessors, the passage concerns the doctrine of the souls who are eager to live in the body of a human being, wherefore they are figuratively known as "daughters of men."[27]

Thus the passage in Genesis is no longer to be read through the Enoch midrash, but rather tropologically as part of Philo's and Origen's theory of the hierarchy of matter and spirit, still loosely connected with the idea of "fall" but no longer causative in any way. Origen wonders further where Celsus heard the part about tears and hot springs. No one, he suggests, would describe hot springs, whose water is fresh, as angels' tears, since tears are naturally salty—unless the angels of Celsus weep only fresh water.

4. Origen on First Principles

We find the second stage of Origen's thinking in his major work on the beginnings and first principles of Christianity, De principiis. The work was composed while he was still in Alexandria between 220 and 231,[28] and it represents his mature and complex thought. Origen was now more alert to the dangers of heresy, by which he always means Gnosticism, and so was more concerned to refute it. Since his own ideas developed within the same philosophical milieu as those of his Gnostic rivals—the Middle Platonism of Alexandria—the points of difference became all the more crucial.

It is in the De principiis that Origen works out his most elaborate version of the Platonic-Philonic theory that the material world originates through a "fall" (descensus = katabolē or katabasis) of spirit into matter, from essence to existence.[29] Indeed, this is the idea from which the very term "Fall" derives, through the mutual influence of the stories of divine and human rebellion and the broadly Platonic context in which the Christian doctrine of sin evolved. But Origen is careful to specify how this doctrine differs from the Gnostic idea of an original darkness, evil in its very nature, and from the parallel idea that matter is inherently evil. For Origen,

---

[27] *Contra Celsum* 5.55, citing Philo, *De gigantibus* 2.2–18. On Origen's use of *Enoch*, see above, n. 12, Ruwett 1943:48–50, Ruwett 1944:157, and Borret (ed.) 1967–76: vol. 3, 146–55.

[28] According to Eusebius, *Ecclesiastical History* 6.24. See Harl et al. (eds.) 1976:7.

[29] Origen, *De princ.* 3.5.4; cf. Pelikan 1971:96, and above, n. 12.

all rational creatures, heavenly powers and men alike, fall not by their nature but by their will. The cause of this prehistoric disturbance is thus, by implication, a rebel; he is not created such. He is evil not in essence but by accident, so to speak. Just as all matter will one day be reconverted into its spiritual essence, so the devil himself will one day lose his evil attributes.[30] Fortunately Origen finds that the texts by which he can prove his theory of evil contain key words to refute the Gnostic claims.

Origen begins his important section on rational creatures (all levels from the highest "powers" to the various degrees of mankind) by posing a question designed to refute his Gnostic adversaries. Has God, he asks, created some of his creatures immutable, holy and happy, others utterly incapable of progressing toward the good, and a third group able to turn good or bad? No, he responds, and his method of argument is a standard *reductio ad absurdum*, leading to the conclusion that "it is absurd to attribute the cause of their sin to their creator rather than to their own will."[31] All creatures, therefore, even the good angels, have their positions in the universal hierarchy by their own merit and not by their inherent nature. But Origen would not expect his audience to accept this theory on the basis of its logic alone, so he turns our attention to the holy scriptures for evidence on "such difficult matters." He looks for clarification especially on the matter of the evil powers, and he finds it in Ezekiel and Isaiah, the very passages that, we have seen, contain vestiges of the ancient rebel myth.

The hyperbolic language of Ezekiel 28.11–19 makes it clear, Origen says, that the words must be understood not simply of a man but of a higher power who fell from on high and was thrown down to the lower and bad places. He claims that this example will show in a most striking manner that these adversary and evil powers were not created thus by their nature but changed from better to worse and turned themselves toward evil. Blessed powers too do not have the kind of nature that would prevent them from taking on the opposite attributes if they wish, if they are negligent, and if they do not carefully maintain their blessed state. For the "Prince of Tyre" was "perfect," was in "the paradise of God," "crowned with beauty."

Origen shows himself to be alert to the figurative nature of the language here, although he attributes it to a cause different from the one we argued

---

[30] *De princ.* 2.3.3; see also Daniélou 1948:215–16, Laporte 1970, and J. B. Russell 1981:126–27, and cf. *Homilies on Joshua* 8.4, where Origen quotes 1 Cor. 15.26, identifying the devil with death as "the last enemy."

[31] *De princ.* 1.5.3.

earlier. If we had only the first part of the chapter in Ezekiel, we might take the words to refer literally to the Prince of Tyre, but the extravagance of the metaphors in the second part, a vestige of Israel's mythological heritage, clearly demonstrate to Origen that Ezekiel is talking about an angelic power. Perhaps, he suggests, it is not a question of the real Tyre, or of its guardian angel, or Watcher, but rather of "the city of Tyre understood in the spiritual sense"—by which he means, although he refrains from arguing the doctrine here, the world as it is constituted by the Fall, the "this world" of the New Testament, over which "the prince of this world" (whether the devil himself or another evil power) holds sway.

Similarly, no earthly king could really be intended by the lavish and dramatic language of Isaiah about Lucifer, the morning star. And conveniently, since he is said to have the nature of light, the Lucifer passage belies the Gnostic theory and absolves God from having made him dark, or evil in his own nature. Origen quotes the Isaiah passage, and continues:

> Evidently by these words is he shown to have fallen from heaven, who formerly was Lucifer, and who used to arise in the morning. If, as some think, he was a being of darkness, how can he be said to have been the light-bringer before? Or how could he arise in the morning, who had in himself nothing of that light?[32]

That this being should have formerly been the light-bringer is vital to Origen's anti-Gnostic case. The language of light and darkness is common to orthodox and heretic alike, but what counts for this quarrel is the original state of being.

Origen continues with his key point, evoking the light imagery of the New Testament and converting it to his own argument: since Gnostics claim to be Christians, what better way to refute them than by quoting Christ himself against them? The passage is an excellent instance of Origen's range and method.

> Even the Savior himself teaches us about the nature of the devil when he says, "Behold I see Satan fall from heaven like lightning" [Luke 10.18]. Obviously there was a time when he was light. But our Lord, who is "the truth," likewise compares his own glorious coming to lightning, when he says, "As lightning flashes from one end of the sky to the other, so also will be the coming of the son of Man" [Matt. 24.27]. So he compares this being also to lightning, and says that he has fallen from heaven, in order to show

---

[32] *De princ.* 1.5.5.

us that he too had been at one time in heaven, and had had a place among the saints, and enjoyed a share in the light, the light which makes the angels of light, just as the disciples are called by the Lord "the light of the world" [Matt. 5.14]. This is the way, then, in which that being once existed as light before he committed a sin and fell to this place, and his glory was turned into dust [Isa. 14.11], which is the mark of the wicked, as the prophet also says; whence too he was called "the prince of this world," i.e., of this earthly habitation. He exercises power over those who were obedient to his wickedness, since "all the world (by which I understand this earthly place) lies in the power of the Evil One" [1 John 5.19], which is to say, in the Apostate. That this being is an apostate [i.e., renegade], the Lord also tells us in the Book of Job: "Can you draw out the apostate dragon [Leviathan] with a hook?" [Job 41.1]. It is certain that this dragon we should understand in the sense of the devil.

Read in this way, the words of Christ give Origen the necessary touchstone with which to interpret several key Old Testament texts and thus oppose the Gnostic view of creation. The Old Testament texts do contain vestiges of the combat tradition, and it is to Origen's credit that he notices the fact and revitalizes this language, even if he has to doctor the text of Job a little by interpolating the word "apostate." Henceforth, then, the rebel angel myth, rediscovered in the texts of Ezekiel and Isaiah, effectively replaces the lustful angels, the Watchers, as the cause of evil. But it is significant that Origen, in discussing the meaning of the Prince of Tyre, should have hesitated between assigning him to the Watcher category or to the "prince of this world" doctrine. For Origen the two stories, of lustful angels or ambitious rebel, are variants of the same fundamental narrative about the Apostate. Origen's main interest is not to establish Satan's motive but to insist on his original nature as light.[33] So the traces of the Watcher story continue to cling to the rediscovered rebel myth, even though Ezekiel and Isaiah have now become the key texts with which to oppose the Gnostic cosmogony.

5. Celsus and Pagan Allegory

The third stage of Origen's thought about the devil is to be found in his long *apologia* for Christianity written against the philosopher Celsus, whose attack had been published toward the end of the second century

---

[33] Compare the conclusion of his argument here (1.5.5), which further insists on this point and so shows that "no creature is immutable."

A.D.[34] Although Origen's defense, the *Contra Celsum*, was written near the end of his life, long after he had left Alexandria and settled in Caesarea, the work shows the fruits of Origen's early intellectual training, for now the opponent is not a Christian heresy that gets the story wrong but a pagan philosopher who lays his axe to the very roots of the Christian doctrine itself.[35]

Celsus' own book does not survive, but the extensive quotations that Origen includes in his own text allow us to reconstruct with some confidence the chief arguments Celsus had used. One of his chief points of attack was the Christian teaching about the devil, which Celsus takes to be a misinterpretation of the Greek combat myth tradition. There are two reasons for this misunderstanding, as Celsus sees it: one, the need of a sorcerer (Christ) to take precautions against possible rivals (he must claim that they are all false teachers inspired by Satan); two, the ludicrous story of the redemption, which confuses the divine myths of combat with tales of demon possession. What Celsus attacks is a central feature of the Christian narrative we have been studying, its linking of the traditional combat language with the New Testament ideas of demon possession, sorcery, and false teaching. These combat myths, he says, "are not like the tales which tell of a devil who is a demon, or, as they say more truthfully, a rival sorcerer with opposing views."[36] This is the key sentence in Celsus' attack, and it is the task of Origen's defense to refute it. What Celsus would separate—the combat tradition and the other Christian tales—Origen has to bind more firmly together.[37]

Celsus' attack depends on the Platonic and Stoic tradition of reinterpreting myth by allegory. He is appalled that the Christians should still take those myths of combat literally, and he quickly points to the problem. The dignity and power of God is impugned if we imagine a being opposed to him, who prevents him from doing what he will. In essence this is a flaw in the conception of God, the flaw of all metaphysical dualism, as

[34] On the date and provenance of Celsus' ideas, chiefly Platonic and Stoic, see Chadwick 1953:ix–xiii and Borret (ed.) 1967–76:vol. 1, 183–207.

[35] Origen is also still keen to defend the faith against Gnosticism, since Celsus at times equates Gnostic and Catholic doctrine (e.g., *Contra Celsum* 6.28: Celsus "ought to have known that those who espoused the cause of the serpent . . . are so far from being Christians that they bring as many accusations against Jesus as Celsus himself").

[36] Origen, *Contra Celsum* 6.42. Again the translation follows Chadwick 1953 closely.

[37] On their idea of the struggle with demons and exorcism, which both Celsus and Origen believed in, see also Harnack 1904:165, 177–80.

Plato had argued. Christian ignorance of philosophical allegory ("divine enigmas") leads to blasphemy:

> They make a being opposed to God, calling him "devil" or, in the Hebrew tongue, "Satan." These ideas are definitely of mortal origin, and it is blasphemous to claim that when the greatest God wishes to help men, he has a being opposed to him, and so is impotent [*adunatei*]. So the son of God is defeated by the devil, and punished by him, so that he may teach us also to despise the punishments he inflicts on us. He predicts that even Satan himself will appear, just as he has, and will manifest great and amazing works, usurping the glory of God. We must not be deceived nor turn away to Satan, but must believe in him alone. All this is blatantly the utterance of a sorcerer out for profit and taking precautions against possible rivals to his opinions.[38]

Celsus here shows himself to be aware that in Christian teaching the combat myth is linked both with Christ's crucifixion and the human struggle against evil powers or demons. It is this important link that he tries to break by ridicule: "All this is ludicrous. In my view, God ought to have punished the devil. Certainly he should not have pronounced threats against the men whom the devil attacked."

Celsus did apparently give an account of the "enigmas" the Christians have misunderstood in their teaching about Satan. "The ancients," he says, "speak in enigmatic terms [*ainittesthai*] about a sort of divine war." Heraclitus, for example, says, "But one must know that war is a mutual thing, and justice is strife, and that all things come into being by strife and necessity."[39] To begin his list of "ancients" with a philosophical statement rather than a genuine myth, as Celsus does, is typical of the allegorical method of interpretation. War or strife are Heraclitus' regular metaphors for what he took to be the state of universal flux. It is a little surprising to find the fragment here in a Platonic-Stoic context, since Celsus is clearly arguing for the permanent superiority of what is good to what is bad. But then Heraclitus too had long been converted into a good Academician. Celsus continues by citing Pherecydes, "who was far earlier than Heraclitus." The myth in question is the battle of Kronos and Ophioneus for possession of the heavens. The same meaning is implied by the "mysteries which affirm that the Titans and Giants fought with the gods, and in the mysteries of the Egyptians which tell of Typhon and Horus and Osiris."

---

[38] *Contra Celsum* 6.42; cf. Plato, *Politicus* 270A.
[39] Diels-Krantz Fragment B80, in Kirk and Raven 1966:214.

Origen complains that Celsus does not explain the profound meaning of these myths, but he must have been well aware of what Celsus was getting at. Celsus says quite enough in the next few lines, but the most complete contemporary account is in Plutarch:

> The fact is that the creation and constitution of this world is complex, resulting, as it does, from opposing influences, which, however, are not of equal strength, but the predominance rests with the better. Yet it is impossible for the bad to be completely eradicated, since it is innate, in large amount, in the body and likewise in the soul of the universe, and is always fighting a hard fight against the better. So in the soul Intelligence and Reason, the Ruler and Lord of all that is good, is Osiris, and in earth and wind and water and the heavens and stars that which is ordered, established, and healthy, as evidenced by the seasons, temperatures, and cycles of revolution, is the efflux of Osiris and his reflected image. But Typhon is that part of the soul which is impressionable, impulsive, irrational, and truculent, and of the bodily or material part, that which is destructible, diseased, and disorderly as evidenced by abnormal seasons and temperatures, and by observations of the sun and disappearances of the moon—outbursts, as it were, and unruly actions on the part of Typhon.[40]

Celsus confirms that this is the kind of interpretation he has in mind when he goes on to adduce the fall of the Homeric Hephaestus as a further instance of "the same truths taught by Heraclitus and Pherecydes and those who teach the mysteries of the Titans and the Giants." He quotes two passages, one from the end of the first book of the *Iliad*, when Hephaestus reminds Hera how he had tried once to defend her, but Zeus took him by the foot and hurled him out of the divine threshold, the other the amplification or variation of this story in *Iliad* 15.18–24. Zeus there reminds Hera of Hephaestus' fall, which according to this speech took place during the struggle of Zeus and Hera over the fate of Heracles. Zeus hung Hera up in the heaven with two anvils suspended from her legs and unbreakable golden chains around her arms. The gods tried to set her free, but whenever one attacked, Zeus would catch him and throw him down from Olympus until he fell, barely able to move, on the earth. Now none of this, of course, happened literally. Rather, says Celsus, we are to understand Zeus' speech as addressed to matter (a point made already by citation from Chrysippus at 4.48). It means (*ainittesthai*) that:

---

[40] Plutarch, *Moralia* 371 A–B, quoted by Chadwick 1953:358. See other references in Borret 1967–78: vol. 3, 27, and below, Chapter 25.5 n. 37.

In the beginning was chaos, but God divided it in certain proportions, bound it together, and ordered it, and that he cast out all the daemons round it which were arrogant, inflicting on them the punishment of being sent down here to earth. Pherecydes understood these words of Homer in this way, saying: "Beneath that land is the land of Tartarus, and it is guarded by the daughters of Boreas, the Harpies and Thyella; there Zeus casts out any of the gods if ever one becomes arrogant." Such ideas are also expressed by the robe of Athena which is seen by every spectator at the procession of the Panathenaea. For it indicates that a goddess, who has no mother and is undefiled, overcomes those born of earth who are overbold.

Celsus here presents Greek literature as if it were a kind of Parthenon frieze, a succession of illustrations of, or comments on, the doctrine of the power of order and spirit over matter and rebellious passion. It is Hesiod, in fact, who has Hephaestus thrown down to Tartarus (*Theogony* 868), but all three—Homer, Hesiod, and Pherecydes—are for Celsus expounding the same doctrine, as is the robe of Athena with its representation of the battle with the giants.

We argued earlier that several of these passages show traces of a myth in which Hephaestus, rather than Prometheus or the Titans, is the adversary of Zeus and that the myth is probably connected with the Near Eastern rebel, allomorphs of whom appear in Isaiah, in the Ugaritic tablets, and in the story of Phaethon.[41] Thus, in this respect at least, Origen may be closer to the truth than Celsus when he develops his own theory of the relation of these various myths to each other. He had already adapted the rebel angel to his cosmogony in order to counter the Gnostic doctrine of original darkness, and he now reasserts the whole story, the whole Christian combat myth, in order to oppose the Celsian allegory. He argues that all these myths are connected because they all refer, even the Greek myths, to the same figure: Satan.

6. Origen's Reply to Celsus

Origen has three main arguments to refute Celsus. First he insists that the writings of Moses, which refer to the adversary in four separate places, are older than the Greek texts, yes, even older than Homer. This was a common claim among Christian apologists and is surprisingly, as archaeological research has shown, at least partly correct. Origen argues that the

[41] See above, Chapters 3 and 6.

Greek texts derive from Moses; specifically, the serpent in Paradise is the original of Pherecydes' Ophioneus. He collects the biblical passages that mention this original adversary figure, and there are many besides the books of Moses. The second argument offers, in terms that Celsus or his like would be able to comprehend and approve, a brief philosophical discourse about the nature and origin of evil. The key passage refers to the Platonic doctrine, derived from the *Phaedrus*, about those who lose their wings: "The Adversary is the first of all beings that were in peace and lived in blessedness who lost his wings and fell from the blessed state."[42] The implication is clear that even Plato is ultimately derivative of the biblical account and did not fully understand it. Origen's third argument takes up the question of false teaching, so scathingly dismissed by Celsus, and defends, through expounding the doctrine of the Antichrist, the Christian warning against deception by the devil. Celsus is himself one of those so deceived, and so Origen's whole apology becomes itself a part of the struggle with the father of lies.

Origen begins his defense, then, by accusing Celsus of being in error: the Christian narrative is not a distortion of philosophical truth. Rather, Celsus' version of the Greek tradition is but an echo of Moses:

> Consider whether he who accuses us of making quite blasphemous errors, and of having been led to depart from the true meaning of the divine enigmas, does not obviously make a mistake himself, since he has failed to realize that it is the writings of Moses, far older than Heraclitus and Pherecydes, older even than Homer, which first expounded [*eisēgage*] the doctrine/story [*logon*] of this wicked one and how he fell from the heavens. For some such story [*toiauta·tina*] is suggested [*ainissetai*] by the serpent [*ophis*], the source of Pherecydes' Ophioneus, who was the cause of the man's expulsion from the divine paradise, and who deceived the female race with the promise [*epangelia*] of divine power and more. And it is said that the man followed her.[43]

For the first time in such explicit if tentative terms the Genesis serpent (and not simply "that old serpent," *ho palaios ophis*, of Revelation) is identified with the adversary. Origen had alluded in the *De principiis* to the devil's inspiration of the serpent,[44] but now the serpent virtually becomes

[42] *Contra Celsum* 6.44.

[43] *Contra Celsum* 6.43.

[44] *De princ.* 3.2.1. The source, quoted also in Jude 9, is variously known as the *Ascension of Moses*, the *Assumption of Moses*, or the *Testament of Moses*. See above, Chapter 13, Charles (ed.) 1913: vol. 2, 408, and Stone (ed.) 1984:344–49.

Satan, since this allows Origen to argue for the priority of Moses over Pherecydes. Once again, then, the quarrel with an opponent helps the church to develop its own teaching.

Origen continues with another point he had made in the earlier work, the identity of "the destroyer" of Exodus 12.23, who smote the Egyptians but spared the Israelites during the Passover. "Who else could he be but the one who is the cause of destruction to those who obey him, who do not resist and struggle against his wickedness?" In this case, Origen's argument fudges the issue a little, since in the text of the Exodus verse (which, of course, Moses wrote) this "destroyer" is clearly under the power of the Lord, who plans the whole operation and who "will not suffer the destroyer to come into your houses and smite you." What Origen means is that on this one occasion the Lord intervened specifically to direct the normal activities of Satan, the destroyer or exterminating angel.

The next passage Origen cites is equally revealing, for it confirms the interpretive tradition in which Origen is working. Chapter 16 of Leviticus, we have seen, was converted by the *Book of Enoch* into an allusion to the fallen Watcher angel, Azazel or Asael. The "Parables of Enoch" had aligned Asael and Satan.[45] Origen now identifies them.

> And further, the averter [*apopompaios*] in Leviticus, whom the Hebrew text calls Azazel, is none other than he. The one on whom the lot fell had to be sent forth into the desert and offered in sacrifice to avert evil [*apotropiazesthai*]. For all who through their sin belong to the portion of evil [*tou cheironos*], being enemies of the people of God's portion, are deserted by God.

The play on the word *eremos*, desert, here is developed from Origen's earlier *Homilies on Leviticus* (9.4–5), where the Yom Kippur rite is used to point a moral rather than to develop a theory of Satan. It is read in the light of Deuteronomy 32.7–43, about those who abandon the inheritance of Jacob for strange gods and about the vengeance of the Lord upon his enemies. Here that reading becomes one more in a list of allusions to the combat of the devil and his people with the people of God. No longer concerned with the purification of God's people by elimination of those who do not follow him, the Leviticus and Deuteronomy passages become episodes in the struggle of God with Azazel-Satan.

Origen continues with a brief remark on the "sons of Belial" in Judges 19.22 and 20.13. The passage to which he alludes is a variant of the Sodom

[45] See above, Chapter 10.3.

and Gomorrah story, and the casual and common curse on "the sons of Belial" becomes now an occasion for Origen to identify Belial and Satan. "Who other than he can be the one whose sons they are said to be because of their wickedness?"

Now Origen comes to the Book of Job:

> Apart from these passages, it is clearly stated in the book of Job, even earlier than Moses himself, that "the devil" [*diabolos*] stands near God and asks for power against Job that he may afflict him with very severe calamities. . . . Moreover, in the last chapters of Job, where the Lord spoke to Job through a whirlwind and clouds . . . , it is possible to find several passages on the serpent-dragon [*peri drakontos*].

Job, then, demonstrates the validity of the Christian reading of scripture. Celsus might well have replied that the Job passages, as we have seen earlier, show nothing of the sort. But Origen insists that they refer to the Christian teaching about the devil as the serpent-dragon and to "the war waged by the power of the serpent-dragon against us."[46] It is especially interesting that he quotes the Leviathan passages from the end of Job as referring to the adversary, since they do in fact allude to a form of the Canaanite sea enemy: "Can you draw out Leviathan with a hook? . . . Remember the battle, don't try again."[47] Thus the language of the Canaanite combat myths is here revitalized for Origen's quarrel with Celsus and transmitted, as an allusion to God's struggle with Satan-Leviathan, to the subsequent Christian tradition.

Origen is scrupulous in citing only passages from the Old Testament, rather than the New Testament story of the temptation of the Savior by this same devil, in order, he says, "that I may not appear to reply to Celsus with arguments drawn from more recent scriptures." Of course, that would play into Celsus' hands, because the basis of the argument has been the relative antiquity of the texts: Moses is older than Homer, and Job is even older than Moses. But it is clear from the position of his remark in the text that Origen himself understood the temptation story in the same way as the trials of Job. He would like to be able to explain the typological parallel between the Old and New Testaments but refrains in deference to the ideas of his antagonist.

The passages Origen has cited so far are, in his view, indications of the nature and character of the adversary, but none of them tells us how he

---

[46] *De princ.* 3.2.1.
[47] Job 41.1–8, in Pope 1965:266–79. See above, Chapter 2.8.

came into being. He therefore concludes his list with a reminder of the two passages which he had explained in detail before (in the *De principiis*). He then tells us, in brief, what they mean, and his language, with its significant allusion to Plato, is very revealing:

> I have not yet mentioned also the passages from Ezekiel which are apparently [*hōs peri*] about the Pharaoh or Nebuchadnezzar or the prince of Tyre, nor the passage from Isaiah in which a lament is sung for the king of Babylon. From these passages one could learn a lot about evil, what sort of origin and genesis it had, and how that evil came to exist from some who lost their wings and followed the example of the first being who lost his wings.

Origen goes on to explain this passage more fully along the lines of his earlier argument. All rational creatures are good only insofar as they receive good by their Creator's beneficence; they are good by accident and not by substance or nature or essence. Some creatures may therefore neglect to partake of "the living bread and the true drink." This is what he means by "wings," for he goes on to say: "Nourished and refreshed by these [i.e., the living bread and the true drink], the wing is restored, even as the most wise Solomon says about the man who is rich with the true wealth, 'For he made for himself wings as an eagle and returns to the house of his leader.' " To lose one's wings, then, is to neglect God.

> It was necessary, then, that God, who knows how to use for a needful end even the consequences of evil, should assign those who became evil in this way to a special place in the universe, and to establish a "gymnasium" of virtue for those who wished to strive "lawfully" [2 Tim. 2.5] in order to recapture virtue.

The idea of the world as a great university for training in goodness is charming and characteristic of Origen, and it helps to explain why God should allow evil to exist in the first place.

Origen then expounds the meaning of the term Satan. "The word Satan in Hebrew (or *Satanas* in the more Hellenic fashion) means "opponent" (*antikeimenos*) when translated into Greek." Origen thus shows himself alert to the root meaning of Satan as "obstacle" or "opponent." He is alluding also to 2 Thessalonians 2.4, where the word *antikeimenos* is used of "the man of sin, the son of perdition, who *opposes* and exalts himself above all that is called God," that is, the Antichrist, whom Origen explains in the following section as "son of Satan," in the figurative sense.[48]

[48] On the Antichrist, see above, Chapters 13, 14.6, and on "son of Satan," see Chapters 12.6 and 17.1, and J. B. Russell 1981:106.

He goes on to explain how the word "Satan" may be used both generally and specifically:

> Everyone who has chosen evil and to lead an evil life, doing everything contrary to virtue, is a Satan, that is, an opponent of the son of God who is righteousness, truth and wisdom. But in the strict sense [*kurioteron*] the Opponent is the first of all beings who were in peace and blessedness who lost his wings and fell from the blessed state. According to Ezekiel he walked blameless [*amōmos*] in all his ways, until iniquity [*anomia*] was found in him, and being "a seal of likeness and a crown of beauty" in the paradise of God he became sated with good things and came to destruction, as the word tells us which mysteriously says to him: "Thou didst become destruction and shalt not exist for ever."

The expression "sated with good things," *korestheis tōn agathōn*, is the only hint here of a personal motive for the fall of Satan. Origen is concerned only to oppose the imputation that the devil does not exist (Ezek. 28.19), which is the basis of Celsus' attack. But elsewhere in Origen we get no help either on this question which would exercise the later tradition. Certainly, it seems as if pride ought to be the cause of the Fall, since the passages from Ezekiel and Isaiah are adduced as accounts of the event. But Origen's mind is subtler than many of those who would later take up the story he here sets forth, and although he mentions the wings so often that he may have had in mind the story of Icarus, what he clearly alludes to, as his opponent would recognize, is the Platonic doctrine expounded in the *Phaedrus*. In spite of the citation from "Solomon" (Prov. 23.5) about the wings of the eagle, the basis of Origen's thinking here is the Platonic doctrine of the "winged soul."

Nowhere is Origen's affinity with his opponents clearer than in the doctrine about the immortality of the soul, derived ultimately from the *Phaedo* and the *Phaedrus* but interpreted now in the light of the philosophical speculation that we know as Middle Platonism.[49] The soul's immortality is the most important Greek idea to have influenced Christianity, one of the features that have made it so different from normative Judaism, and the idea is shared among Christian, heretic, and pagan alike in Origen's intellectual milieu. So we find in Origen an elaborate doctrine of the soul, both in its precosmic state and in its continuing existence beyond the present aeon, which helps to explain the peculiar Origenian variant of the rebel myth.

[49] See Dillon 1977 for a full discussion.

The text that Origen, in common with the other Middle Platonists of various tendencies, took to be the most important was the "myth" of the charioteer in the *Phaedrus*, especially its powerful idea of the "winged soul." Says Socrates:

> Soul, when it is perfect and winged flies up in the air and ranges through the whole world. But the soul which has lost its wings is carried along until it can grasp something solid, when it settles down, takes on an earthly body . . . , and the whole, composed of soul and body, is called a living being and has the name of mortal.[50]

Socrates then explains why the soul loses its wings:

> By its nature, the power of the wing is to soar upward and carry up what is heavy to the place where the race of the gods lives. For more than the things of the body, it has a share in the divine, in beauty, wisdom, goodness and all such qualities. By these, then, the wingedness of the soul is nourished and grows, but by baseness and badness and those opposite qualities, it is consumed and destroyed.

Socrates next describes the world of the gods, led by Zeus in his winged chariot, where all goes well. By contrast, the human chariots drive all in great confusion, dragged down by the unruly horse, "trampling upon and crashing into each other, each striving to overtake. So there is great confusion and rivalry and sweating where, by the incompetence [*kakia*] of the drivers, many are lamed and many have their wings broken" (248b). All the souls are trying to get to "the plain of truth," wherein lies the best pasture for the soul's wing, but a certain unfortunate soul is "unable to follow after God and cannot see [*mē idē*]. Through some mischance [*syntychia*] this soul is filled with forgetfulness and evil [*kakia*] and grows heavy; then it loses its wings and falls to earth."

Origen sees human life in these terms, and even includes the ideas of metempsychosis and rebirth in successive ages, from the same passage of the *Phaedrus*, in his conception of the career of a soul. His idea of creation, derived from the *Timaeus* via Philo and widespread in the Middle Platonic milieu of Alexandria, is the precosmic descent of the soul into matter. He expounds the doctrine thus, and it is clear that his whole cosmology depends on it:

> Before the aeons, all spirits [*noes*] were pure, demons, souls and angels, serving God and fulfilling his commandments. The devil who was one of

[50] Plato, *Phaedrus* 246c.

them, having free will, wanted to oppose God and God threw him out. All the other powers fell with him and the ones who had sinned a lot became demons, the others who had sinned less, angels, those who sinned even less, archangels: thus each received his lot according to his own sin. Only those souls were left who had not sinned enough to become demons, nor so lightly as to be angels. God therefore made the present world and bound the soul to the body in order to punish it.[51]

Thus the fall is universal for Origen, and so a condition of the creation. From it derive not only the bad angels who spend their time trying to draw man away from the truth, and the middle category of souls who become men and who receive help in their efforts to recover the original state of blessedness, but also the good angels and the stars, the celestial beings whom God allies with himself in his work of universal redemption. The devil was the first to fall, through his rebellion or forgetfulness of what is good,[52] but all the other powers fell with him.[53]

On the one hand, then, Origen's teaching about Satan follows the basic line of the Christian combat myth. On the other hand, it is situated within the context of Alexandrian Middle Platonism. The combination may perhaps have occasioned some of the unease with which Origen presents the teaching. It certainly accounts for his peculiar but widely influential story of the original fall of the devil, and thus the idea of the redemption as the resurrection of the soul and its recovery of the original Paradise, fusing Ezekiel and Genesis, the devil's fall and Adam's, celestial history and human history, into one grand cosmic myth. The first text that explicitly situates the original fall of the devil within the Christian narrative is thus a mixture of the primitive Christian myth and Platonic theory. The adversary as precosmic rebel we owe, via Origen's comments on Ezekiel and Isaiah, to Plato. But Plato would not have recognized him.

[51] *De princ.* 1.8.1–4 and 1.6.1–3; cf. 2.8.3, 3.2.5; see also Daniélou 1948:212–14.

[52] *De princ.* 1.5.5, 2.8.3, 2.9.2; cf. *Contra Celsum* 6.45 and Chadwick 1953:362n.

[53] Rufinus' Latin version of 1.6.2 adds "some stayed in their first state," words that do not appear in the corresponding Greek fragment and that show the anxiety of the church to eliminate Origen's heretical views (Daniélou 1948:214). See, however, Crouzel and Simonetti (eds.) 1967–78: vol. 2, p. 89, commenting on *De princ.* 1.5.5.

Part Five

AUGUSTINE AND THE STRUCTURE OF

CHRISTIAN MYTHOLOGY

TWENTY-TWO

AUGUSTINE: THE TASK AND
THE OPPONENTS

T HROUGH the efforts of the early fathers like Irenaeus, Tertullian, and Origen, the church had by the end of the third century A.D. developed several cosmological myths with which to explain the Pauline story of fall and redemption and to combat the heretical views of the Gnostics. Yet this very diversity could become a problem in the face of an elaborate and unified cosmology, such as the new religion of Manichaeism, a more successful and, from the orthodox point of view, a more virulent form of Gnosticism. The struggle with Manichaeism, however, eventually produced the greatest and most forceful personality among the church fathers, and in his writings a comprehensive version of the Christian combat myth was bequeathed to the Middle Ages. We shall first review the situation Augustine inherited, and then summarize the Manichaean views.

1. *Christian Variations of Fall and Redemption*

Although philosophical and theological debate had taken the problems of the combat myth to elaborate and complex levels of speculation, the essential plot remained intact and continually available to the popular mind. A key ingredient in the development of monasticism, for example, was the idea of a struggle with the devil (or some monstrous substitute). Among many examples, the following reflects most fully the various themes we have been following in this book. A certain Benus, a fourth-century monk in Egypt, had a special reputation as a holy man.

> At one time, a certain beast that is called a hippopotamus was laying waste the neighboring countryside, and the farmer folk asked [Benus] and he went to the place, and when he saw the monstrous creature he said to her, "I command thee, in the name of Jesus Christ, lay waste this land no more." And she fled as though an Angel gave chase, and was no more seen.[1]

[1] Waddle 1942:45–46; cf. Le Goff 1977. See also Appendix, and now Bokser 1985.

This story, or its essential framework, is Tale-Type 300 adapted to the local Egyptian conditions. A hippopotamus instead of Huwawa or the demons of the gospels, an authoritative voice rather than hand weapons, as normal in the biblical tradition—but the death-dealing monster who tyrannizes the people is the same as the figure who informs the more complex versions of the plot.

The idea that the Christian redemption means liberation from the tyrant was quickly and universally accepted within the church. But considerable variation was possible within this basic plot, since no canonized version of the total myth existed. This situation had its advantages. Each Christian could have his personal experience of the devil and his wiles—in lust, pride, envy, or disobedience—and however much the experiences differed from each other, they could all be incorporated within the general idea.

At one end of the plot there was much debate about how (or how far) the crucifixion had achieved liberation and victory over the devil. Ignatius espoused the deceit and secrecy idea, according to which the incarnation and death of the Christ-God took place unbeknownst to Satan, who presumably thought of Jesus as a mere man.[2] The more elaborate forms of this idea, in Origen and Gregory of Nyssa, echo Job's God and the ancient combat language of Leviathan: "The Divine Being concealed himself within the veil of [human] nature, that, just as is the case with greedy fish, the hook of the Deity might be swallowed along with the bait of the flesh."[3] In this language the force and the guile variants of the combat plot are curiously combined.

The ransom theory of a transaction between Christ and Satan had, as we have seen, a long vogue, and even Anselm, whose "satisfaction" version of redemption ultimately replaced it, still preserved the combat language and the recapitulation doctrine as a part of his theory: "As the devil had conquered man by the tasting of a tree, to which he persuaded him, so by the suffering endured on a tree, which he inflicted, should he, by a man be conquered."[4]

At the other end of the plot, the origin of the tyrant and his power were

[2] Ignatius, *Letter to the Ephesians* 19.1; cf. 1 Cor. 2.8.

[3] Gregory of Nyssa, *Great Catechism* 21–26, in Schaff 1892: vol. 5, 491–96. See Patrides 1966:133 and J. B. Russell 1981:84, 192–93. Cf. Job 41.1; Augustine, *Sermones* 130.2; and Gregory the Great, *Moralia* 33.14: "Christ made, as it were, a kind of hook of himself for the death of the devil."

[4] Anselm, *Cur Deus homo?* 1.3. On the ransom vs. sacrifice theories of atonement, see esp. Aulén 1969 and also Young 1973 and J. B. Russell 1981:82–85.

similarly argued. The story of the lustful Watchers maintained itself for a while because its theme clearly corresponded to the most easily recognized of the cardinal sins. Lactantius, for example, adapted the Watchers to a more comprehensive narrative about the origin of evil. For him, the devil was an active force, younger brother of Christ and jealous, who passed from good to evil by his own will. The idea of the two brothers works out in strong narrative terms the theory of two spirits we met at Qumran, in Persian belief, or indeed in Jewish-Christian tradition. One of the brothers, by a common allusion, is like the right hand of God, while the other—and this is the first time the narrative logic is pushed so far—is like the left hand. All good derives from one, all evil from the other, and they are in constant battle. God then made the angels, but as with many writers who retained the Watcher story, the subsequent chronology is difficult to sort out.[5] The material world is created just in time for the devil to lead Adam and Eve to fall and Cain, his special protégé, to the fratricide that he himself would like to commit. The Watcher angels fell later, at the time of the flood, tempted by the devil into lust for women. There are now two classes of demons: heavenly ones (Satan and the fallen angels) and earthly demons (the giant offspring). The net result is that Satan and his satellites and ministers have many ways, including paganism, persecution, and perversity, to keep the combat going. In Lactantius' view, such evils are necessary, since "if no evil existed, there would be no danger, and thus no basis for wisdom."[6] Such a view could persist, however, without the Watcher story. Once Satan's fall was so radically separated from it, and once the idea of the ambitious rebel became available through commentary on Ezekiel and Isaiah, the Watcher story itself would eventually be forgotten, though the element of lust, which had formed the bridge to the Eden story, would continue to influence the idea of the Fall.

The Eden tale itself was still open to rather differing interpretations, both allegorical and literal. The serpent was not necessarily Satan, even now, and if he was, no widely agreed story accounted for his hostile presence in the garden or for his own fall. The chronology of events was equally uncertain, and so it was difficult to imagine a coherent narrative structure. Augustine found ways to resolve all these problems, and he did

[5] Lactantius, *Divine Institutes* 2.9, cf. 4.8, where both Christ and the angels are spirits, the "breathings" of God, but contrast with 4.6, where the angels are made much later. See above, Introduction, n. 28, and cf. Watts 1963. For the Jewish-Christian affinities, see J. B. Russell 1981:150.

[6] Lactantius, *De ira Dei* 13. For the Watchers, see *Divine Institutes* 2.15.

so chiefly by connecting his own experience with the biblical narratives through the idea of sin. This concept owed a clear debt both to Neoplatonism and to the Irenaean theory of apostasy, and just as Irenaeus had conceived the idea to oppose the heresies of Gnosticism, so Augustine was led to his comprehensive theory of sin by the need to oppose the heresy that the Gnostic tendency had become in his own day—Manichaeism.

2. *Manichaeism: The Divided Cosmos*

The apocalyptic myth of a cosmic struggle between two independent spirits, one good and one evil, eventually hardened into the most extreme form of dualism that the church ever spawned. The system of Mani was not only explicitly dualist, like the Qumran or New Testament worldviews, in its ethical and eschatological teachings: for Mani the division of light and darkness had existed as separate cosmic principles from the beginning of the universe. The system he devised was a new revelation to supersede three previous religions he recognized as precursors—Buddhism, Zoroastrianism, and Christianity. Its heart was an elaborate myth, strongly Gnostic in mood and imagery, of cosmic exile and salvation. Stripped of its detailed embroidery, the central principle recurred often in the sectarian history of medieval Christendom and its dualist heresies.[7]

Though Mani's parents may have been Persians, he was born in Assyria around A.D. 216 and grew up partly among a Jewish-Christian Gnostic group, the Elchasites. He adapted the Jewish "Book of Giants," extending the already remarkable syncretism of that Enochic work, with its allusions to Gilgamesh and Huwawa, to form a cosmological system that incorporated Buddhist and Zoroastrian ideas but that looked chiefly to Jewish and Gnostic Christianity of the Syrian kind, to Bardaisan of Edessa and to Marcion.[8] Apart from the *Book of Giants*, which seems to have been written in Middle Persian (although published in six or seven languages), Mani's other six major books were composed in what was probably his native tongue, an Aramaic closely related to Syriac. He borrowed the Pauline title of "Apostle of Jesus Christ," but his new system was to be a

---

[7] For surveys, see Loos 1974, Cohn 1975, and J. B. Russell 1985.

[8] Above, Chapter 10.1. For Mani's syncretism, see Henning 1943–46:52–55, Widengren 1946:179, Widengren 1965:43–68, Puech 1949:69–70, Bauer 1972:22–32, Greenfield and Stone 1977, Gruenwald 1983, and Stone (ed.) 1984:450–52. On the "Book of Giants," see now the argument of Stroumsa 1984:161–67 in favor of a Gnostic intermediary.

universal religion to supersede Christianity and to spread "the hope of life" to East and West alike.

So successful was Mani that in the one direction the Roman emperor Diocletian was forced to issue an edict against his followers in 297 claiming that the system "has infected the whole of our world like the poison of a malevolent snake," while records of Manichaeism have been found, in the other direction from its Middle Eastern origins, as far afield as Chinese Turkestan. Nor was it only the Romans who found the religion dangerous to their dominance. Mani himself was executed, in 276, at the instigation of the Mazdaist clergy in the service of the "Great King" of the Persian Empire, for inciting many apostasies from the ruling Sassanid dynasty's form of Zoroastrianism. And once the empire had become an Islamic province, still the Abbasid caliphate of the ninth and tenth centuries found it necessary to persecute the followers of this "doctor from Babylon," whom they called by the old *pehlevi* name *Zindiks*, corruptors of the law (*Zend*).[9] For the "orthodox" among the Christian communities too, Mani and his followers were a threat. Eusebius of Caesarea, like the hated Roman emperor, called Mani a poisonous snake, and the vital but mysterious "Ambrosiaster," from whom Augustine learned so much and who was intimate with the Roman senatorial class, thought of Manichaeism as a Christian heresy. It is he who cites the Diocletian edict while commenting on the following choice text (2 Tim. 6–8): "This is the sort of men who creep into houses, and lead captive silly women, laden with sins, led away with divers lusts, ever learning and never able to come to the knowledge of the truth. Just as Jannes and Jambres opposed Moses, so do these men also resist the truth."[10]

A Manichaean catechism outlines the three stages of their cosmic myth: "We know (1) what is said to have been before there was earth and heaven; we know (2) why God and Satan fought, how Light and Darkness mingled, and who is said to have created heaven and earth; we know (3) why eventually earth and heaven shall pass away, and how Light and Darkness shall be separated from each other, and what shall happen thereafter."[11] The myth explains that originally Light and Darkness, Good and Evil, or God and Matter were separate. The Darkness seethed within itself, fulfilling its need for hate and strife against itself. But at some point

[9] P. Brown 1969:92–95.

[10] Eusebius, *Ecclesiastical History* 8, 31; "Ambrosiaster," *Commentarius ad II ep. Tim. III.* 6, both quoted in P. Brown 1969:98.

[11] Quoted in Jonas 1970:209.

the powers within the Darkness came to its outer boundaries and perceived the Light. They were immediately seized with envy and jealousy,
and in desire for the better they opened the attack. The Light was forced
by this attack to take action, but the peaceable world could find no way
with which to repel the attack—no weapons, nothing warlike or aggressive. God was therefore forced to create a new divine hypostasis more
suitable for combat, the figure called the Primal Man. The Persian Manichaeans called this figure "Ormazd," which in the Zoroastrian system
was the name of the god of light himself (Ahura Mazda), the opponent of
Ahriman, the god of darkness. The existence of this precosmic god Anthropos, or Man, was one of the major Gnostic secrets, a key mythological element in the metaphysic of salvation.[12]

The Primal Man, God's first begotten, was defeated, however, and Satan devoured part of his light. As a result, the parts of Darkness and Light
were mixed together for the first time. The devourer was also affected by
what he devoured, for Light began to act as a poison on him—some versions even make the defeat a deliberate sacrifice to procure this end. Thus
the immediate threat to Light was converted into a delayed victory. The
five assistants of Primal Man were also devoured (and eventually became
the stuff of *psyche*, soul, which acts as a barrier within man, corrupted as
it is by its material environment but protecting the *pneuma*, spirit, the
original Light). Meanwhile Primal Man was himself rescued by the redeemer, the spirit of light—an event which was for the Manichaean what
the crucifixion was to a Pauline Christian: the symbolic archetype and
guarantee of his salvation. One Manichaean, on meeting another, would
repeat the gesture by which the forces of Light reached into Darkness and
saved the primal sacrifice—that is, they shook hands.

The other parts of Light, however, which now form the soul, were too
closely mixed with Darkness, so that another ruse was necessary following this cosmic battle—the creation of the visible world. The whole cosmos was created for redemption in order to unmix what had been mixed,
like the seeds of Psyche's task. The mixed parts were taken by the Living
Spirit (another manifestation of Light) and made into matter and soul-
stuff. Thus all the parts of nature around us come from the impure cadav-
ers of the powers of evil—"the world is an embodiment of the Arch-Ah-
riman."[13] The world so created was a prison for the powers of darkness
and a place of purification for the soul-stuff, likewise but temporarily im-

---

[12] See above, Chapters 12 and 18, and Irenaeus, *Adv. haer.* 1.12.4, 1.30.1.
[13] Persian Manichaean text quoted in Jonas 1970:224.

prisoned. So creation itself, when properly understood, was a redemptive ploy of God, not of a Satanic demiurge.

The enemy now thinks up a truly devilish countertrick to prevent the Light from being separated, since this would mean the final defeat of Darkness, once it had conceived this proud desire for the Light. Having thus caught sight of the divine form, the Prince of Darkness decides to create a more effective prison for the divine Light, something made in its own image (Gen. 1.27). He therefore creates Adam and Eve to entrap permanently a particularly large part of the Light. Man now becomes the major battlefield of the two forces, exactly as he had been for Zarathustra, for the Qumran Jews, or for the writers of the possession stories in the gospels. But this common human experience of division may be differently interpreted, and to gain release from the struggle, each of the redemption religions requires one to know the right story. In the Manichaean account, Light is seeking its own restoration, and Darkness is seeking its very survival.

Eve has the special purpose of seducing Adam and making reproduction the most formidable device in Satan's armory, since it disperses the Light and prolongs the captivity indefinitely: "the whole world was filled with their lust." It thus becomes desperately important for the powers of Light to warn Adam. A messenger is sent, called Jesus, but Adam "falls asleep," Eve appears to him, and it is too late. Consequently, Jesus as "serpent" shows Adam the tree of knowledge, so that he can begin the process of the salvation of Light from this further degradation. This revelation was renewed by Seth, Enoch, Noah, Buddha, Zarathustra, Jesus Christ, and now the final messenger, Mani.

The cosmic myth will reach its conclusion in the last time, as the following apocalyptic psalm makes clear:

> In a moment the Living Spirit will come . . . he will succour the Light. But the counsel of death and the Darkness he will shut up in the dwelling that was established for it, that it might be bound for ever. There is no other means to bind the Enemy save this means; for he will not be received to the Light because he is a stranger to it; nor again can he be left in his land of Darkness, lest he may wage a war greater than the first. A new Aeon will be built in the place of the world that shall dissolve, that in it the powers of Light may reign, because they have performed and fulfilled the will of the Father entire, they have subdued the hated one. . . . This is the Knowledge of Mani, let us worship him and bless him.[14]

[14] Psalm quoted in Jonas 1970:235. On this Coptic collection of Manichaean psalms, almost contemporary with Augustine, see also P. Brown 1967:46.

The Manichaean system, it will be evident, shows remarkable parallels to myths we have referred to earlier. Apart from the obvious resonance with the Qumran texts (the battle of the sons of Light and Darkness), it adapts, for example, the Babylonian idea that the world is made from the body of Tiamat and that man is made from her consort Kingu's blood, a motif echoed also in Snorri's account of Scandinavian mythology and transformed in the Orphic context into a myth that Dionysus was devoured by the Titans and mankind fashioned from the resulting mixture.[15] In retrospect, "mixing" looks like the most influential idea developed in the Yahwistic, Enoch, and Gnostic traditions. Each stage of the Manichaean plot is a repetition with variation of the initial situation, the desire of darkness for light or mixing.

In some of their forms, these opening moves in the cosmogonic myth are derived directly from the lustful Watchers of the Enoch books. Indeed, the sons of darkness are actually referred to by their Aramaic title, ʿirin, Watchers, as well as by the Greek translation, egrēgoroi.[16] In Mani's adaptation, the chief difference is that the myth has been definitely pushed back to cosmogony, so that now rebellion and creation are the same story. We can recognize a Gnostic transformation of the Watcher myth, for example, in the following episode. The divine Messenger sails in his light ship (the moon) across to the middle of the heavens, and there "revealed his forms, male and female, and was seen by all the archons, the sons of Darkness, males and females. And at the sight of the Messenger, who was beautiful in all his forms, all the archons became filled with lust for him, the males for the form of the female, and the females for the form of the male."[17] The male archons, excitable crew that they are, ejaculate at the sight, and the spilled sperm, now called "sin," which is actually some of the light they have been holding back on, falls to earth.

Here another even more archaic complex of motifs occurs in Manichaean transformation: the rebellion of the sea, the beast, and the trees. Some of the sperm falls in the sea ("the moist part" of the earth), where it becomes "a hateful beast in the likeness of Sakla, the Prince of Darkness." A "great rebellion" springs from it, and Adamas, the Primal Man and

---

[15] ANET 66–69 (*Enuma Eliš*, Tablet IV, lines 129–43, VI, lines 5–33); see J. Harrison 1922:490–500; Young 1966:35; S. Thompson 1955–58: Motifs A625, 1200, 2611. On the garments of light in Gnostic contexts, see Puech 1978: vol. 2, 118–22. On "mixing," see above, Chapters 6 and 8, and Layton (ed.) 1981: vol. 1, 734–56.

[16] Henning 1977: vol. 1, 341. See above, Chapter 8 n. 18.

[17] A. V. W. Jackson 1932:241.

champion of Light, is sent to fight and kill it. The other part falls on dry land, five trees spring up, and the sin becomes their fruit.[18] The trees are thus linked to Adam and Eve but symbolically represent vegetal life in general, while the beast in the sea is animal life. Together they make up the living world of rebellious, lust-generated matter that so repels the fastidious Manichee. The beast is to be rejected, since he will reproduce himself through lust, but the trees acquire other connotations from the myth tradition. Their fruit, the "sin," is a concentrated source of light, given its origin, and so a good Manichaean will eat vegetables and fruit, but not meat, in order to reincorporate the light particles.

In the following brief passage, taken from the prototype of Christian attacks on Mani, Hegemonius' *Acta Archelai*, we find most of our basic myths amalgamated into Mani's system: "Hence also some of the angels, refusing to obey God's counsel, resisted his will; and one of them fell like a flash of lightning upon the earth [becoming the devil], while others, beset by the serpent-dragon [*a dracone*], united with the daughters of men."[19] The various echoes are a sign of Mani's syncretism, but they also testify to the persistence of ancient myth in Gnostic guise. And, although it was the most extreme of the various ascetic and dualist systems that flourished in the centuries that gave birth to Christianity, Mani's mythological scheme continued to reappear, under the names of various "heresies"— Paulician, Bogomile, Cathar, Waldensian—since it provided the only fully reasoned defense of the ascetic, world-despising tendency that was partially absorbed into Christianity without its accompanying justification. The monastic life of the Manichaean elect within their established churches, modeled perhaps on Buddhist practice, had a strong impact on the Christian monastic orders.[20] And the most important and brilliant of all the church fathers, Augustine, spent nine years of his life as a follower of this system.

---

[18] Stroumsa 1984:156–58, citing the recently published Cologne Mani Codex; cf. Milik 1976:320–36, Gruenwald 1983.

[19] Hegemonius, *Acta Archelai* 36.3, quoted in Stroumsa 1984:29.

[20] A. V. W. Jackson 1932:225–40; Henning 1943–46:53.

TWENTY-THREE

MANICHAEAN DUALISM AND AUGUSTINIAN DIALECTIC

1. Heresy and Opposition

FOR THE spiritually tormented young man that we get to know in the first books of Augustine's *Confessions*, the piety and asceticism of the Manichaean elect held a strong appeal. The elaborately rationalized myth that showed that the inner man, the spirit, was untarnished and a part of the divine substance offered an especially attractive system of belief to a young intellectual troubled by the demands of the flesh. "I have known my soul and the body that lies upon it, that they have been enemies since the creation," says the Manichaean Psalmbook.[1] Both God and the young man's soul were thus protected from guilty implications. Neither was responsible for evil, and both were part of a cosmic redemptive scheme.

Though this myth preserved the innocence of the deity, the more mature Augustine realized that it left him powerless to redeem more than a small part of the cosmos or of a human self. It thus divided both cosmos and self irrevocably. A Manichaean could never be a whole being, and it was just this wholeness that Augustine sought. Though the Manichaean system apparently relieved him of responsibility ("not I was sinning, but some other nature within me," as Paul put it), Augustine rejected it because "in truth I was a complete whole: it was my impiety that divided me against myself."[2] Augustine's theory of sin was, paradoxically, the way in which he learned to understand this wholeness.

Like its Manichaean counterpart, this theory had to be a complete explanation both of the individual psychology of the believer and of the cosmos in which he found himself. For the orthodox Christian, such an account of the cosmic structure had to be chiefly an exegesis of the scriptures in which this structure was revealed, and especially of the first three chapters of Genesis. Out of the need to construct a satisfactory understanding of his own sinful nature, Augustine was thus led to apply his enormous

---

[1] Quoted in P. Brown 1967:49.
[2] Augustine, *Confessions* 8.10; the translation is normally Warner 1963.

intellectual powers to the very problems of interpretation that faced the earlier fathers of the church. The theory of sin, both cosmic and personal, was to be the means by which he resolved them.

The importance of Augustine's early Manichaean experience to the development of his spiritual understanding may be gauged by the persistence and frequency with which he attacked the heresy throughout the rest of his life. He wrote eight complete works specifically directed against the Manichaeans, including the immense *Reply to Faustus*, besides the scattered and often lengthy refutations in other works like the *Confessions* or *City of God*.[3] This was far more than the amount of space or energy he devoted to the other heretics—Donatists, Arians, even the Pelagians—who engaged his attention. No doubt this was partly the result of his own psychological need to repudiate his sinful past. But the preoccupation with Manichaeism derived also from the dialectical nature of his thought. Just as the earliest Christians had been driven to refine their doctrines by the need to oppose the Gnostic heresy, so Augustine often defined his own views in opposition to the teaching of Mani.

The works that Augustine devoted exclusively to attacking Manichaeism were all written during the first half of his new life as a Christian. The basis of those attacks was the teachings of the church interpreted through the spectacles of Neoplatonists, especially Plotinus. Between the years 400 and 406, however, Augustine underwent a profound change in his understanding of man's spiritual condition, and possibly because of a recent acquaintance with the Neoplatonist Porphyry's attack on Christianity repudiated much of his earlier Platonism.[4] The opponents of Augustine delighted in following out the contradictions in his doctrine that the change caused, and forced him to elaborate but often futile attempts to reconcile his former and his later opinions. The Pelagian opponents of his later years would eagerly and ingenuously point out Pelagian passages from the Neoplatonic era of his attacks on Manichaeism or accuse him of the Manichaean heresy when he attacked themselves.

Many defenders of Augustine, taking their cue from his own *Retractions*, attempt to marry the earlier and the later positions in order to reveal the supposed consistency beneath the surface fluctuations of opinion. Unfortunately, one then ends up with yet another dogmatic theologian stat-

[3] The anti-Manichaean writings are conveniently collected in Zycha (ed.) 1891–92.

[4] TeSelle 1970:185–266. Augustine always calls Porphyry "*doctissimus*" and "the most notable pagan philosopher" (P. Brown 1967:91, 268). On Augustine's Platonism, see Armstrong 1972.

ing and restating the same body of abstract principles, a thinker shorn of the vibrant context that gave life and direction to his thought. No one was more aware than the writer of the *Confessions* that the context of a man's life shapes his character and beliefs, so it is at best a pity to present a blood-less but consistent dogmatist instead of the controversial and brilliant rhetorician.

Rhetoric was the training and much of the joy of Augustine, and he ev-idently appreciated an occasion for the use and display of his hard-won rhetorical powers. He thrived on opposition, as did the church itself.

> Surely it is the process of refuting heretics that brings to light the mind of your church and the content of sound teaching. There must be heresies, in order that those who are tested and proved genuine might be manifested amidst the weak.[5]

The last sentence here is a paraphrase of Paul's words to the Corinthians: "For there must be heresies among you, that those who are genuine may be recognized." The idea that heresies were a test or proof of faith fitted well with Augustine's training in dialectic and rhetoric, but the church has not always followed the tolerant precepts of these teachers. Augustine himself, faced with the noble and high-minded Donatists or generously optimistic Pelagians, forgot his own words once he became powerful in the narrow-minded African church of his birth. It has become a just in-dictment of institutional Christianity that Augustine's *"Cogite intrare"* (Force them to join us) has been often more widely heard and acted upon than his *"Tolle, lege"* (Take and read).[6]

Like Paul, Irenaeus, or Origen before him, Augustine was clearly one of those intellectuals who discover what they believe in the vigorous en-counter with another belief, especially with one that is so close to their own unarticulated faith that the very proximity threatens their peace. The need to oppose accounts in turn for his resistance to the faith of Monica, his Christian mother, in Ciceronian and Manichaean rationalism, the joy with which he embraced Christ and the fervor of his rejection of Mani, and the return to a thoroughly Christianized Manichaeism on his hostile encounter with Pelagianism.

Augustine's picture of the devil owes a great deal to the struggle with a succession of opponents. The picture depends upon his theory of sin, and

---

[5] *Confessions* 7.19, my trans. See 1 Cor. 11.19, discussed above, Chapter 14.3, and below, Chapter 25.2

[6] P. Brown 1967:33–34; Nigg 1962:116–17; Rist 1972:243–48.

in order to grasp this theory we must take account of the important changes through which it passed as his thought developed. At each stage he was engaged in a dialogue. He was concerned not only to construct a coherent system that would explain the tension between man and God and the complicated relationship of psychology to cosmology, but also eager to refute a heresy by a superior philosophical argument.

2. *The Theory of Sin*

Augustine's theory of sin evolved first out of his opposition to the Manichaean views he had so recently espoused. The actual center of the theory was the distinction between sin and evil. For Augustine, sin precedes and is the cause of evil; for Mani, evil causes sin. Indeed, for Mani both sin and evil are manifestations of the power of darkness—symbolically a more inclusive, prior, and as Augustine recognized in Genesis, a more imaginatively effective term.

The core of the early theory of sin and its correlate, virtue, was not the nature of human action considered in itself but the end to which one acts. He attacked the asceticism of the Manichaeans by reminding them of that "vile miscreant," Catiline, who could endure cold, thirst, and hunger— all "to gratify his fierce and ungoverned passions."[7] Asceticism in itself was no virtue. Why, even the Manichaeans themselves (he tells us in a typical use of the opponents' argument against themselves), when told how many Catholic women were virgins, would reply, "So are mules." Virtue was human action directed toward God, sin was action directed toward the self.

At the same time, Augustine also tried to refute the Manichaean and generally Gnostic notion that matter itself is evil. He firmly insisted that evil is corruption, not substance. If the poison of a scorpion's sting were in itself evil, for example, then the scorpon itself would suffer most. Rather, what we call evil is merely the disagreement of the elements and humors with each other, and we should not call it evil at all. "What is truly and properly an evil is hurtful both always and to all." Yet hellebore, for example, is sometimes a food, sometimes a medicine, as well as a poison.

We who live in air die under earth or under water, while innumerable animals creep alive in sand or loose earth, and fish die in our air. Fire consumes

---

[7] *De moribus* 2.13.27, trans. in Schaff (ed.) 1887: vol. 4, 76.

our bodies, but, when suitably applied, it both restores from cold and expels diseases without number.[8]

If the Manichaeans were right, then fire, air, earth, and water could never do any good. The basis of Augustine's argument here is an optimistic and entirely Greek respect for the created cosmos, its beauty and order. Indeed, in an early treatise, *De pulchro et apto*, his first complete work, now lost but referred to in the *Confessions*,[9] he apparently described the glories of nature in largely Platonic terms. Though this attitude never left Augustine completely, it was severely modified when he came to contemplate later "the sufferings of new-born babies."[10]

This early line of argument, attractive as it was to the recent convert, only goes to prove that evil is not matter. Augustine still had to account for suffering and sin. His early attempt to do so was the notion of *consuetudo*, the power of custom or habit. By this means he opposed the Manichaean theory of the presence of evil in man. Augustine's major concern in this anti-Manichaean phase was to show that man himself, not a celestial power, is responsible for sin, that "sinning takes place only by an exercise of the will."[11] Man may freely choose whether or not to sin. The will is free.

Later, however, his views were profoundly altered, and Augustine came to see the inadequacy of this theory to his own felt experience. He had to admit the bondage of the will, despite his continued opposition to Manichaeism. Though he attempted to defend his earlier statement, together with the similar notions set forth in his treatise *De libero arbitrio*, against the Pelagian charge that he had reversed himself, his defense produces such complicated Latin that it has resisted the best efforts of translators and interpreters alike. He had forgotten the dialectical nature of his own thought. The most charitable comment on this passage of the *Retractions* is probably that of his Victorian translator and admirer, Alfred Henry Newman:

> His efforts to show the consistency of this earlier with his later modes of thought are to be pronounced only partially successful. The fact is that in the anti-Manichaean time he went too far in maintaining the absolute freedom of the will and the impossibility of sin apart from personal will in the

[8] *De moribus* 2.8.12–13.
[9] *Confessions* 4.13–15. See Courcelle 1950.
[10] P. Brown 1967:393–96. See Hick 1966:43–95 for a review of these theories.
[11] *De duabus animabus* 10.14.

sinner; while in the anti-Pelagian time he ventured too near to the fatalism that he so earnestly combatted in the Manichaeans.[12]

The major change in Augustine's thought, and one that has affected the entire subsequent history of the church, was the invention of the doctrine of original sin. Intellectually the theory was derived from his reading of Ambrosiaster's commentary on Paul, and although the controversy with the Donatists sharpened the focus of Augustine's thinking on the point,[13] it must have coincided with a profound emotional change. He thought he read the idea in Paul's language at Romans 5.12: "Sin came into the world through one man and death through sin, and so death spread to all men in that [because] all men sinned, *eph' hōi pantes hēmarton.*" The last phrase Augustine persistently mistranslates as *in quo omnes peccaverunt*, in whom [Adam] all men sinned.[14] He refers to Ambrose as his authority for arguing that all men born of sexual intercourse are thereby tainted with original guilt, but the idea of the solidarity between all men and Adam is probably influenced by both the Stoic and Neoplatonic notion of "*spermatikoi logoi*," seedlike words, which are all contained in the divine Logos,[15] and even more by the Gnostic and Manichaean idea, contained in the Adam book tradition, of the Primal Man, or the god Anthropos, Man. Augustine insists on the idea that all seed is Adam's seed and so guilty of Adam's sin.

The theory of inherited guilt, and the correlative theories of predestination and the bondage of the will, now made Augustine's position very hard to distinguish, at least existentially, from the Manichaean. The difference lay only in the story of origins. Adam's sin, not primal darkness or God's fallibility, was the original cause. The result was a world very like the Manichaean, ruled by a dark tyrant whose power was evident in the inevitability of sin.[16]

The mistrust of the body, evident throughout Augustine's life, in the *Confessions* as well as the anti-Pelagian tracts, comes very close to Mani's position that man should abstain from sexual contact because that is how evil is passed along. Pelagian opponents who accused Augustine of Man-

---

[12] Schaff 1887: vol. 4, 102n.

[13] TeSelle 1970:256–66; P. Brown 1967:233–43.

[14] Rom. 5.12; Augustine, *De nuptiis et concupiscentia* 1.3.8, 2.5.15; *Contra Julianum* 1.3.10, 1.4.11. See Patrides 1966:97–101, Te Selle 1970:158–65, and Rist 1972:230–35, who rather belittles the shift in Augustine's thought.

[15] Rist 1972:231.

[16] *City of God* 20.8.41; *Contra Julianum* 6.21.67. See P. Brown 1967:244, 395.

ichaeism and defended the goodness of human sexuality had a strong case. Augustine maintained throughout the Pelagian controversy that the purest of Christian marriages could easily be polluted by the venial sin of sexual desire. The Pelagian attack stung him, however, to repeat his old argument that sinless sex was the property of man and woman before the Fall. Then the body's members were under the control of the will and did not uncannily rise (or fall), as they do under the present dispensation. He also developed a more elegantly scholastic series of distinctions to clarify his differences from Manichaean asceticism. Concupiscence might well be equivalent to original sin, he argued, but "only if it is seen as something within the soul."[17] What makes it sin, apparently, is not the desire itself—after all, animals have that, and it is natural—but the privation of love involved. The soul turns inevitably away from God when it inclines to the gratification of the body, and the proper Platonic ordering of the elements of the soul is disturbed. It is the sense of shame that makes it sin or, to put it scholastically, the material element in original sin is concupiscence but the formal element (what makes it sin) is guilt, the sense that one is turning away from God. One then views the gift of God, the body and the self, as greater than the giver.

Augustine thus justified and extended his central idea, based on the Platonic model and parallel to the Irenaean idea of apostasy, that all sins are subsumed within the first sin: pride.[18] But the problem that the Pelagians raised is equally important: once we have a theory of inherited guilt, original sin, then every human act becomes sinful, whatever its putative object. What then can man do about this? Augustine's answer is frightening, profound, and desperate. Like the author of Job he answers: nothing. Unlike Job, however, he believes in a God who does more than afflict—a good God who offers prevenient grace.

3. The City of Sin and the City of Grace

"He cast upon them the fierceness of his anger, wrath, indignation and trouble, by sending evil angels among them." Augustine quoted these words of Psalm 78 in two of his attacks on the young and brilliant Pelagian, Julian of Eclanum.[19] This dreadful sense of human bondage brought

---

[17] Contra Julianum 3.10.22. See TeSelle 1970:316–18.

[18] De libero arbitrio 3.76; City of God 14.13.1. See TeSelle 1970:109–11 and Rist 1972: 241–43.

[19] Ps. 78.49; Contra Julianum 5.3.8, 6.8.31.

Augustine, and the church after him, very close to the Manichaean and generally Gnostic view of the cosmos as a prison. It mattered little to Julian that this terrifying vision was, for Augustine, the punishment by an angry God for the unspeakable crime of Adam, not the outcome of the war of the two kingdoms. For Julian, human life was essentially the same in both the Manichaean and the Augustinian views: horrible suffering and domination by evil angels.

Though the controversy with Julian was cut short by Augustine's sudden death, its outcome had already been decided. The world-view set forth earlier in the *City of God* would dominate medieval Christendom.[20] Despite the gloomy Manichaean pessimism that a Pelagian could read there, this work was an effort to counter both the Platonic (and Pelagian) and the Manichaean tendencies in Christian tradition. To the Manichaeans Augustine offered a complex theory of evil as the negation of good; to the Pelagians he emphasized the power of sin. Here at last—or so the Latin church came to feel—was a coherent Christian system, a cosmology that would outdo the Manichaean in speculative subtlety and the just recognition of evil yet at the same time preserve the Greek (and Jewish) sense of the created beauty of the universe and the goodness of the material of which it is made.

By means of this system, Augustine brought to its culmination the narrative tradition that Paul had initiated by setting the fall of Adam next to the Redemption. He was deeply influenced by Ambrosiaster's commentary on Paul and by Irenaeus' development of the Pauline theory of correspondence between these two poles of the Christian mythology. We have considered at length some of the difficulties that faced the church in articulating this crucial correspondence, in particular the problem posed by the double Pauline theory of redemption. Was it Adam's sin or the devil's tyranny that occasioned Christ's mission? The key to the Augustinian resolution of the problem was frank acceptance of the theory that "all men, even new-born infants, are involved in the common destiny of the human race, entirely apart from their own decisions."[21] What the common destiny of the race meant, since Adam fell, was bondage to the devil. The first letter of John, we saw, alludes to the birth of Cain from the devil. What Augustine found there was a spiritual allegory of Adam's ancestry:

[20] P. Brown 1967:340–97; see also Hick 1966:96–102.
[21] TeSelle 1970:258.

Adam was created by God, but when he consented to the devil he was born
of the devil, and all whom he begot were like himself. We are born with
desire, and even before we add our own guilt we are born of that damnation. . . . Therefore there are two births, that of Adam and that of Christ,
the one casting us down to death, the other raising us up to life; the one
bearing with it sin, the other freeing us from sin.[22]

Just as Adam was twice born, of God and of the devil, so all Christians, in
the doctrine of John's gospel, must be twice born. One birth, the physical
birth, is of the devil ("*inter faeces et urinam nascimur*"); the second, the spiritual birth of baptism in Christ, is of grace.

So Augustine was able to preserve and articulate the dialectical tension
at the heart of Christianity, and the cosmic system he created depends on
this tension: a monotheistic faith in an evidently divided universe. Once
he became a Christian, Augustine insisted on a monist universe created
and sustained by the power of the one true God. Yet at the same time he
was drawn repeatedly to emphasize the split in the nature of things. He
even came to teach that this split between light and darkness, between the
good and evil angels, took place on the very first day of creation when
God, according to the fourth verse of Genesis, "divided the light from the
darkness." Since these first verses of Genesis describe the actions of God,
Augustine has to be very sure that he does not impute the creation of evil
to God. What God made was the angels, and their substance, like everything else created by God, as the text of Genesis often insists, was good.
Some of these angels, however, whether created equal with the others or
not, turned away, and were thus themselves responsible for their punishment in darkness. So when he discusses the "Fiat Lux" passage, Augustine writes:

"The true Light, which lighteth every man that cometh into the world"
[John 1.9]—this Light lighteth also every pure angel, that he may be light
not in himself, but in God; from whom if an angel turn away, he becomes
impure, as are all those who are called unclean spirits, and are no longer
light in the Lord, but darkness in themselves, being deprived of the participation of Light eternal. For evil has no positive nature; but the loss of good
has received the name "evil."[23]

The first evil will had no efficient cause, but a deficient one, since it loved
its own power and not the giver of that power. It was thus deficient in
love.

[22] *Tractatus in Johannis evangelium* 4.11. See above, Chapter 17.1.
[23] *City of God* 11.9. Quotations are from the translation of Dods 1950.

In the grand scheme of the *City of God*, this division becomes the origin of the two cities, the heavenly and the earthly, whose contrary natures and tendencies explain the whole of cosmic and human history.[24] Despite the strong debt to Manichaeism,[25] this opposition preserves and extends the ethical and eschatological dualism of Paul, and denies the ultimate cosmological dualism of Mani. The metaphor of two cities, like the Irenaean idea of apostasy as a state of mind, enables Augustine to avoid both the total opposition of body and spirit of the Gnostic heresy, and also the dangerous helplessness implicit in the popular idea of a cosmic redemptive battle fought out literally between Christ and Satan. The two cities are two universal tendencies in human and cosmic history.[26] In this way Augustine could preserve the importance of Paul's theory that redemption is liberation, without obscuring the central idea that what we are liberated from is ourselves.

What distinguishes this Augustinian dualism from the Manichaean is essentially the account of the origin of things. On the one hand is a lapsed monism, on the other an original duality. But the Valentinian myth of the demiurge tells a similar story of a divine being whose ambition led him astray, so Augustine also insists on a second or divine perspective, according to which the apparent duality of the earthly city may be seen as a part of the divine, and already fully unified, structure. Even hell *fits*. Most of the time we are bound by the dualistic perspective of the earthly city we inhabit and so cannot see the role of sin in the total scheme. But we are also granted moments of illumination, of grace, which assure us even of the beneficence of evil according to the divine and eternal pattern. From this point of view there is no real battle between opposing forces since the substance of the one apparent force, evil, is illusory.

Not only is this an extremely powerful illusion, however, but it is even a necessary illusion for the present constitution of human life in the earthly city. It is at this point that, the Pelagians argued, Augustine contradicts himself. Though evil as substance may be illusory, its effects are very real, leading even to eternal damnation. What is more, argued Augustine, we are born with a sinful nature, in bondage to sin, and only grace can liberate us. Our own efforts are worth nothing, since they originate in sin. Many people are predestined, like the fallen angels, never to escape this illusion, so that for them the earthly city—a temporary abode for the elect who experience grace—becomes an eternal hell. Like the two births of the Chris-

[24] *City of God* 11.19–20.
[25] Adam 1952, but cf. Rist 1972 and J. B. Russell 1981:196–208.
[26] P. Brown 1967:320.

tian, these people die two deaths: one to the body, the second to God. Ever since the first day of creation, their separation from the light is eternal.[27]

To the Pelagian, or to the unsympathetic modern, Augustine's position may seem like no more than an ugly and ultimately untenable compromise between doctrines of his opponents. To the Pelagian he argued the inescapable reality of sin, the bondage imposed by the earthly perspective, the separation from God; to the Manichaean he argued the insubstantiality of evil, the divine perspective, derived mostly from the Neoplatonic tradition. Indeed, ever since this paradox was first fully enunciated by Augustine, Christian culture has been continually tempted to separate yet again the two linked perspectives; to argue, like the liberal seventeenth-century churchmen among whom the anonymous *Letter of Resolution Concerning Origen* of 1661 stirred a sympathetic response, that hell and the devil were not eternal;[28] or, like the many medieval and strongly Manichaean heretics, Bogomils, Paulicians, Cathars, to argue that the world itself was damned together with all, or almost all, its inhabitants[29]—a position that had at times its attractions for Augustine and for Calvin. Yet one could argue that the church has kept its power because it retained both perspectives:

> The two complementary ideas at the very core of Christian culture—that humanity was basically saved by Christ's coming, and that since the exile from Paradise every human being is basically condemned if we consider his natural status alone and set grace aside—should be considered jointly . . . in order to counteract the jaunty optimism or the despair that could result if they were dealt with separately.[30]

Once Augustine first developed the theory of original sin, sometime between 400 and 406,[31] he was deeply concerned with keeping both dangers constantly in view. The twin threats of despair and of excessive optimism would be continually denounced until the end of his life. Both these dangerous emotional states derive, he believed, from a misapprehension of the relationship of man and God. It was through the doctrine of sin and grace that he tried to articulate the correct relationship and thus transform

---

[27] See below, Chapter 25, but also the general discussion in Hick 1966.
[28] Walker 1964:124–26.
[29] Nigg 1962:177–91; Loos 1974.
[30] Kolakowski 1974:8.
[31] Courcelle 1950; TeSelle 1970:258–66.

these psychological states. The idea of sin was necessary to counter the perverse idea that evil had any independent substance; the idea of grace was essential to oppose the notion that man could be saved by his own efforts. Both heresies denied the distance of man from God and thus failed to read correctly the situation of man within the cosmic structure. The heretics misunderstood the relationship of psychology to cosmology.

It was Augustine's early contact with the Manichaeans which had led him to perceive the importance of this relationship. Once he had undergone the psychological change described in the *Confessions*, he had to reassess the cosmology in which he had previously believed; the Manichaean cosmology no longer corresponded to psychological truth. But he now understood also the error that had led him to be a Manichaean "Auditor" for nine years. It was the same error that had caused the fall of the angel and the fall of man: the illusion that the soul and God have the same nature. This assumption of equality with God is the typical form of pride. Even in the *City of God*, written many years after he abandoned the Manichaean church, he continued to denounce it for this error, the real source of all its other misapprehensions:

> The Manichaeans would not drivel, or rather rave, in such a style as this, if they believed the nature of God to be, as it is, unchangeable and absolutely incorruptible, and subject to no injury; and if moreover they held in Christian sobriety, that the soul which has shown itself capable of being altered for the worse by its own will, and of being corrupted by sin, and so, of being deprived of the light of eternal truth—that this soul, I say, is not a part of God, nor of the same nature as God, but is created by him, and is far different from its creator.[32]

Because they have turned from God to the self, and believe they find the divine (and evil) substance in themselves, they are blind to the distance that separates them from God. Their doctrine prevents them from understanding the world from any but the fallen point of view, sunk as they are in darkness. They cannot experience the goodness of God and the illumination that it brings. The Christian and the Manichaean points of view are the equivalent of the two cities, the heavenly and the earthly, the eternal and the temporal, the world of God and the world of Satan.

Evil appears to have substance only while man is ensnared in the earthly, self-centered point of view. If he can let go of the self and turn back toward God, then the substance of evil naturally evaporates. "For no

[32] *City of God* 11.22.

nature at all is evil; this is a name for nothing but the want of good."[33]
Conversion is a vision, accorded by God's grace, which makes possible
this second, cosmic point of view. Once he is thus enlightened, Augustine
can understand that everything, even darkness and sin, has its place within
the divine structure. Evil, which had before seemed equal with good, is
now seen to be a function of the selfish will and has its use.

> Even the wicked will is a strong proof of the goodness of [the devil's] na-
> ture. But God, as he is the supremely good Creator of good natures, so is
> he of evil wills the most just ruler; so that, while they make an evil use of
> good natures, He makes a good use even of evil wills. Accordingly, He
> caused the devil (good by God's creation, wicked by his own will) to be cast
> down from his high position, and to become the mockery of his angels—
> that is, He caused his temptation to benefit those whom he wishes to injure
> by them.[34]

Similarly man's evil, sin, becomes the grounds for the reception of grace.

The theory of sin and grace, with its concomitant doctrines of the two
points of view and the two cities, the heavenly and the earthly, the divine
and the merely human, did not come all at once to Augustine. He developed it only with great difficulty out of his constant wrestling with Manichaeism, and his gradual understanding of the story of his own life. Until
he could understand the structure of his life and its relationship to the
structure of sin and grace, of light and darkness, that operates everywhere
and at once, he was always in danger either of Pelagian optimism or Manichaean pessimism. Even when he had found the way to reconcile the two
in an understanding of the entire cosmic pattern, it was still possible to
misinterpret his writings in one direction or the other, even for the two
points of view to get confused yet again. The very nature of controversy
is to force the participants to an extreme statement of their point of view
which endangers, though it may not destroy, the balance of the dialectic.

[33] *City of God*, cf. 14.13. See also Rist 1972:233–35. For a different but often persuasive
view, see J. B. Russell 1981:200–208.
[34] *City of God* 11.17.

TWENTY-FOUR

AUGUSTINE'S CONFESSIONS:

THE TWO TREES

At some point before or during the writing of the *Confessions*, Augustine came to see that grace was the key both to his own life and to the cosmic structure. He was thus led to reinterpret his own earlier conversion to Christianity in the light of this new understanding. He now saw his own movement through sin to grace as a recapitulation in miniature of the narrative pattern always at work in the cosmos—the liberation from the bondage of the two wills by "prevenient grace descending." The two points of view he had held in his life, the pagan, or earthly, and the regenerate, transformed view that grace had given him—"the renewing of my mind," as he puts it—were now, he saw, related to each other in the same way that the fall of Satan was related, in the cosmic scheme, to the divine gift of Christ, the light that came into the darkness. The light had always been there, but for a time-bound and sin-bound world it appeared to come, by means of the divine sign of the cross, at a particular time in history, the moment when the call was heard. This intuition enabled him to write the *Confessions*. But this new understanding of the workings of grace brought with it a chastening sense of the distance that separates man from God without grace and wrought a profound change in Augustine's life—virtually a new conversion—and forced him to revise deeply his earlier optimistic and Neoplatonizing version of the Christian story. He had found a way to reconcile the disparate world-views of Manichaeism and Platonism, of what became later the earthly and the heavenly cities, but only at the expense of his personal strength, the overconfidence of his earlier Platonic rejection of Mani and his followers.

Several scholars have suggested either that Augustine's account of his conversion—the famous "*Tolle, lege*" episode—is largely a fabrication or at best that he misremembers his own recent past. Louis Gourdon apparently convinced William James that the account was "premature," that the conversion was to Neoplatonic spiritualism and only a halfway stage to Christianity.[1] More recently, Pierre Courcelle has argued that the elaborate stylization of the narrative, with its references to Hercules at the crossroads, a conventional Stoic theme, casts doubt upon its accuracy.[2]

Accurate or not, what we need to see in this story of his life is precisely that: a narrative solution to a serious psychological and theological crisis. "How shall I *tell* it?" he asks.[3] Augustine found a way to tell his own story that was also, he thought, the way the cosmic story was always being told by God. His own life and the cosmic myth had the same narrative structure. Hence his insistence on the power of grace, for his own moment of insight recapitulated the original and continuing action of God. What happened to Augustine beneath the fig tree was, in his own narrative view, not simply the emotional release, a function of psychological mechanisms, that William James read there. It was a moment of grace, the acceptance of the divine gift through the inspired words of Paul. Grace reached out into his sin and called forth his will out of its bondage. Light came into the darkness, the Word was made flesh, and the divine and the human were reunited yet again. All falls into place, and he has understood the divine structure.

> Why is it that in our part of the creation there is this alternation of defeat and progress, of hurt and reconciliation? Is this the rhythm that you gave to the world when from the highest of the heavens to the lowest things of earth, from the beginning to the end of the ages, from the angel to the worm, you allotted appropriate places and times to good things of every kind and to all your righteous works? (8.3)

Just so, his own conversion has been preceded by his mistakes, both the preliminary illumination of his Neoplatonic phase, recounted in Book Seven, and the Manichaean error—denounced yet again immediately before he tells the fig-tree story. The gift of grace has enabled him to understand the place in his life of the Manichaean heresy. It was the error that led him to the truth.

The structure of the conversion scene follows this progression. Driven by the tumult in his heart, he moves out into the garden, symbolically parallel both to Eden and to Gethsemane. His friend Alypius follows.

---

[1] W. James 1961:147.

[2] Courcelle 1952. Apart from the objections listed in O'Meara 1980:183, Courcelle's view of the relation of autobiography to narrative is rather naive.

[3] Augustine, *Confessions* 13.7. Subsequent references in this chapter are included in the text. The translation, again, is Warner 1963.

There he finds himself, like a yogi, capable of performing many unusual bodily movements, yet he is struck by the resistance of his soul to his will:

> It was easier for my body to obey the slightest intimation of the soul's will that the limbs should be put immediately in motion than it was for the soul to give obedience to itself so as to carry out by the mere act of willing what was its own great will. (8.8)

The mind orders itself to will, and it cannot. He prays for enlightenment to understand this absurdity. He finds that there are two wills, both incomplete: "Neither my will nor my unwillingness was whole and entire." Immediately he feels the threat of the old dualist error, but now he has the insight to refute it.

> Let them perish from your presence, God, as perish empty talkers and seducers of the soul, who, having observed that there are two wills in the act of deliberating, conclude from this that we have in us two minds of two different natures, one good and one evil. They themselves are truly evil when they hold these opinions, and they are just as capable of becoming good if they will realize the truth and agree with the truth, so that your apostle may say to them, "Ye were sometimes darkness, but now light in the Lord." But these people, by imagining that the nature of the soul is what God is, want to be light, not in the Lord, but in themselves, and the result is that they have become an even deeper darkness, since in their appalling arrogance they have gone further away from you. (8.10)

He is now able to transcend the error by the simple act of attributing it to himself. As he put it earlier at the moment of his preliminary illumination, he had tried by his own strength and had not understood the message of Christ's weakness. If sin originates in the failure of will, in the division of the self, one cannot look to one's self for the strength to overcome it. That is the Satanic error. Both wills originate not in some external substance but in the self.

> It was the same "I" throughout. But neither my will nor my unwillingness was whole and entire. So I fought with myself and was torn apart by myself. It was against my will that this tearing apart took place, but this was not an indication that I had another mind of a different nature; it was simply the punishment which I was suffering in my own mind. It was not I, therefore, who caused it, but the sin that dwells in me, and being a son of Adam, I was suffering for his sin which was more freely committed. (8.10)

He continues to refute the Manichaeans with a series of rational arguments enlightened by his knowledge of the source of this error. Then he
returns to more detail about the nature of his own divided self, his own
particular problem with lust. Finally comes the "huge storm which rose
up within me bringing with it a huge downpour of tears." Then the
child's voice, like the voice of grace, chanting "*Tolle, lege,*" and the words
of grace he reads in Paul.[4]

No longer is he the battleground of an eternal warfare between alien
substances. The pattern has changed through the renewing of his mind.
The substance of evil, the illusion of self-sufficiency, has evaporated, and
now the Manichaeans are seen as *empty* talkers. The new pattern is a
movement, a progression like the shape of this description, from error to
truth, from darkness to light, from sin to grace.

Augustine continues in the second part of the *Confessions* to argue that
this same divine pattern is at work on the cosmic level. His analysis of the
first five verses of Genesis, the account of the creation on the first day, expounds the same relationship of finite nature to the grace of God that we
have seen in the account of his conversion. The "Fiat Lux" of the first day
is God's call to the spiritual creation to turn toward himself and be illumined. The division of light from darkness is the separation of those who
respond to the call from those who reject it. Eventually this verse of Genesis will become, in the *City of God*, the archetype of human and angelic
history, the moment when the two cities were founded: the heavenly city
that responds to grace, and the earthly city that by the fall of the demons
draws the human race into its territory.[5]

But here in the *Confessions* Augustine is concerned to show the relationship to the pattern he has perceived in his own life. He meditates on the
darkness of the deep and the Spirit moving above it, and it becomes an
image of conversion, "dark in respect to the flux and the disorder of its
spiritual formlessness, until it became converted to Him from whom it
received its humble degree of life and by His illumination became a life of
beauty" (13.5). He continues a little later:

> So from the beginning was the Spirit borne preeminent above the waters.
> To whom can I tell it, and how can I tell of the weight of concupiscence
> dragging us toward that steep abyss, and of how charity raises us up by your
> spirit which was borne above the waters? To whom shall I tell it? How shall

4 For various efforts to explain this phrase, see O'Meara 1980:183–85.
5 *City of God* 11 and 12, exp. 11.19–90. See below, Chapter 25.

I tell it? For it is not in space that we sink down and are raised up again. The experience is very like this, but at the same time quite unlike. There are affections, there are loves, there is the uncleanness of our spirit flowing away downward in love of care and distraction, and there is your sanctity raising us upward in the love of freedom from care, so that to you we may lift up our hearts, where your Spirit is borne above the waters, and come to that supereminent peace, when our soul shall have passed through the waters that are without substance.

These two levels of divine activity are both implied in the words of Genesis, and the relationship becomes explicit in "Let us make man in our own image." Man is thus included in the cosmic structure and will he, nill he follows its pattern in imitation of God. Augustine's conversion has given him the insight by which he may understand both the course of his own life and the course of the universe as it is described in Genesis: he may "judge all things." Indeed, that is what is demanded of him, as he sees it, by the words "Let us make man in our own image." Now that "his mind has been renewed" he can look back upon the sins that preceded his conversion, including his dismal Manichaean period, and perceive their relationship to the whole, to the whole self he is now becoming, and to the whole world, which he can now begin to comprehend. He can see their place in the story.

He makes the connections explicit several times: "With regard to us there is a distinction of time when it is said 'We were darkness and we shall be made light.' " (13.10) The creation of light and darkness was, however, simultaneous, and it is only the phrasing, conforming to our time-bound state, that makes it sound as if darkness came first. In the same way, light was ever present in Augustine's darkness, but only now does he know that. "The angel fell, the soul of man fell, and they showed us the abyss in that deep darkness, the abyss for the whole spiritual creation, if from the beginning you had not said Let there be light." He continues, referring clearly to the theme that has dominated the book, the movement from darkness to light:

> For even in that miserable restlessness of spirits who fall away from you and discover their own darkness, bared of the garment of your light, you show us clearly enough how noble a thing is the rational creature which you have made, which for its peace and happiness can be contented with nothing less than you, and so cannot be contented with itself. For you, our God, will lighten our darkness. (13.8)

The autobiographical part of the *Confessions* is a *recollection* (10.11), a gathering together for himself of the events of his past that he experienced as separate, unrelated, dispersed, but which he now understands to have followed an order, a sequence that imitates the divine order. As Augustine tells the story of his own past, he oscillates between the two points of view, the enlightened and the dark, the present and the past, now immersed by the act of memory in the dark feel of past events, now praying to the illuminating God. Sin is relived through grace, in a renewed mind.

The first and second parts of the work, the human and the cosmic, are divided from and linked to each other by the long meditation of Book Ten. Here Augustine praises and examines the newly discovered relation of the mind to God, of time to eternity, of a man's memory to the timeless God who is discovered, somehow, beyond it (10.17). Memory is the great treasure palace in which are stored not only the external experiences of life or the ideas a man has thought and the information he has learned, but also inner light, the rational soul itself which enables us both to arrange the contents of memory and to perceive the great model according to which the organization may operate, the mind of God. Memory is the great transforming power once it is graced. The graced mind can begin, as Augustine begins in the second part of the *Confessions*, to extend itself, to comprehend the universal pattern perceived first in the particular life. Personal memory transcends personal time and becomes an image of the timeless, what was for Augustine the eternal present in the mind of God. The fallen past is redeemed and transformed by memory, as sin is redeemed by grace.

Following his divine model, the Christian scriptures, Augustine recollects his life according to the structure of sin and grace. In order to reveal the correspondence between the tree of knowledge with which the biblical story of man begins and the tree of life with which (in the final chapter of the Book of Revelation) the story ends, Augustine carefully organizes his own life around two equally symbolic trees: a pear tree and a fig tree. The episode of the pear tree, when he steals its fruit "solely for the joy I took in sinning, in the theft itself," is placed near the beginning of the work. The episode of the fig tree beneath which he suffers the transformation is placed carefully near the end of the autobiography.[6] The whole account of the passage between the two trees thus becomes a symbolic de-

---

[6] *Confessions* 2.4, 8.12, there being one chapter of autobiography on either end. See above, Chapter 16, and for the ambivalence of the tree motif in connection with the combat plot, see Chapters 1.3 and 10.1.

scription of the universal course of life, since the Fall: the movement downward, into the self, into sin and darkness—through the darkness, now confessed—to the light which had always, it turns out, been reaching downward to rescue the one lost. Hence the great moment of contrition, the flood of tears and the voice beneath the fig tree, is continually anticipated by other moments, glimmerings of the truth. As we read the book we are in continual expectation of this moment—the book is designed for us to expect it. Yet it comes only when it must, according to the inevitability of its own place in the divine and human plot.

There are several such anticipations, moments in which Augustine offers us the final illumination only to leave it incomplete until the time is ready, building for the reader and recollecting for himself the same tension, the almost unbearable desperation, which is necessary for genuine transformation. Of these moments the most significant is also the last before the final conversion (7.9). The difference between this moment and the genuine moment is central to an understanding of the work. At this point Augustine offers us the whole intellectual structure he worked out after the illumination, yet he refuses us the illumination itself. Just when we expect the present meditation to coincide with the moment of grace in his life, he draws back and says instead, "But this was not the way I thought then." The difference, as we learn from the description of the great moment itself, is chiefly an emotional one. Capable as his intellect was of receiving the gift, his emotional nature was still too protected, too haughtily self-reliant. Only when that sense of independence is broken can the divine power flood in. Only then can a man truly receive the divine sacrifice as it was and continues to be offered. In the end one does not understand the Incarnation with the mind, even in the flash of illumination. One receives it only in abandon, in emotional breakdown, in giving up.

> And then in the flash of a trembling glance, my mind arrived at That Which Is. Now indeed I saw your invisible things understood by the things which are made, but I had not the power to keep my eye steadily fixed. . . .
> I tried to find a way of gaining the strength necessary for enjoying you, but I could not find it until I embraced that Mediator between God and men . . . calling to me and saying I am the way, the truth, and the life, and mingling with our flesh that food which I lacked strength to take. (7.17–18)

He lacked the power, the strength to stay fixed, because he had not yet fully felt his own weakness: "I tried . . . ," but the strength comes only in weakness: "I was not humble enough to possess Jesus in his humility as my God, nor did I know what lesson was taught by his weakness."

Nevertheless, it was then that he understood the structure of sin, even if he was not yet equipped to experience the power of grace. The illumination is genuine but partial. It is the experience of loss, of separation, of distance from God—the experience of Paradise lost—without yet the experience of mystic union that complements and completes it. He understands the structure, but that structure is a barrier to its own removal, to the moment of its evaporation. He is still in time, not eternity. He returns to himself.

> With you to guide me, I entered into the innermost part of myself, and I was able to do this because you were my helper. I entered and I saw with my soul's eye (such as it was) an unchangeable light shining above this eye of my soul and above my mind. . . . (He who knows truth knows that light, and he who knows that light knows eternity. Love knows it.) . . . When I first knew you, you raised me up so that I could see that there was something to see and that I still lacked the ability to see it. And you beat back the weakness of my sight, blazing upon me with your rays, and I trembled in love and in dread, and I found that I was far distant from you, in a region of total unlikeness as if I were hearing your voice from on high saying: "I am the food of grown men. Grow and you shall feed upon me. And you will not, as with the food of the body, change me into yourself, but you will be changed into me." (7.10)

The words in parentheses in this passage are a comment from the point of view of the later regenerated self. The rest is the account of this partial truth, from which he still must grow. Yet he can now understand the place of apparent evil: "To you then there is no such thing as evil. And the same is true not only of you but of your whole creation, since there is nothing outside it to break in and corrupt the order you have imposed on it." Thus he disposes, finally, of the Manichaean universe. Instead, he explains now, in some parts of the universe

> there are some things which are considered evil because they do not harmonize with other parts; yet with still other parts they do harmonize and are good and they are good in themselves. And all these things which do not fit in with each other do fit in with that lower part of creation we call the earth, which has its own cloudy and windy sky which again is fitting to it. . . . For things from the earth show that you are to be praised—dragons and all deeps, fire, hail, snow, ice, and stormy wind, which fulfill thy work. . . .
>
> It is the mark of an unsound mind to be displeased with any single thing in your creation, and so it was with me, when I was displeased with many

of the things which you had made. And because my soul dared not be dis-
pleased with my God, I refused to admit that whatever did displease it was
yours. And from this point it had gone on to hold the view that there are
two substances, and here it found no rest and only talked perversely. (7.13–
14)

A way has been found to let go of the Manichaean heresy that had seemed
so natural, a way to let go of the substance of evil upon which that doctrine was founded. In the same way, as the whole book reveals, a way was
found to let go of the impulse to sin, to pass beyond it to the universal
structure of which it is part. All men, he sees, pass this way, through sin,
and some are granted the gift that awaits on the way—grace and absolution. Through sin, the tree of the knowledge of good and evil, the pear
tree—to grace, the cross, the tree of life, the fig tree.

The substantiality of evil is an illusion, and with it the notion that the
devil can achieve his own purposes, since everything, insofar as it runs
away from God, fails of its purpose, though it continues to form a part of
God's great purpose. Augustine could not, of course, maintain this divine, eternal viewpoint. As soon as one loses it—as one must when the
moment of illumination is over, however much the memory may strive
to retain it—evil recovers its substance and power. Man always slips back
into sin; the Fall is ever recurrent. And yet the memory can retain at least
the knowledge of the structure, even when it has lost the immediate presence of the source of the structure. Grace is as present as sin.[7] The oscillation of Augustine's thought always tries to maintain the simultaneous
presence of both parts of the paradox, even if they can truly merge only
in moments of the greatest understanding. If the Pelagian, or Platonic,
Augustine threatens dominance, he will dig for the Manichaean, descending into his darkness. If the Manichaean darkness becomes too enticing,
then he will summon the Pelagian.

In the early development of Christianity, of which the Augustinian
synthesis is the culmination, the role of Satan is crucial to the avoiding of
both errors. If Neoplatonic or Pelagian optimism gains too much appeal,
if one basks too readily in the divine benevolence, then one can turn to the
doctrine that the world is in fact ruled by Satan, the prince of darkness,
the doctrine from which all these other teachings stem. On the other
hand, if the Manichaean gloom gets too dark, then the church remembers

[7] In his last work, Augustine notes that the angels, unsupported by God's help, might fall
as Satan had fallen and become a new race of devils (*Opus imperfectum contra Julianum* 5.57).
See Rist 1972:233.

the teaching about the origin and fate of Satan, that he is not an eternally existing principle, but created—that Satan is himself ruled and thwarted, and that man is granted access to the divine.

For this reason, the *Confessions* contains not only a personal autobiography but an account of the origin of the whole system of which his life is merely a mirror. The same pattern is at work in the cosmos. Both parts of Augustine's work celebrate the majesty of God and the creation of this divine structure of which sin is a part. Cosmology and psychology are two ways to approach the same mystery. Just as the intuition of their connection with each other had enabled Augustine to write the *Confessions*, so the shape of the book itself connects the two. And it is the connection itself that redeems. Gnosticism or Manichaeism were based on this same connection, but their understanding of both parts was perverse.[8] The *Confessions* sets out to correct their errors and to oppose an equally self-consistent and total picture to the Manichaean, but one which will have the advantage of incorporating the central doctrine of Christianity omitted by Mani—the Word made flesh. The first part of the *Confessions* is Augustine's answer to Manichaean psychology. The second part, following the great meditation on memory and mind, the faculty by means of which the link of cosmos and psyche is perceived, is his answer to the Gnostic and Manichaean distortions of the cosmos. It takes, naturally enough in view of the Gnostic impact, the form of a commentary on Genesis.

[8] On Gnosticism as the cosmic projection or justification of personal and psychological dramas, see Jonas 1970:34–86, 241–87. See also Burkitt 1932 and Dodds 1965:13–20, whose approaches perhaps fall foul of psychologism. A more balanced view will include the political aspect; see Pagels 1979, 1983.

TWENTY-FIVE

AUGUSTINE AND GENESIS

T HE FIRST of Augustine's several commentaries on Genesis was an attack on the Manichaeans (*De Genesi contra Manichaeos*), written in 388–389, some two years after his conversion. Thereafter he wrote an unfinished commentary, a complete commentary in twelve books (*De Genesi ad litteram*), and several extended commentaries in other works, the most important of which are the long passages in the *Confessions* and the *City of God*. In each of these subsequent commentaries he continues to denounce the Manichaean heresies, and he even argues that their heresies are foretold figuratively in the text of Genesis itself.[1] The need for such a commentary was thus the same as that which inspired the earlier fathers: the need to refute heresy and also account for it within the narrative system. Out of the separate doctrines of his predecessors he built a complex myth that, with minor revisions, would dominate the church henceforth. Like the Gnostics generally, Augustine believed that a knowledge of origins was essential to the correct understanding of one's own life, but unlike them he believed that Genesis was the conscious expression of God's will, not the devil's, and that diligent thought could bring him, insofar as man can, to understand that will.[2]

Only by a full account of the divine structure—the two cities and their origins—could Augustine resolve the paradox that evil is only the absence of good, a voluntary turning away from God to the self (and especially to the body), and yet that evil personified could take action, the very action that led the rest of us into the power of evil. What he needed to do was not so much to account logically and rationally for the problem of evil—that, after all, was the root of the whole Manichaean fallacy, and as Augustine well knew, the source of its appeal to him in his earlier years. What he needed, what he felt the church needed, was a narrative that would interpret the will of God.

---

[1] *De Genesi contra Manichaeos* 2.26.
[2] *City of God* 12.6–7.

1. *Ambrose on Eden*

A brief comparison with Augustine's own teacher, Ambrose, who also
developed an exegesis of Genesis, will demonstrate both how disparate
were the interpretations still current and thus how far the church needed
to go before it could achieve the synthesis for which Augustine was responsible. Ambrose was mainly content to reiterate the allegorical interpretation common ever since Origen incorporated it from Philo. There
had been a premundane descent of spiritual energy into the physical
world, but whereas for the Gnostics the "fall" of man was the beginning
of salvation, it was for Philo a further descent, this time into physical bodies—the newly acquired "clothes" or animal skins of Adam and Eve. The
body itself was thus the punishment of sin.[3] This makes the Creation itself
what it was for Valentinian Gnostics and for Mani: a means of restraining
evil within physical limits. Augustine was eager to reject this possibility,
since according to the doctrine he found in Genesis the creation was
wholly good. For Augustine, it was not the flesh itself but its mortality
which was the punishment of sin.[4]

According to Ambrose's version of Philo (whom he does not name
since he had not been a Christian), the sin itself "had been committed by
the man as a result of the pleasure of the senses. . . . There was one before
us who . . . saw in the woman sensation, what the Greeks call *aisthēsis*,
and in the man who was deceived the mind, what the Greeks call *nous*."[5]
Ambrose agreed with this analysis. For Philo, the tree of knowledge was
"prudence, the virtue that occupies the middle position"[6] and which God
could not possibly have forbidden. The Fall thus had nothing to do with
any forbidden fruit, since, as the Alexandrian tradition taught, the faculty
of distinguishing good from evil had been present from the creation. Ambrose offered a weak emendation of Philo at this point:

> Since God knew that that man's affections, once endued with knowledge,
> would more readily incline toward craft than toward perfect prudence . . .
> he wished to expel craft from Paradise, and . . . to put there the desire of life
> and the discipline of piety. Therefore he commanded man to eat of every

---

[3] Philo, *Quaestiones et solutiones in Genesim* 1.53; cf. Origen, *Contra Celsum* 4.40. See
above, Chapter 21.

[4] Augustine attacks Origen, e.g., in *City of God* 11.23.

[5] Ambrose, *De paradiso* 1.5–6; 11.51. For Philo and Origen, see above, Chapter 21 nn.
23–27.

[6] Philo, *De opificio mundi* 54. See the analysis of J. M. Evans 1968:70–74, which I have used
shamelessly in this section.

tree which is in Paradise, but that of the tree of knowledge of good and evil he should not eat.[7]

This vague notion of craft (*ars*, with its double connotations of skill and deceit) did little to solve the problems of the Genesis narrative and in no way related to the rest of the allegorical interpretation. Ambrose himself was clearly content. Not so Augustine.

2. Augustine on Eden: The Anti-Manichaean Genesis

Augustine held, in part, to the allegorical approach of Ambrose, but he revised the major implications of the narrative to put the violation of the tree back at the center. It still symbolizes man's middle state, but it becomes again, once it has been tasted, the tree of the knowledge of good and evil. The reason Adam and Eve eat it is pride. Adam and Eve recover in this early Augustinian version their literal identities as complete human beings rather than aspects of the soul, even though the setting of their experience remains allegorical. Eden is the "life of the blessed." That life is lost as soon as the blessed soul turns away from God and in upon itself in the desire to enjoy its own power.

> And the tree of the knowledge of good and evil also signifies the middle state of the soul and its ordained wholeness, for this tree also was planted in the middle of paradise. It is called the tree of the knowledge of good and evil for this reason: if a soul which ought to be reaching forward to what is ahead—that is, to God—and forgetting that which is behind (Phil. 3.13)—that is the pleasures of the body—leaves God and turns in upon itself, and desires to enjoy its own power as if without God, pride swells up within, which is the beginning of every sin. And when the punishment for this sin follows, it learns by experience the difference between the good it has left and the evil into which it has fallen. And to that soul this will be the experience of having tasted of the fruit of the tree of the discernment of good and evil.[8]

This concept of sin was born out of Augustine's contact with the Milanese circle of Neoplatonists. We have seen how Origen's myth of the angelic fall grew out of his Platonic thought, and a similar process seems to have taken place in Augustine's mind, but with the difference that he applies his

---

[7] Ambrose, *Epistles* 45.3–8.
[8] Augustine, *De Genesi contra Manichaeos* 2.9, my trans.

theory of sin first to the fall of Adam before he extends it to include the
angel. Plotinus, himself a reformed Gnostic, had explained as follows:

> What can it be that has brought the souls to forget the father, that world, to
> ignore at once themselves and it? The evil that has overtaken them has its
> source in self-will [*tolma*], in the entry into the sphere of process, and in the
> primal differentiation with the desire for self-ownership.[9]

That is, sin consists in a desire to be independent of God, a theory that
Augustine develops at length and in light of which he reads the first three
chapters of Genesis. The theory gives him a reply to the Manichaean idea
of the two souls of man and to the corresponding idea of two independent
principles, Light and Darkness.[10]

Thus the tree in the garden ceases to be evil or poisonous in the material
sense; it becomes symbolic of the sin, which is pride. The fruit of the tree
is the experience of knowing the difference between what the soul had and
what it now is. The punishment is inevitable because it is itself the experience—"of good lost and evil got," as Milton put it. "Nessun maggior
dolore che ricordarsi del tempo felice Nella miseria," as Dante's Paolo and
Francesca discover in hell. Augustine thus integrated the allegorical with
the literal interpretation of the story, bringing back the tree of knowledge
into the Platonic and Philonic idea that sin is the turning away from God
to the self, from the spiritual to the carnal. "It desires to enjoy its own
power as if without God, pride swells up within, which is the beginning
of every sin."

But Augustine's most significant revision of his teacher's interpretation
of the Fall lies not in the nature of the sin so much as in the author of it.
For Philo and Ambrose the serpent who tempts in Genesis was not Satan
or a fallen angel. He was interpreted according to the allegorical legacy of
the Watcher myth to be "the pleasure of the senses." Augustine retained
through his doctrine of concupiscence the symbolic connection of the Fall
with sensual appetite, but the serpent himself he identified with Satan.
Several earlier fathers, following the hint in Revelation 12.9, had already
suggested this identification—Origen especially, Basil, and John
Chrysostom[11]—but it was by no means general doctrine, as Ambrose's
version reveals. What led Augustine to insist upon it, as with Irenaeus or

---

[9] Plotinus, *Enneades* 5.1.1; cf. 2.9.6. See Rist 1972:242. For Augustine's Platonism, see
P. Brown 1967:88–127 and Armstrong 1972. On *tolma*, see Dillon in Layton (ed.) 1981: vol.
1, 362, cf. 375.

[10] *De duabus animabus contra Manichaeos* was written during the next three years (389–92).
See P. Brown 1967:74.

[11] See above, Chapters 16, 19, and 21.

Origen before, was his need to answer his opponents with a power as great as the one they contended had created man's evil condition. Following the methods of his training in rhetoric and dialectic, Augustine took over the major weapon of his opponents and used it against them.

The composite figure of Satan, the New Testament's tempter of Jesus and eschatological tyrant, had been identified by the Gnostics with the Yahweh of Genesis. Augustine retained the scope and power of this tyrant but identified him not with the creator but with his opponent in Genesis, the serpent. And he was able to tell a convincing story that made the integration complete.

Augustine's first attempt to identify the serpent, in the anti-Manichaean Genesis commentary, reveals the inherent difficulties of the effort to bring together literal and allegorical interpretive methods. His main problem at this stage was to explain how there could be a literal devil in an allegorical paradise, which according to his interpretation was "the life of the blessed."

> The serpent signifies the devil, who was certainly not simple [as the life of blessedness is simple]. For he is said to be wiser than all the beasts, which figuratively implies the devil's cunning. It is not said that the serpent was in Paradise, but that the serpent was among the beasts whom God made. For Paradise, as I said before, means the life of the blessed, in which there was now no serpent, because he was already the devil; and he had fallen from his own blessedness, because he did not stand in the truth.

He goes on to wrestle with a problem we have noted in the Adam books: the ontological status of the devil-serpent, and how he could speak to Eve.

> No more should it be wondered at how he could speak to the woman, since she was in Paradise and he was not; for either she was not in Paradise as in a place, but rather as in the state of blessedness: or even if there is such a place as is called Paradise, in which Adam and his wife corporally lived, should we then understand the entrance of the devil in a corporal sense? Not at all like this; rather in a spiritual sense, as the apostle says, "According to the prince of the power of the air, the spirit who works in the children of disobedience" (Eph. 2.2). Did he then appear to them visibly, or as if in a physical place gain access to those in whom he works? Not at all, but in wonderful ways he suggests whatever he can through their thoughts. These suggestions they resist, and truly say what the apostle also said: "For we are not ignorant of his cunning" (2 Cor. 2.11).[12]

---

[12] *De Genesi contra Manichaeos* 2.14. For the devil-serpent as both inside and outside Paradise, see above, Chapter 12.5; and for Judas, see Chapter 17.2.

And another proof-text, already a significant step in the New Testament context, now confirms this view. "For how did he gain access to Judas, when he persuaded him to betray the Lord? Was it in a place, or did he appear to him through his eyes? No, it was thus, as it is written, that he entered into his heart" (Luke 22.3). So that important episode, the entry of Satan into Judas, by which the gospel writers had elevated the human story to the proportions of the cosmic combat, now becomes also the link between cosmic and human levels at the beginnings of the plot.

The description continues with the kind of insight into universal meaning which would later inform the *Confessions*:

> Even now nothing different happens in one of us, when someone falls into sin, than what happened in those three, the serpent, the woman, and the man. For first comes a suggestion, whether through thought, or through the bodily senses, by sight, or touch, or hearing, or taste, or smell. When the suggestion is made, if our cupidity does not move us to sin, then the cunning of the serpent will be excluded. If this movement happens, however, then we will have been persuaded, just as the woman was.

The story of Eden is, in the manner of liturgical myth, reenacted continually in the life of every Christian as the devil continues to insinuate himself by suggestion.

The noticeable reluctance in this passage to treat the story entirely as a literal, physical event, despite the requirement that God's word be historically accurate, was due in part to the defensive posture of the church in general and of Augustine in particular: the simple, earthy tale must be protected from the sophisticated ridicule of philosophers or heretics. Philo and Ambrose both used allegory in this manner. Augustine, however, was able, like Origen, to transform the simple identifications of literal fact with moral reference that allegory required into an elaborate and much more sophisticated system of figural and symbolic meanings.

Even in the confusion of this early text, for example, the symbolic interpretation has enabled Augustine to bring together two parts of the devil's story that the church had not yet successfully integrated: the serpent and the prince. The serpent of Genesis can now be seen as the symbolic equivalent of the "prince of the power of the air" in Ephesians. They both work in the same way, invisibly, within the soul of "the children of disobedience." These children, like Judas, are all sinners, and thus *a fortiori* Adam and Eve were infected by the same power.

As Augustine developed this symbolic method of interpretation, he

saw that it could explain several other difficult biblical texts. A single
symbolic system could be constructed (it was already there, in his view)
to which all the various clues of the scriptures and the patristic commentaries could lead him. The allegorical approach could not also include the
literal events of the narrative; the very existence of the allegory meant that
the stories of scripture were not event but metaphor. Another way must
be found to avoid the difficulties of literal serpents in allegorical gardens.

But the new symbolic approach did not abandon the allegory so much
as include it within a richer, more inclusive and more flexible system. The
new system included both the allegories of Ambrose and the figural and
typological meanings that Justin, Irenaeus, and Origen had provided
from the prophecies and visions of the inspired voices, Isaiah, Ezekiel, and
John of Patmos. All were modes by which the mind might be transformed, avenues for the Light that had illumined the world at its creation,
returned to redeem it, and continued to shine for the eager believer. The
system of symbolic interpretation was not fully developed until Augustine worked at *De doctrina Christiana*. The idea of a language of signs there
set forth was the result of his painful meditations on the effects of the Fall.
Adam and Eve found that now they could communicate only by the
clumsy method of language and gesture. A dislocation of consciousness
produced the distance between the inquiring intellect and the object of its
search. The word of God was veiled, in order to exercise the seeker. This
veil, the language of sign and symbol, was both the distance of the mind
from God and the avenue by which the philosophic searcher might reach
him.[13] All the biblical texts, with which the theory of signs is chiefly concerned, suggest elusive but accessible implications. These symbolic
meanings can then be shifted around until they form together a coherent
figurative system.

Under the figural aspect the story of Adam becomes several different
tales at once. Adam, a type of the man who thereafter leaves his father and
mother and cleaves to his wife (Gen. 3.24), becomes Christ, who left his
Father and came into the world (John 16.28) "not in the turning away of
sin, as the apostates relinquish God, but by appearing as a man among

---

[13] Markus 1972 and B. D. Jackson 1972 both stress the originality of Augustine's theory
of signs, whether as a view of language or as a means of scriptural hermeneutics. The theory
is chiefly set forth in *De doctrina Christiana* 2.31.48—2.39.59, written during 396 and 397,
although the work was not completed until 426; see Robertson 1958. My argument suggests
that we find the beginnings of the theory already in *De Genesi contra Manichaeos*, from which
the next quotations are taken. See also *De Genesi ad litteram* 8.2.5.

men, when the Word was made flesh, and living among us."[14] All the biblical texts thus point not only to the single truth of charity but also to the
same process: light continues to shine in darkness.

By extension of this argument, the temptation episode becomes also an
archetype of the relation between truth and heresy, itself a continuing
process. The serpent is the devil, but he is also, what is symbolically the
same thing, the Manichaean threat to the unity of the Christian "beatam
vitam."

> If only we too would enjoy every tree of paradise, that is, spiritual delights
> . . . and not touch the tree planted in the middle of paradise, the tree of the
> knowledge of good and evil. That is, if only we would not take pride in our
> own nature, which is of the middle, as I said before, lest, deceived, we ex
> perience the difference between the simple catholic faith and the fallacies of
> the heretics. For thus we come to the discernment of good and evil. "There
> must be heresies," says [Paul], "that what is proved may be made manifest
> among you."[15]

As in the *Confessions*, this Pauline warrant opens the way for much ink to
be flung at the heretics.

> For that serpent, according to the prophetic meaning of the text, signifies
> the poison of the heretics, and especially of those Manichaeans and whoever
> attacks the Old Testament. For there is no more obvious prophecy I think,
> than those heretics in that serpent, or rather that he should be shunned in
> them. For no one more brazenly or fulsomely promises the knowledge of
> good and evil. And in man himself, just as in the tree planted in the middle
> of Paradise, they presume to be the ones to demonstrate this discernment.

So Augustine shows himself aware that Manichaeism was one more
Gnostic religion, one more in the series that Paul had warned the Corinthians against. Claims to impart special or secret knowledge are the same
as the devil's.

> Take even those words, "Ye shall be as gods." Is this not the claim of the
> heretics, when through their proud vanity they try to persuade others to the
> same pride and affirm that the soul is naturally that which only God is? And
> to whom does the opening of the eyes of the flesh apply more than to those
> who leave the inner light of wisdom and drive men to adore that sun which
> is seen by the eyes of the flesh? Indeed, all heretics in general deceive with

[14] *De Genesi contra Manichaeos* 2.24.27.
[15] Ibid., 2.25–26.

the promise of knowledge, and attack those whom they find with a simple faith. . . . They do not listen to the Apostle who says: "I fear that as the serpent seduced Eve in his cunning, so also your senses will be corrupted" (2 Cor. 11.3). Therefore I think that those heretics are prefigured in this prophecy. . . . This serpent, that is, this error of the heretics against which the Apostle thus warned us, . . . this error crawls on its breast and belly and eats the earth.

Its breast, Augustine suggests, is pride, which puffs the heretics up; its belly represents carnal desire, which they falsely attribute not to themselves but to the powers of darkness; they eat the earth in their curiosity to search out spiritual secrets with an earthly eye. The figural or prophetic method thus allows Augustine to extend the doctrine of Irenaeus that the heretics reenact the first apostasy and are under the control of the devil. It says so right there in Genesis. The relationship is also reciprocal. The devil, the serpent of Genesis, prefigures those who turn away later from Christ and the church. As Paul warned, the serpent is still at work.

When he describes the sentence passed on the Genesis serpent, Augustine again goes to the New Testament for his explication. Both the devil and man were punished by getting what they wanted. But the purpose of the punishment was different for man and devil. For man the punishment is a "correction" so that he may know the extent of his separation from the initial blessedness he enjoyed and the prospects of future bliss once he had earned angelic status.[16] For Satan, however, the punishment is eternal, though it also acts as a warning to man. As Augustine describes the fallen state of the devil, he draws upon other scriptural texts to elucidate the meager words of Genesis and fits them to his developing cosmic and symbolic structure. Satan, he says, gets precisely what he sought: power. But he is unhappy in the power he gets, for he knows what he has lost.

Now the serpent is not interrogated, but receives his punishment first, because he could not confess his sin, nor had any way to excuse himself. The actual damnation of the devil is not mentioned now; this is reserved for the last judgment, about which the Lord speaks when he says: "Go into eternal fire, which is prepared for the devil and his angels" (Matt. 25.41). But this punishment is mentioned as a warning to us. For his punishment is to hold in his power those who defy the precepts of God. This is what is set forth in those words by which sentence is passed on him; and it is a greater punishment in that he now enjoys such a miserable power, who before he fell used

[16] Ibid., 2.28, and cf. *De Genesi ad litteram* 11.11.

to rejoice in the sublime truth in which he did not stand. And therefore even the cattle are placed over him, not in the sense that they have power, but in that they preserve their own nature, because cattle have not lost any celestial blessedness—they never had any—but live out their life in the nature they have received.[17]

Augustine seems here to lose track of which text he is interpreting—Genesis or Matthew. What he is trying to do, clearly, is link the powerful New Testament prince with the Old Testament serpent. Though he manages here to explain this current role of the devil as prince of sinners, he would soon realize that he also needed to account for the devil's own fall.

3. The Sin of Satan: The "Literal" Genesis

In this early work, Augustine left several of the implications of his story undeveloped. But in the long twelve-book commentary, *De Genesi ad litteram* (written between 401 and 414), and then in *City of God*, he draws out all the meanings of the text as the complex symbolic system of the cosmos becomes increasingly clear to him. The key to the system remains the theory of sin, with its origins in pride, but this sin is continuous in the universe since the first day. It is the devil's, Adam's, the heretics', all men's.

The most spectacular extension of the anti-Manichaean Genesis commentary occurs in Book Eleven of the new "Commentary According to the Letter." Ostensibly an interpretation of the end of the second and the third chapters of Genesis—the Yahwist's story of Adam and the Fall—it is largely an account not of the Fall of man but of the idea of "fall" in general, and especially the fall of the angel. The Eden story is now precisely located within a symbolic moral system and a complete cosmic plot. Augustine takes issue, for example, with the idea, still current in the church since the Adam books and their Gnostic progeny were adapted by Irenaeus, that the devil fell through envy of man because he was created in the image of God. Yet he finds a way to rearrange the events so as to include envy within his synthesis, just as the Fall of man could still include the important sin of lust.

> But envy follows pride, it does not precede it: for envy is not the cause of pride, but pride is the cause of envy. Therefore, since pride is the love of one's own excellence, whereas envy is hatred for the happiness of another, it is sufficiently obvious which is born from which. For it is through love of

[17] *De Genesi contra Manichaeos* 2.17.

his own excellence that someone envies either his equals, because they *are* equal with him, or his inferiors, because they may become his equals, or his superiors, because he is not their equal. By pride, then, comes envy, not through envy pride.[18]

Thus the envious angel of Irenaeus must have been already fallen, through pride, when he tempted Adam and Eve. Pride, the first and major continuing sin, has become what apostasy was for Irenaeus, a universal state of being.

Once the moral theory of sin has led Augustine to separate the fall of Satan from the Fall of man, since pride precedes envy, he then has to locate the devil's apostasy both literally at some previous time and symbolically within the cosmic system he is constructing to answer the heretics. He has several scriptural clues from which to work, yet they appear to contradict each other in one respect: whether or not the devil ever enjoyed the blessed life of an angel before he fell. Whereas Isaiah and Ezekiel, as Origen and Tertullian had shown, both seem to suggest that Lucifer did enjoy the light before his rebellion, a crucial passage in John's gospel (8.44) appears to suggest that he did not. The text reads:

Ye are of your father the devil, and the lusts of your father ye will do. He was a murderer from the beginning, and abode not in the truth, because there is no truth in him. When he lies, he speaks according to his own nature: for he is a liar, and the father of lies.

Similarly, the first letter of John reads: "He that committeth sin is of the devil; for the devil sinneth from the beginning. For this purpose the Son of God was manifested, that he might destroy the works of the devil."[19] Augustine's several attempts to deal with this apparent contradiction in scripture provide a useful guide to the difficulties he faced in the construction of his symbolic narrative. The amount of space he devotes to them is a measure of his need to oppose the Manichaean heresy yet still include a powerful evil force within the plot. At first he is inclined to accept Isaiah at face value and interpret John to fit it. Then he decides that John is right and that Isaiah must be interpreted. Finally, he reverts to the literal interpretation of Isaiah and a very subtle interpretation of John.

In the series of sermons on John, Augustine quotes Isaiah to show that the words "the devil did not stand in the truth" mean he once enjoyed the

---

[18] *De Genesi ad litteram* 11.14.

[19] 1 John 3.8 (KJV). For the Johannine context, see above, Chapters 17.1 and 23.3. See also Dahl 1964 and R. E. Brown 1966:254–68.

radiance of reflected wisdom but then became dark: "Lucifer qui mane oriebatur, cecidit."[20] Soon, however, when he writes the Genesis commentary, he decides that the devil never stood in the truth and that the Isaiah passage, together with its correlate in Ezekiel, must be understood to apply not so much to Satan himself as to the human beings who followed him. The important word *cecidit* still applies to Satan—"He would not have fallen if he was made such"—but the rest of the passage refers to his followers, in particular the heretics who have abandoned the light of the church for the darkness of apostasy. The figurative meaning of the Isaiah passage is thus an extension of Irenaeus' idea of apostasy as a continuing state of mind:

> Thus "Lucifer who rose in the morning and fell" may be understood of the tribe of apostates from Christ and from the church; for they lost the light they bore and were converted to darkness, in the same way as converts to God cross from darkness into light, that is, they who were darkness become light.
> . . . Thence fell all the heretics, whether by an open and physical separation, or whether, in a hidden and spiritual (though it is manifest in a corporeal) way, they are converted to their own vomit (2 Pet. 2.22).[21]

To be converted to one's own vomit is not a particularly delightful prospect, and the strength of the metaphor measures the intensity of Augustine's opposition to heretics and also the power of a leader who could induce such a conversion. What it means, of course, is the idea, derived from the Platonic tradition, that sin is the love of one's own excellence, or pride.

Once the Isaiah and Ezekiel passages have been so interpreted, however, Augustine must go to great lengths to preserve the John passage from a heretical interpretation. His elaborate argument turns on the meaning of the word *initio* (beginning). At all costs it must not be allowed to imply that the devil was created with a sinful nature.

> When pride threw the devil down, so that he perverted his own good nature with a corrupt will, scripture does not say. But reason makes it obvious that

---

[20] *Tractatus in Johannis evangelicum* 3.7. For a similar analysis, see TeSelle 1970:235. The Latin of the Vulgate reads "et in veritate non stetit."

[21] *De Genesi ad litteram* 11.23–25. I translate *portabat* as "bore" because of the ironic reference to Lucifer, the lightbearer, although the later meaning of *portare*, to wear clothes, is clearly relevant to the passage also, but the pun is untranslatable. Compare *Confessions* 13.8, quoted above, Chapter 24 and n. 10, in the translation of Warner 1963, "spirits who fall away from you and discover their own darkness, bared of the garment of your light"—a brave stab with a different English pun.

it must have been before [man's fall], and because of pride, that he envied man. For it is clear to anyone who looks into the matter that pride is not born from envy, but rather envy from pride. Yet we should not vainly imagine that the devil fell from the beginning [*initio*] of time through pride, nor that there was any previous time in which he lived with the holy angels peaceful and blessed. Rather, from the very beginning [*exordio*] of the creature he turned away [*apostatasse*] from his creator. This is what the Lord says: "He was a murderer from the beginning [*initio*], and stood not in the truth" (John 8.44). We should understand "from the beginning" in both clauses, not only that he was a murderer, but also that he stood not in the truth. He was a murderer from the beginning which brought it about that a man could die, for before there was one who might die, he could not be killed. Therefore the devil was a murderer from the beginning, because he killed the first man, before whom there were no men. But he also stood not in the truth, and this was from the beginning of his own creation, he who might have stood if he had willed to stand.[22]

These two beginnings out of one word in John apply to the two falls. This particular passage might have been easier to interpret if there had been only one fall, as there was for Irenaeus, but the moral and Platonic theory of the priority of pride to envy precludes that solution. Having largely abandoned the Isaiah and Ezekiel references for the moment, Augustine is mainly concerned with denying the possibility that the devil was such from the absolute "beginning"; that would impute the creation of evil to God. So grammatical analysis had also to be cosmology.[23]

Augustine soon felt, however, that this ingenious analysis of John was not sufficient to counter the Manichaean idea of an independent evil principle from "the beginning" of time. He therefore reverted to Origen's interpretation of Isaiah and Ezekiel as a gloss on the text of John. Yet despite this realignment of the texts, his discussion of the John passage becomes even less convincing while more rhetorically elaborate. In *City of God*, he discusses the original state of the angels, and while still unable to decide whether they were all created equal, he insists that the fallen angels once enjoyed perfection. He reiterates his own argument from the Genesis commentary that the word *initio* should be understood in two senses: one, that the devil was a murderer from the beginning of mankind; two, that he did not abide in the truth from the beginning of his creation. He does not, however, mention that this had been his own position; it is merely

---

[22] *De Genesi ad litteram* 11.16.

[23] Compare the similar "correction" of biblical phrasing at *Confessions* 13.10, commenting on Gen. 1.2–4, referred to above, Chapter 24.

"anyone who adopts this position." But at least, he continues, this hypothetical "anyone"

> disagrees with those heretics the Manichaeans, and with any other pestilential sect that may suppose that the devil has derived from some adverse evil principle a nature proper to himself. These persons are so befouled by error, that, although they acknowledge with ourselves the authority of the gospels, they do not notice that the Lord did not say "The devil was naturally a stranger to the truth," but "The devil abode not in the truth," by which He meant us to understand that he had fallen from the truth, in which, if he had abode, he would have become a partaker of it, and have remained in blessedness along with the holy angels.[24]

He continues to expound the John passage, this time assuring us not only that there is nothing suspicious about the text but also that the Lord even added the potentially confusing explanation to enlighten us. A disinterested critic might have asked why the Lord chose to add "The devil abode not in the truth because the truth was not in him." Simply a matter of an unusual turn of phrase, says the master rhetorician:

> Moreover, as if we had been inquiring why the devil did not abide in the truth, our Lord subjoins the reason, saying, "because the truth is not in him." Now it would be in him had he abode in it. But the phraseology is unusual. For, as the words stand, "He abode not in the truth, because the truth is not in him," it seems as if the truth's not being in him were the cause of his not abiding in it; whereas his not abiding in the truth is rather the cause of its not being in him.

Augustine cites a similar expression from a psalm and dismisses the problem. Yet he has been led, in the course of his analysis, to reverse the plain meaning of the text, all to protect God from heretics. Sin causes evil, not evil sin, and if it looks the other way around, that is because of our sinful nature, which is such that we impute evil even to God, when it is really sin we should impute to ourselves and Satan.

And if this explication is not enough, then we have also, he says, the prophetic proofs to support us and to defend God:

> As for what John says about the devil, "The devil sinneth from the beginning," they who suppose it is meant thereby that the devil was made with a sinful nature, misunderstand it; for if sin be natural it is not sin at all. And how do they answer the prophetic proofs—either what Isaiah says when he represents the devil under the person of the king of Babylon, "How art thou

[24] *City of God* 11.14, trans. Dods 1950:359.

fallen, O Lucifer, son of the morning!" or what Ezekiel says, "Thou hast been in Eden, the garden of God; every precious stone was thy covering," where it is meant that he was some time without sin; for a little after it is still more explicitly said, "Thou wast perfect in thy ways"?

Augustine's wavering over these important texts is a sign of the continuing influence of Manichaeism. He has to allow power to evil yet still insist on the primacy of sin. Given a cosmos into which evil entered through sin on the first day of creation, when God divided the light from the darkness, it would be extremely easy, as the Manichaeans did, to get the story wrong. Even one day could make all the difference, and he had himself known the power of error.

The Augustinian system, different by one day from the Manichaean, could now be used against the rival sects in two distinct ways. First, since Augustine had relocated the beginnings of evil within the soul and since the devil himself had no body, he could oppose the Manichaean materialism according to which flesh itself was evil. Second, he has been able to justify both God and Adam. For Mani, God was virtually impotent in his purity, and even when attacked he lacked a source of power to oppose the darkness. And Adam was mostly evil, though with a spark of goodness within. In Augustine's myth God himself had never been violated, and the creation was still within his power. And Adam himself had been created nearly perfect, at least by current standards. Augustine could thus ignore the difficulties resulting from Irenaeus' childlike Adam.[25] So perfect a creature as Adam could fall because the serpent was Satan and because Adam, in his perfection, was free.[26]

The purpose of Augustine's long explication of John's word *initio* was to assert not merely a small time change from the Manichaean system but a different myth of creation. For Mani, creation and evil were simultaneous. For Augustine, creation, both angelic and human, was good but soon corrupted. Yet the need to oppose the Manichaean myth had led Augustine to incorporate much of the enemy's system, partly to defend the church and partly to convince himself that he had a more complete explanation for the "mixture" of good and evil in the world that both he and Mani insisted upon.

The Adamic myth and its Satanic serpent were also vital in Augustine's quarrel with the Pelagians, men who, he felt, had no genuine appreciation of the myth of the Fall, though at least they believed it to be the expression

[25] See above, Chapter 19.2.
[26] Rist 1972:229–34.

of God's will. Adam's sin, they felt, had hurt nò one but himself, and each child is not born with the weight of original sin but innocent. Baptism does not remit sins; it merely gives entry into God's kingdom, a position Augustine had himself shared at an earlier period.[27] Augustine countered what he felt was the foolish optimism of the Pelagians, that all men can work out their own salvation, by insisting once again on the gravity of what happened in Eden, that sin was transmitted by sexual intercourse to all men and that the devil had tremendous power over all of us as a result of that sin. He went so far that the Pelagians accused him of Manichaean fatalism, of the kind of automatic relationship between sin and damnation that Mani had propounded between evil and life itself. Augustine was forced to respond, to insist that the devil is the author of all sin but that we are not therefore automatically damned:

> Although the devil is the author and source of all sins, still it is not *every* sin that makes children of the devil, for the children of God also sin: "If they say that they have no sins they deceive themselves and the truth is not in them" (1 John 1.8). But they sin by virtue of that condition by which they are still children of this world, while by that grace by which they are children of God they do not sin: "Everyone who is born of God does not sin" (1 John 3.9).[28]

The contradiction was already in John, and Augustine's explication does little to solve it. What he must do, he finds, is back away from attributing too much power to the devil. Instead, he makes the idea of sin more important and thus allows for a mixture of good and evil in each man, even in those who are "children of God."

The adversary still has enormous power in this version of Christian combat, but, like Paul, Augustine has turned its setting inward and so found a way to overcome, if hesitantly, its deterministic implications. "The Devil is not to be blamed for everything: there are times when a man is his own devil."[29]

4. Augustine's Eve

The Augustinian synthesis gave the monotheist religion a cosmic structure that could both account for evil and include the ethical dualism that

---

[27] *De libero arbitrio* 3.23.66. See above, Chapter 23, and TeSelle 1970:282.
[28] *Contra duas epistolas Pelagianorum* 3.3.4–5. See above, Chapter 17.1.
[29] Quoted in P. Brown 1967:245.

was so important to the writers of the New Testament. Augustine realized that it had, in fact, been this ethical dualism, the divided will of man, that caused the illusion of metaphysical dualism he was opposing. His insistence on ethical dualism, that sin causes evil, led to a position that would have important consequences for medieval Christendom. The devil's own sin might have been enormous and irrevocable, but it was Eve who introduced sin to mankind. If the devil as the personification of a cosmic evil power had to be originally excluded from the Christian system, then much of the hatred that this power might have evoked was turned on the woman. She was, according to Augustine's own moral system, in which pride comes before the Fall, already sinful.

> There was already in her mind a certain love of her own power and a certain proud self-presumption which needed to be defeated and humiliated through the temptation. Otherwise she would not have believed these words and imagined that she was denied something good and useful.[30]

Adam, on the other hand, is treated differently. Genesis is silent about how Adam was persuaded to eat too. "And she gave it to her husband with her, perhaps even with persuasive words which Scripture, being silent, leaves to be understood. Or possibly there was no need to persuade the man, when he saw that she was not dead from the fruit?" This concentration of the sin itself upon Eve is, we have seen, a common enough reading of the story,[31] but Genesis says she is deceived, not proud. And the eating itself is the sin, not her prior state of mind.

Later Augustine would modify this antifeminism while maintaining his insistence on the inward and spiritual nature of the sin. He includes Adam too in his censure and writes in the *City of God* that both were already sinful when they tasted the fruit:

> The wicked deed . . . was committed by persons who were already wicked. . . . The devil, then, would not have begun by an open and obvious sin to tempt man into doing something which God had forbidden, had not man already begun to seek satisfaction in himself and, consequently, to take pleasure in the words "Ye shall be as Gods."[32]

Augustine has apparently been so concerned to locate the cause of the divided universe in the moral nature of man that, in these passages, he dis-

---

[30] *De Genesi ad litteram* 11.30.
[31] See above, Chapter 11.
[32] *City of God* 14.13.

credits his original integrity and thus, by implication, the benevolence and justice of his creator. However, the flaw in man's nature is attributed not directly to God but to the fact of man's (and the angels') creation *ex nihilo*.[33]

Augustine's difficulties with the beginning, *initio*, both at the cosmic level and the human level, may be seen as a variant of the narrative problems that ensue from the two possibilities for the motivating incident of Propp's general scheme—Lack or Villainy. The theory of sin, in spite of its extensive theological elaboration, fits well the notion of "Lack," while the "Villainy," in Augustine's story, is the positive power of action attributed to the devil. We have seen how, at the earliest stage of the ancient combat plot, the two possibilities could alternate for the beginning of the Gilgamesh story in its various Sumerian or Assyrian forms. We may wonder, now, at the extraordinary ingenuity with which Augustine has found a place for both within his comprehensive story of redemption. Yet we should note also that in his final inability to unravel what was essentially an insoluble problem he has come close to impugning the story's divine author.

5. Opposition and Conversion: God's Plot

Creation from nothing, and so the tendency to fall back toward original nonbeing, is a slender thread upon which to hang the defense of the creator's benevolence and justice. Indeed, for Augustine, we know, nothingness is the equivalent of or substitute for the Manichaean evil. However the two theories may differ metaphysically, original darkness and original nothingness look suspiciously similar in their narrative roles. But the distinction was not Augustine's sole defense of the divine goodness. It was only an aspect of the much grander scheme to which he had come by the meditations recorded in the *Confessions*—the structure of God's plot to bring good out of evil. Only from the worldly perspective does the combat of God with Satan appear to be the truth about the world. In fact, their relation is that of conversion, not opposition.

The medieval church, and then Luther and Calvin, inherited from Augustine, whenever they cared to notice it, a subtly transformed version of the Christian combat myth. The opposition of Satan, the adversary, to God now became in this benevolent vision an accurate but partial view of

---

[33] Ibid. Cf. Rist 1972:233, Pelikan 1971:298–303.

the cosmos. It was accurate because pride, the turning to the self, is always recurrent, but it was partial because behind it another and very different pattern was discernible. As God converted Saul to Paul and sent him to open the eyes of others, to bring them from darkness to light, from the power of Satan to God, so the adversary relation is revealed as itself satanic, while behind it is the more inclusive pattern that converts it.

On the strength of this Augustinian plot, John Donne, for example, could go so far as to preach in a sermon that "it is useful to fall into any manifest sin."[34] The basis of this view was the story that Augustine had told in his *Confessions*, the fundamentally well-made plot he described elsewhere:

> The works of God are so wisely and exquisitely contrived that, when an angelic and human creature sins, that is, does not what God wished it to do but what itself wished, yet by that very will of the creature whereby it does what the Creator did not will, it fulfills what he willed—God as supremely good, putting even evils to good use.[35]

Angelic and human levels and cosmic and earthly plots have finally become equivalents of each other, brought together through the theory of sin. And sin itself is part of the benign structure of the universe, benign at least for those who experience grace. This glimpse of the divine structure is what finally enabled Augustine to accord such power to evil—God permits it to have so much power because God himself is so much more, indeed infinitely, powerful. The need to believe in the infinite power of God and the smallness of man is what drove Augustine originally—if we may believe the *Confessions* and the major thrust of his anti-Manichaean writings—to oppose ancient myth in its Manichaean form, that God had been defeated by the Darkness in their first encounter, or that God was only partially responsible for the creation. Now a more subtle but also a more exalted monotheism than the belief of Second Isaiah, whose God claimed to create evil, provided the way out of this extreme satanic heresy.

In the end, Augustine's cosmos is just as divided within itself as the Manichaean cosmos, but he has been able to account for this split within a monist system. Furthermore, the way out of the city of sin is granted by the very structure of the journey we make through it: God is able to bring good out of evil. At the end of his attack on the Manichaean interpretation of Genesis, he summarizes in the form of a dialogue with heresy the

---

[34] Donne, *Eighty Sermons*, 1680:171, quoted in Lovejoy 1937.
[35] Augustine, *Enchiridion* 100.

theological interpretation of the old myth at which the church, after so long a trial, had now arrived:

> What do these heretics hold who attack the Old Testament scriptures? Let them ask the questions according to their method, and let us answer as God deigns to give us answers.
>
> Why did God make man, they ask, if he knew he was going to sin? Because even from a sinner he could make many good things, regulating him according to the management of his justice, and because man's sin was no obstacle to God. If he had not sinned, there would be no death; because he did sin, other mortals are corrected by his sin. For nothing so recalls man from sin as the thought of his imminent death.
>
> So he should have made man, they say, so as not to sin. No, he should not have done this; rather, man is made so that he would not sin if he did not want to.

Then these hypothetical heretics take another, familiar, tack:

> Then he should not have made woman, they say. This is to say that good should not have come into being, for even she is some good, so much good, in fact, that the apostle says she is a glory to man; all things come from God.
>
> Again they say, Who made the devil? He himself, for the devil was made not by his nature but by sin.
>
> Well then, they say, God should not have made him if he knew that he would sin. Why indeed should he not have made him, when through his justice and providence he corrects so many through the malice of the devil? Or perhaps you have not heard the apostle Paul tell us, "Them I have handed over to Satan, so they may learn not to blaspheme" [1 Tim. 1.20]? And of himself he says, "Lest I should be puffed up with the greatness of revelations, the thorn of the flesh was given me, that angel of Satan who beats me" (2 Cor. 12.7).
>
> Then, they say, is the devil good because he is useful? Not at all. The devil is evil to a great degree, but God is good and omnipotent, who even out of malice works so many good and just things. Only to the devil's evil will should we impute the attempt to do evil, not to the providence of God, who from evil makes good.[36]

In this dialogue with the heretics who attack scripture, we see a thorough transformation of the Christian combat myth into philosophical debate. Out of evil God brings good, just as out of heretics' errors he brings the version of the redemptive story that Augustine's work could now be-

---

[36] *De Genesi contra Manichaeos* 2.28.

queath to the Middle Ages and to the Reformed churches of the Renaissance. Out of this Augustinian synthesis would eventually grow the grandest vision of this cosmic plot, Milton's *Paradise Lost*, in which Satan's plot is finally converted by god's (or Milton's) more inclusive plot and in which Satan's errors teach the reader new truths.

The composers of the Gilgamesh epic, the *Enuma Eliš*, or the *Theogony*, working in their ancient oral/aural traditions, had woven inherited tales into new poems. In a similar way, Augustine manipulated the various narratives of the classical and Judeo-Christian traditions into a new mythology, working as storytellers do on several levels at once. How conscious was he, for example, of its history when he used the word *"tyfus"* so often? As a Greek loan-word, it sticks out oddly from his elegant Latin. Yet its meaning is very Augustinian: pride or arrogance. For example at *Confessions* 3.3, a devil-filled section, he writes, "Gaudebam superbe et tumebam *tyfo*," accusing his own vanity as a young and enthusiastic student of rhetoric—"I was pleased with myself, proud and swelling with arrogance." Did he know that the word began as Typhon or Typhoeus, the giant adversary of Zeus in Hesiod? Almost certainly he knew Plato's moralization and play with the name. In the *Phaedrus* 229e–230a Socrates announces his scorn for those who rationalize myths. He prefers self-examination, on the Delphic principle, he says, to see whether "I am a wild beast more complex than Typhon or more puffed up with the fumes of pride [*epitethumenon*], or whether I am a simpler being . . . not puffed up [*atuphou*]." Socrates is playing on the root meanings of "wind" (whence "typhoon") and "smoke" in order to draw his moral: myths can be used as mirrors. A long tradition thereafter used the word in this or similar senses. Arnobius, for example, called any heretical opponent of Christianity *typhus*.[37] Converting Typhon into the "fumes" or "empty wind" of pride is a typical and revealing move of Augustine's. It prepared the way for Luther's version of the combat and allows this book to find its end in its beginning.[38]

The cosmic myth of Satan's fall Augustine has reimagined in the terms provided by Israel's long history of rebelliousness, beginning with Adam's sin, and especially by the moment when God intervened directly in human history, the ordinary province of legend, to transform that history into myth. The scriptures, themselves an instance of the long process of

[37] Courcelles 1984:350 cites this and the other examples given.
[38] See also Milton, *Paradise Lost*, 1, 199–237, for Typhon and the association with "stench and smoke."

composition (literally: putting together), were now reread from that new redemptive point of view, what we called above the symbolic method, and thus each episode, when placed in this new sacred mythology, could be read as a rehearsal or recapitulation of the whole plot.

The effort to tell this new story had begun with Paul's reassessment of the apocalyptic combat myth in the light of his severe rabbinic view of the law. In Augustine's system, Satan and the combat he provoked had now become a useful tool for the schoolmaster who would correct his erring pupils. The death-dealing adversary of the ancient combat myth had become the windy and deluded opponent of God, and Satan's vice-gerent, death, was now God's way of recalling man from sin. The enemy himself was now the means of conversion.

APPENDIX

METHODS AND TERMS

O UR CENTURY has seen remarkable developments in the study of traditional narrative forms, of the kind explored in this book. Many of
these developments are discussed in footnotes, but some deserve special
remarks here: questions of classification, formal and structural analysis,
and oral-formulaic composition.

1. Classification of Traditional Narrative

Tales themselves spread much farther and faster than any of the people
who do the telling. Folklorists, largely inspired by Scandinavian scholarship, have long been writing monographs on the diffusion of folktale
types around the globe. The tales of the Kind and Unkind Girl, Cinderella, or Cupid and Psyche are only the best-known instances of tales told
from England to China and the Americas.[1] The names and situations and
the secondary elaborations change, but the basic plot of the type remains
recognizably intact. European folktales were classified by Anti Aarne in
1910 in *Verzeichnis der Märchentypen*, a work updated by Stith Thompson
in 1964. This should be distinguished from Thompson's six-volume *Motif
Index of Folk Literature*.[2]

The combat narratives of the ancient world have been classified by Fontenrose 1959 in the manner of the tale-type index. This monumental and
erudite work was undeservedly greeted with a brief and contemptuous review by Samuel Kramer,[3] whose own indefatigable work as both editor
and popularizer of Sumerian texts has won wide recognition. Unfortunately, Kramer did not grasp the importance of the book's folkloristic
classifications nor of its understanding of how and why stories become
popular and spread beyond national boundaries. However, Fontenrose

---

[1] W. Roberts 1958, Rooth 1951, Swahn 1955.

[2] Aarne and Thompson 1964; S. Thompson 1955–58. For a general introduction, see
S. Thompson 1946, Dundes (ed.) 1965, or Lüthi 1968.

[3] Kramer 1961. Contrast Burke 1968 and Yarbro-Collins 1976:57–67, where it forms the
point of reference for an analysis of Revelation. See above, Chapter 13.

rarely mentions Satan, and the book was written without benefit of Propp's ideas.

Fontenrose presents several useful lists of the elements common to different myths (although his lists do not quite agree with each other). There is a list of "themes" (ten in all) with various subcategories of each, and the book closes with a helpful index of those same themes and the corresponding numbers in Thompson's motif index (though Fontenrose explains that his "theme" is a somewhat larger category than Thompson's "motif"). But the list of themes is subject to many of the same criticisms made of Thompson's index.[4] Some of the themes are characteristics of the Enemy (or Champion), some are event themes (e.g., 7f, "The Enemy Fled During Combat"), while another whole category (9) refers to the means by which the Enemy is overcome. The logic of the scheme is loose. Why, for example, are 10a, "He Punished the Enemy," and 10b, "He Celebrated His Victory," subcategories of the same theme, while 6, "A Champion Appeared to Face Him," and 7, "The Champion Fought the Enemy," get categories all to themselves?[5] The system as a whole suffers by comparison with Propp's, in which each "Function" is an incident of the plot rather than a characteristic of someone's personality or an item in the furniture of the tale.

Fontenrose tries to compensate for such difficulties by offering two further lists and various tables. One is a list of "plot components," a term that is not defined but that suggests an effort at formalist analysis along Proppian lines. These plot-components, however, are also called "general features," and again the logic of this scheme is unclear. But the book offers an invaluable group of tables that show the occurrence in each myth analyzed of these various themes and plot components, and from these tables it is possible to construct the basic plot of the myths according to Propp-like principles.

The Proppian approach is described more fully below, but an illustration will clarify the similarities and differences between the two kinds of analysis. Of the four subtypes of the combat myth which Fontenrose discerns, one can be shown to correspond closely to the relevant section of Propp, but the actual model for this summary is the Aarne-Thompson tale-type index. Comparison with AT 300 (the Dragon-Slayer) yields in-

---

[4] S. Thompson 1955–58. On the limitations of motif categories, see Armstrong in Maranda (ed.) 1972:173–93, Dundes (ed.) 1965:207–15, and Propp 1968:8–9.

[5] Fontenrose 1959:262–65; cf. Gaster 1961:150–51 and above, Introduction n. 26.

teresting results. Fontenrose's Subtype IV reads as follows, and I add the appropriate Proppian number and the relevant subdivision of AT 300.

1. The death-god or a demon or specter controls and/or terrorizes a land [Propp 8; AT 300 III, Motif G346. Devastating monster. Lays waste to the land].

2. He (the demon may be female, in which case appropriate changes of gender must be made)
   a. seizes the young of man and beast [8.1, 8.6; II, S262. Periodic sacrifices to a monster] and/or
   b. demands that young women be given to him [8.8, 8.15, 8.16; II. B11.10. Sacrifice of human being to dragon] and/or
   c. imposes heavy tribute [8.5] and/or
   d. kills everyone who comes his road, frequently by forcing him at hazard of his life into contest with him [8.14, 8.18, 8.19].

3. The champion [9 and 10; IC]
   a. through love of the victim [9 and 10; II, T68.1. Princess offered as prize to rescuer] and/or
   b. desiring to save the victim [9.3, 9.4 and 10] or
   c. acting under a superior's orders [9.1, 9.12] or
   d. desiring on his own to rid the land of its bane [9.3, 10 and 11],

4. a. descends into the lower world [11 and 15] or
   b. enters into or waits at cave, lair, or tomb [15; IV. D1975. Dragon-fighter's magic sleep. While waiting for fight with dragon, hero falls into magic sleep] and

5. fights [16; IVf. B11.11. Fight with dragon] and kills [18] the enemy, accomplishing his purpose [19; R111.1.3. Rescue of princess (maiden) from dragon].

The analysis clearly corresponds to Parts II–IV (Sacrifice, Dragon, and Fight) of AT 300, but it takes no account of I (Hero and His Dogs, Propp's Donor Sequence, 12–14) or V–VII (Tongue, Imposter, Recognition, Propp 17.23–29). Yet one of the narratives that Fontenrose includes within this subtype is the Perseus and Andromeda tale (p. 303), which also provided some of Aarne's and Thompson's material for AT 300.[6] Therefore, both omitted sequences were in fact present in Fontenrose's material—he simply ignored them. Typical in this respect is the Sumerian tale of Gilgamesh and Huwawa, and since this tale is also an instance of Fon-

[6] Strictly speaking, what Aarne and Thompson used was Hartland 1894–96, an analysis of the Perseus tradition that includes much extraneous material culled from the world's folktales. See Aarne and Thompson 1964:89.

tenrose's Subtype IV, the omission of Propp's sequences is a flaw in the analysis.

Because Fontenrose's various themes and plot components are unsystematically derived and depend so heavily on the personal characteristics of the actors (a limitation from which Propp's model is free), it is clear that we need a more rigorous but still flexible model for the ancient combat narratives, based on the event principle of Propp's functions.

2. Propp on Morphological Analysis

The classification of tale-types was made more manageable when Vladimir Propp argued that many of them shared a common formal structure. Following Propp's lead, scholars have been applying his ideas, with modifications, to the narratives of the ancient world. Many well-known tales, such as the *Odyssey* or "David and Goliath," have been shown to fit the essential Proppian sequence.[7] This has caused controversy, even consternation, in some circles, but it does mean that ancient narrative types may now be discussed in the same terms as the tales that folklorists have more frequently taken as their province.

The tales among which Propp discovered a common plot structure were all genetically related to each other, since the tale-type index includes only those tales told among the European peasantry (whereas Thompson's motif index has a claim to global relevance). So the question whether the recognition of formal similarities implies any historical link does not arise in practice. The same is true of the narratives studied in this book, which share parallel kinds of formal similarities. There are historical connections, usually demonstrable, among all the cultures whose combat narratives we discuss here. Indeed, successive ancient empires frequently adopted the myths of their predecessors, though perhaps with the names changed. The Hittite borrowings from the Asianic Hurrians, for example, and their joint or independent adaptations from their Semitic neighbors, provided an important channel by which the narratives of the Near East were transmitted to Indo-European-speaking people and so to the Greeks.[8] (We should not, therefore, follow Indo-European linguists or the overzealous followers of Georges Dumézil in ignoring Semitic and

---

[7] Propp 1968, first published in Russian in 1928. See also Damon 1969, Limet 1972, Alster 1975, Jason 1979, and now Propp 1984.

[8] Gurney 1954; Page 1959; Wais 1952.

other influence on early Indo-European mythology.[9]) The Hebrew adaptation of Canaanite myths, especially under the Davidic monarchy, is
an important stage in the narrative tradition of the adversary. And the secular Gilgamesh tradition, to take one more example, was widespread
throughout the ancient world. It is not surprising that a fragment of the
epic was unearthed at Megiddo in Palestine, that his name appears on an
Aramaic fragment from Qumran, or that reflexes of the Gilgamesh epic,
particularly the relation of hero and Enkidu, should have been discerned
in the Homeric tradition.[10]

Propp has been both praised and blamed for the key concept in his
method, the idea of "Function"—praised because the concept liberated
narrative studies from the nineteenth-century legacy of preoccupation
with character and of atomistic studies of "themes" or "motifs," but
blamed because the concept demands too rigid an adherence to the superficial sequence of events. As Lévi-Strauss, Greimas, and other French
Structuralists have pointed out, for example, many of Propp's separate
Functions are better understood as transformations of each other, or
rather of an underlying impulse that may be "realized" in a variety of
ways. For example, testings of the hero, overcoming difficult tasks, even
the actual combat itself, though differentiated according to their consequences in Propp's system, are more usefully conceived as paradigmatic
variants.[11]

In spite of the theoretical problems, the great advance of Propp's
method of analysis was that it enables us to recognize and account for obvious similarities among different tale-types. What the index calls "Tales
of the Supernatural Adversary" turn out to be remarkably similar to
"Tales of the Stupid Ogre," and this parallel has a special relevance to the
adversary tradition, whether the Sumerian Huwawa or the Christian
devil. Propp himself was aware that his system would apply to kinds of
tale other than those called "Tales of Magic," Types 300–749 in the Aarne
and Thompson index: "Quite a large number of legends, individual tales
about animals, and isolated novellae display the same structure."[12] This is
because the tales of the index are often grouped according to their principal characters, but by Propp's method tales become comparable whether
they have animals or ogres as chief agents. AT 9 and AT 1030 have the same

[9] See, e.g., Boedeker 1974, Littleton 1973:198–200, and esp. Dumézil 1945.
[10] D. W. Thomas (ed.) 1967:319; Milik 1976:308; Gresseth 1975; Nagler 1977.
[11] Lévi-Strauss 1960; Greimas 1970; Meletinsky 1971; Culler 1975:213; Turner 1977.
[12] Propp 1968:99, and see now Propp 1984:xxvii, 39–47.

plot, although one is classified as an animal tale and the other as a tale of the stupid ogre.[13] Propp was also aware, although he did not specify further, "that a similar construction is displayed by a number of very archaic myths, some of which present this structure in an amazingly pure form."[14]

3. *The Combat Plot*

Table 1 provides a structural outline, following Propp's idea, of the combat plot as it applies to the material brought together in this book. Most of Propp's central sequence, from Function 8 (Villainy) to Functions 19 and 20 (Lack Liquidated and Hero Returns), appears fairly constantly. The preliminary sequence, concerned with the initiating activities of the villain (Functions 1–7), is often present too, but I have preferred to eliminate it from the schema because, as will be clear from Chapter 6.1 on the rebel variant, I consider this sequence an elaboration of the initial motivating incident. I have also suppressed Propp's concluding sequence, which has to do with the struggles of the returning hero for recognition of his status. Although present in the Christian narratives, where the stigmata correspond to Propp's Functions 17 and 27, this sequence is generally not relevant in the hero legends or myths to which my schema chiefly applies, since the hero is already known as such to his community, frequently as its king or god. Finally, the schema takes into account the structuralist critiques but maintains the essential concept of "function," a narrative slot that may be filled by a wide range of particular incidents. The table is keyed to Propp and Fontenrose as well as to the summary of the Dragon-Slayer folktale in the Aarne and Thompson index.

Each of the twelve features of the schema in the table represents a significant incident in the plot structure of most ancient combat narratives. Some are always present (e.g., Villainy, Battle, Victory, Triumph), for without them the narrative would not be a combat, but others may at times be absent or attenuated without changing the basic structure and character of the narrative. This applies especially to features η–θ–ι (Enemy Ascendant, Hero Recovers, Battle Rejoined), which therefore deserve special comment.

One of the most important elements Fontenrose discerned in his mate-

[13] Dundes 1962b:98–99, and introduction to Propp 1968:xiv.
[14] Propp 1968:100, and see now Propp 1984:100–123.

rial was the frequency with which the hero is initially defeated or even killed (his Theme 8 and Plot Component E, my ζ), a principle of plot construction which Hollywood and television drama continue to exploit. So important and widespread a component deserves a separate Propp-like slot, and this initial defeat also entails a further slot for the resultant ascendancy of the enemy, and then a third for the recovery of the hero. Often, as in the Christian version, a new hero, the god's son, will fill this slot in the narrative. In Propp's terms, the initial defeat begins a new "move" of the plot, but the result is often a kind of double plot in which the second and successful combat is seen in terms of the first. My schema therefore indicates that features η–θ–ι are a transformation of or inversion (in the structuralist sense) of α–β–ϵ. Indeed, some variants of this second combat attract other features of the narrative: the hero recovers his potency (or wakes up) through the help of a friend or relative, a new donor incident, and then a fresh journey takes place. In that case, the second combat will actually be of the type α^2–β^2–γ^2–δ^2–ϵ^2, a fully realized form of the initial sequence. My system of notation thus grants separate status to important events such as the defeat of the hero (which for Lévi-Strauss would be merely an inversion of his victory), but it also allows for the possibility of paradigmatic transformations, of the repetition with variation which is the essence of story-telling. But the system is neither rigidly sequential like Propp's, nor does it ignore the syntax of narrative, like Lévi-Strauss and his followers.[15]

In adapting Propp for our purposes, we must bear in mind certain definite differences between folktales and hero legends or myths. The folktale hero owes no specific allegiance to a community, although such a bond may well be forged in the course of his adventures (he ends up marrying the king's daughter, for example). But the hero of legend or myth is usually pictured as the representative of his people (he is already their king or god, for example), and this relationship is often portrayed as the selection of the hero by the divine council or as the hero's response to their problems. In the sequence of events, the hero "emerges" from the group and so becomes a genuine culture hero.[16] Thus many folktales of the Proppian type contain a "donor sequence," an episode in which the hero is tested by a supernatural agent at the beginning of his journey and then receives a magic agent of some kind (he gives an old man his meager ra-

---

[15] See discussion in Fischer 1963:288, Dundes in Propp 1968:xxi, and Turner 1977:122.
[16] Dundes 1964; Meletinsky 1971:268; Jason 1977. See Introduction n. 19.

TABLE I. *Schema of Combat Myths*

	α	β	γ	δ	ε	ζ
Forsyth	Lack/Villainy	Hero emerges/prepares to act	Donor/Consultation	Journey	Battle	Defeat
Propp	8	9–10(11)	12–14	15(11)	16	(6, 12.4)
Fontenrose Themes	1–5(7g)	6			7	8
Plot components	A–C	D				E
AT 300 (The Dragon-Slayer)	II & III	Ia–c	Id–h		IVf	IVb, IVc
HUWAWA	(1) Name (2) Rivers clogged	Decision to go to "the Land"	Enkidu, companions Utu	Journey to forest	Cuts trees	Sleep
LABBU	People lament	Tishpak accepts	Sin gives weapons		War general	Preliminary defeat
YAMM (cf. Shilyat Leviathan, Tannin)	Challenge (gods cower)	Baal accepts	Kothar	Journey to palace	"Driver" strikes	
MOT	Challenge	Baal accepts	Kothar	Journey to Land of Death	Fight "like buffalo, snakes"	Baal killed (chewed)
ANZU	Tablet stolen	Many offers	Ninurta chosen	Goes forth	Attacks	Repelled by Tablet
AZAG	Hail or sickness	Ninurta	Sharur	Goes forth	Attacks	Repelled
APSU	Apsu will destroy, gods lament	Ea accepts	"Magic circle"		Ea recites spell	
TIAMAT	Challenge (Kingu)	Marduk born / Marduk emerges	Ea gives powers / Gods grant supreme power and weapons	Ea goes forth / Marduk goes forth	Attacks	Ea defeated
TITANS	Attack	Zeus	Cyclopes give thunder		Attack	Ten-year standoff
TYPHON	Challenge	Zeus accepts		Goes forth	Mt. Casius	Zeus' "sinews" severed

η (α²)	θ (β²)	ι (ε²)	κ	λ	μ
Enemy ascendant	Hero recovers/ New hero	Battle rejoined	Victory	Enemy punished	Triumph
(7, 8)	(9–11)	16	18	30	19, 27, 29, 31
8, 4, 5g F	6 G	7 H	9 H	10a H	10b–d I
III, VIe	IVc–e, VId	IVf–g	(V)	Va	VII
Terror	Wakes	Attacks trees	Huwawa helpless	Huwawa beheaded	Enlil scene
		Storm	Arrow	Labbu killed	Banquet Kingship
			Victory	Yamm killed or subdued	Palace built
Mot rules	Anat rescues Baal (β² + γ²)	Anat attacks Mot (gore)	Anat/Baal seize Mot	Mot cut to pieces, scattered	Exult (Baal king)
Ninurta leaves	Ea helps (β² + γ²)	Winds attack wings	Ninurta over-powers Anzu	Throat cut, skull crushed	Kingship
Ninurta flees		New attack	Waters overcome	Waters harnessed, stones judged	Ninurt establishes order
			Apsu sleeps	Apsu killed	Shrine established in "Apsu"
Misery among gods	Ea gives power to Marduk	Single combat	Winds and arrow	Tiamat split	Kingship, order
	Hundred-Handers help	Terrible strife	Titans thrown down	Titans imprisoned	Zeus rules
	Zeus recovers in cave	Thunderbolts and chariot	Zeus victor	Typhon chained or buried	Zeus rules

[continued overleaf]

TABLE 1. *Schema of Combat Myths* (cont.)

	α	β	γ	δ	ε	ζ
SEMIHAZAH– ASAEL	Watcher conspiracy– descent	God hears lament of earth	God sends Michael, Raphael	Michael, Raphael come to earth	Announce punishment / Giants kill each other	
MASTEMA [Satan]	Watchers (Corruption)	Noah appeal (plants)	God angry	Michael, Raphael sent	Giants kill each other (Flood)	Only 9/10ths punished
BELIAL	Dominion of Belial	Qumran sect, Teacher of Righteous- ness	Michael, others, sent by God	Desert home	Sons of Light vs. Darkness	Seven reverses (War Scroll)
SATAN	Rebellion	Messiah	God sends him	Incarna- tion (descent of Re- deemer)	Struggle with "powers and demons"	Crucifixion

tions or helps some animals in distress). But in the myths and legends of the ancient Near East, this sequence is often replaced by a "consultation episode," a meeting of the divine council or elders or an appeal to the hero from the gods.

There is a corresponding class difference between folktale and myth or legend. The tales of Propp's corpus were the product of peasant societies, while our texts of the ancient myths come from schools closely connected to the ruling class. Thus, while the folktale may often be interpreted as a fantasy that offers various compensations for powerlessness, the heroic poems with which we are initially concerned usually raise matters of state and try to resolve them. The hero is thus a representative of the state in a way that would be odd for a Jack or an Ivan. This sometimes leads to in- teresting duplication of motives. In the Sumerian Gilgamesh tale, for ex- ample, the hero first decides on his mission simply to make a name for himself, but we later learn that his city is in a bad way: the rivers are clogged with corpses and the people are suffering. The motivating inci- dent is thus both a "lack" (of heroic stature) and "villainy" (if the city's problems are to be attributed to the monster's depredations).

Like the folktales analyzed by Propp, the combat narratives generally

$\eta\,(\alpha^2)$	$\theta\,(\beta^2)$	$\iota\,(\varepsilon^2)$	κ	λ	μ
Demons continue depredations (α^2)	(Michael-Raphael)	[Human history] End-time battle	World destroyed	Rebel chained, abyss or fire	New earth
Continue "under Satan"		Human history	Purification	"No more Satan"	Peace and joy
Belial must rule a little while	New assault	Final battle, End-time	Michael wins	Belial consigned to fire	New earth
Descent into hell	Resurrection	History continues	End-time, Parousia	Satan chained, fire, abyss	Redemption or New earth

begin with a statement of the fundamental situation, a conflict or opposition of some kind, which determines the subsequent events and which the champion's victory will "liquidate." Such a beginning becomes specifically a combat myth at the moment when the initial situation, Propp's "lack," is attributed to the agency of the enemy figure. Often enough this may be achieved by a simple enumeration of the enemy's characteristics—he is greedy, tyrannical, lustful, and so forth. But often too there is an actual attack, or at least a specific problem caused by the enemy's presence—he dries up rivers or clogs them with dead bodies, bars the trade routes, prevents growth, or generally causes the mayhem that leads him (or her) to be a representative of chaos in cosmogonic variants of the pattern. This fundamental opposition may exist at many levels of experience: political (tyranny versus orderly government), religious (the gods are divided), economic (absence of a necessary product, such as wood or water, which the enemy keeps to himself), familial (older vs. younger generation, in which case Freudian insights, with the monster as fantasy father, become explicit), personal (fame versus obscurity), metaphysical (chaos vs. orderly organization of the universe), and of course ethical. Such oppositions will be expressed in the narrative by such images as light/dark, city/

forest (culture/nature), sleep/wake, death/life, pollution/purification, lack/abundance, and monster/human. Finally, the whole narrative will present a basic opposition of before and after (when the enemy rules, chaos/now the king rules, order).[17] The socio-psychological function of the narrative will be the effort to organize these oppositions into some sort of acceptable, if temporary, structure. The success of this effort will be represented as the triumph of the hero, and the narrative or unacceptable aspects of the polarity projected onto the defeated enemy.

The Propp-like schema is not vital to my argument in this book. I use it simply to establish the kinds of parallels I am looking for in ancient narrative traditions, to overcome the myopia of overspecialized scholarship which often resists accepting similarities in other cultural traditions in favor of an understandable but occasionally pedantic insistence on difference or uniqueness (a special weakness among theologians of rival religious persuasions), and also to provide the reader with some sense of what this book does not do. I am not, for example, seeking grand but unconscious archetypes in widely disparate cultures. (I do not consider the religious or mythological traditions of China or Australia, or even the connection with Indian systems, except to mention an occasional reflex or the possible impact of Buddhism on Gnosticism.) And although I have learned much from the brilliant work of Dumézil, I am not persuaded by his grand Indo-European structure.[18]

The Proppian schema drops from sight as the book moves forward in time to the Judeo-Christian writings, where there is no need to establish cultural parallels and where the historical connections are well documented. The problems of establishing what the Christian myth was are discussed in the text, and the schema in Table 1 includes possible analyses of the Satan story only to suggest the potential parallels with earlier myths, not as a definitive account of what was a constantly shifting narrative with a dynamically unstable structure allowing for great paradigmatic (or allegorical) variation.[19]

[17] Burke 1968:387; Lévi-Strauss 1967.

[18] Dumézil has proved most useful to those scholars working on Scandinavian mythology. See, e.g., Turville-Petrie 1964 and Haugen 1970. Cf. Melia 1974 and Littleton 1973.

[19] Maranda and Maranda (eds.) 1971 and Barthes et al. 1974 offer further theoretical discussion. See now Anatoly Liberman in Propp 1984:ix–lxxxi.

4. Oral-Formulaic Poetry

The references to oral poetry in the earlier chapters of this book will raise questions, or even ire, among some Assyriologists and so call for brief explanation. The Parry-Lord theory of oral composition, applied initially both to Homeric epics and to Slavic epics, has now been extended with modifications to other areas of ancient narrative tradition—to biblical narratives, to the Ugaritic texts, and with some reluctance to Babylonian and Sumerian material. I cannot here argue the grounds upon which I find the modified theory persuasive, although some of them are alluded to in the text. The reader is referred to the footnotes for relevant literature, in particular to the dialogue between German and American Homerists on the subject.[20] The following remarks simply review the more significant implications for the Gilgamesh tradition.

What scholars once referred to as "translations" from one tongue to another are often, from this point of view, separate adaptations of epic and mythical narratives in related oral traditions. Variations among the different language versions of one narrative may be more satisfactorily explained on such a theory, although no doubt some of the texts, most notably the late Assyrian recensions of Babylonian poetry like the Gilgamesh epic, are scholarly transcriptions. Ashurbanipal, we know, sent out teams of scholars to preserve and transcribe the literature of the past for his great library at Nineveh. It is true also that many of the texts Ashurbanipal's scholars discovered in their searches had themselves been preserved as school texts, which will explain many textual and lexical variants. But the closer a narrative is to actual oral tradition, and in our case that is very close, the more relevant and informative become the achievements of oral theory and of folklore scholarship. Formulaic language, repetition of substantial sections from one part of a poem to another, composition by theme and type-scene, even ring-composition, are all characteristics of oral epic that are found abundantly in the Sumerian material.[21] Therefore the common practice among cuneiform specialists of establishing a "composite" text must yield to the careful comparison of

[20] Fenik (ed.) 1978. On the application of oral theory to Ugaritic texts, see Cross 1973:112–13. For the biblical tradition, see Gunn 1974, Anderson 1975, Culley 1976, Walker (ed.) 1979, and Alter 1981. See also Chapter 1 nn. 3, 49, and 50 and now Foley 1985 and the new journal *Oral Tradition*.

[21] Limet 1972:16–21; Alster 1972:16–27, 36–44.

variants familiar to folklorists. A composite text of a Sumerian poem will have little more value than a composite version of a Hopi myth for the field worker alert to the variations among the clans and from one performance to another.[22] The application of oral epic theory, coupled with the folklorist's awareness of how and why tales become popular and spread beyond national boundaries, must now be as seriously considered for other ancient Near Eastern literature as it has been for the Bible.

The situation facing Sumerologists is summarized thus by van Dijk:

> Les textes pullulent de variantes, parfois très substantielles, de transpositions et d'insertions, qui empêchent de les réduire à un texte composite. Il semble que la transmission du récit ait reposé en grande partie sur la tradition orale des conteurs populaires et des maîtres d'écoles qui ont usé d'une grande liberté en dictant le texte à leurs élèves. Ainsi s'explique le fait que des recensions très divergentes, contemporaines de ce texte, ont été retrouvées dans le même endroit.[23]

If this is an accurate statement of the ancient situation, then we have several levels of oral transmission: the popular storyteller, the oral epic poet (ignored by van Dijk), and the teacher who "dictates" (or retells?) the story to his pupils as they learn to write the complex cuneiform script and often an alien or archaic language. Each stage will produce its own kinds of variation, but all make the knowledge of oral transmission an essential part of the scholar's equipment.

In the past, the model for editing cuneiform texts has been the collation of medieval manuscripts and ancient papyrus fragments of classical texts, and the assumption behind this enterprise has been the possibility that one could thus recover from the accumulated scribal errors of centuries what the author actually wrote. But in the case of oral poetry, there is no such thing as a fixed text, for each performance is unique, even when there is considerable interaction with written forms. If very divergent recensions are often found in the same place, then we have a *prima facie* case for oral composition and transmission. A composite text, made up of fragments from scattered archaeological sites, and sometimes, as in the case of the Gilgamesh epic, in different languages, will satisfy our own desire for a complete story, but it will not tell us how the story went in any actual per-

---

[22] Eggan 1950:79: "The origin legends of the same clan from different villages show major contradictions and . . . even within the same village the stories of associate clans did not always correspond." Cf. Falkenstein 1960:70–71, and see now Tigay 1982.

[23] Van Dijk in Garelli (ed.) 1960:69.

formance. Above all, it does not allow for the enormous range of variation between one performance and another, and which is actually demonstrable for the Gilgamesh tradition. We are lucky in that enough of the Gilgamesh material has survived for us to reconstruct at least some of the probable versions current between five and three thousand years ago.

At some point in each tradition, it is clear, poetic narratives were written down and then fixed in scribal tradition. They were often then handed down within the school system, which trained scribes in the different cuneiform writing system. Most variants thereafter seem to be due often to mishearing a standard text dictated by the teacher, probably from memory, or less often to misreading a sign. Yet dictating from memory may often produce significant variation itself and is indeed a common method of oral "composition," as Finnegan has shown.[24] No doubt there was little scope for free variation in the scribal schools, since the whole point was to learn the writing method accurately. But one must allow for a continuum between exact copying and oral composition even when the texts had become, in one particular context, standard and so hallowed.

[24] Finnegan 1977:16–24, 73–77.

BIBLIOGRAPHY AND REFERENCES

AARNE, Anti, and THOMPSON, Stith. 1964. *Types of the Folktale*. Helsinki. Academia Scientiarum Fennica.

ADAM, A. 1952. "Der Manichäische Ursprung von den Zwei Reichen bei Augustin." *Theologische Literaturzeitung* 77:385–90.

AHARONI, Yohanan. 1976. "Nothing Early and Nothing Late: Rewriting Israel's Conquest." *Biblical Archaeologist* 39:55–76.

ALBRIGHT, William F. 1950. "The Psalm of Habakkuk." In *Studies in Old Testament Prophecy*, edited by H. H. Rowley, pp. 1–18. Edinburgh: T. & T. Clark.

—— 1957. *From the Stone Age to Christianity: Monotheism and the Historical Process.* 2nd ed. New York: Doubleday.

ALEXANDER, P. S. 1972. "The Targumim and Early Exegesis of 'Sons of God' in Genesis 6." *Journal of Jewish Studies* 23:60–71.

ALSTER, Bendt. 1972. *Dumuzi's Dream: Aspects of Oral Poetry in a Sumerian Myth.* Copenhagen: Akademisk Forlag.

—— 1975. "On the Interpretation of the Sumerian Myth 'Inanna and Enki.' " *Zeitschrift für Assyriologie* 64:20–24.

ALTER, Robert. 1981. *The Art of Biblical Narrative*. New York: Basic Books.

ALTMANN, A. 1944. "The Gnostic Background of the Rabbinic Adam Legends." *Jewish Quarterly Review* 35:371–89.

AMIET, Pierre. 1953. "Les combats mythologiques dans l'art mésopotamien du troisième et du début du second millénaire." *Revue archéologique* 42:129–64.

ANDERSON, Bernhard W. 1962. "Exodus Typology in Second Isaiah." In *Israel's Prophetic Heritage*, edited by Bernhard W. Anderson and W. Harrelson, pp. 177–95. New York: Harper and Row.

—— 1967. *Creation Versus Chaos: The Reinterpretation of Mythical Symbolism in the Bible.* New York: Association Press.

—— 1970. "Myth and the Biblical Tradition." *Theology Today* 27:44–62.

—— 1975. *Understanding the Old Testament.* Englewood Cliffs, N.J.: Prentice-Hall.

—— 1978. "The Interpretation of Genesis 1–11." *Journal of Biblical Literature* 97: 23–39.

ARMSTRONG, A. H. 1972. "St. Augustine and Christian Platonism." In *Augustine: A Collection of Critical Essays*, edited by R. S. Markus, pp. 3–37. New York: Doubleday Anchor.

ASTOUR, Michael C. 1967. *Helleno-Semitica: An Ethnic and Cultural Study in West-Semitic Impact on Mycenaean Greece.* Leiden: Brill.

AUERBACH, Erich. 1953. *Mimesis*. Princeton: Princeton University Press.

AULÉN, Gustav. 1969 (1st ed. 1931). *Christus Victor*. New York: Macmillan.

BAMBERGER, Bernard J. 1952. *Fallen Angels*. Philadelphia: Jewish Publication Society of America.

BARC, B. 1981. "Samaèl-Saklas-Yaldabaôth. Recherche sur la genèse d'un mythe gnostique." In *Colloque International sur les textes de Nag Hammadi, Québec 22–25 août 1978*, edited by B. Barc, pp. 123–50. Quebec and Louvain: Laval University Press.

BARC, B., ed. 1981. *Colloque International sur les textes de Nag Hammadi, Québec 22–25 août 1978*. Quebec and Louvain: Laval University Press.

BARR, J. 1974. "Philo of Byblos." *Bulletin of the John Rylands Library* 57:17–68.

BARRETT, C. K. 1973. *A Commentary on the Second Epistle to the Corinthians*. London: A. & C. Black.

—— 1983. "Gnosis and the Apocalypse of John." In *The New Testament and Gnosis: Essays in Honour of R. McL. Wilson*, edited by A. H. B. Logan and A. J. M. Wedderburn, pp. 125–37. Edinburgh: T. & T. Clark.

BARTH, Markus. 1974. *Ephesians*. 2 vols. New York: Doubleday Anchor.

BARTHÉLEMY, D., and MILIK, J. T. 1955. *Qumran Cave I*. Discoveries in the Judaean Desert 1. Oxford: Clarendon Press.

BARTHELMUS, R. 1979. *Heroentum in Israel und seiner Umwelt*. Zurich: Theologischer Verlag.

BARTHES, Roland, et al. 1974. *Structural Analysis and Biblical Exegesis*. Pittsburgh: Pickwick.

BARTON, George A. 1893. "Tiamat." *Journal of the American Oriental Society* 15: 1–27.

BARTSCH, H. W., ed. 1961. *Kerygma and Myth*. New York: Harper and Row.

BASCOM, William. 1957, 1958. "The Myth-Ritual Theory." *Journal of American Folklore* 70:103–14, 359–61; 71:79–80, 152–56.

—— 1965. "The Forms of Folklore: Prose Narratives." *Journal of American Folklore* 78:3–20.

BAUER, Walter. 1972 (1st ed. 1934). *Orthodoxy and Heresy in Earliest Christianity*. London: SCM Press.

BAUMGARTEN, A. I. 1981. *The Phoenician History of Philo of Byblos*. Leiden: Brill.

BAUMGARTEN, J. 1975. *Paulus und die Apokalyptik*. Neukirchen-Vluyn: Neukirchener Verlag.

BEASLEY-MURRAY, G. R. 1983. "The Interpretation of Daniel 7." *Catholic Bible Quarterly* 45:44–58.

BECKWITH, R. T. 1981. "The Earliest Enoch Literature and Its Calendar: Marks of Their Origin, Date, and Motivation." *Revue de Qumran* 10.39:365–404.

BEN AMOS, D. 1969. "Analytical Categories and Ethnic Genres." *Genre* 2:295–301.

BENEDICT, Ruth. 1935. *Zuni Mythology*. 2 vols. New York: Columbia University Press.

BERLIN, Adele. 1981. *Enmerkar and Ensuhkesdanna*. Leiden: Brill.

BEST, E. 1965. *The Temptation and the Passion: The Markan Soteriology*. Cambridge: Cambridge University Press.

BETZ, Hans Dieter. 1979. *Galatians*. Philadelphia: Westminster.

BIANCHI, Ugo. 1978. "Docetism: A Peculiar Theory About the Ambivalence of the Presence of the Divine." In *Selected Essays on Gnosticism, Dualism, and Mysteriosophy*, pp. 303–11. Leiden: Brill.

BIANCHI, Ugo, ed. 1967. *Le origini delle gnosticismo: Colloquio di Messina 13–18 aprile 1966*. Leiden: Brill.

BIDNEY, David. 1967. "The Concept of Myth." *Theoretical Anthropology* 2:286–326.

BLACK, Matthew. 1985. *The Book of Enoch*. Leiden: Brill.

BLACK, Matthew, ed. 1970. *Apocalypsis Henochi Graece*. Leiden: Brill.

BLACKMAN, Edwin C. 1948. *Marcion and His Influence*. London: S.P.C.K.

BOEDEKER, Deborah. 1974. *Aphrodite's Entry into Greek Epic*. Leiden: Brill.

BOHANNAN, Laura. 1966. "Shakespeare in the Bush." *Natural History* 75:28–33.

BOKSER, Baruch M. 1985. "Wonder Working and the Rabbinic Tradition." *Journal for the Study of Judaism* 16:42–92.

BOLTE, Johannes, and POLIVKA, Georg. 1913–32. *Anmerkungen zu den Kinder- und Hausmärchen des Brüder Grimm*. 5 vols. Leipzig: Dieterich.

BOMAN, Thorlief. 1960. *Hebrew Thought Compared with Greek*. London: SCM Press.

BOOTH, Wayne. 1974. *A Rhetoric of Irony*. Chicago: University of Chicago Press.

BORNKAMM, G. 1961. *Die Vorgeschichte des Sogenannten Zweiten Korintherbriefs*. Heidelberg: C. Winter.

—— 1966 (1st ed. 1952). *Das Ende des Gesetzes: Paulusstudien, Gesammelte Aufsätze*. Munich: C. Kaiser.

—— 1971. *Paul*. 2 vols. New York: Harper and Row.

BORRET, Marcel, ed. 1967–76. *Origène: Contre Celse*. 5 vols. Paris: Editions du Cerf.

BORSCH, F. H. 1967. *The Son of Man in Myth and History*. Philadelphia: Fortress.

BOURKE, J. G. 1891. *Scatalogic Rites of All Nations*. Washington, D.C.: Lowdermilk.

BOUSSET, Wilhelm. 1896. *The Antichrist Legend*. London: AMS Press (reprint).

BOWKER, John. 1969. *The Targums and Rabbinic Literature*. Cambridge: Cambridge University Press.

BOYD, James W. 1975. *Satan and Mara: Christian and Buddhist Symbols of Evil*. Leiden: Brill.

BRANDENBURGER, E. 1962. *Adam und Christos*. Neukirchen: Neukirchener Verlag.

BRANDON, S.G.F. 1963. "The Devil in Faith and History." *History Today* 13:468–78.

BREASTED, James. 1933. *The Dawn of Conscience*. New York: Scribner's.

BRÉMOND, Claude. 1966. "La logique des possibles narratifs." *Communications* 8:60–76.

—— 1970. "Morphology of the French Folktale." *Semiotica* 2:247–76.

BRIGGS, Katherine. 1964. "The Folds of Folklore." *Shakespeare Survey* 17:165–78.

BRIGHT, John. 1972. *A History of Israel*. Philadelphia: Westminster.

BROWN, C. S. 1966. "Odysseus and Polyphemos: The Name and the Curse." *Comparative Literature* 18:193–202.

BROWN, Norman O. 1970. *Life Against Death*. Middletown, Conn.: Wesleyan University Press.

BROWN, Peter. 1967. *Augustine of Hippo*. Berkeley: University of California.

—— 1969. "The Diffusion of Manichaeism in the Roman Empire." *Journal of Roman Studies* 59:92–103.

BROWN, Raymond E. 1965. *New Testament Essays*. Milwaukee: Bruce.

—— 1966. *The Gospel According to John*. Anchor Bible. New York: Doubleday.

—— 1982. *The Epistles of John*. Anchor Bible. New York: Doubleday.

BRUCE, F. F. 1982. *The Epistle to the Galatians*. Grand Rapids, Mich.: Eerdmans.

BRUNDAGE, B. C. 1958. "Hercules the Levantine: A Comprehensive View." *Journal of Near Eastern Studies* 17:225–36.

BRUNO DE JÉSUS-MARIE, ed. 1952. *Satan: Essays Collected and Translated from "Etudes Carmélitaines."* New York: Sheed and Ward.

BRUNS, Gerald L. 1984. "Canon and Power in the Hebrew Scriptures." In *Canons*, edited by Robert von Hallberg, pp. 65–83. Chicago: University of Chicago Press.

BUBER, Martin. 1952. *Good and Evil*. New York: Scribner's.

BULTMANN, Rudolph. 1951, 1955. *Theology of the New Testament*. 2 vols. New York: Scribner's.

—— 1957. *History and Eschatology*. New York: Harper and Row.

—— 1958a (4th ed., Eng. trans., 1968). *Die Geschichte der synoptischen Tradition*. Göttingen: Vandenhoeck and Ruprecht.

—— 1958b. *Jesus Christ and Mythology*. New York: Scribner's.

BURKE, Kenneth. 1968. *Language as Symbolic Action*. Berkeley: University of California Press.

—— 1970. *The Rhetoric of Religion: Studies in Logology*. Berkeley: University of California Press.

BURKITT, F. C. 1932. *Church and Gnosis*. London: AMS Press.

BURROWS, Millar. 1958. *More Light on the Dead Sea Scrolls*. London: Secker and Warburg.

—— 1968 (1st ed. 1955). *The Dead Sea Scrolls*. New York: Viking.

BUTLER, Elizabeth M. 1952. *The Fortunes of Faust*. Cambridge: Cambridge University Press.

BUTTERWORTH, Edric A. S. 1970. *The Tree at the Navel of the Earth*. Berlin: De Gruyter.

BYNUM, David E. 1978. *The Daemon in the Wood: A Study of Oral Narrative Patterns*. Cambridge, Mass.: Harvard University Press.

CAIRD, G. B. 1956. *Principalities and Powers: A Study in Pauline Theology*. Oxford: Clarendon.

—— 1966. *A Commentary on the Revelation of St. John the Divine*. London: A. & C. Black.

CAMPBELL, Edward F., Jr., and FREEDMAN, David Noel, eds. 1970. *The Biblical Archaeologist Reader 3*. New York: Doubleday Anchor.

CAQUOT, A. 1958. "Le dieu *'Attr* et les textes de Ras Shamra." *Syria* 35:45–60.

CAQUOT, A., and SZNYCER, M. 1970. "Textes ougaritiques." In *Les religions du Proche-Orient asiatique*. Paris: Fayard-Denoël.

—— 1974. *Textes ougaritiques*. Vol. 1: *Mythes et legendes*. Paris: Editions du Cerf.

CARGILL-THOMPSON, W.D.J. 1980. *Studies in the Reformation*. London: Athlone.

CARR, Wesley. 1981. *Angels and Principalities*. Cambridge: Cambridge University Press.

CARROLL, Robert P. 1979a. "Twilight of Prophesy or Dawn of Apocalyptic?" *Journal for the Study of the Old Testament* 14:3–35.

—— 1979b. *When Prophecy Failed: Cognitive Dissonance in the Prophetic Traditions of the Old Testament*. New York: Seabury.

CARSCH, Henry. 1968. "The Role of the Devil in Grimms' Tales." *Social Research* 35:466–99.

CARTER-PHILIPS, F. 1978. "Heracles." *Classical World* 71:431–40.

CARUS, Paul. 1974 (1st ed. 1899). *The History of the Devil and the Idea of Evil*. Chicago: Open Court.

CASSUTO, Umberto. 1961–64. *A Commentary on the Book of Genesis*. 2 vols. Jerusalem: Magnes.

CHADWICK, Henry. 1966. *Early Christian Thought and the Classical Tradition: Studies in Justin, Clement, and Origen*. Oxford: Clarendon.

—— 1953. *Origen: Contra Celsum*. Cambridge: Cambridge University Press.

CHADWICK, Henry M., and CHADWICK, Nora K. 1932. *The Growth of Literature*. 2 vols. Cambridge: Cambridge University Press.

CHARLES, R. H., ed. 1893. *The Book of Enoch*. Oxford: Clarendon.

—— 1913. *The Apocrypha and the Pseudepigrapha of the Old Testament*. 2 vols. Oxford: Clarendon.

CHARLESWORTH, James H. 1976. *The Pseudepigrapha and Modern Research*. Missoula, Mont.: Scholars Press.

CHARLESWORTH, James H., ed. 1983. *The Old Testament Pseudepigrapha*. Vol. 1. London: Darton, Longman, and Todd.

CHEYNE, T. K. 1895. Review of *Shöpfung und Chaos* by Hermann Gunkel. *Critical Review* 5:256–66.

CHILDS, Brevard S. 1959. "The Enemy from the North and the Chaos Tradition." *Journal of Biblical Literature* 78:187–98.

CHILDS, Brevard S. 1960. *Myth and Reality in the Old Testament.* London: SCM Press.

—— 1970. "A Traditio-Historical Study of the Reed Sea Tradition." *Vetus Testamentum* 20:406–18.

—— 1974. *The Book of Exodus.* Philadelphia: Westminster.

CLADER, Linda Lee. 1976. *Helen: The Evolution from Divine to Heroic in Greek Epic Tradition.* Leiden: Brill.

CLAPHAM, Lynn R. 1969. "Sanchuniathon: The First Two Cycles." Ph.D. diss., Harvard University.

CLARKE, Ernest G., ed. 1973. *The Wisdom of Solomon.* Cambridge: Cambridge University Press.

CLEMENTS, R. E. 1977. Review of *Das überlieferungeschichtliche Problem des Pentateuch* by R. Rentdorff. *Journal for the Study of the Old Testament* 3:46–56.

—— 1980. *Isaiah and the Deliverance of Jerusalem.* Sheffield, Eng.: JSOT.

CLIFFORD, Richard J. 1972. *The Cosmic Mountain in Canaan and the Old Testament.* Cambridge, Mass.: Harvard University Press.

CLINES, D.J.A. 1979. "The Significance of the 'Sons of God' Episode." *Journal for the Study of the Old Testament* 13:33–46.

COATS, George W. 1967. "The Traditio-Historical Character of the Reed Sea Motif." *Vetus Testamentum* 17:253–62.

COCHRANE, Charles N. 1957. *Christianity and Classical Culture.* New York: Oxford University Press.

COHEN, Percy. 1969. "Theories of Myth." *Man,* N.S. 4:337–53.

COHN, Norman. 1975. *Europe's Inner Demons.* London: Chatto.

—— 1977. *The Pursuit of the Millennium.* Oxford: Oxford University Press.

COLLINS, J. J. 1975. "The Mythology of the Holy War in Daniel and the Qumran War Scroll." *Vetus Testamentum* 25:496–512.

—— 1978. "Methodological Issues in the Study of I Enoch." *Society of Biblical Literature Seminar Papers* 5:315–22.

—— 1981. "Patterns of Eschatology at Qumran." In *Traditions in Transformation,* edited by B. Halpern and J. D. Levinson, pp. 351–75. Winona Lake, Ind.: Eisenbrauns.

COLLINS, J. J., ed. 1979. *Apocalypse: Morphology of a Genre.* Missoula, Mont.: Scholars Press.

CONZELMANN, Hans. 1969. *An Outline of the Theology of the New Testament.* New York: Harper and Row.

—— 1973. *History of Primitive Christianity.* Nashville: Abingdon.

—— 1975. *I Corinthians.* Philadelphia: Fortress.

COOPER, Alan. 1983. "Psalm 24.7–10: Mythology and Exegesis." *Journal of Biblical Literature* 102:37–60.

COURCELLE, Pierre. 1950. *Recherches sur les confessions de Saint Augustin.* Paris: Boccard.

—— 1952. "Source chrétienne et allusions païennes de l'épisode du 'Tolle, lege.' " *Revue d'histoire et de philosophie religieuse* 32:171–200.

—— 1984. *Opuscula Selecta*. Paris: Etudes Augustiniennes.

COURT, John M. 1979. *Myth and History in the Book of Revelation*. London: S.P.C.K.

CRANFIELD, C.E.B. 1979. *The Epistle to the Romans*. 2 vols. Edinburgh: T. & T. Clark.

CROSS, F. L., ed. 1955. *The Jung Codex, A Newly Discovered Gnostic Papyrus: Three Studies by H. C. Puech, G. Quispel, W. C. Van Unnik*. London: Mowbray.

CROSS, Frank Moore. 1953. "The Council of Yahweh in Second Isaiah." *Journal of Near Eastern Studies* 12:274–77.

—— 1973. *Canaanite Myth and Hebrew Epic*. Cambridge, Mass.: Harvard University Press.

CROSS, Frank Moore, and TALMON, Shemayuhu, eds. 1975. *Qumran and the History of the Biblical Text*. Cambridge, Mass.: Harvard University Press.

CROUZEL, Henri, and SIMONETTI, Manlio, eds. 1978–84. *Origène: Traité des Principes*. Paris: Editions du Cerf.

CULLER, Jonathan. 1975. *Structuralist Poetics*. Ithaca, N.Y.: Cornell University Press.

CULLEY, R. C. 1976. *Studies in the Structure of Hebrew Narrative*. Philadelphia: Fortress.

CULLMANN, Oscar. 1957. *The State in the New Testament*. London: SCM Press.

—— 1962. *Christ and Time*. London: SCM Press.

CUSHMAN, L. W. 1900. *The Devil and the Vice in English Dramatic Literature Before Shakespeare*. Halle a.S.: Niemeyer.

DAHL, N. A. 1964. "Der Erstgeborene Satans und der Vater des Teufels (Polyk. 7.1 und Joh. 8.44)." In *Apophoreta: Festschrift für Ernst Haenchen*, pp. 70–84. Berlin: Töpelmann.

—— 1981. "The Arrogant Archon and the Lewd Sophia: Jewish Traditions in Gnostic Revolt." In *The Rediscovery of Gnosticism*, edited by B. Layton, vol. 2, pp. 689–712. Leiden: Brill.

DAHOOD, Mitchell. 1966. *Psalms 1–50*. Anchor Bible. New York: Doubleday.

—— 1969. *Psalms 51–100*. Anchor Bible. New York: Doubleday.

—— 1970. *Psalms 101–150*. Anchor Bible. New York: Doubleday.

DAMON, Philip. 1969. "Dilation and Displacement in the *Odyssey*." *Pacific Coast Philology* 5:49–53.

—— 1980. "The Middle of Things: Narrative Patterns in the Iliad, Roland, and Beowulf." In *Old English Literature in Context: Ten Essays*, edited by John Niles. Cambridge: Cambridge University Press.

DANIÉLOU, J. 1948. *Le génie du Christianisme I: Origène*. Paris: La Table Ronde.

—— 1950. *Sacramentum Futuri*. Paris: Beauchesne.

DARDEL, Eric. 1954. "The Mythic." *Diogenes* 7:33–51.

DAVENPORT, Gene L. 1971. *The Eschatology of the Book of Jubilees*. Leiden: Brill.

DAVIDSON, R. 1973. *Genesis 1–11*. Cambridge: Cambridge University Press.

DAY, John. 1985. *God's Conflict with the Dragon and the Sea*. Cambridge: Cambridge University Press.

DELCOR, M. 1971. *Le livre de Daniel*. Paris: Gabalda.

—— 1976. "Le mythe de la chute des anges et l'origine des géants comme explication du mal dans le monde dans l'apocalyptique juive: Histoire des traditions." *Revue de l'histoire des religions* 190:3–53.

DENIS, Albert-Marie. 1970. *Introduction aux pseudépigraphes grecques*. Leiden: Brill.

DE ROUGEMONT, Denis. 1944. *The Devil's Share*. New York: Bollingen.

DETIENNE, Marcel. 1958. "La legende pythagoricienne d'Helène." *Revue de l'histoire des religions* 152:128–52.

DE VRIES, J. 1961. *Forschungsgeschichte der Mythologie*. Freiburg and Munich: Alber.

DEXINGER, Ferdinand. 1966. *Sturz der Göttersöhne oder Engel vor der Sintflut? Versuch eines Neuverständnisses von Genesis 6.2–4*. Vienna: Herder.

DHORME, P. 1919. "Les traditions babyloniennes sur les origines." *Revue biblique* 28:350–71.

DIBELIUS, Martin. 1909. *Die Geisterwelt im Glauben des Paulus*. Göttingen: Vandenhoeck and Ruprecht.

—— 1935 (1st ed. 1919). *From Tradition to Gospel*. New York: Scribner's.

DIETRICH, B. C. 1974. *Origins of Greek Religion*. Berlin: De Gruyter.

DIGGLE, James. 1978. *Euripides: Phaethon*. Cambridge: Cambridge University Press.

DILLON, John. 1977. *The Middle Platonists*. London: Duckworth.

DIMANT, Devorah. 1978. "1 Enoch 6–11: A Methodological Perspective." *Society of Biblical Literature Seminar Papers* 5:323–39.

DION, Roger. 1969. *Les anthropophages de l'Odyssée, cyclopes et laestrygons*. Paris: Vion.

DODD, C. H. 1932. *The Epistle of Paul to the Romans*. London: Hodder and Stoughton.

—— 1935. *The Bible and the Greeks*. London: Hodder and Stoughton.

—— 1953. "The Mind of Paul." In *New Testament Studies*, pp. 83–128. Manchester, Eng.: Manchester University Press.

DODDS, E. R. 1965. *Pagan and Christian in an Age of Anxiety*. Cambridge: Cambridge University Press.

DODS, Marcus, trans. 1950. *Augustine: The City of God*. New York: Modern Library.

DÖLGER, Franz-Joseph. 1929–34. "Der Kampf mit dem Agypter in der Perpetua-Vision: Das Martyrium als Kampf mit dem Teufel." In Dölger's *Antike und Christentum*, vol. 3, pp. 177–88. Münster: Aschendorff.

DORESSE, J. 1960. *The Secret Books of the Egyptian Gnostics*. New York: Viking.

DORSON, Richard M. 1965. "The Eclipse of Solar Mythology." In *Myth: A Sym-*

posium, edited by Thomas A. Sebeok, pp. 25–63. Bloomington: Indiana University Press.

DORSON, Richard M., ed. 1968. *Peasant Customs and Savage Myths: Selections from the British Folklorists*. Chicago: University of Chicago Press.

DOTY, William G. 1972. *Contemporary New Testament Interpretation*. Englewood Cliffs, N.J.: Prentice-Hall.

DRESDEN, Michael J. 1961. "Mythology of Ancient Iran." In *Mythologies of the Ancient World*, edited by Samuel N. Kramer, pp. 331–64. New York: Doubleday Anchor.

DRIVER, G. R. 1956a. *Canaanite Myths and Legends*. Edinburgh: T. & T. Clark.

—— 1956b. "Mythical Monsters in the Old Testament." In *Studi Orientalistici in onore di Giorgio Levi della Vida*, vol. 1, pp. 234–49. Rome: Instituto per l'Oriente.

DRIVER, S. R. 1907. *The Book of Genesis*. London: Methuen.

—— 1925. *An Introduction to the Literature of the Old Testament*. New York: Scribner's.

DRURY, John. 1976. *Tradition and Design in Luke's Gospel*. London: Darton, Longman, and Todd.

DUCHESNE-GUILLEMIN, Jacques. 1953. *Ormazd et Ahriman*. Paris: Presses Universitaires de France.

—— 1958. *The Western Response to Zoroaster*. Oxford: Clarendon.

—— 1963. *The Hymns of Zarathustra*. Boston: Beacon Press.

DUMÉZIL, Georges. 1945. *Naissance d'archanges: Essai sur la formation de la théologie zoroastrienne (Jupiter, Mars, Quirinus III)*. Paris: Gallimard.

DUMONT, Louis. 1972. "A Structural Definition of a Folk Deity of Tamil Nad: Aiyanar, the Lord." In *A Reader in Comparative Religion*, edited by William A. Lessa and E. Z. Vogt, pp. 189–95. New York: Harper and Row.

DUNDES, Alan. 1962a. "Earth-Diver: Creation of the Mythopoeic Male." *American Anthropologist* 64:1032–51.

—— 1962b. "From Etic to Emic Units in the Structural Study of Folktales." *Journal of American Folklore* 75:95–105.

—— 1964. *Morphology of North American Indian Folktales*. Folklore Fellows Communications 195. Helsinki.

—— 1975. *Analytical Essays in Folklore*. The Hague: Mouton.

—— 1976a. "A Psychoanalytic Study of the Bullroarer." *Man*, N.S. 2:220–38.

—— 1976b. "Structuralism and Folklore." *Studia Fenica* 20:75–93.

—— 1976c. "To Love My Father All: A Psychoanalytic Study of the Folktale Source of *King Lear*." *Southern Folklore Quarterly* 40:353–66.

—— 1977. *The Hero Pattern and the Life of Jesus*. Berkeley, Calif.: Centre for Hermeneutical Studies.

DUNDES, Alan, ed. 1965. *The Study of Folklore*. Englewood Cliffs, N.J.: Prentice-Hall.

EGGAN, Fred. 1950. *Social Organization of the Western Pueblo*. Chicago: University of Chicago Press.

EICHRODT, Walther. 1962. "In the Beginning." In *Israel's Prophetic Heritage*, edited by Bernhard W. Anderson and W. Harrelson, pp. 1–10. New York: Harper and Row.

—— 1970. *Ezekiel: A Commentary*. Philadelphia: Westminster.

EISSFELDT, Otto. 1932. *Baal Zaphon, Zeus Kasios und der Durchzug der Israeliten durchs Meer*. Halle: Niemeyer.

ELIADE, Mircea. 1959. *Cosmos and History*. New York: Harper and Row.

ELLIS, E. Earle. 1975. "Paul and His Opponents: Trends in Research." In *Christianity, Judaism, and Other Greco-Roman Cults*, edited by Jacob Neusner, vol. 1, pp. 264–98. Leiden: Brill.

ELLIS, Peter. 1968. *The Yahwist: The Bible's First Theologian*. Notre Dame, Ind.: Fides.

EMERTON, J. A. 1971. "The Riddle of Genesis xiv." *Vetus Testamentum* 21:403–39.

—— 1982. "Leviathan and *ltn*: The Vocalization of the Ugaritic Word for the Dragon." *Vetus Testamentum* 32:327–31.

ERIKSON, Erik H. 1958. *Young Man Luther*. New York: Norton.

ETHERIDGE, J. W. 1968 (1st ed. 1862). *The Targums of Onkelos and Jonathan ben Uzziel on the Pentateuch, with the Fragments of the Jerusalem Targum: Genesis and Exodus*. New York: Ktav.

EVANS, Ernest. 1972. *Tertullian: Adversus Marcionem*. Oxford: Clarendon.

EVANS, J. Martin. 1968. *"Paradise Lost" and the Genesis Tradition*. Oxford: Clarendon.

EVELYN-WHITE, Hugh G., ed. 1914. *Hesiod, the Homeric Hymns, and Homerica*. Loeb Classical Library. Cambridge, Mass.: Harvard University Press.

FALKENSTEIN, Adam. 1960. "Zur Überlieferung des Epos von Gilgameš und Huwawa." *Journal of Near Eastern Studies* 69:65–71.

FALLON, F. T. 1978. *The Enthronement of Sabaoth: Jewish Elements in Gnostic Creation Myths*. Leiden: Brill.

FARRER, Austin. 1951. *A Study in Mark*. London: Dacre.

FELDMAN, Burton, and RICHARDSON, Robert D., eds. 1972. *The Rise of Modern Mythology: 1680–1860*. Bloomington: Indiana University Press.

FELL, John L. 1977. "Vladimir Propp in Hollywood." *Film Quarterly* 30:19–28.

FENIK, Bernard, ed. 1978. *Homer: Tradition and Originality*. Leiden: Brill.

FENTON, John C. 1978. "Controversy in the New Testament." *Studia Biblica* 3 (*Journal for the Study of the New Testament*, Supplementary Series 3):97–110.

FINET, André, ed. 1973. *La voix de l'opposition en Mesopotamie*. Brussels: Comité belge de recherche en Mésopotamie.

FINNEGAN, Ruth. 1967. *Limba Stories and Story-Telling*. Oxford: Oxford University Press.

—— 1977. *Oral Poetry*. Cambridge: Cambridge University Press.

FIRTH, Raymond. 1963. "Offering and Sacrifice: Problems of Organisation." *Journal of the Royal Anthropological Institute* 93:12–24.

FISCHER, John L. 1963. "The Sociopsychological Analysis of Folktales." *Current Anthropology* 4:235–95.

FITZMYER, J. A. 1971. *The Genesis Apocryphon of Qumran Cave I: A Commentary*. Rome: Pontifical Biblical Institute.

—— 1974. *Essays on the Semitic Background of the New Testament*. Missoula, Mont.: Scholars Press.

FLUSSER, D. 1953. "The Apocryphal Book of *Ascensio Isaiae* and the Dead Sea Sect." *Israel Exploration Journal* 3:30–47.

FÖRSTER, Werner. 1964. *From the Exile to Christ: A Historical Introduction to Palestinian Judaism*. Philadelphia: Fortress.

FÖRSTER, Werner, ed. 1972. *Gnosis: A Selection of Gnostic Texts*. 2 vols. Oxford: Clarendon.

FOLEY, John M. 1985. *Oral-Formulaic Theory and Research: An Introduction and Annotated Bibliography*. New York: Garland.

FONTENROSE, Joseph. 1945. "Philemon, Lot, and Lycaon." *University of California Publications in Classical Philology* 13:93–120.

—— 1959. *Python: A Study in Delphic Myth*. Berkeley: University of California Press.

—— 1966. *The Ritual Theory of Myth*. Berkeley: University of California Press.

FORD, J. Massyngberde. 1975. *Revelation*. Anchor Bible. New York: Doubleday.

FORSYTH, Neil. 1979. "The Allurement Scene: A Typical Pattern in Greek Oral Epic." *California Studies in Classical Antiquity* 13:107–20.

—— 1981. "Huwawa and His Trees: A Narrative and Cultural Analysis." *Acta Sumerologica* 3:13–29.

—— 1985. "Having Done All to Stand: Biblical and Classical Allusion in *Paradise Regained*." *Milton Studies* 22:199–214.

FOUCAULT, Michel. 1969. "Qu'est-ce qu'un auteur?" *Bulletin de la Société Française de la Philosophie* 63:73–95.

FOWLER, Alastair, ed. 1971. *John Milton: Paradise Lost*. London: Longman.

FRAME, Douglas. 1977. *The Myth of Return in Early Greek Epic*. New Haven: Yale University Press.

FRANKFORT, Henri. 1934. "Gods and Myths on Sargonid Seals." *Iraq* 1:2–29.

—— 1939. *Cylinder Seals*. London: Macmillan.

FRAZER, James G. 1919. *Folklore in the Old Testament*. 3 vols. London: Macmillan.

FREI, Hans. 1974. *The Eclipse of Biblical Narrative*. New Haven: Yale University Press.

FRIDRICHSEN, Anton. 1931. "The Conflict of Jesus with the Unclean Spirits." *Theology* 22:122–35.

FRIEDMAN, Jerome. 1978. *Michael Servetus: A Case Study in Total Heresy*. Geneva: Droz.

FROIDEVAUX, L. M., ed. 1959. *Irénée de Lyon: Démonstration de la Prédication Apostolique*. Sources Crétiennes. Paris: Editions du Cerf.

FRYE, Northrop. 1957. *Anatomy of Criticism*. Princeton: Princeton University Press.

—— 1983. *The Great Code: The Bible and Literature*. New York: Harcourt Brace Jovanovich.

FRYE, R. N. 1975. "Qumran and Iran: The State of Studies." *Christianity, Judaism, and Other Greco-Roman Cults*, edited by Jacob Neusner, vol. 1, pp. 107–73. Leiden: Brill.

FULLER, R. H. 1962. *The New Testament in Current Study*. New York: Scribner's.

GAISSER, Julia H. 1969. "Adaptation of Traditional Material in the Glaucus-Diomedes Episode." *Transactions of the American Philological Association* 100:165–76.

GARÇON, Maurice, and VINCHON, Jean. 1930. *The Devil: A Historical, Critical, and Medical Study*. New York: Dutton.

GARELLI, Paul, ed. 1960. *Gilgameš et sa légende*. Cahiers du Groupe François-Thureau-Dangin 1. Paris: C. Klincksieck.

GASTER, Theodore H. 1952. "The Egyptian 'Story of Astarte' and the Ugaritic Poem of Baal." *Bibliotheca Orientalis* 9:82–85.

—— 1961. *Thespis: Ritual, Myth, and Drama in the Ancient Near East*. New York: Doubleday Anchor.

—— 1963. "Demon, Demonology." In *Interpreter's Dictionary of the Bible*, edited by G. A. Buttrick et al., vol. 1, pp. 202–9. Nashville: Abingdon.

—— 1964. *The Dead Sea Scriptures*. New York: Doubleday Anchor.

—— 1971. "Belial." In *Encyclopedia Judaica*, vol. 4, pp. 427–28. Jerusalem: Keter.

GELB, I. J. 1963. *A Study of Writing*. Chicago: University of Chicago Press.

GEORGI, Dieter. 1964. *Die Gegner des Paulus im 2. Korintherbrief*. Neukirchen-Vluyn: Neukirchener.

GIBB, John, and MONTGOMERY, William. 1972. *Augustinus: Confessiones*. Cambridge: Cambridge University Press.

GINZBERG, Louis. 1910–38. *Legends of the Jews*. 7 vols. Philadelphia: Jewish Publication Society.

GLASSON, T. F. 1961. *Greek Influence in Jewish Eschatology*. London: S.P.C.K.

GLENN, Justin. 1971. "The Polyphemos Folktale and Homer's Kyklopeia." *Classical Journal* 102:131–81.

GOETZE, A. 1969. "Hittite Myths, Epics, and Legends." In *Ancient Near Eastern Texts in Relation to the Old Testament*, edited by James B. Pritchard (3rd ed.). Princeton: Princeton University Press.

GOODSPEED, Edgar J. 1927. *The Formation of the New Testament*. Chicago: University of Chicago Press.

—— 1938. *The Apocrypha*. Chicago: University of Chicago Press.

GORDIS, Robert. 1965. *The Book of God and Man: A Study of Job*. Chicago: University of Chicago Press.

—— 1971. *Poets, Prophets, and Sages: Essays in Biblical Interpretation*. Bloomington, Ind.: Indiana University Press.

—— 1978. *The Book of Job: Text, Translation, and Commentary*. New York: Jewish Theological Seminary of America.

GORDON, Cyrus H. 1949. *Ugaritic Literature: A Comprehensive Translation of the Poetic and Prose Texts*. Rome: Pontifical Biblical Institute.

—— 1955. *Ugaritic Manual*. Analecta Orientalia 35. Rome: Pontifical Biblical Institute.

—— 1961. "Canaanite Mythology. In *Mythologies of the Ancient World*, edited by Samuel N. Kramer, pp. 181–217. New York: Doubleday Anchor.

—— 1962. *Before the Bible: The Common Background of Greek and Hebrew Civilisations*. London: Collins.

—— 1966. "Leviathan: A Symbol of Evil." In *Biblical Motifs*, edited by A. Altmann, pp. 1–9. Cambridge, Mass.: Harvard University Press.

GOTTWALD, Norman K. 1959. *A Light to the Nations*. New York: Harper and Row.

—— 1979. *The Tribes of Yahweh*. Maryknoll, N.Y.: Orbis.

GRAF, Arturo. 1931 (1st ed. 1899). *The Story of the Devil*. London: Macmillan.

GRANT, Robert M. 1959. *Gnosticism and Early Christianity*. New York: Columbia University Press.

—— 1960. *The Secret Sayings of Jesus*. Garden City, N.Y.: Doubleday.

—— 1965. *The Formation of the New Testament*. New York: Harper and Row.

GRANT, Robert M., ed. 1961. *Gnosticism: A Sourcebook of Heretical Writings from the Early Christian Period*. New York: Harper and Row.

GRAVES, Robert, and PATAI, Raphael. 1964. *Hebrew Myths: The Book of Genesis*. Garden City, N.Y.: Doubleday.

GRAY, John. 1965. *The Legacy of Canaan*. Leiden: Brill.

GREENFIELD, Jonas. 1973. "Prolegomena" to Hugh Odeburg's *3 Enoch*. New York: Ktav.

GREENFIELD, Jonas, and STONE, M. E. 1977. "The Enochic Pentateuch and the Date of the Similitudes." *Harvard Theological Review* 70:51–65.

GREIMAS, A. J. 1970. *Du Sens*. Paris: Seuil.

—— 1971. "The Interpretation of Myth: Theory and Practice." In *Structural Analysis of Oral Tradition*, edited by Pierre and E. K. Maranda. Philadelphia: University of Pennsylvania Press.

GRELOT, Pierre. 1956. "Isaie XIV. 12–15 et son arrière-plan mythologique." *Revue de l'histoire des religions* 149:18–48.

—— 1958a. "La géographie mythique d'Hénoch et ses sources orientales." *Revue biblique* 65:33–69.

GRELOT, Pierre. 1958b. "La légende d'Hénoch dans les Apocryphes et dans la Bible: Origine et signification." *Revue des sciences religieuses* 46:5–26, 181–210.

GRESSETH, G. K. 1975. "The Gilgamesh Epic and Homer." *Classical Journal* 70: 1–19.

GRIFFITHS, J. Gwyn. 1960. *The Conflict of Horus and Seth.* Liverpool: Liverpool University Press.

GRIMAL, Pierre, ed. 1965. *Larousse World Mythology.* New York: Putnam.

GRUENWALD, I. 1983. "Manichaeism and Judaism in Light of the Cologne Mani Codex." *Zeitschrift für Papyrologie und Epigraphik* 50:29–45.

GÜTERBOCK, H. C. 1948. "The Hittite Version of the Hurrian Kumarbi Myth: Oriental Forerunners of Hesiod." *American Journal of Archaeology* 52:123–34.

—— 1952. *The Song of Ullikummi.* New Haven: Yale University Press.

GUNKEL, Hermann. 1895. *Schöpfung und Chaos in Urzeit und Endzeit: eine religionsgeschichtliche Untersuchung über Gen. 1 und Ap. Joh. 12.* Göttingen: Vandenhoeck and Ruprecht.

—— 1910. *Genesis: Übersetzt und Erklärt.* Göttingen: Vandenhoeck and Ruprecht.

GUNN, David. 1974. "Narrative Patterns and Oral Tradition in Judges and Samuel." *Vetus Testamentum* 24:286–317.

GURNEY, Oliver R. 1954. *The Hittites.* Harmondsworth: Penguin.

—— 1962. "Tammuz Reconsidered: Some Recent Developments." *Journal of Semitic Studies* 7:147–58.

—— 1972. "The Tale of the Poor Man of Nippur and Its Folktale Parallels." *Anatolian Studies* 22:149–58.

HAAG, Herbert. 1974. *Teufelsglaube.* Tübingen: Katzmann.

HABEL, Norman. 1971. *Literary Criticism of the Old Testament.* Philadelphia: Fortress.

HALLO, W. W. 1968. *The Exaltation of Inanna.* New Haven: Yale University Press.

HAMERTON-KELLY, R. G. 1970. "The Temple and the Origins of Jewish Apocalyptic." *Vetus Testamentum* 20:1–15.

HANSEN, J. 1975. "Gilgamesh, Humbaba, and the Land of the Erin Trees." *Iraq* 37:23–35.

HANSON, A. T. 1966. *The Pastoral Letters.* Cambridge: Cambridge University Press.

—— 1974. *Studies in Paul's Technique and Theology.* London: S.P.C.K.

HANSON, Paul D. 1975. *The Dawn of Apocalyptic.* Philadelphia: Fortress.

—— 1977. "Rebellion in Heaven: Azazel and Euhemeristic Heroes in I Enoch 6–11." *Journal of Biblical Literature* 96:195–233.

HARL, Margarite, DORIVAL, Gilles, and LE BOULLUEC, Alain, eds. 1976. *Origène: Traité des Principes.* Paris: Etudes Augustiniennes.

HARNACK, Adolf. 1904. *The Expansion of Christianity in the First Three Centuries.* 2 vols. New York and London: Putnam.

HARRISON, Jane. 1922. *Prolegomena to the Study of Greek Religion*. Cambridge: Cambridge University Press.

HARRISON, R. K. 1969. *Introduction to the Old Testament*. Grand Rapids: Eerdmans.

HARTLAND, E. S. 1894–96. *The Legend of Perseus*. 3 vols. London: D. Nutt, for the Folklore Society.

HARTMANN, Lars. 1966. *Prophecy Interpreted: The Formation of Some Jewish Apocalyptic Texts and of the Eschatological Discourse Mark Thirteen*. Lund: Gleerup.

HARTWELL, Kathleen. 1929. *Lactantius and Milton*. Cambridge, Mass.: Harvard University Press.

HATTO, A. T. 1972. *The Niebelungenleid*. Baltimore: Penguin.

HAUGEN, Einar. 1970. "The Mythic Structure of the Ancient Scandinavians." In *Structuralism: A Reader*, edited by Michael Lane. New York: Basic Books.

HAY, D. M. 1973. *Glory at the Right Hand: Psalm 110 in Early Christianity*. Nashville: Abingdon.

HEIDEL, Alexander. 1949. *The Gilgamesh Epic and Old Testament Parallels*. Chicago: University of Chicago Press.

—— 1963. *The Babylonian Genesis: The Story of Creation*. Chicago: University of Chicago Press.

HELMBOLD, A. 1967. *The Nag Hammadi Gnostic Texts and the Bible*. Grand Rapids: Eerdmans.

HENDERSON, Ian. 1952. *Myth in the New Testament*. Studies in Biblical Theology 7. London: SCM Press.

HENDERSON, Joseph L., and OAKES, Maud. 1963. *The Wisdom of the Serpent*. New York: Braziller.

HENGEL, M. 1974. *Judaism and Hellenism*. 2 vols. Philadelphia: Fortress.

HENNECKE, E., and SCHNEEMELCHER, W. 1963–65. *New Testament Apocrypha*. 2 vols. Philadelphia: Westminster.

HENNING, W. B. 1977 [1934]. "Ein Manichäisches Henochbuch." Reprinted in *Selected Papers*, vol. 1, pp. 336–45. Leiden: Brill.

—— 1943–46, 1977. "The Book of the Giants." *Bulletin of the School of Oriental and African Studies* 11 (1943–46): 52–74. Reprinted in *Selected Papers*, vol. 2, pp. 115–36. Leiden: Brill.

HERDNER, A., ed. 1963. *Corpus des tablettes cunéiformes alphabétiques*. 2 vols. Paris: Imprimerie Nationale. = CTA.

HICK, John. 1966. *Evil and the God of Love*. New York: Harper and Row.

HICK, John, ed. 1977. *The Myth of God Incarnate*. London: SCM Press.

HILLERS, Delbert R., and McCALL, Marsh Jr. 1976. "Homeric Dictated Texts: A Re-examination of Some Near Eastern Evidence." *Harvard Studies in Classical Philology* 80:19–23.

HOMANS, George C. 1941. "Anxiety and Ritual: The Theories of Malinowski and Radcliffe-Brown." *American Anthropologist* 43:164–72.

HOOKE, Samuel H. 1963. *Middle Eastern Mythology*. Harmondsworth: Penguin.

HOOKE, Samuel H., ed. 1958. *Myth, Ritual, and Kingship*. Oxford: Clarendon.

HOOKER, Morna D. 1983. Review of *Angels and Principalities* by Wesley Carr. *Journal of Theological Studies* 34:606–9.

HOPKINS, Clark. 1934. "Assyrian Elements in the Perseus-Gorgon Story." *American Journal of Archaeology* 38:341–58.

HORSLEY, R. A. 1980. "Gnosis in Corinth: I Corinthians 8.1–16." *New Testament Studies* 27:32–51.

HORTON, Fred L. 1976. *The Melchizedek Tradition*. Cambridge: Cambridge University Press.

HOW, W. W., and WELLS, J. 1928. *A Commentary on Herodotus*. 2 vols. Oxford: Clarendon.

HRUŠKA, B. 1975. *Der Mythenadler Anzu in Literatur und Vorstellung des alten Mesopotamien*. Budapest: ELTE.

HUGHES, P. E. 1962. *Paul's Second Epistle to the Corinthians*. Grand Rapids: Eerdmans.

HUMBERT, Paul. 1958. *Opuscules d'un Hebraïsant*. Neuchâtel: Université de Neuchâtel.

HYMAN, Stanley E. 1960. Review of *Python: A Study in Delphic Myth* by Joseph Fontenrose. *Carleton Miscellany* 1:124–27.

JACKSON, A. V. Williams. 1932. *Researches in Manichaeism, with Special Reference to the Turfan Fragments*. New York: Columbia University Press.

JACKSON, B. Darrell. 1972. "The Theory of Signs in St. Augustine's *De Doctrina Christiana*." In *Augustine: A Collection of Critical Essays*, edited by R. A. Markus, pp. 92–147. New York: Doubleday Anchor.

JACOBSEN, Thorkild. 1939. *The Sumerian King List*. Assyriological Studies 11. Chicago: University of Chicago Press.

—— 1946. "Sumerian Mythology: A Review Article." *Journal of Near Eastern Studies* 5:128–52.

—— 1968. "The Battle Between Marduk and Tiamat." *Journal of the American Oriental Society* 88:104–08.

—— 1970. *Toward the Image of Tammuz and Other Essays*. Cambridge, Mass.: Harvard University Press.

—— 1976. *Treasures of Darkness: A History of Mesopotamian Religion*. New Haven: Yale University Press.

JAMES, Montague Rhodes. 1953 (1st ed. 1924). *The Apocryphal New Testament*. Oxford: Clarendon.

JAMES, William. 1961 (1st ed. 1901). *Varieties of Religious Experience*. New York: Collier.

JASON, Heda. 1969. "A Multi-Dimensional Approach to Oral Literature." *Current Anthropology* 10:413–26.

—— 1977. "A Model for Narrative Structure in Oral Literature." In *Patterns in Oral Literature*, edited by Heda Jason and D. Segal, pp. 99–140. The Hague: Mouton.

—— 1979. "The Story of David and Goliath: A Folk Epic?" *Biblica* 60:36–70.

JASPERS, Karl, and BULTMANN, Rudolf. 1958. *Myth and Christianity: An Inquiry into the Possibility of Religion Without Myth*. New York: Noonday.

JEREMIAS, J. 1955. *The Parables of Jesus*. New York: Scribner's.

—— 1971. *New Testament Theology*. London: SCM Press.

JERVELL, J. 1960. *Imago Dei: Gen.1.26f. im Spätjudentum, in der Gnosis und in den paulinischen Briefen*. Göttingen: Vandenhoeck and Ruprecht.

JEWETT, E. H. 1890. *Diabology: The Person and Kingdom of Satan*. New York: T. Whittaker.

JOINES, K. R. 1975. "The Serpent in Genesis 3." *Zeitschrift für die alttestamentliche Wissenschaft* 88:1–11.

JONAS, Hans. 1970. *The Gnostic Religion: The Message of the Alien God and the Beginnings of Christianity*. Boston: Beacon Press.

JONES, Ernest. 1951. *On the Nightmare*. New York: Liveright.

JONES, John. 1962. *On Aristotle and Greek Tragedy*. London: Chatto and Windus.

JUNG, Leo. 1926. *Fallen Angels in Jewish, Christian, and Mohammedan Literature*. Philadelphia: Dropsie College.

KÄSEMANN, Ernst. 1964. *Essays on New Testament Themes*. London: SCM Press.

—— 1980. *Commentary on Romans*. London: SCM Press.

KAISER, Otto. 1974. *Isaiah 13–39: A Commentary*. Philadelphia: Westminster.

KAPELRUD, A. S. 1974. "The Mythological Features in Genesis Chapter 1 and the Author's Intentions." *Vetus Testamentum* 24:178–86.

KASKE, Robert E. 1971. "*Beowulf* and the Book of Enoch." *Speculum* 46:421–31.

KAUFMANN, Yehezkel. 1960. *The Religion of Israel*. Chicago: University of Chicago Press.

KEE, Howard Clark. 1968. "The Terminology of St. Mark's Exorcism Stories." *New Testament Studies* 14:232–46.

—— 1974. "Satan, Magic, and Salvation in the Testament of Job." In *Society of Biblical Literature Seminar Papers*, edited by G. Macrae, vol. 1, pp. 53–76. Cambridge, Mass.: SBL.

—— 1977. *Jesus in History: An Approach to the Study of the Gospels*. New York: Harcourt Brace Jovanovich.

KEE, Howard Clark, ed. 1973. *The Origins of Christianity: Sources and Documents*. Englewood Cliffs, N.J.: Prentice-Hall.

KELLER, C. A. 1977. "Der Problem des Bösen in Apokalyptik und Gnostik." In *Gnosis and Gnosticism*, edited by M. Kraus, pp. 70–90. Leiden: Brill.

KELLY, Henry Ansgar. 1964. "The Devil in the Desert." *Catholic Bible Quarterly* 26:190–220.

—— 1974. *The Devil, Demonology, and Witchcraft*. New York: Doubleday.

KELLY, Henry Ansgar. 1979. "The Struggle Against Satan in the Liturgies of Baptism and Easter." *Chronica* 24:9–20.

—— 1985. *The Devil at Baptism*. Ithaca: Cornell University Press.

KELLY, J.N.D. 1960. *Early Christian Doctrines*. London: A. & C. Black.

—— 1969. *A Commentary on the Epistles of Peter and Jude*. London: A. & C. Black.

KERMODE, Frank. 1979. *The Genesis of Secrecy*. Cambridge, Mass.: Harvard University Press.

KIKAWADA, Isaac M. 1974. "The Shape of Genesis 11.1–9." In *Rhetorical Criticism: Essays in Honor of James Muilenberg*, edited by Jared J. Jackson and M. Kessler, pp. 18–32. Pittsburgh: Pickwick.

—— 1975. "Literary Convention of the Primeval History." *Annual of the Japanese Biblical Institute* 1:1–21.

KILMER, Anne D. 1972. "The Mesopotamian Concept of Overpopulation and Its Solution as Reflected in Mythology." *Orientalia* 41:160–77.

KIPPENBERG, H. G. 1971. *Garizim und Synagoge*. Berlin: De Gruyter.

KIRK, G. S. 1970. *Myth: Its Meaning and Function in Ancient and Other Cultures*. Berkeley: University of California Press.

—— 1974. *The Nature of Greek Myths*. Harmondsworth: Penguin.

KIRK, G. S., and RAVEN, John E. 1966. *The Presocratic Philosophers*. Cambridge: Cambridge University Press.

KITTEL, Gerhard (with G. Friedrich), ed. 1951–76 (Eng. trans.). *Theological Dictionary of the New Testament*. 10 vols. Grand Rapids: Eerdmans. Published in German as *Theologisches Wörterbuch zum Neuen Testament* (Stuttgart: Kohlhammer, 1933–79).

KLIBANSKY, Raymond, PANOVSKY, Erwin, and SAXL, Fritz. 1964. *Saturn and Melancholy*. New York: Basic Books.

KLIJN, A.F.J. *Seth in Jewish, Christian, and Gnostic Literature*. Leiden: Brill.

KLUCKHOHN, Clyde. 1942. "Myths and Rituals: A General Theory." *Harvard Theological Review* 35:45–79.

KLUGER, Rivkah Schärf. 1967. *Satan in the Old Testament*. Evanston, Ill.: Northwestern University Press.

KNIBB, Michael A. 1978. *The Ethiopic Book of Enoch*. 2 vols. Oxford: Clarendon.

—— 1979. "The Date of the Parables of Enoch: A Critical Review." *New Testament Studies* 25:345–59.

KNOX, Bernard. 1968. "Silent Reading in Antiquity." *Greek, Roman, and Byzantine Studies* 9:421–36.

KOLAKOWSKI, Leszek. 1974. "Can the Devil Be Saved? A Marxist Answer." *Encounter* 43:7–13.

KRAELING, E. G. 1947. "The Significance and Origin of Genesis 6.1–4." *Journal of Near Eastern Studies* 6:193–208.

KRAMER, Samuel N. 1938. *Gilgamesh and the Huluppu Tree*. Assyriological Studies 10. Chicago: University of Chicago Press.

—— 1944. "The Epic of Gilgamesh and Its Sumerian Sources: A Study in Literary Evolution." *Journal of the American Oriental Society* 64:7–23.

—— 1947. "Gilgamesh and the Land of the Living." *Journal of Cuneiform Studies* 1:3–46.

—— 1949. "Gilgamesh and Agga." *American Journal of Archaeology* 53:1–18.

—— 1959. *History Begins at Sumer.* New York: Doubleday Anchor.

—— 1961. Review of *Python: A Study in Delphic Myth* by Joseph Fontenrose. *American Journal of Archaeology* 65:405.

—— 1972 (1st ed. 1944). *Sumerian Mythology.* Philadelphia: University of Pennsylvania Press.

KRAMER, Samuel N., ed. 1961. *Mythologies of the Ancient World.* New York: Doubleday Anchor.

KRAUSE, Martin, ed. 1977. *Gnosis and Gnosticism.* Nag Hammadi Studies 8. Leiden: Brill.

LAESSOE, J. 1953. "Literary and Oral Tradition in Ancient Mesopotamia." In *Studia Orientalia Ioanni Pedersen dicata,* pp. 204–13. Hauniae: E. Munksgaard.

LAMBERT, W. G. 1960. *Babylonian Wisdom Literature.* Oxford: Clarendon.

—— 1963. "The Great Battle of the Mesopotamian Religious Year: The Conflict in the Akitu House." *Iraq* 25:189–90.

—— 1964. "The Reign of Nebuchadnezzar I." In *The Seed of Wisdom,* edited by W. S. McCullough. Toronto: University of Toronto Press.

—— 1965. "A New Look at the Babylonian Background of Genesis." *Journal of Theological Studies* 16:287–300.

—— 1978. *The Background of Jewish Apocalyptic.* London: Athlone.

LAMBERT, W. G., and MILLARD, A. R. 1969. *The Atrahasis Epic.* Oxford: Clarendon.

LAMBERT, W. G., and WALCOT, Peter. 1965. "A New Babylonian Theogony and Hesiod." *Kadmos* 4:64–72.

LANDSBERGER, B. 1961. "Einige unerkannt gebliebene oder verkannte Nomina des Akkadischen." *Wiener Zeitschrift für die Kunde des Morgenlandes* 57:1–23.

LANGDON, S. 1923. *The Babylonian Epic of Creation Restored from the Recently Recovered Tablets of Assur.* Oxford: Clarendon.

LANGTON, Edward. 1942. *Good and Evil Spirits: A Study of the Jewish and Christian Doctrine, Its Origin and Development.* New York: Macmillan.

—— 1946. *Satan, a Portrait: A Study of the Character of Satan Through All the Ages.* London: Skeffington.

—— 1949. *Essentials of Demonology: A Study of the Jewish and Christian Doctrine, Its Origin and Development.* London: Epworth.

LAPORTE, J. 1970. "La Chute chez Philon et Origène." In *Kyriakon: Festschrift Johannes Quasten,* vol. 1, pp. 320–55. Münster: Aschendorff.

LATTIMORE, Richmond. 1962. "Why the Devil Is the Devil." *Proceedings of the American Philosophical Society* 106:427–29.

LATTIMORE, Richmond. 1964. *Story Patterns in Greek Tragedy*. Ann Arbor: University of Michigan Press.

LAWLOR, H. J. 1897. "Early Citations from the Book of Enoch." *Journal of Philology* 25:164–225.

LAWRENCE, William W. 1912. "The Haunted Mere in Beowulf." *Publications of the Modern Language Association* 27:208–45.

LAWSON, John. 1948. *The Biblical Theology of St. Irenaeus*. London: Epworth.

LAYTON, B., ed. 1981. *The Rediscovery of Gnosticism: Proceedings of the International Conference on Gnosticism at Yale, 1978*. 2 vols. Leiden: Brill.

LEACH, Edmund. 1970 (1969). *Genesis as Myth and Other Essays*. London: Cape.

—— 1972. "Pulleyar and the Lord Buddha: An Aspect of Religious Syncretism in Ceylon." In *A Reader in Comparative Religion*, edited by William A. Lessa and E. Z. Vogt, pp. 302–13. New York: Harper and Row.

LEE, J. Y. 1970. "Interpreting the Demonic Powers in Pauline Thought." *Novum Testamentum* 12:54–72.

LE GOFF, Jacques. 1977. "Culture ecclésiastique et culture folklorique au Moyen Age: Saint Marcel de Paris et le dragon." In *Pour un autre Moyen Age*, pp. 236–79. Paris: Gallimard.

LEIVESTAD, R. 1954. *Christ the Conqueror: Ideas of Conflict and Victory in the New Testament*. London: S.P.C.K.

LERNER, Robert. 1972. *The Heresy of the Free Spirit*. Berkeley: University of California Press.

LESSA, William A., and VOGT, E. Z., eds. 1972. *A Reader in Comparative Religion*. New York: Harper and Row.

LÉVI-STRAUSS, Claude. 1960. "L'analyse morphologique des contes russes." *International Journal of Slavic Linguistics and Poetics* 3:122–49.

—— 1964–70. *Mythologies*. 4 vols. Paris: Plon.

—— 1967. "The Story of Asdiwal." In *The Structural Study of Myth and Totemism*, edited by Edmund Leach, pp. 1–47. London: Tavistock.

LEVY, G. Rachel. 1934. "The Oriental Origin of Herakles." *Journal of Hellenic Studies* 54:40–53.

—— 1953. *The Sword from the Rock: An Investigation into the Origins of Epic Literature and the Development of the Hero*. London: Faber and Faber.

LEWIS, Edwin. 1948. *The Creator and the Adversary*. New York: Abingdon-Cokesbury.

LEWIS, Jack P. 1968. *A Study of the Interpretation of Noah and the Flood in Jewish and Christian Literature*. Leiden: Brill.

LIMET, H. 1972. "Les chants épiques sumeriens." *Revue belge de philologie et d'histoire* 50:3–19.

LINCOLN, A. T. 1981. *Paradise Now and Not Yet*. Cambridge: Cambridge University Press.

LINFORTH, Ivan M. 1941. *The Arts of Orpheus*. Berkeley: University of California Press.

LING, Trevor A. 1961. *The Significance of Satan: New Testament Demonology and Its Contemporary Relevance*. London: S.P.C.K.

LIPINSKI, E. 1971. "El's Abode: Mythological Traditions Related to Mt. Hermon and to the Mountains of Armenia." *Orientalia Lovaniensia Periodica* 2:15–41.

LITTLETON, C. Scott. 1969a. "Is the Kingship in Heaven Theme Indo-European?" In *Indo-European and the Indo-Europeans*, edited by G. Cardona. Philadelphia: University of Pennsylvania Press.

—— 1969b. "Lévi-Strauss and the Kingship in Heaven: A Structural Analysis of a Widespread Theogonic Theme." *Journal of the Folklore Institute* 6:70–84.

—— 1973. *The New Comparative Mythology*. Berkeley: University of California Press.

LODS, Adolphe. 1927. "La chute des anges: origine et portée de cette speculation." *Revue d'histoire et de philosophie religieuses* 7:295–315.

LOEWENSTAMM, Samuel E. 1972. "The Killing of Mot in Ugaritic Myth." *Orientalia* 41:378–82.

LOGAN, A.H.B., and WEDDERBURN, A.J.M. 1983. *The New Testament and Gnosis: Essays in Honour of Robert McL. Wilson*. Edinburgh: T. & T. Clark.

LOHSE, Eduard. 1971. *Colossians and Philemon*. Philadelphia: Fortress.

LONG, Charles P. 1963. *Alpha: The Myths of Creation*. Toronto: University of Toronto.

LOOS, Milan. 1974. *Dualist Heresy in the Middle Ages*. Prague: Akademia.

LORD, Albert. 1965. *The Singer of Tales*. New York: Harper and Row.

—— 1974. "Perspectives on Recent Work in Oral Literature." *Forum for Modern Language Studies* 10.

LOSSKY, Vladimir. 1957. *The Mystical Theology of the Eastern Church*. Cambridge: James Clarke.

LOVEJOY, Arthur C. 1937. "Milton and the Paradox of the Fortunate Fall." *English Literary History* 4:161–79.

LÜTHI, Max. 1968. *Märchen*. Stuttgart: Metzler.

LUKE, J. T. 1977. "Abraham and the Iron Age." *Journal for the Study of the Old Testament* 4:35–47.

LUOMALA, Katherine. 1940. *Oceanic, American Indian, and African Myths of Snaring the Sun*. Honolulu: Bishop Museum.

McCUE, James F. 1979. "Orthodoxy and Heresy: Walter Bauer and the Valentinians." *Vigiliae Christianae* 33:118–30.

MacCULLOUGH, John A. 1930. *The Harrowing of Hell: A Comparative Study of an Early Christian Doctrine*. Edinburgh: T. & T. Clarke.

MacDONALD, J. 1964. *The Theology of the Samaritans*. London: SCM Press.

McEVENUE, Sean. 1971. *The Narrative Style of the Priestly Writer*. Rome: Pontifical Biblical Institute.

McHugh, Michael P. 1972. "Satan and Saint Ambrose." *Classical Folia* 26:94–106.

McKay, J. W. 1970. "Helel and the Dawn-Goddess." *Vetus Testamentum* 20:451–64.

McKenzie, John L. 1956. "Mythological Allusions in Ezekiel 28.12–18." *Journal of Biblical Literature* 75:322–27.

—— 1968. *Second Isaiah.* New York: Doubleday Anchor.

MacRae, G. W. 1965. "The Coptic Gnostic Apocalypse of Adam." *Heythrop Journal* 6:27–35.

—— 1970. "The Jewish Background of the Gnostic Sophia Myth." *Novum Testamentum* 12:86–101.

—— 1972. "The Apocalypse of Adam Reconsidered." *Society of Biblical Literature Seminar Papers,* vol. 2, pp. 573–79. Missoula, Mont.: Scholars Press.

Mair, Lucy. 1969. *Witchcraft.* New York: McGraw-Hill.

Mallowan, M.E.L. 1964. "Noah's Flood Reconsidered." *Iraq* 26:62–82.

Maranda, Pierre, ed. 1972. *Mythology: Selected Readings.* Harmondsworth: Penguin.

Maranda, Pierre, and Maranda, E. K., eds. 1971. *Structural Analysis of Oral Tradition.* Philadelphia: University of Pennsylvania Press.

Markus, R. A. 1972. "St. Augustine on Signs." In *Augustine,* edited by R. A. Markus, pp. 61–91. New York: Doubleday Anchor.

Markus, R. A., ed. 1972. *Augustine: A Collection of Critical Essays.* New York: Doubleday Anchor.

Marwick, Max, ed. 1970. *Witchcraft and Sorcery.* Harmondsworth: Penguin.

Masters, R.E.L. 1974. *Eros and Evil.* Harmondsworth: Penguin.

Maunder, Mrs. A.S.D. 1918. "The Date and Place of Writing of the Slavonic Book of Enoch." *The Observatory* 41:309–16.

May, Harry S. 1971. "The Daimonic in Jewish History; or, the Garden of Eden Revisited." *Zeitschrift für Religions- und Geistesgeschichte* 23:205–19.

May, Herbert G. 1937. "Some Aspects of Solar Worship at Jerusalem." *Zeitschrift für die alttestamentliche Wissenschaft* 14:269–81.

—— 1955. "Some Cosmic Connotations of *mayim rabbīm*, 'Many Waters,' " *Journal of Biblical Literature* 74:9–21.

—— 1963. "Cosmological Reference in the Qumran Doctrine of the Two Spirits and in Old Testament Imagery." *Journal of Biblical Literature* 82:1–14.

Meletinsky, E. M. 1971. "Structural-Typological Analysis of Folktales." *Genre* 4:249–79.

Melia, Daniel. 1974. "Parallel Versions of 'The Boyhood Deeds of Cuchulain.' " *Forum for Modern Language Studies* 10:211–26.

Mendenhall, George E. 1955, 1970. *Law and Covenant in Israel and the Ancient Near East.* Pittsburgh: Biblical Colloquium. Reprinted in *The Biblical Archaeol-*

ogist Reader, edited by E. F. Campbell and D. N. Freedman, vol. 3, pp. 3–53. New York: Doubleday Anchor.

MERRILL, Eugene H. 1975. *Qumran and Predestination*. Leiden: Brill.

MILIK, J. T. 1971. "Problèmes de la littérature hénochique à la lumière des fragments araméens de Qûmran." *Harvard Theological Review* 64:335–49.

—— 1972. "Milkî-Sedeq et Milkî-Reša dans les anciens écrits juifs et chrétiens." *Journal of Jewish Studies* 23:95–144.

—— 1976. *The Books of Enoch: Aramaic Fragments from Qumran Cave 4*. Oxford: Clarendon.

MILLER, Patrick D. 1967. "El the Warrior." *Harvard Theological Review* 60:411–31.

—— 1973. *The Divine Warrior in Early Israel*. Cambridge, Mass.: Harvard University Press.

MINEAR, Paul S. 1960. *Eyes of Faith*. St. Louis: Bethany Press.

MITTON, C. L. 1976. *Ephesians*. London: Clarendon.

MOORE, George F. 1927–30. *Judaism in the First Centuries of the Christian Era*. 3 vols. Cambridge, Mass.: Harvard University Press.

MORAN, William L. 1971. Review of *The Atrahasis Epic* by W. G. Lambert and A. R. Millard. *Biblica* 52:57–61.

MORRISON, C. D. 1960. *The Powers That Be: Earthly Rulers and Demonic Powers in Romans 13.1–7*. London: SMC Press.

MOULE, C.F.D. 1963. *An Idiom Book of New Testament Greek*. Cambridge: Cambridge University Press.

—— 1964. "The Influence of Circumstances on the Use of Eschatological Terms." *Journal of Theological Studies* 15:1–19.

MOUNCE, Robert H. 1977. *The Book of Revelation*. Grand Rapids: Eerdmans.

MÜLLER, G. 1958. "Origenes und die Apokatastasis." *Theologische Zeitschrift* 14:174–90.

MUNZ, Peter. 1973. *When the Golden Bough Breaks: Structuralism or Typology?* London: Routledge and Kegan Paul.

MURPHY-O'CONNOR, J., ed. 1968. *Paul and Qumran*. London: Chapman.

MURRAY, Margaret A. 1931. *The God of the Witches*. Oxford: Clarendon.

MYERS, Jacob M. 1965. *I Chronicles*. New York: Doubleday Anchor.

NAGEL, Georges. 1950. "A propos des rapports du psaume 104 avec les textes égyptiens." *Festschrift für Alfred Bertholet*, edited by O. Eissfeldt. Tübingen: J.B.C. Mohr.

NAGLER, Michael N. 1975. *Spontaneity and Tradition: A Study in the Oral Art of Homer*. Berkeley: University of California Press.

—— 1977. "Dread Goddess Endowed with Speech." *Archetypal News* 3:21–37.

NAGY, Gregory. 1973. "Phaethon, Sappho's Phaon, and the White Rock of Leucas." *Harvard Studies in Classical Philology* 77:137–77.

—— 1979. *The Best of the Achaeans*. Baltimore: Johns Hopkins University Press.

NAIDOFF, Bruce. 1978. "A Man to Work the Soil: A New Interpretation of Genesis 2–3." *Journal for the Study of the Old Testament* 5:2–14.

NATHORST, Bertel. 1969. *Formal or Structural Studies of Traditional Tales: The Usefulness of Some Methodological Proposals Advanced by Vladimir Propp, Alan Dundes, Claude Lévi-Strauss and Edmund Leach.* Stockholm Studies in Comparative Religion 9. Stockholm: Almqvist and Wiksell.

NEUGEBAUER, O. 1981. *The "Astronomical" Chapters of the Ethiopic Book of Enoch (72–82).* Copenhagen: Royal Danish Academy. Reprinted in Matthew Black, *The Book of Enoch* (Leiden: Brill, 1985).

NEWSOM, C. A. 1980. "The Development of 1 Enoch 6–19: Cosmology and Judgement." *Catholic Bible Quarterly* 42:310–29.

NICKELSBURG, George W. E. 1977. "Apocalyptic and Myth in 1 Enoch 6–11." *Journal of Biblical Literature* 96:383–405.

—— 1981. "Some Related Traditions in the Apocalypse of Adam, the Book of Adam and Eve, and 1 Enoch." In *The Rediscovery of Gnosticism*, edited by B. Layton, vol. 2, pp. 515–39. Leiden: Brill.

NIELSEN, Eduard. 1954. *Oral Tradition: A Modern Problem in Old Testament Studies.* Naperville, Ill.: Allenson.

NIGG, Walter. 1962. *The Heretics.* New York: Knopf.

NINEHAM, Dennis. 1963. *Saint Mark.* Harmondsworth: Penguin.

NOCK, Arthur Darby. 1933. *Conversion: The Old and New in Religion from Alexander the Great to Augustine of Hippo.* Oxford: Oxford University Press.

NOTH, Martin. 1966. *The Old Testament World.* Philadelphia: Fortress.

OBENDIECK, Hans. 1931. *Der Teufel bei Martin Luther.* Berlin: Furche.

ODEBURG, Hugh. 1973 (1st ed. 1928). *3 Enoch.* New York: Ktav.

ODEN, Robert A. 1976. "The Persistence of Canaanite Religion." *Biblical Archaeologist* 39:31–36.

O'FLAHERTY, Wendy D. 1976. *The Origins of Evil in Hindu Mythology.* Berkeley: University of California Press.

OGDEN, S. M. 1961. *Christ Without Myth.* New York: Harper and Row.

OINAS, Felix, J., ed. 1978. *Heroic Epic and Saga.* Bloomington: Indiana University Press.

O'MEARA, John J. 1980 (1st ed. 1954). *The Young Augustine.* London: Longman.

ONG, Walter. 1982. *Orality and Literacy.* London: Methuen.

OPPENHEIM, A. Leo. 1949. "The Golden Garments of the Gods." *Journal of Near Eastern Studies* 8:172–93.

—— 1964. *Ancient Mesopotamia: Portrait of a Dead Civilization.* Chicago: University of Chicago Press.

ORTUTAY, Gyula. 1959. "Principles of Oral Transmission of Folk Culture." *Acta Ethnographica* 8:175–221.

OSTEN-SACKEN, Peter von der. 1969. *Gott und Belial.* Göttingen: Vandenhoeck and Ruprecht.

OTTO, Rudolf. 1923. *The Idea of the Holy*. Oxford: Oxford University Press.

PAGE, Denys L. 1959. *History and the Homeric Iliad*. Berkeley: University of California Press.

PAGELS, Elaine. 1975. *The Gnostic Paul*. Philadelphia: Fortress.

—— 1976. "The Demiurge and His Archons: A Gnostic View of the Bishops and Presbyters?" *Harvard Theological Review* 69:301–24.

—— 1979. *The Gnostic Gospels*. New York: Random House.

—— 1983. "Adam and Eve, Christ and the Church." In *The New Testament and Gnosis: Essays in Honour of R. McL. Wilson*, edited by A.H.B. Logan and A.J.M. Wedderburn, pp. 146–75. Edinburgh: T. & T. Clarke.

PALLIS, Marco. 1974. "Is There a Problem of Evil?" In *The Sword of Gnosis*, edited by Jacob Needleman, pp. 230–52. Harmondsworth: Penguin.

PALMER, P. M., and MORE, R. P., eds. 1936. *The Sources of the Faust Tradition*. Oxford: Oxford University Press.

PAPINI, Giovanni. 1955. *The Devil*. London: Eyre and Spottiswoode.

PARRY, Adam, ed. 1971. *The Making of Homeric Verse: Collected Papers of Milman Parry*. Oxford: Clarendon.

PATRICK, J. Max. 1967. *The Prose of John Milton*. New York: Doubleday Anchor.

PATRIDES, C. A. 1966. *Milton and the Christian Tradition*. Oxford: Clarendon.

—— 1967. "The Salvation of Satan." *Journal of the History of Ideas* 28:467–78.

PEABODY, Berkley. 1975. *The Winged Word: A Study of the Technique of Ancient Greek Oral Composition as Seen Principally Through Hesiod's Works and Days*. Albany: State University of New York.

PEAKE, A. S. 1919. *A Commentary on the Bible*. London: Nelson.

PEARSON, Birger A. 1969. "A Reminiscence of Classical Myth at II Peter 2.4." *Greek, Roman, and Byzantine Studies* 10:72–75.

—— 1972. "Jewish Haggadic Traditions in the *Testimony of Truth*." In *Ex Orbe Religionum: Studia Geo Widengren Oblata*, vol. 1, pp. 457–70. Leiden: Brill.

—— 1980. "Jewish Elements in Gnosticism and the Development of Gnostic Self-Definition." In *Jewish and Christian Self-Definition*, edited by E. P. Sanders, pp. 151–60, 240–45. London: SCM Press.

—— 1981. "The Figure of Seth in Gnostic Literature." In *The Rediscovery of Gnosticism*, edited by B. Layton, vol. 2, pp. 472–514. Leiden: Brill.

—— 1983. "Philo, Gnosis, and the New Testament." In *New Testament and Gnosis: Essays in Honour of R. McL. Wilson*, pp. 73–89. Edinburgh: T. & T. Clarke.

PEARSON, Birger A., ed. 1975. *Religious Syncretism in Antiquity*. Missoula, Mont.: Scholars Press.

PEDERSEN, Johannes. 1926, 1940. *Israel: Its Life and Culture*, 4 vols. London: Oxford University Press.

PELIKAN, Jaroslav. 1971. *The Christian Tradition*, vol. 1: *The Emergence of the Catholic Tradition (100–600)*. Chicago: University of Chicago Press.

PERKINS, Pheme. 1977. "Apocalypse of Adam: The Genre and Function of a Gnostic Apocalypse." *Catholic Bible Quarterly* 39:382–95.

PERRIN, Norman. 1974. *The New Testament: An Introduction*. New York: Harcourt Brace Jovanovich.

PETERSEN, David L. 1979. "Genesis 6.1–4: Yahweh and the Organisation of the Cosmos." *Journal for the Study of the Old Testament* 13:47–64.

PÉTREMENT, Simone. 1946. *Le dualisme dans l'histoire de la philosophie et des religions*. Paris: Gallimard.

—— 1947. *Le dualisme chez Platon, les gnostiques et les manichéens*. Paris: Presses Universitaires de France.

PETTAZONI, R. 1954. *Essays on the History of Religions*. Leiden: Brill.

PETTINATO, Giovanni. 1976. "The Royal Archives of Tell Mardikh-Ebla." *Biblical Archaeologist* 39:44–52.

PFEIFFER, Robert H. 1927. "The Priority of Job over Isaiah 40–55." *Journal of Biblical Literature* 46:202–6.

—— 1948. *Introduction to the Old Testament*. New York: Harper and Brothers.

PINES, S. 1970. "Eschatology and the Concept of Time in the Slavonic Book of Enoch." In *Types of Redemption: Studies in the History of Religion* 18, edited by R. J. Werblowsky and C. J. Bleeker, pp. 72–87. Chicago: University of Chicago Press.

POPE, Marvin H. 1955. *El in the Ugaritic Texts*. Leiden: Brill.

—— 1965. *Job*. New York: Doubleday Anchor.

—— 1966. "Baal-Zaphon and Zeus Casios." *Journal of Biblical Literature* 85:455–69.

—— 1972. *The Song of Songs*. New York: Doubleday Anchor.

PRITCHARD, James B., ed. 1969. *Ancient Near Eastern Texts in Relation to the Old Testament*. 3rd ed. Princeton: Princeton University Press. = ANET.

PROPP, Vladimir. 1968 (1st ed. 1928). *Morphology of the Folktale*. Austin: University of Texas Press.

—— 1984. *Theory and History of Folklore*. Edited by Anatoly Liberman. Minneapolis: University of Minnesota Press.

PUECH, H.-C. 1949. *Le manichéisme: Son fondateur, sa doctrine*. Paris: Civilisations du Sud.

—— 1978. *En quête de la Gnose*. 2 vols. Paris: Gallimard.

QUINN, Esther C. 1962. *The Quest of Seth for the Oil of Life*. Chicago: University of Chicago Press.

QUISPEL, Gilles. 1974. *Gnostic Studies I*. Amsterdam: Nederlands Historisch-Archaeologisch Institut.

—— 1983. "Judaism, Judaic Christianity and Gnosis." In *The New Testament and Gnosis: Essays in Honour of R. McL. Wilson*, edited by A.H.B. Logan and A. J. Wedderburn, pp. 46–68. Edinburgh: T. & T. Clarke.

RAD, Gerhard von. 1962. *Old Testament Theology*, vol. 1. New York: Harper and Row.

—— 1966. *Deuteronomy: A Commentary*. Philadelphia: Westminster.

—— 1972. *Genesis: A Commentary*. Philadelphia: Westminster.

RÄISÄNEN, Heikki. 1980. "Paul's Theological Difficulties with the Law." *Studia Biblica 1978* (*Journal for the Study of the Old Testament Supplementary Series* 3) 3:301–20.

RANK, Otto. 1959. *The Myth of the Birth of the Hero*. New York: Vintage.

RASHDALL, H. 1919. *The Idea of Atonement in Christian Theology*. London: Macmillan.

RAST, Walter E. 1972. *Tradition History and the Old Testament*. Philadelphia: Fortress.

REICKE, Bo. 1964. *The Epistles of James, Peter, and Jude*. New York: Doubleday Anchor.

RENTDORFF, R. 1977a. *Das überlieferungeschichtliche Problem des Pentateuch*. Berlin: De Gruyter.

—— 1977b. "The 'Yahwist' as Theologian?" *Journal for the Study of the Old Testament* 3:2–9.

REVARD, Stella P. 1980. *The War in Heaven: Paradise Lost and the Tradition of Satan's Rebellion*. Ithaca, N.Y.: Cornell University Press.

RICHARDSON, Cyril C., ed. 1970. *Early Christian Fathers*. New York: Macmillan.

RICOEUR, Paul. 1967. *The Symbolism of Evil*. Boston: Beacon Press.

—— 1975. "Biblical Hermeneutics." *Semeia* 4:39–51.

RIST, John M. 1972. "Augustine on Free Will and Predestination." In *Augustine*, edited by R. A. Markus, pp. 218–52. New York: Doubleday Anchor.

ROBBINS, Frank E. 1912. *The Hexaemeral Literature: A Study of the Greek and Latin Commentaries on Genesis*. Chicago: University of Chicago Press.

ROBBINS, Russell H. 1960. *Encyclopedia of Witchcraft and Demonology*. New York: Crown.

ROBERT, Charles. 1895. "Les fils de Dieu et les filles des hommes." *Revue biblique* 4:340–75, 525–52.

ROBERTS, Warren. 1958. *The Tale of the Kind and Unkind Girls*. Berlin: De Gruyter.

ROBERTSON, D. W. 1958. *Augustine: On Christian Doctrine*. New York: Modern Library.

ROBINSON, James T., ed. 1977. *The Nag Hammadi Library in English*. Leiden: Brill.

ROBINSON, James T., et al., eds. 1973–83. *The Nag Hammadi Library*. 18 vols. to date. Leiden: Brill.

ROGERSON, J. 1970. "Structural Anthropology and the Old Testament." *Bulletin of the School of Oriental and African Studies* 33:490–500.

ROOTH, Anna Birgitta. 1951. *The Cinderella Cycle*. Lund: Gleerup.

—— 1962. *The Raven and the Carcass: Investigation of a Motif in the Deluge Myth in Europe, Asia, and North America*. Helsinki: Suomalainen Tiedeakademia.

ROUSSEAU, Adelin, and DOUTRELEAU, Louis, eds. 1965–82. *Irénée de Lyon, Contre les Hérésies*. 5 two-part vols. Sources Chrétiennes. Paris: Editions du Cerf.

ROUSSEAU, F. 1971. *L'Apocalypse et le milieu prophétique du Nouveau Testament*. Tournai: Desclée.

ROUX, Georges. 1966. *Ancient Iraq*. Harmondsworth: Penguin.

ROWLEY, H. H. 1944. *The Relevance of Apocalyptic: A Study of Jewish and Christian Apocalypses from Daniel to the Revelation*. New York: Association Press.

ROZELAAR, Marc. 1952. "The Song of the Sea." *Vetus Testamentum* 2:221–28.

RUBINSTEIN, A. 1967. "Observations on the Slavonic Book of Enoch." *Journal of Jewish Studies* 13:1–21.

RUDHARDT, Jean. 1971. *La thème de l'eau primordiale dans la mythologie grecque*. Berne: Francke.

RUDOLPH, Kurt. 1969, 1971. "Gnosis und Gnostizismus, ein Forschungsbericht." *Theologisches Revue* 34 (1969): 121–75, 181–231; 36 (1971): 1–61, 89–124.

—— 1978. *Die Gnosis: Wesen und Geschichte einer spätantiken Religion*. Göttingen: Vandenhoeck and Ruprecht.

RUDWIN, Maximilian. 1921. *Devil Stories*. New York: Knopf.

—— 1931. *The Devil in Legend and Literature*. Chicago: Open Court. Reprint 1973.

RUSSELL, D. S. 1964. *The Method and Message of Jewish Apocalyptic*. Philadelphia: Westminster.

RUSSELL, Jeffrey Burton. 1977. *The Devil: Perceptions of Evil from Antiquity to Primitive Christianity*. Ithaca, N.Y.: Cornell University Press.

—— 1981. *Satan: The Early Christian Tradition*. Ithaca, N.Y.: Cornell University Press.

—— 1985. *Lucifer: The Devil in the Middle Ages*. Ithaca, N.Y.: Cornell University Press.

RUWETT, J. 1943. "Les 'Antilegomena' dans l'oeuvre d'Origène." *Biblica* 24: 48–60.

—— 1944. "Les apocryphes dans l'oeuvre d'Origène." *Biblica* 25:151–62.

SANDERS, E. P. 1977. *Paul and Palestinian Judaism*. Philadelphia: Fortress; London: SCM Press.

SANDERS, James A. 1977. "Torah and Paul." In *God's Christ and His People: Studies in Honour of N. A. Dahl*, edited by Jacob Jervell and Wayne A. Meeks, pp. 132–40. Oslo: Universitetsforlaget.

—— 1981. "Text and Canon: Old Testament and New." In *Mélanges Dominique Barthélemy*, edited by P. Casetti et al., pp. 373–94. Fribourg: Editions Universitaires.

SANDERS, J. T. 1971. *The New Testament Christological Hymns*. Cambridge: Cambridge University Press.

SANMARTIN, J. 1978. "Die ug. Basis NSS und das 'Nest' des B'I (KTU 1.3IVIf)." *Ugarit-Forschungen* 10:449–50.

SASSON, Jack M. 1972. "Some Literary Motifs in the Composition of the Gilgamesh Epic." *Studies in Philology* 69:259–73.

SCHAFF, Philip, ed. 1886–88 (1st series), 1890–94 (2nd series). 30 vols. *A Select Library of Nicene and Post-Nicene Fathers*. Buffalo: Christian Literature Co.

SCHENKE, H.-M. 1962. *Der Gott "Mensch" in der Gnosis*. Göttingen: Vandenhoeck and Ruprecht.

SCHLIER, Heinrich. 1959. *Mächte und Gewalten im Neuen Testament*. Freiburg im Breisgau: Herder.

SCHMID, H. H. 1976. *Der sogenannte Jahwist*. Zurich: Theologischer Verlag.

SCHMIDT, K. L. 1951. "Lucifer als gefallene Engelmacht." *Theologische Zeitschrift* 7:161–79.

SCHMITHALS, Walter. 1971. *Gnosticism in Corinth*. Nashville: Abingdon.

—— 1972. *Paul and the Gnostics*. Nashville: Abingdon.

SCHNIEWIND, J. 1951. "Die Archonten dieses Aons: 1 Kor. 2.6–8." In *Nachgelassene Reden und Aufsätze*, pp. 104–17. Berlin: De Gruyter.

SCHOEPS, Hans J. 1961. *Paul: The Theology of the Apostle in the Light of Jewish Religious History*. Philadelphia: Westminster.

—— 1964. *Theologie und Geschichte des Judenchristentums*. Tübingen: Mohr.

SCHOLEM, Gershom. 1960. *Major Trends in Jewish Mysticism*. New York: Schocken.

—— 1962. *Ursprung und Anfänge der Kabbala*. Berlin: De Gruyter.

SCHOLER, David M. 1971. *Nag Hammadi Bibliography 1948–1969*. Leiden: Brill.

SCHÜTZ, J. H. 1975. *Paul and the Anatomy of Apostolic Authority*. Cambridge: Cambridge University Press.

SCOBIE, C.H.H. 1973. "The Origin and Development of Samaritan Christianity." *New Testament Studies* 19:390–411.

SEGAL, Alan F. 1977. *Two Powers in Heaven: Early Rabbinic Reports About Christianity and Gnosticism*. Leiden: Brill.

SERVICE, Elman R. 1975. *The Origins of the State and Civilization*. New York: Norton.

SHAFFER, Aaron. 1984. "Gilgamesh, the Cedar Forest and Mesopotamian History." In *Studies in Literature from the Ancient Near East: S. N. Kramer Festschrift*. New Haven: American Oriental Society.

SHARPE, J. L. 1973. "Second Adam in The Apocalypse of Moses." *Catholic Bible Quarterly* 35:35–46.

SHELLRUDE, G. M. 1981. "The Apocalypse of Adam: Evidence for a Christian Gnostic Provenance." In *Gnosis and Gnosticism*, edited by Martin Krause. Leiden: Brill.

SIECKE, Ernst. 1978 *Drachenkämpfe als Mythus, Saga, Märchen*. New York: Ayer. (Reprint of 1907 ed.)

SMITH, Grafton Elliot. 1919. *The Evolution of the Dragon*. Manchester: Manchester University Press.

SMITH, J. R. 1975. "Wisdom and Apocalypse." In *Religious Syncretism in Antiquity*, edited by Birger A. Pearson. Missoula, Mont.: Scholars Press.

SMITH, Morton, and HADAS, Moses. 1965. *Heroes and Gods*. New York: Harper and Row.

SMITH, W. Robertson. 1889. *Lectures on the Religion of the Semites*. New York: Appleton.

SOUTER, Alexander, ed. 1947. *Novum Testamentum Graece*. Oxford: Clarendon.

SPEISER, E. A. 1964. *Genesis*. New York: Doubleday Anchor.

STAROBINSKI, Jean. 1971. "Le démoniaque de Gérasa: Analyse littéraire de Marc 5.1–10." In *Analyse structurale et exégèse biblique*, by Roland Barthes et al. Neuchâtel: Delachaux et Niestlé.

—— 1974. "Le combat avec Légion." In *Trois Fureurs*, pp. 73–126. Paris: Gallimard.

STOLZ, Benjamin A., and SHANNON, Richard S., eds. 1976. *Oral Literature and the Formula*. Ann Arbor: University of Michigan Press.

STONE, Michael E. 1978. "The Book of Enoch and Judaism in the Third Century B.C.E." *Catholic Bible Quarterly* 40:479–92.

STONE, Michael E., ed. 1984. *Jewish Writings of the Second Temple Period*. Philadelphia: Fortress; Assen: Van Gorcum.

STRACK, H. L., and BILLERBECK, P. 1922–61. *Kommentar zum Neuen Testament aus Talmud und Midrasch*. 6 vols. Munich: Beck.

STRAUSS, David F. 1973 (1st ed. 1835). *The Life of Jesus Critically Examined*. London: SCM Press.

STROUMSA, Gedaliahu A. G. 1984. *Another Seed: Studies in Gnostic Mythology*. Leiden: Brill.

SUMMERS, Montague. 1973 (1st ed. 1926). *The History of Witchcraft and Demonology*. London: Routledge and Kegan Paul.

SUTER, D. W. 1979. "Fallen Angel, Fallen Priest: The Problem of Family Purity in I Enoch 6–16." *Hebrew Union College Annual* 50:115–35.

SWAHN, J. O. 1955. *The Tale of Cupid and Psyche*. Lund: Gleerup.

TALBERT, Charles H. 1975. *Literary Patterns, Theological Themes, and the Genre of Luke-Acts*. Missoula, Mont.: Scholars Press.

—— 1976. "The Myth of a Descending-Ascending Redeemer in Mediterranean Antiquity." *New Testament Studies* 22:418–40.

TARDIEU, Michel. 1974. *Trois mythes gnostiques: Adam, Eros et les animaux d'Egypte dans un écrit de Nag Hammadi (II, 5)*. Paris: Etudes Augustiniennes.

TEDLOCK, Dennis. 1970. *Finding the Center: Narrative Poetry of the Zuni Indians*. New York: Doubleday Anchor.

—— 1972. "On the Translation of Style in Oral Narrative." In *Towards New Perspectives in Folklore*, edited by A. Paredes and R. Bauman. Austin: University of Texas Press.

TENNANT, F. R. 1903. *The Sources of the Doctrines of the Fall and Original Sin.* Cambridge: Cambridge University Press.

TESELLE, Eugene. 1970. *Augustine the Theologian.* New York: Herder and Herder.

TEYSSÈDRE, Bernard. 1985a. *Le Diable et l'Enfer au temps de Jésus.* Paris: Albin Michel.

—— 1985b. *Naissance du Diable: De Babylone aux grottes de la mer morte.* Paris: Albin Michel.

THOMAS, D. Winton. 1963. "*Beli'al* in the Old Testament." In *Biblical and Patristic Studies in Memory of R. P. Casey.* Freiburg im Breisgau: Herder.

THOMAS, D. Winton, ed. 1967. *Archaeology and Old Testament Study.* Oxford: Clarendon.

THOMAS, Keith. 1978. *Religion and the Decline of Magic.* Harmondsworth: Penguin.

THOMPSON, R. Campbell. 1930. *The Epic of Gilgamesh: Text, Translation, and Notes.* Oxford: Clarendon.

THOMPSON, Stith. 1946. *The Folktale.* New York: Dryden.

—— 1955–58. *Motif Index of Folk Literature.* 6 vols. Bloomington: Indiana University Press.

THOMPSON, Thomas L. 1974. *The Historicity of the Patriarchal Narratives.* Berlin: De Gruyter.

THRALL, Margaret. 1983. "Super-Apostles, Servants of Christ, Servants of Satan." *Journal for the Study of the New Testament* 6:42–57.

TIGAY, Jeffrey H. 1977. "Was There an Integrated Gilgamesh Epic in the Old Babylonian Period?" In *Essays on the Ancient Near East in Honor of J. J. Finkelstein,* edited by Maria DeJongh Ellis, pp. 215–18. Hamden, Conn.: Archon.

—— 1982. *The Evolution of the Gilgamesh Epic.* Philadelphia: University of Pennsylvania Press.

TILLICH, Paul. 1948. *The Protestant Era.* Chicago: University of Chicago Press.

TODOROV, Tzvetan, ed. 1965. *Théorie de la littérature: Textes des formalistes russes.* Paris: Seuil.

TORREY, Charles C. 1945. *The Apocryphal Literature: A Brief Introduction.* New Haven: Yale University Press.

TRACHTENBERG, Joshua. 1943. *The Devil and the Jews.* New Haven: Yale University Press.

TROELTSCH, Ernst. 1960 (1st ed. 1911). *The Social Teachings of the Christian Churches.* 2 vols. Chicago: University of Chicago Press.

TURMEL, Joseph (pseud. Father Louis Coulange). 1929. *Life of the Devil.* London: Knopf.

TURNER, H.E.W. 1954. *The Pattern of Christian Truth.* London: Mowbray.

TURNER, Terence S. 1977. "Narrative Structure and Mythopoesis: A Critique and Reformation of Structuralist Concepts of Myth, Narrative, and Poetics." *Arethusa* 10:103–67.

TUR-SINAI, N. H. (Harry Torczyner). 1957. *The Book of Job: A New Commentary*. Jerusalem: Kiryath Sepher.

TURVILLE-PETRIE, E.O.G. 1964. *Myth and Religion of the North*. New York: Holt, Rinehart, and Winston.

UTLEY, Francis Lee. 1957. "Abraham Lincoln's 'When Adam Was Created.' " In *Studies in Folklore*, edited by W. E. Richmond, pp. 187–212. Bloomington: Indiana University Press.

—— 1974. "The Migration of Folktales: Four Channels to the Americas." *Current Anthropology* 15:5–27.

VAILLANT, André. 1952. *Le livre des secrets d'Hénoch: Texte slave et traduction française*. Paris: Institut d'Etudes Slaves.

VAN BUREN, E. Douglas. 1934. "The God Ningizzida." *Iraq* 1:60–89.

—— 1946. "The Dragon in Ancient Mesopotamia." *Orientalia* 15:1–20.

VAN DER KAM, J. 1978. "Enoch Traditions in Jubilees and Other Second Century Sources." *Society of Biblical Literature Seminar Papers* 5:229–51.

VAN GRONINGEN, G. 1967. *First Century Gnosticism*. Leiden: Brill.

VAN SETERS, J. 1975. *Abraham in History and Tradition*. New Haven: Yale University Press.

VAWTER, Bruce. 1963. " 'And He Shall Come Again with Glory': Paul and Christian Apocalypse." In *Studiorum Paulinorum Congress 1961*, pp. 143–50. Rome: Pontifical Biblical Institute.

—— 1977. *On Genesis: A New Reading*. New York: Doubleday.

VERMES, G. 1958. "Baptism and Jewish Exegesis." *New Testament Studies* 4:413–38.

—— 1970. "Bible and Midrash: Early Old Testament Exegesis." In *The Cambridge History of the Bible*, vol. 1, pp. 199–231. Cambridge: Cambridge University Press.

—— 1975. *The Dead Sea Scrolls in English*. 2nd ed. Harmondsworth: Penguin.

VERNANT, J.-P. 1965. *Mythe et pensée chez les Grecques*. Paris: Maspero.

—— 1966. "Le mythe hésiodique des races." *Revue de philosophie* 40:247–81.

VIAN, Francis. 1952. *La guerre des géants: Le mythe avant l'époque hellenistique*. Paris: Thèse de Lettres.

—— 1960. "Le mythe de Typhée et les problèmes de ses origines orientales." In *Eléments orientaux dans la religion grecque ancienne*, pp. 17–37. Paris: Presses Universitaires de France.

VICKERS, Brian. 1973. *Towards Greek Tragedy*. Harlow, Essex: Longmans.

VIRROLEAUD, Charles. 1941. "Le roi Keret et son fils." *Syria* 22:105–36, 197–217.

VIRROLEAUD, Charles, ed. 1957. *Le palais royale d'Ugarit*, vol. 2. Paris: Imprimerie Nationale.

WADDLE, Helen. 1942. *The Desert Fathers*. New York: Sheed and Ward.

WAIS, Kurt. 1952. "Ullikummi, Hrungnir, Armilus und Verwandte." In *Edda, Skalden, Saga: Festschrift Felix Genzmer*, pp. 211–61, 325–31. Heidelberg: Winter Universitäts Verlag.

WAKEMAN, Mary K. 1973. *God's Battle with the Monster: A Study in Biblical Im-agery*. Leiden: Brill.

WALCOT, Peter. 1966. *Hesiod and the Near East*. Cardiff: University of Wales.

WALKER, D. P. 1964. *The Decline of Hell*. Chicago: University of Chicago Press.

WALKER, William O., ed. 1979. *The Relationship Among the Gospels: An Interdis-ciplinary Dialogue*. San Antonio: Trinity University Press.

WALLACE, Howard. 1948. "Leviathan and the Beast in Revelation." *Biblical Ar-chaeologist* 11:61–68.

WALSH, J. 1977. "Genesis 2.4b–3.24: A Synchronous Approach." *Journal of Bib-lical Literature* 96:161–77.

WARNER, Rex, trans. 1963. *The Confessions of St. Augustine*. New York: New American Library.

WATTS, Alan W. 1963. *The Two Hands of God: The Myths of Polarity*. New York: Braziller.

WEBSTER, T.B.L. 1958. *From Mycenae to Homer*. London: Methuen.

WEST, M. L. 1966. *Hesiod's Theogony*. Oxford: Clarendon.

—— 1971. *Early Greek Philosophy and the Orient*. Oxford: Clarendon.

—— 1978. *Hesiod's Works and Days*. Oxford: Clarendon.

WHITE, H. 1975. "French Structuralism and Old Testament Narrative Analysis: Roland Barthes." *Semeia* 3:99–127.

WICKHAM, L. R. 1974. "The Sons of God and the Daughters of Men: Genesis 6.2 in Early Christian Exegesis." *Language and Meaning: Oudtestamentische Studien* 19:135–47.

WIDENGREN, Geo. 1946. "Mesopotamian Elements in Manichaeism." *Upsala Universitets Arsskrift* 3.

—— 1951. "The King and the Tree of Life in Ancient Near Eastern Religion." *Up-sala Universitets Arsskrift* 4.

—— 1965. *Mani and Manichaeism*. London: Holt, Rinehart, and Winston.

—— 1973. *The Gnostic Attitude*. Santa Barbara, Calif.: Institute of Religious Stud-ies.

WILKE, Claus. 1969. "*ku-li*," *Zeitschrift für Assyriologie* 59:98–99.

WILLCOCK, M. M. 1964. "Mythological Paradeigmata in the *Iliad*." *Classical Quarterly*, N.S. 14:141–54.

WILLIAMS, N. P. 1927. *The Ideas of the Fall and of Original Sin*. London: Long-mans.

WILLIAMSON, H.G.M. 1977. *Israel in the Book of Chronicles*. Cambridge: Cam-bridge University Press.

WILSON, John A. 1951. *The Culture of Ancient Egypt*. Chicago: University of Chi-cago Press.

WILSON, R. McL. 1958. *The Gnostic Problem*. London: Mowbray.

—— 1968. *Gnosis and the New Testament*. Oxford: Blackwell.

WINSTON, D. 1966. "The Iranian Component in the Bible, Aprocrypha, and Qumran." *History of Religions* 5:183–216.

WISEMAN, D. J. 1975. "A Gilgamesh Epic Fragment from Nimrud." *Iraq* 37:159–63.

WISSE, F. 1981. "The Opponents in the New Testament in the Light of the Nag Hammadi Writings." In *Colloque International sur les Textes de Nag Hammadi*, edited by Bernard Barc. Quebec: Laval; Louvain: Peeters.

—— 1983. "Prolegomena to the Study of the New Testament and Gnosis." In *New Testament and Gnosis: Essays in Honour of R. McL. Wilson*, pp. 138–45. Edinburgh: T. & T. Clarke.

WOLLEN, Peter. 1976. "North by North-West: A Morphological Analysis." *Film Forum* 1.

WOODS, Barbara Allen. 1959. *The Devil in Dog-Form*. Berkeley: University of California Publications in Folklore 11.

WOODS, Richard. 1973. *The Devil*. Chicago: Thomas More Press.

WRIGHT, Will. 1975. *Six Guns and Society: A Structural Study of the Western*. Berkeley: University of California Press.

YADIN, Yigael. 1962. *The Scroll of the War of the Sons of Light Against the Sons of Darkness*. Oxford: Oxford University Press.

YARBRO-COLLINS, Adela. 1976. *The Combat Myth in the Book of Revelation*. Missoula, Mont.: Scholars Press.

—— 1981. "Myth and History in the Book of Revelation: The Problem of Its Date." In *Traditions in Transformation*, edited by Bruce Halpern and Jon D. Levinson, pp. 377–403. Winona Lake, Ind.: Eisenbrauns.

YATES, Frances. 1969. *Giordano Bruno and the Hermetic Tradition*. New York: Vintage.

YATES, Roy. 1977. "Jesus and the Demonic in the Synoptic Gospels." *Irish Theological Quarterly* 44:39–57.

YOUNG, Frances M. 1973. "Insight or Incoherence: The Greek Fathers on Good and Evil." *Journal of Ecclesiastical History* 24:113–26.

YOUNG, Jean I. 1966. *The Prose Edda of Snorri Sturlusson*. Berkeley: University of California Press.

ZAEHNER, Robert C. 1955. *Zurvan: A Zoroastrian Dilemma*. Oxford: Clarendon.

—— 1956. *The Teachings of the Magi*. New York: Macmillan.

—— 1961. *The Dawn and Twilight of Zoroastrianism*. London: Wiedenfeld and Nicolson.

ZANDEE, Jan. 1964. "Gnostic Ideas on the Fall and Salvation." *Numen* 11:13–74.

ZIMMERLI, Walther. 1983. *Ezekiel 2: A Commentary on the Book of the Prophet Ezekiel, Chapters 25–48*. Philadelphia: Fortress.

ZWEIG, Paul. 1968. *The Heresy of Self-Love: A Study of Subversive Individualism*. New York: Basic Books.

ZYCHA, J., ed. 1891–92. *Corpus Scriptorum Ecclesiasticorum Latinorum*, vol. 25. Vienna: Akademie der wissenschaften.

INDEX

Modern scholars and other references from the footnotes have been included here only when explicitly discussed.

A

Abaddon, 65

Abel, 14, 230

Abelard, 338 n. 11

Abibalos, 69

Abomination of Desolation, 279

Abraham, 276

Absalom, David and, 119, 315

abyssos, 252

Achilles, 11, 66, 70, 79, 81–82, 253, 287

Achitophel, 315

Acta Archelai, 395

Acts: *2.34, 7.55–56* (Psalm 110), 263; *6* (Nicholas), 313; *10.38* (Jesus' life), 296; *26* (Paul), 275

Adad (Irrigator), 52

Adam: ancestry of, 403–404; Augustine and, 421–35; Christ and, 302, 340; Fall and, 198, 278; Gnosticism, 232, 236–42, 329–31; in Irenaeus, 339–48; Manichaeism, 393–94; Origen and, 364–65; original wisdom of, 225–27; in Pauline letters, 277–79, 301–302; rebellion myth and, 304–305; Satan's envy, 237–42; three sons of, 230; Watcher myth and, 217–18. *See also* Adam books

Adamas (Anthropos), 230, 401

Adam books, general, 221–47, 277, 343. *See also Apocalypse of Adam; Apocalypse of Moses*; "Book of Adam"; *Penitence of Adam; Vita Adae et Evae*

Adapa, 141 n. 70

Adversary: ambivalence of, 161, 176–77, 304, 321; in Book of Job, 114; exorcism and, 291–93; function in plot, 5–6, 11, 25, 45, 445–52; in Hesiod, 68, 77–87; Irenaeus's theory, 337; law and, 272–76; as rebel, 124–46, 370; rebel angel and, 189–90, 193–98, 358; Satan as, 4–6, 114, 122–23, 188–90, 210–11, 233–47, 251, 254, 267, 271–72, 275, 288, 293–97, 304–306, 314–17, 363–67, 374, 377–81, 427, 434–36; as tempter, 233–34; as ty-

rant, 139, 145. *See also* Death; Dragon; Sea; Waters

Aelian, 42

Aeschylus, 125, 132; Prometheus myth, 87, 176

Aeshma Daeva, 206

Agent provocateur, 121–22, 304–305

Ahab, 112

Ahriman, 109 n. 3, 296, 392

Ahura Mazda, 108–109, 392

Aiyanar, 5

Akhenaton, 47, 55–58

Alexander the Great, 170

Allegory: Augustine and, 423–25; in Ezekiel, 195–96; myths interpreted by, 87, 367–68, 373–74; in Revelation, 255

Ambrose, 401; on Eden, 420–21

Ambrosiaster, 391, 403

Anat, 46, 60–62, 252–54

Angel of Light, 192–211, 268–69; Moses and Aaron, 198. *See also* Light; Radiance

Angels: as messengers, 111–12; punishment of rebellious, 178–79; radiance of, 214, 237, 242, 268, 350; sinful angels and women, 152–59, 161, 163–72, 233–34; stars and, 252; wickedness of, 169–70. *See also* Rebel myth; Watcher Angels

Angra Mainyu, 109 n. 3

Animal Apocalypse, 180–81

Anselm, 337–38, 366–67, 388

Antaeus, 253 n. 15

Antichrist, 169 n. 25, 210–11, 321; in Johannine letters, 312; Origen, 377, 380; Pauline tradition, 279–81; Polycarp, 314; Revelation, 252 n. 10; Roman Empire as, 255

Antifeminism: Augustine on, 434–36; in Enoch books, 181; in Judaism, 157–58; theological dilemmas and, 212–18; in Yahwist, 155–56

Antiochus Epiphanes, 279

Anu, 52, 128

Library of Congress Cataloging-in-Publication Data

FORSYTH, NEIL, 1944–
THE OLD ENEMY.

BIBLIOGRAPHY: P.   INCLUDES INDEX.
I. DEVIL—COMPARATIVE STUDIES. 2. DEVIL—
HISTORY OF DOCTRINES. 3. DEVIL IN LITERATURE—
HISTORY AND CRITICISM. I. TITLE.
BL480.F67 1987   809'.93351   87–2316
ISBN 0–691–06712–0 (ALK. PAPER)